Other Great Guides for Your Trip:

Frommer's Spain

Spain For Dummies

Frommer's Spain's Best-Loved Driving Tours

Frommer's Europe

Frommer's Europe from $70 a Day

Frommer's Gay & Lesbian Europe

Frommer's Europe's Greatest Driving Tours

Europe For Dummies

Hanging Out in Europe

Frommer's Road Atlas Europe

Here's what the critics say about Frommer's:

"Amazingly easy to use. Very portable, very complete."
— *Booklist*

♦

"The only mainstream guide to list specific prices. The Walter Cronkite of guidebooks—with all that implies."
— *Travel & Leisure*

♦

"Complete, concise, and filled with useful information."
— *New York Daily News*

♦

"Hotel information is close to encyclopedic."
— *Des Moines Sunday Register*

♦

"Detailed, accurate, and easy-to-read information for all price ranges."
— *Glamour Magazine*

Barcelona, Madrid & Seville

3rd Edition

by Darwin Porter & Danforth Prince

IDG Books Worldwide, Inc.
An International Data Group Company
Foster City, CA • Chicago, IL • Indianapolis, IN • New York, NY

ABOUT THE AUTHORS

North Carolina-born **Darwin Porter** and Ohio native **Danforth Prince** are the coauthors of several best-selling Frommer's guides—notably Spain, England, France, Italy, and Germany. Porter, who worked in television advertising and is a former bureau chief for the *Miami Herald,* wrote the first-ever Frommer's guide to Spain while still a student. Prince, who began his association with Porter in 1982, worked for the Paris bureau of the *New York Times.* Both writers have made countless annual trips through the cities of Barcelona, Madrid, and Seville and through the countryside of Spain to share their discoveries with you.

IDG BOOKS WORLDWIDE, INC.

An International Data Group Company
909 Third Avenue
New York, NY 10022

Find us online at **www.frommers.com**

ISBN 0-7645-6167-7
ISSN 1090-5499

Editor: Matthew Garcia
Production Editor: Cara Buitron
Photo Editor: Richard Fox
Design by Michele Laseau
Staff Cartographer: Elizabeth Puhl
Production by IDG Books Indianapolis Production Department
Front cover photo: Antoni Gaudí's Casa Batlló in Barcelona

SPECIAL SALES

For general information on IDG Books Worldwide's books in the U.S., please call our Consumer Customer Service Department at 1-800-762-2974. For reseller information, including discounts, bulk sales, customized editions, and premium sales, please call our Reseller Consumer Service Department at 1-800-434-3422.

Manufactured in the United States of America.

5 4 3 2 1

Contents

List of Maps vii

1 **Introducing Barcelona, Madrid & Seville** **1**

1 Frommer's Favorite Barcelona Experiences 2

2 Frommer's Favorite Madrid Experiences 3

3 Frommer's Favorite Seville Experiences 5

4 Best Barcelona Hotel Bets 7

5 Best Barcelona Restaurant Bets 9

6 Best Madrid Hotel Bets 10

7 Best Madrid Restaurant Bets 12

8 Best Seville Hotel Bets 14

9 Best Seville Restaurant Bets 15

2 **Planning a Trip to Barcelona, Madrid & Seville** **17**

1 Visitor Information & Entry Requirements 17

2 Money 20

The Spanish Peseta 21

3 When to Go 22

Calendar of Events: Barcelona, Madrid & Seville 23

4 Health & Insurance 25

5 Tips for Travelers with Special Needs 26

6 Getting There 29

3 **Settling into Barcelona** **37**

1 Orientation 38

Neighborhoods in Brief 41

The Barcelona Card 43

2 Getting Around 43

Fast Facts: Barcelona 46

3 Where to Stay 49

Family-Friendly Hotels 54

4 Where to Dine 63

Family-Friendly Restaurants 71

Fast Food & Picnic Fare 81

4 **Exploring Barcelona** **83**

1 In & Around the Ciutat Vella (Old City) 83

2 In the Eixample 87

3 In & Around the Parc de la Ciutadella 88

4 In & Around the Parc de Montjuïc 89

5 In La Barceloneta & the Harbor 90

6 Outside the City Center 91

7 Parks & Gardens 92

8 Especially for Kids 94

9 Architectural Standouts 94

Walking Tour—The Gothic Quarter 95

10 Organized Tours 100

11 Shopping 101

12 Barcelona After Dark 106

13 Side Trips from Barcelona 114

5   Settling into Madrid   121

1 Orientation 122
   Neighborhoods in Brief 124
2 Getting Around 124
   Fast Facts: Madrid 125
3 Where to Stay 131

   Family-Friendly Hotels 145
4 Where to Dine 150
   An Early-Evening Tapeo 151
   Family-Friendly Restaurants 159
   Picnics, Madrid Style 178

6   Exploring Madrid   180

1 The Major Museums 180
2 Near the Plaza Mayor &
   Puerta del Sol 184
3 Along Paseo del Prado 185
4 Near the Gran Vía & Plaza de
   España 186
5 In Chamartín, Chueca &
   Salamanca 187
6 Outside the City Center 188
7 Parks & Gardens 189

8 Especially for Kids 190
9 Special-Interest Sightseeing 191
   *Walking Tour—Hapsburg
   Madrid* 192
10 Organized Tours 195
11 Shopping 195
12 Madrid After Dark 202
   The Sultry Sound of Flamenco 207

7   Side Trips from Madrid   214

1 Toledo 214
2 Aranjuez 228

3 San Lorenzo de El Escorial 230
4 Segovia 234

8   Seville   241

1 Orientation 241
   Neighborhoods in Brief 243
2 Getting Around 244
   Fast Facts: Seville 244
3 Where to Stay 245
   Family-Friendly Hotels 249
4 Where to Dine 255
   Family-Friendly Restaurants 256
   Food on the Run 259

5 Exploring Seville 260
6 Especially for Kids 265
   *Walking Tour—The Old
   City* 265
7 Organized Tours 270
8 Shopping 271
9 Seville After Dark 274
10 Side Trips from Seville 277
   The Legacy of al-Andalus 280

Appendix A: Barcelona, Madrid & Seville in Depth   285

1 The Cities Today 285
2 A Look at the Past 288
3 Architecture 101 292
   The Spectacle of Death 294

4 The Cuisine: Tapas, Paella &
   Sangría 297
   From Vineyards to the Bodegas 300

Appendix B: Basic Phrases & Vocabulary   302

 Appendix C: Menu Savvy   304

 Index   305

General Index   305

Barcelona Accommodations
Index   310

Madrid Accommodations
Index   311

Seville Accommodations
Index   311

Barcelona Restaurant Index   311

Madrid Restaurant Index   312

Seville Restaurant Index   312

List of Maps

Barcelona Metro   45

Central Barcelona Accommodations   50

Central Barcelona Dining   64

Central Barcelona Attractions   84

Walking Tour—The Gothic Quarter   97

Barcelona Environs   115

Madrid Metro   126

Central Madrid Accommodations   134

Central Madrid Dining   152

Central Madrid Attractions   182

Walking Tour—Hapsburg Madrid   193

Madrid Environs   215

Toledo   218

Seville Accommodations   247

Seville Dining   257

Seville Attractions   263

Walking Tour—The Old City   267

Seville Environs   279

An Invitation to the Reader

In researching this book we discovered many wonderful places—hotels, restaurants, shops, and more. We're sure you'll find others. Please tell us about them, so we can share the information with your fellow travelers in upcoming editions. If you were disappointed with a recommendation, we'd love to know that, too. Please write to:

Frommer's Barcelona, Madrid & Seville, 3rd Edition
IDG Books Worldwide, Inc.
909 Third Avenue
New York, NY 10022

An Additional Note

Please be advised that travel information is subject to change at any time—and this is especially true of prices. We therefore suggest that you write or call ahead for confirmation when making your travel plans. The authors, editors, and publisher cannot be held responsible for the experiences of readers while traveling. Your safety is important to us, however, so we encourage you to stay alert and be aware of your surroundings. Keep a close eye on cameras, purses, and wallets, all favorite targets of thieves and pickpockets.

What the Symbols Mean

✪ Frommer's Favorites

Our favorite places and experiences—outstanding for quality, value, or both.

The following abbreviations are used for credit cards:

AE	American Express	EC	Eurocard
CB	Carte Blanche	JCB	Japan Credit Bank
DC	Diners Club	MC	MasterCard
DISC	Discover	V	Visa
ER	EnRoute		

Find Frommer's Online

www.frommers.com offers up-to-the-minute listings on almost 200 cities around the globe—including the latest bargains and candid, personal articles updated daily by Arthur Frommer himself. No other Web site offers such comprehensive and timely coverage of the world of travel.

Introducing Barcelona, Madrid & Seville

Although these three cities are remarkably different in texture and attractions, each is evocative of the region it presides over: Barcelona, capital of Catalonia; Madrid, capital of Castile (and the entire country); and Seville, capital of Andalusia. To walk their streets, to sample their cuisine, to view their monuments, to taste and observe their daily life: These are reasons enough to visit Spain. If you do miss the rest of the country, it would be a pity; but if you at least manage the cities covered in this guide, you'll have found a window on the three different worlds that best exemplify Spain: Catalonia, Castile, and Andalusia.

Barcelona, progressive and industrial, is the most European of Spanish cities, yet also Mediterranean in both climate and atmosphere. Catalans often speak of their "schizophrenia"—that is, the tension caused by their desires both to maintain the traditional and to embrace the new.

Though the city's palm tree-lined streets may seem languid, there's activity aplenty as Barcelona races to keep up with other major cities in Europe. Economic vigor is one part of the mix—one-fourth of the country's goods are manufactured here—but 21st-century Barcelona is also a place to have fun and relax. Never before have there been so many good restaurants, hotels, nightclubs, and new attractions.

Since the 1992 Olympics, the city has undergone a veritable renaissance, sprucing up its buildings and improving its tourist facilities at a rate equaled by no other city in Spain, not even Madrid.

Speaking of the capital city: Once staid, almost seedy in its decay, Madrid has burst upon the European scene with newfound enthusiasm for the modern world. Lively at all hours, the city appears to be recovering from a long and dreary sleep, determined to stay up every minute of the day and night for fear of missing out on anything.

It's true that Madrid doesn't match the great attractions and architecture of London, Paris, or Rome, but it does have the Prado and its stellar art galleries. It offers visitors a fascinating nightlife scene, great restaurants, and deluxe hotels, and it's within striking distance of some of the country's best day trips, including Toledo, Segovia, and El Escorial. Neither Barcelona nor Seville can be used as a base for such a diverse array of attractions.

Heading south, the temperature rises and the pace slows as we approach Seville, center of world attention during the 1992 Expo. It doesn't boast the great art museums of Barcelona or Madrid, but it does possess a stunning cathedral, along with truly incomparable Moorish architecture. Orange and palm trees line its streets, where lovely vistas await at every turn. Chances are you won't be singing in the rain, as Seville is dry, dusty, and hot—in fact, it's the hottest city in Iberia.

Famed for its Easter festivities, when hooded and robed penitents march through the streets, Seville follows those events with its April Fair, a week of celebrations. Sevillanos ride on horseback looking like stage extras from *Carmen,* and the entire city celebrates with food, wine, and bullfights, followed by nightly flamenco dancing and the region's own special dance, the *Sevillano.* Almost any time of the year is ideal for a visit to Andalusia's capital, although we prefer the spring or fall. Seville's cathedral is one of the finest in Spain; the Alcazar evokes memories of a great Moorish civilization; and the Museo de Bellas Artes has one of the country's best art collections. But Seville offers much more: Visitors can enjoy the sensory pleasures of Andalusia itself.

1 Frommer's Favorite Barcelona Experiences

- **Wandering the Crooked Streets of the Gothic Quarter.** Long before Madrid was founded, the kingdom of Catalonia was a bastion of art and architecture. Whether the Barri Gòtic, as it's called in Catalán, is truly Gothic is the subject of endless debate, but the Ciutat Vella, or old city, of Barcelona is one of the most evocative sites in Spain. Its richly textured streets, with their gurgling fountains, vintage stores, and ancient fortifications, inspired such artists as Pablo Picasso (a museum of whose work is found here) and Joan Miró (who was born in this neighborhood). Stop in at Sala Parés, Spain's oldest art gallery, at carrer Petritxol 5 (☎ **93-318-70-20**)—one of the birthplaces of Catalán modernism. See chapter 4.

- **Watching the Sardana.** The national dance of Catalonia is performed at noon in the Plaça de Sant Jaume, in front of the cathedral. Nothing is more folkloric than this street dance played out against the backdrop of a *cobla,* or brass band. The dance may have originated in one of the Greek islands, and then been brought to Barcelona by sailors. It may even have come from Sardinia (hence the name). But regardless of its point of origin, the *Sardana* remains uniquely Catalán. See chapter 4.

- **Strolling Along Les Rambles.** Les Rambles cuts through the heart of Barcelona's oldest district, beginning at the Plaça de Catalunya and running toward the sea. A tree-lined boulevard, it's the most famous street in Spain—and a lot more intriguing than Madrid's dull Gran Vía. The street is democratic, bringing together buskers, shop owners, tourists, drag queens, and drug dealers—mixed in with hotels, cafes, porno houses, newsstands, and flower stalls. It's composed of five different Ramblas or Rambles (either term is correct). Late at night, the scene on Spain's most charismatic street evokes the writings about Barcelona by Jean Genet. See chapter 4.

- **Drinking Cava in a *Xampanyería.*** Enjoy a glass of bubbly, Barcelona style. Cataláns swear that their *cavas* taste better than French champagne. After the staid Franco years, *xampanyerías* (champagne bars) literally burst onto the Barcelona nightlife scene; many stay open until the wee hours of the morning. You can select *brut* or *brut nature* (brut is slightly sweeter). Try any of these popular brands, which also happen to be the best: Mestres, Parxet, Torello, Recaredo, Gramona, or Mont-Marçal. See chapter 4.

- **Exploring the Museu Picasso.** Examine the evolution of a genius from the age of 14. Barcelona's most popular attraction, housed in three Gothic mansions, spans Picasso's long, multifaceted career, taking in the blue period, cubism, and beyond. Of special interest are the paintings in the Barcelona section from the years 1895 to 1897, when he lived in the Catalán capital. See works by Picasso-as-copyist (he re-created Velázquez's famous portrait of Philip IV) and admire the portraits, especially the one he painted of his aunt, *Retrato de la Tía Pepa* (*Portrait of Aunt Pepa*). In the *Caballo Corneado* (*Gored Horse*) charcoal drawing, you can see the beginnings of cubism. See chapter 4.

- **Going Gaga Over Gaudí.** No architect in Europe was as fantastical as Antoni Gaudí y Cornet, the foremost proponent of Catalán *modernismo.* Barcelona is studded with the works of this extraordinary artist—in fact, UNESCO now lists all his creations among the World Trust Properties. This eccentric genius conceived buildings as "visions." A recluse and a celibate bachelor, as well as a fervent Catalán nationalist, he lived out his own fantasy. Nothing is more stunning than his Sagrada Família, Barcelona's best-known landmark, a cathedral on which Gaudí labored for the last 43 years of his life, before he was tragically killed by a tram in 1926. The landmark cathedral was never completed. In Barcelona, the question is not "to be or not to be," but "to finish or not to finish." Believe it or not, they're still working on it. If it's ever finished, "The Sacred Family" will be Europe's largest cathedral. See chapter 4.

- **Experiencing the Bodega Bohemia.** This Barcelona institution, just off the Rambles, is a cabaret extraordinaire. A talent showcase for theatrical personalities of yesteryear, this bodega has been going strong since 1893. The performers are past their prime—indeed, many of the showgirls look old enough to have entertained troops in the Spanish-American war—but they've mastered the theatrical tricks of the trade and still know how to deliver a great show. The raucous audience is consistently filled with people who boo, catcall, cheer, and scream with laughter. At the Bodega Bohemia, it's still a hot night in the old town. See chapter 4.

- **Walking the Harbor Front.** A major port of call for international cruise ships, Spain's largest port boasts a pedestrian promenade with benches, contemporary bridges, palm trees, and some of the city's finest (and priciest) restaurants. Begin at the Moll de la Fusta, or "Wooden Wharf," where the Barri Gòtic meets the harbor. Continue along the beach of Barceloneta to the Port Vell, or Olympic port. This is the site of Platja Barcelona, a beach constructed for the 1992 Olympic games. If you're hungry, head for one of the several excellent restaurants at the yacht basin, or one of the modest cafes serving Spanish tapas. Panoramic views of the sea unfold before you. It's a great way to spend an afternoon or early evening. See the accompanying walking tour in chapter 4.

2 Frommer's Favorite Madrid Experiences

- **Sitting in *Sol* or *Sombra* at the Bullfights.** With origins as old as pagan Spain, the art of bullfighting is the expression of Iberian temperament and passions. Detractors object to the sport as cruel, bloody, violent, hot, and savage. Aficionados, however, understand bullfighting as a microcosm of death, catharsis, and rebirth. These philosophical underpinnings may not be immediately apparent, but if you strive to understand the bullfight, it can be one of the most evocative and memorable events in Spain. Head for the *plaza de toros* (bullring) in Madrid. Tickets are either *sol* (sunny side) or *sombra* (in the shade); you'll pay more to get out of the sun. Observe how the feverish crowds appreciate the ballet of the *banderilleros,* the thundering fury of the bull, the arrogance of the matador—all leading to "death in the afternoon." See chapter 6.

- **Seeing the Masterpieces at the Prado.** It's one of the world's premier art museums, ranking with the Louvre. The Prado is home to some 4,000 masterpieces, many of them acquired by Spanish kings. The wealth of Spanish art is staggering—everything from Goya's *Naked Maja* to the celebrated *Las Meninas* (*The Maids of Honor*) by Velázquez (our favorite). Masterpiece after masterpiece unfolds before your eyes: You can imagine your fate in Hieronymus Bosch's *Garden of Earthly Delights* or recoil from the horror of Goya's *Disasters of War* etchings. When the Spanish artistic soul gets too dark, escape to the Italian salons and view canvases by Caravaggio, Fra Angelico, and Botticelli. Be warned, though, that a quick run-through won't suffice: It would take a lifetime to savor the Prado's wonders. See chapter 6.

- **Feasting on Tapas in the Tascas.** Tapas, those bite-size portions washed down with wine, beer, or sherry, are reason enough to go to Madrid! Spanish tapas are so good their once-secret recipes have been broadcast around the world, but they always taste better at home. A *tapeo* is akin to a London pub crawl—you travel from one tapas bar to another. Each has a different specialty. Tapas bars, called *tascas,* are a quintessential Spanish experience, be it in Galicia, Andalusia, Catalonia, or Castile. Originally tapas were cured ham or *chorizo* (spicy sausage). Today they are likely to include everything—*gambas* (deep-fried shrimp), anchovies marinated in vinegar, stuffed peppers, a cool, spicy gazpacho, or hake salad. To go really native, try lamb's sweetbreads or bulls' testicles. These dazzling spreads will hold you over until the fashionable 10pm dining hour. The best streets for your tasca crawl include Ventura de la Vega, the area around Plaza de Santa Ana or Plaza de Santa Bárbara, Cava Baja, or calle de Cuchilleros. See chapter 6.

- **Lounging in an Outdoor Cafe.** In sultry summertime, Madrileños come alive on their *terrazas.* The drinking and good times can go on until dawn. In glamorous hangouts or on lowly street corners, the cafe scene takes place mainly along an axis shaped by the Paseo de la Castellana, Paseo del Prado, and Paseo de Recoletos. Wander up and down the boulevards and select a spot that appeals to you. For traditional atmosphere, the terrazas at Playa Mayor win out. See chapter 6.

- **Shopping the Rastro.** Madrid's flea market represents a tradition that's 500 years old. Savvy shoppers arrive before 7am every Sunday to beat the rush and claim the best merchandise. The teeming place doesn't really get going until about 9am, and then it's shoulder-to-shoulder stretching down calle Riberia de Curtidores. Real or fake antiques, secondhand clothing, porno films, Franco-era furniture, paintings (endless copies of Velázquez), bullfight posters, old books, religious relics, and plenty of just plain junk, including motorcycles from World War II, are for sale. These streets also contain some of the finest permanent antique shops in Madrid. But beware: Pickpockets are out in full force. More than a few mugging victims have later found their purses here for resale—thoroughly emptied, of course. See chapter 6.

- **Sunday Strolling in the Retiro.** Spread across 350 cool acres in sweltering Madrid, Parque de Retiro was originally designed as the gardens of Buen Retiro palace, occupied by Philip IV in the 1630s. In 1767 Charles III opened part of the gardens to the general public. Only after the collapse of Isabella II's monarchy in 1868 did the park become available to all Madrileños. Statues dot the grounds (a towering 1902 monument to Alfonso XII presides over the lake), which also contain some 15,000 trees, a rose garden, and a few art galleries. The best time for a stroll is Sunday morning before lunch, when vendors hawk their wares, magicians perform their acts, and fortune-tellers read tarot cards. You can even rent a boat and laze away the morning on the lake. See chapter 6.

- **Nursing a Drink at Chicote.** The 1930s interior at Madrid's most famous bar looks the same as it did during the Civil War. Shells might have been flying along the Gran Vía, but the international press corps covering the war drank on. After the war, the crowd of regulars included major writers, artists, and actors. By the late 1960s it had degenerated into a pickup bar frequented by prostitutes. But today it has regained the *joie de vivre* of yore and is one of the smart, sophisticated spots to rendezvous in Madrid. See chapter 6.

- **Experiencing the Movida.** We can't tell you exactly how to go about this. Just go to Madrid—the *movida* will seek you out. Very roughly translated as the "shift" or the "movement," movida characterizes post-Franco life in Madrid, after Madrileños threw off the yoke of dictatorship and repression. In a larger context, the movida is a cultural renaissance affecting all aspects of local life, encompassing a wide range of social projects and progressive causes. Movida is best experienced around midnight, when the town just starts to wake up; the action centers around hipper-than-thou places with names like Bar Cock. Madrileños hop from club to club as if they're afraid they'll miss out on something if they stay in one place too long. To truly catch a whiff of movida, head for the lively nightlife areas of Chueca, Huertas, and Malasaña, and the big clubs around calle Arenal. See chapter 6.

3 Frommer's Favorite Seville Experiences

- **Getting Caught Up in the Passions of Flamenco.** It's best heard in some old tavern, in a neighborhood like the Barrio de Triana in Seville. From the lowliest *taberna* to the poshest nightclub, you can hear the staccato heel clicking, foot stomping, castanet rattling, hand clapping, and sultry guitar and tambourine sound. Some say its origins lie deep in Asia, but the Spanish gypsy has given the art form, which dramatizes inner conflict and pain, an original style. Performed by a great artist, flamenco can tear your heart out with its soulful and throaty singing. See chapter 8.

- **Celebrating *Semana Santa* (Holy Week).** Since the 16th century, the city's processions and celebrations at Easter have been the biggest and most elaborate in Spain. Solemn evening processions take place each day of the week before Easter, organized by *codafrías,* or religious brotherhoods. Members of various codafrías dress as penitents in hoods, capes, and masks—a little spooky. Huge platforms, called *pasos,* are carried on their shoulders, and religious statues are paraded through the streets. But it's not all solemn; Sevillanos indulge in almost pagan celebrations of singing, eating, and drinking, too. With hardly enough time for a breather, Semana Santa segues into Feria de Abril, a 6-day festival of bullfights, street dancing, parades, fireworks, and flamenco performances. See chapter 8.

- **Strolling Through Barrio Santa Cruz.** Wandering this area of whitewashed houses, winding streets, and artisans' shops is one of the scenic adventures of a trip to Seville. In the Middle Ages the barrio was the home of Seville's Jewish community. Enter at calle de Mateus Gago, which intersects with the monumental realm of Plaza de la Virgen de los Reyes, and plunge right in. The neighborhood is filled with restaurants and tascas, so you can take a break whenever you choose. Most historic figures of Seville have passed through this barrio, although few traces of its former Jewish heritage remain. All the former synagogues have been turned into churches, including Santa Maria la Blanca, with Murillo's *Last Supper.* Go during the day—the risk of mugging is high at night. See chapter 8.

• **Discovering the Mysteries of Casa de Pilatos.** This palace for the marqués de Tarifa, completed in 1540, was partially modeled on the House of Pontius Pilate, which the marqués had visited in Jerusalem. It's a riot of Mudéjar design: textured wood ceilings, carved stucco filigree, brightly patterned tiles, a Plateresque portal, a central patio with Moorish arches, a Gothic balustrade, and a bubbling fountain. There's nothing else quite like it in Seville. It's still the home of the duque de Medinaceli, who sequesters himself in a private wing when visitors come to call. See chapter 8.

• **Climbing La Giralda.** All that remains of the former Almohad mosque is La Giralda, a 20-story bell tower that you can climb on a clear day to see olive groves in a 360° view around Seville. It was once the minaret of a great Moorish mosque; so intrigued were conquering Christians with its ingenious *sebka* rhomboid brick pattern that they spared the tower and incorporated it into the design of the cathedral they built on the site. The "Apples of Yanmur," the golden spheres with which the Almohads crowned the tower in the 1100s, are long gone. Today the 308-foot tower is topped by a belfry, a lantern, and a revolving statue dedicated to the Christian religion. It's quite a climb to the top, but the view from this remarkable monument is worth the effort. See chapter 8.

• **Shopping Along Calle Sierpes.** A narrow pedestrian street in the heart of Seville, calle Sierpes is lined with everything from chic boutiques to innumerable pricey fan shops. The bevy of sidewalk cafes on hand allows you to take a break and watch the action. Back in Franco-era Spain, a popular saying of Sevillanos (male, of course) was, "The three finest pleasures a man can know are to be young, to be in Sevilla, and to stand in Sierpes at dusk when the girls are passing." The saying might still be true, though in today's Spain it could be said by ladies admiring the young men. Cervantes reputedly began work on *Don Quixote* in a royal prison that once stood on this street. All that's left is a plaque commemorating the poet. See chapter 8.

• **Visiting El Arenal and Triana.** El Arenal and Triana were Seville's 17th-century seafaring quarters, immortalized by such writers as Cervantes, Lope de Vega, and Quevedo. As the site of the 12-sided Torre del Oro, a "gold tower" constructed by the Almohads in 1220, El Arenal draws the most visitors. (The tower was once covered in gold tiles.) Stroll along Marqués de Contadero, which stretches from the banks of the Guadalquivir River to the base of the Torre del Oro. From here you can take a tiled boardwalk to the Plaza de Toros, one of the most famous bullrings in Spain, home to the great school of *tauromaquia.* Seville's most important museum, the Museo Provincial de Bellas Artes, is also here, with an impressive collection of works by Seville painters, including Murillo. Across the river, Triana was once Seville's gypsy quarter, home to potters and tile makers; gentrification has now jacked up real-estate values. At calle Betis, a terraced riverside promenade, enjoy a panoramic view of the city skyline. See chapter 8.

• **Attending the Opera in Seville.** Seville has been the setting for some of the world's best-loved operas—Bizet's *Carmen,* Donizetti's *La Favorita,* Beethoven's *Fidelio,* Verdi's *La Forza del Destino,* Mozart's *The Marriage of Figaro,* and Rossini's *The Barber of Seville.* Ironically, it wasn't until 1991 that Seville got its own opera house—the Teatro de la Maestranza at Núñez de Balboa, which quickly became one of the world's premier venues for operatic performances.

Although you may hear *The Barber of Seville* performed everywhere from Milan to New York, it always sounds better in its hometown. See chapter 8.

4 Best Barcelona Hotel Bets

- **Best Historic Hotel:** When the great hotelier César Ritz founded the **Hotel Ritz** (☎ 93-318-52-00) in 1919, it was immediately considered the grande dame of Barcelona hotels. Although the term may seem dated, the sentiment still holds true in this case. It's Barcelona's traditional and authentic old-world favorite, ranking along with the Ritz in Madrid for prestige. Although there's great competition in Barcelona's luxury hotel market, the rich and famous still show up on the doorstep of the glamorous, thoroughly renovated Hotel Ritz. See chapter 3.
- **Best for Business Travelers:** It's not the grandest hotel in town, but the 12-story **Barcelona Hilton** (☎ 800/445-8667 in the U.S. and Canada, or 93-495-77-77), near the main soccer stadium, has a state-of-the-art business center and four floors of executive rooms, one reserved exclusively for women. Guest rooms have bedside controls and security locks; rapid checkout means you'll get to the airport on time; and the highly professional staff can help connect you with the movers and shakers in Barcelona with whom you'll be doing business. See chapter 3.
- **Best for a Romantic Getaway:** Barcelona isn't exactly a summer resort town, but the **Claris** (☎ 800/888-4747 in the U.S., or 93-487-62-62), which some regard as the best hotel in the city, offers such luxury and comfort that it should suffice. This beautifully restored 19th-century palace boasts a Japanese water garden and a rooftop pool. Even its duplex configurations—separating sleeping from living areas—add to the private, romantic ambience. The owners' collection of Egyptian and Indian artifacts creates an exotic flavor. The most romantic (also expensive) public area in the hotel is Caviar Caspa, a pocket of posh set among cozy, intimate surroundings. See chapter 3.
- **Best Fashionable Hotel:** The **Hotel Arts** (☎ 800/241-3333 in the U.S., or 93-221-10-70), the only hotel in Europe commanded by the prestigious Ritz-Carlton group, is the place to stay for the fashionable and for those who want to be. The 44-story glass-and-steel tower has a dramatic seafront location, and the view from the open-air pool is simply splendid. It's a glamorous and chic rendezvous. See chapter 3.
- **Best Hotel Lobby for Pretending You're Rich:** There's the Ritz, of course (see above), but the **Avenida Palace** (☎ 93-301-96-00) recaptures some of the city's long-ago glamour. Set in an old stone palace, this longtime favorite has a rich, historic atmosphere. It boasts one of the plushest lobbies in the world, with glittering chandeliers, red carpeting (the only color to use, of course), and a curving marble staircase fancy enough to make you feel like a Morgan, Ford, or Getty of yesteryear. See chapter 3.
- **Best for Families:** In the Barri Gòtic opposite the cathedral, the **Hotel Colón** (☎ 800/845-0636 in the U.S., or 93-301-14-04) has long been a favorite thanks to its choice location near many of the major sights of Barcelona. The traditional hotel has a Spanish-style lobby and high-ceilinged rooms in a part of town usually known for accommodations with small, dark bedrooms. Families should try for one of the nine sixth-floor units with spacious terraces. Baby-sitting can be arranged, and families can avail themselves of the relatively speedy laundry service. See chapter 3.

- **Best Moderately Priced Hotel:** Cited for its good value, the **Hotel Regencia Colón** (☎ 93-318-98-58) is a sibling of the Colón (see above). It enjoys the same remarkable location in the Barri Gòtic near the cathedral, but charges far less for the privilege of staying here. Updated in 1991, it offers good housekeeping and roomy comfort. Antiques are used here and there to create a warm, welcoming atmosphere, and many rooms have such amenities as big closets and private safes. See chapter 3.

- **Best Budget Hotel:** Long popular with Frommer's readers, the **Hotel Continental** (☎ 93-301-25-70) occupies the top two floors of a building opening onto the upper Rambles. A choice location for sightseeing, it also offers modern rooms that, though hardly the grandest in town, sometimes open onto half-moon balconies overlooking the most famous boulevard in Spain. The hotel is not only a good value for Barcelona, but its buffet breakfast is also exceedingly generous. See chapter 3.

- **Best B&B:** For the price, the **Hostal Levante** (☎ 93-317-95-65) is a rather good-size B&B with a total of 38 decent and well-kept rooms. Of course, only seven of them contain a private bathroom, but those down the hall are generally kept immaculate. It's a viable alternative for those hoping to keep costs low in a very high-priced city. You'll also save money on sightseeing; the hotel is only a brief stroll from Plaça de Sant Jaume, which is in the exact center of the Barri Gòtic. See chapter 3.

- **Best Service:** Many hotels in its price range are better than the **Princesa Sofía** (☎ 93-330-71-11), but the manager at this HUSA chain entry has hired one of the best, most professional, and most polite staffs in town (and nearly everyone speaks English). Even though the hotel is gargantuan, they somehow seem to address personal problems carefully and to fulfill requests quickly and efficiently without ever losing their cool. The Sofía's business service facilities are on par with those of the Barcelona Hilton. See chapter 3.

- **Best Location:** There's the Colón and its sibling, the Regencia Colón (see above), but there's also **Le Meridien Barcelona** (☎ 800/543-4300 in the U.S., or 93-318-62-00), the only five-star hotel in the old town. Former guests may remember it as the seedy Hotel Manila, but it was completely renovated in 1988 and is now one of the city's leading hotels. Handsomely furnished and decorated, Le Meridien is just steps from the Rambles. You can literally walk out your door and be involved in Barcelona street life within a minute. The Colón is still a better location for those who want to be in the heart of the old quarter, but for the Rambles and its dozens of restaurants and attractions, Le Meridien is the stellar choice. See chapter 3.

- **Best Hotel Health Club:** Massive but plush, the **Princesa Sofía** (☎ 93-330-71-11) provides an attractive mixture of formal service in a hypermodern format, with a design placing great emphasis on such American-style amenities as the health club. Consequently, what you'll find one level below the lobby manages to incorporate everything you'd find at a well-run California gym, with a Catalán staff that really seems to care about the state of your physical well-being. Views from the exercise bikes and treadmills encompass a verdant garden and a very large outdoor pool measuring about 80 feet in length. This Americanized health club is open only to hotel guests. An American-style restaurant serves cool drinks, light meals, and salads in the hotel's garden, midway between the pool and the health club. See chapter 3.

- **Best Hotel Pool:** The 44-story **Hotel Arts** (☎ 800/241-3333 in the U.S., or 93-221-10-00) soars above a position close to the edge of the sea, adjacent to the harbor used for Olympic sailing events. Part of the hotel's allure derives from its azure-colored outdoor pool, the focal point of the second floor, which excels in both functional and aesthetic capacities. No one will mind if you aggressively swim several laps, but for sitting there's an alfresco restaurant, the Marina, that serves party-colored drinks and flavorful food throughout the day and evening. Water buffs appreciate the pool's proximity to the beach, and as such, can alternate between fresh and saltwater swimming. See chapter 3.

- **Best Views:** The **Rey Juan Carlos I** (☎ 800/448 8355 in the U.S., or 93-448-08-08), which made its debut in 1993, is a 17-story marble-and-glass tower built around the most dramatic atrium in town. The glass-bubble elevators are worth riding for the panoramic view of Barcelona alone. Not only that, but the hotel offers interior balconies as well. Even more vistas unfold from the hotel's big outdoor swimming pool and sundeck, which are set in a large garden. See chapter 3.

5 Best Barcelona Restaurant Bets

- **Best View:** Part of the fun of going to Barcelona is dining with a view of the water, and **Can Costa** (☎ 93-221-59-03) not only offers that but also serves up some of the city's most succulent seafood. It has prospered since the eve of World War II, luring patrons who came to sample traditional recipes from the best baby squid in town to a classic Valencian shellfish paella. See chapter 3.

- **Best Decor:** Once **Beltxenea** (☎ 93-215-30-24) was a chic, elegant apartment in the Eixample, but in 1987 it was converted into a restaurant. The dining rooms still retain the atmosphere of exclusivity and elegance, and these days, the restaurant serves some of the best Basque cookery in Catalonia. See chapter 3.

- **Best Value:** The most celebrated restaurant in La Boquería, the covered food market of Barcelona, is **Garduña** (☎ 93-302-43-23). Originally a hotel, it was converted into a restaurant in the 1970s, today serving artists, writers, actors, and others in a blue-collar atmosphere. The food is super-fresh; you get hearty seafood medleys here at prices far below what most other restaurants charge. It also offers one of the best fixed-price menus in town. See chapter 3.

- **Best Catalán Cuisine: Los Caracoles** (☎ 93-302-31-85), below Plaça Reial, is the old favorite in town; despite the fact that it's a tourist haunt, it serves delectable local cuisine. It has been Barcelona's most colorful and popular restaurant since 1835. Everybody from Richard Nixon to John Wayne has sampled its spit-roasted chicken and the namesake snails. There's nothing else quite like it in town. See chapter 3.

- **Best Seafood:** On the main thoroughfare of Gràcia is **Botafumeiro** (☎ 93-218-42-30), where you get the city's best array of seafood. The chief attraction is mariscos Botafumeiro, a myriad selection of the best shellfish in Spain, with one plate arriving right after the other. The fresh fish is flown daily to Barcelona, often from the coast of Galicia, where the restaurant owner comes from. See chapter 3.

- **Best Continental Cuisine:** In this chic part of town, chef Josep Bullick of **La Dama** (☎ 93-202-06-86) turns out a delectable cuisine that rivals many of the top restaurants of Paris. After sampling such dishes as the langoustine salad with orange vinegar, you'll be won over by his bold innovative cuisine. Peerless ingredients and a faultless technique produce such dishes as roast fillet of goat, which may not sound appetizing, but in this chef's hands it becomes a dish of wonder. See chapter 3.

- **Best French Cuisine: Jaume de Provença** (☎ 93-430-00-29) boasts modern French cuisine that's often perfumed with the delicate spices and aromas of Provence. Chef Jaume Bargués enjoys a well-earned reputation as one of Barcelona's finest chefs. Haute cuisine is handled here with deft hands, and imagination and vision go into the constantly changing menus that depend on what's the best and the freshest in any given season. See chapter 3.
- **Best for Creative Cuisine:** Red-haired Mey Hofmann, daughter of a German father and a Catalán mother, lures the most discriminating palates to **Restaurant Hofmann** (☎ 93-319-58-89), in the Barri Gòtic. Her cuisine is the city's most creative, a perfect medley of dishes inspired by both Catalonia and neighboring France. Everything from her *fine tarte* with deboned sardines to her ragout of crayfish with green risotto tastes superb, each dish inventive and based on market-fresh ingredients. See chapter 3.
- **Best Wine List: Neichel** (☎ 93-203-84-08) enjoys a dedicated loyal following, drawn not only to Jean-Louis Neichel's French and Catalán cuisine, but also to the best wine list in the city—a medley of the finest vintages from both France and Catalonia, as well as throughout Spain. The sommelier helpfully guides you to the perfect wine for your meal, which might include fillet of sea bass in a sea urchin cream sauce. He doesn't push the most expensive selections, either. See chapter 3.
- **Best for Late-Night Dining:** The good food at **Els Quatre Gats** (☎ 93-302-41-40) is prepared in an unpretentious style of Catalán cookery called *cucina de mercat* (based on whatever looks fresh at the market that day). This is the most legendary cafe in Barcelona, patronized by the likes of Picasso when he was wandering around the port at the tender age of 18. In the heart of the Barri Gòtic, it becomes particularly animated late at night, serving food and drink until 2am. See chapter 3.
- **Best Picnic Fare:** There's no better place for the makings of a picnic than the **Mercat de la Boquería,** in the center of the Rambles. Also known as the Mercat de Sant Josep, it's one of the world's most extensive produce markets, an attraction in its own right. Dating from 1914, it offers aisle upon aisle of attractively displayed produce from both sea and land. Many of the ingredients are already cooked and prepared, and can be packed for you to carry along in your picnic basket. See chapter 3.
- **Best Local Favorite:** Since 1836, **7 Portes** (☎ 93-319-30-33) has been feeding locals its several variations of paella, including versions with rabbit or with sardines. It offers one of the most extensive menus in Barcelona, and is a classic, mellow place with waiters wearing long white aprons.

6 Best Madrid Hotel Bets

- **Best Historic Hotel:** Inaugurated by Alfonso XIII in 1910, the **Ritz** (☎ 800/225-5843 in the U.S. and Canada, or 91-701-67-67), the gathering place of Madrid society, is still the capital's leading luxury choice. This Edwardian hotel is mellower than ever before, the old haughtiness of former management gone with the wind—it long ago rescinded its policy of not allowing movie stars as guests. The rich and famous continue to parade through its portals; today in the lobby you're likely to encounter nearly anyone, from the secretary-general of NATO to Paloma Picasso. See chapter 5.

- **Best for Business Travelers:** The concierge at the **Park Hyatt Villa Magna** (☎ **800/223-1234** in the U.S. and Canada, or 91-587-12-34) is one of the most skillful in Madrid, well versed in procuring virtually anything a traveler could conceivably need during a trip to the Spanish capital. One floor below lobby level, this five-star hotel's business center is well stocked with access to translators, word processors, fax machines, and photocopiers. There's a branch of Hertz car rental on the premises, and enough stylish conference rooms (staffed with butlers and stocked with caviar if the nature of your business meeting calls for it) to provide a place for any sales or executive meeting. See chapter 5.

- **Best for a Romantic Getaway:** The **Santo Mauro Hotel** (☎ 91-319-69-00) opened in 1991 in a villa built in 1894 for the duke of Santo Mauro. The lavish property has an ageless grace, although it has been brought up to a state-of-the-art condition. In good weather guests retreat to a beautiful garden pavilion and enjoy many facilities such as a gym and indoor pool. It's resort-like in nature, although situated in Madrid. If you can afford it, go for one of the suites with a fireplace. See chapter 5.

- **Best Fashionable Hotel:** A former rundown apartment house, the **Hotel Villa Real** (☎ 91-420-37-67) has blossomed into a fashionable address, opposite the Cortes and next to the Palace Hotel. This is a 19th-century building of classic French architecture. Some of the town's most important movers and shakers can be found in the cocktail bar. A chic rendezvous patronized by the cognoscenti of Spain, it's where you'd invite the duchess of Alba for tea. See chapter 5.

- **Best Hotel Lobby for Pretending You're Rich:** The **Palace Hotel** (☎ 800/325-3535 in the U.S., 800/325-3589 in Canada, or 91-360-80-00), between the Prado and the Cortes, is a Victorian wedding cake of a place. To sit and people-watch in this lobby—the grandest belle époque lobby in Madrid—is to be at the epicenter of Spanish political life. Head for the dazzling stained-glass cupola of the main rotunda lounge, and take in the fanciful ceiling frescoes and the custom-made carpets along the way. See chapter 5.

- **Best for Families:** The family-friendly, chain-run **Novotel Madrid** (☎ 800/221-4542 in the U.S. and Canada, or 91-724-76-00) on the outskirts of town is a good place for the whole clan. Rates are reasonable, and the bedrooms can easily be arranged to sleep children. There's also a pool, and the breakfast buffet is one of the most generous in Madrid. Children 15 and under stay free in their parents' room. See chapter 5.

- **Best Moderately Priced Hotel:** Built in 1966 and still going strong, the reasonably priced **Gran Hotel Colón** (☎ 91-573-59-00) is west of Retiro Park in a relatively safe area of Madrid that's easily connected to the center by subway. It's well maintained and kept up-to-date, offering well-designed bedrooms with comfortably traditional furnishings. See chapter 5.

- **Best Budget Hotel: Hostal Cervantes** (☎ 91-429-27-45) is a family-run hotel that has long been a favorite with Frommer's readers. Reached by a tiny birdcage-style elevator, the hostal is conveniently located near such fabled and pricey citadels as the Palace Hotel—but rates here are amazingly reasonable. True, it's a bit spartan and no breakfast is served, but for the location and the price it's virtually unbeatable. See chapter 5.

- **Best B&B:** Of the numerous budget accommodations housed in a single 19th-century building on the Gran Vía (the main street of Madrid), the **Hostal-Residencia Continental** (☎ 91-521-46-40) is the best. Located on the building's third and fourth floors, this long-established B&B has comfortable, tidy, and recently renovated rooms. See chapter 5.

- **Best Service:** There are grander hotels in Madrid, but it's hard to find a staff as highly motivated, professional, and efficient as the one at the **Castellana Inter-Continental Hotel** (☎ 800/327-0200 in the U.S., or 91-310-02-00). Room service is offered around the clock, and the staff is adept at solving your Madrid-related problems. Nothing seems to make them lose their cool, even when there's a long line at the desk. See chapter 5.
- **Best Location:** The **Gran Hotel Reina Victoria** (☎ 91-531-45-00) is for those who want to be in the heart of Old Madrid, within easy walking distance of all those midtown Hemingway haunts. Dozens of the finest tapas bars are literally at your doorstep, and you can walk among the flower vendors, cigarette peddlers, and lottery-ticket hawkers, enjoying an atmosphere that's missing from the newer and more modern section of Madrid. See chapter 5.
- **Best Hotel Health Club:** The **Ritz** (☎ 800/225-5843 in the U.S. and Canada, or 91-701-67-67) is not only the most historic hotel in Madrid, but it's also got a state-of-the-art fitness center on its top floor. The 1,727-square-foot gym over-looks the Prado Museum, Los Jerónimos Church, and the tree-lined Paseo del Prado. All Ritz guests have complimentary use of most of the center's services and facilities, which include English-speaking professional trainers, the latest exercise equipment, saunas, UVA rays, dressing rooms, showers, lockers, and an outside jogging trail that's open March to October. See chapter 5.
- **Best Hotel Pool:** The swimming pool at the **Meliá Castilla** (☎ 800/336-3542 in the U.S., or 91-567-50-00) isn't the largest in Madrid, but because of the hotel's location in the heart of the city's business district, and because it's an oasis of good service and greenery in an otherwise congested neighborhood, it's a favorite. Set in the center of the hotel's courtyard, with 15 carefully manicured stories rising around it, the pool offers cool refreshments from a nearby bar, snacks and platters from the nearby restaurant, and a welcome calm and quiet after a day navigating the crowds of central Madrid. It's open only to residents of the hotel from April to October. See chapter 5.
- **Best Views:** Often called the Waldorf-Astoria of Spain, the 26-story **Crowne Plaza Madrid City Centre** (☎ 91-547-12-00) has been one of Madrid's massive landmarks since 1953. From its bedroom windows you'll have views of the city skyline. Try for one of the units on the eighth floor with a balcony. See chapter 5.

7 Best Madrid Restaurant Bets

- **Best for a Romantic Dinner:** El Amparo (☎ 91-431-64-56) sits in one of Madrid's most elegant enclaves, with cascading vines on its facade. You can dine grandly, enjoying not only the romantic ambience but also some of the finest food in the city. A sloping skylight bathes the interior with sunlight during the day, and at night lanterns cast soft, flattering glows, making you and your date look luscious. See chapter 5.
- **Best for a Business Lunch:** For decades the influential leaders of Madrid have come to Jockey (☎ 91-319-24-35) to combine power lunches with one of the true gastronomic experiences in Madrid. In spite of increased competition, Jockey is still among the favorite rendezvous sites for heads of state, international celebrities, and diplomats. It's the perfect place to close that business deal with your Spanish partner—he or she will be impressed with your selection. See chapter 5.
- **Best for a Celebration:** At night the whole area around Plaza Mayor becomes one giant Spanish fiesta, with singers, guitar players, and bands of roving

students serenading for their sangría and tapas money. Since 1884 it has always been party night at **Los Galayos** (☎ **91-366-30-28**) too, with tables and chairs set out on the sidewalk for people-watching. The food's good as well—everything from suckling pig to roast lamb. See chapter 5.

- **Best View:** The cafe tables on the terrace of the **Café de Oriente** (☎ **91-541-39-74**) afford one of the most panoramic views in Madrid—a view that takes in everything from the Palacio Real (Royal Palace) to the Teatro Real. Diplomats, even royalty, have patronized this place, known for its good food and attractive belle époque decor, which includes banquettes and regal paneling. See chapter 5.
- **Best Decor:** **Las Cuatro Estaciones** (☎ **91-553-63-05**) has the most spectacular floral displays in Madrid. These flowers, naturally, change with the seasons, so you never know what you'll see when you arrive to dine. The entrance might be filled with hydrangeas, chrysanthemums, or poinsettias. The food is equally superb, but it's the stunningly modern and inviting decor that makes Las Cuatro Estaciones the perfect place for a lavish dinner on the town. See chapter 5.
- **Best for Kids: Foster's Hollywood** (☎ **91-435-61-28**) wins almost handsdown. Since 1971 it has lured kids with Tex-Mex selections, one of the juiciest hamburgers in town, and what a *New York Times* reporter found to be "probably the best onion rings in the world." The atmosphere is fun too, evoking a movie studio with props. See chapter 5.
- **Best Basque Cuisine:** Some food critics regard **Zalacaín** (☎ **91-561-48-40**) as the best restaurant in Madrid. Its name comes from Pio Baroja's 1909 novel, *Zalacaín El Aventuero,* but its cuisine comes straight from heaven. When the maître d' suggests a main dish of cheeks of hake, you might turn away in horror—until you try it. Whatever is served here is sure to be among the finest food you'll taste in Spain—all the foie gras and truffles you desire, but many innovative dishes to tempt the palate as well. See chapter 5.
- **Best American Cuisine:** Not everything on the menu at **La Gamella** (☎ **91-532-45-09**) is American, but what there is here is choice, inspired by California. Owner Dick Stephens, a former choreographer, now runs this prestigious restaurant in the house where the Spanish philosopher Ortega y Gasset was born. Even the king and queen of Spain have tasted the savory fare, which includes everything from an all-American cheesecake to a Caesar salad with strips of marinated anchovies. It's also known for serving what one food critic called, "the only edible hamburger in Madrid," and that palate had tasted the hamburger at Foster's Hollywood (see above). See chapter 5.
- **Best Continental Cuisine:** Although the chef at **El Mentidero de la Villa** (☎ **91-308-12-85**) roams the world for culinary inspirations, much of the cookery is firmly rooted in French cuisine. Continental favorites are updated here and given new twists and flavors, sometimes betraying a Japanese influence. From France come the most perfect noisettes of veal (flavored with fresh tarragon) that you're likely to be served in Spain. Even the Spanish dishes have been brought up-to-date and are lighter and subtler in flavor. See chapter 5.
- **Best Seafood:** On the northern edges of Madrid, **El Cabo Mayor** (☎ **91-350-87-76**) consistently serves the finest and freshest seafood in the country. Members of the royal family are likely to come here for their favorite seafood treats, which might be a savory kettle of fish soup from Cantabria (a province between the Basque country and Asturias), or stewed sea bream flavored with thyme. Even the atmosphere is nautically inspired. See chapter 5.

- **Best Steakhouse:** Spanish steaks at their finest are offered at **Casa Paco** (☎ 91-366-31-66). Señor Paco was the first in Madrid to sear steaks in boiling oil before serving, so that the almost-raw meat continues to cook on the plate, preserving the natural juices. This Old Town favorite also has plenty of atmosphere, and has long been a celebrity favorite as well. See chapter 5.
- **Best Roast Suckling Pig:** Even hard-to-please Hemingway agreed: The roast suckling pig served at **Sobrino de Botín** (☎ 91-366-42-17) since 1725 is the best and most aromatic dish in the Old Town. You'd have to travel to Segovia (home of the specialty) for better fare than this. Under time-aged beams, you can wash down your meal with Valdepeñas or Aragón wine. See chapter 5.
- **Best Wine List:** Although it may no longer be considered the finest restaurant in Madrid, as it once was, **Horcher** (☎ 91-532-35-96) does have one of the city's most laudable wine lists. The cuisine is also just as good as it ever was, but there's so much competition these days that other shining stars have toppled Horcher from its throne. Nevertheless, its wine cellars have won praise from kings and gourmands throughout Europe. It offers not only Spain's best vintages but also those from the rest of the continent. Trust the sommelier: He's one of the best in the business, and his advice is virtually always spot-on. See chapter 5.

8 Best Seville Hotel Bets

- **Best Historic Hotel:** The **Hotel Alfonso XIII** (☎ 800/221-2340 in the U.S. and Canada, or 95-422-28-50), a reproduction of a Spanish palace, opened in 1929 for the Iberoamerican Exposition and was completely remodeled for Expo '92. It has hosted all the leading stars, politicians, and luminaries who have come through Seville over the years—everyone from Jackie Onassis to Grace Kelly to Spain's most famous matadors. It remains the grandest period piece in Andalusia, with an ornate lobby filled with pillars and coffered ceilings. See chapter 8.
- **Best for a Romantic Getaway:** On a hillside in the hamlet of Sanlúcar, 12 miles south of Seville, is the **Hacienda Benazuza** (☎ 95-570-33-44). This manor house on 40 acres boasts one of the most romantic and tranquil settings in all of Andalusia. Operated since 1992 by Basque entrepreneurs, this delightful retreat, with elegant rooms, reflecting pools, and landscaped gardens, offers welcome relief after hot, dusty Seville. See chapter 8.
- **Best for Families:** The **Hotel Doña María** (☎ 95-422-49-90), just steps from the cathedral, is best for families that want a central location so they can walk to all of Seville's major attractions. The hotel is a winner in its own right, with a swimming pool on the upper floor. Many of the rooms are large enough to accommodate families traveling together. Overall, it's a gracious choice with a helpful staff. See chapter 8.
- **Best Moderately Priced Hotel:** The **Residencia y Restaurant Fernando III** (☎ 95-421-77-08) is in Barrio de Santa Cruz, the old Jewish ghetto, reached along a maze of narrow streets. Although the four-story hotel is modern and commercial, its many Andalusian touches convey a cozy atmosphere. The English-speaking staff is helpful and efficient, making this a winning choice. See chapter 8.
- **Best Budget Hotel:** Murillo (☎ 95-421-60-95), in the heart of the Barrio de Santa Cruz, is named after the artist, who used to live in the district. It's close to the gardens of the Alcázar, within walking distance of all of Seville's major attractions. The functional rooms are a good value. This has been the old-quarter favorite of budgeteers for decades. See chapter 8.

- **Best Service:** Seville's most efficient staff—each member polite, professional, and helpful—operates in the **Hotel Inglaterra** (☎ 95-422-49-70), in the heart of town three blocks north of the bullring. Employees welcome guests (most often in English) with friendly smiles; there's 24-hour room service, and every wish (within reason) is fulfilled speedily and efficiently. See chapter 8.
- **Best Location:** The **Bécquer** (☎ 95-422-89-00) enjoys an excellent location, three blocks west of the bullring and two blocks north of the river, in the heart of Seville. Many of the city's best restaurants and attractions can be reached by foot, and numerous tapas bars line the streets surrounding the hotel. The Museo de Bellas Artes is also nearby. See chapter 8.
- **Best Hotel Health Club:** Although Seville's hoteliers were late in discovering the world demand for health clubs in hotels, the **Hotel Meliá Sevilla** (☎ 800/ 336-3542 in the U.S., or 95-442-15-11) responded to the challenge and opened the most professional facility. The staff is very skilled, guiding you through the hotel's array of facilities, ranging from the best sauna and whirlpool in town to a gym and squash courts. There's also a pool. See chapter 8.
- **Best Restoration:** In the historic core of the city, **Casa Imperial** (☎ 95-450-03-00) is a hotel of charm and grace, lovingly restored. In the 15th century, it was the home of the butler to the Marquis of Tarifa, and he lived very well indeed in a setting of sparkling chandeliers and beamed ceilings. See chapter 8.
- **Best Secret Address:** Diners know that the **Taverna del Alabardero** (☎ 95-456-06-37) is one of the city's best restaurants, but those in-the-know also realize it's one of the most charming places to stay in Seville. This restored 19th-century mansion has only seven bedrooms, but they are choice and comfortable, each spaciously and individually decorated in an Andalusian style. See chapter 8.
- **Best Hotel Pool:** On the Isla de la Cartuja, accessible by the Puerta Itálica, **Grand Hotel Barcelo** (☎ 95-446-22-22) was built on the site where Expo '92 took place. Its well-maintained, state-of-the-art outdoor swimming pool is the best in town. It's surrounded by gardens, making it an inviting oasis in the often sweltering heat of Seville. See chapter 8.

9 Best Seville Restaurant Bets

- **Best Andalusian Cuisine:** A small, cozy restaurant, close to the cathedral, **Enrique Becerra** (☎ 95-421-30-49) is a whitewashed house with wrought-iron window grilles that offers the city's best array of traditional Andalusian home-cooked dishes. Other restaurants are more innovative, but Enrique Becerra sticks fast to Sevillian tradition, both in decor and in menu offerings. Try, for example, *jarrete de ternera a la cazuela* (a regional veal stew). Every time-tested favorite is launched by a soothing bowl of gazpacho, and washed down with sangría. See chapter 8.
- **Best Continental Cuisine:** Seville has no finer dining selection than **Egaña Oriza** (☎ 95-422-72-11), located in a restored mansion adjacent to Murillo Park. A chic Basque enclave of nouvelle cuisine, Egaña Oriza features a few Basque specialties, but most of the dishes are rooted in the continental style. The food is innovative and beautifully prepared: Instead of the typical gazpacho with vegetables and olive oil, the preparation here includes succulent Sanlúcar prawns. Steak, for example, comes with foie gras in a grape sauce. See chapter 8.
- **Best Italian Cuisine:** In spite of the name, the **Pizzería San Marco** (☎ 95-421-43-90) serves not just pizza, but a wide array of delectable Italian specialties: among them chicken Parmesan, various forms of scaloppine, and some savory pastas. The cookery has both flavor and flair. See chapter 8.

- **Best Modern Cuisine: Taverna del Alabardero** (☎ 95-456-06-37) serves an Andalusian cuisine, but it's a nouvelle one, imaginatively updated and creative in presentation. Dishes have flair and flavor, everything from spicy peppers stuffed with the pulverized thigh of a bull to an Andalusian white fish set on a compote of aromatic tomatoes flavored with fresh coriander. It's even hosted the king and queen of Spain. The tavern is also a restaurant *avec chambres,* renting seven beautifully and traditionally furnished bedrooms. See chapter 8.
- **Best Pizza:** The **Pizzería San Marco** wins again; see "Best Italian Cuisine," above. See chapter 8.
- **Best Seafood: La Isla** (☎ 95-421-26-31), in the Arenal district, is the place to go for the freshest fish. Though Seville is inland, fish is rushed to the restaurant from the Huelva or Cádiz coasts, and more exotic catches are flown in from Galicia, in the northwest. Many of the fish dishes are based on traditional Galician cooking methods. The *parrillada de mariscos y pescados,* a fish and seafood grill for two people, is the best dish on the menu. See chapter 8.
- **Best Fast Food:** The **Cervecería Giralda** (☎ 95-422-74-35) serves not only the best fast food in town, but it's also the most conveniently located eatery, lying near such attractions as the cathedral, the Alcázar, and Giralda Tower. If you're in a hurry, ask for one of the *platos combinados* (combination plates), which are most filling and are served quickly without a long wait. See chapter 8.
- **Best View:** The **Río Grande** (☎ 95-427-39-56) is a classic Sevillian restaurant with large terraces opening onto the Guadalquivir River. Near Plaza de Cuba in front of the Torre del Oro, it has the most panoramic view in town. Although many diners find the vista absorbing, the restaurant's Andalusian cuisine is also delightful, prepared with old-fashioned care. Here are all the matador favorites— everything from bull tail Andalusian to garlic-chicken Giralda, the latter dish dedicated to the tower adjoining the cathedral. See chapter 8.
- **Best for Kids:** Next door to the more fabled Río Grande, the multilevel **El Puerto** (☎ 95-427-17-25) also has an alfresco terrace opening onto the river. It features the most reasonably priced *cubiertos* (fixed-price menus) in town. Fresh seafood is a special treat here. There's also a cafeteria bar. See chapter 8.
- **Best Outdoor Dining:** See the **Río Grande** ("Best View," above) and **Hostería del Laurel** ("Best Local Favorite," below). See chapter 8.
- **Best Local Favorite:** In the heart of the Barrio de Santa Cruz, the **Hostería del Laurel** (☎ 95-422-02-95) is one of the most enduring restaurants in town, long popular with visitors and locals alike. In summer patrons can dine on an outdoor terrace on the square. The decor is old-fashioned—white walls, leather-backed chairs, and heavy wooden tables. The food is traditional Spanish fare, with many Andalusian specialties. See chapter 8.
- **Best Spot to Meet a Matador: El Burladero,** in the Hotel Tryp Colón (☎ 95-422-29-00), is the local favorite of visiting matadors. The bullring in Seville often draws the country's biggest stars. They like to relax and unwind here in a setting devoted to the memorabilia of their trade. Photographs adorning the walls trace the history of bullfighting. Even the name of the restaurant comes from the wooden barricades in the ring where bullfighters can escape the charge of an enraged bull. See chapter 8.

Planning a Trip to Barcelona, Madrid & Seville

This chapter is devoted to the where, when, and how of your trip—the advance planning required to get it together and take it on the road.

1 Visitor Information & Entry Requirements

VISITOR INFORMATION

TOURIST OFFICES You can begin your info search with Spain's tourist offices located in the following places:

In the United States For information before you go, contact the **Tourist Office of Spain,** 666 Fifth Ave., 5th Floor, New York, NY 10103 (☎ 212/265-8822). It can provide sightseeing information, events calendars, train and ferry schedules, and more. Elsewhere in the United States, branches of the Tourist Office of Spain are located at: 8383 Wilshire Blvd., Suite 956, Beverly Hills, CA 90211 (☎ 323/658-7188); 845 N. Michigan Ave., Suite 915E, Chicago, IL 60611 (☎ 312/642-1992); and 1221 Brickell Ave., Suite 1850, Miami, FL 33131 (☎ 305/358-1992).

In Canada Contact the **Tourist Office of Spain,** 102 Bloor St. W., 14th Floor, Toronto, Ontario M5S 1M9, Canada (☎ 416/961-3131).

In Great Britain Write to the **Spanish National Tourist Office,** 22–23 Manchester Square, London W1M 5AP (☎ 020/7486-8077).

WEB SITES On the Net you can find lots of great information at the following sites:

Spain in General Tourist Office of Spain (www.okspain.org), **All About Spain** (www.red2000.com), **Cybersp@in** (www.cyberspain.com).

Barcelona **Barcelona: A Different Point of View** (http://members.xroom.com/barcy), **Barcelona Prestige** (www.bcn-guide.com), **Time Out: Barcelona** (www.timeout.com/barcelona), **Transports Metropolitans de Barcelona** (www.tmb.net/weleng.htm).

Madrid **Madrid by All About Spain** (www.red2000.com/spain/madrid), **Madridman** (www.madridman.com), **Time Out: Madrid** (www.timeout.com/madrid), **Soft Guide Madrid** (www.softguides.com/index_madrid.html), **Web Madrid** (www.webmadrid.com).

Seville   Sevilla On Line (www.sol.com), **Andalucia.com** (www.andalucia.com), **Andalucia: There's Only One** (www.andalucia.org).

ENTRY REQUIREMENTS

PASSPORTS   A valid passport is all that an American, British, Canadian, or New Zealand citizen needs to enter Spain, and one can be secured as follows. (Australians, however, need a visa—see below.)

In the United States   You can apply for passports in person at one of 13 regional offices or by mail. To apply, you'll need a passport application form, available at U.S. post offices and federal court offices, and proof of citizenship, such as a birth certificate or naturalization papers; an expired passport is also accepted. First-time applicants for passports pay $60 ($40 if under 18 years of age). Persons 18 or older who have an expired passport that's not more than 12 years old can reapply by mail. The old passport must be submitted along with new photographs and a pink renewal form (DSP-82).

If your expired passport is more than 12 years old, or if it was granted to you before your 16th birthday, you must apply in person. The fee is $40. Call ☎ **202/647-0518** at any time for information. You can also write to Passport Service, Office of Correspondence, Department of State, 1111 19th St., NW, Suite 510, Washington, DC 20522-1075. Information can also be obtained on the Internet at **http://travel. state.gov** or by calling the **National Passport Information Center (NPIC)** at ☎ **900/225-5674.** The cost is 35¢ per minute for 24-hour automated service, or $1.05 per minute 9am to 3pm for live operator service.

In Canada   Citizens may go to one of 28 regional offices located in major cities. Alternatively, you can mail your application to the Passport Office, External Affairs and International Trade Canada, Ottawa, ON K1A 0G3. Post offices have application forms. Passports cost C$60, and proof of Canadian citizenship is required, along with two signed identical passport-size photographs. Passports are valid for five years. For more information, call ☎ **800/567-6868.**

In Great Britain   British subjects may apply to one of the regional offices in Liverpool, Newport, Glasgow, Peterborough, Belfast, or London. You can also apply in person at a main post office. The fee is £21, and the passport is good for 10 years. Two photos must accompany the application. For more information regarding fees, documentation requirements, and to ask for an emergency passport, telephone the London Passport office at ☎ **020/7271-3000.**

In Australia   Citizens may apply at the nearest post office. Provincial capitals and other major cities have passport offices. Application fees are subject to review every three months. Call ☎ **02/13-12-32** for the latest information. Australians must pay for a departure tax stamp costing A$20 at a post office or airport; children 11 and under are exempt. Australian citizens will also need a visa to enter Spain. Apply at a Spanish consulate well before departure time. Spanish consulates are located at 31 Market St., Sydney, NSW 2000 (☎ **02/9261-2433**), and at 766 Elizabeth St., Melbourne, VIC 3000 (☎ **03/9347-1966**).

In New Zealand   Citizens may go to their nearest consulate or passport office to obtain an application, which may be filed in person or by mail. To obtain a 10-year passport, proof of citizenship is required, plus a fee of NZ$80. Passports are processed at the New Zealand Passport Office, Documents of National Identity Division, Department of Internal Affairs, P.O. Box 10-526, Wellington (☎ **0800/ 22-50-50**).

In Ireland   Contact the passport office at Setna Centre, Molesworth St., Dublin 2 (☎ **01/671-16-33**). The charge is IR£45. Applications are sent by mail. Irish citizens living in North America can contact the Irish Embassy, 2234 Massachusetts Ave., NW, Washington, DC 20008 (☎ **202/462-3939**). The embassy can issue a new passport or direct you to one of three North American consulates that have jurisdiction over a particular region; the charge is US$80.

CUSTOMS   You can take into Spain most personal effects and the following items duty-free: two still cameras and 10 rolls of film per camera, tobacco for personal use, 1 liter each of liquor and wine, a portable radio, a tape recorder, a typewriter, a bicycle, sports equipment, fishing gear, and two hunting weapons with 100 cartridges each.

Returning to Your Home Country   Returning **U.S. citizens** who have been away for 48 hours or more are allowed to bring back, once every 30 days, US$400 worth of merchandise duty-free. You'll be charged a flat rate of 10% duty on the next US$1,000 worth of purchases. Be sure to have your receipts handy. On gifts, the duty-free limit is US$100. For more specific guidance, write to the **U.S. Customs Service,** P.O. Box 7407, Washington, DC 20044 (☎ **202/927-6724**), requesting the free pamphlet *Know Before You Go.* You can also download the pamphlet from the Internet at **www.customs.ustreas.gov/ travel/kbygo.htm**.

Citizens of **Canada** can write for the booklet *I Declare,* issued by **Revenue Canada,** 2265 St. Laurent Blvd., Ottawa K1G 4KE (☎ **800/461-9999** or 506/636-5064). Canada allows its citizens a C$750 exemption, and you are allowed to bring back duty-free 200 cigarettes, 2.2 pounds of tobacco, 40 imperial ounces (1.2 qt.) of liquor, and 50 cigars. In addition, you are allowed to mail gifts to Canada from abroad at the rate of C$60 a day, provided they are unsolicited and aren't alcohol or tobacco (write on the package: "Unsolicited gift, under $60 value"). All valuables should be declared on the Y-38 Form before departure from Canada, including serial numbers of, for example, expensive foreign cameras that you already own. *Note:* The C$750 exemption can be used only once a year and only after an absence of at least 7 days.

If you're a citizen of the **United Kingdom,** you can buy wine, spirits, or cigarettes in an ordinary shop in any other European Union country and bring home *almost* as much as you like. (U.K. Customs and Excise does set theoretical limits.) But if you buy your goods in a duty-free shop, then the old rules still apply—you're allowed to bring home 200 cigarettes and 2 liters of table wine, plus 1 liter of spirits or 2 liters of fortified wine. If you're returning home from a non-EU country, the same allowances apply, and you must declare any goods in excess of these allowances. British customs tends to be strict and complicated in its requirements. For details, get in touch with **Her Majesty's Customs and Excise Office,** Dorset House, Stamford Street, London SE1 9PY (☎ **020/8910-3744;** fax 020/7202-4131).

The duty-free allowance in **Australia** is A$400 or, for those under 18, A$200. Australian citizens are allowed to mail gifts to Australia from abroad duty-free to a limit of A$200 per parcel. There are no other restrictions on unsolicited gifts; however, you could be subject to a customs investigation if you send multiple parcels of the same gift to the same address. Upon returning to Australia, citizens can bring in 250 cigarettes or 250 grams of loose tobacco, and 1,125 milliliters of alcohol. If you're returning with valuable goods you already own, such as foreign-made cameras, you should file form B263. A helpful brochure, available from Australian consulates or customs offices, is *Know Before You Go.* For more information, contact **Australian Customs Services,** GPO Box 8, Sydney NSW 2001 (☎ **02/9213-2000**).

The duty-free allowance for **New Zealand** is NZ$700. New Zealanders are allowed to mail gifts to New Zealand from abroad duty-free to a limit of NZ$70 per parcel. Beware of sending multiple parcels of the same gift to the same address; a customs investigation could await your return home. Citizens over 17 years of age can bring in

200 cigarettes, or 50 cigars, or 250 grams of tobacco (or a mixture of all three if their combined weight doesn't exceed 250 grams); plus 4.5 liters of wine and beer, or 1.125 liters of liquor. New Zealand currency does not carry import or export restrictions. Fill out a certificate of export, listing the valuables you are taking out of the country; that way, you can bring them back without paying duty. Most questions are answered in a free pamphlet available at New Zealand consulates and Customs offices: *New Zealand Customs Guide for Travellers,* Notice no. 4. For more information, contact **New Zealand Customs,** 50 Anzac Ave., P.O. Box 29, Auckland (☎ **9/ 359-66-55**).

Ireland allows its citizens to bring in 200 cigarettes or 100 cigarillos or 50 cigars or 250 grams (8.8 oz.) of tobacco, plus 1 liter (1.1 qt.) of liquor exceeding 22% by volume (such as whisky, brandy, gin, rum, or vodka), or 2 liters of distilled beverages and spirits with a wine or alcoholic base of an alcoholic strength not exceeding 22% by volume, plus 2 liters of other wine and 50 grams (1.8 oz.) of perfume. Other allowances include duty-free goods to a value of IR£73 (US$116.80) per person or IR£36.50 (US$58.40) per person for travelers under 15 years of age. For more information, contact **The Revenue Commissioners,** Dublin Castle, Dublin 2 (☎ **01/ 679-27-77**).

2 Money

CURRENCY

The basic unit of Spanish currency is the **peseta** (abbreviated **pta.**), currently worth about 6/10 of a cent in U.S. currency. One dollar was worth about 165 pesetas at press time. Coins come in 1, 5, 25, 50, 100, 200, and 500 pesetas. Notes are issued in 500, 1,000, 5,000, and 10,000 pesetas.

Many hotels in Spain don't accept dollar- or pound-denominated checks; those that do will almost certainly charge for the conversion. In some cases, they'll accept countersigned traveler's checks or a credit card, but if you're prepaying a deposit on hotel reservations, it's cheaper and easier to pay with a check drawn on a Spanish bank.

This can be arranged by a large commercial bank or by a specialist such as **Ruesch International,** 700 11th St. NW, 4th Floor, Washington, DC 20001-4507 (☎ **800/ 424-2923**), which performs a wide variety of conversion-related tasks, usually for only US$5 to US$15 per transaction.

If you need a check payable in pesetas, call Ruesch's toll-free number, describe what you need, and note the transaction number given to you. Mail your dollar-denominated personal check (payable to Ruesch International) to the address above. Upon receiving this, the company will mail a check denominated in pesetas for the financial equivalent, minus the US$2 charge. The company can also help you with many different kinds of wire transfers and conversions of VAT (value-added tax, known as IVA in Spain), refund checks, and also will mail brochures and information packets on request. Brits can contact **Ruesch International Ltd.,** 18 Saville Row, London W1X 2AD (☎ **0171/734-2300**).

ATM NETWORKS

PLUS, Cirrus, and other networks connecting automated-teller machines operate in Spain. If your bank card has been programmed with a PIN (personal identification number), it is likely that you can use your card at ATMs abroad to withdraw money directly from your home bank account. Check with your bank to see if your PIN code must be reprogrammed for usage in Spain. Before leaving, always determine the frequency limits for withdrawals, and what fees, if any, your bank will assess. For Cirrus locations abroad, call ☎ **800/424-7787** or check MasterCard's Web site at

The Spanish Peseta

For American Readers   At this writing, US$1 = approximately 165 pesetas (or 1 peseta = $^6/_{10}$ of 1 U.S. cent). This was the rate of exchange used to calculate the dollar equivalents given throughout this edition.

For British Readers   At this writing, £1 = approximately 265 pesetas (or 1 peseta = $^4/_{10}$ of 1 pence). This was the rate of exchange used to calculate the pound values in the table below.

The Euro   At this writing, one euro = approximately 166 pesetas. Although it wasn't in particularly widespread use at the time of the compilation of this chart, look for an increasing emphasis on the euro and its applicability to daily life within Spain.

Note: Because the exchange rate fluctuates from time to time according to a complicated roster of political and economic factors, this table should be used only as a general guide.

Peseta	U.S.$	U.K.£	Euro	Peseta	U.S.$	U.K.£	Euro
50	0.30	0.20	0.30	10,000	60.00	40.00	60.00
100	0.60	0.40	0.60	15,000	90.00	60.00	90.00
300	1.80	1.20	1.80	20,000	120.00	80.00	120.00
500	3.00	2.00	3.00	25,000	150.00	100.00	150.00
700	4.20	2.80	4.20	30,000	180.00	120.00	180.00
1,000	6.00	4.00	6.00	35,000	210.00	140.00	210.00
1,500	9.00	6.00	9.00	40,000	240.00	160.00	240.00
2,000	12.00	8.00	12.00	45,000	270.00	180.00	270.00
3,000	18.00	12.00	18.00	50,000	300.00	200.00	300.00
4,000	24.00	16.00	24.00	100,000	600.00	400.00	600.00
5,000	30.00	20.00	30.00	125,000	750.00	500.00	600.00
7,500	45.00	30.00	45.00	150,000	900.00	600.00	900.00

www.mastercard.com. For PLUS usage abroad, contact your local bank or check Visa's Web site at www.visa.com.

TRAVELER'S CHECKS

Although ATM usage is becoming increasingly commonplace, many people prefer the security of traveler's checks. Purchase them before leaving home and arrange to carry some ready cash (usually about US$250, depending on your needs). In the event of theft, if the checks are properly documented, the value of your checks will be refunded. Most large banks sell traveler's checks, charging fees that average between 1% and 2% of the value of the checks you buy, although some out-of-the-way banks, in rare instances, have charged as much as 7%. If your bank wants more than a 2% commission, call the traveler's check issuers directly for the address of outlets where this commission will cost less.

   American Express (☎ **800/221-8472** in the U.S. and Canada) is one of the largest and most immediately recognized issuers of traveler's checks. No commission is charged to members of the AAA and to holders of certain types of American Express credit cards. The company issues checks denominated in U.S. dollars, Canadian dollars, and British pounds, among other currencies. The vast majority of checks sold in North America are denominated in U.S. dollars. For questions or problems that arise outside the United States or Canada, contact any of the company's many regional representatives.

Citicorp (☎ **800/336-8472** in the U.S. and Canada, or 813/623-1709, collect, from other parts of the world) issues checks in U.S. dollars as well as British pounds. **Thomas Cook** (☎ **800/223-7373** in the U.S., or 609/987-7300, collect, from other parts of the world) issues MasterCard traveler's checks denominated in U.S. dollars, British pounds, Spanish pesetas, and Australian dollars. Depending on individual banking laws in each of the various states, some of these currencies may not be available in every outlet. **Interpayment Services** (☎ **800/221-2426** in the U.S. and Canada, or 212/858-8500 from most other parts of the world) sells Visa checks sponsored by a consortium of member banks and the Thomas Cook organization. Traveler's checks can be denominated in U.S. or Canadian dollars or British pounds.

CREDIT CARDS

American Express, Visa, and **Diners Club** are widely recognized in Spain. If you see the **EuroCard** or **Access** sign on an establishment, it means that it accepts **Master-Card. Discover** cards are accepted only in the United States.

3 When to Go

CLIMATE

Spring and fall are ideal times to visit any of these cities. May and October are the best months, in terms of both weather and crowds. In our view, however, the balmy month of May (with an average temperature of 61°F) is the most glorious time for making your own discovery of Barcelona, Madrid, or Seville.

In summer it's hot, hot, and hotter still, with the cities in Castile (Madrid) and Andalusia (Seville and Córdoba) stewing up the most scalding brew. Madrid has dry heat; the temperature can hover around 84° in July, 75° in September. Seville has the dubious reputation of being the hottest part of Spain in July and August, often baking under *average* temperatures as high as 93°.

Barcelona, cooler in temperature, is often quite humid. The overcrowded Costa Brava has temperatures around 81° in July and August.

August remains the major vacation month in Europe. The traffic from France, the Netherlands, and Germany to Spain becomes a veritable migration, and low-cost hotels along the coastal areas are virtually impossible to find. To compound the problem, many restaurants and shops also decide that it's time for a vacation, thereby limiting the visitor's selections for both dining and shopping.

HOLIDAYS

Holidays include January 1 (New Year's Day), January 6 (Feast of the Epiphany), March 19 (Feast of St. Joseph), Good Friday, Easter Monday, May 1 (May Day), June 10 (Corpus Christi), June 29 (Feast of St. Peter and St. Paul), July 25 (Feast of St. James), August 15 (Feast of the Assumption), October 12 (Spain's National Day), November 1 (All Saints' Day), December 8 (Immaculate Conception), and December 25 (Christmas).

No matter how large or small, every city or town in Spain also celebrates its local saint's day. In Madrid it's May 15 (St. Isidro). You'll rarely know what the local holidays are in your next destination in Spain. Try to keep money on hand, because you may arrive in town only to find banks and stores closed. In some cases, intercity bus services are suspended on holidays.

Calendar of Events: Barcelona, Madrid & Seville

The dates given below may not be precise. Sometimes the exact days may not be announced until six weeks before the actual festival. Check with the National Tourist Office of Spain (see "Visitor Information," at the beginning of this chapter) if you're planning to attend a specific event.

January

- **Three Kings Day (Día de los Reyes),** Barcelona. Parades are staged throughout the main arteries of old Barcelona in anticipation of the Feast of the Epiphany (January 6). Parades usually take place on January 5 or 6.

February

- **ARCO** (Madrid's International Contemporary Art Fair), Madrid. One of the biggest draws on Spain's cultural calendar, this exhibit showcases the best in contemporary art from Europe and America. At the Crystal Pavilion of the Casa de Campo, the exhibition draws galleries from throughout Europe, the Americas, Australia, and Asia, who bring with them the works of regional and internationally known artists. To buy tickets, you can contact El Corte Ingles at ☎ **91-418-88-00,** or Madrid Rock at ☎ **91-547-24-23.** The cost is between 5,000 ptas. (US$30) and 6,000 ptas. (US$36). You can get schedules from the tourist office closer to the event. Dates vary, but usually mid-February.

- **Madrid Carnaval.** The carnival kicks off with a big parade along the Paseo de la Castellana, culminating in a masked ball at the Círculo de Bellas Artes on the following night. Fancy-dress competitions last until February 28, when the festivities end with a tear-jerking "burial of a sardine" at the Fuente de los Pajaritos in the Casa de Campo. This is followed that evening by a concert in the Plaza Mayor. Call ☎ **91-429-31-77** for more information. Dates vary.

- **Salon de Anticuarios en Barcelona.** This giant antiques fair is usually held from late February to mid-March in the Feria de Barcelona.

March

- **Marathon Catalunya,** Barcelona. This annual marathon begins in Mataró, winds its way through the city, and ends at the Olympic Stadium in Montjuïc. Usually in mid-March.

April

- **Bullfights.** Holy week traditionally kicks off the season all over Spain, especially in Madrid and Seville. Although not as popular in Barcelona as in the rest of the country, this national pastime affords the visitor an unparalleled insight into the Spanish temperament.

- ✪ **Semana Santa (Holy Week),** Seville. Though many of the country's smaller towns stage similar celebrations, the festivities in Seville are by far the most elaborate. From Palm Sunday until Easter Sunday, a series of processions with hooded penitents moves to the piercing wail of the *saeta,* a love song to the Virgin or Christ. *Pasos* (heavy floats) bear images of the Virgin or Christ. Make hotel reservations way in advance. Call the Seville Office of Tourism for details (☎ **95-422-14-04**). Mid-April.

- ✪ **Feria de Sevilla (Seville Fair).** This is the most celebrated week of revelry in the country, with all-night flamenco dancing, merrymaking in *casetas* (entertainment booths), bullfights, horseback riding, flower-decked coaches, and dancing in the streets. You'll need to reserve a hotel early for this one. For general information and exact festival dates, contact the Office of Tourism in Seville (☎ **95-422-14-04**). Mid-April.

- **Festivat de Sant Jordi** and **Parades de Libres I Roses,** Barcelona. On the feast day of Catalonia's patron saint, Sant Jordi, citizens of Barcelona shower each other with books and roses. April 23.

May

○ **Fiesta de San Isidro,** Madrid. Madrileños run wild with a 10-day celebration honoring their city's patron saint. Food fairs, Castilian folkloric events, street parades, parties, music, dances, bullfights, and other festivities mark the occasion. Make hotel reservations early. Expect crowds and traffic (and beware of pickpockets). For information, write to Oficina Municipal de Información y Turismo, Plaza Mayor, 3, 28014 Madrid, or call ☎ 91-429-31-77. May 12 to 21.

- **Fira del Libre de Barcelona.** This annual book fair is located primarily on the Passeig de Grácia in Barcelona. Late May to early June.

June

- **Corpus Christi,** all over Spain. A major holiday on the Spanish calendar, this event is marked by big processions, especially in such cathedral cities as Toledo, Málaga, Seville, and Granada. June 14.

- **Verbena de Sant Joan,** Barcelona. This traditional festival occupies all Cataláns. Barcelona literally "lights up," with fireworks, bonfires, and dances until dawn. The highlight of the festival is the fireworks show at Montjuïc. Dates vary.

July

- **Veranos de la Villa,** Madrid. Called "the summer binge" of Madrid, this program presents folkloric dancing, pop music, classical music, zarzuelas, and flamenco at various venues throughout the city. Open-air cinema is a feature in the Parque del Retiro. Ask at the various tourist offices for complete details (the program changes every summer). Sometimes admission is charged, but often these events are free. Mid-July until the end of August.

August

- **Fiestas of Lavapiés and La Paloma,** Madrid. These two fiestas begin with the Lavapiés on August 1 and continue through the hectic La Paloma celebration on August 15, the day of the Virgen de la Paloma. Thousands of people race through the narrow streets. Apartment dwellers hurl buckets of cold water onto the crowds below to cool them off. Children's games, floats, music, flamenco, and zarzuelas, along with street fairs, mark the occasion. For more information, call ☎ 91-429-31-77. August 1 to 15.

September

- **Diada,** Barcelona. This is the most significant festival in Catalonia. It celebrates the region's autonomy from the rest of Spain, following years of repression under the dictator Franco. Demonstrations and flag-waving events take place. The *senyera,* the flag of Catalonia, is much in evidence. Not your typical tourist fare, but interesting nevertheless. September 11.

- **Fiesta de la Mercé,** Barcelona. The city abounds with various musical and theatrical performances in honor of one of the city's patron saints, the Virgin de la Mercé. Shows are staged throughout Barcelona. A pageant and fireworks display signal the end of the festival. Week of September 25.

October

○ **Autumn Festival,** Madrid. Both Spanish and international artists participate in this cultural program, with a series of operatic, ballet, dance, music, and theatrical performances. From Strasbourg to Tokyo, this event is a premier attraction, yet ticket prices are reasonable. Make hotel reservations early, and for tickets write to **Festival de Otoño,** Plaza de España, 8, 28008 Madrid (☎ **91-580-25-75**). Late October to late November.

- **Grape Harvest Festival,** Jerez de la Frontera. The major wine festival in Andalusia honors the famous sherry of Jerez, with 5 days of processions, flamenco dancing, bullfights, livestock on parade, and, of course, sherry drinking. For information, call ☎ **956-333-11-50.** Mid-October (dates vary).

November

- **All Saints' Day,** Seville. This holy day is celebrated all over Spain, but the citizens of Seville show a certain fervor in lamenting the souls of the dead, as family and friends place wreaths and garlands on their graves. November 1.
- **Festival Internacional de Jazz de Barcelona.** The festival lasts all month, and locations for this jazz festival change yearly. For information, call ☎ **93-304-34-21.**

December

- **Día de los Santos Inocentes,** Seville. Another countrywide holiday celebrated with particular gusto in sunny Seville. On this day, the Spanish play many practical jokes and in general do *loco* things to one another—it's the Spanish equivalent of April Fools' Day. December 28.

4 Health & Insurance

HEALTH

Barcelona, Madrid, and Seville shouldn't pose any major health hazards. The overly rich cuisine—garlic, olive oil, and wine—may give some travelers mild diarrhea, so take along some anti-diarrhea medicine, moderate your eating habits, and, even though the water is generally safe, drink bottled water only. Fish and shellfish from the horrendously polluted Mediterranean should only be eaten cooked.

If you need a doctor, ask your hotel to locate one for you. You can also obtain a list of English-speaking doctors in Spain from the **International Association for Medical Assistance to Travelers (IAMAT),** in the United States at 417 Center St., Lewiston, NY 14092 (☎ **716/754-4883**); and in Canada at 40 Regal Rd., Guelph, ON N1K 1B5 (☎ **519/836-0102**).

If you have a chronic medical condition, talk to your doctor before taking an international trip. He or she may have specific advice to give you. For conditions such as epilepsy, heart problems, and diabetes, wear a Medic Alert Identification Tag; it immediately alerts any doctor to the nature of your condition and provides a 24-hour hotline phone number, enabling a foreign doctor to obtain medical records for you. The initial membership costs $35, and there is a $15 annual fee. Contact the **Medic Alert Foundation,** 2323 Colorado, Turlock, CA 95381-1009 (☎ **800/825-3785**).

Take all vital medicines with you in your carry-on luggage, and bring enough to last you during your stay. Also bring copies of each prescription written with the generic name, not the brand name, of the drug you're taking. It's a good idea to bring a sunscreen with a high SPF, since the sun can be intense, especially in Seville.

INSURANCE

Before purchasing any additional insurance, check your homeowner's, automobile, and medical insurance policies, as well as the insurance provided by your credit-card companies and auto and travel clubs. You may have adequate off-premises theft coverage; your credit-card company may even provide cancellation coverage if the ticket is paid for with its card.

Remember: Medicare only covers U.S. citizens traveling in Mexico and Canada. Also note that to submit any claim you must always have thorough documentation, including all receipts, police reports, medical records, and such.

If you're prepaying for your vacation or are taking a charter or any other flight that has cancellation penalties, look into cancellation insurance. Most companies listed below offer insurance packages that include provisions for lost luggage, medical coverage, emergency evacuation, accidental death, and trip cancellation. Call for policy specifics.

Among the firms to try are **Travel Guard International,** 1145 Clark St., Stevens Point, WI 54481 (☎ **800/826-1300**); **Travelex** (Tele-Trip), Mutual of Omaha Plaza, Omaha, NE 68175 (☎ **800/228-9792**); **MEDEX International,** c/o Wallach & Co., 107 W. Federal St. (P.O. Box 480), Middleburg, VA 22117-0480 (☎ **888/ MEDEX-00** or 410/453-6300); **Access America,** 6600 W. Broad St., Richmond, VA 23230 (☎ **800/284-8300**); **Travel Assistance International** by Worldwide Assistance Services, Inc., 1133 15th St. NW, Suite 400, Washington, DC 20005 (☎ **800/821-2828** or 202/828-5894); and **Travel Insured International, Inc.,** P.O. Box 280568, East Hartford, CT 06128-0568 (☎ **800/243-3174** in the U.S., or 860/528-7663).

5 Tips for Travelers with Special Needs

FOR TRAVELERS WITH DISABILITIES

Because of Spain's many hills and endless flights of stairs, visitors with disabilities may have difficulty getting around the country. But conditions are slowly improving: Newer hotels are more sensitive to the needs of persons with disabilities, and the more expensive restaurants are generally wheelchair-accessible. However, since most places have very limited, if any, facilities for people with disabilities, consider taking an organized tour specifically designed to accommodate such travelers.

For the names and addresses of such tour operators as well as other related information, contact the **Society for the Advancement of Travel for the Handicapped,** 347 Fifth Ave., New York, NY 10016 (☎ **212/447-7284**). Annual membership dues are $45, or $30 for seniors and students.

You can also obtain a free copy of *Air Transportation of Handicapped Persons,* published by the U.S. Department of Transportation. Write for Free Advisory Circular No. AC12032, Distribution Unit, U.S. Department of Transportation, Publications Division, M-4332, Washington, DC 20590.

For the blind or visually impaired, the best source is the **American Foundation for the Blind,** 15 W. 16th St., New York, NY 10011 (☎ **800/232-5463** to order information kits and supplies, or 212/502-7600). It offers information on travel and various requirements for the transport and border formalities for Seeing Eye dogs. It also issues identification cards to those who are legally blind.

One of the best organizations serving the needs of persons with disabilities (wheelchairs and walkers) is **Flying Wheels Travel,** 143 West Bridge, P.O. Box 382, Owatonna, MN 55060 (☎ **800/535-6790** or 507/451-5005), which offers various escorted tours and cruises internationally.

For a $35 annual fee, consider joining **Mobility International USA,** P.O. Box 10767, Eugene, OR 97440 (☎ **541/343-1284** voice & TDD). It answers questions on various destinations and also offers discounts on videos, publications, and programs it sponsors.

If you're flying around Spain, the airline and ground staff will help you on and off planes and reserve seats for you with sufficient legroom, but it is essential to arrange for this assistance *in advance* by contacting your airline.

For British Travelers with Disabilities   The annual vacation guide *Holidays and Travel Abroad* costs £5 from **Royal Association for Disability and Rehabilitation** (RADAR), Unit 12, City Forum, 250 City Rd., London EC1V 8AF (☎ **020/ 7250-3222**). RADAR also provides a number of information packets on such subjects as sports and outdoor vacations, insurance, financial arrangements for persons with disabilities, and accommodations in nursing care units for groups or for the elderly. Each of these fact sheets is available for £2. Both the fact sheets and the holiday guides can be mailed outside the United Kingdom for a nominal postage fee.

Another good service is the **Holiday Care Service,** 2nd Floor Imperial Buildings, Victoria Road, Horley, Surrey RH6 7PZ (☎ **01293/774-535;** fax 01293/784-647), a national charity that advises on accessible accommodations for elderly people or those with disabilities. Annual membership costs £15 (U.K. residents) and £30 (abroad). Once you're a member, you can receive a newsletter and access to a free reservations network for hotels throughout Britain and, to a lesser degree, Europe and the rest of the world.

FOR GAYS & LESBIANS

In 1978 Spain legalized homosexuality among consenting adults. In April 1995, the parliament of Spain banned discrimination based on sexual orientation. Madrid and Barcelona are the major gay centers of the country. The leading gay resort is Sitges, south of Barcelona.

To learn about gay and lesbian travel in Spain, you can secure publications or join data-dispensing organizations before you go. *Frommer's Gay & Lesbian Europe* has fabulous chapters on both Madrid and Barcelona, as well as Sitges and Ibiza. Men can order *Spartacus,* the international gay guide, or *Odysseus 2001: The International Gay Travel Planner,* a guide to international gay accommodations. Both lesbians and gay men might want to pick up a copy of *Gay Travel A to Z,* which provides general information as well as listings for bars, hotels, restaurants, and places of interest for gay travelers throughout the world.

Our World, 1104 N. Nova Rd., Suite 251, Daytona Beach, FL 32117 (☎ **904/ 441-5367**), is a magazine devoted to options and bargains for gay and lesbian travel worldwide. It costs $35 for 10 issues. *Out and About,* 8 W. 19th St., Suite 401, New York, NY 10011 (☎ **800/929-2268**), has been hailed for its "straight" reporting about gay travel. It profiles the best gay or gay-friendly hotels, gyms, clubs, and other places, with coverage of destinations throughout the world. It costs $49 a year for 10 information-packed issues. It aims for the most upscale gay male traveler, and has been praised by everybody from *Travel & Leisure* to the *New York Times.*

The **International Gay Travel Association (IGTA),** 4331 N. Federal, Suite 304, Ft. Lauderdale, FL 33308 (☎ **800/448-8550** or 954/776-2626), encourages gay and lesbian travel worldwide. With around 1,200 member agencies, it specializes in networking travelers with the appropriate gay-friendly service organization or tour specialist. It offers a quarterly newsletter, marketing mailings, and a membership directory that is updated four times a year. Travel agents who are IGTA members will be tied into this organization's vast information resources.

FOR SENIORS

Many discounts are available for seniors, but often you need to be a member of an association to obtain them.

For information before you go, write for the free booklet, *101 Tips for the Mature Traveler,* available from **Grand Circle Travel,** 347 Congress St., Suite 3A, Boston, MA 02210 (☎ **800/221-2610** or 617/350-7500).

One of the most dynamic travel organizations for seniors is **Elderhostel,** 75 Federal St., Boston, MA (☎ **877/426-8056**). Established in 1975, it operates an array of programs throughout Europe, including Spain. Most courses last around three weeks and are a good value, since they include airfare, accommodations in student dormitories or modest inns, all meals, and tuition. Courses involve no homework, are not graded, and are often liberal arts-oriented. These are not luxury vacations, but they are fun and fulfilling. Participants must be at least 60 years old. A companion must be at least 50 years old; spouses may participate regardless of age.

SAGA International Holidays, 222 Berkeley St., Boston, MA 02116 (☎ **800/ 343-0273**), runs tours for seniors 50 and older. Many tours are all-inclusive; all cover air transfers and accommodations. Insurance, both baggage and medical, is also included in the net price of the tours.

In the United States, the best organization to join is the **American Association of Retired Persons (AARP),** 601 E St. NW, Washington, DC 20049 (☎ **800/ 424-3410** or 202/434-AARP). Members are offered discounts on car rentals, hotels, and airfares. The association's group travel is provided by the AARP Travel Experience from American Express. Tours may be purchased through any American Express office or travel agent or by calling ☎ **800/241-1700.**

Information is also available from the **National Council of Senior Citizens,** 8403 Colesville Rd., Suite 1200, Silver Spring, MD 20910 (☎ **301/578-8800**), which charges $12 per person or per couple. You receive a monthly newsletter, part of which is devoted to travel tips; reduced discounts on hotel and auto rentals are available.

Uniworld, 16000 Ventura Blvd., Encino, CA 91436 (☎ **800/733-7820** or 818/382-7820), specializes in single tours for the mature person. It arranges for you to share an accommodation with another single person or gets you a low-priced single supplement. Uniworld specializes in travel to certain districts of England, France, Spain, Italy, and Scandinavia.

For British Seniors   Located opposite Platform 2 in Victoria Station, London SW1V 1JY, **Wasteels** (☎ **020/7834-7066**) currently provides a Rail Europe Senior Card to those over 60. It costs £5 for any British citizen with government-issued proof of age and £16 for anyone with a certificate of age not issued by the British government. With this card, discounts are sometimes available on certain trains within Britain and throughout the rest of Europe. Wasteel's main office is just around the corner from Victoria Station, at 120 Wilton Rd., London SW1 V1J (☎ **020/7834-7066**).

FOR STUDENTS

America's largest student, youth, and budget travel group, **Council Travel** has more than 60 offices worldwide, including the main office at 205 E. 42nd St., New York, NY 10017-5706 (☎ **800/2-COUNCIL**); call them to find the location nearest you. It also sells a number of publications for young people considering traveling abroad. Send $1 in postage for a copy of *Student Travels* magazine, which provides information on all of Council Travel's services as well as on programs and publications of the Council on International Educational Exchange.

The most commonly accepted form of ID is also an "open sesame" to bargains. An **International Student Identity Card (ISIC)** gets you such benefits as special student airfares to Europe, medical insurance, and many special discounts. In Spain the card secures you free entrance into state museums, monuments, and archaeological sights. Domestic train fares in Spain are also reduced for students. The card, which costs $20, is available at Council Travel offices nationwide, as well as on hundreds of college and university campuses across the country. Proof of student status and a passport-size photograph (2 in. by 2 in.) are necessary. For the ISIC-issuing office nearest you, contact the **Council on International Educational Exchange,** 205 E. 42nd St., New York, NY 10017 (☎ **212/822-2700**).

For British Students   One organization, **USIT Campus,** 52 Grosvenor Gardens, London SW1W 0AG (☎ **020/7730-3402**), provides a wealth of information and special offers for the student traveler, ranging from route planning to flight insurance, including rail cards. The **International Student Identity Card (ISIC)** is an internationally recognized proof of student status that will entitle you to savings on flights, sightseeing, food, and accommodations. It costs only £5 and is well worth the price. Always show your ISIC when booking a trip—you may not get a discount without it.

6 Getting There

BY PLANE

Any information about fares or even flights in the highly volatile airline industry is not written in stone; even travel agencies with banks of computers have a hard time keeping abreast of last-minute discounts and schedule changes. For up-to-the-minute information, including a list of the carriers that fly to Barcelona and Madrid, check with a travel agent or the individual airlines.

THE MAJOR AIRLINES

FROM NORTH AMERICA   Flights to Barcelona and Madrid from the U.S. East Coast take 6 to 7 hours, depending on the season and prevailing winds.

The national carrier of Spain, **Iberia Airlines** (☎ 800/772-4642; www. iberia.com), offers more routes to and within Spain than any other airline, with nonstop service to Madrid from both New York and Miami. From Miami, Iberia takes off for at least eight destinations in Mexico and Central America, and in cooperation with its air partner, Ladeco (an airline based in Chile), to dozens of destinations throughout South America as well. Iberia also flies from Los Angeles to Madrid, with a brief stop in Miami. Iberia offers service to Madrid through Montréal two and three times a week, depending on the season. Also available are attractive rates on fly/drive programs within Iberia and Europe.

Iberia's fares are lowest if you reserve an APEX (advance-purchase excursion) ticket at least 21 days in advance, schedule your return 7 to 30 days after your departure, and leave and return between Monday and Thursday. Iberia does not offer direct flights to Barcelona or Seville; all passengers must transfer planes in Madrid. Fares, which are subject to change, are lower during off-season. Most transatlantic flights are on carefully maintained 747s and DC-10s, and in-flight services reflect Spanish traditions, values, and cuisine.

A noteworthy cost-cutting option is Iberia's Europass. Available only to passengers who simultaneously arrange for transatlantic passage on Iberia and a minimum of two additional flights, it allows passage on any flight within Iberia's European or Mediterranean dominion for US$250 for the first two flights and US$125 for each additional flight. This is especially attractive for passengers wishing to combine trips to Spain with, for example, visits to such far-flung destinations as Cairo, Tel Aviv, Istanbul, Moscow, and Munich. For details, ask Iberia's phone representative.

Iberia's main Spain-based competitor is **Air Europa** (☎ 888/238-7672; www. g-air-europa.es), which offers nonstop service from New York's JFK Airport to Madrid, with continuing service to major cities within Spain. Fares are competitive.

Employee-owned **Trans World Airlines** (☎ **800/221-2000;** www.twa.com) operates separate daily nonstop flights to both Barcelona and Madrid from JFK. Like its competitors, TWA offers access to its trip-planning service (in this case, the Getaway Vacation desk) and can arrange fly/drive holidays, land packages at Spanish hotels, and escorted motorcoach tours.

American Airlines (☎ **800/433-7300;** www.aa.com) offers daily nonstop service to Madrid from its massive hub in Miami, with excellent connections from there to the rest of the airline's impressive North and South American network.

Delta (☎ **800/241-4141;** www.delta.com) maintains daily nonstop service from Atlanta (centerpiece of its worldwide network) to Madrid, with continuing service (and no change of equipment) to Barcelona. Delta's Dream Vacation department maintains access to fly/drive programs, land packages, and escorted bus tours through the Iberian peninsula. Delta also offers daily nonstop service between New York's JFK and Barcelona's El Prat airports.

Since 1991, **United Airlines** (☎ **800/538-2929;** www.ual.com) has flown passengers nonstop every day to Madrid from Washington. United also offers fly/drive programs and escorted motorcoach tours.

Continental Airlines (☎ **800/231-0856;** www.continental.com) offers between six and seven nonstop flights per week, depending on the season, to Madrid from Newark, New Jersey, an airport many New York residents prefer.

US Airways (☎ **800/428-4322;** www.usairways.com) offers daily nonstop service between Philadelphia and Madrid. US Airways offers connections to Philadelphia from more than 50 cities throughout the United States, Canada, and the Bahamas.

Most U.S.-based carriers offer service solely to Madrid; once in Madrid, Spain's airline, Iberia, offers low fares to cities throughout the country.

FROM GREAT BRITAIN The two major carriers that fly between the United Kingdom and Spain are **British Airways (BA)** (☎ **0345/222-747,** or 020/8759-5511 in London; www.british-airways.com) and **Iberia** (☎ **020/7830-0011** in London). In spite of the frequency of their routes, however, we suspect most vacationing Brits fly charter (see below).

More than a dozen daily flights, on either BA or Iberia, depart from both London's Heathrow and Gatwick airports. The Midlands is served by flights from Manchester and Birmingham, two major airports that can also be used by Scots flying to Spain. Approximately seven flights a day go between London and Madrid, with at least six to Barcelona (trip time: 2 to 2¹/₂ hours). From either the Madrid airport or the Barcelona airport, you can tap into Iberia's domestic network—flying, for example, to Seville or the Costa del Sol (centered at the Málaga airport). The best air deals on scheduled flights from the United Kingdom are those requiring a Saturday night stopover.

GOOD-VALUE CHOICES

Most airlines divide their year roughly into seasonal slots, with the least expensive fares between November 1 and March 14. The shoulder season (spring and early fall) is only slightly more expensive—and includes October, which many veteran tourists consider the ideal time to visit Spain. Summer, of course, is the most expensive time.

SPECIAL PROMOTIONAL FARES Many airlines occasionally offer promotional fares to Europe. To take advantage of this, you need to have a good travel agent or to do a lot of shopping or calling around yourself to learn what's available at the time of your intended trip.

CHARTER FLIGHTS   A charter flight is one reserved months in advance for a one-time-only transit to a predetermined destination. For reasons of economy, some travelers choose this option.

Before paying for a charter, check the restrictions on your ticket or contract. You may be asked to purchase a tour package and pay far in advance. You'll pay a stiff penalty (or forfeit the ticket entirely) if you cancel. Charters are sometimes canceled if the tickets don't sell out. In some cases the charter-ticket seller will offer you an insurance policy for your own legitimate cancellation (proving illness with a hospital certificate, or having a death in the family, for example).

There is no way to predict whether a charter or a bucket-shop flight (see below) will be cheaper. You'll have to investigate this at the time of your trip. Charter operators and bucket shops used to perform separate functions, but today many perform both functions.

Among charter-flight operators is **Council Charter,** a subsidiary of the Council on International Educational Exchange (CIEE), 205 E. 42nd St., New York, NY 10017 (☎ **212/822-2700**). This outfit can arrange charter seats to most major European cities, including Madrid, on regularly scheduled aircraft.

One of the biggest New York charter operators is **Travac,** 989 Sixth Ave., 16th Floor, New York, NY 10018 (☎ **800/TRAV-800** or 212/563-3303).

Be warned: Some charter companies have proved unreliable in the past.

BUCKET SHOPS   Bucket shops—or consolidators, as they're also called—exist in many forms. In their purest sense, they act as a clearinghouse for blocks of tickets that airlines discount and consign during normally slow periods of air travel. Ticket prices vary, sometimes going for as much as 35% off full fare. Terms of payment can be anywhere from 45 days before departure to the last minute.

Bucket shops abound from coast to coast, but just to get you started, here are some recommendations. (Look also for ads in your local newspaper travel section.)

In New York, try **TFI Tours International,** 34 W. 32nd St., 12th Floor, New York, NY 10001 (☎ **800/745-8000** or 212/736-1140), which offers service to cities worldwide, including Madrid and Barcelona.

For the Midwest, explore the possibilities of **Travel Avenue,** 10 S. Riverside Plaza, Suite 1404, Chicago, IL 60606 (☎ **800/333-3335**), a national agency whose headquarters are here. Its tickets are often cheaper than those sold by most shops.

One of the biggest U.S. consolidators is **Travac,** 989 Sixth Ave., New York, NY 10018 (☎ **800/TRAV-800** or 212/563-3303), which offers discounted seats throughout the United States to most cities in Europe, including Madrid, on TWA, United, Delta, and other major airlines.

UniTravel, 1177 N. Warson Rd., St. Louis, MO 63132 (☎ **800/325-2222**), offers tickets to Madrid and elsewhere in Europe at prices that may be lower than what airlines charge if you order tickets directly from them. Unitravel is best suited to providing discounts for passengers who want (or need) to get to Europe on short notice.

You can also try **1-800-FLY-4-LESS,** a discount domestic and international airline ticketing service. Travelers unable to buy their tickets three weeks in advance can use this service to obtain low discounted fares with no advance purchase requirements. This nationwide airline reservation and ticketing service specializes in finding only the lowest fares.

A final option, suitable for clients with flexible travel plans, is available through **Airhitch,** 2641 Broadway, 3rd Floor, Suite 100, New York, NY 10025 (☎ **800/326-2009,** or 212/864-2000). If you let Airhitch know which 5 consecutive days you're available to fly to Europe, they will agree to fly you there within those 5 days.

Airhitch arranges for departure from any of three U.S. regions (the East Coast, West Coast, and Midwest/Southeast); they try, but cannot guarantee, to fly you from and to the cities of your choice.

REBATORS   Another competitor in the low-cost airfare market, rebators pass along to the passenger part of their commission, although many assess a fee for their services. Most rebators offer discounts that range from 10% to 25%, plus a $25 handling charge. Although not the same as travel agents, they sometimes offer similar services, including discounted land arrangements and car rentals.

One major rebator is **Travel Avenue,** 10 S. Riverside Plaza, Suite 1404, Chicago, IL 60606 (☎ **800/333-3335** or 312/876-1116).

TRAVEL CLUBS   Another possibility for low-cost air travel is the travel club, which supplies an unsold inventory of tickets offering discounts of 20% to 60%.

After you pay an annual fee, you are given a hot line number to call to find out what discounts are available. Many discounts become available several days, sometimes as much as a month, before departure—so you have to be fairly flexible.

The best of these clubs include the following: **Moment's Notice,** 7301 New Utrecht Ave., Brooklyn, NY 11228 (☎ **718/234-6295;** www.moments-notice.com), has a 24-hour members' hot line (regular toll charges) and a $25 yearly fee. **Travelers Advantage,** 3033 S. Parker Rd., Suite 900, Aurora, CO 80014 (☎ **800/433-9383**), offers members, for $49, a catalog (issued quarterly), maps, discounts at select hotels, and a 5% cash bonus on purchases. **Encore Travel Club,** 4501 Forbes Blvd., Lanham, MD 20706 (☎ **800/638-8976**), charges $59.95 a year for membership and offers up to a 50% discount at more than 4,000 hotels, sometimes during off-peak periods; it also offers substantial discounts on airfare, cruises, and car rentals through its volume-purchase plans. Membership includes a travel package outlining the company's many services and use of a toll-free telephone number for advice and information.

TRAVEL WEB SITES   In this information age, more savvy travelers are finding excellent deals by searching the Internet. Increasingly, travel agencies and companies are using the Web as a medium to offer everything from vacations to plane reservations to budget airline tickets on major carriers.

Here are some sites for planning and booking travel. They offer domestic and international flight, hotel, and rental-car bookings, plus news, destination information, and deals on cruises and vacation packages.

Now incorporating Preview Travel, ✪ **Travelocity** (www.travelocity.com; www. previewtravel.com; www.frommers.travelocity.com), is Frommer's online travel planning/booking partner. It uses the SABRE system to offer reservations and tickets for more than 400 airlines, plus reservations and purchase capabilities for more than 45,000 hotels and 50 car-rental companies. An exclusive feature of the SABRE system is its Low Fare Search Engine, which automatically searches for the three lowest-priced itineraries based on a traveler's criteria. Last-minute deals and consolidator fares are included in the search. If you book with Travelocity, you can select specific seats for your flights with online seat maps and also view diagrams of the most popular commercial aircraft. Its hotel finder provides street-level location maps and photos of selected hotels. With the Fare Watcher e-mail feature, you can select up to five routes and receive e-mail notices when the fare changes by $25 or more. Travelocity's Destination Guide includes updated information on some 260 destinations worldwide— supplied by Frommer's.

Expedia (expedia.com) is Travelocity's major competitor. It offers several ways of obtaining the best possible fares: Flight Price Matcher service allows your preferred airline to match an available fare with a competitor; a comprehensive Fare Compare area shows the differences in fare categories and airlines; and Fare Calendar helps you plan your trip around the best possible fares. Its main limitation is that like many online databases, Expedia focuses on the major airlines and hotel chains, so don't expect to find too many budget airlines or one-of-a-kind B&Bs here.

TRIP.com (www.trip.com) began as a site geared toward business travelers, but its innovative features and highly personalized approach have broadened its appeal to leisure travelers as well. It's the leading travel site for those using mobile devices to access Internet travel information. TRIP.com includes a trip-planning function that provides the average and lowest fare for the route requested, in addition to the current available fare. An on-site "newsstand" features breaking news on airfare sales and other travel specials. Among its most popular features are Flight TRACKER and intelliTRIP. Flight TRACKER allows users to track any commercial flight en route to its destination anywhere in the United States., while accessing real-time FAA-based flight monitoring data. intelliTRIP is a travel search tool that allows users to identify the best airline, hotel, and rental-car rates in less than 90 seconds. In addition, the site offers e-mail notification of flight delays, plus city resource guides, currency converters, and a weekly e-mail newsletter of fare updates, travel tips, and traveler forums.

Yahoo! Travel (www.travel.yahoo.com) is currently the most popular of the Internet information portals, and its travel site is a comprehensive mix of online booking, daily travel news, and destination information. The Best Fares area offers what its name promises, plus provides feedback on refining your search if you have flexibility in travel dates or times. There is also an active section of Message Boards for discussions on travel in general and specific destinations.

For last-minute deals and other online bargains, try these sites: **1travel.com** (www.1travel.com), **Cheap Tickets** (www.cheaptickets.com), **Last Minute Travel** (www.lastminutetravel.com), **Moment's Notice** (www.moments-notice.com), **Priceline** (www.travel.priceline.com), **Smarter Living** (www.smarterliving.com), and **Web Flyer** (www.webflyer.com).

TIPS FOR BRITISH TRAVELERS

A regular fare from the United Kingdom to Spain is extremely high, so savvy Brits usually call a travel agent for a deal—either a charter flight or some special air-travel promotion. These so-called deals are almost always available, due to great interest in Spain as a tourist destination. Another way to keep costs down is an APEX (Advance Payment Excursion) ticket. Alternatively, a PEX (public excursion fare) ticket offers a discount without the strict booking restrictions. You might also ask the airlines about a Eurobudget ticket, which has restrictions or length-of-stay requirements.

British periodicals are always full of classified advertisements touting "slashed" fares to Spain. Good sources include the London-based magazine *Time Out,* the daily travel section of London's *Evening Standard,* and the Sunday edition of almost any newspaper.

Most vacationing Brits looking for air-flight bargains go charter. Delays can be frequent (some last 2 whole days and nights), and departures are often at inconvenient hours. Booking conditions can also be severe, and one must read the fine print carefully and deal with only a reputable travel agent. Stays rarely last a month, and booking must sometimes be made at least a month in advance, although a 2-week period is sometimes possible.

Charter flights leave from most British regional airports for various destinations (for example, Málaga), bypassing the congestion at the Madrid airports. Figure on saving approximately 10% to 15% off regularly scheduled flight tickets. Recommended companies include **Trailfinders** (☎ **020/7937-5400** in London) and **Avro Tours** (☎ **020/8715-0000** in London).

In London, many bucket shops around Victoria Station and Earls Court offer low fares. Make sure the company you deal with is a member of the IATA, ABTA, or ATOL. These umbrella organizations will help you out if anything goes wrong.

CEEFAX, a British television information service included on many home and hotel TVs, runs details of package holidays and flights to Europe and beyond. Just switch to your CEEFAX channel to find a menu of listings that includes travel information.

BY TRAIN

If you're already in Europe, you may want to go to Spain by train, especially if you have a Eurailpass. Even if you don't, the cost is moderate. Rail passengers who visit from Britain or France should make *couchette* and sleeper reservations as far in advance as possible, especially during the peak summer season.

Since Spain's rail tracks are of a wider gauge than those used for French trains (except for the TALGO and Trans-Europe-Express trains), you'll probably have to change trains at the border unless you're on an express train (see below). For long journeys on Spanish rails, seat and sleeper reservations are mandatory.

The most comfortable and the fastest trains in Spain are the TER, TALGO, and Electrotren. However, you pay a supplement to ride on these fast trains. Both first- and second-class fares are sold on Spanish trains. Tickets can be purchased in either the United States or Canada at the nearest office of FrenchRail or from any reputable travel agent. Confirmation of your reservation will take about a week.

If you want your car carried, you must travel Auto-Expreso in Spain. This type of auto transport can be booked only through travel agents or rail offices once you arrive in Europe.

To go from London to Spain by rail, you'll need to change not only the train but also the rail terminus in Paris. In Paris it's worth the extra bucks to purchase a TALGO express or a "Puerta del Sol" express—that way, you can avoid having to change trains once again at the Spanish border. Trip time from London to Paris is about 6 hours; from Paris to Madrid, about 15 hours or so, which includes 2 hours spent in Paris changing trains and stations. Many rail passes are available in the United Kingdom for travel in Europe. Stop in at **Wasteels,** at Victoria Station, opposite platform 2, London, SW1V 1JZ (☎ **020/7834-7066**), which can help you find the best option for the trip you're planning.

BY BUS

Bus travel to Spain is possible but not popular—it's quite slow. But coach services do operate regularly from major capitals of Western Europe to Madrid and Barcelona, from which bus connections can be made to Seville. The busiest routes are from London and are run by **Eurolines Limited,** 52 Grosvenor Gardens, London SW1W 0AU (☎ **0990/143-219** or 020/7730-8235). The journey from London's Victoria Station to Madrid is provided by two services: Service 180 is an express from Victoria Station to Madrid, departing London daily at 9pm, arriving in Madrid the following day at 9:30pm; and Service 181 leaves London at 9pm on the first day, arriving in Madrid at 12:30am on the third day.

Other bus trips can be arranged from London to Barcelona, Alicante, Benidorm, and Marbella.

Julia Tours of Barcelona (☎ **93-490-40-00** in Barcelona or 01582/40-4511 in Britain) operates a coach that departs from London's Victoria Station on Monday, Wednesday, and Saturday. It leaves London at 11am and arrives in Barcelona the following morning at 11am. On Wednesday the bus leaves at 9:30am and gets into Barcelona at 11:45am. An English-speaking staff in Barcelona can make reservations for you and supply more details.

BY CAR

If you're touring the rest of Europe in a rented car, you might, for an added cost, be allowed to drop off your vehicle in a major city such as Madrid or Barcelona.

Motor approaches to Spain are across France via expressways. The most popular border crossing is east of Biarritz. For the best route to Madrid, take the E70 west of Bilbao; then cut south on the E804 to the junction with the E05, which heads southwest to Burgos. Bypass Burgos and continue south on the route to Madrid, which is also known as the N-I.

To get to Barcelona from the north, take the A7 or the E9 to A18; from the Costa Brava, take the A19 heading southwest; and from the south, enter Barcelona on the A16.

If you're driving from Madrid to Seville, connect with the E90 and head southwest toward Mérida; from there, head south on the E803 to Seville. For an alternative route, head south on the E5 to Córdoba. After exploring Córdoba, continue southwest on the E5; this highway will take you to Seville.

If you're driving from Britain, make sure you have a cross-Channel reservation, as traffic tends to be very heavy, especially in summer. The major ferry crossings connect Dover and Folkestone with Dunkirk. Newhaven is connected with Dieppe, and the British city of Portsmouth with Roscoff. One of the fastest crossings is by Hovercraft from Dover to Boulogne or Calais. It costs more than the ferry, but it takes only about half an hour.

You can also take the "Chunnel," the underwater Channel Tunnel linking Britain (Folkestone) and France (Calais) by road and rail—a great engineering feat that was first envisioned by Napoléon way back in 1802. Travel time between the English and French highway systems is about 1 hour.

BY ORGANIZED TOUR

Some people prefer having a tour operator make all their travel arrangements. There are many such companies, each offering transportation to and within Spain, pre-arranged accommodations, and such extras as bilingual tour guides and lectures. Often these tours to Spain include excursions to Morocco or Portugal.

Some of the most unusual tours are run by **Abercrombie & Kent International,** 1520 Kensington Rd., Oak Brook, IL 60521 (☎ **800/323-7308** in the U.S., or 020/7730-9600), a Chicago-based company that specializes in glamorous tours around the world. It offers deluxe 13- or 19-day tours of the Iberian Peninsula by train. Guests stay in fine hotels, ranging from a late medieval palace to the exquisite Alfonso XIII in Seville. Despite all the extras that are included, these trips cost less than any personally arranged tours with equivalent facilities and services. A 13-day tour is US$4,795 per person; a 19-day tour is US$7,195. Single supplements range from US$948 for 13 days to US$1,461 for 19 days. Airfare is extra.

American Express Vacations, P.O. Box 1525, Fort Lauderdale, FL 33302 (☎ **800/241-1700** in the U.S. and Canada), offers some of the most comprehensive programs available to Spain, including Madrid as the major stopover.

Trafalgar Tours, 11 E. 26th St., Suite 1300, New York, NY 10010 (☎ **800/ 626-6604** or 212/689-8977), features two 10-day tours of southern Spain. The itineraries are identical, but the prices differ according to season. Tours include visits to

Granada, Seville, and Córdoba, as well as free time on the Costa del Sol. One of the most popular offerings is a 16-day trip called "The Best of Spain," with Saturday departures. Land-only packages cost US$1,335; land and air packages go from US$1,905 to US$2,115. Another choice, "Spanish Discovery," departs on Friday from April 3 to December 27. Land-only packages cost from US$799; land plus airfare costs from US$1,500 to US$1,630.

Insight International's "Highlights of Spain" is a 10-day tour that begins in Barcelona, sweeps along the southern and eastern coasts, and concludes in Madrid. Sights of interest include Seville, the peaks of the Sierra Nevada, and Cervantes's famed plains of La Mancha. The cost ranges from US$1,863 to US$2,023, and includes airfare, accommodations, and some meals. Tours run weekly, April 7 to November 26. For information, contact your travel agent or Insight International (☎ 800/582-8380).

Alternative Travel Group Ltd., 69–71 Banbury Rd., Oxford OX2 6PE, UK (☎ 018/6531-0399), organizes walking and cycling holidays, plus wine tours in Spain, Italy, and France. Tours explore the scenic countryside and medieval towns of each country. If you'd like a brochure outlining the tours, call ☎ **018/6531-5663.**

Settling into Barcelona 3

Blessed with rich and fertile soil, an excellent harbor, and a hard-working population, Barcelona has always prospered. At a time when Madrid was still a dusty and unknown Castilian backwater, Barcelona was a powerful, diverse capital, one influenced more by the Mediterranean empires that conquered it than by the cultures of the arid Iberian plains to the west. Carthage, Rome, and Charlemagne-era France each overran Catalonia, and each left an indelible mark on the region's identity.

The Catalán people have clung fiercely to their unique culture and language—both of which, earlier in this century, Franco systematically tried to eradicate. But Catalonia has endured, becoming a semi-autonomous region of Spain (with Catalán its official language). And Barcelona, the region's lodestar, has truly come into its own. The city's most powerful monuments open a window onto its history: the intricately carved edifices that comprise the medieval Gothic Quarter; the curvilinear *modernisme* (Catalán art nouveau) that inspired Gaudí's Sagrada Familia; and the seminal surrealist works of Picasso and Miró, found in museums that peg Barcelona as a crucial incubator for 20th-century art.

As if those attractions weren't enough, Barcelona is on the doorstep of some of the great playgrounds and vacation retreats of Europe: the Balearic Islands to the east, the Costa Brava (Wild Coast) to the north, the Penedés wine country to the west, the Roman city of Tarragona, the monastery at Montserrat, and such Costa Dorada resort towns as Sitges, to the south.

Despite its allure, Barcelona grapples with problems common to many major cities: the increasing polarization of rich and poor, a rising tide of drug abuse, and an escalating crime rate, mostly theft. But in reaction to a rash of negative publicity, city authorities have, with some degree of success, brought crime under control, at least within the tourist zones.

A revitalized Barcelona eagerly prepared for and welcomed thousands of visitors as part of the 1992 Summer Olympic Games. But the action didn't end when the last medal was handed out. Barcelona turned its multimillion-dollar building projects into permanently expanded facilities for sports and tourism. Its modern US$150 million terminal at El Prat de Llobregat Airport can accommodate 12 million passengers a year; and ever-pragmatic Barcelona moved into the 21st century with a restructuring program called "Post Olympic."

1 Orientation

GETTING THERE

BY PLANE   During the months before the 1992 Olympics, airlines scrambled to provide nonstop transatlantic service to Barcelona. In the post-Olympic world, however, most passengers must first change aircraft in Madrid. The only exceptions are **TWA** (☎ 800/221-2000; www.twa.com) and **Delta** (☎ 800/241-4141; www.delta.com). Passengers originating in such European capitals as London, Paris, and Rome can fly nonstop to Barcelona (usually on their national airlines), but most passengers, for whatever reason, opt for transit through Madrid. For more information on flying into Madrid, refer to "Getting There" in chapter 2.

Within Spain, the most likely carrier is **Iberia** (☎ 800/772-4642; www.iberia.com), which offers peak-hour shuttle flights at 15-minute intervals between Madrid and Barcelona. Service from Madrid to Barcelona at less congested times of the day averages around one flight every 30 to 40 minutes. Iberia also offers flights between Barcelona and Valencia, Granada, Seville, and Bilbao. Within Barcelona, you can arrange ticketing at **Iberia,** Plaça de Espanya, s/n (☎ 93-325-73-58) or Disputacío 258 (☎ 93-401-33-81). Generally cheaper than Iberia, both **Air Europa** (☎ 93-298-33-28; www.g-air-europa.es) and **Spanair** (☎ 93-298-33-62; www.spanair.com) run shuttles between Madrid and Barcelona. Frequency of shuttle flights depends on demand, with more in the early morning and late afternoon.

El Prat de Llobregat, 08820 Prat de Llobregat (☎ 93-298-38-38), the Barcelona airport, is 7½ miles (12km) southwest of the city. The route to the center of town is carefully marked. A train runs daily between the airport and Barcelona's Estació Central de Barcelona-Sants from 6:14am (the first airport departure) to 10:44pm (the last city departure). The 21-minute trip costs 305 pesetas (US$1.85) Monday to Friday and 350 pesetas (US$2.10) Saturday and Sunday. If your hotel is near Plaça de Catalunya, you might opt instead for an Aerobús that runs daily every 15 minutes between 5:30am and 10pm. The fare is 475 pesetas (US$2.85). A taxi from the airport into central Barcelona will cost 3,000 to 3,500 pesetas (US$18 to US$21).

BY TRAIN   A train called the Barcelona-TALGO provides rail service between Paris and Barcelona in 11½ hours. For many other connections from the mainland of Europe, it's necessary to change trains at Port Bou, on the French-Spanish border. Most trains issue seat and sleeper reservations.

Trains departing from the **Estació de França,** Avenida Marqués de l'Argentera (metro: Barceloneta, L3), cover long distances within Spain as well as international routes, carrying a total of 20,000 passengers daily. Express night trains serve Paris, Zurich, Milan, and Geneva. Every international route served by the state-owned RENFE railway company uses the Estació de França, including some of its most luxurious express trains, such as the *Pau Casals* and the *TALGO Catalán.*

This modernized 1929 station includes a huge screen with updated information on train departures and arrivals, personalized ticket dispatching, a passenger attention center, a tourism information center, showers, internal baggage control, a first-aid center, and kiosks for hotel reservations and car rentals. But it is much more than a departure point: The station has an elegant restaurant, a cafeteria, a book-and-record store, a jazz club, and even a disco. Estació de França is just steps away from Ciutadella Park, the zoo, and the port and is near Vila Olímpica.

From this station you can book tickets to the major cities of Spain: Madrid (5 TALGOS trains per day, 7 hours; and 3 *rápidos,* 10 hours), Seville (2 trains daily, 10½ hours), and Valencia (11 daily, 4 hours).

RENFE also has a terminal at **Estació Central de Barcelona-Sants,** Plaça de Països Catalánes (metro: Sants-Estació).

For general RENFE information, call ☎ **902-24-01-02.**

BY BUS   Bus travel to Barcelona is possible but not popular—it's pretty slow. **Eurolines Limited,** Grosvenor Gardens, London SW1W 0AU (☎ **0990/143-219** or 020/7730-8235), can arrange your trip from London to Barcelona. **Enatcar,** Estació del Nord in Barcelona (☎ **93-245-25-28**), can arrange service to southern France and Italy, and **Linebús,** also found at the Estació del Nord (☎ **93-265-07-00**), offers six bus trips a week to Paris. **Julià Via,** carrer Viriato (☎ **93-490-40-00**), operates four buses a week to Frankfurt, Germany, and another four per week to Marseille, France.

Enatcar, Estació del Nord (☎ **93-245-25-28**), operates 14 buses per day to Madrid (trip time: 8 hours) and 9 buses per day to Valencia (trip time: 4½ hours). A one-way ticket to Madrid costs 3,200 pesetas (US$19.20); to Valencia, 2,900 pesetas (US$17.40). For bus travel to one of the beach resorts along the Costa Brava, go to **Sarfa,** Estació del Nord (☎ **93-265-11-58**), which operates buses from Barcelona to such resorts as Tossa de Mar. Trip time is usually 2 hours.

BY CAR   **From France** (the usual European road approach to Barcelona), the major access route is at the eastern end of the Pyrenees. You have a choice of the express highway (**E-15**) or the more scenic coastal road. *But be warned:* If you take the scenic coastal road in July and August, you'll often encounter bumper-to-bumper traffic. From France, you can also approach Barcelona via Toulouse. Cross the border into Spain at Puigcerdá (frontier stations are here), near the principality of Andorra. From here, take the **N-152** to Barcelona.

From Madrid, take the **N-2** to Zaragoza, then the **A-2** to El Vendrell, followed by the **A-7** motorway to Barcelona. **From the Costa Blanca** or **Costa del Sol,** follow the **E-15** north from Valencia along the eastern Mediterranean coast.

BY FERRY   **Transmediterránea,** Moll Sant Bertran s/n (☎ **93-295-91-00**), operates daily voyages to the Balearic island of Majorca (trip time: 8 hours) and also to Minorca (trip time: 9 hours). In summer, it's important to have a reservation as far in advance as possible, due to overcrowding.

VISITOR INFORMATION

Barcelona has two types of tourist offices. The local government office deals with Spain in general and Catalunya in particular, with basic information about Barcelona. This organization has an office at the airport, **El Prat de Llobregat** (☎ **93-478-47-04**), which you'll pass as you clear customs. Summer hours are Monday to Saturday 9:30am to 8:30pm; off-season hours are Monday to Saturday 9:30am to 8pm; year-round, it's open Sunday 9:30 to 3pm. There's another large office in the center of Barcelona at the **Palau de Rubert,** Passeig de Gràcia, 107 (☎ **93-238-40-40**), where there are often exhibitions. It's open daily 10am to 7pm.

The other organization, the **Oficina de Informació de Turisme de Barcelona,** Plaça de Catalunya, 17-S (☎ **93-304-34-21,** or 906-30-12-82 from inside Spain), deals exclusively with Barcelona. The staff can help you make hotel reservations in person and by telephone (☎ **93-304-34-34**). This is also where you can obtain detailed information about the city and the Barcelona card for tourist discounts. The office is open daily 9am to 9pm. The same organization has an office at the **Estació Central de Barcelona-Sants** (Sants railway station), Plaça Päisos Catalánes (no phone; metro: Sants-Estació). In summer it's open daily 8am to 8pm; off-season, Monday to Friday 8am to 8pm, Saturday and Sunday 8am to 2pm.

For more information on what's taking place in the city, call ☎ **010** Monday to Friday 7am to 11pm and Saturday 9am to 2pm.

CITY LAYOUT

MAIN SQUARES, STREETS & ARTERIES   Plaça de Catalunya (Plaza de Cataluña in Spanish) is the city's heart; the world-famous **Rambles** (Ramblas) are its arteries. Les Rambles begin at the Plaça Portal de la Pau, with its 164-foot-high monument to Columbus and a panoramic view of the port, and stretch north to the Plaça de Catalunya, with its fountains and trees. Along this wide promenade you'll find bookshops and newsstands, stalls selling birds and flowers, and benches or cafe tables and chairs, where you can sit and watch the passing parade.

At the end of the Rambles is the **Barri Xinés** (Barrio Chino or Chinese Quarter), which has enjoyed notoriety as a haven of prostitution and drugs, populated in Jean Genet's *The Thief's Journal* by "whores, thieves, pimps, and beggars." Still a dangerous district, it is best viewed during the day, if at all.

Off the Rambles lies **Plaça Reial** (Plaza Real), the most harmoniously proportioned square in Barcelona. Come here on Sunday morning to see the stamp and coin collectors peddle their wares.

The major wide boulevards of Barcelona are the **Avinguda** (Avenida) **Diagonal** and **Passeig** (Paseo) **de Colom,** and an elegant shopping street, the **Passeig de Gràcia.**

A short walk from the Rambles will take you to the **Passeig del Moll de la Fusta,** a waterfront promenade developed in the 1990s, with some of the best (but not the cheapest) restaurants in Barcelona. If you can't afford the high prices, come here at least for a drink in the open air and to take in a view of the harbor.

To the east is the old port of the city, called **La Barceloneta,** which dates from the 18th century. This strip of land between the port and the sea has traditionally been a good place for seafood.

Barri Gòtic (Barrio Gótico, Gothic Quarter in English) lies to the east of the Rambles. This is the site of the city's oldest buildings, including the cathedral.

North of Plaça de Catalunya, the **Eixample** unfolds. An area of wide boulevards, in contrast to the labyrinthine Gothic Quarter, it contains two major roads leading out of Barcelona, the Avinguda Diagonal and Gran Vía de les Corts Catalánes. Another major neighborhood, working-class **Gràcia,** lies north of the Eixample.

Montjuïc, one of the mountains of Barcelona, begins at Plaça d'Espanya, a traffic rotary, just beyond which are Barcelona's famous fountains. Montjuïc was the setting for the principal events of the 1992 Summer Olympic Games. The other mountain is **Tibidabo,** in the northwest, which boasts great views of the city and the Mediterranean. It contains an amusement park.

FINDING AN ADDRESS/MAPS   Finding an address in Barcelona can be a problem. The city is characterized by long boulevards and a complicated maze of narrow, twisting streets. Therefore, knowing the street number is all-important. If you see the designation *s/n* it means that the building has no number (*sin número*). Therefore, it's crucial to learn the cross street if you're seeking a specific address.

The rule about street numbers is that there is no rule. On most streets, numbering begins on one side and runs up that side until the end, then runs in the opposite direction on the other side. Therefore, number 40 could be opposite 408. But there are many exceptions. Sometimes street numbers on buildings in the older quarters have been obscured by the patina of time.

Arm yourself with a good map before setting out. Those given away free by tourist offices and hotels aren't adequate, since they don't label the little streets. The best map for exploring Barcelona, published by **Falk,** is available at most bookstores and newsstands, such as those found along the Rambles. This pocket map includes all the streets, along with an index of how to find them.

Neighborhoods in Brief

Barri Gòtic   The Gothic Quarter rises to the north of Passeig de Colom, with its **Columbus Monument,** and is bordered on its east by a major artery, Via Laietana, which begins at La Barceloneta at Plaça d'Antoni López and runs north to Plaça d'Urquinaona. Les Rambles forms the western border of the Gothic Quarter, and on the northern edge is the Ronda de Sant Pere, which intersects with **Plaça de Catalunya** and the **Passeig de Gràcia.** The heart of this medieval quarter is the **Plaça de Sant Jaume,** which was a major crossroads in the old Roman city. Many of the structures in the old section are ancient, including the ruins of a Roman temple dedicated to Augustus. Antique stores, restaurants, cafes, museums, some hotels, and bookstores fill the place today. It's also the headquarters of the **Generalitat,** seat of the Catalán government.

Les Rambles   The most famous promenade in Spain, ranking with Madrid's Paseo del Prado, was once a drainage channel. These days, street entertainers, flower vendors, news vendors, cafe patrons, and strollers flow along its length. This gradual 1-mile descent toward the sea has often been called "a metaphor for life," because of its bustling scene that is a combination of cosmopolitanism and crude vitality—in all, a rich, dazzling human spectacle. Les Rambles (Las Ramblas) is actually composed of five different sections, each a particular *rambla,* with names like Rambla de Canaletes, Rambla dels Estudis, Rambla de Sant Josep, Rambla dels Caputxins, and Rambla de Santa Mònica. The pedestrian esplanade is shaded as it makes its way from the Plaça de Catalunya to the port—all the way to the Columbus Monument. Along the way you'll pass the **Gran Teatre del Liceu,** on Rambla dels Caputxins, one of the most magnificent opera houses in the world until it caught fire in 1994. Miró created a sidewalk mosaic at the Plaça de la Boquería. During the stagnation of the Franco era, this street grew seedier and seedier. But the opening of the Ramada Renaissance hotel and the restoration of many buildings have brought energy and hope for the street.

Barri Xinés (El Raval)   Despite the name, this isn't "Chinatown," as most people assume—in fact, historians are unsure just how the neighborhood got its name. For decades it's had an unsavory reputation, known for its houses of prostitution. Franco outlawed prostitution in 1956, but apparently no one ever told the denizens of this district of narrow, often murky old streets and dark corners. Nighttime can be dangerous, so exercise caution; still, most visitors like to take a quick look to see what all the excitement is about. Just off Les Rambles, the area lies primarily between the waterfront and carrer de l'Hospital. Although it's got a long way to go, Barri Xinés is undergoing tremendous change that began with the preparation for the 1992 Olympics. Barcelona has launched a program of urban renewal that has led to the destruction of some of the seedier parts of the barrio. The opening of the **Museu d'Art Contemporani** at Plaça dels Angels—designed by the noted American architect Richard Meier—has led to a revitalization of the area and the opening of a lot more art galleries. The official name that Barcelona has given to the district is **El Raval.**

Barri de la Ribera   Another neighborhood that stagnated for years but is now well into a renaissance, the Barri de la Ribera is adjacent to the Barri Gòtic, going east to Passeig de Picasso, which borders the Parc de la Ciutadella. The centerpiece of this district is the **Museu Picasso,** housed in the 15th-century Palau Agüilar, at Montcada, 15. Numerous art galleries have opened around the museum, and the old quarter is fashionable. Many mansions in this area were built at the time of one of the major maritime expansions in Barcelona's history, principally in the 1200s and 1300s. Most of these grand homes still stand along **Carrer de Montcada** and other nearby streets.

La Barceloneta and the Harbor   Although Barcelona was founded on seagoing tradition, its waterfront was in decay for years. Today, it's bursting with activity along the waterfront promenade, **Passeig del Moll de la Fusta.** The best way to get a bird's-eye view of the area is to take an elevator to the top of the Columbus Monument in Plaça Portal de la Pau.

In the vicinity of the monument were the **Reials Drassanes,** or royal shipyards, a booming place of industry during Barcelona's maritime heyday in the Middle Ages. Years before Columbus landed in the New World, ships sailed the world from here, flying the traditional yellow-and-red flag of Catalonia.

To the east lies a mainly artificial peninsula called **La Barceloneta** (Little Barcelona), formerly a fishing district, dating mainly from the 18th century. It's now filled with seafood restaurants. The blocks here are long and surprisingly narrow—architects planned them that way so that each room in every building fronted a street. Many bus lines terminate at the Passeig Nacional here, site of the **Barcelona Aquarium.**

Eixample   To the north of the Plaça de Catalunya lies the Eixample, or Ensanche, the section of Barcelona that grew beyond the old medieval walls. This great period of enlargement (*eixample* in Catalán), came mainly in the 19th century. Avenues form a grid of perpendicular streets, cut across by a majestic boulevard—**Passeig de Gràcia,** a posh shopping street ideal for leisurely promenades. The area's main traffic artery is **Avinguda Diagonal,** which links the expressway and the heart of this congested city.

The Eixample was the center of Barcelona's *modernisme* movement, and it possesses some of the most original buildings any architect ever designed—not just those by Gaudí, but by others as well. Gaudí's Sagrada Familia is one of the major attractions.

Montjuïc and Tibidabo   Montjuïc, called Hill of the Jews after a Jewish necropolis there, gained prominence in 1929 as the site of the World's Fair and again in 1992 as the site of the Summer Olympic Games. Its major attractions are the Joan Miró museum, the Olympic installations, and the **Poble Espanyol** (Spanish Village), a 5-acre site constructed for the World's Fair, where examples of Spanish art and architecture are displayed against the backdrop of a traditional Spanish village. Tibidabo (1,650 feet) is where you should go for your final look at Barcelona. On a clear day you can see the mountains of Majorca (the largest and most famous of the Balearic Islands). Reached by train, tram, and cable car, Tibidabo is the most popular Sunday excursion in Barcelona.

Pedralbes   Pedralbes is where wealthy Barcelonans live, some in stylish blocks of apartment houses, others in 19th-century villas behind ornamental fences, and still others in stunning *modernisme* structures. Set in a park, the **Palau de Pedralbes** (at Avinguda Diagonal, 686) was constructed in the 1920s as a gift from the city to Alfonxo XIII, the grandfather of today's King Juan Carlos. The king abdicated and fled in 1931, never making much use of the palace. Today it has a new life, housing a museum of carriages and a group of European paintings called the **Colecció Cambó.**

Vila Olímpica   This seafront property contains the tallest buildings in the city. The revitalized site, in the post-Olympic Games era, is the setting for numerous showrooms for imported cars, designer clothing stores, restaurants, and business offices. The "village" was where the athletes lived during the 1992 games. A regular city-in-miniature is taking shape, complete with banks, art galleries, nightclubs, bars, even pastry shops.

The Barcelona Card

An ideal way to appreciate Barcelona better and save money at the same time is with the Barcelona card. It's definitely a bargain if you'll stay in the city for more than an afternoon and do any sightseeing at all. For 24 hours it costs 2,500 pesetas (US$15) for adults, 2,000 pesetas (US$12) for children 6 to 15. For 48 hours it is 3,000 pesetas (US$18) for adults, 2,500 pesetas (US$15) for children, for 72 hours, 3,500 pesetas (US$21) and 3,000 pesetas (US$18).

The card offers visitors many advantages. The 24-hour card covers 10 free journeys on the metro or bus, and the 48- and 72-hour cards offer unlimited travel on all public transport. Cardholders receive 25% discounts on the Tombbus (which runs along the best shopping route in central Barcelona) and the Tibibus (to the Fun Fair on Mount Tibidabo). On airport and tourist buses, fares are reduced by 15%.

Culture vultures with the card get discounts of 30% to 50% in 28 museums. Eleven theaters and shows grant a 10% to 25% discount, which also applies at 16 leisure and night venues. Barcelona is famous for its designers, whose work ranges from clothes to ceramics. With this card you get a 12% discount at 23 leading stores. Finally, there is an 8% discount in 11 restaurants. The cards specify where they can be used. They're for sale at the tourist offices at the airport, at Sants station, and in the Plaça de Catalunya (see "Visitor Information," above).

2 Getting Around

To save money on public transportation, buy one of two transportation cards, each good for 10 trips: **Tarjeta T-1,** costing 795 pesetas (US$4.75), is good for the metro and the bus; **Tarjeta T-2,** for 760 pesetas (US$4.55), is good on everything but the bus.

Passes (*abonos temporales*) are available at the office of **Transports Metropolita de Barcelona,** Plaça de la Universitat, open Monday to Friday 8am to 7pm and Saturday 8am to 1pm.

To save money on sightseeing tours during summer, take a ride on **Bus Turistic,** which passes by 24 of the most popular sights. You can get on and off the bus as you please and also ride the Tibidabo funicular and the Montjuïc cable car and funicular for the price of a single ticket. Tickets, which may be purchased on the bus or at the tourist office at Plaça de Catalunya, cost 1,800 pesetas (US$10.80) for 1 day or 2,300 pesetas (US$13.80) for 2 days.

BY SUBWAY

Barcelona's metro system consists of five main lines; it crisscrosses the city more frequently and with greater efficiency than the bus network. Two commuter trains also service the city, fanning out to the suburbs. Service is Monday to Friday 5am to 11pm, Saturday 5am to 1am, and Sunday and holidays 6am to 1am. A one-way fare is 140 pesetas (US85¢). The entrance to each metro station is marked with a red diamond. The major station for all subway lines is **Plaça de Catalunya.**

BY BUS

Some 50 bus lines traverse the city, and as always, you don't want to ride them at rush hour. The driver issues a ticket as you board at the front. Most buses operate daily

6:30am to 10pm; some night buses go along the principal arteries 11pm to 4am. Buses are color-coded—red ones cut through the city center during the day, and yellow ones do the job at night. A one-way fare is 145 pesetas (US85¢).

BY TAXI

Each yellow-and-black taxi bears the letters SP (*servicio público*) on both its front and its rear. A lit green light on the roof and a "Libre" sign in the window indicate that the taxi is free to pick up passengers. The basic rate begins at 300 pesetas (US$1.80). Check to make sure you're not paying the fare of a previously departed passenger; taxi drivers have been known to "forget" to turn back the meter. For each additional kilometer in slow-moving traffic, you are assessed 110 to 120 pesetas (US65¢ to US70¢). Supplements might also be added—150 pesetas (US90¢) for a large suitcase that is placed in the trunk, for instance. Rides to the airport carry a supplement of 300 pesetas (US$1.80). For a taxi, call ☎ **93-330-08-04.**

BY CAR

Driving is frustrating in congested Barcelona, and it's potentially dangerous. Besides, it's unlikely that you'd ever find a place to park. Try other means of getting around. Save your car rentals for 1-day excursions from the Catalonian capital to such places as Sitges and Tarragona to the south, Montserrat to the west, or the resorts of the Costa Brava to the north.

All three of the major U.S.-based car-rental firms are represented in Barcelona, both at the airport and often (except for Budget) at downtown offices. The company with the longest hours and some of the most favorable rates is the airport office of **Budget** (☎ **93-298-35-00**), open Monday to Friday (without a midday break) 7am to midnight.

Other contenders include **Avis,** carrer de Casanova, 209 (☎ **93-209-95-33**), open Monday to Friday 8am to 1pm and 4 to 7pm, and Saturday 8am to 1pm. **Hertz** maintains its office at Tuset, 10 (☎ **93-217-80-76**); it's open Monday to Friday 8am to 2pm and 4 to 7pm, and Saturday 9am to 1pm. Both Hertz and Avis are closed on Sunday, forcing clients of those companies to trek out to the airport to pick up or return their cars; however, after-hours arrangements can be made by request.

Remember that it's usually cheaper and easier to arrange your car rental before leaving North America by calling one of the firms' toll-free numbers.

BY FUNICULAR & RAIL LINK

At some point in your journey, you may want to visit Tibidabo or Montjuïc (or both). A train called **Tramvía Blau** (Blue Streetcar) goes from Plaça Kennedy to the bottom of the funicular to Tibidabo. It operates every 15 to 20 minutes from 9:05am to 9:35pm on weekends only. The fare is 300 pesetas (US$1.80) one way, 450 pesetas (US$2.70) round-trip. During the week, buses run from the Plaça Kennedy to the bottom of the funicular from approximately 7am to 9:30pm daily. The bus costs 145 pesetas (US85¢) one way.

At the end of the run, you can go the rest of the way by funicular to the top, at 1,650 feet, for a stunning panoramic view of Barcelona. The funicular operates only when the Fun Fair at Tibidabo is open. Opening times vary according to the time of year and the weather conditions. As a rule, the funicular starts operating 20 minutes before the Fun Fair opens, then every half an hour. During peak visiting hours, it runs every 15 minutes. The fare is 300 pesetas (US$1.80) one way, 400 pesetas (US$2.40) round-trip.

Barcelona Metro

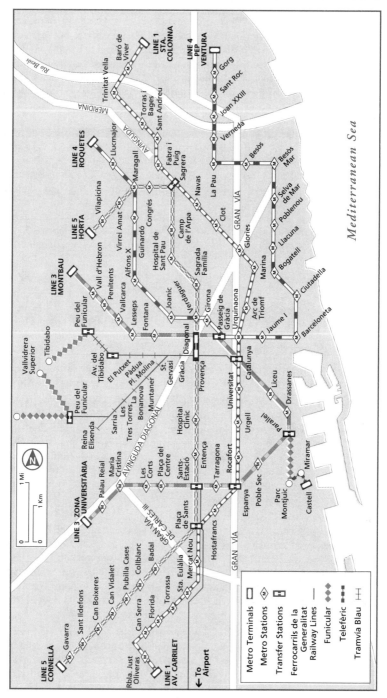

The **Tibibus** (☎ 93-211-79-42) goes from the Plaça de Catalunya, in the center of the city, to Tibidabo from June 24 to September 15, Tuesday to Sunday, and on every weekend out of season. It runs every 30 minutes 10:30am to 6:30pm and sometimes 8:30pm, depending on when the park closes. The one-way fare is 270 pesetas (US$1.60). To reach Montjuïc, the site of the 1992 Olympics, take the **Montjuïc funicular** (☎ 93-318-70-74). It links with subway line 3 at Paral-lel. The funicular operates June 13 to September 30 daily 11am to 10pm. In winter it operates daily 10:45am to 8pm. The round-trip fare is 600 pesetas (US$3.60).

A **cable car** linking the upper part of the Montjuïc funicular with Castell de Montjuïc is in service in winter, daily 11:15am to 6:30pm (until 7:30pm on weekends). The one-way fare is 400 pesetas (US$2.40); the round-trip fare is 600 pesetas (US$3.60) for adults, 500 pesetas (US$3) for children. From June 28 to September 15 and holidays it operates Monday to Friday 11:15am to 8pm, until 9pm on weekends.

The **Montjuïc telèferic** (cable car) runs from Barceloneta to Montjuïc. Service from June 20 through September 15 is daily 10:30am to 7pm, and noon to 5pm in winter. The fare is 1,000 pesetas (US$6) one way, 1,200 pesetas (US$7.20) round-trip.

Fast Facts: Barcelona

American Express   For your mail or banking needs, the American Express office in Barcelona is at Passeig de Gràcia, 101 (☎ 93-217-00-70; metro: Diagonal), near the corner of carrer del Rosselló. It's open Monday to Friday 10am to 6pm and Saturday 9:30am to noon.

Baby-Sitters   Most major hotels can arrange for baby-sitters with adequate notice. You'll have to make a special request for an English-speaking baby-sitter.

Bookstores   The best selection of English-language books, including travel maps and guides, is at LAIE, Pau Claris, 85 (☎ 93-318-17-39; metro: Plaça de Catalunya or Urquinaona), 1 block from the Gran Vía de les Corts Catalánes. It's open Monday to Friday 10am to 9pm and Saturday 10:30am to 9pm. The bookshop has an upstairs cafe with international newspapers and a little terrace, serving breakfast, lunch (salad bar), even dinners. The cafe is open Monday to Saturday 9am to 1am. The shop also presents cultural events, including art exhibits and literary presentations.

Consulates   The **U.S. Consulate,** Reina Elisenda, 23 (☎ 93-280-22-27; train: Reina Elisenda), is open Monday to Friday 9am to 12:30pm and 3 to 5pm. The **Canadian Consulate,** Passeig de Gràcia, 77, 3rd floor (☎ 93-215-07-04; metro: Passeig de Gràcia), is open Monday to Friday 10am to noon. The **U.K. Consulate,** Avinguda Diagonal, 477 (☎ 93-366-62-00; metro: Hospital Clinic), is open Monday to Friday 9:30am to 1:30pm and 4 to 5pm. The **Australian Consulate** is at Gran Vía Carlos III, 98, 9th floor (☎ 93-330-94-96; metro: María Cristina), and is open Monday to Friday 10am to noon.

Currency Exchange   Most banks will exchange currency Monday to Friday 8:30am to 2pm and Saturday 8:30am to 1pm. Saturday hours are not valid in summer. A major *oficina de cambio* (exchange office) is at the Estació Central de Barcelona-Sants, the principal rail station for Barcelona. It's open Monday to Saturday 8:30am to 10pm, Sunday 8:30am to 2pm and 4:30 to 10pm. Exchange offices are also available at Barcelona's airport, El Prat de Llobregat, open daily 7am to 11pm.

Dentists   Call Clínica Dental Beonadex, Paseo Bona Nova, 69, 3rd Floor (☎ 93-418-44-33), for an appointment. It's open Monday 3 to 9pm and Tuesday to Friday 8am to 3pm.

Doctors   See "Hospitals," below.

Drugstores   The most central one is Farmacía Manuel Nadal i Casas, Rambla de Canaletes, 121 (☎ 93-317-49-42; metro: Plaça de Catalunya), open daily 9am to 1:30pm and 4:30 to 10pm. Various pharmacies take turns staying open late at night. Pharmacies that aren't open post the names and addresses of the pharmacies in the area that are open.

Emergencies   In case of fire, call ☎ 080; for the police, ☎ 092; and for an ambulance, ☎ 061.

Hospitals   Barcelona has many hospitals and clinics, including the Hospital Clínic and the Hospital de la Santa Creu i Sant Pau, at the intersection of carrer Cartagena and carrer Sant Antoni Maria Claret (☎ 93-291-90-00; metro: Hospital de Sant Pau).

Internet Access   El Café de Internet, Avenida de las Corts Catalánes, 656 (☎ 93-412-19-15; e-mail: JordiCarcellaChoia@sevicom.es), is open daily 9am to midnight.

Laundry   Ask at your hotel for the one nearest you, or try one of the following: Lavandería Brasilia, Avinguda Meridiana, 322 (☎ 93-352-72-05; metro: Plaça de Catalunya), is open Monday to Friday 9:30am to 1:30pm and 4 to 8pm. Also centrally located is Lavandería Yolanda, carrer Carma, 114 (☎ 93-329-43-68; metro: Liceu, at Les Rambles); it's open Monday to Friday 9am to 1:30pm and 4 to 8pm, Saturday 9am to 1:30pm.

Newspapers & Magazines   The *International Herald-Tribune* is sold at major hotels and nearly all the news kiosks along Les Rambles. Sometimes you can also obtain copies of *USA Today* or one of the London newspapers, such as the *Times*. The two leading daily newspapers of Barcelona, which often list cultural events, are *El Periódico* and *La Vanguardia*.

Police   In an emergency, dial ☎ 092.

Post Office   The main post office is at Plaça d'Antoni López (☎ 93-318-38-31; metro: Jaume I). It's open Monday to Friday 8am to 10pm and on Saturday 8am to 8pm.

Radio & TV   If your hotel room has a radio or a TV set (unlikely in budget accommodations), you can often get Britain's BBC World Service. Deluxe and some first-class hotels subscribe to CNN. Two national TV channels (1 and 2) transmit broadcasts in Spanish, and two regional channels (3 and 33) broadcast in Catalán; there are also some private TV channels, such as Canal +. If you're listening to radio, tune in to the Spanish music program, "Segunda Programa," with everything from classical music to jazz (nights only).

Rest Rooms   Some public rest rooms are available, including those at popular tourist spots, such as Tibidabo and Montjuïc. You'll also find rest rooms at the major museums of Barcelona, at all train stations and airports, and at metro stations. The major department stores, such as El Corté Ingles, also have good rest rooms. Otherwise, out on the streets you may be a bit hard-pressed. Sanitation is questionable in some of the public facilities. If you use the facilities of a cafe or tavern, it's customary to make a small purchase at the bar, even if only a glass of mineral water.

Safety   Be particularly careful with cameras, purses, and wallets, all favorite targets of thieves and pickpockets in Barcelona; particularly on the world-famous Rambles. The southern part of Les Rambles, near the waterfront, is the most dangerous section, especially at night. Proceed with caution.

Taxes   If you're not a European Union (EU) resident and you make purchases in Spain worth more than 15,000 pesetas (US$90), you can get a tax refund. (The internal tax, known as VAT [value-added tax] in most of Europe, is called IVA in Spain.) Depending on the goods, the rate usually ranges from 7% to 16% of the total worth of your merchandise. Luxury items are taxed at 33%.

To get this refund, you must complete three copies of a form that the store will give you, detailing the nature of your purchase and its value. Citizens of non-EU countries show the purchase and the form to the Spanish Customs Office. The shop is supposed to refund the amount due you. Inquire at the time of purchase how they will do so and discuss in what currency your refund will arrive.

Telegrams & Telex   These can be sent at the main post office (see p. 47). You can also send telex and fax messages at all major and many budget hotels.

Telephones   If you don't speak Spanish, you may find it easier to telephone from your hotel, but remember that this is often very expensive because hotels impose a surcharge on every operator-assisted call. In some cases this can be as high as 40% or more. On the street, phone booths (known as *cabinas*) have dialing instructions in English; you can make local calls by inserting a 25 peseta coin for 3 minutes.

In Spain many smaller establishments, especially bars, discos, and a few informal restaurants, don't have phones. Further, many summer-only bars and discos secure a phone for the season only, then get a new number the next season. Many attractions, such as small churches or even minor museums, have no staff to receive inquiries from the public.

In 1998, all telephone numbers in Spain changed to a nine-digit system instead of the six- or seven-digit method used previously. Each number is now preceded by its provincial code for local, national, and international calls. For example, when calling to Barcelona from Barcelona or another province within Spain, telephone customers must dial 93-123-45-67.

To call Spain from another country, first dial the international long-distance code (011) plus the country code (34), followed by the 9-digit number. Hence, when calling Barcelona from the United States, dial (011-34) 93-123-45-67.

To make an international call from Spain, you must dial 07, followed by the country code, the area code, and the telephone number.

When in Spain, the access number for an **AT&T** calling card is ☎ **1-800-callATT.** The access number for **Sprint** is ☎ **800/888-0013.**

More information is also available on the Teléfonica Web site at www.telefonica.es.

Tipping   Don't overtip. The government requires restaurants and hotels to include their service charges—usually 15% of the bill. However, that doesn't mean you should skip out of a place without dispensing some extra pesetas. The following are some guidelines:

Your hotel porter should get 75 pesetas (US45¢) per bag and never less than 100 pesetas (US60¢), even if you have only one suitcase. Maids should be given 150 pesetas (US90¢) per day, more if you're generous. Tip doormen 125 pesetas (US75¢) for assisting with baggage and 50 pesetas (US30¢) for calling a cab. In top-ranking hotels the concierge will often submit a separate bill, showing charges for newspapers and other services; if he or she has been particularly help-ful, tip extra. For cab drivers, add about 10% to the fare as shown on the meter. At airports, such as Barajas in Madrid and major terminals, the porter who han-dles your luggage will present you with a fixed-charge bill.

In both restaurants and nightclubs, a 15% service charge is added to the bill. To that, add another 3% to 5% tip, depending on the quality of the service. Waiters in deluxe restaurants and nightclubs are accustomed to the extra 5%, which means you'll end up tipping 20%. If that seems excessive, you must remember that the initial service charge reflected in the fixed price is distributed among all the help.

Barbers and hairdressers expect a 10% to 15% tip. Tour guides expect 200 pesetas (US$1.20), although a tip is not mandatory. Theater and bullfight ush-ers get from 50 to 75 pesetas (US30¢ to US45¢).

3 Where to Stay

The hotel offerings in Barcelona have never been better or as plentiful as they are now. In the wake of the 1992 Olympics, old palaces were restored and converted into hotels, and long-seedy and tarnished hotels were renovated in time for the games. The result is an abundance of good hotels in all price ranges. Along with Madrid, Barcelona still ranks as one of the most expensive cities in Spain, but the tariffs charged by its first-class and deluxe hotels are completely in line with other major cities of continental Europe, and reasonable in price when stacked up against such cities as Paris and London. A favorable exchange rate in relation to the U.S. dollar also makes these prices more affordable.

Safety is an important factor to consider when choosing a hotel in Barcelona. Some of the least expensive hotels are not in good locations. A popular area for the budget-conscious traveler is the **Barri Gòtic** (Gothic Quarter), located in the heart of town. You'll live and eat less expensively here than in any other part of Barcelona—but you should be careful when returning to your hotel late at night.

More modern, but also more expensive, accommodations can be found north of the Barri Gòtic in the **Eixample district,** centered around the metro stops Plaça de Catalunya and Universitat. Although many buildings are *modernista,* from the first two decades of this century, sometimes the elevators and plumbing tend to be of the same vintage. The Eixample is a desirable and safe neighborhood, especially along its wide boulevards. Noise is the only problem you might encounter.

Farther north still, above the Avinguda Diagonal, you'll enter the **Gràcia area,** where you can enjoy distinctively Catalán neighborhood life. You'll be a bit away from the main attractions, but they can be reached easily by public transportation.

Many of Barcelona's hotels were built before the invention of the automobile, and even those built later rarely found space for a garage. When parking is available at the hotel, the price is indicated; otherwise, the hotel staff will direct you to a garage some-where in the general vicinity. Expect to pay upwards of 2,000 pesetas (US$14) for 24 hours; you might as well park your car, as you can't see traffic-congested Barcelona comfortably by automobile—rely on your trusty feet and public transportation instead.

CIUTAT VELLA

The Ciutat Vella ("Old City" in Catalán) forms the monumental center of Barcelona, taking in Les Rambles, Plaça de Sant Jaume, Via Laietana, Passeig Nacional, and Pas-seig de Colom. In its older structures it contains some of the city's best hotel bargains. Most of the glamorous and more expensive hotels are in Sur Diagonal (see p. 57).

Central Barcelona Accommodations

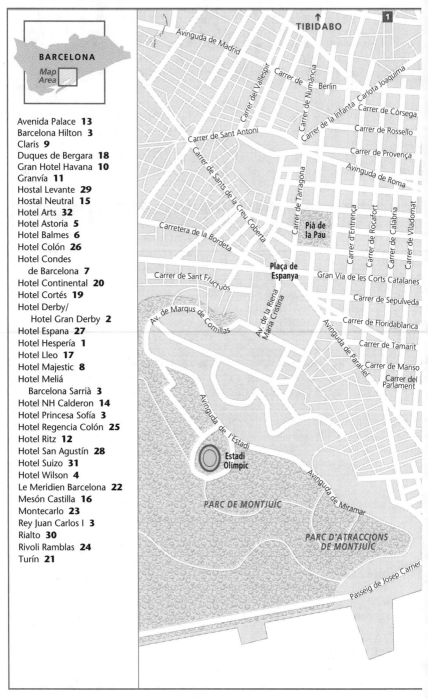

Avenida Palace **13**
Barcelona Hilton **3**
Claris **9**
Duques de Bergara **18**
Gran Hotel Havana **10**
Granvía **11**
Hostal Levante **29**
Hostal Neutral **15**
Hotel Arts **32**
Hotel Astoria **5**
Hotel Balmes **6**
Hotel Colón **26**
Hotel Condes
    de Barcelona **7**
Hotel Continental **20**
Hotel Cortés **19**
Hotel Derby/
    Hotel Gran Derby **2**
Hotel Espana **27**
Hotel Hespería **1**
Hotel Lleo **17**
Hotel Majestic **8**
Hotel Meliá
    Barcelona Sarrià **3**
Hotel NH Calderon **14**
Hotel Princesa Sofía **3**
Hotel Regencia Colón **25**
Hotel Ritz **12**
Hotel San Agustín **28**
Hotel Suizo **31**
Hotel Wilson **4**
Le Meridien Barcelona **22**
Mesón Castilla **16**
Montecarlo **23**
Rey Juan Carlos I **3**
Rialto **30**
Rivoli Ramblas **24**
Turín **21**

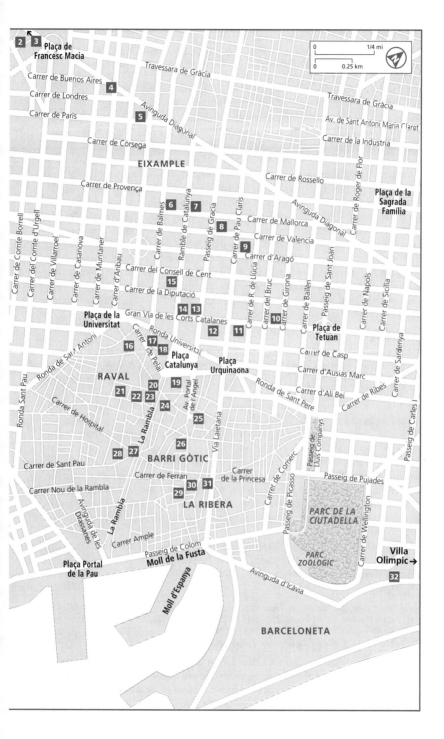

Plaça de Francesc Macia

Carrer de Buenos Aires

Carrer de Londres

Carrer de Paris

Travessara de Gràcia

Avinguda Diagonal

Carrer de Còrsega

EIXAMPLE

Carrer de Provença

Carrer de Rossello

Travessara de Gràcia

Av. de Sant Antoni Maria Claret

Carrer de la Industria

Carrer de Roger de Flor

Plaça de la Sagrada Família

Avinguda Diagonal

Carrer de Mallorca

Carrer de Valencia

Carrer d'Aragó

Carrer de Comte Borrell

Carrer del Comte d'Urgell

Carrer de Villarroel

Carrer de Casanova

Carrer de Muntaner

Carrer d'Aribau

Carrer de Balmes

Rambla de Catalunya

Passeig de Gràcia

Carrer de Pau Claris

Carrer de R. de Llúcia

Carrer del Bruc

Carrer de Girona

Carrer de Bailèn

Passeig de Sant Joan

Carrer de Napols

Carrer de Sicilia

Carrer del Consell de Cent

Carrer de la Diputació

Gran Vía de les Corts Catalanes

Plaça de la Universitat

Ronda Universitat

Carrer de Pelai

Plaça Catalunya

Plaça Urquinaona

Plaça de Tetuan

Carrer de Casp

Carrer d'Ausias Marc

Carrer de Sardenya

Ronda de Sant Antoni

Ronda de Sant Pere

Carrer d'Ali Bei

Carrer de Ribes

Passeig de Carles I

RAVAL

Ronda Sant Pau

Carrer de Hospital

Carrer de Sant Pau

La Rambla

Av. Portal de l'Angel

Via Laietana

BARRI GÒTIC

Carrer de Ferran

Carrer Nou de la Rambla

Avinguda de les Drassanes

La Rambla

Carrer Ample

Carrer de la Princesa

Carrer de Comerc

LA RIBERA

Passeig de Picasso

Passeig de Lluís Companys

PARC DE LA CIUTADELLA

Passeig de Pujades

Carrer de Wellington

Villa Olimpic →

Plaça Portal de la Pau

Passeig de Colom

Moll de la Fusta

Moll d'Espanya

PARC ZOOLOGIC

Avinguda d'Icàvia

BARCELONETA

0   1/4 mi

0   0.25 km

Very Expensive

✪ **Le Meridien Barcelona.** Les Rambles, 111, 08002 Barcelona. ☎ **800/543-4300** in the U.S., or 93-318-62-00. Fax 93-301-77-76. www.meridienbarcelona.com. E-mail: lemeridien@meridienbarcelona.com. 205 units. A/C MINIBAR TV TEL. 42,000–52,000 ptas. (US$252–US$312) double; from 65,000 ptas. (US$390) suite. AE, DC, MC, V. Parking 2,000 ptas. (US$12). Metro: Liceu or Plaça de Catalunya.

This is the finest hotel in the old town of Barcelona, a fact to which guests such as Michael Jackson can surely attest. It is superior in both amenities and comfort to its two closest rivals in the area: Colón and Rivoli Ramblas. Built in 1956, in the darkest days of the Franco regime, it was for years called the Hotel Manila and remained a lackluster choice. Then it was completely renovated and opened as the Ramada Renaissance in 1988. Finally, in 1991, the French-owned Meridien chain took over. It's now a medley of artful pastels and tasteful decorating. Guest rooms are spacious and comfortable, with such amenities as extra-large beds, heated bathroom floors, in-house videos, hair dryers, two phones, and double-glazed windows. (However, that doesn't prevent noise from Les Rambles from penetrating the rooms.) The Renaissance Club—an executive floor popular with businesspeople—provides extra amenities.

Dining/Diversions: A chic lobby bar, open daily 7 to 11pm, has live piano music. The main restaurant, **Le Patio,** serves fine continental and Catalán cuisine.

Amenities: 24-hour room service, laundry, concierge, baby-sitting, business center, rooms for people with disabilities, small gym.

Expensive

Hotel Colón. Avinguda de la Catedral, 7, 08002 Barcelona. ☎ **800/845-0636** in the U.S., or 93-301-14-04. Fax 93-317-29-15. E-mail: colon@nexus.es. 148 units. A/C MINIBAR TV TEL. 26,000–40,000 ptas. (US$156–US$240) double; from 46,000 ptas. (US$276) suite. AE, DC, MC, V. Bus: 16, 17, 19, or 45.

The Colón is an appropriate choice if you plan to spend a lot of time exploring Barcelona's medieval neighborhoods. Blessed with what might be the most dramatic location in the city, immediately opposite the main entrance to the cathedral, this hotel sits behind a dignified neoclassical facade graced with carved pilasters and ornamental wrought-iron balustrades. Inside, you'll find conservative and slightly old-fashioned public spaces, a helpful staff, and guest rooms filled with comfortable furniture and, despite recent renovations, an appealingly dowdy charm. Although not all rooms have views, all have private bathrooms; the units in back are quieter. Sixth-floor rooms with balconies overlooking the square are the most desirable; some of the lower rooms are rather dark.

Dining/Diversions: The hotel maintains two well-recommended restaurants, the **Grill** (for continental specialties) and **Carabela** (for Catalán specialties).

Amenities: Concierge, room service (24 hours), laundry/valet, limousine, baby-sitting.

Hotel NH Calderón. Rambla de Catalunya, 26, 08007 Barcelona. ☎ **93-301-00-00.** Fax 93-412-41-93. www.nh-hoteles.es. 283 units. A/C MINIBAR TV TEL. Mon–Thurs 26,100 ptas. (US$156.60) double, Fri–Sun 22,500 ptas. (US$135) double. AE, DC, MC, V. Parking 2,000 ptas. (US$12). Metro: Passeig de Gràcia or Plaça de Catalunya.

Efficient, well-maintained, and well-staffed with a multilingual corps of employees, this hotel will deliver exactly what it promises: safe and comfortable accommodations in a well-conceived, standardized format that's akin to many other modern hotels around the world. Originally built in the 1960s in a high-rise, 10-story style that wasn't particularly imaginative, this hotel was greatly improved in the early 1990s after its acquisition by NH, with frequent renovations ever since. Accommodations contain comfortable, contemporary-looking furnishings with hints of high-tech design, good lighting, lots of varnished hardwood, and colorful fabrics.

Dining/Diversions: The hotel has a formal restaurant serving both a Catalonian and international cuisine. It also has a bar often filled with businesspersons.

Amenities: Health club, sauna, open-air swimming pool on the roof.

Rivoli Ramblas. Les Rambles, 128, 08002 Barcelona. ☎ **93-302-66-43.** Fax 93-318-87-60. E-mail: rivoli@alba.mssl.es. 87 units. A/C MINIBAR TV TEL. 33,000 ptas. (US$198) double; from 85,000 ptas. (US$510) suite. Rates include breakfast. AE, DC, MC, V. Metro: Plaça de Catalunya or Liceu.

Behind a dignified, art deco townhouse on the upper section of the Rambles, a block south of the Plaça de Catalunya, this recently renovated hotel incorporates many fine examples of avant-garde Catalán design into its stylish interior. The Colón has more tradition and style, and the Meridien more modern comfort; this is choice number three in the old town. Still, the public rooms glisten with polished marble and a pristinely contrived minimalism. Guest rooms are carpeted, soundproof, and elegant, although rather cramped for the price. Along with safety deposit boxes and private bathrooms, guest rooms boast such electronic amenities as VCRs, radios, and TVs with satellite hookups.

Dining/Diversions: Le Brut Restaurant serves regional, Spanish, and international dishes. **The Blue Moon** cocktail bar features piano music and a soothingly high-tech design. A rooftop terrace, decked with flowers and suitable for coffee or drinks, offers a view over the rooftops of one of Barcelona's most architecturally interesting neighborhoods.

Amenities: Concierge, room service, baby-sitting, laundry/valet, small health club/ fitness center, sauna, solarium, car rentals, shopping boutiques.

MODERATE

✪ **Duques de Bergara.** Bergara, 11. ☎ **93-301-51-51.** Fax 93-317-34-42. 149 units. A/C MINIBAR TV TEL. 26,000 ptas. (US$156) double; 34,000 ptas. (US$204) triple. AE, DC, MC, V. Public parking nearby 3,000 ptas. (US$18). Metro: Plaça de Catalunya.

This upscale hotel occupies what was originally built in 1899 as the private townhouse of the Duke of Bergara. In 1998, the original five-story structure was more than doubled in size with the addition of a new seven-story tower, where bedrooms are outfitted with the same conservatively traditional comforts that appear within units in the older wing. Public areas manage to artfully contain most of the paneling, stained glass, and decorative accessories originally installed by the modernista architect who designed the place, Emilio Salas i Cortes, a professor of the movement's greatest luminary, Gaudí. In the hotel's reception area, look for stained-glass panels containing the heraldic coat of arms of the building's original occupant and namesake, the Duke of Bergara.

On the premises are a restaurant (El Duc, reviewed on p. 69), bar, cafe, and outdoor swimming pool that functions as something of a social center throughout the afternoon and early evening.

Hotel Lleó. Pelal, 22–24, 08001 Barcelona. ☎ **93-318-13-12.** Fax 93-412-26-57. www. hotel-lleo.es. 80 units. A/C MINIBAR TV TEL. 18,500 ptas. (US$111) double. AE, DC, MC, V. Parking 3,000 ptas. (US$18) nearby. Metro: Plaça de Catalunya or Plaça de la Universitat.

Solid, well run, and conservative, this hotel occupies an 1840s building on a busy commercial street in one of the most central neighborhoods in town. Completely renovated in 1992 in time for the Olympics, it offers clean, streamlined, and comfortable bedrooms, each equipped with a lockbox and comfortable, functional furniture. There is a restaurant. For the price, this is a good, standard, functional choice, but not a lot more.

ⓘ   Family-Friendly Hotels

Hotel Colón *(see p. 52)*   Opposite the cathedral in the Gothic Quarter, this hotel has been compared to a country home. Families ask for and often get spacious rooms.

Hotel Hespería *(see p. 62)*   At the northern edge of the city, this hotel has gardens and a safe neighborhood setting. The rooms are generous enough in size for an extra bed.

Hotel Princesa Sofía *(see p. 58)*   Although primarily a business-oriented hotel, the Princesa Sofía has excellent baby-sitting services, as well as two pools (one indoor and one outdoor), making it ideal for the business traveler and his or her family.

✪ **Hotel Regencia Colón.** Sagristans, 13–17, 08002 Barcelona. ☎ **93-318-98-58.** Fax 93-317-28-22. 55 units. A/C MINIBAR TV TEL. 18,000 ptas. (US$108) double; 20,500 ptas. (US$123) triple. AE, DC, MC, V. Metro: Plaça de Catalunya or Urquinaona.

This stately stone six-story building stands directly behind the more prestigious, superior, and more expensive Hotel Colón—both lie in the shadow of the cathedral. The Regencia Colón is attractive to tour groups. The formal lobby seems a bit dour, but the well-maintained rooms are comfortable and often spacious, albeit worn. All units are insulated against sound, and 40 of them have full tub baths (the remainder have showers). All have piped-in music. The hotel's location at the edge of the Barri Gòtic is a plus. Considering what you get for the reasonable prices charged, the hotel is a good value for Barcelona.

Montecarlo. Les Rambles, 124, 08002 Barcelona. ☎ **93-412-04-04.** Fax 93-318-73-23. E-mail: montecarlobcn@abaforum.es. 74 units. A/C MINIBAR TV TEL. 18,000–23,000 ptas. (US$108–US$138) double; 26,500 ptas. (US$159) triple. AE, DC, MC, V. Parking 2,000 ptas. (US$12). Metro: Plaça de Catalunya.

This hotel, beside the wide and sloping promenade of the Rambles, was originally built around 200 years ago as an opulent and aristocratic private home, with comfort superior to such previously recommended competitors as the Lleó. In the 1930s, it was transformed into the unpretentious hotel you'll find today. Each of the bedrooms is comfortably decorated, most of them renovated around 1989. Double-glazed windows help keep out some of the noise. Public areas include some of the building's original decorative touches, such as carved doors, a baronial fireplace, and crystal chandeliers.

INEXPENSIVE

Granvía. Gran Vía de les Corts Catalánes, 642, 08007 Barcelona. ☎ **93-318-19-00.** Fax 93-318-99-97. 50 units. A/C MINIBAR TV TEL. 13,500 ptas. (US$81) double. AE, DC, MC, V. Parking 2,300 ptas. (US$13.80). Metro: Plaça de Catalunya.

A grand hotel on one of the most fashionable boulevards in Barcelona, the Granvía has public rooms that reflect the opulence of the 1860s—chandeliers, gilt mirrors, and French provincial furniture—and a grand balustraded staircase. It's your best choice if you want to feel like royalty. Although the traditional guest rooms contain interesting antique reproductions, they are comfortable rather than luxurious. Expect fancifully shaped headboards and pastel-colored chenille bedspreads along with upholstery that could use refreshing. The courtyard, which has a fountain and palm trees, is set with tables for alfresco drinks; continental breakfast is served in the garden room off the courtyard. Centrally heated in the winter, the hotel has one drawback: street noise, which might disturb the light sleeper.

✪ **Hostal Levante.** Baïxada de Sant Miguel, 2, 08002 Barcelona. ☎ **93-317-95-65.** E-mail: hotellevante@mixmail.com. 38 units. 5,500 ptas. (US$33) double without bathroom, 6,500 ptas. (US$39) double with bathroom. MC, V. Metro: Liceu or Jaume I.

This is one of the nicest and most reasonably priced places to stay in Barcelona. In a quiet, imposing building more than two centuries old, it stands just a short distance from Plaça de Sant Jaume, in the center of the Barri Gòtic. The units are clean and comfortable, and there's central heating. The staff speaks English. No meals are served.

Hostal Neutral. Rambla de Catalunya, 42, 08007 Barcelona. ☎ **93-487-63-90.** Fax 93-487-40-28. 35 units. TEL. 5,600–6,500 ptas. (US$33.60–US$39) double; 7,600 ptas. (US$45.60) triple. MC, V. Metro: Passeig de Gràcia.

An older pension, but very recommendable, this hostel has a reputation for cleanliness and efficiency. As the name suggests, the small rooms here are neutral—but comfortable nevertheless, although furnished with a medley of odds and ends. Colorful antique floor tiling brightens some of the high-ceilinged rooms. Breakfast is served in a salon with a coffered ceiling, and there's a large TV room nearby. English is spoken. The entrance is one flight up.

Hotel Continental. Rambla de Canaletes, 138, 08002 Barcelona. ☎ **93-301-25-70.** Fax 93-302-73-60. www.hotelcontinental.com. E-mail: ramblas@hotelcontinental.com. 35 units. MINIBAR TV TEL. 10,700–13,500 ptas. (US$64.20–US$81) double; 15,500 ptas. (US$93) triple; 18,000 ptas. (US$108) quad. Rates include buffet breakfast. AE, DC, MC, V. Metro: Plaça de Catalunya.

This hotel is on the upper two floors of a commercial building in a safer section of the upper Rambles. The flowery, slightly faded reception area is clean and accented with 19th-century statues. The rooms are pleasant and modern, and 10 have semicircular balconies overlooking the Rambles. Though the decor in some of the bedrooms shouts "Laura Ashley gone mad," everything is clean and comfortable. Amenities include safe-deposit boxes and hair dryers. A buffet breakfast is served daily 6am to noon.

Hotel Cortés. Santa Ana, 25, 08002 Barcelona. ☎ **93-317-91-12.** Fax 93-302-78-70. 46 units. TV TEL. 9,300 ptas. (US$55.80) double. Rates include breakfast. AE, DC, MC, V. Metro: Plaça de Catalunya.

A short walk from the cathedral, the Cortés was originally built around 1910 and, like many of its competitors in Barcelona, was thoroughly renovated in time for the 1992 Olympics. It competes effectively against the Continental. Guest rooms are scattered over five floors, and about half overlook a quiet central courtyard (the other half open onto the street). The hotel's ground floor contains a simple, unpretentious restaurant and bar, where breakfast is served and where you can enjoy a beer throughout the day and night.

Hotel España. Carrer Sant Pau, 11, 08002 Barcelona. ☎ **93-318-17-58.** Fax 93-317-11-34. 60 units. TEL. 10,800 ptas. (US$64.80) double. AE, DC, MC, V. Metro: Liceu or Drassanes.

Although the rooms at this cost-conscious hotel have none of the architectural grandeur of Barcelona's modernist age, they're well-scrubbed, comfortably sized, functional, and outfitted with furniture and accessories derived from the hotel's most recent renovation in 1992. The building itself is a relic of the city's turn-of-the-century splendor, constructed in 1902 by fabled architect Domenech I Montaner, designer and architect of the Palau de la Música. There's an elevator that can carry you up the building's four floors; a facade that still evokes the past; and a hard-working staff that's comfortable with foreign, non-Spanish-speaking visitors. The lower Rambla, near which this hotel sits, evokes either cultural fascination or indignation, depending on how urbanized you are, but overall, it's an acceptable and well-managed choice at a relatively reasonable price. There's a restaurant on the premises, the España, open daily for lunch and dinner, that serves food and drink to locals and hotel residents alike.

Hotel San Agustín. Plaça de San Agustín, 3, 08001 Barcelona. ☎ **93-318-16-58.** Fax 93-317-29-28. 76 units. A/C TV TEL. 15,000 ptas. (US$90) double; 18,500 ptas. (US$111) triple; 22,000–25,000 ptas. (US$132–US$150) quad; 29,000 ptas. (US$174) 2-room family unit. Rates include breakfast. AE, DC, MC, V. Metro: Liceu.

This tastefully renovated five-story hotel stands in the center of the old city, near the covered produce markets overlooking the brick walls of an unfinished Romanesque church. Guest rooms are comfortable and modern, with such amenities as piped-in music and private safes. Some units are specially equipped for persons with disabilities. The hotel also runs a good restaurant offering reasonably priced meals.

Hotel Suizo. Plaça de l'Angel, 12, 08010 Barcelona. ☎ **93-310-61-08.** Fax 93-315-04-61. www.gargallo-hotels.com. E-mail: reserve@gargallo-hotels.com. 50 units. A/C MINIBAR TV TEL. 18,500 ptas. (US$111) double. AE, DC, MC, V. Parking 3,000 ptas. (US$18) nearby. Metro: Jaume I.

A few blocks from the cathedral in a 19th-century building, the Hotel Suizo has an elaborate belle époque-style bar where drinks and snacks are served. A Gargallo hotel, it's a sibling of the Rialto (see below). The Suizo doesn't have the roomy hallways of the Rialto, but its public rooms are more attractively furnished and inviting. The reception area is pleasantly modern. Guest rooms have antique-patterned wallpaper, Spanish furniture, and private bathrooms. The staff is polite and helpful.

✪ **Mesón Castilla.** Valldoncella, 5, 08002 Barcelona. ☎ **93-318-21-82.** Fax 93-412-40-20. 56 units. A/C TEL. 15,000 ptas. (US$90) double. V. Parking 2,500 ptas. (US$15). Metro: Plaça de Catalunya or Universitat.

This two-star hotel, in a former apartment building, has a Castilian facade, with a wealth of art nouveau detailing, and its high-ceilinged lobby is filled with cabriole-legged chairs. Owned and operated by the Spanish hotel chain HUSA, the Castilla is clean, charming, and well maintained. Its nearest rival is the Regencia Colón, to which it is comparable in atmosphere and government ratings. It is far superior to either the Cortés or the Continental. The rooms are comfortable—beds have ornate Catalán-style headboards—and some open onto large terraces. Breakfast is the only meal served, but it is a fine buffet, with ham, cheese, and eggs. One reader found the location of the hotel "fantastic," right in the center of Barcelona, close to the Rambles.

Rialto. Ferran, 40–42, 08002 Barcelona. ☎ **93-318-52-12.** Fax 93-318-53-12. www. gargallo-hotels.com. E-mail: reserve@gargallo-hotels.com. 163 units. A/C MINIBAR TEL. 18,500 ptas. (US$111) double. AE, DC, MC, V. Parking 3,000 ptas. (US$18) nearby. Metro: Jaume I.

One of the best choices in the Barri Gòtic, this hotel is part of the Gargallo chain, which also owns the Hotel Suizo. The three-star Rialto is furnished with Catalán flair and style. Completely overhauled in 1985, it offers clean, well-maintained, and comfortably furnished guest rooms with private bathrooms. The hotel has a cafeteria.

Turín. Carrer Pintor Fortuny, 9–11, 08001 Barcelona. ☎ **93-302-48-12.** Fax 93-302-10-05. www.hotelturin@icab.es. E-mail: hotelturin@teleline.es. 60 units. A/C TV TEL. 17,000 ptas. (US$102) double; 20,500 ptas. (US$123) triple. AE, DC, MC, V. Parking 2,000 ptas. (US$12). Metro: Plaça de Catalunya.

This neat and well-run three-star hotel is in a terra-cotta grillwork building located in a shopping district. It offers small, streamlined accommodations with balconies. An elevator will take you to your room. The Turín also has a restaurant specializing in grilled meats and fresh fish. It's a clean, safe choice, comparable to the Lleó, but in its price range inferior in atmosphere to the Mesón Castilla.

SUR DIAGONAL
VERY EXPENSIVE

✪ **Barcelona Hilton.** Avinguda Diagonal, 589, 08014 Barcelona. ☎ **800/445-8667** in the U.S. and Canada, or 93-495-77-77. Fax 93-495-77-00. www.hilton.com. E-mail: barcelona@hilton.com. 287 units. A/C MINIBAR TV TEL. 32,000 ptas. (US$192) double; from 44,000 ptas. (US$264) suite. Rates include breakfast. AE, DC, MC, V. Parking 3,000 ptas. (US$18). Metro: María Cristina.

Opened in 1990 as one of the most publicized hotels in Barcelona, this five-star property lies in a desirable position on one of the most famous and elegant boulevards. Opposite the gates to the fairgrounds of Barcelona (beyond that, to the Olympic Stadium), this is a huge seven-floor corner structure, with a massive tower placed on top of it. It hides behind a rather lackluster white marble facade. The lobby is sleek with lots of marble, and public lounges are furnished with black leather and velvet chairs. Most guest rooms are large and finely equipped, although none are set aside for nonsmokers. Furnishings are standard Hilton, but with suitable amenities such as private safes. Bathrooms are also well equipped with such features as large mirrors and hair dryers.

Dining/Diversions: The **Restaurant Cristal Garden** serves well-prepared international and Spanish menus in a relaxed but polished setting. A bar/lounge lies nearby. Night owls head for a popular local disco, Up & Down, a short walk from the hotel.

Amenities: 24-hour room service, concierge, laundry/valet, translation and secretarial services, express checkout, limousine service, baby-sitting. The hotel maintains a cooperative relationship with a well-equipped health club half a mile away. Tennis courts are a mile away, and the hotel can arrange golf at a course 16 miles away. Shopping boutiques and a news kiosk are on the premises.

✪ **Claris.** Carrer de Pau Claris, 150, 08009 Barcelona. ☎ **800/888-4747** in the U.S., or 93-487-62-62. Fax 93-215-79-70. www.derbyhotels.es. E-mail: info@derbyhotels.es. 120 units. A/C MINIBAR TV TEL. Mon–Thurs 42,000 ptas. (US$252) double; from 50,000 ptas. (US$300) suite. Fri–Sun 28,000 ptas. (US$168) double; from 35,000 ptas. (US$210) suite. Fri–Sun rates include breakfast. AE, DC, MC, V. Parking 2,250 ptas. (US$13.50). Metro: Passeig de Gràcia.

One of the most unusual hotels built in Barcelona since the 1930s, this postmodern hotel is the only five-star grand luxe lodging in the city center. It incorporates vast quantities of teak, marble, steel, and glass with the historically important facade of a landmark 19th-century building (the Verdruna Palace). Although we prefer the Ritz (see below), many hotel critics hail the Claris as the stellar choice in Barcelona. It opened in 1992 in time for the Barcelona Olympics. Its seven stories include a swimming pool and garden on the roof, a small museum of Egyptian antiquities from the owner's valuable collection on the second floor, and two restaurants, one of which specializes in different brands of caviar. Each of the guest rooms is painted an iconoclastic shade of blue-violet and combines unusual art objects with state-of-the-art electronic accessories. (Art objects, depending on the inspiration of the decorator, include Turkish kilims, English antiques, Hindu sculptures, Egyptian stone carvings, and engravings inspired by Napóleon's campaigns in Egypt.) Committed to celebrating the many facets of Catalán culture, the hotel's owner and developer, art collector Jordi Clos, named his hotel after the 19th-century Catalán writer Pau Claris.

Dining/Diversions: On site is the **Restaurante Claris,** where Catalán meals in the Ampurdán style are served. Also on the premises is a restaurant sponsored by the international caviar emporium, **Caviar Caspa,** where sturgeon eggs from many different distributors compete for gastronomic attention with an array of smoked meats, smoked fish, and bubbly wines. The restaurant's forte is light but elegant lunches and suppers.

Amenities: Room service, laundry/valet, baby-sitting, swimming pool, sauna, currency exchange.

Hotel Princesa Sofía. Plaça de Pius XII, 4, 08028 Barcelona. ☎ 93-330-71-11. Fax 93-508-10-01. www.interconti.com. E-mail: barcelona@interconti.com. 500 units. A/C MINIBAR TV TEL. 38,000–48,000 ptas. (US$228–US$288) double; from 70,000 ptas. (US$420) suite. AE, DC, MC, V. Parking 2,600 ptas. (US$15.60). Metro: Palau Reial or María Cristina.

About 2 miles (3km) northwest of Barcelona's historic center, the bustling high-rise Princesa Sofía is the city's busiest, most business-oriented modern hotel. It's much better than the Hilton. Although it opened as a five-star hotel, its new four-star government rating is more accurate. The hotel was built in 1975 and renovated in the early 1990s. Packed with glamorous touches, the Princesa Sofía hosts dozens of daily conferences and social events. Guest rooms contain comfortable traditional furniture, often with a vaguely British feel. Rooms, usually midsize, are well appointed, with private safes, thick carpeting, and king-size beds with quality mattresses. The tiled bathrooms have thick towels, hair dryers, and dual marble vanities.

Dining/Diversions: Le Gourmet serves lackluster continental and Catalán meals. **L'Empordá** is slightly less expensive, and a coffee shop, **El Snack 2002,** is open until midnight. There's also a bar, and a branch of **Régine's** disco.

Amenities: 24-hour room service, laundry and valet, concierge, baby-sitting. In-house Iberia Airlines branch, boutique, barber and hairdresser, car rentals. Amply equipped gym and health club, sauna, indoor and outdoor swimming pools. Extensive conference and meeting facilities, an unusually well-managed business center offering translation (English and French) and secretarial services.

✪ **Hotel Ritz.** Gran Vía de les Corts Catalánes, 668, 08010 Barcelona. ☎ **93-318-52-00.** Fax 93-318-01-48. www.ritzbcn.com. E-mail: ritz@ritzbcn.com. 125 units. A/C MINIBAR TV TEL. 40,000–60,000 ptas. (US$240–US$360) double; 55,000–220,000 ptas. (US$330–US$1,320) suite. AE, DC, MC, V. Parking 3,500 ptas. (US$21). Metro: Passeig de Gràcia.

Acknowledged by many as the finest, most prestigious, and most architecturally distinguished hotel in Barcelona, the art deco Ritz was built in 1919. Richly remodeled during the late 1980s (and suffering a brief name change to HUSA Palace during the '90s), it has welcomed more millionaires, famous people, and aristocrats—with their official and unofficial consorts—than any other hotel in the region. One of the finest features is the cream-and-gilt neoclassical lobby, whose marble floors and potted palms are flooded with sunlight from an overhead glass canopy, and where afternoon tea is served to the strains of a string quartet. Guest rooms are as formal, high-ceilinged, and richly outfitted as you'd expect, some with Regency furniture; bathrooms are accented with mosaics and bathtubs inspired by those in ancient Rome.

Dining/Diversions: The elegant **Restaurante Diana** serves French and Catalán cuisine amid soaring ceilings, crystal chandeliers, and formally dressed waiters (see "Dining," below, for the complete review). Nearby lies the elegantly paneled **Bar Parilla,** where music from a grand piano will soothe your frazzled nerves while you enjoy the deep leather upholstery and gilded cove moldings.

Amenities: 24-hour room service, laundry, limousine service, concierge, baby-sitting, business center, car rentals, handful of shopping kiosks and boutiques.

Rey Juan Carlos I. Avinguda Diagonal, 661, 08028 Barcelona. ☎ **800/448-8355** in the U.S., or 93-448-08-08. Fax 93-364-32-64. www.hilton.com. 432 units. A/C MINIBAR TV TEL. 46,000 ptas. (US$276) double; 70,000 ptas. (US$420) suite. Occasional weekend discounts. AE, DC, MC, V. Free parking. Metro: Zona Universitària.

Named for the Spanish king, who attended its opening and who has visited it several times since, this five-star choice competes effectively against the Ritz, Claris, and Hotel Arts. Opened just before the Olympics, it rises 17 stories from a position at the northern end of the Diagonal, within a prestigious neighborhood known for corporate headquarters, banks, and upscale stores. Note that it's a bit removed, however, from many of Barcelona's top-flight attractions. The design includes a soaring inner atrium, at one end of which a bank of glass-sided elevators glide silently up and down. Guest rooms contain many electronic extras, conservatively comfortable furnishings, and in many cases, views out over Barcelona to the sea.

Dining/Diversions: The hotel's most elegant restaurant is **Chez Vous,** a glamorous and panoramic room with impeccable service and French/Catalán meals. Saturday night, a dinner dance offers a live orchestra accompanied by a set-price menu. There's also a Japanese restaurant, **Kokoro,** and the **Café Polo,** which serves an endless series of buffets at lunch and dinner. The gardens surrounding the hotel contain fountains, flowering shrubs, and the **Café Terraza.**

Amenities: 24-hour room service, laundry, concierge staff, swimming pool, health club, jogging track, men's and women's hairdresser, car-rental facilities, business center.

EXPENSIVE

Avenida Palace. Gran Vía de les Corts Catalánes, 605 (at Passeig de Gràcia), 08007 Barcelona. ☎ **93-301-96-00.** Fax 93-318-12-34. 160 units. A/C MINIBAR TV TEL. 31,000 ptas. (US$186) double; 50,000–72,000 ptas. (US$300–US$432) suite. AE, DC, MC, V. Metro: Plaça de Catalunya or Passeig de Gràcia.

Set in an enviable 19th-century neighborhood filled with elegant shops and apartment buildings, this hotel lies behind a pair of mock-fortified towers that were built (like the hotel) in 1952. Despite its relative modernity, it evokes an old-world sense of charm, thanks to the attentive staff, the scattering of flowers and antiques, and the 1950s-era accessories that fill its well-upholstered public rooms. Guest rooms, all with private bathrooms, are solidly traditional and quiet, and some are set aside for non-smokers, a rarity in Spain.

Dining/Diversions: This hotel has an elegantly proportioned dining room, **El Restaurante Pinateca,** which serves lunch and dinner Monday to Friday. A bar/lounge contains potted palms, some interesting antiques, and a sense of graciousness.

Amenities: Concierge, translation and secretarial services, currency exchange, hairdresser/barber, room service, express checkout, baby-sitting.

Gran Hotel Havana. Gran Vía de les Corts Catalánes, 647, 08010 Barcelona. ☎ **93-412-11-15.** Fax 93-412-26-11. www.hoteles-silken.com. E-mail: silken@hotels-silken.com. 145 units. A/C MINIBAR TV TEL. 25,000 ptas. (US$150) double. AE, DC, MC, V. Parking 2,200 ptas. (US$13.20). Metro: Diagonal.

Civic leaders and architects alike praise this hotel as an example of a sophisticated recycling of a historic monument. It was built in the 1870s as an almost obscenely large private home, then converted into a hotel (Havana) in the 1950s. In 1991, in anticipation of a flood of visitors for the Barcelona Olympic Games, its six-story interior was gutted and rebuilt in a minimalist, high-tech style whose blues and grays emulate the colors of the nearby sea. With postmodern Milan as inspiration, the midsize comfortable rooms have an absolute lack of decorative frippery, with a strong emphasis on geometric shapes and ample use of marble, especially in the bathrooms and the public areas. The staff is hard-working and multilingual.

Dining/Diversions: The hotel has a very respectable restaurant, serving an international and regional cuisine, but you'll find far better food outside your door. There is also a business-type of bar.

Amenities: Room service, baby-sitting, laundry/dry cleaning, concierge.

✪ **Hotel Condes de Barcelona.** Passeig de Gràcia, 73–75, 08008 Barcelona. ☎ **93-488-22-00.** Fax 93-467-47-81. www.condesdebarcelona.com. E-mail: cbhotel@ condesdebarcelona. com. 183 units. A/C MINIBAR TV TEL. 30,000 ptas. (US$180) double; 56,000–65,000 ptas. (US$336–US$390) suite. AE, DC, MC, V. Parking 2,000 ptas. (US$12). Metro: Passeig de Gràcia.

Located off the architecturally splendid Passeig de Gràcia, this four-star hotel, originally designed to be a private villa (1895), is one of Barcelona's most glamorous. Business was so good, it opened a 74-room extension, which regrettably lacks the élan of the original core. It boasts a unique neomedieval facade, influenced by Gaudí's *modernista* movement. During a recent renovation, just enough hints of high-tech furnishings were added to make the lobby exciting, but everything else has the original opulence. The curved lobby-level bar and its adjacent restaurant add a touch of art deco. All the comfortable guest rooms, in salmon, green, or peach color schemes, have marble bathrooms, reproductions of Spanish paintings, and soundproof windows. Some rooms are already beginning to show a post-Olympian wear and tear.

Dining/Diversions: In times past you might have seen the late Conde de Barcelona, father of King Juan Carlos, passing through on the way to a refreshing snack in the **Café Condal,** featuring regional dishes. Guests at the piano bar have included, on occasion, the Baron von Thyssen and his Catalán wife, who sold much of their fabulous art collection to the government to create a museum in Madrid.

Amenities: Laundry, baby-sitting, room service, outdoor swimming pool.

Hotel Majestic. Passeig de Gràcia, 68, 08007 Barcelona. ☎ **93-488-17-17.** Fax 93-488-18-80. www.hotelmajestic.es. E-mail: recepcion@hotelmajestic.es. 322 units. A/C MINIBAR TV TEL. 36,000 ptas. (US$216) double; 50,000–70,000 ptas. (US$300–US$420) suite. AE, DC, MC, V. Parking 2,200 ptas. (US$13.20). Metro: Urquinaona.

The Majestic functioned as one of Barcelona's most visible landmarks beginning in the 1920s, when it was built in a sought-after location within a 10-minute walk from Plaça Catalunya. In the early 1990s, it was radically renovated and upgraded into a four-star format that retained the dignified stateliness of the public areas, but added a sense of color and contemporary drama to each of the bedrooms. Today, these are each outfitted in a different, usually monochromatic color scheme, with carpets, artwork, and upholsteries that a team of decorators labored over for months. The staff is hardworking and conscientious, albeit sometimes swamped with tour buses containing dozens of clients arriving all at once.

Dining/Diversions: The hotel has two restaurants, the most celebrated of which is the **Drolma,** attracting hip foodies from within the city. The **Salon Condado** is more ordinary, serving breakfasts and often dinners for groups traveling together. The hotel also has a bar.

Amenities: Room service, laundry/dry cleaning, concierge, baby-sitting, swimming pool, gym, and sauna.

Hotel Meliá Barcelona Sarrià. Avinguda Sarrià, 50, 08029 Barcelona. ☎ **800/336-3542** in the U.S., or 93-410-60-60. Fax 93-321-51-79. 314 units. A/C MINIBAR TV TEL. 32,000 ptas. (US$192) double; from 42,000 ptas. (US$252) suite. AE, DC, MC, V. Parking 2,450 ptas. (US$14.70). Metro: Hospital Clínic.

Located just a block away from the junction of Avinguda Sarría and Avinguda Diagonal, right in the modern business heart of Barcelona, this five-star hotel opened in 1976. Some of its rooms were renovated as late as 1993, but others are beginning to look a bit worn. It offers comfortably upholstered and carpeted guest rooms in a neutral international modern style. The hotel, a member of the nationwide Spanish chain Meliá, caters to both the business traveler and the vacationer.

Dining/Diversions: A restaurant serves both Catalán and international dishes, and a cocktail bar provides drinks and piano music six nights a week.

Amenities: Concierge, 24-hour room service, laundry/valet, executive floor, private parking, baby-sitting, business center, one of the best-equipped health clubs in Barcelona.

Hotel Balmes. Carrer Mallorca, 216, 08008 Barcelona. ☎ **93-451-19-14.** Fax 93-451-00-49. www.derbyhotels.es. E-mail: info@derbyhotels.es. 92 units. A/C MINIBAR TV TEL. 24,400 ptas. (US$146.40) double. AE, DC, MC, V. Parking 2,000 ptas. (US$12). Metro: Diagonal.

Set within a seven-story building from the late 1980s, this chain hotel successfully combines a conservative and well-conceived decor with modern accessories and a well-trained staff. Bedrooms are vaguely English in their inspiration, but with a warmly monochromatic color scheme of yellows and browns, marble-trimmed bathrooms, and enough space to allow residents, many of whom are in Barcelona as part of business trips, to live and work comfortably. If you're looking for a maximum of peace and quiet, rooms overlooking the back of the hotel—site of an outdoor swimming pool and a small garden—are quieter and calmer than those facing the busy street. There's a bar on the premises, but the in-house restaurant follows only a limited schedule, serving breakfast daily, and lunch Monday to Friday. Other than that, no meals are served.

Hotel Derby/Hotel Gran Derby. Carrer Loreto, 21–25 and 28, 08029 Barcelona. ☎ **93-322-32-15.** Fax 93-410-08-62. www.derbyhotels.es. E-mail: info@derbyhotels.es. 151 units. A/C MINIBAR TV TEL. Hotel Derby 30,000 ptas. (US$180) double; Grand Derby 32,000 ptas. (US$192) junior suite. AE, DC, MC, V. Parking 2,250 ptas. (US$13.50). Metro: Hospital Clínic.

Divided into two separate buildings, these twin hotels (owned and managed by the same corporation, which also operates the Astoria, below) are in a tranquil neighborhood about 2 blocks south of the busy intersection of the Avinguda Diagonal and Avinguda Sarría. The Derby offers 111 conventional hotel rooms, whereas the Gran Derby (across the street) contains 40 suites, many of which have small balconies overlooking a flowered courtyard. (All drinking, dining, and entertainment facilities lie in the larger of the two establishments, the Derby.) A team of English-inspired designers imported a British aesthetic into these hotels, and the pleasing results include well-oiled hardwood panels, soft lighting, and comfortably upholstered armchairs. Less British in feel than the public rooms, guest rooms and suites are outfitted with simple furniture in a variety of decorative styles, each comfortable and quiet.

Although the hotel does not have a full-fledged restaurant, it contains a dignified but unpretentious coffee shop, The Times, which serves Spanish, British, and international food. The Scotch Bar, an upscale watering hole, has won several Spanish awards for the diversity of its cocktails.

INEXPENSIVE

✪ **Hotel Astoria.** París, 203, 08036 Barcelona. ☎ **93-209-83-11.** Fax 93-202-30-08. www.derbyhotels.es. E-mail: info@derbyhotels.es. 117 units. A/C MINIBAR TV TEL. 22,000 ptas. (US$132) double. AE, DC, MC, V. Parking nearby 1,800 ptas. (US$10.80). Metro: Diagonal.

One of our favorite hotels, and an excellent value, the Astoria is located near the upper part of the Rambles, near the Diagonal. It has an art deco facade that makes it appear older than it is. The high ceilings, geometric designs, and brass-studded detailing in the public rooms could be Moorish or Andalusian. Each of the comfortable guest rooms is soundproofed; half have been renovated with slick louvered closets and glistening white paint. The more old-fashioned rooms have warm textures of exposed cedar and elegant, pristine modern accessories. If you'd like an American-style buffet breakfast, the Astoria is one of the best bets in town. Its buffet offers eggs, bacon, juice, fried potatoes, even pancakes.

NORTE DIAGONAL
MODERATE

Hotel Hespería. Los Vergós, 20, 08017 Barcelona. ☎ **93-204-55-51.** Fax 93-204-43-92. www.hoteles-hesperia.es. 134 units. A/C MINIBAR TV TEL. 22,000 ptas. (US$132) double. AE, DC, MC, V. Parking 1,750 ptas. (US$10.50). Metro: Tres Torres.

This hotel, on the northern edge of the city, a 10-minute taxi ride from the center, is surrounded by the verdant gardens of one of Barcelona's most pleasant residential neighborhoods. Built in the late 1980s, the hotel was renovated before the 1992 Olympics. You'll pass a Japanese rock garden to reach the stone-floored reception area, with its adjacent bar. Sunlight floods the monochromatic guest rooms—all doubles, although singles can be rented at the prices above. The uniformed staff offers fine service. A restaurant on the premises serves a regional cuisine.

Hotel Wilson. Avinguda Diagonal, 568, 08021 Barcelona. ☎ **93-209-25-11.** Fax 93-200-83-70. www.husa.es. E-mail: depcomcen@husa.es. 57 units. A/C MINIBAR TV TEL. 18,000 ptas. (US$108) double; 25,000 ptas. (US$150) suite. Parking 2,000 ptas. (US$12). AE, DC, DISC, MC, V. Metro: Diagonal.

Set in a neighborhood rich with architectural curiosities, this comfortable hotel is a member of the nationwide HUSA chain. The small lobby isn't indicative of the rest of the building, which on the second floor opens into a large and sunny coffee shop/bar/TV lounge. The guest rooms are well kept, generally spacious, and furnished in a traditional style, a color-coordinated medley of pastels. Laundry services are provided.

VILA OLÍMPICA
VERY EXPENSIVE

✪ **Hotel Arts.** Carrer de la Marina, 19–21, 08005 Barcelona. ☎ **800/241-3333** in the U.S., or 93-221-10-00. Fax 93-221-10-70. www.ritzcarlton.com. 482 units. A/C MINIBAR TV TEL. 55,000–80,000 ptas. (US$330–US$480) double; 75,000 ptas. (US$450) suite. AE, CB, DC, MC, V. Parking 3,200 ptas. (US$19.20). Metro: Ciutadella-Vila Olímpica.

This is the only hotel in Europe managed by the opulent Ritz-Carlton chain, the first of what the company hopes will be a string of hotels across the European continent. It occupies 33 floors of one of the tallest buildings in Spain, and one of Barcelona's only skyscrapers, a 44-floor postmodern tower whose upper floors contain the private condominiums of some of the country's most gossiped-about aristocrats and financiers. Views are straight out over the sea from this location about 1½ miles southwest of Barcelona's historic core, adjacent to the sea and the Olympic Village. Although some rooms were occupied by athletes and Olympic administrators in 1992, the hotel didn't become fully operational until 1994. Its decor is contemporary and elegant, with a large lobby sheathed in slabs of soft gray and yellow marble, and guest rooms outfitted in pastel shades of yellow or blue. Rooms have sweeping views over the skyline of Barcelona and the Mediterranean. The staff is youthful, well trained, polite, and hardworking.

Dining/Diversions: Three in-house restaurants include the **Newport Room,** which pays homage to new American cuisine and the seafaring pleasures of New England; the **Café Veranda,** a light and airy indoor/outdoor restaurant; and the **Goyesca,** which serves Spanish food and shellfish.

Amenities: 24-hour room service, laundry, concierge staff who can arrange almost anything, fitness center, outdoor pool, business center. Adjacent to the hotel is an upscale cluster of many different luxury boutiques operated by the Japanese retailer Sogo.

4 Where to Dine

Finding an economical restaurant in Barcelona is easier than finding an inexpensive, safe hotel. There are sometimes as many as eight spots on a block, if you include tapas bars as well as restaurants. Reservations are seldom needed, except in the most expensive and popular places.

Barri Gòtic offers the cheapest meals. There are also many low-cost restaurants in and around the carrer de Montcada, site of the Picasso museum. Dining rooms in the Eixample tend to be more formal, more expensive, and less adventurous.

However, if you can afford to dine in first-class and deluxe restaurants, you'll find some of the grandest culinary experiences in Europe here. The widely diversified Catalán cuisine reaches its pinnacle in Barcelona, and many of the finest dishes feature fresh seafood. But you don't get just Catalán fare here, as the city is also rich in the cuisines of all the major regions of Spain, including Castile and Andalusia. Because of Barcelona's proximity to France, many of the finer restaurants also serve French or French-inspired dishes, the latter often with a distinctly Catalán flavor.

CIUTAT VELLA
EXPENSIVE

✪ **Agut d'Avignon.** Trinitat, 3 (at carrer d'Avinyó). ☎ **93-302-60-34.** Reservations required. Main courses 2,000–5,000 ptas. (US$12–US$30). AE, DC, MC, V. Daily 1–4:30pm and 9pm–12:30am. Metro: Jaume I or Liceu. CATALÁN.

Founded in 1962, one of our favorite restaurants in Barcelona is located near the Plaça Reial, in a tiny alleyway (the cross street is calle d'Avinyó). The restaurant explosion in Barcelona has toppled Agut d'Avignon from its once supreme position, but it's still going strong and has a dedicated following. The restaurant attracts the leading politicians, writers, journalists, financiers, industrialists, and artists of Barcelona—even the king and various ministers of the cabinet, along with the visiting presidents from other countries. Since 1983, the restaurant has been run by Mercedes Giralt Salinas and her son, Javier Falagán Giralt. A small 19th-century vestibule leads into the multilevel dining area, which has two balconies and a main hall; on the whole it evokes a hunting lodge. You might need help translating the Catalán menu. Specialties are prepared according to traditional recipes and are likely to include acorn squash soup served in its shell, fisherman stew with garlic toast, haddock stuffed with shellfish, sole with *nyoca* (a medley of different nuts), large shrimps with aioli (a garlic mayonnaise sauce), duck with figs, and fillet beef steak in a sherry sauce.

Casa Leopoldo. Sant Rafael, 24. ☎ **93-441-30-14.** Reservations required. Main courses 1,800–6,000 ptas. (US$10.80–US$36); fixed-price menu 5,500 ptas. (US$33). AE, DC, MC, V. Tues–Sun 1:30–4pm; Tues–Sat 9–11pm. Closed Aug and Easter week. Metro: Liceu. SEAFOOD.

An excursion through the somewhat seedy streets of the Barri Xinés is part of the experience of coming to this restaurant, though at night it's safer to come by taxi. This

Central Barcelona Dining

Agua **46**
Agut **35**
Agut d'Avignon **32**
Alt Heidelberg **20**
Balsa **7**
Bar del Pi **49**
Bar Turó **4**
Beltxenea **17**
Biocenter **22**
Bodega la Plata **38**
Bodegueta **13**
Botafumeiro **8**
Brasserie Flo **57**
Buena Brasa **18**
El Caballito Blanco **16**
Café de L'Academia **48**
Café Vienna **21**
Campanas **37**
Can Costa **45**
Can Culleretes **30**
Can Isidre **29**
Can Majó **44**
Can La María **19**
Can Pescallunes **55**
Los Caracoles **33**
Casa Alfonso **58**
Casa Calvert **59**
Casa Leopoldo **28**
Casa Tejada **6**
Chicago Pizza Pie Factory **14**
La Cuineta **50**
La Dama **10**
Dentellière **40**
Restau Diana **60**
El Duc **20**
Dulcinea **25**
Egipte **23**
Els 4 Gats **54**
Gaig **62**
Garduña **27**
Jamón Jamón **5**
Jarra **39**
Jaume de Provença **2**
Kentucky Fried Chicken **31**
Llauna **1**
L'Olive **11**
Mercat de la Boquería **26**
Neichel **3**
Nou Celler **51**
Pitarra **36**
Pla de la Garsa **52**
Quo Vadis **24**
Ramonet **42**
Reno **9**
Restaurant Hofmann **53**

Rey de la Gamba **43**
Roig Robí **12**
Rosalert **61**
Rosca **56**
7 Portes **41**
Seynor Parellada **47**
Talaia Mar **46**
Tragaluz **15**
El Túnel **34**
Via Veneto **3**

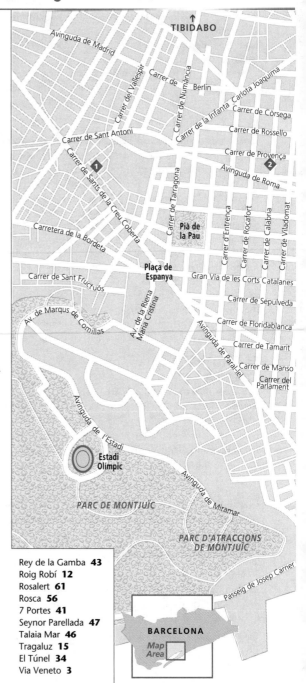

EIXAMPLE

Plaça de Francesc Macia

Carrer de Buenos Aires

Carrer de Londres

Carrer de Paris

Travessara de Gràcia

Travessara de Gràcia

Av. de Sant Antoni Maria Claret

Carrer de la Industria

Avinguda Diagonal

Carrer de Còrsega

Carrer de Provença

Carrer de Rosselló

Plaça de la Sagrada Família

Carrer de Roger de Flor

Avinguda Diagonal

Carrer de Mallorca

Carrer de Valencia

Carrer d'Aragó

Carrer de Balmes

Ramble de Catalunya

Passeig de Gràcia

Carrer de Pau Claris

Carrer de R. de Llúcia

Carrer del Bruc

Carrer de Girona

Carrer de Bailèn

Passeig de Sant Joan

Carrer de Napóls

Carrer de Sicilia

Carrer del Consell de Cent

Carrer de la Diputació

Carrer de Comte Borrell

Carrer del Comte d'Urgell

Carrer de Villarroel

Carrer de Casanova

Carrer de Muntaner

Carrer d'Aribau

Plaça de la Universitat

Gran Via de les Corts Catalanes

Plaça de Tetuan

Ronda Universitat

Ronda de Sant Antoni

Carrer de Pelai

Plaça Catalunya

Plaça Urquinaona

Carrer de Casp

Carrer de Saxdenya

RAVAL

Carrer d'Ausias Marc

Ronda de Sant Pere

Carrer d'Ali Bei

Carrer de Ribes

Ronda Sant Pau

Carrer de Hospital

Av. Portal de l'Angel

BARRI GÒTIC

Via Laietana

Carrer de Sant Pau

Passeig de Lluís Companys

Passeig de Carles I

Carrer Nou de la Rambla

La Rambla

Carrer de Ferran

Carrer de la Princesa

Carrer de Comerç

Passeig de Pujades

LA RIBERA

PARC DE LA CIUTADELLA

Carrer de Picasso

Carrer de Wellington

Avinguda de les Drassanes

Carrer Ample

Passeig de Colom

Moll de la Fusta

PARC ZOOLOGIC

Villa Olimpic

Plaça Portal de la Pau

Moll d'Espanya

Avinguda d'Icavia

BARCELONETA

65

colorful restaurant, founded in 1939, has some of the freshest seafood in town and caters to a loyal clientele. There's a popular stand-up tapas bar in front, then two dining rooms, one slightly more formal than the other. Specialties include eel with shrimp, barnacles, cuttlefish, seafood soup with shellfish, and deep-fried inch-long eels.

Quo Vadis. Carme, 7. ☎ **93-302-40-72.** Reservations recommended. Main courses 1,500–3,500 ptas. (US$9–US$21); *menú del día* 4,000 ptas. (US$24). DC, MC, V. Mon–Sat 1:15–4pm and 8:30–11:30pm. Metro: Liceu. SPANISH/CONTINENTAL.

Elegant and impeccable, this is one of the finest restaurants in Barcelona. Within a century-old building near the open stalls of the Boquería food market, it was established in 1967 and has done a discreet but thriving business ever since. Seating is within any of four different dining rooms, each decorated with exposed paneling and a veneer of conservative charm. Personalized culinary creations include a ragout of seasonal mushrooms; fried goose liver with prunes; fillet of beef with wine sauce; a wide variety of fish, grilled or, in some cases, flambéed; and a wide choice of desserts made with seasonal fruits imported from all over Spain.

Restaurant Hoffmann. Argenteria, 74–78. ☎ **93-319-58-89.** Reservations recommended. Main courses 2,200–4,500 ptas. (US$13.20–US$27); fixed-price lunch (includes wine and coffee) 4,800 ptas. (US$28.80); tasting menu 7,500 ptas. (US$45). AE, DC, MC, V. Mon–Fri 1:30–3:30pm and 9–11:30pm. Metro: Jaume I. CATALAN/FRENCH/INTERNATIONAL.

This restaurant in the Barri Gòtic has suddenly become one of the most famous in Barcelona, partly because of its creative cuisine, partly because of its close association with a well-respected training school for future employees of Catalonia's hotel and restaurant industry. The culinary and entrepreneurial force behind it all is Mey Hoffmann, the red-haired offspring of a German father and Catalán mother, whose interior decor reflects her own personality and sense of whimsy. Expect to find masses of verdant plants and fresh flowers, old photographs, dramatic oil paintings, and through the windows, views of the facade of one of Barcelona's most beloved Gothic churches, Santa María del Mar. During clement weather, tables are also set up within a trio of separate courtyards, rich with the detailing of the 18th-century building that surrounds it. Menu items change every two months and are often concocted from French ingredients. Examples include a superb version of *fine tarte* with deboned sardines, foie gras wrapped in puff pastry, baked John Dory with new potatoes and ratatouille, a ragout of crayfish with green risotto, a succulent version of pigs' feet with eggplant, and rack of lamb with grilled baby vegetables. Especially flavorful, if you appreciate beef, is a fillet steak cooked in Rioja wine and served with a confit of shallots and a gratin of potatoes. Fondant of chocolate makes a worthy dessert.

MODERATE

Agut. Gignas, 16. ☎ **93-315-17-09.** Reservations required. Main courses 2,800–3,200 ptas. (US$16.80–US$19.20); fixed-price lunch 1,200–1,600 ptas. (US$7.20–US$9.60). MC, V. Tues–Sun 1:30–4pm and Tues–Sat 9pm–midnight. Closed Aug. Metro: Jaime 1. CATALÁN.

In a historic building in the Barri Xinés, three blocks from the harbor front, Agut epitomizes the bohemian atmosphere surrounding this fairly seedy area. For three-quarters of a century, this has been a family-run business, with Maria Agut Garcia the current reigning empress. Don't confuse Agut with the more famous Agut d'Avignon nearby. The aura is still of the 40s and 50s, with a cozy little bar to the right as you enter. Paintings on the walls are from well-known Catalán artists from the 40s to the 60s. The cuisine is solid and time-tested fare; vigorous cookery served at moderate prices. Begin with *mil hojas de butifarra amb zets* or layers of pastry filled with Catalán sausage and mushrooms, or else the *terrine de albergines amb fortmage de cabra* (terrine of eggplant with goat's cheese gratinée). One of our favorite dishes is *soufle de rape amb gambes* (soufflé of monkfish with shrimp). For gastronomes only, try the *pie de cerdo relleno con foie amb truffles* (pork feet stuffed with duck liver and truffles). For dessert, if you order *sortido*, you'll get a combination plate with an assortment of the small homemade cakes of the house.

Brasserie Flo Jonqueras, 10. ☎ **93-319-31-02.** Reservations recommended. Main courses 1,800–3,600 ptas. (US$10.80–US$21.60); fixed-price menu 3,000 ptas. (US$18). AE, DC, MC, V. Mon–Thurs 1–4pm and 8:30pm–midnight, Fri–Sun 1–4pm and 8:30pm–1am. Metro: Urquinaona. FRENCH/INTERNATIONAL.

In a former textiles factory, this handsomely restored warehouse was opened as a restaurant in 1982 by a French group. It is as close as Barcelona gets to an Alsace brasserie. The art deco dining room has been compared to one on a transatlantic steamer at the turn of the century—spacious, palm-filled, comfortable, and air-conditioned. Start off with the fresh foie gras. The specialty is a large plate of *choucroute* (sauerkraut) served with a steamed ham hock. Also good are the shrimp in garlic, salmon tartare with vodka, black rice, and stuffed sole with spinach. These dishes, each familiar fare, are nevertheless solid, satisfying, and filling.

Can Culleretes. Quintana, 5. ☎ **93-317-64-85.** Reservations recommended. Main courses 1,200–2,200 ptas. (US$7.20–US$13.20); *menú del día* 2,300 ptas. (US$13.80). MC, V. Tues–Sun 1:30–4pm, Tues–Sat 9–11pm. Closed 3 weeks in July. Metro: Liceu. Bus: 14 or 59. CATALÁN.

Founded in 1786 as a *pastelería* (pastry shop) in the Barri Gòtic, this oldest of Barcelona restaurants still retains many original architectural features. All three dining rooms are decorated in Catalán style, with tile dadoes and wrought-iron chandeliers. The well-prepared food features authentic dishes of northeastern Spain, including sole Roman style, *zarzuela a la marinera* (shellfish medley), cannelloni, and paella. From October to January, special game dishes are available, including *perdiz* (partridge). Signed photographs of celebrities, flamenco artists, and bullfighters who have visited this place decorate the walls.

Can Pescallunes. Carrer Magdalenas, 23. ☎ **93-318-54-83.** Reservations required for lunch. Main courses 2,000–3,500 ptas. (US$12–US$21). AE, DC, MC, V. Mon–Fri 1–3:30pm and 8:30–10:30pm. Metro: Urquinaona. FRENCH/CATALÁN.

With the look, feel, and menu of a French bistro, this 10-table restaurant is a short walk from the cathedral. It opened in 1980 in this turn-of-the-century building where an elaborate street lantern marks the entrance. Richly flavorful specialties are *rape* (monkfish, pronounced *rah*-pay) with clams and tomatoes, a smooth vichyssoise, chateaubriand with béarnaise sauce, sole cooked in cider, steak tartare, and dessert crepes with Cointreau. The specials change daily, and the prices remain a model of temperance.

Egipte. Les Rambles, 79. ☎ **93-317-74-80.** Reservations recommended. Main courses 1,400–2,500 ptas. (US$8.40–US$15); fixed-price menu 1,200–2,000 ptas. (US$7.20–US$12). AE, DC, MC, V. Daily 1–4pm and 8pm–midnight. Metro: Liceu. CATALÁN/SPANISH.

A favorite among the locals, this tiny place, located right behind the central marketplace, jumps day and night. The excellent menu includes spinach *vol-au-vent* (traditionally served with an egg on top), *lengua de ternera* (tongue), and *berengeras* (stuffed eggplant), a chef's specialty. The local favorite is codfish in cream sauce. The ingredients are fresh, and the price is right. Expect hearty market food and a total lack of pretension.

Els Quatre Gats. Montsió, 3. ☎ **93-302-41-40.** Reservations required Sat–Sun. Main courses 1,400–3,000 ptas. (US$8.40–US$18); fixed-price menu (Mon–Sat) 1,800 ptas. (US$10.80). AE, MC, V. Daily 1–4pm; Mon–Sat 7:30pm–midnight. Cafe daily 8am–2am. Metro: Plaça de Catalunya. CATALÁN.

A Barcelona legend since 1897, the "Four Cats" was a favorite of Picasso, Rusinyol, and other artists who once hung their works on its walls. Located on a narrow cobblestone street near the cathedral, the fin de siècle cafe was the setting for poetry readings by Joan Maragall, piano recitals by Isaac Albéniz and Ernie Granados, and murals by Ramón Casas. It was a base for members of the *modernisme* movement and played a major role in the intellectual and bohemian life of the city. In Catalán slang, the name of the restaurant translates as "just a few people."

Today a bar that's become a popular meeting place in the heart of the Barri Gòtic, it was long ago restored but retains its fine old look. The fixed-price menu, offered every day but Sunday, rates as one of the better bargains in town, considering the locale. The good food is prepared in an unpretentious style of Catalán cooking called *cuina de mercat* (based on whatever looks fresh at the market that day). The constantly changing menu reflects the seasons. No hot food is served on Sunday.

La Cuineta. Paradis, 4. ☎ **93-315-01-11.** Reservations recommended. Main courses 2,000–3,200 ptas. (US$12–US$19.20); fixed–price menu 3,200 ptas. (US$19.20). AE, DC, MC, V. Daily 1–4pm and 8pm–midnight. Metro: Jaume I. CATALÁN.

A well-established restaurant near the center of the Catalán government, this is a culinary highlight of the Barri Gòtic. The restaurant is decorated in typical regional style and favors local cuisine. The fixed-price menu is a good value, or you can order à la carte. The most expensive appetizer is *bellota* (acorn-fed ham), but we suggest that you settle instead for a market-fresh Catalán dish, such as *favas* (broad beans) stewed with *butifarra,* a tasty, spicy local sausage.

✪ **Los Caracoles.** Escudellers, 14. ☎ **93-302-31-85.** Reservations required. Main courses 1,800–8,000 ptas. (US$10.80–US$48). AE, DC, MC, V. Daily 1pm–midnight. Metro: Drassanes. CATALÁN/SPANISH.

Set in a labyrinth of narrow cobblestone streets, Los Caracoles is the port's most colorful and popular restaurant—and has been since 1835. It has won acclaim for its spit-roasted chicken as well as for its namesake, snails. A long, angular bar is up front, with a two-level restaurant in back. You can watch the busy preparations in the kitchen, where dried herbs, smoked ham shanks, and garlic bouquets hang from the ceiling. In summer, tables are placed outside. The excellent food features all sorts of Spanish and Catalán specialties. Everybody from Richard Nixon to John Wayne has stopped in, and Salvador Dalí was a devoted patron. Today's clientele may not be as legendary, but hordes keep coming to dine. Tourists often make this their number-one restaurant stop in Barcelona, but it's no tourist trap—Los Caracoles delivers the same aromatic and robust food it always did. We doubt if it has ever updated a recipe—the cookery is the way it was. If you avoid the very expensive fresh shellfish dishes, you'll find most offerings are at the lower end of the price scale.

INEXPENSIVE

Biocenter. Pintor Fortuny, 25. ☎ **93-301-45-83.** Main courses 672–1,000 ptas. (US$4.05–US$6); fixed-price menu 1,200 ptas. (US$7.20). No credit cards. Bar Mon–Sat 9am–5pm; food Mon–Sat 1–5pm. Metro: Plaça de Catalunya. VEGETARIAN.

This is the largest and best-known vegetarian restaurant in Barcelona, the creation of Catalonia-born entrepreneur Pep Cañameras, who is likely to be directing the service from his position behind the bar in front. Many clients, vegetarians or not, congregate over drinks in the front room. Some continue on for meals in one of two ground-floor dining rooms, whose walls are decorated with the paintings and artworks of the owner and his colleagues. There's a salad bar, an array of vegetarian casseroles, such soups as gazpacho or lentil, and a changing selection of seasonal vegetables. No meat or fish of any kind are served.

Café de L'Academia. Carrer Lledó, 1 (Barri Gòtic), Plaça Sant Just. ☎ **93-315-00-26.** Reservations required. Main courses 1,000–1,700 ptas. (US$6–US$10.20); fixed-price menu (lunch only) 1,275 ptas. (US$7.65). Set dinner 3,500 ptas. (US$21). AE, MC, V. Mon–Fri 9am–noon, 1:15–4pm, and 9pm–midnight. Closed last 2 weeks in Aug. Metro: Jaume 1. CATALÁN/MEDITERRANEAN.

In the center of Barri Gòtic, only a short walk from Plaça Sant Jaume, this 28-table restaurant looks expensive but is really one of the best and most affordable in the medieval city. The building dates from the 15th century, although the restaurant was only founded in the mid-1980s. Its owner, Jordí Casteldi, offers an elegant atmosphere in a setting of brown stone walls and ancient wooden columns. At a small bar you can peruse the menu and study the wines offered. The menu is varied and the dishes always well prepared. Usually dishes of this quality cost three times as much in Barcelona. The chef is proud of his "kitchen of the market," suggesting that only the freshest ingredients from the day's shopping are featured. Try such delights as *lassanye de butifarra I ceps* (lasagna with Catalán sausage and flap mushrooms), *bacalla gratinado i musselina de carofes* (salt cod gratinée with an artichoke mousse), or *terrina d'berengeras amb formtage de cabra* (terrine of eggplant with goat cheese). A specialty, and a delectable one at that, is *codorniz rellena en cebollitas tiernas y foie de pato* (partridge stuffed with tender onions and duck liver).

✪ El Duc. In the Duques de Bergara, Bergara, 11. ☎ **93-301-51-51.** Reservations recommended. Main courses 1,200–2,200 ptas. (US$7.20–US$13.20); fixed-price menu (Mon–Fri only) 2,500 ptas. (US$15). AE, DC, MC, V. Daily 1–4pm and 8–11pm. Metro: Plaça de Catalunya. CATALÁN

Set on the lobby level of the previously recommended hotel, within a compound whose oldest section was designed by Emilio Salas i Cortes, an early mentor of Gaudí, this is a well-managed and competent restaurant serving food that's a lot better than what's offered in the dining rooms of many competing hotels. Adjacent to the Plaça de Catalunya, it offers conservative but flavorful dishes that include prawn cocktails, goose-liver pâté, margret of duckling in fruit sauce, tenderloin of beef "Café de Paris," grilled entrecôte, and fried fish. Ingredients are very fresh, and the chefs more than competent. They add flavor to every dish without destroying the natural taste. For such an elegant enclave, the prices are extremely reasonable.

✪ Garduña. Morera, 17. ☎ **93-302-43-23.** Reservations recommended. Main courses 1,200–3,800 ptas. (US$7.20–US$22.80); fixed-price lunch 1,200–1,800 ptas. (US$7.20–US$10.80); fixed-price dinner 1,800 ptas. (US$10.80). AE, DC, MC, V. Mon–Sat 1–4pm and 8pm–midnight. Metro: Liceu. CATALÁN.

This is the most famous restaurant within Barcelona's covered food market, La Boquería. Originally conceived as a hotel, it eliminated its bedrooms in the 1970s and has concentrated on food ever since. Battered, somewhat ramshackle, and a bit claustrophobic, it nevertheless enjoys a fashionable reputation among actors, sculptors, writers, and painters who appreciate a blue-collar atmosphere that might have been designated as bohemian in an earlier era. Because of its position near the back of the market, you'll pass endless rows of fresh produce, cheeses, and meats before you reach it, a fact that adds to its allure. You can dine downstairs, near a crowded bar, or a bit more formally upstairs. Food is ultra-fresh (the chefs certainly don't have to travel far for the ingredients) and might include "hors d'oeuvres of the sea," cannelloni Rossini, grilled hake with herbs, *rape* (monkfish) *marinera,* paella, brochettes of veal, seafood rice, or a *zarzuela* (stew) of fresh fish with spices.

La Dentellière. Carrer Ample, 26. ☎ **93-319-68-21.** Reservations recommended. Main courses 1,000–1,500 ptas. (US$6–US$9); fixed-price lunch 1,100 ptas. (US$6.60); fixed-price dinner 2,500 ptas. (US$15). MC, V. Tues–Sat 1:30–4pm and 8:30–11pm. Metro: Drassanes. FRENCH.

Charming, and steeped in the French aesthetic, this bistro occupies a 200-year-old historic building in the heart of the Barri Gòtic. Inside, you'll find a small corner of provincial France, thanks to the dedicated effort of Evelyne, the France-born writer/owner. Beneath the centuries-old ceiling beams, in a pair of antique-strewn dining rooms noted for their slightly cramped tables, you'll order from an imaginative menu that includes a lasagna made from strips of salted codfish, peppers, and tomato sauce; and a delectable carpaccio of fillet of beef with pistachios, lemon juice, vinaigrette, and Parmesan cheese. The wine list is particularly imaginative, with worthy vintages mostly from France and Spain.

La Rosca. Juliá Portet, 6. ☎ **93-302-51-73.** Main courses 2,500–2,800 ptas. (US$15–US$16.80); fixed-price menu 1,000 ptas. (US$6). No credit cards. Sun–Fri 9am–4pm and 8pm–midnight. Closed Aug 20–30. Metro: Urquinaona and Catalunya. CATALÁN/SPANISH.

For more than half a century Don Alberto Vellve, the owner, has welcomed customers into this little Barri Gòtic eatery, close to Plaça de Catalunya. On a short street, the place is easy to miss, except to some of its devotees who have been coming here for decades. Go here if you'd like to see the type of place where people dined inexpensively in the Franco era. A mixture of Catalán and modern Spanish cuisine is served in this small rustic house that has high ceilings and white walls. The decor has nostalgic touches such as old bullfighting posters and pictures of Barcelona in the mid–20th century. There are 60 unadorned tables, which diners fill quickly to take advantage of the cheap three-course luncheon menu. Dig into such hearty fare as veal stew or assorted grilled fish and shellfish. Baby squid is cooked in its own ink, and one of the best and most typical dishes is white beans sautéed with ham and Catalán sausage. For a true treat, ask for the *rape a la planate* or grilled monkfish.

Nou Celler. Princesa, 16. ☎ **93-310-47-73.** Reservations required. Main courses 850–2,200 ptas. (US$5.10–US$13.20); fixed-price lunch menu 1,000–1,300 ptas. (US$6–US$7.80). MC, V. Sun–Fri 8:30am–1:30pm. Closed June 23–July 23. Metro: Jaume I. CATALÁN/SPANISH.

Near the Picasso Museum, this establishment is perfect for either a bodega-type meal or a cup of coffee. Country artifacts hang from the beamed ceiling and plaster walls. The back entrance, at Barra de Ferro, 3, is at the quieter end of the place, where dozens of original artworks are arranged into a collage. The dining room offers such Franco-era food as fish soup, Catalán soup, *zarzuela* (a medley of seafood), paella, hake, and other classic dishes.

Pitarra. Avinyó, 56. ☎ **93-301-16-47.** Reservations required. Main courses 1,200–2,000 ptas. (US$7.20–US$12); fixed-price lunch 1,500 ptas. (US$9). AE, DC, MC, V. Mon–Sat 1–4pm and 8:30–11pm. Closed Aug 3–30. Metro: Liceu. CATALÁN.

Founded in 1890, this restaurant in the Barri Gòtic was named after the 19th-century Catalán playwright who lived and wrote his plays and poetry here in the back room. Try the grilled fish chowder or a Catalán salad, followed by grilled salmon or squid Málaga style. Valencian paella is another specialty. The cuisine does not even pretend to be imaginative, but instead adheres strictly to time-tested recipes—"the type of food we ate when growing up," in the words of one diner.

ⓕ Family-Friendly Restaurants

Dulcinea *(see p. 82)*   This makes a great refueling stop any time of the day— guaranteed to satisfy any chocoholic.

Fast-Food Places *(see p. 81)*   Burger King, the Chicago Pizza Pie Factory, and Kentucky Fried Chicken are good bets for familiar fast food that the kids will enjoy.

Garduña *(see p. 69)*   This is the best known restaurant in Barcelona's covered food market, La Boquería. Kids love to go to this battered and ramshackle place, which not only serves good and inexpensive food, but also allows visitors to experience the aura of one of Spain's most bustling food markets. The choice of food items is so wide and varied, there's something here to please everyone.

Poble Espanyol *(see p. 42)*   A good introduction to Spanish food. All the restaurants in the "Spanish Village" serve comparable food at comparable prices—let the kids choose what to eat.

Pla de la Garsa. Assaonadors, 13. ☎ **93-315-24-13.** Reservations recommended for weekends. Main courses 900–2,000 ptas. (US$5.40–US$12); fixed-price menu (lunch) 1,200 ptas. (US$7.20). AE, DC, MC, V. Mon–Sat 1:15–3:45pm and 8pm–midnight, Sun 1:30–4pm. Metro: Jaume 1. CATALÁN/MEDITERRANEAN.

In Barrio Ribera, close to the cathedral, this historic building has been fully renovated but still retains some 19th-century fittings such as a cast-iron spiral staircase diners ascend to reach another dining area upstairs. However, the ground floor is more interesting. Here you'll encounter the owner, Ignacio Sulle, an antiques collector who has filled his establishment with an intriguing collection of objets d'art. He boasts one of the city's best wine lists, and features a daily array of traditional Catalán and Mediterranean favorite dishes, and is also known for his variety of French cheese. Every dish has a special something that raises it to a gastronomic height. Begin with one of the pâtés, especially the goose, or else a confit of duck thighs. You can also order meat and fish pâtés. One surprise is a terrine with black olives and anchovies. For a main course, try the perfectly seasoned beef bourguignonne or *fabetes fregides amb menta i pernil* (beans with meat and diced Serrano ham). The cheese selection is one of the finest we've found in town, especially bountiful in Catalán goat cheese, including Serrat Gros from the Pyrénées.

Senyor Parellada. Carrer Argentaria, 37. ☎ **93-310-50-94.** Reservations recommended. Main courses 750–2,300 ptas. (US$4.50–US$13.80). AE, MC, V. Mon–Sat 1–3:30pm and 9–10:30pm. Metro: Jaume I. CATALÁN.

The glossy, contemporary-looking interior of this place is in distinct contrast to a battered-looking facade of a building that's at least a century old. Inside, within a pair of lemon-yellow and blue dining rooms, you'll be confronted with a choice of menu items that include Italian-style cannelloni, stuffed cabbage, codfish "as it was prepared by the monks of the Poblet monastery," baked monkfish with mustard and garlic sauce, roasted duck served with figs, and roasted rack of lamb with red-wine sauce. Patrons flock faithfully to this bistro, knowing they'll be served a traditional cuisine of northeast Spain with fine local products. The chefs seem to know how to coax the most flavor out of the premium ingredients.

SUR DIAGONAL
VERY EXPENSIVE

Beltxenea. Majorca, 275. ☎ **93-215-30-24.** Reservations recommended. Main courses 2,600–5,500 ptas. (US$15.60–US$33); tasting menu 7,500 ptas. (US$45). AE, DC, MC, V. Mon–Fri 1:30–4pm, Mon–Sat 8:30–11:30pm. Closed 2 weeks in Aug. Metro: Passeig de Gràcia. BASQUE/FRENCH.

Set in a structure originally designed in the late 19th century as an Eixample apartment building, this restaurant celebrates the nuances and subtleties of Basque cuisine. Since the Basques are noted as the finest chefs in Spain, this is a grand cuisine indeed—and in this case, it's served in one of the most elegantly and comfortably furnished restaurants in Barcelona. Save a visit here for that special night—it's worth the money. Within a dignified dining room with parquet floors and nautical accessories, you can enjoy a meal that marries the inspiration of the chef and the availability of fresh ingredients. Examples include hake served either fried with garlic or garnished with clams and served with fish broth; well-prepared, succulent roast lamb or grilled rabbit; and excellent desserts. Summer dining is possible outside in the formal garden.

✪ **Jaume de Provença.** Provença, 88. ☎ **93-430-00-29.** Reservations recommended. Main courses 2,200–7,000 ptas. (US$13.20–US$42). AE, DC, MC, V. Tues–Sun 1–4pm; Tues–Sat 9–11:30pm. Closed Easter week, Aug. Metro: Entença. CATALÁN/FRENCH.

Located a few steps away from the Estació Central de Barcelona-Sants railway station at the western end of the Eixample, this is a small, cozy, and personalized spot with a country-rustic decor. It is the only restaurant along the Diagonal that can compare to La Dama (see below). The young-at-heart clientele is served by a polite and hardworking staff. Named after its owner/chef Jaume Bargués, it features modern interpretations of traditional Catalán and southern French cuisine. Examples include a gratin of clams with spinach, a salad of two different species of lobster, foie gras and truffles, pigs' trotters with plums and truffles, crabmeat lasagna, cod with saffron sauce, sole with mushrooms in a port-wine sauce, and a dessert specialty of orange mousse, whose presentation is an artistic statement in its own right. This establishment, incidentally, was launched during the 1940s by Jaume's forebears, who acquiesced to their talented offspring's new and successful culinary theories.

✪ **La Dama.** Diagonal, 423. ☎ **93-202-06-86.** Reservations required. Main courses 3,000–4,000 ptas. (US$18–US$24); fixed-price menu 6,500–9,000 ptas. (US$39–US$54). AE, DC, MC, V. Daily 1:30–3:30pm and 8:30–11:30pm. Metro: Provença. CATALÁN/INTERNATIONAL.

This is one of the few restaurants in Barcelona that deserves, and gets, a Michelin star. Located a floor above street level in one of the grandly iconoclastic 19th-century buildings for which Barcelona is famous, this stylish and well-managed restaurant serves a clientele of local residents and civic dignitaries with impeccable taste and confidence. You'll take an art-nouveau elevator (or the sinuous stairs) up one flight to reach the dining room. The specialties might include salmon steak served with vinegar derived from *cava* (sparkling wine) and onions, cream-of-potato soup flavored with caviar, a salad of crayfish with orange-flavored vinegar, an abundant seasonal platter of autumn mushrooms, and succulent preparations of lamb, fish, shellfish, beef, goat, and veal. The building that contains the restaurant, designed by Manuel Sayrach, is 3 blocks west of the intersection of Avinguda Diagonal and Passeig de Grácia.

EXPENSIVE

Can Isidre. Les Flors, 12. ☎ **93-441-11-39.** Reservations required. Main courses 2,200–5,000 ptas. (US$13.20–US$30). AE, DC, MC, V. Mon–Sat 1:30–4pm and 8:30–11:30pm. Closed Sat–Sun June–Aug. Metro: Paral-lel. CATALÁN.

In spite of its seedy location (take a cab at night!), this is perhaps the most sophisticated Catalán bistro in Barcelona, drawing such patrons as King Juan Carlos and Queen Sofía. Opened in 1970, it was also visited by Julio Iglesias and the famous Catalonian band leader Xavier Cugat. Isidre Gironés and his wife, Montserrat, are known for fresh Catalán cuisine. Flowers and artwork decorate the restaurant, and the array of food is beautifully prepared and served. Try spider crabs and shrimp, a gourmand salad with foie gras, sweetbreads with port and flap mushrooms, or carpaccio of veal in Harry's Bar style. The selection of Spanish and Catalán wines is excellent.

✪ **Casa Calvet.** Carrer Casp, 48. ☎ **93-412-40-12.** Reservations recommended. Main courses 2,050–3,300 ptas. (US$12.30–US$19.80). AE, MC, V. Mon–Sat 1–4pm and 7–11:30pm. Metro: Castro. CATALÁN/CONTINENTAL.

This is one of the most visible and popular restaurants of the Eixample district, with a reputation and cachet that has attracted everyone from the Mayor of Barcelona to Queen Sofía and her daughter, the Infanta Cristina. The setting is on the ground floor of one of the great modernist apartment buildings of Barcelona, a stained-glass and wood-trimmed fantasy designed by Antoni Gaudí in 1899. The menu is sophisticated, reflecting influences from both Catalonia and nearby France. Examples include fresh pan-fried duck liver served in a bitter orange sauce, ravioli stuffed with oysters and clams and served in a sparkling cava sauce, and grilled fillet of pork with chestnuts and cider sauce.

Restaurante Diana. In the Hotel Ritz, Gran Vía de les Corts Catalánes, 668. ☎ **93-318-52-00.** Reservations recommended. Main courses 2,950–4,500 ptas. (US$17.70–US$27); fixed-price menu 3,865–5,130 ptas. (US$23.20–US$30.80) Mon–Fri, 7,650 ptas. (US$45.90) Sat–Sun. AE, DC, MC, V. Daily 1:30–4pm and 8:30–11pm. Metro: Arc del Triomf. FRENCH.

At least part of the allure of dining here involves the chance to visit the most legendary hotel in Barcelona. Located on the lobby level of the Ritz, the restaurant is filled with French furnishings and accessories amid a gilt-and-blue color scheme. The polite and well-trained staff serves such dishes as seafood salad flavored with saffron; fillets of sole layered with lobster; filet mignon braised in cognac, cream, and peppercorn sauce; turbot in white-wine sauce; and a wide array of delectable desserts. The cuisine is of a high international standard, although the restaurant doesn't quite reach the sublime culinary experience of La Dama or Jaume de Provença (see above).

MODERATE

La Buena Brasa. Aribau, 159. ☎ **93-410-47-83.** Reservations recommended. Main courses 1,500–2,000 ptas. (US$9–US$12). MC, V. Daily noon–5pm and 8pm–midnight. Metro: Diagonal. MEDITERRANEAN.

The name of this restaurant translates as "the good charcoal grill," which certainly provides a clue as to what the house specialties will be. The owner, José Luis Iglesias, welcomes a host of discerning Barcelona professional people who come not for the glamorous surroundings, but for the market-fresh cuisine. You might begin with a selection of tapas ranging from smoked salmon to pâtés. Or try *esqueixada* (shredded salt-dried cod in a vinaigrette of oil and vinegar given extra flavor by onions and tomatoes), or an *escalivada* mixing fresh eggplant, red peppers, and onions cooked on hot coals and served with anchovies. Other excellent dishes include *arroz y bacalao frito con pimientos y ajos tiernos* (rice with fried salt cod, peppers, and tender garlic), and calcots a la Brasa (a local variety of grilled spring onion). Most diners come here for the grilled meats, especially rabbit, goat, and lamb. The best dessert is an excellent *tarta al whisky* or whisky cake.

L'Olive. Muntaner, 171 (corner of Corsega). ☎ **93-430-90-27.** Reservations recommended. Main courses 1,500–2,600 ptas. (US$9–US$15.60). *Menú completo* 4,500 ptas. (US$27). AE, DC, MC, V. Daily 1–4pm and Mon–Sat 8:30pm–midnight. Metro: Muntaner and Hospital Clínic. CATALÁN/SPANISH.

You assume that this restaurant is named for the olive that figures so prominently in its cuisine, but actually it's named for the owner, Josep Olive. You can be born with no more apt a name for a Mediterranean restaurateur. In the Eixample, the building is designed in a modern Catalán style with walls adorned with reproductions of famous Spanish paintings by Miró, Dalí, and Picasso. The tables are topped in marble, the floors impeccably polished. There are sections on both floors where it's possible to have some privacy, and overall the feeling is one of elegance with a touch of intimacy. You won't be disappointed by anything on the menu, especially *bacalla cache* (raw salt cod) or *filet de vedella al vi negre al forn* (veal fillets cooked in the oven in a red-wine sauce), and especially the *salsa magret* of duck with strawberry sauce. One specialty is *amanida de col llombarda amb seitons* (a salad of finely shredded red cabbage that has been parboiled in sherry vinegar and tossed with a purée of olive oil and a small fish similar to white anchovies). Monkfish flavored with roasted garlic is always a palate pleaser, and you can finish with a *crema catalán* (a flan), or one of the delicious Catalán pastries.

✪ **Rosalert.** Avenida Diagonal, 301. ☎ **93-207-10-19.** Main courses 1,500–2,000 ptas. (US$9–US$12). *Menú completo* 6,000 ptas. (US$36). AE, DC, MC, V. Tues–Sun 9am–6pm and 8pm–2am. Closed Aug 10–30. Metro: Verdaguer/Sagrada Familia. CATALÁN/SEAFOOD.

At the corner of Carrer Napols, close to La Sagrada Família, this restaurant has been the domain of Jordí Alert for more than four decades. He specializes in *comida de mar a la plancha* (grilled seafood) in a typical setting of hardwood floors and tile-covered walls. The seafood or shellfish are grilled on a heated iron plate without any additives. There is no more awesome glass tank of live crustacea in Barcelona. You choose your meal and the poor victim is extracted with a net and thrown on the grill. Of course, you'll find all the typical offerings: tiny octopus, succulent mussels, fat shrimp, calamares, fresh oysters, and langoustines. If you're daring you can order such unusual seafood as *dátils* ("dates" in English), a delicious shellfish whose shape resembles that of a date. Begin with one of the freshly made tapas such as salt cod in vinaigrette or broad beans laced with garlic and virgin olive oil. Your best bet might be the *parrillada* or assorted fish and shellfish from the grill. One of the best offerings is turbot cooked on the grill with potatoes and fresh mushrooms.

Talaia Mar. Marina, 16 (Port Maritim). ☎ **93-221-90-90.** Reservations recommended. Main courses 1,950–3,550 ptas. (US$11.70–US$21.30). AE, DC, MC, V. Daily 1:30–4pm and 8pm–midnight. Metro: Via Olimpica. SEAFOOD/INTERNATIONAL.

Some architects have compared the form of this avant-garde restaurant to a postmodern *mirador* (glassed-in bay window) whose panoramic view faces the port of Barcelona and the open sea. Established in 1992 with a half-moon interior, it's more stylish and sleek than many of its nearby competitors, with a cuisine that's hip, well conceived, and based on fresh ingredients. Look for a wide variety of grilled fish, many of them hauled in fresh from deep offshore waters that morning, and served as simply as possible, sometimes only with lemon or butter sauce. Shellfish are prominently displayed in cases as part of a meal's theatricality; roasted pork and lamb are always a worthwhile choice.

INEXPENSIVE

Ca La María. Tallers, 76. ☎ **93-318-89-93.** Reservations recommended Sat–Sun. Main courses 1,200–1,600 ptas. (US$7.20–US$9.60). AE, DC, MC, V. Mon–Sun 1:30–4pm; Tues–Sat 8:30–11pm. Metro: Universitat. CATALÁN.

This small blue-and-green-tiled bistro (only 18 tables) is on a quiet square opposite a Byzantine-style church near the Plaça de la Universitat. This is not a place for haute cuisine. Look for the constantly changing daily specials. A bit battered in looks, the restaurant serves endearingly homelike food—providing you grew up in a family of Catalán cooks. Despite their simple origins, these dishes are often surprisingly tasty, as exemplified by the baby squid with onions and tomatoes, anglerfish with burnt garlic, and a veal sirloin cooked to taste.

El Caballito Blanco. Mallorca, 196. ☎ **93-453-10-33.** Main courses 1,000–3,900 ptas. (US$6–US$23.40). AE, MC, V. Tues–Sun 1–3:45pm, Tues–Sat 9–10:45pm. Closed Aug. Metro: Hospital Clínic. SEAFOOD/INTERNATIONAL.

This old Barcelona standby famous for its seafood has long been popular among locals. The fluorescent-lit dining area does not offer much atmosphere, but the food is good, varied, and relatively inexpensive unless you order the lobster. The "Little White Horse," in the Passeig de Gràcia area, features a huge selection, including monkfish, mussels marinara, and shrimp with garlic. If you don't want fish, try the grilled lamb cutlets. Several different pâtés and salads are offered. There's a bar to the left of the dining area.

Tragaluz. Pasaje Concepción, 5, Eixample. ☎ **93-487-01-96.** Reservations recommended. Main courses 1,500–3,500 ptas. (US$9–US$21). AE, MC, V. Daily 1:30–4pm and 8:30pm–midnight. Metro: Diagonale or Provença. MEDITERRANEAN.

Named after the turn-of-the-century modernist building that contains it, this well-respected restaurant has three very contemporary-looking, mostly beige dining rooms on three separate floors. Menu items are derived from fresh ingredients that vary with the season. Depending on the month of your visit, you might find terrine of duck liver, Santurce-style hake (with garlic and herbs), fillet of sole stuffed with red peppers, and beef tenderloin in a Rioja wine sauce. One of the best desserts is a semi-soft slice of deliberately underbaked chocolate cake. Diners seeking low-fat dishes will find solace here, as will vegetarians. The vegetables served are the best and freshest on the market that day. You'll also find a sushi restaurant downstairs. Most dishes are at the lower end of the price scale.

NORTE DIAGONAL
VERY EXPENSIVE

✪ **Botafumeiro.** Gran de Gràcia, 81. ☎ **93-218-42-30.** Reservations recommended for dining rooms. Main courses 3,200–6,000 ptas. (US$19.20–US$36). AE, DC, MC, V. Daily 1pm–1am. Metro: Enrique Quiroga. SEAFOOD.

Although the competition is severe, this classic *marisquería* consistently puts Barcelona's finest seafood on the table. Much of the allure of this place comes from the attention to detail paid by the white-jacketed staff, who will prepare a setting at the establishment's bar for anyone who prefers to dine there. If you do choose to venture to the rear, you'll find a series of attractive dining rooms outfitted with light-grained panels, white napery, polished brass, potted plants, and paintings by Galician artists.

These rooms are noted for the ease with which business deals are arranged during the lunch hour, when international business-types make it their rendezvous of choice. The king of Spain is occasionally a patron.

The menu includes the most legendary seafood in Barcelona, prepared ultra-fresh in a glistening, modern kitchen that's visible from parts of the dining room. The restaurant prides itself on its fresh and saltwater fish, clams, mussels, lobster, crayfish, scallops, and several varieties of crustaceans that you may never have seen before. Stored live in holding tanks or in enormous crates near the restaurant's entrance, many of the creatures are flown in daily from Galicia, home of owner Moncho Neira. In contrast to the 100-or-so fish dishes (which might include *zarzuelas*, paellas, and grills), the menu lists only four or five meat dishes, including three kinds of steak, veal, and a traditional version of pork with turnips. The wine list offers a wide array of *cavas* from Catalonia and highly drinkable choices from Galicia.

✪ **Gaig.** Passeig de Maragall, 402. ☎ **93-429-10-17.** Reservations recommended. Main courses 5,000–6,000 ptas. (US$30–US$36); menu gastronómico 8,850 ptas. (US$53.10). AE, DC, MC, V. Tues–Sun 1:30–4pm and 9–11pm, Sun 1:30–4pm. Closed 3 weeks in Aug. Metro: Horta. MODERN CATALÁN.

One of the shining culinary showcases of Barcelona, Gaig was founded some 130 years ago by the great-grandmother of the present owner, Carlos Gaig. Back then it was known as a *fonda* or small inn for travelers. Despite the age of the building, the interior design is both modern and luxurious, having recently been restyled by well-known designers. The restaurant is celebrated locally for the quality and freshness of its food, purchased daily at the Boquería market in the heart of the old city. If you order a meal with eggs, they will have been contributed by chickens seen wandering about an outdoor patio where summer dining takes place. The cuisine centers on traditional Catalán recipes transformed to suit more modern palates. Among the best dishes to order are *arroz del delta con pichon y zetas* (delta rice with partridge and mushrooms), *rape asado a la catalána* (grilled monkfish with local herbs), and *els petits filet de vedella amb prunes i pinyons* (small veal fillets with prunes and pine nuts). One of the tastiest dishes is marinated roast pork thigh. Desserts include *crema de Sant Joseph* (a warm flan with wild strawberries), homemade chocolates, and a selection of *tartes*.

EXPENSIVE

✪ **Neichel.** Pedralbes, 16. ☎ **93-203-84-08.** Reservations required. Main courses 2,500–4,200 ptas. (US$15–US$25.20). AE, MC, V. Mon–Fri 1:30–3:30pm; Mon–Sat 8:30–11pm. Closed holidays and Aug. Metro: Palau Reial or María Cristina. FRENCH/MEDITERRANEAN.

Owned and operated by Alsatian-born Jean Louis Neichel, who has been called "the most brilliant ambassador French cuisine has ever had within Spain," this restaurant serves a clientele best described as stratospheric. Outfitted in cool gray and pastels, with its main decoration derived from a bank of windows opening onto greenery, Neichel is almost obsessively concerned with gastronomy.

Your meal might include a mosaic of foie gras with vegetables, strips of salmon marinated in sesame and served with *escabeche* (vinaigrette) sauce, a prize-winning terrine of sea crab floating on a lavishly decorated bed of cold seafood sauce, escalope of turbot served with *coulis* (purée) of sea urchins, fricassée of Bresse chicken served with spiny lobsters, Spanish milk-fed lamb served with the juice of Boletus mushrooms, rack of lamb gratinéed within an herb-flavored pastry crust, and an array of well-flavored game birds obtained in season from hunters throughout Catalonia and France. Both the European cheeses and the changing array of freshly made desserts are spectacular.

Reno. Tuset, 27. ☎ **93-200-91-29.** Reservations required. Main courses 1,400–3,800 ptas. (US$8.40–US$22.80). AE, DC, MC, V. Sun–Fri 1–4pm; Sun–Sat 8:30–11:30pm. Metro: Diagonal. CATALÁN/FRENCH.

One of the finest and most enduring haute cuisine restaurants in Barcelona, Reno boasts an impeccably mannered staff (formal but not intimidating) and an understated modern decor accented with black leather and oversized mirrors. A discreet row of sidewalk-to-ceiling windows hung with fine-mesh lace shelters diners from prying eyes on the octagonal plaza outside. Specialties, influenced by the seasons and by the traditions of France, might include partridge simmered in wine or port sauce, assorted smoked fish (each painstakingly smoked on the premises), fillet of sole either stuffed with foie gras and truffles or grilled with anchovy sauce, Catalán-style civet of lobster, roast duck with a sauce of honey and sherry vinegar, and an appetizing array of pastries wheeled from table to table on a trolley. Dessert might also be one of several kinds of crepes flambéed at your table. The restaurant, incidentally, was established in the 1950s by the present owner's father.

Roig Robí. Séneca, 20. ☎ **93-218-92-22.** Reservations required. Main courses 2,200–4,500 ptas. (US$13.20–US$27); fixed-price menu 7,500 ptas. (US$45). AE, DC, MC, V. Mon–Fri 1:30–4pm; Mon–Sat 9–11pm. Metro: Diagonal. CATALÁN.

This restaurant, whose name translated from Catalán means "ruby red" (the color of a perfectly aged Rioja), serves excellent food from an imaginative kitchen. A warm welcome keeps patrons coming back here, although we're not as excited about this restaurant as we once were. It remains, however, one of the city's most dependable choices. Begin by ordering an apéritif from the L-shaped oak bar. Then head down a long corridor to a pair of flower-filled dining rooms. In warm weather, glass doors open onto a walled courtyard, ringed with cascades of ivy and shaded with willows and mimosa. Menu items include fresh beans with pine-nut sauce, hake al Roig Robí, fresh mushroom salad with green beans and fresh tomatoes, shellfish from Costa Brava, ravioli stuffed with spring herbs, chicken stuffed with foie gras, and a cockscomb salad—the latter a dish too adventuresome for many palates.

✪ **Via Veneto.** Ganduxer, 10. ☎ **93-200-72-44.** Reservations required. Main courses 2,500–4,500 ptas. (US$15–US$27). AE, DC, MC, V. Mon–Fri 1:15–4pm; Mon–Sat 8:45pm–midnight. Closed Aug 1–20. Metro: La Bonanova. INTERNATIONAL.

With a soothing and dignified decor of calming colors and baroque swirls, this restaurant is known for its solid respectability and consistently well prepared cuisine. A short walk from the Plaça de Francesc Macia, it offers such dishes as a tartare of fresh fish with caviar, roasted salt cod with potatoes, veal kidney with truffle sauce, loin of roast suckling pig with baby vegetables of the season, and fillet steak served in a brandy, cream, and peppercorn sauce. Innovative and imaginative Catalán recipes are always being created here. The cuisine is finely crafted based on superb local products, and there's a wide array of wines to accompany any meal. Dessert might be a richly textured combination of melted chocolate, cherries, Armagnac, and vanilla ice cream.

MOLL DE LA FUSTA & BARCELONETA
EXPENSIVE

✪ **Can Costa.** Passeig Don Joan de Borbò, 70. ☎ **93-221-59-03.** Reservations recommended. Main courses 2,000–5,500 ptas. (US$12–US$33). AE, MC, V. Daily 12:30–4pm; Mon–Sat 8–11:30pm. Metro: Barceloneta. SEAFOOD.

One of the most long-lived seafood restaurants in this seafaring town is Can Costa, an emporium of fish and shellfish whose big windows overlook the water. Originally established in the late 1930s, it has two busy dining rooms, a uniformed, well-seasoned staff, and an outdoor terrace where clients can take advantage of the streaming sunlight and harbor-front breezes. Fresh seafood rules the menu here, prepared according to traditional recipes. They include the best baby squid in town—sautéed in a flash so that it has an almost grilled flavor, and is rarely overcooked or too rubbery. A chef's specialty that has endured through many a season is *fideuá de peix,* which is equivalent to a classic Valencian shellfish paella, except in this case, noodles are used in lieu of rice. All the desserts are homemade by the kitchen staff daily.

Can Majó. Almirante Aixada, 23. ☎ **93-221-54-55.** Reservations recommended. Main courses 2,000–3,800 ptas. (US$12–US$22.80); fixed-price menu 6,000 ptas. (US$36). AE, MC, V. Tues–Sun 1:30–4:30pm and 9–11:30pm. Metro: Barceloneta. SEAFOOD.

Located in the old fishing quarter of Barceloneta, Can Majó attracts many people from the fancier quarters, who journey down here for a great seafood dinner. The Suárez-Majó family welcomes you; they're still operating a business where their grandmother first opened a bar. Try a house specialty, *pelada* (Catalán for *paella*), perhaps starting with *entremeses* (hors d'oeuvres), from which you can select barnacles, oysters, prawns, whelks, clams, and crab—whatever was caught that day. The clams with white beans are recommended. The classic all-vegetable gazpacho comes with fresh mussels and shrimp.

Ramonet. Carrer Maquinista, 17. ☎ **93-319-30-64.** Reservations recommended. Main courses 2,500–4,200 ptas. (US$15–US$25.20); fixed-price menu 4,800–7,000 ptas. (US$28.80–US$42). AE, DC, MC, V. Daily 10am–4pm and 8pm–midnight. Usually closed Aug 10–Sept 10. Metro: Barceloneta. SEAFOOD.

Located in a Catalán-style villa near the seaport, this rather expensive restaurant serves a large variety of fresh seafood, and has done so since 1763. The front room, with stand-up tables for seafood tapas, beer, and regional wine, is often crowded. In the two dining rooms in back, lined with wooden tables, you can choose from a wide variety of fish—shrimp, hake, and monkfish are almost always available. Other specialties include a portion of pungent anchovies, grilled mushrooms, black rice, braised artichokes, and a tortilla with spinach and beans. Mussels "from the beach" are also sold.

MODERATE

Agua. Passeig Maritim de la Barceloneta, 30 (Pot Marítim). ☎ **93-225-12-72.** Reservations recommended. Main courses 950–2,250 ptas. (US$5.70–US$13.50). AE, MC, V. Daily 1:30–4:30pm and 8:30pm–midnight (1am on Fri–Sat). Metro: Ciudadela. CATALÁN/SEAFOOD.

It bustles, it's hip, and it serves well-prepared fish and shellfish in a hypermodern setting that overlooks the beach. A terrace beckons anyone who wants an in-your-face view of the water, but if the wind is blowing with a bit too much chill, you can retreat into the big-windowed blue-and-yellow dining room. Here, amid display cases with the catch of the day, you can order heaping portions of meats and fish that are grilled over an open fire. Excellent examples include grilled versions of chicken, fish, shrimp, crayfish, and an especially succulent version of stuffed squid. Most of these are served with as little culinary fanfare, and as few sauces, as possible, allowing the freshness and flavor of the raw ingredients to shine through the char-grilled coatings. Risottos, some of them studded with fresh clams and herbs, are usually winners, with many versions suitable for vegetarians.

El Túnel. Ample, 33–35. ☎ **93-315-27-59.** Reservations recommended for lunch. Main courses 1,500–2,500 ptas. (US$9–US$15). MC, V. Tues–Thurs 6pm–midnight; Fri–Sat 6pm–1:30am. Closed Aug. Metro: San Jaume. SPANISH.

This long-established restaurant, located near the general post office, features delectable fish soup, cannelloni with truffles, kidney beans with shrimp, roast kid, fish stew, and fillet of beef with peppers. The food is uncomplicated but delicious. The service is eager, the wine cellar extensive.

○ **7 Portes.** Passeig d'Isabel II, 14. ☎ **93-319-30-33.** Reservations required. Main courses 3,000–4,500 ptas. (US$18–US$27). AE, DC, MC, V. Daily 1pm–midnight. Metro: Barceloneta. SEAFOOD.

This is a lunchtime favorite for businesspeople (the Stock Exchange is across the way) and an evening favorite for many in the know clients who have made it their preferred restaurant in Catalonia. It's been going since 1836. The restaurant's name means "Seven Doors," and it really does have seven doors. These open onto as many rooms, with smaller dining salons on the next landing. A festive and elegant place, it has a high-ceilinged main dining room, numerous gilt-framed mirrors, and a black-and-white marble floor. Waiters wear the long, white aprons of the belle epoque era. Regional dishes, served in enormous portions, include fresh herring with onions and potatoes, a different paella daily (sometimes with shellfish, for example, or with rabbit), and a wide array of fresh fish, succulent oysters, and an herb-laden stew of black beans with pork or white beans with sausage.

NEAR ESTACIÓN DE SANTS
INEXPENSIVE

La Llauna. Plaça D'Osca, 2. ☎ **93-422-32-25.** Reservations recommended on weekends. Main courses 800–3,000 ptas. (US$4.80–US$18); menú del día (at lunch) 1,700 ptas. (US$10.20). MC, V. Thur–Tues 1–4pm and 8pm–midnight. Metro: Plaça de Sants and Estación de Sants. CATALÁN.

The name of this restaurant is a reference to the pot in which *calcots* are cooked. Available only in the spring, this rare dish is similar to a spring onion but twice or more the size with an almost meaty taste. It isn't easy to find this delicacy in Barcelona, but this restaurant specializes in them, cooked over an open charcoal grill. In the Sant area, it has two floors for diners, each decorated in a Catalán rustic style with white walls and posters of Mediterranean and local country life. Prices are very reasonable. The menu includes well-prepared regional dishes based on fresh, local products. Locals begin with *pa amb tomaquet* or toasted bread with tomatoes and olive oil, going on to sample such hearty fare as various grilled meats with fried potatoes or *gambas a la Llauna o con conejo* (shrimp or rabbit with *calcots* in wine sauce).

WEST OF TIBIDABO

La Balsa. Infanta Isabel, 4. ☎ **93-211-50-48.** Reservations required. Main courses 2,200–3,500 ptas. (US$13.20–US$21); fixed-price lunch 3,000 ptas. (US$18); fixed-price dinner 6,500–7,000 ptas. (US$39–US$42). AE, MC, V. Tues–Sat 2–3:30pm; Mon–Sat 9–11:30pm. Closed Easter week. No buffet in Aug. INTERNATIONAL.

Perched on the uppermost level of a circular tower originally built as a water cistern, La Balsa offers a view over most of the surrounding cityscape. To reach it you must climb up to what was originally the structure's rooftop. Glassed-in walls, awnings, and a verdant mass of potted plants create the decor. You're likely to be greeted by owner and founder Mercedes López before being seated. Menu items emerge from a cramped but well-organized kitchen several floors below. (The waiters here are reputedly the most athletic in Barcelona because they must run up and down the stairs carrying steaming platters.) Often booked several days in advance, the restaurant serves such dishes as a salad of broad beans (*judías verdes*) with strips of salmon in lemon-flavored vinaigrette, stewed veal with wild mushrooms, a salad of warm lentils with anchovies, pickled fresh salmon with chives, undercooked magret (breast) of duck served with fresh and lightly poached foie gras, and baked hake (flown in frequently from faraway

Galicia) prepared in squid-ink sauce. The restaurant is 1¼ miles north of the city's heart, in the Tibidabo district, close to the Science Museum (Museu de la Ciència). The neighborhood is one of the greenbelts of Barcelona.

TASCAS

The bars listed below are known for their tapas; for further recommendations, refer to the "Barcelona After Dark" section of chapter 4.

Alt Heidelberg. Ronda Universitat, 5. ☎ **93-318-10-32.** Tapas 250–750 ptas. (US$1.50–US$4.50); combination plates 1,000–1,450 ptas. (US$6–US$8.70). MC, V. Mon–Fri 8am–1:30am, Sat–Sun noon–2am. Metro: Universitat. GERMAN/TAPAS.

Since the 1930s, this has been an institution in Barcelona, offering German beer on tap, a good selection of German sausages, and Spanish tapas. You can also enjoy full meals here—sauerkraut garni is a specialty.

Bar del Pi. Plaça Sant Josep Oriol, 1. ☎ **93-302-21-23.** Tapas 250–600 ptas. (US$1.50–US$3.60). No credit cards. Mon–Fri 9am–11pm, Sat 9:30am–10pm, Sun 10am–10pm. Metro: Liceu. TAPAS.

One of the most famous bars in the Barri Gòtic, this establishment is midway between two medieval squares, opening onto the church of Pi. You can sit inside at one of the cramped bentwood tables or stand at the crowded bar. In warm weather, take a table beneath the single plane tree on this landmark square. The selection of tapas is limited; most visitors come to drink coffee, beer, or wine. The plaza, which people spill out onto, usually draws an interesting group of young bohemian sorts and travelers.

✪ **Bar Turó.** Tenor Viñas, 1. ☎ **93-200-69-53.** Tapas 300–1,500 ptas. (US$1.80–US$9). MC, V. Sun–Thurs 9am–1am, Fri–Sat 9am–3am. Metro: Maria Cristina. TAPAS.

Set in an affluent residential neighborhood north of the old town, Bar Turó serves some of the best tapas in town. In summer you can either sit outside or retreat to the narrow confines of the inside bar. There you can select from about 20 different kinds of tapas, including Russian salad, fried squid, and Serrano ham.

Bodega la Plata. Mercè, 28. ☎ **93-315-10-09.** Tapas 250–1,000 ptas. (US$1.50–US$6). No credit cards. Mon–Sat 10am–11pm. Metro: Barceloneta. TAPAS.

Established in the 1920s, and part of a trio of famous bodegas on this narrow medieval street, La Plata occupies a corner building whose two open sides allow richly aromatic cooking odors to permeate the neighborhood. This bodega has a marble-topped bar and overcrowded tables. The culinary specialty is *raciones* (small plates) of deep-fried sardines (head and all). You can make a meal with two servings of these, coupled with the house's tomato, onion, and fresh anchovy salad.

Bodegueta. Rambla de Catalunya, 100. ☎ **93-215-48-94.** Tapas from 250 ptas. (US$1.50). No credit cards. Mon–Sat 8am–1:45am, Sun 7pm–1:30am. Metro: Diagonal. TAPAS.

Founded in 1940, this old wine tavern specializes in Catalán sausage meats. Everything can be washed down with inexpensive Spanish wines. Beer costs 125 to 195 pesetas (US90¢ to US$1.35); wine goes for 100 pesetas (US70¢).

Casa Alfonso. Roger de Lluria, 6. ☎ **93-301-97-83.** Tapas 1,200–2,500 ptas. (US$7.20–US$15). No credit cards. Mon–Tues 9am–10pm, Wed–Sat 9am–1am. Metro: Urquinaona. TAPAS.

Spaniards love their ham, which comes in a great many forms. The best of the best is *jamon Jabugo*, the only kind sold at this traditional establishment. Entire hams hang

---

Fast Food & Picnic Fare

The **Chicago Pizza Pie Factory,** calle de Provença, 300 (☎ **93-215-94-15;** metro: Passeig de Gràcia), offers pizzas for 1,250 to 3,800 pesetas (US$7.50 to US$22.80), the latter big enough for four. It's open daily 1pm to 1am; happy hour runs 5 to 9pm.

Café Viena, Rambla dels Estudis, 115 (☎ **93-317-14-92;** metro: Plaça de Catalunya), is Barcelona's most elegant fast-food place. Waiters wearing Viennese vests serve croissants with Roquefort for breakfast and, later in the day, toasted ham sandwiches, hamburgers with onions, and pasta with tomato sauce. Meals cost from 1,600 pesetas (US$9.60). Service is Monday to Saturday 8:30am to 1am, Sunday 9am to 11pm.

The best place to buy the makings for a picnic is ✪ **Mercat de la Boquería,** in the center of the Rambles (metro: Liceu). This is the old marketplace of Barcelona. You'll jostle elbows with butchers and fishmongers in bloodied smocks and see salespeople selling cheeses and sausages. Much of the food is uncooked, but hundreds of items are already prepared, and you can even buy a bottle of wine or mineral water.

Now for where to have your picnic: Right in the heart of Barcelona is the **Parc de la Ciutadella** (see "Parks & Gardens" in chapter 4), at the southeast section of the district known as the Barri de la Ribera, site of the Picasso Museum. After lunch, take the kids to the park zoo and later go out on the lake in a rented rowboat. It's more scenic to picnic in **Montjuïc,** site of several events at the 1992 Summer Olympics. After your picnic, you can enjoy the amusement park, take in the Miró museum, or walk through the Poble Espanyol, a re-created Spanish village.

---

from steel braces. They're taken down, carved, and trimmed before you into paper-thin slices. This particular form of cured ham, generically called *jamon serrano,* comes from pigs fed acorns in Huelva, in deepest Andalusia. Devotees of all things porcine will ascend to piggy-flavored heaven.

✪ **Casa Tejada.** Tenor Viñas, 3. ☎ **93-200-73-41.** Tapas 350–2,500 ptas. (US$2.10–US$15). MC, V. Daily 9am–2am. Metro: Muntaner. TAPAS.

Covered with rough stucco and decorated with hanging hams, Casa Tejada (established in 1964) offers some of Barcelona's best tapas. Arranged behind a glass display case, they include such dishes as marinated fresh tuna, German-style potato salad, five preparations of squid (including one that's stuffed), and ham salad. For variety, quantity, and quality, this place is hard to beat. There's outdoor dining in summer.

La Jarra. Mercè, 9. ☎ **93-315-17-59.** Tapas 350–600 ptas. (US$2.10–US$3.60). No credit cards. Thurs–Tues 11am–1am. Metro: Barceloneta. TAPAS.

Established in the 1950s, La Jarra occupies a tile-covered L-shaped room that's somewhat bleak in appearance, yet residents claim it is one of the most authentic tapas bars in the old town. You can order a *ración* (portion) of marinated mushrooms or well-seasoned artichokes Rioja style, but the culinary star is the ever-present haunch of *jamón canario* (Canary Island ham), which is carved before your eyes into lean, succulent morsels served with boiled potatoes, olive oil, and lots of salt. It resembles roast pork in flavor and appearance.

Las Campanas (Casa Marcos). Mercè, 21. ☎ **93-315-06-09.** Tapas 150–1,250 ptas. (US90¢–US$7.50). No credit cards. Thurs–Tues 12:30am–4pm and 7pm–2am. Metro: Jaume I. TAPAS.

No sign marks the restaurant—from the street Las Campanas looks like a storehouse for cured hams and wine bottles. At a long and narrow stand-up bar, patrons flock here for a chorizo, which is then pinioned between two pieces of bread. Sausages are usually eaten with beer or red wine. The place opened in 1952, and nothing has changed since. A tape recorder plays nostalgic favorites, everything from Edith Piaf to the Andrews Sisters.

Rey de la Gamba. Joan de Borbò, 48–53. ☎ **93-221-75-98.** Tapas 550–10,000 ptas. (US$3.30–US$60). MC, V. Daily 11am–1am. Metro: Barceloneta. SHELLFISH.

The name of this place means "king of prawns," but the restaurant could also be called the House of Mussels since it sells more of that shellfish. In the old fishing village of Barceloneta, dating from the 18th century, this place packs them in, especially on weekends. A wide array of seafood is sold, along with cured ham—the combination is considered a tradition.

DESSERT

Dulcinea. Via Petrixol, 2. ☎ **93-302-68-24.** Cup of chocolate 400–600 ptas. (US$2.40–US$3.60). No credit cards. Daily 9am–1pm and 4:30–9pm. Closed Aug. Metro: Liceu. CHOCOLATE.

At this, the most famous chocolate shop in Barcelona, established in 1941, the specialty is *melindros* (sugar-topped soft-sided biscuits), which the regulars who flock here love to dunk into the very thick hot chocolate—so thick, in fact, that imbibing it feels like eating a melted chocolate bar. A cup of hot chocolate with cream costs 450 pesetas (US$2.70), and a *ración* of chocolate-flavored *churros* (a deep-fried pastry) goes for 150 pesetas (US90¢).

Exploring Barcelona 4

Long a Mediterranean center of commerce, Barcelona is also one of the focal points of European tourism, a role sparked by the 1992 Olympic Games. Spain's second-largest city is also its most cosmopolitan and avant-garde.

Because of its rich history, Barcelona is filled with landmark buildings and world-class museums. These include Antoni Gaudí's famed Sagrada Família, the Museu Picasso, the Gothic cathedral, and Les Rambles, the famous tree-lined promenade cutting through the heart of the old quarter.

The capital of Catalonia, Barcelona sits at the northeast end of the Costa Brava, Spain's gateway to the Mediterranean. A half-hour flight east will land you on any of the Balearic Islands—fast-paced Majorca, rowdy Ibiza, or sleepy Minorca. (For more information on the Balearic Islands, consult *Frommer's Spain.*) You can also branch out from Barcelona to one of the sites of interest in its environs, including the beaches of Sitges, the monastery at Montserrat, and the Penedés vineyards (see "Side Trips from Barcelona," later in this chapter).

To begin, however, you'll want to take in the artistic and intellectual aura of this unique seafaring city. Residents take justifiable pride in their Catalán heritage, and they are eager to share it with you. Many of these sights can be covered on foot, and this chapter includes three walking tours.

An array of nightlife (Barcelona is a *big* bar town), shopping possibilities, and sports programs are also covered in this chapter, along with some organized tours, special events, and trips to Catalonia's wine country. It makes for some serious sightseeing; you'll need plenty of time to take it all in.

1 In & Around the Ciutat Vella (Old City)

The ✪ **Barri Gòtic** is the old aristocratic quarter of Barcelona, parts of which have survived from the Middle Ages. Spend at least 2 to 3 hours exploring its narrow streets and squares, which continue to form a vibrant, lively neighborhood today. Start by walking up the carrer del Carme, east of Les Rambles. A nighttime stroll takes on added drama, but exercise caution.

The buildings, for the most part, are austere and sober, the cathedral being the crowning achievement. Roman ruins and the vestiges of 3rd-century walls add further interest. This area is intricately detailed

Central Barcelona Attractions

Casa Amatller **17**
Casa de L'Ardiaca **34**
Casa Batlló **16**
Casa Lleó Morera **18**
Casa Milà **13**
Casa-Museu Gaudí **9**
Castell de la Ciutat/
  Ayuntamiento **36**
Castell de Montjuïc **1**
Castell de Tres Dragons **28**
Catedral de Barcelona **35**
Center of Contemporary
  Culture of Barcelona **19**
Fundació Antoni Tàpies **15**
Fundació Joan Miró **3**
Galeria Olímpica **2**
Gran Teatre del Liceu **21**
L'Aquarium de Barcelona **37**
Mirador de Colón **23**
Monastir de Pedrables **10**
Monument à Colom **23**
Museu Arqueològic **4**
Museu Barbier-Mueller
  Art Precolombí **30**
Museu d'Art
  Contemporain
  de Barcelona **20**
Museu d'Art Modern **25**
Museu de la Ciència **10**
Museu de les Arts
  Decoratives **8**
Museu Egipci
  de Barcelona **14**
Museu Frederic Marès **32**
Museu Geològie **27**
Museu d'Historia de
  la Ciutat **34**
Museu Marítim **23**
Museu Nacional d'Art
  de Catalunya **5**
Museu Picasso **29**
Museu Tèxtil i
  d'Indumentària **31**
Palau Güell **22**
Palau Reial
  (Royal Palace) **33**
Parc de Joan Miró **7**
Parc de la Ciutadella **26**
Parc Güell **11**
Parc Zoologic **24**
Poble Espanyol **6**
Sagrada Família **12**
Torre de Collserola **9**

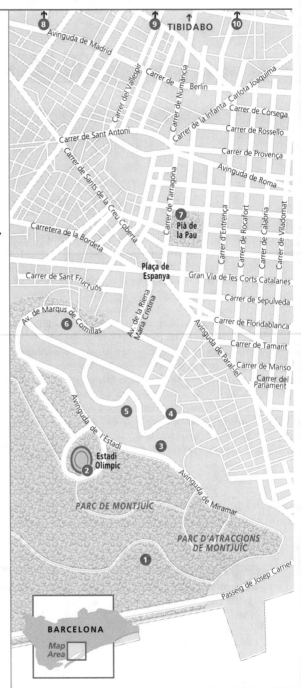

and filled with many attractions that are easy to miss. For a tour of the Barri Gòtic, see the Walking Tour later in this chapter.

○ **Catedral de Barcelona.** Plaça de la Seu, s/n. ☎ **93-315-15-54.** Free admission to cathedral; museum, 100 ptas. (US60¢). Cathedral, daily 8am–1:30pm and 4–7:30pm; cloister museum, daily 10am–1pm. Metro: Jaume I.

Barcelona's cathedral stands as a celebrated example of Catalonian Gothic architecture. Except for the 19th-century west facade, the basilica was begun at the end of the 13th century and completed in the mid–15th century. The three naves, cleaned and illuminated, have splendid Gothic details. With its large bell towers, blending of medieval and Renaissance styles, beautiful cloister, high altar, side chapels, sculptured choir, and Gothic arches, it ranks as one of the most impressive cathedrals in Spain. Vaulted galleries in the cloister surround a garden of magnolias, medlars, and palm trees; the galleries are further enhanced by forged iron grilles. The historian Cirici called this the loveliest oasis in Barcelona. The cloister, illuminated on Saturdays and fiesta days, also contains a museum of medieval art. The most notable work displayed is the 15th-century *La Pietat* of Bartolomé Bermejo. At noon on Sunday you can see the *sardana*, a Catalonian folk dance, performed in front of the cathedral.

Center of Contemporary Culture of Barcelona (CCCB). Montalegre, 5. ☎ **93-306-41-00.** Admission 600 ptas. (US$3.60) adults, 400 ptas. (US$2.40) students and seniors over 65, free for children under 16. Tues and Thurs–Fri 11am–2pm and 6–8pm, Wed and Sat 11am–8pm, Sun 11am–7pm. Metro: Catalunya.

Located in the Ciutat Vella, the Center of Contemporary Culture of Barcelona takes the city itself as its subject. It explores Barcelona's culture, history, and present role as a modern European city.

Museu d'Art Contemporani de Barcelona. Plaça dels Angels, 1. ☎ **93-412-08-10.** Admission 750 ptas. (US$4.50) adults, 500 ptas. (US$3) students, free for children. Tues–Sat 11am–7:30pm, Sun 10am–3pm. Metro: Plaça de Catalunya.

A soaring, glistening white edifice in Barcelona's once-shabby but on-the-rebound Raval district, the Museum of Contemporary Art is to Barcelona what the Pompidou Center is to Paris. Designed by the American architect Richard Meier, the building itself is a work of art, manipulating sunlight to offer brilliant, natural interior lighting. On display in the 74,000 square feet of exhibit space are the works of such modern luminaries as Tápies, Klee, Miró, and many others. The museum has a library, bookstore, and cafeteria.

Museu d'Història de la Ciutat. Plaça del Rei. ☎ **93-315-11-11.** Admission 700 ptas. (US$4.20) adults, 500 ptas. (US$3) children and students. Tues–Sat 10am–2pm and 4–8pm, Sun 10am–2pm. Bus: 16, 17, 19, 22, or 45.

Connected to the Royal Palace (see below), this museum traces the history of the city from its early days as a Roman colony to its role as the city of the 1992 Summer Olympics. The museum is housed in a mansion from the 1400s called the Padellás House. Many of the exhibits date from Roman days, with much else from medieval times.

Museu Frederic Marès. Plaça de Sant Iú, 5–6. ☎ **93-310-58-00.** Admission 300 ptas. (US$1.80) adults, free for children 12 and under. Tues and Thurs 10am–5pm; Wed, Fri, and Sat 10am–7pm; Sun 10am–2pm. Metro: Jaume I. Bus: 17, 19, or 45.

One of the biggest repositories of medieval sculpture in the region is the Frederic Marès Museum, located just behind the cathedral. It's housed in an ancient palace whose interior courtyards, chiseled stone, and soaring ceilings are impressive in their own right, an ideal setting for the hundreds of polychrome sculptures. The sculpture section dates from pre-Roman times to the 20th century. Also housed in the same building is the Museu Sentimental, a collection of everyday items that help to illustrate life in Barcelona during the past two centuries. Admission to both museums is included in the ticket price.

Palau Reial (Royal Palace). Plaça del Rei. ☎ **93-315-11-11.** Admission 700 ptas. (US$4.20). Summer, Tues–Sat 10am–8pm; off-season, Tues–Sat 10am–2pm and 4–8pm; year-round Sun 10am–2pm. Bus: 16, 17, 19, 22, or 45.

The former palace of the counts of Barcelona, this later became the residence of the kings of Aragón. It is believed that Columbus was received here by Isabella and Ferdinand when he returned from his first voyage to the New World. Here, some believe, the monarchs got their first look at a Native American. The Saló del Tinell, a banquet hall with a wood-paneled ceiling held up by half a dozen arches, dates from the 14th century. Rising five stories above the hall is the Torre del Reí Martí, a series of porticoed galleries.

Museu Barbier-Mueller Art Precolombí. Carrer de Montcada, 12–14. ☎ **93-310-45-16.** Admission 500 ptas. (US$3) adults, 250 ptas. (US$1.50) students, free for children under 12. Free to all first Sat of every month. Tues–Sat 10am–8pm, Sun and holidays 10am–3pm. Metro: Jaume I. Bus: 14, 17, 19, 39, 40, 45, or 51.

Inaugurated by Queen Sofía in 1997, this is one of the most important collections of pre-Columbian art in the world. In the restored Palacio Nadal, built during the Middle Ages, the collection contains almost 6,000 pieces of tribal and ancient art. Josef Mueller (1887–1977) acquired the first pieces by 1908. Pre-Columbian cultures created religious, funerary, and ornamental objects of great stylistic variety with relatively simple means. Stone sculpture and ceramic objects are especially outstanding. For example, the Olmecs, who settled on the Gulf of Mexico at the beginning of the first millennium B.C., executed notable monumental sculpture in stone and magnificent figures in jade. Many exhibits focus on the Mayan culture, the most homogenous and widespread of its time, dating from 1000 B.C. Mayan artisans mastered painting, ceramics, and sculpture. Note also the work by the pottery makers of the Lower Amazon, particularly those from the island of Marajó.

2 In the Eixample

Fundació Antoni Tàpies. Aragó, 255. ☎ **93-487-03-15.** Admission 700 ptas. (US$4.20) adults, 350 ptas. (US$2.10) students, free for children under 11. Tues–Sun 11am–8pm. Metro: Passeig de Gràcia.

When it opened in 1990, this became the third Barcelona museum devoted to the work of a single artist. In 1984 the Catalán artist Antoni Tàpies set up a foundation bearing his name, and the city of Barcelona donated an ideal site: the old Montaner i Simon publishing house near the Passeig de Gràcia in the 19th-century Eixample district. One of the landmark buildings of Barcelona, the brick-and-iron structure was built between 1881 and 1884 by that exponent of Catalán Art Nouveau, architect Lluís Domènech i Montaner. The core of the museum is a collection of works by Tàpies (most contributed by the artist himself), covering the different stages of his career as it evolved into abstract expressionism. Here you can see the entire spectrum of mediums in which he worked: painting, assemblage, sculpture, drawing, and ceramics. His associations with Picasso and Miró are apparent. The largest of all the works by Tàpies is on top of the building itself: a controversial gigantic sculpture made from 9,000 feet of metal wiring and tubing, entitled *Cloud and Chair*.

Museu Egipci de Barcelona. Calle València, 284. ☎ **93-488-01-88.** Admission 900 ptas. (US$5.40) adults, 700 ptas. (US$4.20) students and children. Mon–Sat 10am–2pm and 4–8pm, Sun 10am–2pm. Guided tours Sat. Closed holidays. Metro: Passeig de Gràcia.

Spain's only museum dedicated specifically to Egyptology contains more than 250 pieces from founder Jordi Clos's personal collection. On display are sarcophagi, jewelry, hieroglyphics, and various sculptures and artworks. Exhibits pay close attention to the everyday life of ancient Egyptians, including details regarding education, social customs, religion, and food. The museum possesses its own lab for restorations. A library with more than 3,000 works is open to the public.

✪ **La Sagrada Família.** Majorca, 401. ☎ **93-207-30-31.** Admission (includes video) 800 ptas. (US$4.80). Elevator to the top (about 200 feet) 200 ptas. (US$1.20). Daily, Nov–Feb 9am–6pm; Mar and Sept–Oct, 9am–7pm; Apr and Aug, 9am–8pm. Metro: Sagrada Família.

Gaudí's incomplete masterpiece is one of the more idiosyncratic creations of Spain— if you have time to see only one Catalán landmark, make it this one. Begun in 1882 and still incomplete at Gaudí's death in 1926, this incredible church—the Church of the Holy Family—is a bizarre wonder. The languid, amorphous structure embodies the essence of Gaudí's style, which some have described as art nouveau run rampant. Work continues on the structure, but without any sure idea of what Gaudí intended. Some say that the church will be completed by the mid–21st century. The crypt of the cathedral features a small museum of the architect's scale models. Photographs show the progress (or lack thereof) of construction on the building; there are even photos of Gaudí's funeral.

3 In & Around the Parc de la Ciutadella

Museu d'Art Modern. Plaça d'Armes, Parc de la Ciutadella. ☎ **93-319-57-28.** Admission 500 ptas. (US$3) adults, 250 ptas. (US$1.50) youths 8–21, free for children under 8. Tues–Sat 10am–7pm, Sun 10am–2:30pm. Closed Jan 1, Dec 25. Metro: Arc de Triomf. Bus: 14, 16, 17, 39, 40, 41, 51, 57, 59, or 64.

This museum shares a wing of the Palau de la Ciutadella with the Catalonian parliament. Constructed in the 1700s, it was once used as an arsenal, forming part of Barcelona's defenses. It later became a royal residence before being turned into a museum early in the last century. Its collection focuses on the early 20th century and features the work of Catalán artists, including Martí Alsina, Vayreda, Casas, Fortuny, and Rusiñol. The collection also encompasses some 19th-century Romantic and neoclassical works, as well as *modernista* furniture (including designs by architect Puig i Cadafalch).

✪ **Museu Picasso.** Montcada, 15–19. ☎ **93-319-63-10.** Admission 700 ptas. (US$4.20) adults, 400 ptas. (US$2.40) students and people under 25, free for children under 13. Tues–Sat 10am–8pm, Sun 10am–3pm. Metro: Jaume I.

Two old palaces on a medieval street have been converted into this museum housing works by Pablo Picasso, who donated some 2,500 of his paintings, engravings, and drawings in 1970. Picasso was particularly fond of Barcelona, the city where he spent much of his formative youth. In fact, some of the paintings were done when Picasso was only 9 years old. One portrait, dating from 1896, depicts his stern aunt, Tía Pepa. Another, completed when Picasso was 16, depicts *Science and Charity* (his father was the model for the doctor). Many of the works, especially the early paintings, show the artist's debt to van Gogh, El Greco, and Rembrandt; a famous series, *Las Meninas* (1957), is said to "impersonate" the work of Velázquez. From Picasso's blue period, the *La Vie* drawings are the most interesting. His notebooks contain many sketches of Barcelona scenes.

You Paid What?

47,000 hotels, 700 airlines, 50 rental car companies. And a few million ways to save money.

Travelocity.com
A Sabre Company

Go Virtually Anywhere.

AOL Keyword: Travel

Will you have enough stories to tell your grandchildren?

Yahoo! Travel

Taking the Bull by the Horns

Cataláns don't pursue bullfighting with as much fervor as do the Castilians of Madrid. Nevertheless, you may want to attend a *corrida* in Barcelona. Bullfights are held April to September, usually Sunday at 6:30pm at the Plaça de Toros Monumental, Gran Vía de les Corts Catalánes (☎ **93-245-58-04**). Purchase tickets (1,800 to 6,500 ptas./US$10.80 to US$39) in advance from the office at Muntaner, 24 (☎ **93-453-38-21**).

4 In & Around the Parc de Montjuïc

Fundació Joan Miró. Plaça de Neptú, Parc de Montjuïc. ☎ **93-329-19-08.** Admission 800 ptas. (US$4.80) adults, 450 ptas. (US$2.70) students, free for children under 15. June–Sept, Tues–Wed and Fri–Sat 10am–8pm, Thurs 10am–9:30pm, Sun 10am–2:30pm; Nov–May, Tues–Wed and Fri–Sat 11am–7pm, Thurs 10am–9:30pm, Sun 10am–2:30pm. Bus: 50 at Plaça d'Espanya.

Born in 1893, Joan Miró went on to become one of Spain's greatest painters, known for his whimsical abstract forms and brilliant colors. Some 10,000 works by this Catalán surrealist, including paintings, graphics, and sculptures, have been collected here. The foundation building has been greatly expanded in recent years, following the design of Catalán architect Josep Lluís Sert, a close personal friend of Miró. An exhibition in a modern wing charts (in a variety of media) Miró's complete artistic evolution, from his first drawings at the age of 8 to his last works. Temporary exhibitions on contemporary art are also frequently shown.

Galería Olímpica. Passeig Olimpic, s/n, lower level. ☎ **93-426-06-60.** Admission 400 ptas. (US$2.40) adults, 170 ptas. (US$1) children. Apr–Sept, Tues–Sat 10am–1pm and 4–8pm, Sun 10am–2pm; Oct–Mar, Tues–Sat 10am–1pm and 4–6pm, Sun 10am–2pm. Metro: Espanya. Bus: 50.

An enthusiastic celebration of the 1992 Olympic Games in Barcelona, this is one of the few museums in Europe exclusively devoted to sports and sports statistics. Its exhibits include photos, costumes, and memorabilia, with heavy emphasis on the pageantry, the number of visitors who attended, and the fame the events brought to Barcelona. Of interest to statisticians, civic planners, and sports buffs, the gallery has audiovisual information about the building programs that prepared the city for the onslaught of visitors. There are also conference facilities, an auditorium, video recordings of athletic events, and archives. In the cellar of the Olympic Stadium's southeastern perimeter, the museum is most easily reached by entering the stadium's southern gate (Porta Sud).

Museu Arqueològic de Catalunya. Passeig de Santa Madrona, 39–41, Parc de Montjuïc. ☎ **93-423-21-49.** Admission 400 ptas. (US$2.40) adults, 300 ptas. (US$1.80) students, free for children. Tues–Sat 9:30am–7pm, Sun 10am–2:30pm. Metro: Espanya. Bus: 55.

Occupying the former Palace of Graphic Arts, built for the 1929 World's Fair, the Museu Arqueològic reflects the long history of this Mediterranean port city, beginning with prehistoric Iberian artifacts. The collection includes articles from the Greek, Roman (glass, ceramics, mosaics, bronzes), and Carthaginian periods. Some of the more interesting relics were excavated in the ancient Greco-Roman city of Empúries in Catalonia; other parts of the collection came from the Balearic Islands.

✪ **Museu Nacional d'Art de Catalunya.** Palau Nacional, Parc de Montjuïc. ☎ **93-622-03-60.** Admission 800 ptas. (US$4.80) adults, 400 ptas. (US$2.40) youths 7–20, free for children under 7. Tues–Wed and Fri–Sat 10am–7pm, Thurs 10am–9pm, Sun 10am–2:30pm. Metro: Espanya.

This museum is the major depository of Catalán art. With massive renovations recently completed, the National Art Museum of Catalonia is perhaps the most important center for Romanesque art in the world. More than 100 pieces, including sculptures, icons, and frescoes, are on display. The highlight of the museum is the collection of murals from various Romanesque churches. The frescoes and murals are displayed in apses, much as in the churches in which they were found. Each is placed in sequential order, providing the viewer with a tour of Romanesque art from its primitive beginnings to the more advanced, late Romanesque and early Gothic era.

Poble Espanyol. Marqués de Comillas, Parc de Montjuïc. ☎ **93-508-63-00.** Admission 975 ptas. (US$5.85) adults, 525 ptas. (US$3.15) children 7–12, free for children under 7. Audiovisual hall free. Mon 9am–8pm, Tues–Thurs 9am–2am, Fri–Sat 9am–4am, Sun 9am–midnight. Metro: Espanya. Bus: 13 or 50.

In this re-created Spanish village built for the 1929 World's Fair, various regional architectural styles, from the Levante to Galicia, are reproduced—in all, 115 life-size reproductions of buildings and monuments, ranging from the 10th through the 20th centuries. At the entranceway, for example, stands a facsimile of the gateway to the walled city of Ávila. The center of the village has an outdoor cafe where you can sit and have drinks. Numerous shops sell crafts and souvenir items from all of the provinces, and in some of them you can see artists at work, printing fabric and blowing glass. Ever since the 1992 Olympics, the village has offered 14 restaurants of varying styles, one disco, and eight musical bars. In addition, visitors can see an audiovisual presentation about Barcelona and Catalonia in general. Many families delight in the faux Spanish atmosphere here, though more discriminating visitors find it a bit of a tourist trap—overly commercialized and somewhat cheesy. It's a matter of personal taste.

5 In La Barceloneta & the Harbor

Mirador de Colón. Portal de la Pau. ☎ **93-302-52-24.** Admission 250 ptas. (US$1.50) adults, 150 ptas. (US90¢) children 4–12, free for children under 4. Sept 25–March, Mon–Fri 10am–2pm and 3:30–6:30pm, Sat–Sun and holidays 10am–6:30pm; Apr–May, Mon–Fri 10am–2pm and 3:30–7:30pm, Sat–Sun 10am–7:30pm. June–Sept 24, daily 9am–8:30pm. Closed Jan 1, Jan 6, Dec 25–26. Metro: Drassanes. Bus: 14, 18, 36, 57, 59, or 64.

This monument to Christopher Columbus was erected at the Barcelona harbor on the occasion of the Universal Exhibition of 1888. It consists of three parts, the first being a circular structure, raised by four stairways (19$^{1}/_{2}$ feet wide) and eight iron heraldic lions. On the plinth are eight bronze bas-reliefs depicting Columbus's principal feats. (The originals were destroyed; these are copies.) The second part is the base of the column, consisting of an eight-sided polygon, four sides of which act as buttresses; each side contains sculptures. The third part is the 167-foot column, which is Corinthian in style. The capital boasts representations of Europe, Asia, Africa, and America—all linked together. Finally, over a princely crown and a hemisphere recalling the newly discovered part of the globe, is a 25-foot-high bronze statue of Columbus—pointing, ostensibly, to the New World—by Rafael Ataché. Inside the iron column, an elevator ascends to the *mirador*. From here, a panoramic view of Barcelona and its harbor unfolds.

L'Aquarium de Barcelona. Port Vell. ☎ **93-221-74-74.** Admission 1,400 ptas. (US$8.40) adults, 950 ptas. (US$5.70) children 4–12 and students, free for children under 4. June–Aug daily 9:30am–11pm; Sept daily 9:30am–9:30pm; Oct–May daily 9:30am–9pm. Metro: Drassanes or Barceloneta.

One of the most impressive testimonials to sea life anywhere opened in 1996 in Barcelona's Port Vell, a 10-minute walk from the bottom of the Rambles. The largest aquarium in Europe, it contains 21 glass tanks positioned along either side of a wide curving corridor. Each tank depicts a different marine habitat, with emphasis on everything from multicolored fish and corals to seagoing worms to sharks. The highlight is a huge "oceanarium" representative of the Mediterranean as a self-sustaining ecosystem. You view it from the inside of a glass-roofed, glass-sided tunnel that runs along its entire length, making fish, eels, and sharks appear to swim around you.

Museu Marítim. Avinguda de las Drassanes, s/n. ☎ **93-318-32-45.** Admission 800 ptas. (US$4.80) adults, 400 ptas. (US$2.40) children 7–17 and seniors, free for children under 7. Tues–Sat 10am–7pm. Closed holidays. Metro: Drassanes. Bus: 14, 18, 36, 38, 57, 59, 64, or 91.

Located in the former Royal Shipyards (Drassanes Reials), this 13th-century Gothic complex was used for the construction of ships for the Catalán-Aragonese rulers. The most outstanding exhibition here is a reconstruction of *La Galería Real* of Don Juan of Austria, a lavish royal galley. Another special exhibit features a map by Gabriel de Vallseca that was owned by explorer Amerigo Vespucci.

6 Outside the City Center

Museu de la Ciència (Science Museum). Teodor Roviralta, 55. ☎ **93-212-60-50.** Admission to museum and planetarium, 750 ptas. (US$4.50) adults, 650 ptas. (US$3.90) children under 17. Museum only 500 ptas. (US$3) adults, 350 ptas. (US$2.10) children. Planetarium only 250 ptas. (US$1.50). Tues–Sun 10am–8pm. Bus: 17, 22, 58, or 73.

Museu de la Ciència of the La Caixa Foundation is one of the most popular museums in Barcelona, with more than 500,000 people visiting annually. Its modern design and hands-on activities have made it the most important science museum in Spain and a major cultural attraction.

Visitors can touch, listen, watch, and participate in a variety of hands-on exhibits. From the beauty of marine life to the magic of holograms, the museum offers a world of science to discover. Ride on a human gyroscope, hear a friend whisper from 65 feet (20m) away, feel an earthquake, or use the tools of a scientist to examine intricate life forms with microscopes and video cameras.

More than 300 exhibits explore the wonders of science, from optics to space travel to the life sciences. In the "Optics and Perception" exhibits, visitors can interact with prisms, lenses, and holograms and walk inside a kaleidoscope. In the "Living Planet" area, baby sharks swim, a tornado swirls, and plants magically change their form when touched.

In the "Mechanics" exhibit, visitors can lift an 88-pound (40kg) weight with little effort. The use of lasers and musical instruments provides a fun way to learn about sound and light waves. Throughout the exhibits, there are computers to help you delve deeper into various topics. Visitors can also walk inside a submarine and make weather measurements in a working weather station. For those who want to explore new worlds, there are planetarium shows where the beauty of the night sky surrounds the audience.

The museum is a bit out of the way: To get here, take a bus (see above) at the Plaça Catalunya and go all the way to Avinguda del Tibidabo. Then follow the signs for two blocks, turning left onto carrer Teodor Roviralta, where you'll see the museum. It's right at the southern foothills of Tibidabo in a greenbelt district of Barcelona.

Monestir de Pedralbes. Baixada del Monestir, 9. ☎ **93-203-92-82.** Admission 400 ptas. (US$2.40) adults, 250 ptas. (US$1.50) students and seniors over 64, free for children under 13. Tues–Sun 10am–2pm. Metro: Reina Elisenda. Bus: 22, 63, 64, 75, or 114.

One of the oldest buildings in Pedralbes (the city's wealthiest residential area) is this monastery, founded in 1326 by Elisenda de Montcada, queen of Jaume II. Still a convent, the establishment is also the mausoleum of the queen, who is buried in its Gothic church. Walk through the cloisters, with nearly two dozen arches on each side, rising three stories. A small chapel contains the chief treasure of the monastery, murals by Ferrer Bassa, who was the major artist of Catalonia in the 1300s.

This monastery was a minor attraction of Barcelona until 1993, when 72 paintings and eight sculptures from the famed Thyssen-Bornemisza collection went on permanent display here. Among the more outstanding works of art are Fra Angelico's *The Virgin of Humility* and 20 paintings from the early German Renaissance period. Italian Renaissance paintings range from the end of the 15th century to the middle of the 16th century, as exemplified by works of Dosso Dossi, Lorenzo Lotto, Tintoretto, Veronese, and Titian. The baroque era is also represented, including such old masters as Rubens, Zurbarán, and Velázquez.

Museu de les Arts Decoratives. Palau Reial de Pedralbes, Avinguda Diagonal, 686. ☎ **93-280-50-24.** Admission 400 ptas. (US$2.40). Free 1st Sun of every month. Tues–Sat 10am–7pm, Sun and holidays 10am–3pm. Metro: Palau Reial. Bus: 7, 63, 67, 68, or 75.

Set in a beautiful park, this palace was constructed as a municipal gift to Alfonso XIII. He didn't get to make much use of it, however, as he was forced into exile in 1931. Today it houses a collection of objets d'art, furniture, jewelry, and glassware from the 14th century to the present. More than 200 pieces, all of Spanish origin, are on display.

Torre de Collserola. Carretera de Vallvidrera, Turó de la Vilana. ☎ **93-406-93-54.** Admission 500 ptas. (US$3). Wed–Fri 11am–2:30pm and 3:30–7:30pm, Sat–Sun 11am–8pm. A funicular goes to a point near the tower's parking lot; from here, free minivans make frequent runs up the mountain to the tower's base.

Some city planners hailed this as the most ambitious building project of the 1992 Olympics. When it was perceived that Barcelona lacked a state-of-the-art television transmitter, a team of engineers whipped up plans for a space-age needle. Completed within 24 months of its initiation, it rises 940 feet above the city's highest mountain ridge, the Collserola, beaming TV signals throughout the rest of Europe. Open now as a tourist attraction, the tower offers panoramic views over Catalonia, as well as insight into some of the most bizarre engineering in town. Trussed with cables radiating outward to massive steel anchors, the tower perches delicately atop an alarmingly narrow vertical post only 14 feet wide. A high-speed elevator carries visitors from deep inside the mountain (where there's a cafeteria) to an observation platform 1,820 feet above the Mediterranean.

7 Parks & Gardens

Barcelona isn't just museums; much of its life takes place outside, in its unique parks and gardens, through which you'll want to stroll. The **Parc Güell** (☎ **93-424-38-09**) was begun by Gaudí as a real-estate venture for a friend, the wealthy, well-known Catalán industrialist Count Eusebi Güell, but it was never completed. Only two houses were constructed, but it makes for an interesting excursion nonetheless. The city took over the property in 1926 and turned it into a public park. It's open May to

September, daily 10am to 9pm; October to April, daily 10am to 6pm. Admission is free. To reach the park, take bus no. 24, 25, 31, or 74.

One of the houses, **Casa-Museu Gaudí,** carrer del Carmel, 28 (☎ 93-219-38-11), contains models, furniture, drawings, and other memorabilia of the architect. Gaudí, however, did not design the house—Ramón Berenguer claimed that honor. Admission is 300 pesetas (US$2.10). The museum can be visited Sunday to Friday 10am to 8pm.

Gaudí completed several of the public areas of the park, which today look like a surrealist Disneyland, complete with a mosaic pagoda and a lizard fountain spitting water. Originally he planned to make this a model community of 60 dwellings, somewhat like the arrangement of a Greek theater. A central grand plaza with its market below was built, as well as an undulating bench decorated with ceramic fragments. The bizarre Doric columns of the would-be market are hollow, part of Gaudí's drainage system.

Another attraction, **Tibidabo Mountain,** offers the finest view of Barcelona. A funicular takes you up 1,600 feet to the top. The ideal time to visit this summit (the culmination of the Sierra de Collcerola) north of the port is at sunset, when the city lights are on. An amusement park, with a Ferris wheel swinging over Barcelona, has been opened here. (For more information on this Parc d'Atraccions, see "Especially for Kids," later in this chapter.) There's also a church, called Temple del Sagrat Cor (Sacred Heart), in this carnival-like setting, plus restaurants and mountaintop hotels. From Plaça de Catalunya, take a bus to Avinguda del Tibidabo, where you can board a special bus that will transport you to the funicular. Hop aboard to scale the mountain. The funicular runs daily 7:15am to 9:45pm and costs 400 pesetas (US$2.80) each way.

Located in the south of the city, the mountain park of **Montjuïc** (*Montjuch* in Spanish) has splashing fountains, gardens, outdoor restaurants, and museums, making for quite an outing. The re-created Spanish village, the Poble Espanyol, and the Joan Miró Foundation are also in the park. There are many walks and vantage points for viewing the Barcelona skyline.

The park was the site of several events during the 1992 Summer Olympics. An illuminated fountain display, the **Fuentes Luminosas,** at Plaça de la Font Magica, near Plaça d'Espanya, is on view from 8 to 11pm every Saturday and Sunday October to May, and from 9pm to midnight on Thursday, Saturday, and Sunday June to September. See the individual attractions in the park for their various hours of opening. To reach the top, take bus no. 61 from Plaça d'Espanya or the Montjuïc funicular.

Parc de la Ciutadella, Avinguda Wellington, s/n (☎ 93-225-67-80), gets its name, Park of the Citadel, because it's the site of a former fortress that defended the city. After Philip V won the War of the Spanish Succession (Barcelona was on the losing side), he got his revenge. He ordered that the "traitorous" residential suburb be leveled. In its place rose a citadel. In the mid–19th century it, too, was leveled, though some of the architectural evidence of that past remains in a governor's palace and an arsenal. Today most of the park is filled with lakes, gardens, and promenades, but it includes a **zoo** (see "Especially for Kids," below) and the **Museu d'Art Modern** (see "In & Around the Parc de la Ciutadella," earlier in this chapter). Gaudí is said to have contributed to the monumental fountain in the park when he was a student. The park is open, without charge, daily 8am to 9pm. To reach the park, take the metro to Ciutadella.

Parc de Joan Miró, near Plaça de Espanya, is dedicated to one of the most famous artists of Catalonia and occupies an entire city block. One of the parks, added in the 1990s and one of Barcelona's most popular, it's often called Parc de l'Escorxador (slaughterhouse), a reference to what the park used to be. Its main features are an esplanade and a pond from which a sculpture by Miró, *Woman and Bird,* rises up. Palm, pine, and eucalyptus trees, as well as playgrounds and pergolas, complete the picture. To reach the park, take the metro to Espanya. It's open throughout the day.

8 Especially for Kids

The Catalán people have an obvious affection for children, and although many of the attractions of Barcelona are for adults, there is an entire array of amusements designed for the young and young at heart.

Children ages 3 to 7 have their own special place at the **Museu de la Ciència,** Teodor Roviralta, 55 (☎ **93-212-60-50**). "Clik del Nens" is a science playground. Children walk on a giant piano, make bubbles, lift a hippopotamus, or enter an air tunnel. They observe, experiment, and examine nature in an environment created just for them. Special 1-hour guided sessions are given daily. (For further details, see "Outside the City Center," earlier in this chapter.)

Poble Espanyol, Marqués de Comillas, Parc de Montjuïc (☎ **93-325-78-66**), is described in "In & Around the Parc de Montjuïc," earlier in this chapter. Kids compare a visit here to a Spanish version of Disneyland. Frequent fiestas enliven the place, and it's fun for everybody, young and old.

Parc Zoologic. Parc de la Ciutadella. ☎ **93-225-67-80.** Admission 1,550 ptas. (US$9.30) adults, 975 ptas. (US$5.85) students and children, free for children under 3. Summer, daily 9:30am–7:30pm; off-season, daily 10am–5pm. Metro: Ciutadella.

Modern, with barless enclosures, this ranks as Spain's top zoo. One of the most unusual attractions is the famous albino gorilla, Snowflake (*Copito de Nieve*), the only one of its kind in captivity in the world. The main entrances to the Ciutadella Park are via Passeig de Pujades and Passeig de Picasso.

Parc d'Atraccions (Montjuïc). Parc de Montjuïc. ☎ **93-211-79-42.** Admission 1,200 ptas. (US$7.20); ticket for all rides, 2,500 ptas. (US$15). Oct–Mar, Sat–Sun 11:30am–8pm; Apr–May, Sat–Sun 11am–9pm; June–Sept Mon–Fri 10am–6pm, Sat–Sun noon–9pm. Metro: Paral-lel; then take the funicular.

This place becomes a festival in summer, with open-air concerts and more than three dozen rides for the kids. Everything is set against a wide view of Barcelona and its harbor. Children love the nightly illuminated fountain displays and the music from June 20 to October 4.

Parc d'Atraccions (Tibidabo). Plaça Tibidabo, 3–4, Cumbre del Tibidabo. ☎ **93-211-79-42.** Ticket for all rides 2,400 ptas. (US$14.40) adults, 600 ptas. (US$3.60) adults over 64. May to mid-June, Wed–Sun noon–8pm; mid-June to Sept, Tues–Sun noon–8pm; off-season, Sat–Sun and holidays 11am–8pm. Transit: Bus no. 58 to Avinguda del Tibidabo to Tramvía Blau, then take funicular.

On top of Tibidabo, this park combines the traditional with the modern—rides from the beginning of the century complete with 1990s novelties. In summer the place takes on a carnival-like atmosphere.

9 Architectural Standouts

Architecture enthusiasts will find a wealth of fascinating sights in Barcelona. Primary among them, of course, are the fantastical creations of Antoni Gaudí and his *modernista* cohorts.

Casa Milà. Passeig de Gràcia, 92. ☎ **93-484-59-80.** Tours 600 ptas. (US$3.60) adults, 350 ptas. (US$2.10) students, free children under 12. In Spanish, daily 10am–7:30pm; in English, daily at 6pm. Metro: Diagonal.

Commonly called La Pedrera, Casa Milà is the most famous apartment-house complex in Spain. Antoni Gaudí's imagination went wild when planning its construction; he even included vegetable and fruit shapes in his sculptural designs. Controversial and much criticized upon its completion, today it stands as a classic example of *modernista* architecture. The entire building was restored in 1996. The ironwork around the balconies forms an intricate maze, and the main gate has windowpanes shaped like turtle shells. The rooftop, filled with phantasmagorical chimneys known in Spanish as *espantabrujas* (witch-scarers), affords a view of Gaudí's unfinished cathedral, La Sagrada Família. The Espai Gaudí (Gaudí Space) in the attic has an intriguing multimedia display of the works of this controversial artist.

Casa Amatller. Passeig de Gràcia, 41. ☎ **93-216-01-75.** Free admission, but donations welcome. Thurs 10am, 11am, and noon; you must phone ahead to reserve a time for visitation. Metro: Passeig de Gràcia.

Constructed in a cubical design, with a Flemish-Gothic gable, this building was created by Puig i Cadafalch in 1900. It stands in sharp contrast to its neighbor, the Gaudí-designed Casa Batlló. The architecture of the Casa Amatller, actually imposed on an older structure, is a vision of ceramic, wrought iron, and sculptures. The structure combines grace notes of Flemish Gothic—especially on the finish of the facade—with elements of Catalán architecture. The gable outside is in the Flemish style. Inside, visitors may view the original Gothic-Revival interior, now the headquarters of the Institut Amatller d'Art Hispanic.

Casa Batlló. Passeig de Gràcia, 43. ☎ **93-488-06-66.** Mon–Fri 10am–4pm. Metro: Passeig de Gràcia.

Next door to the Casa Amatller, Casa Batlló was designed by Gaudí in 1905. Using sensuous curves in iron and stone, the architect gave the facade a lavish baroque exuberance. The balconies have been compared to "sculpted waves." The upper part of the facade evokes animal forms, and delicate tiles are spread across the design— a polychromatic exterior extraordinaire. The downstairs building is the headquarters of an insurance company. Many tourists walk inside for a view of Gaudí's interior, which is basically as he designed it. Since this is a place of business, be discreet.

Casa Lleó Morera. Passeig de Gràcia, 35. No phone. Metro: Passeig de Gràcia.

Lying between the carrer del Consell de Cent and the carrer d' Aragó is one of the most famous buildings of the *modernismo* movement. It is one of the trio of structures called the Mançana de la Discòrdia (Block of Discord), a play on words and an allusion to the mythical judgment of Paris. Three of the most famous *modernisme* architects of Barcelona, including Gaudí, competed with their various works along this block. Florid Casa Lleó, designed by Domènech i Montaner in 1905, was revolutionary in its day. That assessment still stands. Today the building is private; no visits to the interior are possible.

Casa de la Ciutat/Ayuntamiento. Plaça de Sant Jaume. ☎ **93-402-70-00.** Sat–Sun 10am–2pm; other times by special arrangement. Metro: Jaume I.

Originally constructed at the end of the 14th century, the building that houses the municipal government is one of the best examples of Gothic civil architecture in the Catalán-Mediterranean style. Across this landmark square from the Palau de la

Generalitat, it has been endlessly renovated and changed since its original construction. Behind a neoclassical facade, the building has a splendid courtyard and staircase. Its major architectural highlights are the 15th-century Salón de Ciento (Room of the 100 Jurors) and the Salón de las Crónicas (Room of the Chronicles), the latter decorated with black marble. The Salón de Ciento, in particular, represents a medley of styles.

Walking Tour—The Gothic Quarter

Start: Plaça Nova.
Finish: Plaça de la Seu.
Time: 3 hours.
Best Times: Any sunny day.
Worst Times: Rush hours (Monday to Saturday 7 to 9am and 5 to 7pm), because of traffic.

Begin at the:

1. **Plaça Nova.** Set within the shadow of the cathedral, this is the largest open-air space in the Gothic Quarter and the usual site of the Barcelona flea market. Opening onto this square is the Portal del Bisbe, a gate flanked by two round towers that have survived from the ancient Roman wall that once stood here. From Plaça Nova, climb the incline of the narrow asphalt-covered street (carrer del Bisbe) lying between these massive walls. On your right, notice the depth of the foundation, which indicates how much the city has risen since the wall was constructed.

   At the approach of the first street, carrer de Santa Llúcia, turn left, noticing the elegant simplicity of the corner building with its Romanesque facade, the:

2. **Capilla de Santa Llúcia** (☎ 93-315-15-54), open daily 9am to 1:15pm and 4 to 6:45pm. The chapel's solidly graceful portal and barrel-vaulted interior were completed in 1268.

   Continue down carrer de Santa Llúcia a few paces, noticing the:

3. **Casa de L'Ardiaca** (Archdeacon's House). Constructed in the 15th century as a residence for Archdeacon Despla, the Gothic building has sculptural reliefs with Renaissance motifs. In its cloister-like courtyard are a fountain and a palm tree. Notice the mail slot, where five swallows and a turtle carved into stone await the arrival of important messages. Since 1919 this building has been home to the **Museu d'Història de la Ciutat (City History Museum).**

   As you exit the Archdeacon's House, continue in the same direction several steps until you reach the:

4. **Plaça de la Seu.** From this square in front of the main entrance to the **Catedral de Barcelona** (see "In & Around the Ciutat Vella," earlier in this chapter), you can stand and admire the facade of Mediterranean Gothic architecture. On each side of Plaça de la Seu, you can see the remains of Roman walls.

   After touring the cathedral, exit from the door you entered and turn right onto carrer dels Comtes, admiring the gargoyles along the way. After about 100 paces, you'll approach the:

5. **Museu Frederic Marés,** on Plaça de Sant Iú. On the lower floors are Punic and Roman artifacts, but most of the museum is devoted to the works of this Catalán sculptor.

   Exit through the same door you entered and continue your promenade in the same direction. You'll pass the portal of the cathedral's side, where the heads of

Walking Tour—The Gothic Quarter

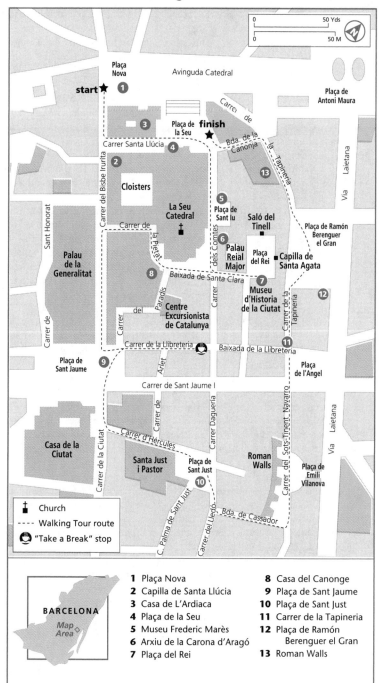

1 Plaça Nova
2 Capilla de Santa Llúcia
3 Casa de L'Ardiaca
4 Plaça de la Seu
5 Museu Frederic Marès
6 Arxiu de la Carona d'Aragó
7 Plaça del Rei
8 Casa del Canonge
9 Plaça de Sant Jaume
10 Plaça de Sant Just
11 Carrer de la Tapineria
12 Plaça de Ramón Berenguer el Gran
13 Roman Walls

two rather abstract angels flank the throne of a seated female saint. A few paces farther, notice the stone facade of the:

6. **Arxiu de la Carona d'Aragó.** This is the archives building of the crown of Aragón. Formerly called Palacio del Lugarteniente (Deputy's Palace), this Gothic building was the work of Antonio Carbonell. On some maps it also appears as the Palacio de los Virreyes (Palace of the Viceroys). The palace contains medieval and royal documents. Enter its courtyard, admiring the century-old grapevines. Then climb the 11 monumental steps to your left, facing a modern bronze sculpture by a Catalán artist. It represents, with a rather abstract dateline and map, the political history and imperial highlights of Catalonia.

As you exit from the courtyard, you'll find yourself back on carrer dels Comtes. Continue in the same direction, turning left at the intersection of Baixada de Santa Clara. This street, in 1 short block, will bring you to one of the most famous squares of the Gothic Quarter:

7. **Plaça del Rei.** The Great Royal Palace, an enlarged building of what was originally the residence of the counts of Barcelona, stands at the bottom of this square. Here at the King's Square you can visit both the **Palau Reial** and the **Museu d'Història de la Ciutat** (see "In & Around the Ciutat Vella," earlier in this chapter). On the right side of the square stands the **Palatine Chapel of Santa Agata,** a 14th-century Gothic temple that is part of the Palau Reial. In this chapel is preserved the altarpiece of the Lord High Constable, a 15th-century work by Jaume Huguet.

Retrace your steps up Baixada de Santa Clara, crossing carrer dels Comtes, and continue straight to carrer de la Pietat, which will skirt the semicircular, massively buttressed rear of the cathedral. With the buttresses of the cathedral's rear to your right, pass the 14th-century:

8. **Casa del Canonge** (House of the Canon), opening onto carrer Arzobispo Irurita. This building was erected in the Gothic style and restored in 1929; escutcheons from the 15th and 16th centuries remain. Notice the heraldic symbols of medieval Barcelona on the building's stone plaques—twin towers supported by winged goats with lion's feet. On the same facade, also notice the depiction of twin angels. The building today is used as a women's training school, the Escola Professional per a la Doña.

Continue walking along carrer de la Pietat, which makes a sudden sharp left. Notice the carved *Pietà* above the Gothic portal leading into the rear of the cathedral. Continue walking straight. One block later, turn left onto carrer del Bisbe and continue downhill. Your path will lead you beneath one of the most charming bridges in Spain. Carved into lacy patterns of stonework, it connects the Casa del Canonge with Palau de la Generalitat.

Continue walking until carrer del Bisbe opens into:

9. **Plaça de Sant Jaume.** In many ways, this plaza is the political heart of Catalán culture. Across this square, constructed at what was once a major junction for two Roman streets, race politicians and bureaucrats intent on Catalonian government affairs. On Sunday evenings you can witness the *sardana,* the national dance of Catalonia. Many bars and restaurants stand on side streets leading from this square.

Standing in the square, with your back to the street you just left (carrer del Bisbe), you'll see, immediately on your right, the Doric portico of the **Palau de la Generalitat,** the parliament of Catalonia. Construction of this exquisite work, with its large courtyard and open-air stairway, along with twin arched galleries in the Catalonian Gothic style, began in the era of Jaume I. A special feature of the building is the Chapel of St. George, constructed in flamboyant Gothic style between 1432 and 1435 and enlarged in 1620 with the addition of vaulting and a cupola with hanging capitals. The back of the building encloses an orangery courtyard begun in 1532. In the Salón Dorado, the Proclamation of the Republic was signed. The palace bell tower houses a carillon on which both old and popular music is played each day at noon. Across the square are the Ionic columns of the **Casa de la Ciutat/Ayuntamiento,** the Town Hall of Barcelona (see "Architectural Standouts," earlier in this chapter).

With your back to carrer del Bisbe, turn left onto the narrow and very ancient carrer de la Llibreteria. Two thousand years ago, this was one of the two roads that marked the Roman center of town. Walk uphill on carrer de la Llibreteria for about 1½ blocks.

☕ TAKE A BREAK **Mesón del Café,** Llibreteria, 16 (☎ **93-315-07-54**), founded in 1909, specializes in coffee and cappuccino. It is one of the oldest coffeehouses in the neighborhood, sometimes crowding 50 people into its tiny precincts. Some regulars perch on stools at the bar and order breakfast. Coffee costs 125 ptas. (US75¢), and a cappuccino goes for 275 ptas. (US$1.65). The cafe is open Monday to Saturday 7am to 11pm.

Retrace your steps along carrer de la Llibreteria and once again enter the Plaça de Sant Jaume. Facing the Town Hall, take the street that parallels its left side, carrer de la Ciutat. Note the elegant stonework on the building's side, which is carved in a style radically different from the building's neoclassical facade. At the first left, turn onto carrer d'Hercules, and walk along it for one block until you enter the quiet, somewhat faded beauty of:

10. **Plaça de Sant Just.** The square is dominated by the entrance to the Església dels Sants Just i Pastor. Above the entrance portal, an enthroned Virgin is flanked by a pair of protective angels. The Latin inscription hails her as *Virgo Nigra et Pulchra, Nostra Patrona Pia* (Black and Beautiful Virgin, Our Holy Patroness). This church dates from the 14th century, although work continued into the 16th. Some authorities claim that the church, in an earlier manifestation of the present structure, is the oldest in Barcelona. Visiting hours are erratic (☎ **93-301-73-33**); you'll find that its doors are usually closed except during Sunday mass.

Opposite the facade of the church, at Plaça de Sant Just, 4, is an aristocratic townhouse covered with faded but still elegant frescoes of angels cavorting among garlands, an example of the artistry, taste, and wealth of a bygone era. With your back to the Virgin, turn right onto the narrow cobblestoned street, carrer del Lledo, which begins at the far end of the square. One short block later, turn left onto Baixada de Cassador. As you descend the steep slope of this narrow street, notice the blue-and-white covering of the House of the Blue Tiles at the bottom of the hill.

Turn left onto carrer del Sots Tinent Navarro. The massive gray-stone wall rising on your left is the base of an ancient Roman fort. Note the red bricks of a 13th-century palace on top of the Roman wall. The solitary Corinthian column rising from the base is another reminder of Barcelona's Roman past.

Continue on to Plaça d'Emili Vilanova. Near the top of the Roman wall, note the pair of delicate columns of a Gothic window. Continue another block to the cross street, carrer Jaume I. Cross it and approach Plaça de l'Angel. Continue walking to the:

11. **Carrer de la Tapineria.** For centuries, Catalonia has been the center of Spain's footwear industry. In medieval times, this was the street of the shoemakers. In fact, the industry is so entrenched that there is even a museum devoted to antique footwear, the **Museu del Calçat Antic,** Plaça Sant Felip Neri, 5 (☎ 93-301-45-33), open Monday to Saturday 11am to 2pm and 4 to 7pm, Sunday 11am to 2pm. Admission is 200 ptas. (US$1.20).

In 1 short block carrer de la Tapineria leads to:

12. **Plaça de Ramón Berenguer el Gran.** An equestrian statue dedicated to this hero (1096–1131) is ringed with the gravel of a semicircular park, whose backdrop is formed by the walls of the ancient Roman fort and, nearby, a Gothic tower.

Traverse the park, crossing in front of the equestrian statue, until you once again reach the edge of the Roman wall as you head toward the park's distant end. Here carrer de la Tapineria will lead you on a path paralleling the ancient:

13. **Roman Walls.** These are one of Barcelona's most important treasures from its past. The walls, known as *Las Murallas* in Spanish, were constructed between A.D. 270 and 310. The walls followed a rectangular course, and were built so that their fortified sections would face the sea. By the 11th and 12th centuries, Barcelona had long outgrown their confines. Jaume I ordered the opening of the Roman Walls, and the burgeoning growth that ensued virtually destroyed them, except for the foundations you see today.

Continue your promenade, but turn left at the narrow Baixada de la Canonja. A short walk down this cobblestone alleyway will return you to **Plaça de la Seu,** not far from where you began this tour.

10 Organized Tours

Pullmantur, Gran Vía de les Corts Catalánes, 635 (☎ 93-317-12-97; metro: Plaça de Catalunya), offers a number of tours and excursions with English-speaking guides. For a preview of the city, you can take a morning tour. They depart from the company's terminal at 9:30am, and take in the cathedral, the Gothic Quarter, Les Rambles, the monument to Columbus, and the Spanish Village and the Olympic Stadium. Tickets cost 4,800 ptas. (US$28.80). An afternoon tour leaves at 3:30pm and visits some of the most outstanding architecture in the Eixample, including Gaudí's Sagrada Família, Parc Güell, and a stop at the Picasso Museum. This tour costs 5,000 ptas. (US$30).

Pullmantur also offers several excursions outside Barcelona. The daily tour of the monastery of Montserrat includes a visit to the Royal Basilica to view the famous sculpture of the Black Virgin. This tour, which costs 6,000 ptas. (US$40.20), departs at 9:30am and returns at 2:30pm to the company's terminal. A full-day Girona–Figueres tour includes a visit to Girona's cathedral and its Jewish quarter, plus a trip to the Dalí museum. This excursion, which costs 12,500 ptas. (US$75), leaves Barcelona at 9am and returns at approximately 6pm. Call ahead—a minimum number of participants is required or the tour isn't conducted.

Another company that offers tours of Barcelona and the surrounding countryside is **Juliatours,** Ronda Universitat, 5 (☎ 93-317-64-54). Itineraries and prices are similar to Pullmantur's. One tour, the "Visita Ciudad Artística," focuses on the city's artistic significance. The tour also passes Casa Lleó Morera, designed in 1905 by Domènech i Montaner in a floral modernist mode, and takes in many of Gaudí's brilliant buildings, including the Casa Milá (La Pedrera) and La Sagrada Família. Also included is a visit to the Museu Picasso or Museu d'Art Modern, depending on the day of your tour. This tour, which leaves at 3:30pm and returns at 6:30pm, costs 5,000 ptas. (US$30).

11 Shopping

Barcelonans look more to Paris and their own sense of design than to Madrid for their fashions and style. *Moda joven* (young fashion) is all the rage in Barcelona.

If your time and budget are limited, you may want to patronize Barcelona's major department store, **El Corte Inglés,** for an overview of Catalán merchandise at reasonable prices. Barcelona is filled with boutiques, but clothing is an expensive item here, even though the city has been a textile center for centuries.

Markets (see below) are very popular in Barcelona and are suitable places to search for good buys.

THE SHOPPING SCENE

If you're a window shopper, stroll along the **Passeig de Gràcia** from the Avinguda Diagonal to the Plaça de Catalunya. Along the way, you'll see some of the most elegant and expensive shops in Barcelona, plus an assortment of splendid turn-of-the-century buildings and cafes, many with outdoor tables. Another prime spot for shopping is the **Ramble de Catalunya** (upper Rambles).

Another shopping expedition is to the **Mercat de la Boquería,** Rambla, 101 (☎ **93-318-25-84**), near carrer del Carme. Here you'll see a wide array of straw bags and regional products, along with a handsome display of the food that you are likely to be eating later in a local restaurant: fruits, vegetables (artfully displayed), breads, cheeses, meats, and fish. Vendors sell their wares Monday to Saturday 7:30am to 9pm.

In the **old quarter,** not far from Plaça de Catalunya, the principal shopping streets are all five Rambles, plus carrer del Pi, carrer de la Palla, and Avinguda Portal de l'Angel, to cite some of the major ones. Moving north in the **Eixample** are Passeig de Catalunya, Passeig de Gràcia, and Rambla de Catalunya. Going even farther north, **Avinguda Diagonal** is a major shopping boulevard. Other prominent shopping streets include Bori i Fontesta, via Augusta, carrer Muntaner, Travessera de Gràcia, and carrer de Balmes.

In general, shopping hours are Monday to Saturday 9am to 8pm. Some smaller shops close 1:30 to 4pm.

The **American Visitors Bureau,** Gran Vía, 59134 (☎ **93-301-01-50**), between Rambla de Catalunya and carrer de Balmes, will pack and ship your purchases and gifts and even handle excess luggage and personal effects. The company also operates a travel agency here, booking flights and hotel accommodations for those needing it. It's open Monday to Friday 9am to 1pm and 4 to 7pm, Saturday 9am to 1pm.

Watch for sales (*rebajas* or *rebaixes* in Catalán) in mid-January, late July, and August. Merchandise is often heavily discounted by stores getting rid of their winter and summer stock.

SHOPPING A TO Z

Barcelona, a city known for its design and fashion, offers a wealth of shopping opportunities. In general, prices tend to be slightly lower than in London, Paris, and Rome.

In addition to modern, attractively designed, and stylish **clothing, shoes** and **decorative objects** are often good buys. In the city of Miró, Tàpies, and Picasso, **art** is a major business, and the reason so many gallery owners from around the world come to visit. You'll find dozens of galleries, especially in the Barri Gòtic and around the Picasso Museum. Barcelona is also noted for its **flea markets,** where good purchases are always available if you search hard enough.

Antiques abound here, but rising prices have put much of them beyond the means of the average shopper. However, the list below includes some shops where you can look, if nothing else. Most shoppers from abroad settle happily for handcrafts, and the city is rich in offerings, ranging from pottery to handmade furniture. Barcelona has been in the business of creating and designing **jewelry** since the 17th century, and its offerings in this field are of the widest possible range—as are the prices.

What follows is only a limited selection of some of the hundreds of shops in Barcelona.

ANTIQUES

El Bulevard des Antiquaris. Passeig de Gràcia, 55. No central phone. Metro: Passeig de Gràcia.

This 70-unit shopping complex, just off one of the town's most aristocratic avenues, has a huge collection of art and antiques assembled in a series of boutiques. There's a cafe/bar on the upper level. In summer, it's open Monday to Friday 9:30am to 8:30pm; in winter, on Monday 4:30 to 8:30pm and Tuesday to Saturday 10:30am to 8:30pm. Some boutiques keep shorter hours.

✪ **Sala d'Art Artur Ramón.** Carrer de la Palla, 25. ☎ **93-302-59-70.** Metro: Jaume I.

One of the finest antique and art dealers in Barcelona can be found in this three-level emporium, which boasts high ceilings and a medieval kind of grace. Set on a narrow flagstone-covered street near Plaça del Pi (the center of the antique district), it stands opposite a tiny square, the Placeta al carrer de la Palla, whose foundations were laid by the Romans. The store, which has been operated by four generations of men named Artur Ramón, contains everything from Romanesque works to Picasso. Prices are high, as you'd expect, for items of quality and lasting value. Open Monday to Saturday 10am to 1:30pm and 5 to 8pm.

✪ **Urbana.** Còrsega, 258. ☎ **93-218-70-36.** Metro: Hospital Sant Pau.

Urbana sells an array of architectural remnants (usually from torn-down mansions), antique furniture, and reproductions of brass hardware. There are antique and reproduction marble mantelpieces, wrought-iron gates and garden seats, even carved wood fireplaces with the *modernisme* look. It's an impressive, albeit costly, array of merchandise rescued from the architectural glory of yesteryear. Open Monday to Friday 10am to 2pm and 5 to 8pm.

CAMERAS

✪ **Casa Arpí.** Rambla dels Caputxins, 38. ☎ **93-301-74-04.** Metro: Liceu.

This is one of the most famous camera shops in Spain. A multilingual staff will guide you to the best buys in new and used cameras, including familiar brand-name products. The firm also does quality processing, ready within 24 to 48 hours. Open Monday to Friday 9am to 2pm and 4 to 8pm, Saturday 9am to 2pm.

DEPARTMENT STORES

El Corte Inglés. Plaça de Catalunya, 14. ☎ **93-302-12-12.** Metro: Plaça de Catalunya.

Just one of the local representatives of the largest and most glamorous department store chain in Spain, this store sells a wide variety of merchandise, ranging from Spanish handcrafts to high-fashion items, from Spanish or Catalán records to food. The store also has restaurants and cafes and offers a number of consumer-related services, such as a travel agent. It has a department that will arrange the mailing of your purchases back home. Open Monday to Friday 10am to 9:30pm.

El Corte Inglés has two other Barcelona locations at Av. Diagonal, 617–619 (☎ **93-419-28-28,** metro: María Cristina); and at Av. Diagonal, 471 (☎ **93-419-20-20,** metro: María Cristina).

DESIGNER HOUSEWARES

✪ **Vinçón.** Passeig de Gràcia, 96. ☎ **93-215-60-50.** Metro: Passeig de Gràcia.

Fernando Amat's Vinçón is the best in the city, with 10,000 products—everything from household items to the best in Spanish contemporary furnishings. Its mission is to purvey items of good design, period. Housed in the former home of artist Ramón Casas—a contemporary of Picasso during his Barcelona stint—with gilded columns and mosaic-inlaid floors, the showroom is filled with the best Spain has, with each item personally selected because of its quality and craft. The always creative window displays alone are worth the trek there: Expect *anything*. Open Monday to Saturday 10am to 1:30pm and 5 to 8pm.

FABRICS & WEAVINGS

Coses de Casa. Plaça de Sant Josep Oriol, 5. ☎ **93-302-73-28.** Metro: Jaume I.

Appealing fabrics and weavings are displayed in this 19th-century store, called simply "Household Items." Many are handwoven in Majorca, their boldly geometric patterns inspired by Arab motifs of centuries ago. The fabric, for the most part, is 50% cotton, 50% linen; much of it would make excellent upholstery material. Open Monday to Friday 9:45am to 1:30pm and 4:30 to 8pm, Saturday 10am to 2pm and 5 to 8pm.

FASHION

Antonio Miró. Consejo de Ciento, 349. ☎ **93-487-06-70.** Metro: Plaça de Catalunya.

This shop is devoted exclusively to the clothing design of Miró, without the Groc label (see below). Before purchasing anything at Groc, you should also survey the wares of this store, which seems even more stylish. Fashionable clothing for both men and women is sold here. Open Monday to Saturday 10am to 2pm and 4:30 to 8pm.

Groc. Ramble de Catalunya, 100. ☎ **93-215-74-74.** Metro: Plaça de Catalunya.

Designs for both women and men are sold here. One of the most stylish shops in Barcelona, it is expensive but filled with high-quality apparel made from the finest of natural fibers. The men's store is downstairs, the women's store one flight up. Open Monday to Saturday 10am to 2pm and 4:30 to 8pm. The men's department is closed Monday 10am to 2pm; the women's department is closed Saturday 4:30 to 8pm. The entire store is closed in August.

GALLERIES

Art Picasso. Tapinería, 10. ☎ **93-310-49-57.** Metro: Jaume I.

Here you can get good lithographic reproductions of works by Picasso, Miró, and Dalí, as well as T-shirts emblazoned with the designs of these masters. Tiles sold here often carry their provocatively painted scenes. Open Monday to Saturday 9:30am to 8pm and Sunday 9:30am to 3pm.

✪ **Sala Parés.** Petritxol, 5. ☎ **93-318-70-20.** Metro: Plaça de Catalunya.

Established in 1840 by the Maragall family, this is an institution among art galleries in the city, recognizing and promoting the work of many Spanish and Catalán painters and sculptors who have gone on to acclaim. Paintings are displayed in a two-story amphitheater, whose high-tech steel balconies are supported by a quartet of steel columns evocative of Gaudí. Exhibitions of the most avant-garde art in Barcelona change about every three weeks. Open Monday to Saturday 10:30am to 2pm and 4:30 to 8:30pm, Sunday 11am to 2pm.

GIFTS

Beardsley. Petritxol, 12. ☎ **93-301-05-76.** Metro: Plaça de Catalunya.

Named after the Victorian English illustrator, this store is on the same street where the works of Picasso and Dalí were exhibited before they became world famous. The wide array of gifts, perhaps the finest selection in Barcelona, includes a little bit of everything—dried flowers, writing supplies, silver dishes, unusual bags and purchases, and lots more. Open Monday to Friday 9:30am to 1:30pm and 4:30 to 8pm, Saturday 10am to 2pm and 5 to 8:30pm.

Bon Original Shop. Plaça de Catalunya, 17-S. ☎ **93-304-31-23.** Metro: Plaça de Catalunya.

Found at the tourist offices, this shop sells a variety of articles inspired by Barcelona and designed so that the visitor can take away an appropriate and often worthy souvenir. A representative range of products are sold, including textiles, ceramics, jewelry, stationery, gift items, and travel-related gear. Open Monday to Saturday 9:30am to 8pm.

LEATHER

Loewe. Passeig de Gràcia, 35. ☎ **93-216-04-00.** Metro: Passeig de Gràcia.

The biggest branch in Barcelona of this prestigious Spanish leather-goods chain is in one of the best-known *modernismo* buildings in the city. Everything is top-notch, from the elegantly spacious showroom to the expensive merchandise to the helpful salespeople. The company exports its goods to branches throughout Asia, Europe, and North America. Open Monday to Saturday 9:30am to 2pm and 4:30 to 8pm.

MARKETS

El Encants antique market is held every Monday, Wednesday, Friday, and Saturday in Plaça de les Glóries Catalánes (metro: Glóries). There are no specific times—go anytime during the day to survey the selection.

Coins and postage stamps are traded and sold in **Plaça Reial** on Sunday 10am to 2pm. The location is off the southern flank of Les Rambles (metro: Drassanes).

A book-and-coin market is held at the **Ronda Sant Antoni** every Sunday 10am to 2pm (metro: Universitat).

MUSIC

Casa Beethoven. Rambles, 97. ☎ **93-301-48-26.** Metro: Liceu.

The most complete collection of sheet music in town can be found here. In a narrow store established in 1920, the collection naturally focuses on the works of Spanish and Catalán composers. Music lovers might make some rare discoveries here. Open Monday to Friday 9am to 1:30pm and 4 to 8pm, Saturday 9am to 1:30pm and 5 to 8pm.

PORCELAIN

Kastoria 2. Avinguda Catedra, 6–8. ☎ **93-310-04-11.** Metro: Plaça de Catalunya.

This large store near the cathedral carries many kinds of leather goods, including purses, suitcases, coats, and jackets. But most people come here to look at its famous Lladró porcelain—they are authorized dealers and have a big selection. Open Monday to Saturday 10am to 2pm and 3 to 8pm and Sunday 10am to 2pm.

POTTERY

Artesana I Coses. Placeta de Montcada, 2. ☎ **93-319-54-13.** Metro: Jaume I.

Here you'll find pottery and porcelain from every major region of Spain. Most of the pieces are heavy and thick-sided—designs in use in the country for centuries. Open Monday to Saturday 10am to 2pm and 4 to 8pm, Sunday 10am to 2pm.

Itaca. Carrer Ferran, 26. ☎ **93-301-30-44.** Metro: Liceu.

This shop carries a wide array of handmade pottery, not only from Catalonia and other parts of Spain, but also from Portugal, Mexico, and Morocco. The merchandise has been selected for its basic purity, integrity, and simplicity. Open Monday to Friday 10am to 2pm and 4:30 to 8pm, Saturday 10am to 2pm and 5 to 8:30pm.

SHOPPING CENTERS & MALLS

The landscape of Barcelona has exploded since the mid-1980s with the construction of several American-style shopping malls, some of which are too far from the city's historic core to be convenient to most foreign visitors. Here's a description, however, of some of the city's best.

Centre Comercial Barcelona Glories. Avenida Diagonal, 208. ☎ **93-486-04-04.** Metro: Glories.

Built in 1995, this is the largest shopping center in downtown Barcelona, a three-story emporium of the good life, based on California models but crammed into a distinctly urban neighborhood. More than 100 shops are here: some posh, others much less so. Although there's a typical shopping-mall anonymity to some aspects of this place, you'll still be able to find virtually anything you might have forgotten while packing for your trip. Open Monday to Saturday 10am to 10pm.

Diagonal Center (Illa). Avinguda Diagonal, 557. ☎ **93-444-00-00.** Metro: María Cristina.

Smaller than the above-mentioned Centre Comercial Barcelona Glories, with about half the number of shops, this two-story mall contains stores devoted to luxury products, as well as a scattering of bars, cafes, and simple but cheerful restaurants favored by office workers and shoppers. Built in the early 1990s, it even has an area devoted to video games, where teenagers can make as much electronic noise as they want while their guardians go shopping. It's open Monday to Saturday 10am to 9pm.

Maremagnum. Moll d'Espanya, s/n. ☎ **93-225-81-00.** Metro: Drassanes.

The best thing about this place is its position adjacent to the waterfront of Barcelona's historic seacoast; it's also well suited to outdoor promenades. Built in the early 1990s near the Columbus Monument, it contains a handful of shops selling touristy items and lots of cafes, bars, and places to sit. You might get the idea that only a few of the people who come here are really interested in shopping, despite the fact that the place defines itself as a shopping mall.

Poble Espanyol. Marqués de Comillas, Parc de Montjuïc. ☎ **93-325-78-66.** Metro: Espanya, then free red double-decker bus to Montjuïc, or Bus 13, which costs 165 ptas. (US$1.15).

This is not technically a shopping mall but a "village" (see "In & Around the Parc de Montjuïc," earlier in this chapter) with about 35 stores selling typical folk crafts from every part of Spain: glassware, leather goods, pottery, paintings, and carvings—you name it. Stores keep various hours, but you can visit any time during the day.

STRAW PRODUCTS

La Manual Alpargatera. Avinyó, 7. ☎ **93-301-01-72.** Metro: Jaume I or Liceu. Turn off Les Rambles at carrer Ferran, walk 2 blocks, and make a right.

In addition to its large inventory of straw products, such as hats and bags, this shop is known mainly for its footwear, called espadrilles (*alpargatas* in Spanish). This basic rope-soled shoe (whose design is said to be 1,000 years old) is made on the premises. Some Cataláns wear only espadrilles when performing the *sardana,* their national dance. Open Monday to Saturday 9:30am to 1:30pm and 4:30 to 8pm.

UMBRELLAS

Julio Gómez. Rambla de Sant Josep (also called Rambla de las Flors), 104. ☎ **93-301-33-26.** Metro: Liceu.

For more than a century, Julio Gómez has sold umbrellas here. In a workshop out back, women labor over these unique umbrellas or lace-trimmed silk or cotton parasols. There are also Spanish fans, walking sticks capped with silver, and other memorabilia, all adding up to an evocative piece of shopping nostalgia. Open Monday to Saturday 9:30am to 1:30pm and 4 to 8pm.

12 Barcelona After Dark

Barcelona comes alive at night—the funicular ride to Tibidabo or the illuminated fountains of Montjuïc are especially popular. During the Franco era, the center of club life was the cabaret-packed district near the south of Les Rambles, an area, incidentally, known for nighttime muggings—so use caution if you go there. But the most fashionable clubs long ago deserted this seedy area and have opened in nearly every major district of the city.

Your best source of local information is a little magazine called *Guía del Ocio,* which previews "La Semana de Barcelona" (This Week in Barcelona). It's in Spanish, but most of its listings will probably be comprehensible. The magazine is sold at virtually every news kiosk along Les Rambles.

Nightlife begins for many Barcelonans with a promenade (*paseo*) along Les Rambles in the early evening, usually from 5 to 7pm. Then things quiet down a bit, until a second surge of energy brings out Les Rambles crowds again, from 9 to 11pm. After that the esplanade clears out quite a bit, but it's always lively.

If you've been scared off by press reports of Les Rambles between the Plaça de Catalunya and the Columbus Monument—though the area's really been cleaned up in the past decade—you'll feel safer along the Ramble de Catalunya, in the Eixample, north of the Plaça de Catalunya. This street and its offshoots are lively at night, with many cafes and bars.

The array of nighttime diversions in Barcelona is staggering. There is something to interest almost everyone and to fit most pocketbooks. For families, the amusement parks are the most-frequented venues. Sometimes locals opt for an evening in the *tascas* (taverns) or pubs, perhaps settling for a bottle of wine at a cafe, an easy and inexpensive way to spend an evening of people-watching. Serious drinking in pubs and cafes begins by 10 or 11pm. But for the most fashionable bars and discos, Barcelonans delay their entrances until at least 1am.

Cultural events are big in the Catalonian repertoire, and the old-fashioned dance halls, too, still survive in some places. Although disco has waned in some parts of the world, it is still going strong in Barcelona. Decaying movie houses, abandoned garages, and long-closed vaudeville theaters have been taken over and restored to become nightlife venues for the after-dark movement that sweeps across the city until dawn.

Flamenco isn't the rage here that it is in Seville and Madrid, but it still has its devotees. The city is also filled with jazz aficionados. Best of all, the old tradition of the music hall with vaudeville lives on in Barcelona.

SPECIAL EVENTS & DISCOUNTS   In summer you'll see plenty of free entertainment just by walking the streets—everything from opera to monkey acts. The Rambles is a particularly good place to watch.

There's almost always a **festival** happening in the city, and many of the events can be enjoyed for free. The tourist office can give you details of when and where. Some **theaters** advertise discount or half-price nights. Check in the weekly *Guía del Ocio*.

THE PERFORMING ARTS

Culture is deeply ingrained in the Catalán soul. The performing arts are strong here— some, in fact, taking place on the street, especially along Les Rambles. Crowds will often gather around a singer or mime. A city square will suddenly come alive on Saturday night with a spontaneous festival—"tempestuous, surging, irrepressible life and brio," is how the writer Rose MacCauley described it.

Long a city of the arts, Barcelona experienced a cultural decline during the Franco years, but now it is filled once again with the best opera, symphonic, and choral music.

CLASSICAL MUSIC

Palau de la Música Catalána. Sant Francesc de Paula, 2. ☎ **93-295-72-00.** Box office Mon–Fri 10am–9pm, Sat 3–9pm.

In a city chock-full of architectural highlights, this one stands out. In 1908 Lluís Domènech i Montaner, a Catalán architect, designed this structure, including stained glass, ceramics, statuary, and ornate lamps, among other elements. It stands today, restored, as a classic example of *modernismo*. Concerts and leading recitals are presented here. The box office is open Monday to Friday 10am to 9pm, Saturday 3 to 9pm.

THEATER

Theater is presented in the Catalán language and therefore will not be of interest to most visitors. For those who do speak the language, or perhaps are fluent in Spanish (even then, though, you're unlikely to understand much of the goings-on), here are some recommendations.

✪ **Gran Teatre del Liceu.** Rambla dels Caputxins. ☎ **93-485-99-00.** Metro: Liceu.

This monument to belle époque extravagance, a 2,700-seat opera house, is one of the grandest theaters in the world. It was designed by the Catalán architect Josep Oriol Mestves. On January 31, 1994, fire gutted the opera house, shocking Catalonians, many of whom regarded this place as the citadel of their culture. The government immediately vowed to rebuild, and the new Liceu was reopened in 1999, well before the millennium deadline set by the cultural czars.

Mercat de Los Flors. Lleida, 59. ☎ **93-426-18-75.** Tickets 1,500–3,000 ptas. (US$9–US$18). Metro: Espanya.

Housed in a building constructed for the 1929 International Exhibition at Montjuïc is this other major Catalán theater. Peter Brook first used it as a theater for a 1983 presentation of *Carmen*. Innovators in drama, dance, and music are showcased here, as are modern dance companies from Europe, including troupes from Italy and France. The 999-seat house also has a restaurant overlooking the rooftops of the city.

Teatre Lliure. Montseny, 47. ☎ **93-218-92-51.** Tickets 2,000–2,500 ptas. (US$12–US$15) Tues–Thurs, 2,500–3,000 ptas. (US$15–US$18) Fri–Sun. Metro: Fontana.

This self-styled free theater is the leading Catalán-language company in Barcelona. Once a workers' union, since 1976 the building has been the headquarters of a theater cooperative. Its directors are famous in Barcelona for their bold presentations here, including works by Bertolt Brecht, Luigi Pirandello, Jean Genet (who wrote about Barcelona), and even Molière and Shakespeare. New dramas by Catalán playwrights are also presented. The house seats from 200 to 350.

Teatre Nacional de Catalunya. Plaça de les Arts, 1. ☎ **93-306-57-00.** Tickets 3,200–3,700 ptas. (US$19.20–US$22.20). Closed Aug. Metro: Monumental.

This leading company is directed by Josep María Flotats, an actor-director who was trained in the tradition of theater repertory, working in such theaters in Paris as the Théâtre de la Villa and the Comédie-Français. He founded his own company in Barcelona, where he presents both classic and contemporary plays.

FLAMENCO

El Tablao de Carmen. Poble Espanyol de Montjuïc. ☎ **93-325-68-95.** Dinner and show, 7,800 ptas. (US$46.80); one drink and show, 4,200 ptas. (US$25.20).

This club provides a highly rated flamenco cabaret in the re-created village. You can go early and explore the village if you wish and even have dinner here. This place has long been a tourist favorite. The club is open Tuesday to Sunday 8pm to past midnight. During the week, it sometimes closes around 1am, but often stays open until 2 or 3am on weekends, depending on business. The first show is always at 9:30pm; the second show Tuesday to Thursday and Sunday is at 11:30pm, on Friday and Saturday at midnight. Reservations are encouraged.

Los Tarantos. Plaça Reial, 17. ☎ **93-318-30-67.** Cover (includes one drink) 1,500 ptas. (US$9). Metro: Liceu.

Established in 1963, this is the oldest flamenco club in Barcelona, with a rigid allegiance to the tenets of Andalusian flamenco. Its roster of artists changes regularly, and are often imported from Seville or Córdoba, stamping out their well-rehearsed passions in ways that make the audience appreciate the nuances of Spain's most intensely controlled dance idiom. No food is served here—instead, the place most resembles a cabaret theater, where up to 120 clients at a time can drink, talk quietly, and savor the nuances of a dance that combines elements from medieval Christian and Muslim traditions. Each show lasts around 1¼ hours. Shows are Monday to Saturday at 10pm and again at midnight.

Tablao Flamenco Cordobés. Les Rambles, 35. ☎ **93-317-66-53.** Dinner and show, 8,000 ptas. (US$48); one drink and show, 4,500 ptas. (US$27). Closed Jan. Metro: Drassanes.

At the southern end of Les Rambles, a short walk from the harbor front, you'll hear the strum of the guitar, the sound of hands clapping rhythmically, and the haunting sound of the flamenco, a tradition here since 1968. Head upstairs to an Andalusian-style room where performances take place with the traditional *cuadro flamenco*—singers, dancers, and guitarist. Cordobés is said to be the best showcase for flamenco in Barcelona. From November 1 to March 31 (except for one week in December), the show with dinner begins at 8:30pm and the show without dinner at 10pm. From April 1 to October 31 and December 25 to December 31, four shows are offered nightly: with dinner at 8pm and 9:45pm, without dinner at 9:30pm and 11:15pm. Reservations are required. It's closed in January.

CABARET

Arnau. Avinguda del Paral-lel, 60. ☎ **93-329-21-04.** Cover (includes one drink) from 2,000 ptas. (US$12). Metro: Paral-lel.

A veteran at surviving the many changes that have affected the worlds of cabaret and entertainment since its heyday in the 1970s, this place has managed to keep up with the times and the demands of the marketplace. Shows mingle touches of Catalán folklore with glitz and glitter, hints of family nostalgia, and doses of melodrama. Two shows are presented Wednesday to Sunday, at 10pm and midnight. Drinks cost from 600 pesetas (US$4.20) each.

Espai Barroc. Carrer Montcada, 20. ☎ **93-310-06-73.** Cover (includes one drink) 2,500 ptas. (US$15). Metro: Jaime I.

One of Barcelona's most culture-conscious nightspots occupies some of the showplace rooms of the Palau Dalmases, a stately palace within the Barri Gòtic that was built in stages between the 13th and 18th centuries. Within a stately looking room that's painted in tones of terra-cotta and lined with grand art objects, you can listen to recorded opera arias and sip glasses of beer or wine. The most appealing night here is Thursday, when, beginning at 11pm, you'll hear a group of 10 singers perform a roster of arias from assorted operas, one of which is invariably *Carmen*. Since its establishment in 1996, the place has thrived, attracting a clientele where it seems that virtually everyone around the bar has at least heard of the world's greatest operas, and some can even discuss them more or less brilliantly. Open Tuesday to Sunday 8pm to 2am.

Luz de Gas. Carrer de Muntaner, 246. ☎ **93-209-77-11.** Cover (includes one drink) 2,000 ptas. (US$12). Bus: 7, 15, 33, 58, or 64.

This theater/cabaret has the hottest Latino jazz in this port city on weekends. On weeknights, there's cabaret. The place is an art nouveau delight, with colored glass lamps and enough voluptuous nudes to please Rubens himself. This club was once a theater, and now its original multiple seating has been turned into different areas, each with its own bar. The lower two levels open onto the dance floor and stage. If you'd like to talk, head for the top tier with its glass enclosure. You'll have to call to see what the lineup is on any given night: jazz, pop, soul, rhythm and blues, salsa, bolero, whatever.

DANCE CLUBS & DISCOS

Bikini. Deu i Mata, 105. ☎ **93-322-00-05.** Cover 1,000–3,000 ptas. (US$6–US$18). Metro: Les Corts.

Set in the basement of a commercial-looking shopping center is this comprehensive and wide-ranging nightlife compound, with at least two venues for dancing in every conceivable genre (including funk, indie, rock-and-roll, and golden-oldie music). There's a separate room for Puerto Rican salsa (the owners refer to it as a "salsoteca") and a large area where fans of emerging musical groups applaud wildly to the music of their favorite band of the minute. The action changes every night of the week, and has even been known to include sophisticated adaptations of conventional tango music. The establishment has provided a showcase for the career ambitions of dozens of youthful singers and rock-and-roll bands. Open Monday to Thursday 7pm to 4:30am, Friday and Saturday 7pm to 6am.

Up and Down. Numancia, 179. ☎ **93-280-29-22.** Cover (includes one drink) 1,000–2,000 ptas. (US$6–US$12). Metro: María Cristina.

The chic atmosphere of this disco attracts the elite of Barcelona, across the generational divide. The more mature patrons, specifically the black-tie, post-opera crowd, head for the upstairs section, leaving the downstairs to the loud music and flaming youth. Up and Down, with a black-and-white decor, is the most cosmopolitan disco in Barcelona, with a carefully planned ambience, impeccable service, and a welcoming atmosphere. Waiters are piquant and sassy. Technically, this is a private club—you can be turned away at the door. The restaurant is open Monday to Saturday 10pm to 2am, serving meals costing from 4,500 pesetas (US$31.50). The disco is open Tuesday to Saturday 12:30am to anytime between 5 and 6:30am, depending on business. Drinks in the disco cost 1,400 pesetas (US$9.80) for a beer or from 1,900 pesetas (US$13.30) for a mixed drink.

JAZZ & BLUES

Barcelona Pipa Club. Plaça Reial, 3. ☎ **93-302-47-32.** Cover (includes one soft drink or beer) 1,000 ptas. (US$6). Metro: Liceu.

If you find the Harlem Jazz Club (see below) small, wait until you get to the "Pipe Club." Long beloved by jazz aficionados, this is for pure devotees. Ring the buzzer and you'll be admitted (at least we hope you will) to a club reached after a climb of two flights up a seedy rundown building. This is hardly a trendy nighttime venue: Instead, it attracts lovers of hot jazz. Five rooms are decorated with displays or photographs of pipes—naturally Sherlock Holmes gets in on the act. Depending on the performer, music ranges from New Orleans jazz to Brazilian rhythms. Jazz is featured Thursday to Sunday 10pm to 5am, although the club with its comfortable bar is open daily during the same hours.

Harlem Jazz Club. Comtessa de Sobradiel, 8. ☎ **93-310-07-55.** One-drink minimum. No cover. Closed Aug. Metro: Jaume.

On a nice street in the Ciutat Vella, this is one of Barcelona's oldest and finest jazz clubs. Live music begins at 9pm and often lasts until the late set at 3am. No matter how many times you've heard "Black Orpheus" or "The Girl from Ipanema," it always sounds new again here. Music is viewed with a certain reverence; no one talks when the performers are on. Even the decor doesn't distract, consisting of black-and-white photographs of jazz greats hanging on the smoke-colored walls. The place is unbelievably small, with only a handful of tables. Live jazz, blues, tango, Brazilian music—the sounds are always fresh. Hours are Tuesday to Thursday 8pm to 4am, Saturday and Sunday until 5am. Closed in August.

Jamboree. Plaça Reial, 17. ☎ **93-301-75-64.** Cover (includes one drink) 1,500–2,000 ptas. (US$9–US$12). Metro: Liceu.

In the heart of the Barri Gòtic, this has long been one of the city's premier venues for good blues and jazz. It varies its musical performances, though, and doesn't feature jazz every night—perhaps a Latin dance band will be scheduled. Sometimes a world-class performer will appear here, but most likely it'll be a younger group. The crowd knows its jazz and seems to demand only the best talent for the evening jazz sessions. On our last visit, we were entertained by an evening of Chicago blues. Shows are at midnight, and the club is open daily 9pm to 5am.

BARS & PUBS

In addition to the bars listed below, several Barcelona tapas bars are recommended in the "Where to Dine" section of chapter 3.

Bar Pastis. Carrer Santa Mònica, 4. ☎ **93-318-79-80.** Metro: Drassanes.

Just off the southern end of Les Rambles, this tiny bar was opened in 1947 by Carme Pericás and Quime Ballester, two Valencianos. They made it a shrine to Edith Piaf, and her songs are still played on an old phonograph in back of the bar. If you look at the dusty art in this dimly lit place, you'll see some of Piaf. But mainly the decor consists of paintings by Quime Ballester, who had a dark, rather morbid vision of the world. You can order four different kinds of pastis in this "corner of Montmartre." Outside the window, check out the view, usually a parade of transvestite hookers. The crowd is likely to include almost anyone, especially people who used to be called "bohemians"; they live on in this bar of yesterday. Live music is performed Sunday to Thursday. Go after 11:30pm. Open Monday, Wednesday, and Thursday 7:30pm to 2:30am, Friday and Saturday 7:30pm to 3am, and Sunday 6:30pm to 1:30am.

Café Bar Padam. Rauric, 9. ☎ **93-302-50-62.** Metro: Liceu.

The tapas served here are derived from time-honored Catalán culinary traditions, but the clientele and decor are modern, hip, and often gay. The bar is on a narrow street in the Ciutat Vella, about 3 blocks east of the Ramble dels Caputxins. The only color in the black-and-white rooms comes from fresh flowers and modern paintings. Tapas include fresh anchovies and tuna, plus cheese platters. Jazz is sometimes featured. Open Monday to Saturday 7pm to 2am.

Cocktail Bar Boadas. Tallers, 1. ☎ **93-318-95-92.** Metro: Plaça de Catalunya.

This intimate and conservative bar is usually filled with regulars. Established in 1933, it lies near the top of Les Rambles. Many visitors stop here for a pre-dinner drink and snack before wandering to one of the district's many restaurants. You can choose from among a wide array of Caribbean rums, Russian vodkas, and English gins—the skilled bartenders know how to mix them all. The place is especially well known for its daiquiris. Open daily noon to 2am.

Cocktelería Boadas. Carrer Taller, 1. ☎ **93-318-95-92.** Metro: Plaça de Catalunya.

At the corner of the Rambles is this bustling cocktail bar where at least part of the fun derives from trying to remember the parade of famous patrons who have come here for a drink or two since the place was established in 1933. The art deco setting might remind you just a bit of the most licentious days of old Havana—that's where the founder of this place got his start before moving back to his family's home turf of Barcelona. Many patrons always order Hemingway's favorite drink, a *mojito* (the Cuban rum equivalent of a mint julep). Open Monday to Saturday 11am to 2am.

Dirty Dick's. Taberna Inglesa. Carrer Marc Aureli, 2. ☎ **93-200-89-52.** Metro: Muntaner.

An English-style pub behind an inwardly curving bay window in a residential part of town, Dirty Dick's has an interior of dark paneling and exposed brick, with banquettes for quiet conversation. If you sit at the bar, you'll be faced with a tempting array of tiny sandwiches that taste as good as they look. The pub is set at the crossing of Vía Augusta, a main thoroughfare leading through the district. Open daily 6pm to 2:30am.

El Born. Passeig del Born, 26. ☎ **93-319-53-33.** Metro: Jaume I.

Facing a rustic-looking square, this place, once a fish store, has been cleverly converted. There are a few tables near the front, but our preferred spot is the inner room, decorated with rattan furniture, ceramic jugs, books, and modern paintings. Music here could be anything from Louis Armstrong to classic rock-and-roll. Dinner can also be had at the upstairs buffet. The room is somewhat cramped, but there you'll find a simple but tasty collection of fish, meat, and vegetable dishes, all carefully laid out; a full dinner without wine costs around 3,000 ptas. (US$18). Beer costs 350 ptas. (US$2.10); wine, 200 ptas. (US$1.20). Open Monday to Thursday 6pm to 2:30am and Friday and Saturday 6pm to 3am.

✪ **Els Quatre Gats.** Montsió, 3. ☎ **93-302-41-40.** Metro: Urquinaona.

In 1897 Pere Romeu and three of his friends, painters Ramón Casas, Santiago Rusiñol, and Miguel Utrillo, opened a cafe for artists and writers at the edge of the Barri Gòtic. Early in the history of the cafe, they staged a one-man show for a young artist, Pablo Picasso, but he didn't sell a single painting. However, Picasso stayed around to design the art nouveau cover of the menu. The cafe folded in 1903, becoming a private club and art school and attracting Joan Miró. In 1978 two Cataláns reopened the cafe in the Casa Martí, a building designed by Josep Puig i Cadafalch, one of the leading architects of *modernismo.* The cafe displays works by major modern Catalán painters, including Tàpies. You can come in to drink coffee, taste some wine, eat a full meal—and even try, if you dare, a potent *Marc de Champagne,* an eau-de-vie distilled from the local cava. The cafe is open daily 8am to 2am. See also the restaurant listing in chapter 3.

✪ **Otto Zutz Club.** Carrer Lincoln, 15. ☎ **93-238-07-22.** Cover 2,000 ptas. (US$12). Metro: Passeig de Gràcia or Fontana.

Boasting a neo-industrial decor, this nightspot is the last word in hip and a magnet for the city's artists and night people. Facetiously named after a German optician and the recipient of millions of pesetas worth of interior drama, it sits behind an angular facade that reminds some visitors of a monument to some mid-20th-century megalomaniac. Built to house a textile factory, the building contains a labyrinth of metal staircases decorated in shades of blue, highlighted with endless spotlights, and warmed with lots of exposed wood. Open Wednesday 10pm to 6am and Thursday and Saturday 11pm to 6am.

Pub 240. Aribau, 240. ☎ **93-209-09-67.** Cover 2,500 ptas. (US$15). Metro: Universitat.

This elegant bar, which bears absolutely no resemblance to an English pub, is arranged in three sections: a bar, a small amphitheater, and a lounge for talking and listening to music. Rock and South American folk music are played here, and the place is jammed almost every night. Open daily 7pm to 5am.

Zig-Zag Bar. Platón, 13. ☎ **93-201-62-07.** Metro: Muntaner.

Favored by actors, models, cinematographers, and photographers, this bar claims to have inaugurated Barcelona's trend toward high-tech minimalism in its watering holes. Owned by the same entrepreneurs who developed the state-of-the-art nightclub Otto Zutz, it offers an unusual chance to see Spain's nightlife in action. Open Monday to Thursday 10pm to 2:30am, Friday and Saturday 10pm to 3am.

CHAMPAGNE BARS

The growing popularity of champagne bars during the 1980s was an indication of Spain's increasing cosmopolitanism. The Cataláns call their own version of champagne *cava.* In Catalán, champagne bars are called *xampanyerías.* These Spanish wines are often excellent, said by some to be better than their French counterparts. With more than 50 companies producing cava in Spain and with each bottling up to a dozen different grades of wine, the best way to learn about Spanish champagne is either to visit the vineyard or to sample the products at a *xampanyería.*

Champagne bars usually open at 7pm and operate into the wee hours of the morning. Tapas are served, ranging from caviar to smoked fish to frozen chocolate truffles. Most establishments sell only a limited array of house *cavas* by the glass—you'll be offered a choice of *brut* or *brut nature* (brut is slightly sweeter). More esoteric cavas must be purchased by the bottle. The most acclaimed brands include Mont-Marçal, Gramona, Mestres, Parxet, Torello, and Recaredo.

Xampanyería Casablanca. Bonavista, 6. ☎ **93-237-63-99.** Metro: Passeig de Gràcia.

Someone had to fashion a champagne bar after the Bogart-Bergman film, and this is it. Four kinds of house cava are served by the glass. The staff also serves a good selection of tapas, especially pâtés. The Casablanca is near the Passeig de Gràcia. Open Sunday to Thursday 6:45pm to 2:30am and Friday and Saturday 6:45pm to 3am.

Xampú Xampany. Gran Via de les Corts Catalanes, 702. ☎ **93-265-04-83.** Metro: Girona.

At the corner of the Plaça de Tetuan, this *xampanyería* offers a variety of hors d'oeuvres in addition to the wine. Abstract paintings, touches of high tech, bouquets of flowers, and a pastel color scheme create the decor. Open daily 6pm to 4am.

GAY & LESBIAN BARS

Arena Classic. Diputació, 233. No phone. Cover Thurs–Fri 600 ptas. (US$3.60), Sat and holidays 1,000 ptas. (US$6). Metro: Universitat.

Attracting a crowd of gay men and lesbians, this club successfully combines '70s and '80s dance music to keep you moving and grooving till the wee hours. Thursdays there's a special party organized by a local lesbian group. Open Thursday to Saturday 11pm to 4am.

El Convento. Carrer Bruniquer, 59 (Plaça Joanic). No phone. Cover (includes one drink) 1,000 ptas. (US$6). Metro: Joanic.

This may be like no disco you've ever seen. The decoration is like a church, with depictions of the Virgin Mary and even candles adding to the ecclesiastical atmosphere. But the clientele consists of mainly young gay males in a party mood. Often shows and organized parties are presented here. A novelty, to say the least. Hours are daily midnight to 6am.

Martin's Disco. Passeig de Gràcia, 130. ☎ **93-218-71-67.** Cover 1,200 ptas. (US$7.20), including first drink. Metro: Passeig de Gràcia.

Behind a pair of unmarked doors, in a neighborhood of art nouveau buildings, this is one of the more popular gay discos in Barcelona. Within a series of all-black rooms, you'll wander through a landscape of men's erotic art, upended oil drums (used as cocktail tables), and the disembodied front-end chassis of yellow cars set amid the angular surfaces of the drinking and dancing areas. Another bar supplies drinks to a large room where films are shown. Open daily 11:30pm to 6am.

Metro. Sepúlveda, 185. No phone. Cover 1,000 ptas. (US$6). Metro: Universitat.

Metro attracts a diverse crowd—from young fashion victims to more rough-and-ready macho types. One dance floor plays contemporary house and dance music, and the other traditional Spanish music mixed with Spanish pop. This is a good opportunity to watch men of all ages dance the Sevillana together in pairs with a surprising degree of grace. One interesting feature appears in the bathrooms, where videos have been installed in quite unexpected places. Open daily midnight to 5am.

Punto BCN. Muntaner, 63–65. No phone. Metro: Eixample.

Barcelona's largest gay bar attracts a mixed crowd of young trendies and foreigners. Always crowded, it's a good base to start out your evening. With every drink you receive free entry to Arena, Arena Classic (see above), and Arena VIP. There is a very popular happy hour on Wednesday 6 to 9pm. On Friday and Saturday there are lots of surprises and giveaways. Open daily 6pm to 2:30am.

A CASINO

Midway between the coastal resorts of Sitges and Villanueva, about 25 miles (40km) southwest of Barcelona and about 2 miles (3km) north of Sitges, stands the **Gran Casino de Barcelona,** Sant Pere (San Pedro) de Ribes (☎ **93-893-36-66**). The major casino in all of Catalonia, it is housed in a villa originally built during the 1800s. Elegant, with gardens, it attracts restaurant clients as well as gamblers. A set menu in the restaurant (reservations recommended) costs 5,000 ptas. (US$30), and drinks go for around 900 ptas. (US$5.40) each. For admission to the casino, you'll pay 550 ptas. (US$3.30) and must show your passport. The casino is open year-round Sunday to Thursday 5pm to 4am, Friday and Saturday 5pm to 5am.

13 Side Trips from Barcelona

The major day trips include those to the beaches of Sitges, the monastery of Montserrat, the Penedés vineyards, and the canonical church in Cardona. Among other popular stopovers are the resorts north of Barcelona along the Costa Brava, which are covered extensively in *Frommer's Spain.*

SITGES

Sitges, 25 miles (40km) south of Barcelona, is one of the most popular resorts of southern Europe. It's especially crowded in summer, mostly with affluent young northern Europeans, many of them gay. For years the resort largely drew prosperous middle-class industrialists from Barcelona, but those staid days have gone; Sitges is as swinging today as Benidorm and Torremolinos down the coast, but nowhere near as tacky.

Sitges has long been known as a city of culture, thanks in part to resident artist, playwright, and Bohemian mystic Santiago Rusiñol. The 19th-century modernismo movement began largely at Sitges, and the town remained the scene of artistic encounters and demonstrations long after the movement waned. Sitges continued as a resort of artists, attracting such giants as Salvador Dalí and poet Federico García Lorca. The Spanish Civil War (1936–39) erased what has come to be called the "golden age" of Sitges. Although other artists and writers arrived in the decades to follow, none had the name or the impact of those who had gone before.

ESSENTIALS

GETTING THERE   By Train   RENFE runs trains from Barcelona-Sants to Sitges, a 30-minute trip, costing 355 ptas. (US$2.15). Call ☎ **93-490-02-02** in Barcelona for information about schedules. Four trains leave Barcelona per hour.

By Car   Sitges is a 45-minute drive from Barcelona along the **C-246,** a coastal road. An express highway, the **A-7,** opened in 1991. The coastal road is more scenic, but it can be extremely slow on weekends because of the heavy traffic, as all of Barcelona seemingly heads for the beaches.

VISITOR INFORMATION   The **tourist office** is at Carrer Sínis Morera, 1 (☎ **93-894-42-51**). June to September 15, it's open daily 9am to 9pm; September 16 to May, hours are Monday to Friday 9am to 2pm and 4 to 6:30pm, and Saturday 10am to 1pm.

SPECIAL EVENTS   The **Carnaval** at Sitges is one of the outstanding events on the Catalán calendar. For more than a century, the town has celebrated the days before the beginning of Lent. Fancy dress, floats, feathered outfits, and sequins all make this an exciting event. The party begins on the Thursday before Lent with the arrival of the king of the Carnestoltes and ends with the Burial of a Sardine on Ash Wednesday. Activities reach their flamboyant best on Sant Bonaventura, where gay people hold their own celebrations.

FUN ON & OFF THE BEACH

The old part of Sitges used to be a fortified medieval enclosure. The castle is now the seat of the town government. The local parish church, called *La Punta* (The Point) and built next to the sea on top of a promontory, presides over an extensive maritime esplanade, where people parade in the early evening. Behind the side of the church are the Museu Cau Ferrat and the Museu Maricel (see below).

Most people are here to hit the beach. The beaches have showers, bathing cabins, and stalls; kiosks rent motorboats and water-sports equipment. Beaches on the eastern end and those inside the town center are the most peaceful—for example, **Aiguadoiç** and **Els Balomins. Playa San Sebastián, Fragata Beach,** and the **"Beach of the Boats"** (below the church and next to the yacht club) are the area's family beaches. A young, happening crowd heads for the **Playa de la Ribera,** to the west.

All along the coast women can and certainly do go topless. Farther west are the most solitary beaches, where the scene grows more racy, especially along the **Playas del Muerto,** where two tiny nude beaches lie between Sitges and Vilanova i la Geltrú. A shuttle bus runs between the cathedral and Golf Terramar. From Golf Terramar, go along the road to the club L'Atlántida, then walk along the railway. The first beach draws nudists of every sexual persuasion, and the second is almost solely gay. Be advised that lots of action takes place in the woods in back of these beaches.

Beaches aside, Sitges has some choice museums, which really shouldn't be missed.

We'll Have a Gay Old Time

Along with Ibiza, Key West, and Mikonos, Sitges has established itself firmly on the "A" list of gay resorts. It's a perfect destination for those who want a ready-made combination of beach and bars, all within a few minutes walk of each other. It also works well as a temporary, calmer alternative to Barcelona, which is about 30 minutes away by train , and so is great for a day trip or a few days out of the city. Off-season, it's pretty quiet on the gay front apart from the carnival in February. Summer, however, is pure hedonism, and the town draws the boys in from all over Europe to the gay beach in the middle of the town in front of the Passeig Maritim. The other beach is nudist and farther out of town between Sitges and Vilanova. The best directions would be to go as far as the Atlantida disco and then follow the train track to the farther of the two beaches.

Museu Cau Ferrat. Carrer del Fonallar. ☎ **93-894-03-64.** Admission 500 ptas. (US$3) adults, 250 ptas. (US$1.50) students, free for children under 16; combination ticket for 3 museums listed 800 ptas. (US$4.80) adults, 400 ptas. (US$2.40) students and children. June 22–Sept 10, Tues–Sat 9:30am–2pm and 4–9pm, Sun 9:30am–2pm; Sept 11–June 21, Tues–Fri 9:30am–2pm and 4–6pm, Sat 9:30am–2pm and 4–8pm, Sun 9:30am–2pm.

The Catalán artist Santiago Rusiñol combined two 16th-century cottages to make this house, where he lived and worked and which upon his death in 1931 he willed to Sitges along with his art collection. More than anyone else, Rusiñol made Sitges a popular resort. The museum collection includes two paintings by El Greco and several small Picassos, including *The Bullfight*. A number of Rusiñol's works are also on display.

Museu Maricel. Carrer del Fonallar. ☎ **93-894-03-64.** Admission 500 ptas. (US$3) adults, 250 ptas. (US$1.50) students, free for children under 16; admission included in combination ticket (see Museu Cau Ferrat, above). June 21–Sept 11, Tues–Sat 9:30am–2pm and 4–8pm, Sun 9:30am–2pm; Sept 12–June 20, Tues–Fri 9:30am–2pm and 4–6pm, Sat 9:30am–2pm and 4–8pm, Sun 9:30am–2pm.

Opened by the king and queen of Spain, Museu Maricel contains art donated by Dr. Jesús Pérez Rosales. The palace, owned by American Charles Deering when it was built right after World War I, is made up of two parts connected by a small bridge. The museum has a good collection of Gothic and Romantic paintings and sculptures, as well as many fine Catalán ceramics. There are also three noteworthy works by Santiago Rebull and an allegorical painting of World War I by José María Sert.

Museu Romàntic ("Can Llopis"). Sant Gaudenci, 1. ☎ **93-894-29-69.** Admission 500 ptas. (US$3) adults, 250 ptas. (US$1.50) students, free for children under 16; admission included in combination ticket (see above). June 21–Sept 11, Tues–Sat 9:30am–2pm and 4–8pm, Sun 9:30am–2pm; Sept 12–June 20, Tues–Fri 9:30am–2pm and 4–6pm, Sat 9:30am–2pm and 4–8pm, Sun 9:30am–2pm.

This museum recreates the daily life of a Sitges land-owning family in the 18th and 19th centuries. The family rooms, furniture, and household objects are most interesting. You'll also find wine cellars, and an important collection of antique dolls (upstairs).

WHERE TO STAY

Hotel Calípolis. Avinguda Sofía, 2–4, 08870 Sitges. ☎ **93-894-15-00.** Fax 93-894-07-64. 170 units. A/C MINIBAR TV TEL. 18,500–23,000 ptas. (US$111–US$138) double; from 32,000 ptas. (US$192) suite. AE, DC, MC, V. Parking 2,000 ptas. (US$12).

This 11-story hotel fits in a gently undulating curve against the resort's beachfront and seaside promenade. The good-size rooms contain expansive balconies, safes, satellite TVs, marble bathrooms, and a comfortably conservative decor of contemporary furniture. Most offer sea views; the remainder offer views of the mountains.

Hotel Platjador. Passeig de la Ribera, 35, 08870 Sitges. ☎ **93-894-50-54.** Fax 93-811-03-84. 60 units. A/C TV TEL. 8,500–15,000 ptas. (US$51–US$90) double. Rates include breakfast. MC, V. Closed Nov–Apr.

One of the best hotels in town, the Platjador, on the esplanade fronting the beach, has comfortably furnished and recently restored rooms, many with big French doors opening onto balconies and sea views. There's also a pool. The dining room, facing the beach, is known for its good cuisine, including gazpacho, paella, fresh fish, and flan for dessert.

San Sebastián Playa, Port Alegre 53, 08070 Sitges. ☎ **93-894-86-76.** Fax 93-894-04-30. www.tryp.es. E-mail: hotel@tryp.es. 51 units. A/C MINIBAR TV TEL. 15,500–19,000 ptas. (US$93–US$114) double; 27,000 ptas. (US$162) suite. AE, DC, MC, V. Parking 1,500 ptas. (US$9).

The best in Sitges, opposite San Sebastián beach, this four-star hotel with its wedding cake facade has been around since 1990. The functional art deco interior is beautiful. A lot of attention has gone into the rooms, which are spacious and comfortable, with such modern conveniences as private safes and fully equipped bathrooms. Each also has a balcony opening onto the sea.

WHERE TO DINE

Chez Jeanette. Sant Pau, 23. ☎ **93-894-00-48.** Reservations recommended. Main courses 1,200–2,650 ptas. (US$7.20–US$15.90); *menú del día* 1,850 ptas. (US$11.10). AE, DC, V. Daily 7–11:30pm, Sat–Sun 1–4pm. Closed Dec 20–Jan 15. INTERNATIONAL.

A Frenchwoman named Jeanette established a Catalán-style restaurant here in 1975. She has since died, but her culinary tradition continues. Patrons flock to the rustic atmosphere created by textured stucco walls and a regional tavern decor. Set back on a restaurant-flanked street a short walk from the beach, it draws both straights and gays. From the standard menu, you can order onion soup, *rape* (monkfish) with whisky, and entrecôte with Roquefort sauce. There are also several *platos del día*. The chef is proudest of his *parilla pescada*, a mixed grill of fresh fish from the Mediterranean.

✪ **Els Quatre Gats.** Sant Pau, 13. ☎ **93-894-19-15.** Reservations recommended. Main courses 3,000–4,500 ptas. (US$18–US$27); *menú del día* 2,500 ptas. (US$15). AE, DC, MC, V. Thurs–Tues 1–4pm and 8–11pm. Closed Nov–Mar. CATALÁN.

When it opened in the early 1960s as a bar/cafe a few steps from the beachfront Passeig de la Ribera., it adopted the name of one of Catalonia's most historic cafes, Els Quatre Gats (see "Barcelona After Dark"). By 1968, the newcomer was firmly established as one of the leading restaurants in Sitges, serving a well-received *cocina del mercado*, based on whatever was fresh and available in the local markets. In a setting accented with paintings and varnished paneling, you can enjoy fresh grilled fish, garlic soup, lamb cutlets with local herbs, roast chicken in wine sauce, and veal kidneys in sherry sauce.

El Velero. Passeig de la Ribera, 38. ☎ **93-894-20-51.** Reservations required. Main courses 1,800–5,000 ptas. (US$10.80–US$30); fixed-price menu 3,000 ptas. (US$18). AE, DC, MC, V. Daily 1:30–4pm and 8:30–11:30pm. SEAFOOD.

This is one of the leading restaurants of Sitges, occupying a position along the beachfront promenade. The most desirable tables are found on the glass greenhouse terrace, opening onto the esplanade, although there is a more glamorous restaurant inside. Try a soup, such as clam and truffle or whitefish, followed by a main dish such as paella marinara (with seafood) or supreme of salmon in pine-nut sauce.

SITGES AFTER DARK

One of the best ways to pass an evening in Sitges is to walk the waterfront esplanade, have a leisurely dinner, then retire at about 11pm to one of the open-air cafes for a nightcap and some serious people-watching. Few local dives can compete with the scene taking place on the streets.

If you're straight, you may have to hunt to find a bar that isn't predominantly gay. There are so many gay bars, in fact, that a map is distributed pinpointing their locales. Nine of them are concentrated on **Carrer Sant Bonaventura** in the center of town, a 5-minute walk from the beach (near the Museu Romàntic). If you grow bored with the action in one place, you just have to walk down the street to find another. Drink prices run about the same in all the clubs.

Mediterráneo, Sant Bonaventura, 6 (no phone), is the largest gay disco/bar. It sports a formal Iberian garden and sleek modern styling. Upstairs in this restored 1690s house just east of the Plaça d'Espanya, there are pool tables and a covered terrace. On summer nights, the place is filled to overflowing. Other gay bars include **Bourbon's,** Sant Bonaventura, 13 (☎ 93-894-33-47), which appeals to a predominately youngish crowd, and **El Candil,** Carrer de la Carreta, 9 (no phone), where the age range is wider and which has a dark room and video shows. **El Horno,** Joan Tarrida, 6 (☎ 93-894-09-09), with slight leather overtones that grow more prominent as the night progresses, opens earlier, at 5:30pm, and also features videos and a dark room.

Another of the town's most popular nightspots, with DJs spinning the latest dance hits, is **Ricky's Disco,** Sant Pau, 25 (☎ 93-894-96-81), which charges a cover of 1,200 ptas. (US$7.20). This place caters to an international mix of gays and straights. It's set back from the beach on a narrow street noted for its inexpensive restaurants and folkloric color. **Trailer,** Angel Vidal, 36 (no phone), is an extremely popular club and the best place to end the night. It closes at 5:30am, and the entry cost of 1,500 ptas. (US$9) includes one drink.

MONTSERRAT

Montserrat is 35 miles (56km) northwest of Barcelona and 368 miles (592km) east of Madrid. The **monastery at Montserrat,** which sits atop a 4,000-foot mountain 7 miles (11km) long and 3¹/₂ miles (5.5km) wide, is one of the most important pilgrimage spots in Spain. It ranks alongside Zaragoza and Santiago de Compostela. Thousands travel here every year to see and touch the medieval statue of *La Moreneta* (The Black Virgin), the patron saint of Catalonia. Many newly married couples flock here for her blessings. Avoid visiting on Sunday, if possible. Thousands of locals pour in, especially if the weather is nice. Remember that the winds blow cold up here; even in summer, visitors should take along warm sweaters, jackets, or coats. In winter, thermal underwear might not be a bad idea.

ESSENTIALS

GETTING THERE   By Train   The best and most exciting way to go is via the Catalán railway—Ferrocarrils de la Generalitat de Catalunya (Manresa line), with five trains a day leaving from the Plaça d'Espanya in Barcelona. The central office is at Plaça de Catalunya, 1 (☎ 93-205-15-15). The train connects with an aerial cableway (*Aeri de Montserrat*), which is included in the rail passage of 1,855 ptas. (US$11.15) round-trip.

By Bus   The train with its funicular tie-in has taken over as the preferred means of transport. However, a long-distance bus service is provided by **Autocars Julià** in Barcelona. Daily service from Barcelona to Montserrat is generally operated, with departures near Estació Central de Barcelona-Sants, Plaça de Països Catalánes. One bus makes the trip at 9am, returning at 5pm; the round-trip ticket costs 1,500 ptas. (US$9). Contact the Julià company at carrer Viriato (☎ **93-490-40-00**).

By Car   Take the **N-2** southwest of Barcelona toward Tarragona, turning west at the junction with the **N-11**. The signposts and exit to Montserrat will be on your right. From the main road, it's 9 miles (14.5km) up to the monastery through eerie rock formations and dramatic scenery.

VISITOR INFORMATION   The **tourist office** is at Plaça de la Creu (☎ **93-877-77-77**). It's open 10am to 1:45pm and 3 to 5:30pm.

SEEING THE SIGHTS

One of the **monastery's** noted attractions is the 50-member ✪ **Escolanía** (boys' choir), one of the oldest and most renowned in Europe, dating from the 13th century. At 1pm daily you can hear them singing *Salve Regina* and the *Virolai* (hymn of Montserrat) in the basilica. The basilica is open daily 8 to 10:30am and noon to 6:30pm. Admission is free. To view the Black Virgin, a statue from the 12th or 13th century, enter the church through a side door to the right. At the Plaça de Santa María you can also visit the **Museu de Montserrat** (☎ **93-877-77-77**), known for its collection of ecclesiastical paintings, including works by Caravaggio and El Greco. Modern Spanish and Catalán artists are also represented (see Picasso's early *El Viejo Pescador,* dating from 1895), as well as works by Dalí and such French impressionists as Monet, Sisley, and Degas. The collection of ancient artifacts is also interesting. And look for the crocodile mummy, which is at least 2,000 years old. The museum is open Monday to Friday 10am to 6pm, Saturday and Sunday 9:30am to 6:30pm; admission is 500 ptas. (US$3) for adults, 300 ptas. (US$1.80) for children and students.

The 9-minute **funicular ride** to the 4,119-foot-high peak, Sant Jeroni, makes for a panoramic trip. The funicular operates about every 20 minutes from April to October, daily 10am to 6:40pm. The cost is 925 ptas. (US$5.55) round-trip. From the top, you'll see not only the whole of Catalonia but also the Pyrenees and the islands of Majorca and Ibiza.

You can also make an excursion to **Santa Cova (Holy Grotto),** the alleged site of the discovery of the Black Virgin. The grotto dates from the 17th century and was built in the shape of a cross. You go halfway by funicular but must complete the trip on foot.

The chapel is open April to October, daily 9am to 6:30pm; off-season hours are daily 10am to 5:30pm. The funicular operates from April to October only, every 15 minutes daily 10am to 7pm, at a cost of 350 ptas. (US$2.10) round-trip.

WHERE TO STAY & DINE

Abat Cisneros. Plaça de Monestir, 08199 Montserrat. ☎ **93-877-77-01.** Fax 93-877-77-24. 56 units. TV TEL. 5,800–10,500 ptas. (US$34.80–US$63) double. AE, DC, MC, V. Parking 450 ptas. (US$2.70).

On the main square, this is a well-maintained modern hotel with few pretensions and a history of family management dating from 1958. Guest rooms are simple and clean. The in-house restaurant offers fixed-price meals for around 2,675 pesetas (US$18.75) per person. Many regional dishes of Catalonia are served.

PENEDÉS WINERIES: HOME OF *CAVA*

From the Penedés wineries comes the famous *cava,* Catalán champagne, which can be sampled in the champagne bars of Barcelona. You can see where this wine originates by journeying 25 miles (40km) from Barcelona, via highway A-2, to Exit 27. There are also daily trains to Sant Sadurní d'Anoia, home to 66 cava firms. Trains depart from Barcelona Sants.

The firm best equipped to receive visitors is **Codorníu** (☎ **93-818-32-32**), the largest producer of cava (some 40 million bottles a year). Codorníu is ideally visited by car because of unreliable public transportation. However, it's sometimes possible to get a taxi from the station at Sant Sadurní d'Anoia.

Groups are welcomed at Codorníu (there must be at least four people present before a tour is conducted). Advance reservations are not necessary. Tours are presented in English, among other languages, and last 1¹/₂ hours; visitors will explore some of the 10 miles (16km) of underground cellars by electric cart. Take a sweater, even on a hot day. A former pressing section has been turned into a museum, exhibiting wine-making instruments through the ages. The museum is housed in a building designed by the great *modernista* architect Puig i Cadafalch—one reason King Juan Carlos has declared the plant a national historic and artistic monument.

The tour ends with a cava tasting. Tours are conducted Monday to Friday 9am to 5pm. Call the number above for more information. The ideal time for a visit is during the autumn grape harvest. Admission is free Monday to Friday, 200 pesetas (US$12) Saturday and Sunday.

CARDONA: CATALÁN CASTLE VILLAGE

Another popular excursion from Barcelona is to Cardona, 60 miles (97km) northwest. Take the N-11 west, then go north on Route 150 to Manresa. Cardona, reached along Route 1410, lies northwest of Manresa, a distance of 20 miles (32km). The home of the dukes of Cardona, the town is known for its canonical church, **Sant Vicenç de Cardona,** placed inside the walls of the castle. The church was consecrated in 1040. The great Catalán architect Josep Puig i Cadafalch wrote, "There are few elements in Catalán architecture of the 12th century that cannot be found in Cardona, and nowhere better harmonized." The church reflects the Lombard style of architecture. The castle (now a parador—see below) was the most important fortress in Catalonia.

Parador Nacional Duques de Cardona. Castillo de Cardona, s/n, 08261 Cardona. ☎ **93-869-12-75.** Fax 93-869-16-36. www.parador.es. 54 units. A/C TV TEL. 16,000–18,500 ptas. (US$96–US$111) double; 20,000 ptas. (US$120) suite. AE, DC, MC, V.

Atop a cone-shaped mountain towering 330 feet over Cardona, this restored castle opened as a four-star parador in 1976. Once the seat of Ludovici Pio (Louis the Pious) and a stronghold against the Moors, it was later expanded by Guifré el Pilós (Wilfred the Hairy). In the 9th century the palace went to Don Ramón Folch, nephew of Charlemagne. The massive fortress proved impregnable to all but the inroads of time, and several ancient buildings in this complex have been restored and made part of the parador. The spacious units, some with minibars, are furnished with hand-carved wood canopied beds and woven bedspreads and curtains. The public rooms boast antique furniture, tapestries, and paintings of various periods. The bar is in a former dungeon, with meals served in the stone-arched medieval dining room. Try the Catalán bouillabaisse, accompanied by wines whose taste would be familiar to the Romans. Service is daily 1 to 4pm and 8 to 10:30pm.

AT&T

AT&T Direct® Service

AT&T Access Numbers

Aruba	800-8000	Czech Rep. ▲	00-42-000-101
Australia ●	**1-800-551-155**	Egypt ● (Cairo) ‡	510-0200
Austria ●	**0800-200-288**	France	0-800-99-0011
Bahamas	1-800-872-2881	Germany	0800-2255-288
Barbados ✦	1-800-872-2881	Greece ●	00-800-1311
Belgium ●	**0-800-100-10**	Guam	1-800-2255-288
Bermuda ✦	1-800-872-2881	Hong Kong	800-96-1111
Cayman Isl ✦	1-800-872-2881	Hungary	06-800-01111
China, PRC ▲	10811	India ✱, ➤	000-117
Costa Rica	0-800-0-114-114	Ireland ✓	1-800-550-000

AT&T

AT&T Direct® Service

AT&T Access Numbers

Aruba	8¤0-8000	Czech Rep. ▲	00-42-000-101
Australia ●	**1-800-551-155**	Egypt ● (Cairo) ‡	510-0200
Austria ●	**0800-¤00-288**	France	0-800-99-0011
Bahamas	1-800-8¨2-2881	Germany	0800-2255-288
Barbados ✦	1-800-8¨2-2881	Greece ●	00-800-1311
Belgium ●	**0-800-100-10**	Guam	1-800-2255-288
Bermuda ✦	1-800-8¨2-2881	Hong Kong	800-96-1111
Cayman Isl ✦	1-800-8¨2-2881	Hungary	06-800-01111
China, PRC ▲	10811	India ✱, ➤	000-117
Costa Rica	0-800-0-114-114	Ireland ✓	1-800-550-000

Israel	1-800-94-94-949	**Philippines**●	105-11
Italy●	172-1011	**Portugal**▲	0800-800-128
Jamaica●	1-800-872-2881	**Singapore**	800-0111-111
Japan●▲	005-39-111	**Spain**	900-99-00-11
Malaysia●	1800-80-0011	**Switzerland**●	0-800-89-0011
Mexico●▽	01-800-288-2872	**Thailand**◄	001-999-111-11
Neth. Ant.○	001-800-872-2881	**Turkey**●	00-800-12277
Netherlands●	0800-022-9111	**U.K.**	0800-89-0011
New Zealand●	000-911	**U.K.**	0800-013-0011
Panama	800-001-0109	**Venezuela**	800-11-120

FOR EASY CALLING WORLDWIDE

1 Just dial the AT&T Access Number for the country you're calling from.
2 Dial the phone number you're calling.   *3* Dial your card number.

For access numbers not listed ask any operator for **AT&T Direct**® Service.
In the U.S. call 1-800-331-1140 for a wallet guide listing all worldwide
AT&T Access Numbers.

Visit our Web site at: www.att.com/traveler
Bold-faced countries permit country-to-country calling outside the U.S.

- ● Public phones may require coin or card deposit to place call.
- ♦ Outside of Cairo, dial "02" first.
- + May not be available from every phone/payphone.
- ▲ Public phones and select hotels.
- ○ Use U.K. access number in N. Ireland.
- ∨ When calling from public phones, use phones marked "Lenso."
- ▽ When calling from public phones, use phones marked "Ladatel."
- ✕ Not available from public phones.
- ▼ Available from phones with international calling capabilities or from most Public Calling Centers.
- ○ From St. Maarten or phones at Bobby's Marina, use 1-800-872-2881.

When placing an international call *from* the U.S., dial 1 800 CALL ATT.

© 1/2000

Israel	1-800-94-94-949	**Philippines**●	105-11
Italy●	172-1011	**Portugal**▲	0800-800-128
Jamaica●	1-800-872-2881	**Singapore**	800-0111-111
Japan●▲	005-39-111	**Spain**	900-99-00-11
Malaysia●	1800-80-0011	**Switzerland**●	0-800-89-0011
Mexico●▽	01-800-288-2872	**Thailand**◄	001-999-111-11
Neth. Ant.○	001-800-872-2881	**Turkey**●	00-800-12277
Netherlands●	0800-022-9111	**U.K.**	0800-89-0011
New Zealand●	000-911	**U.K.**	0800-013-0011
Panama	800-001-0109	**Venezuela**	800-11-120

FOR EASY CALLING WORLDWIDE

1 Just dial the AT&T Access Number for the country you're calling from.
2 Dial the phone number you're calling.   *3* Dial your card number.

For access numbers not listed ask any operator for **AT&T Direct**® Service.
In the U.S. call 1-800-331-1140 for a wallet guide listing all worldwide
AT&T Access Numbers.

Visit our Web site at: www.att.com/traveler
Bold-faced countries permit country-to-country calling outside the U.S.

- ● Public phones may require coin or card deposit to place call.
- ♦ Outside of Cairo, dial "02" first.
- + May not be available from every phone/payphone.
- ▲ Public phones and select hotels.
- ○ Use U.K. access number in N. Ireland.
- ∨ When calling from public phones, use phones marked "Lenso."
- ▽ When calling from public phones, use phones marked "Ladatel."
- ✕ Not available from public phones.
- ▼ Available from phones with international calling capabilities or from most Public Calling Centers.
- ○ From St. Maarten or phones at Bobby's Marina, use 1-800-872-2881.

When placing an international call *from* the U.S., dial 1 800 CALL ATT.

© 1/2000

TIMBUKTU   KALAMAZOO

AT&T Direct® Service

The easy way to call home from anywhere.

Global connection with the AT&T Network

AT&T direct service

For the easy way to call home, take the attached wallet guide.

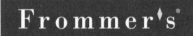

Settling into Madrid **5**

Madrid was conceived, planned, and built when Spain was at the peak of its confidence and power and the city became the solid and dignified seat of a great empire stretching around the world. Monumental Madrid glitters almost as much as Paris, Rome, or London and parties more than any other city. Although it lacks the spectacular Romanesque and Gothic monuments of older Spanish cities, Madrid never fails to convey its own sense of grandeur.

Madrid has the highest altitude of any European capital and its climate can be blisteringly hot in summer but quite cold in winter. Traffic roars down wide boulevards that stretch for miles—from the narrow streets of the city's historic 17th-century core to the ugly concrete suburbs that have spread in recent years.

Don't come to Madrid expecting a city that looks classically Iberian. True, many of the older buildings in the historic core look as Spanish as those you might have encountered in rural towns across the plains of La Mancha. However, a great number of the monuments and palaces mirror the architecture of France—an oddity that reflects the genetic link between the royal families of Spain and France.

Most striking is how the city has blossomed since Franco's demise. Madrid was the epicenter of *la movida* (the movement), a renaissance of the arts after years of dictatorial creative repression. Today, despite stiff competition from such smaller cities as Barcelona and Seville, Madrid still reigns as the country's artistic and creative centerpiece.

More world-class art is on view in the central neighborhood around the stellar Prado than within virtually any other concentrated area in the world: the Caravaggios and Rembrandts at the Thyssen-Bornemisza; the El Grecos and Velázquezes at the Prado itself; and the Dalís and Mirós—not to mention Picasso's wrenching *Guernica*—at the Reina Sofía. Ironically, much of the city's art was collected by 18th-century Spanish monarchs whose artistic sense was frequently more astute than their political savvy.

Regrettably, within the city limits you'll also find sprawling expanses of concrete towers, sometimes paralyzing traffic, a growing incidence of street crime, and entire districts that, as in every other metropolis, bear no historic or cultural interest for the tourist. Many long-time visitors to the city find that its quintessential Spanish feel has subsided somewhat in the face of a Brussels-like "Europeanization" that has occurred since Spain's 1986 induction into the European Union. The city's gems remain the opulence of the **Palacio Real,** the bustle of

El Rastro's flea market, and the sultry fever of late-night flamenco. When urban commotion starts to overwhelm, seek respite in the **Parque del Retiro,** a vast, verdant oasis in the heart of the city a stone's throw from the Prado.

1 Orientation

GETTING THERE

BY PLANE   Madrid's international airport, **Barajas,** is nine miles east of the center and has two terminals—one international, the other domestic—connected by a moving sidewalk. For Barajas Airport information, call ☎ **91-305-83-43.**

Air-conditioned yellow airport buses can take you from the arrival terminal to a bus depot under the Plaza de Colón. You can also get off at stops along the way, provided that your baggage isn't stored in the hold. The fare is 380 pesetas (US$2.30); buses leave every 15 minutes, either to or from the airport.

By taxi, expect to pay 2,500 pesetas (US$15) and up, plus surcharges, for the trip to the airport and for baggage handling. If you take an unmetered limousine, make sure you negotiate a price in advance.

A subway connecting Barajas Airport and central Madrid was completed in 1999, allowing additional ground transportation options. However, the ride involves a change. Take line 8 to Mar de Cristal and switch to line 4; the one-way trip costs 130 pesetas (US80¢).

BY TRAIN   Madrid has three major railway stations: **Atocha** (Avenida Ciudad de Barcelona; metro: Atocha RENFE), for trains to Lisbon, Toledo, Andalusia, and Extremadura; **Chamartín** (in the northern suburbs at Augustín de Foxá, metro: Chamartín), for trains to and from Barcelona, Asturias, Cantabria, Castilla-León, the Basque country, Aragón, Catalonia, Levante (Valencia), Murcia, and the French frontier; and **Estación Príncipe Pío** or Norte (Paseo del Rey 30; metro: Norte), for trains to and from northwest Spain (Salamanca and Galicia). For information about connections from any of these stations, call RENFE (Spanish Railways) at ☎ **91-328-90-20** daily 7am to 11pm.

For tickets, go to the principal office of **RENFE,** Alcalá, 44 (☎ **91-328-90-20;** metro: Banco de España). The office is open Monday to Friday 9am to 8pm.

BY BUS   Madrid has at least eight major bus terminals, including the large **Estacíon Sur de Autobuses,** calle Méndez Alvaro (☎ **91-468-42-00;** metro: Mendez Alvaro). Most buses pass through this station.

BY CAR   All highways within Spain radiate outward from Madrid. The following are the major highways into Madrid, with information on driving distances to the city:

Highways to Madrid

Route	From	Distance to Madrid
N-I	Irún	315 miles (505km)
N-II	Barcelona	389 miles (622km)
N-III	Valencia	217 miles (347km)
N-IV	Cádiz	388 miles (625km)
N-V	Badajoz	254 miles (409km)
N-VI	Galicia	374 miles (598km)

VISITOR INFORMATION

The most convenient **tourist office** is on Duque de Medinaceli 2, Plaza de España (☎ **91-429-31-77;** metro: Plaza de España); it's open Monday to Friday 9am to 7pm and Saturday 9:30am to 1pm. Ask for a street map of the next town on your itinerary, especially if you're driving. The staff here can give you a list of hotels but cannot recommend any particular lodging.

CITY LAYOUT

In modern Spain all roads, rails, and telephone lines lead to Madrid, which has outgrown its previous boundaries and is branching out in all directions.

MAIN ARTERIES & SQUARES   Every new arrival must find the **Gran Vía,** which cuts a winding pathway across the city beginning at **Plaza de España,** where you'll find one of Europe's tallest skyscrapers, the Edificio España. This avenue is home to the largest concentration of shops, hotels, restaurants, and movie houses in the city, with **calle de Serrano** a close runner-up.

South of the Gran Vía lies the **Puerta del Sol,** from which all road distances within Spain are measured. However, its significance has declined, and today it is a prime hunting ground for pickpockets and purse snatchers. **Calle de Alcalá** begins here and runs for 2½ miles.

The **Plaza Mayor** at the heart of Old Madrid is an attraction in itself with its mix of French and Georgian architecture. (Be wary of thieves here, especially late at night.) Pedestrians pass under the arches of the huge square onto the narrow streets of the old town, where you can find some of the capital's most intriguing restaurants and tascas, serving tasty tapas and drinks. On the ground level arcade of the plaza are shops, many selling souvenir hats of turn-of-the-century Spanish sailors or army officers.

The area south of Plaza Mayor—known as *barrios bajos*—is full of narrow cobblestone streets lined with 16th- and 17th-century architecture. From the Plaza, take **Arco de Cuchilleros,** packed with markets, restaurants, flamenco clubs, and taverns, to explore this district.

Gran Vía ends at calle de Alcalá, and at this juncture lies **Plaza de la Cibeles,** with its fountain to Cybele, "the mother of the gods," and what is known as "the cathedral of post offices." From Cibeles, the wide **Paseo de Recoletos** begins a short run to **Plaza de Colón.** From this latter square rolls the serpentine **Paseo de la Castellana,** flanked by expensive shops, apartment buildings, luxury hotels, and foreign embassies.

Heading south from Cibeles is **Paseo del Prado,** where you'll find Spain's major attraction, the Museo del Prado, as well as the Jardín Botánico (Botanical Garden). The *paseo* also leads to the Atocha railway station. To the west of the garden lies **Parque del Retiro,** a magnificent park once reserved for royalty, with restaurants, nightclubs, a rose garden, and two lakes.

FINDING AN ADDRESS   Madrid is a city of grand boulevards extending for long distances and of cramped meandering streets that follow no plan. Finding an address can sometimes be a problem, primarily because of the way buildings are numbered.

On most streets, the numbering begins on one side and runs consecutively until the end, resuming on the other side and going in the opposite direction—rather as a farmer plows a field, up one side and down the other. Thus, number 50 could be opposite number 250. But there are many exceptions to this system of numbering. That's why it's important to know the cross street as well as the number of the address you're looking for. To complicate matters, some addresses don't have a number at all. What they have instead is the designation *s/n*, meaning *sin número* (without number). For example, the address of the Panteón de Goya (Goya's Tomb) is Glorieta de San Antonio de la Florida, s/n (see chapter 6). Note also that in Spain, as in many other European countries, the building number comes after the street name.

STREET MAPS   Arm yourself with a good map before setting out. Falk publishes the best, and it's available at most newsstands and kiosks in Madrid. The free maps given away by tourist offices and hotels aren't really adequate for more than general orientation, as they don't list the maze of little streets that is Old Madrid.

Neighborhoods in Brief

Madrid can be divided into three principal districts—Old Madrid, which holds the most tourist interest; Ensanche, the new district, often with the best shops and hotels; and the periphery, which is of little interest to visitors.

Plaza Mayor/Puerta Del Sol   This is the heart of Old Madrid, often called the tourist zone. Filled with taverns and bars, it is bounded by carrera de San Jerónimo, calle Mayor, Cava de San Miguel, Cava Baja, and calle de la Cruz. From Plaza Mayor, the Arco de Cuchilleros is filled with Castilian restaurants and taverns; more of these traditional spots, called *cuevas,* line the Cava de San Miguel, Cava Alta, and Cava Baja. To the west of this old district is the Manzanares River. Also in this area is Muslim Madrid, which is centered on the Palacio de Oriente and Las Vistillas. What is now Plaza de la Paja was actually the heart of the city and its main marketplace during the medieval period. In 1617 the Plaza Mayor became the hub of Madrid, and it remains the nighttime center of tourist activity, more so than the Puerta del Sol.

The Salamanca Quarter   Ever since Madrid's city walls came tumbling down in the 1860s, the district of Salamanca to the north has been the fashionable address. Calle de Serrano cuts through this neighborhood and is lined with stores and boutiques. Calle de Serrano is also home to the U.S. Embassy.

Gran Vía/Plaza De España   Gran Vía is the city's main street, lined with cinemas, department stores, and the headquarters of banks and corporations. It begins at the Plaza de España, with its bronze figures of Don Quixote and his faithful squire, Sancho Panza.

Argüelles/Moncloa   The university area is bounded by Pintor Rosales, Cea Bermúdez, Bravo Murillo, San Bernardo, and Conde Duque. Students haunt its famous ale houses.

Chueca   This old and decaying area north of the Gran Vía includes the main streets of Hortaleza, Infantas, Barquillo, and San Lucas. It is the center of gay nightlife, with dozens of clubs and cheap restaurants. It can be dangerous at night, although police presence has increased.

Castellana/Recoletos/Paseo del Prado   Not a real city district, this is Madrid's north-south axis, its name changing along the way. The Museo del Prado and some of the city's more expensive hotels are found here. Many restaurants and other hotels are located along its side streets. In summer its large medians serve as home to open-air terraces filled with animated crowds. The most famous cafe is the Gran Café Gijón (see "Where to Dine," later in this chapter).

2 Getting Around

Getting around Madrid is not easy, because everything is spread out. Even many Madrileño taxi drivers, often new arrivals themselves, are unfamiliar with their own city once they're off the main boulevards.

BY SUBWAY

The metro system is quite easy to learn and use. The fare is 145 pesetas (US85¢) for a one-way trip; the central converging point is the Puerta del Sol. The metro operates

6am to 1:30am and you should try to avoid rush hours. For information, call ☎ **91-429-31-77.** You can save money on public transportation by purchasing a 10-trip ticket known as a *bonos*—it costs 680 pesetas (US$4.10).

BY BUS

A bus network also services the city and suburbs, with routes clearly shown at each stop on a schematic diagram. Buses are fast and efficient because they travel along special lanes. Both red and yellow buses charge 145 pesetas (US85¢) per ride.

For 680 pesetas (US$4.10) you can also purchase a 10-trip *bonos* ticket (but without transfers) for Madrid's bus system. It's sold at **Empresa Municipal de Transportes,** Plaza de la Cibeles (☎ **91-406-88-00**), where you can also purchase a guide to the bus routes. The office is open daily 8am to 8:30pm.

BY TAXI

Cab fares are pretty reasonable. When you flag down a taxi, the meter should register 180 pesetas (US$1.10); for every kilometer thereafter, the fare increases by 89 pesetas (US55¢). A supplement is charged for trips to the railway station or the bullring, as well as on Sundays and holidays. The ride to Barajas Airport carries a 400 peseta (US$2.40) surcharge and there is a 160 peseta (US95¢) supplement from railway stations. In addition, there is a 160 peseta (US95¢) supplement on Sundays and holidays, and at night. It's customary to tip at least 10% of the fare.

Warning: Make sure that the meter is turned on when you get into a taxi. Otherwise, some drivers will assess the cost of the ride, and their assessment, you can be sure, will involve higher mathematics.

Also, there are unmetered taxis that hire out for the day or the afternoon. These are legitimate, but some drivers will operate as gypsy cabs. Since they're not metered, they can charge high rates. They are easy to avoid—always take either a black taxi with horizontal red bands or a white one with diagonal red bands instead.

If you take a taxi outside the city limits, the driver is entitled to charge you twice the rate shown on the meter.

To call a taxi, dial ☎ **91-447-51-80.**

BY CAR

Driving in congested Madrid is a nightmare and potentially dangerous. It always feels like rush hour, though theoretically, rush hours are only from 8 to 10am, 1 to 2pm, and 4 to 6pm Monday to Saturday. Parking is next to impossible, except in expensive garages. About the only time you can drive around Madrid with a minimum of hassle is in August, when thousands of Madrileños have taken their automobiles and headed for Spain's vacation oases. Save your car rentals (see "Fast Facts: Madrid," below) for 1-day excursions from the capital. If you drive into Madrid from another city, ask at your hotel for the nearest garage or parking possibility and leave your vehicle there until you're ready to leave.

Fast Facts: Madrid

American Express   For your mail or banking needs, you can go to the American Express office at the corner of Marqués de Cubas and Plaza de las Cortés, 2, across the street from the Palace Hotel (☎ **91-322-55-00** or 91-322-54-24; metro: Gran Vía). Open Monday to Friday 9am to 5:30pm and Saturday 9am to noon.

Madrid Metro

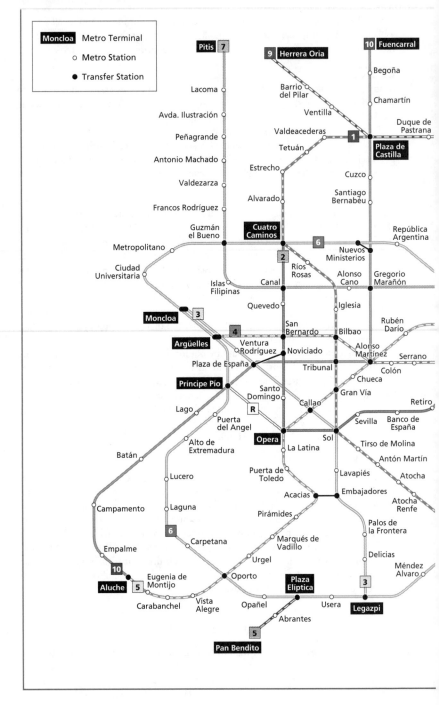

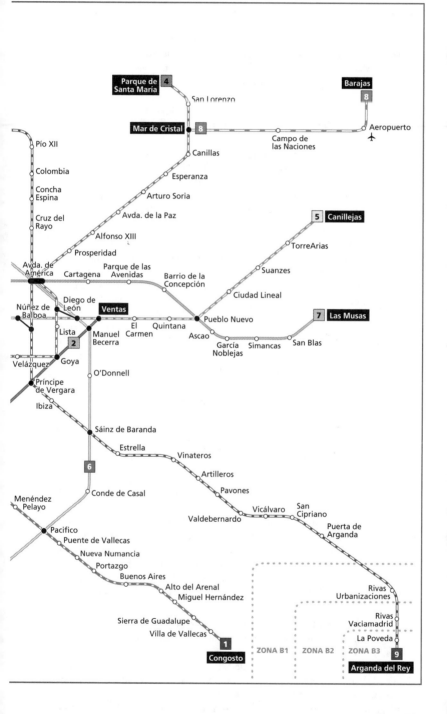

Baby-Sitters   Most major hotels can arrange for baby-sitters, called *canguros* (literally, kangaroos) or *niñeras*. Usually the concierge keeps a list of reliable nursemaids and will contact them for you provided you give adequate notice. Rates vary considerably but are usually fairly reasonable. Although many baby-sitters in Madrid speak English, don't count on it. You may also want to contact La Casa de la Abuela (☎ **91-574-30-94**). Located in the prestigious Barrio Salamanca, this "grandmother's house" is basically a children's hotel and offers child care combined with creative exercises and workshops in a child-friendly environment. It is open year-round and prices vary.

Car Rentals   Should you want to rent a car while in Madrid, you have several choices. In addition to its office at Barajas Airport (☎ 91-393-72-22), **Avis** has a main office in the city center at Gran Vía, 60 (☎ 91-305-48-55). **Hertz,** too, has an office at Barajas Airport (☎ 91-393-72-28), and another in the heart of Madrid in the Edificio España, Gran Vía, 88 (☎ 91-542-58-05). **Budget** maintains its headquarters at Gran Vía, 49 (☎ 91-393-72-16). It's known in Spain as Inter-rent.

Currency Exchange   The currency exchange at Chamartín railway station (metro: Chamartín) is open 24 hours and gives the best rates in the capital. If you exchange money at a bank, ask about the minimum commission charged.

Many banks in Spain still charge a 1% to 2% commission with a minimum charge of 500 pesetas (US$3). However, branches of Banco Central Hispano charge no commission. Branches of El Corte Inglés, the department store chain, offer currency exchange facilities at various rates. You get the worst rates at street kiosks such as Chequepoint, Exact Change, and Cambios-Uno. Although they're handy and charge no commission, their rates are very low. Naturally, American Express offices offer the best rates on their own checks. ATMs are plentiful in Madrid.

Dentists   For an English-speaking dentist, contact the U.S. Embassy, Serrano, 75 (☎ **91-587-22-00**); it maintains a list of dentists who have offered their services to Americans abroad. For dental services, also consult Unidad Médica Anglo-Americana, Conde de Arandá, 1 (☎ **91-435-18-23**). Office hours are Monday to Friday 9am to 8pm and Saturday 10am to 1pm, and there is a 24-hour answering service.

Doctors   For an English-speaking doctor, contact the U.S. Embassy, Serrano, 75 (☎ **91-587-22-00**).

Drugstores   For a late-night pharmacy, dial ☎ **098** or look in the daily newspaper under *Farmacias de Guardia* to learn which drugstores are open after 8pm. Another way to find one is to go to any pharmacy, which, even if closed, will always post a list of nearby pharmacies that are open late that day. Madrid contains hundreds of pharmacies, but one of the most central is Farmacia Gayoso, Arenal 2 (☎ **91-521-28-60;** metro: Puerta del Sol). It is open Monday to Saturday, 24 hours a day.

Embassies & Consulates   If you lose your passport, fall seriously ill, get into legal trouble, or have some other serious problem, your embassy or consulate will probably have the means to provide assistance. These are the Madrid addresses and hours: The **U.S. Embassy,** at calle Serrano, 75 (☎ 91-587-22-00; metro: Núñez de Balboa), is open Monday to Friday 9:30am to noon and 3 to 5pm. The **Canadian Embassy,** Núñez de Balboa, 35 (☎ 91-423-32-50; metro: Velázquez), is open Monday to Friday 9am to 12:30pm. The **U.K. Embassy,**

calle Fernando el Santo, 16 (☎ 91-319-02-00; metro: Colón), is open Monday to Friday 9am to 2pm and 3:30 to 6pm. The **Republic of Ireland Embassy** is at Claudio Coello, 73 (☎ 91-576-35-00; metro: Serrano); it's open Monday to Friday 10am to 2pm. The **Australian Embassy,** Plaza Diego de Ordas 3, Edificio Santa Engracia 120 (☎ 91-441-93-00; metro: Rios Rosas), is open Monday to Thursday 8:30am to 1:30pm and 2:30 to 5pm, and Friday from 8:30am to 2pm. The **New Zealand Embassy** is at Plaza de la Lealtad, 2 (☎ 91-523-02-26; metro: Banco de España); it's open Monday to Friday 9am to 1:30pm and 2:30 to 5:30pm.

Hospitals/Clinics   Unidad Médica Anglo-Americana, Conde de Arandá, 1 (☎ **91-435-18-23;** metro: Usera), is not a hospital but a private outpatient clinic, offering the services of various specialists. This is not an emergency clinic, although someone on the staff is always available. The daily hours are 9am to 8pm. For a real medical emergency, call ☎ **112** for an ambulance.

Internet Access   Head for **Net Café,** San Bernardo, 81 (☎ **91-595-09-99;** e-mail: netcafe@netcafe.es), open daily 11am to 2am, if you've just gotta check your e-mail.

Laundry & Dry Cleaning   Try a self-service facility, Lavandería Donoso Cortés, Donoso Cortés, 17 (☎ **91-446-96-90;** metro: Quevedo); it's open Monday to Friday 9am to 2pm and 3:30 to 8pm, Saturday 9am to 2pm. A good dry-cleaning service is provided by El Corte Inglés department store at calle Preciados, 3 (☎ **91-379-80-00;** metro: Callao), where the staff speaks English.

Luggage Storage & Lockers   These can be found at both the Atocha and Chamartín railway terminals, as well as the major bus station at the Estación Sur de Autobuses, calle Méndez Alvaro (☎ **91-468-42-00;** metro: Méndez Alvaro). Storage is also provided at the air terminal underneath the Plaza de Colón.

Newspapers & Magazines   The Paris-based *International Herald Tribune* is sold at most newsstands in the tourist districts, as is *USA Today,* plus the European editions of *Time* and *Newsweek. Guía del Ocio,* a small magazine sold in newsstands, contains entertainment listings and addresses, though in Spanish only.

Police   In an emergency, dial ☎ **112.**

Post Office   If you don't want to receive your mail at your hotel or the American Express office, direct it to *Lista de Correos* at the central post office in Madrid. To pick up mail, go to the window marked *Lista,* where you'll be asked to show your passport. Madrid's central office is in Palacio de Comunicaciones at Plaza de la Cibeles (☎ **91-396-20-00**).

Radio & TV   On short-wave radio you can hear the Voice of America and the BBC daily. There is also an English-language radio program in Madrid called "Buenos Días" (Good Morning), which airs many useful hints for visitors; it's broadcast Monday to Friday 6 to 8am on 657 megahertz. Radio 80 broadcasts news in English Monday to Saturday 7 to 8am on 89 FM. Some TV programs are broadcast in English in the summer months. Many hotels—but regrettably not most of our budget ones—also bring in satellite TV programs in English.

Rest Rooms   Some public rest rooms are available, including those in the Parque del Retiro and on Plaza de Oriente across from the Palacio Real. Otherwise, you can always go into a bar or tasca, but you should order something. The major department stores, such as Galerías Preciados and El Corte Inglés, have good, clean rest rooms.

Safety   Because of an increasing crime rate in Madrid, the U.S. Embassy has warned visitors to leave valuables in a hotel safe or other secure place when going out. Your passport may be needed, however, as the police often stop foreigners for identification checks. The embassy advises against carrying purses and suggests that you keep valuables in front pockets and carry only enough cash for the day's needs. Be aware of those around you and keep a separate record of your passport number, traveler's check numbers, and credit-card numbers.

Purse snatching is common, and criminals often work in pairs, grabbing purses from pedestrians, cyclists, and even from cars. A popular scam involves one miscreant's smearing the back of the victim's clothing, perhaps with mustard, ice cream, or something worse. An accomplice then pretends to help clean up the mess, all the while picking the victim's pockets.

Every car can be a target, parked or just stopped at a light, so don't leave anything in sight in your vehicle. If a car is standing still, a thief may open the door or break a window in order to snatch a purse or package, even from under the seat. Place valuables in the trunk when you park and always assume that someone is watching to see whether you're putting something away for safekeeping. Keep the car locked while driving.

Taxes   There are no special city taxes for tourists, except for the VAT (value-added tax; known as IVA in Spain) levied nationwide on all goods and services, ranging from 7% to 33%. In Madrid the only city taxes are for home and car owners, which need not concern the casual visitor. For information on how to recover VAT, see "Shopping" in chapter 6.

Telephone   If you don't speak Spanish, you'll find it easier to telephone from your hotel, but remember that this is often very expensive because hotels impose a surcharge on every operator-assisted call. In some cases this can be as high as 40% or more. On the street, phone booths (known as *cabinas*) have dialing instructions in English; you can make local calls by inserting a 25 peseta (US15¢) coin for 3 minutes. In Spain many smaller establishments, especially bars, discos, and a few low-cost restaurants, don't have phones. For long-distance calls, especially transatlantic ones, it may be best to go to the main telephone exchange, Locutorio Gran Vía, Gran Vía, 30; or Locutorio Recoletos, Paseo de Recoletos, 37–41. You may not be lucky enough to find an English-speaking operator, but you can fill out a simple form that will facilitate the placement of your call.

In 1998, all telephone numbers in Spain changed to a nine-digit system. Each number is now preceded by its provincial code for local, national, and international calls. For example, when calling to Madrid from Madrid or another province within Spain, telephone customers must dial 91-123-45-67.

To call Spain from another country, first dial the international long-distance code **011** plus the country code **34,** followed by the 9-digit number. Hence, when calling Madrid from the United States, dial **(011-34)** 91-123-45-67.

To make an international call from Spain, you must dial **07,** followed by the country code, the area code, and the telephone number.

When in Spain, the access number for an **AT&T** calling card is ☎ **1-800-callATT.** The access number for **Sprint** is ☎ **800/888-0013.**

More information is also available on the Teléfonica Web site at **www. telefonica.es**.

3 Where to Stay

Though expensive, Madrid's hotels are among the finest in the world. The city's much-maligned reputation, earned in the days of Franco, is but a long, distant, and unpleasant memory: No more rooms last renovated in 1870 or food that tastes of acidic olive oil left over from the Spanish-American War.

More than 50,000 hotel rooms blanket the city—from *grand luxe* bedchambers fit for a prince to bunker-style beds in the hundreds of neighborhood *hostales* and *pensiones* (low-cost boardinghouses). Three-quarters of our recommendations are modern, yet many guests prefer the landmarks of yesteryear, including those grand old establishments, the Ritz and the Palace (ca. 1910–12). *But beware:* Many older hostelries in Madrid haven't kept abreast of the times; a handful haven't added improvements or overhauled bedrooms substantially since the 1960s.

Traditionally, hotels are clustered around the Atocha Railway Station and the Gran Vía. In our search for the most outstanding hotels, we've downplayed these two popular, but noisy, districts. The newer hotels have been built away from the center, especially on residential streets jutting off from Paseo de la Castellana. Bargain seekers, however, will still find great pickings along the Gran Vía and in the Atocha district.

In inexpensive hotels, be warned that you'll have to carry your bags to and from your room. Don't expect bellboys or doormen in cheaper hotels.

Note: Mention of private bathrooms is made *only* if all the rooms in the hotel in question do *not* come with a bathroom. Also, breakfast is not included in the quoted rates unless otherwise specified. A 7% government room tax is added to all rates.

RESERVATIONS Most hotels require at least a day's deposit before they will reserve a room for you. Preferably, this can be accomplished with an international money order or, if agreed to in advance, with a personal check or credit-card number. You can usually cancel a room reservation one week ahead of time and get a full refund. A few hotel keepers will return your money up to three days before the reservation date, but some will take your deposit and never return it, even if you cancel far in advance. Many budget hotel owners operate on such a narrow margin of profit that they find just buying stamps for airmail replies too expensive by their standards. Therefore, it's important that you enclose a prepaid International Reply Coupon with your payment, especially if you're writing to a budget hotel. Better yet, call and speak directly to the hotel of your choice or send a fax.

If you're booking into a chain hotel, such as a Hyatt or a Forte, you can call toll free in North America and easily make reservations over the phone. Whenever such a service is available, toll-free numbers are indicated in the individual hotel descriptions.

If you arrive without a reservation, begin your search for a room as early in the day as possible. If you arrive late at night, you have to take what you can get, often for a much higher price than you'd like to pay.

RATINGS Spain officially rates its hotels by star designation, from one to five stars. Five stars is the highest rating in Spain, signaling a deluxe establishment complete with all the amenities and the high tariffs associated with such accommodations.

Most of the establishments recommended in this guide are three- and four-star hotels. Hotels granted one and two stars, as well as pensions (guest houses), are less comfortable, with limited plumbing and other physical facilities, although they may be perfectly clean and decent places. The latter category is strictly for dedicated budgeters.

PARKING   As mentioned, this is a serious problem. Few hotels have garages because many buildings turned into hotels were constructed before the invention of the automobile. Street parking is rarely available, and even if it is, you run the risk of having your car broken into. If you're driving into Madrid, most hotels (and most police) will allow you to park in front of the hotel long enough to unload your luggage. Someone on the staff can usually pinpoint the location of the nearest garage in the neighborhood, often giving you a map showing the way—be prepared to walk 2 or 3 blocks to your car. Parking charges given in most hotel listings are the prices these neighborhood garages charge for an average-size vehicle.

NEAR THE PLAZA DE LAS CORTÉS
VERY EXPENSIVE

○ **Hotel Villa Real.** Plaza de las Cortés, 10, 28014 Madrid. ☎ **91-420-37-67.** Fax 91-420-25-47. www.derbyhotels.es. E-mail: info@derbyhotels.es. 115 units. A/C MINIBAR TV TEL. 50,000 ptas. (US$300) double; from 75,000 ptas. (US$450) suite. AE, DC, MC, V. Parking 2,000 ptas. (US$12). Metro: Sevilla, Banco de España.

Until 1989, Villa Real was little more than a run-down 19th-century apartment house auspiciously located across a three-sided park from the Spanish parliament (*Congreso de los Diputados*) between Puerta del Sol and Paseo del Prado. Developers poured billions of pesetas into renovations to produce a stylish hotel today patronized by the cognoscenti of Spain. The eclectic facade is an odd mixture of neoclassical and Aztec motifs; there are footmen and doormen dressed in uniforms of buff and forest green stationed out front. Villa Real's rooms are more consistent in quality than those offered by its neighbor, the Palace (see below), which can have very good or very bad rooms. But Villa Real lacks the mellow charm and patina of the Palace. The interior contains a scattering of modern paintings amid neoclassical moldings and details.

Each of the accommodations offers a TV with video movies and satellite reception, a safe for valuables, soundproofing, a sunken salon filled with leather-upholstered furniture, and built-in furniture accented with burl-wood inlays. Rooms are not imaginatively decorated but are for the most part generous in size, with separate sitting areas and big, bright, and well-equipped bathrooms.

Dining/Diversions: The social center is the high-ceilinged formal bar. The hotel's formal restaurant, **Europa,** serves both lunch and dinner, with Spanish and international cuisine.

Amenities: 24-hour room service, laundry/valet, baby-sitting, express checkout, sauna, foreign currency exchange, business center.

Palace. Plaza de las Cortés, 7, 28014 Madrid. ☎ **800/937-8461** in the U.S. and Canada, or 91-360-80-00. Fax 91-360-81-00. www.palacemadrid.com. 465 units. A/C MINIBAR TV TEL. 63,000–79,000 ptas. (US$378–US$474) double; from 79,000 ptas. (US$474) suite. AE, DC, MC, V. Parking 2,500 ptas. (US$15). Metro: Banco de España.

The Palace, an ornate Victorian wedding cake, is known as the "grand *dueña*" of Spanish hotels. The establishment had an auspicious beginning, inaugurated by King Alfonso XIII in 1912. Covering an entire city block, it faces the Prado and Neptune Fountain, in the historical and artistic area, within walking distance of the main shopping center and the best antiques shops. Some of the city's most intriguing tascas and restaurants are only a short stroll away.

Architecturally, the Palace captures the grand pre-World War I hotel style, with an emphasis on space and comfort. But it doesn't achieve the snobby appeal and chic of its nearby sibling, the Ritz, or even of the Villa Real. One of the largest hotels in Madrid, it retains first-class service. The hotel is air-conditioned with a formal, traditional lobby. The rooms are also conservative and traditional, boasting plenty of space

If You Have an Early Flight

Unless absolutely necessary, it's worth making the journey into Madrid rather than staying at rather bleak Barajas, where the airport is located. If you find that you have to stay, the least expensive option is the **Best Western Villa de Barajas,** av. De Logroño, 331 (☎ **91-329-28-18;** fax 91-329-27-04), where double rooms go for 15,000 ptas. (US$90). Each room has a TV, telephone, and offers 24-hour room service. There is also a restaurant offering traditional Spanish food. The hotel runs a free shuttle bus to and from the airport. The trip takes about 5 minutes.

and large bathrooms with lots of amenities. As was the style when the hotel was built, accommodations vary widely, with the best rooms on the fourth, fifth, and sixth floors. The noisy rooms are on the side; they also lack views. Many rooms appear not to have been renovated for two decades or so.

Dining/Diversions: The elegant **La Cupola** serves Italian specialties along with some of the more famous dishes of Spanish cuisine. Piano music and other entertainment are featured.

Amenities: 24-hour room service, laundry/valet, baby-sitting, express checkout, foreign currency exchange, business center.

INEXPENSIVE

✪ **Hostal Cervantes.** Cervantes, 34, 28014 Madrid. ☎ **91-429-27-45.** Fax 91-429-83-65. 12 units. 6,500 ptas. (US$39) double. No credit cards. Metro: Banco de España.

One of Madrid's most pleasant family-run hotels, the Cervantes has been widely appreciated by our readers for years. You'll take a tiny birdcage-style elevator to the immaculately maintained second floor of this stone-and-brick building. Each accommodation contains a bed and spartan furniture. No breakfast is served, but the owners, the Alfonsos, will direct you to a nearby cafe. The establishment is convenient to the Prado, Retiro Park, and the older sections of Madrid.

NEAR THE PLAZA ESPAÑA
EXPENSIVE

Crowne Plaza Madrid City Centre. Plaza de España, 28013 Madrid. ☎ **800/465-4329** in the U.S., or 91-454-85-00. Fax 91-548-23-89. www.crowneplaza.es. E-mail: reservas@ crowneplaza.es. 306 units. A/C MINIBAR TV TEL. 39,167 ptas. (US$235) double; from 53,410 ptas. (US$320.45) suite. AE, DC, MC, V. Parking 1,600 ptas. (US$9.60). Metro: Plaza de España.

Built in 1953 atop a city garage, the Plaza Hotel could be called the Waldorf-Astoria of Spain. A massive rose-and-white structure, it soars upward to a central tower 26 stories high. It is a landmark visible for miles around and one of the tallest skyscrapers in Europe. Once one of the best hotels in Spain, the Plaza has long since ceased to be a market leader. The hotel's accommodations include conventional doubles as well as luxurious suites, each containing a sitting room and abundant amenities. Each accommodation, regardless of its size, has a marble bathroom. Furniture is usually of a standardized modern style, in harmonized colors. Upper-floor rooms are quieter.

Dining/Diversions: Los Lagos is the breakfast room of the hotel, and a tempting regional Spanish cuisine is offered nightly in the main restaurant, **Mirador de la Plaza de España.** The **Plaza** cocktail bar is a major gathering point for businesspeople.

Amenities: Room service, laundry, money exchange, medical service, hairdresser, shopping arcade, gym, whirlpool, sauna.

Central Madrid Accommodations

Anaco **30**
Aristos **20**
Casón del Tormes **7**
Castellana Inter-Continental
  Hotel **20**
Conde Duque **10**
Crowne Plaza Madrid City
  Centre **11**
Cuzco **20**
Emperatriz **20**
Eurobuilding **20**
Gran Hotel Colón **22**
Gran Hotel Reina Victoria **35**
Gran Hotel Velázquez **21**
Green Hotel el Prado **36**
Hostal Alcázar Regis **12**
Hostal Buenos Aires **13**
Hostal Cervantes **25**
Hostal la Macarena **2**
Hostal la Perla Asturiana **33**
Hostal Nuevo Gaos **16**
Hostal Residencia
  Americano **32**
Hostal Residencia
  Don Diego **21**
Hostal Residencia
  Principado **28**
Hostal-Residencia
  Continental **15**
Hotel Atlántico **14**
Hotel Chamartin **20**
Hotel Claridge **23**
Hotel Escultor **19**
Hotel Francisco I **3**
Hotel Gaudí **29**
Hotel Inglés **39**
Hotel Mercátor **24**
Hotel Nuria **17**
Hotel Opera **5**
Hotel Paris **40**
Hotel Puerta de Toledo **1**
Hotel Residencia Cortezo **34**
Hotel Residencia Lisboa **37**
Hotel Residencia
  Santander **39**
Hotel Santo Domingo **6**
Hotel Villa Real **38**
Husa Princesa **8**
Meliá Castilla **20**
Meliá Madrid Princesa **9**
Miguel Angel **19**
NH Nacional **27**
Novotel Madrid **20**
Palace **38**
Park Hyatt Villa Magna **20**
Residencia Liabeny **31**
Ritz **26**
Santo Mauro Hotel **18**
Tirol **8**
Tryp Ambassador **4**
Wellington **21**

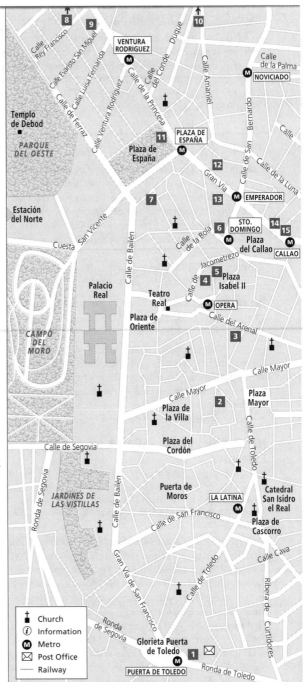

✝ Church
ⓘ Information
Ⓜ Metro
✉ Post Office
--- Railway

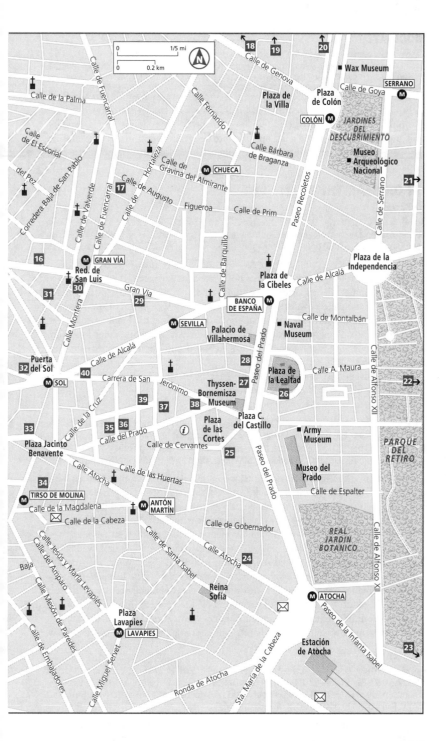

MODERATE

Casón del Tormes. Calle del Río, 7, 28013 Madrid. ☎ **91-541-97-46.** Fax 91-541-18-52.
E-mail: hotormes@infonegocio.com. 63 units. A/C TV TEL. 15,000 ptas. (US$90) double;
18,000 ptas. (US$108) triple. MC, V. Parking 2,100 ptas. (US$12.60). Metro: Plaza de España.

This attractive three-star hotel is around the corner from the Royal Palace and Plaza
de España. Set behind a four-story red brick facade with stone-trimmed windows, it
overlooks a quiet one-way street. The long, narrow lobby contains vertical wooden
paneling, a marble floor, and a bar opening into a separate room. The guest rooms are
not spectacular, but generally roomy and comfortable. Motorists appreciate the public parking lot nearby. Laundry service is provided.

ON OR NEAR THE GRAN VÍA
EXPENSIVE

Hotel Gaudí. Gran Vía, 9, 28013 Madrid. ☎ **91-531-22-22.** Fax 91-531-54-69. www.
hoteles-catalonia.es. E-mail: catalon@hoteles-catalonia.es. 88 units. A/C MINIBAR TV TEL.
26,900 ptas. (US$161.40) double; 40,000 ptas. (US$240) suite. AE, DC, MC, V. Metro: Gran Vía.

In a turn-of-the-century building in the heart of Madrid, this hotel is located in a
landmark Modernist building which has been beautifully restored. It was constructed
in 1898 by Emilio Salas y Cortes, one of the teachers of the great Barcelona architect,
Gaudí. It was completely overhauled and expanded in 1998. Some of the most important attractions of Madrid are within an easy walk, including the Prado, the Thyssen
Museum, and the Plaza Mayor with its rustic taverns. The bedrooms come in a number of sizes, but each is comfortably furnished and beautifully maintained with hair
dryers and safes.

Dining/Diversions: The hotel operates a restaurant serving Spanish and international food, and there is also a separate snack bar.

Amenities: Fitness center, whirlpool, and sauna.

✪ **Hotel Santo Domingo.** Plaza Santo Domingo, 13, 28013 Madrid. ☎ **91-547-98-00.**
Fax 91-547-59-95. 120 units. A/C MINIBAR TV TEL. Mon–Thurs 28,000 ptas. (US$168) double;
Fri–Sun 21,000 ptas. (US$126) double. Breakfast free Sat–Mon mornings; otherwise 1,450 ptas.
(US$8.70) extra. AE, DC, MC, V. Parking 2,500 ptas. (US$15). Metro: Santo Domingo.

This is a stylish, carefully decorated hotel whose five floors rise from a position adjacent to the Gran Vía, a 2-minute walk from the Plaza de España. It was inaugurated
in 1994, when an older building was radically gutted and reconfigured into the comfortable modern structure you see today. Guest rooms are each decorated individually,
in a style that's just a wee bit different from that of its neighbor, in pastel-derived
shades of pink, green, blue, and yellow. Some units contain gold damask wall cover-
ings, faux-tortoiseshell desks, and striped satin bedspreads. Bathrooms are generally
spacious and outfitted with ceramics and gray marble slabs. The best units are the
fifth-floor doubles, especially those with furnished balconies and views over the tile
roofs of Old Madrid. Each is carefully soundproofed to guard against noises from the
street and from its neighbors and contains phones with personal answering machines.
There's a bar and a restaurant in the hotel's lobby, serving lunch and dinner every day.

MODERATE

Hotel Atlántico. Gran Vía, 38, 28013 Madrid. ☎ **800/528-1234** in the U.S. and Canada, or
91-522-64-80. Fax 91-531-02-10. www.hotel-atlantico.com. E-mail: hatlantico@mad.servicom.es.
80 units. A/C MINIBAR TV TEL. 20,000 ptas. (US$120) double. Rates include breakfast. AE, DC,
MC, V. Parking 2,000 ptas. (US$12). Metro: Gran Vía.

Refurbished in stages between the late 1980s and 1994, this hotel occupies five floors
of a grand turn-of-the-century building on one of Madrid's most impressive avenues.

Established in 1989 as a Best Western affiliate, it offers security boxes in relatively unadorned but well-maintained guest rooms, which have been insulated against noise. Accommodations are rather small. The hotel contains an English-inspired bar serving drinks and snacks that's open 24 hours a day.

Residencia Liabeny. Salud, 3, 28013 Madrid. ☎ **91-531-90-00.** Fax 91-532-74-21. 222 units. A/C MINIBAR TV TEL. 16,000 ptas. (US$96) double; 18,000–23,000 ptas. (US$108–US$138) triple. AE, MC, V. Parking 1,500 ptas. (US$9). Metro: Puerta del Sol or Gran Vía.

The Liabeny, behind a stone-sheathed, austere rectangular facade, is in a prime location midway between the tourist highlights of the Gran Vía and Puerta del Sol. Named after the original owner of the hotel, it contains seven floors of comfortable, contemporary guest rooms, which even though newly redecorated are a bit too pristine for our taste. The cocktail bar is more warming, although in a rather macho style, and the dining room is strictly for convenience. A coffee shop is also on the premises, and good laundry service and rather personalized attention from the staff add to the appeal of the place.

INEXPENSIVE

Anaco. Tres Cruces, 3, 28013 Madrid. ☎ **91-522-46-04.** Fax 91-531-64-84. 39 units. A/C TV TEL. 10,000–12,500 ptas. (US$60–US$75) double; 14,000–17,000 ptas. (US$84–US$102) triple. AE, DC, MC, V. Parking 1,500 ptas. (US$9). Metro: Gran Vía, Callao, or Puerta del Sol.

A modest yet modern hotel, the Anaco is just off the main shopping thoroughfare, the Gran Vía. Opening onto a tree-shaded plaza, it attracts those seeking a clean resting place. The guest rooms are compact and contemporary, with built-in headboards, reading lamps, and lounge chairs. *A useful tip:* Ask for one of the five terraced rooms on the top floor, which rent at no extra charge. The hotel has a bar/cafeteria/restaurant open daily. English is spoken here. Nearby is a municipally operated garage.

Green Hotel El Prado. Calle Prado, 11, 28014 Madrid. ☎ **91-369-02-34.** Fax 91-429-28-29. E-mail: prado@green-hoteles.com. 45 units. 16,200–21,750 ptas. (US$102.05–US$137.05) double. AE, MC, V. Metro: Plaza Santa Ana.

You might get the feeling that this hotel is both overbooked and understaffed. But it has comfortable rooms, relatively reasonable rates, and a well-scrubbed interior that's less than a decade old. You'll register in a somewhat claustrophobic lobby, then head upstairs to a room that's cozy and not overly large, and sleekly outfitted with contemporary-looking, full-grained walls and partitions. Other than breakfast, no meals are served.

Hostal Alcázar Regis. Gran Vía, 61, 28013 Madrid. ☎ **91-547-93-17.** 25 units. 6,500 ptas. (US$39) double; 8,500 ptas. (US$51) triple. No credit cards. Metro: Plaza de España or Santo Domingo.

Conveniently located in the midst of Madrid's best shops is this post–World War II building, complete with a circular Greek-style temple as its crown. On the building's fifth floor, you'll find long and pleasant public rooms, wood paneling, lead glass windows, parquet floors, crystal chandeliers, and high-ceilinged guest rooms, each with a new bathroom.

Hostal Buenos Aires. Gran Vía, 61, 28013 Madrid. ☎ **91-542-01-02.** Fax 91-542-28-69. 25 units. A/C TV TEL. 8,000 ptas. (US$48) double. AE, DC, MC, V. Metro: Plaza de España or Santo Domingo. Bus: 1, 2, or 44.

To reach this place, you pass through a marble-covered street-floor lobby within a 1955 building, then take the elevator to the second floor. The hostal occupies two floors; one of its best features is a wood-sheathed cafe/bar that's open 24 hours a day.

Guest rooms are comfortable, modern, and clean, although a bit small, with safety deposit boxes, balconies, and hair dryers.

Hostal Nuevo Gaos. Calle Mesonero Romanos, 14, 28013 Madrid. ☎ **91-532-71-07.** 23 units. A/C TV TEL. 7,500–8,500 ptas. (US$45–US$51) double. AE, DC, MC, V. Parking 1,500 ptas. (US$9). Metro: Callao or Gran Vía.

On the second, third, and fourth floors of a 1930s building just off the Gran Vía, this *residencia* offers guests the chance to enjoy a comfortable standard of living at moderate rates. The place lies directly north of Puerta del Sol, across the street from the popular flamenco club Torre Bermejas. Breakfast can be taken at a nearby cafe.

✪ **Hostal-Residencia Continental.** Gran Vía, 44, 28013 Madrid. ☎ **91-521-46-40.** Fax 91-521-46-49. www.hostalcontinental.com. E-mail: continental@mundivia.es. 29 units. TV TEL. 6,206 ptas. (US$37.25) double. AE, DC, MC, V. Parking 2,500 ptas. (US$15) nearby. Metro: Callao. Bus: 1, 2, 36, or 46.

Sprawling over the third and fourth floors of Gran Vía, 44, this hostal is a bit more expensive than the other accommodations in the building, but the rooms are comfortable, tidy, and renovated, and the desk clerk speaks English. The Continental is in a virtual house of budget hotels, a 19th-century building filled exclusively with small hotels and pensions. If no room is available at the Continental, you can ring the doorbells of the other establishments because the entire building is a good bet for the budget tourist. No breakfast is served.

Hotel Nuria. Fuencarral, 52, 28004 Madrid. ☎ **91-531-92-08.** Fax 91-532-90-05. 80 units. TV TEL. 6,640 ptas. (US$39.85) double. Rates include breakfast. AE, DC, MC, V. Metro: Gran Vía or Tribunal. Bus: 3, 7, or 40.

Hotel Nuria, just three blocks from the Gran Vía, has some guest rooms with especially interesting views of the capital. Furnishings are simple and functional. A bar, restaurant, and TV lounge are available to guests. The hotel was last renovated in 1986.

NEAR THE PUERTA DEL SOL
EXPENSIVE

✪ **Gran Hotel Reina Victoria.** Plaza Santa Ana, 14, 28012 Madrid. ☎ **91-531-45-00.** Fax 91-522-03-07. www.trynet.com. E-mail: invasuie@trynet.com. 201 units. A/C MINIBAR TV TEL. From 30,000 ptas. (US$180) double; from 65,000 ptas. (US$390) suite. AE, DC, MC, V. Parking 1,750 ptas. (US$10.50). Metro: Tirso de Molina or Puerta del Sol.

This establishment is about as important to the legends of Madrid as the famous bullfighter Manolete himself. He used to stay here, giving lavish parties in one of the reception rooms and attracting mobs in the square below when he went out on his balcony for morning coffee. Since the recent renovation and upgrading of this property by Spain's Tryp Hotel Group, it's less staid and more impressive than ever.

Originally built in 1923 and named after the grandmother of the present king of Spain, Juan Carlos, the hotel sits behind an ornate and eclectic stone facade, which the Spanish government protects as a historic monument. Although it's located in a congested and noisy neighborhood in the center of town, the Reina Victoria opens onto its own sloping plaza, once a meeting place for 17th-century intellectuals. Today the area is usually filled with flower vendors, older people reclining in the mid-afternoon sun, and young people resting between bouts at the dozens of neighborhood tapas bars.

Each of the hotel's guest rooms contains sound-resistant insulation, a safe for valuables, and a private bathroom with many amenities.

Dining/Diversions: Guests enjoy the hotel's stylish and popular lobby bar, the **Manuel Gonzalez Manolete;** the lavishly displayed bullfighting memorabilia and potent drinks add another attraction to an already memorable hotel. The in-house restaurant is **El Ruedo.**

Amenities: 24-hour room service, concierge, baby-sitting. Because of the hotel's position in one of Madrid's most interesting neighborhoods, almost anything is available within a few minutes' walk.

Tryp Ambassador. Cuesta Santo Domingo, 5 and 7, 28013 Madrid. ☎ **91-541-67-00.** Fax 91-559-10-40. E-mail: ambassador@trypnet.com. 182 units. A/C MINIBAR TV TEL. 28,000 ptas. (US$168) double; from 38,000 ptas. (US$228) suite. AE, DC, MC, V. Metro: Opera or Santo Domingo.

In the early 1990s, the well-respected Tryp hotel chain renovated and massively enlarged—with the construction of a severely dignified annex—the late-19th-century palace of the dukes of Granada. The result today is a lavishly restored, four-story historic hotel, with suitably grand public areas, that's interconnected via a sunny lobby to a six-story annex that contains about 60% of the establishment's guest rooms. Regardless of their location within the much-expanded premises, units are conservatively modern, and outfitted in a combination of white and salmon accented with touches of mahogany.

Dining/Diversions: There's a restaurant on the premises, **El Madroño,** with a greenhouse-style bar lavishly filled with plants and caged exotic birds.

Amenities: Room service, dry cleaning/laundry, concierge, baby-sitting.

MODERATE

✪ **Hotel Opera.** Cuesta de Santo Domingo, 2, 28013 Madrid. ☎ **91-541-28-00.** Fax 91-541-69-23. E-mail: hotelopera@phoenix.net. 79 units. A/C TV TEL. 15,000 ptas. (US$90) double. AE, DC, MC, V. Parking 2,000 ptas. (US$12). Metro: Opera.

Don't judge this little discovery by its dreary gray facade or its narrow little windows; it livens up considerably once you enter. Set close to the royal palace and the opera house, this hotel isn't regal, but it offers first-rate comfort and a warm welcome from its English-speaking staff. Guest rooms range from medium in size to surprisingly spacious, each fitted with first-rate furnishings, including twin or double beds. Bathrooms are also excellent, clad in marble with dual basins. The hotel's lovely El Café de la Opera is a popular rendezvous point, even if you're not a guest. It's adorned with fabric-covered walls and horse-y art. The Opera remains one of Madrid's relatively undiscovered boutique hotels.

INEXPENSIVE

✪ **Hostal la Macarena.** Cava de San Miguel, 8, 28005 Madrid. ☎ **91-365-92-21.** Fax 91-364-27-57. 25 units. TEL. 8,000 ptas. (US$48) double; 10,000 ptas. (US$60) triple; 13,000 ptas. (US$78) quad. MC, V. Metro: Puerta del Sol, Opera, or La Latina.

Known for its reasonable prices and praised by readers for the warmth of its reception, this unpretentious, clean hostal is run by the Ricardo González family. Its 19th-century facade, accented with belle époque patterns, stands in ornate contrast to the chiseled simplicity of the ancient buildings facing it. The location is one of the hostal's assets: It's on a street (an admittedly noisy one) immediately behind Plaza Mayor, near one of the best clusters of *tascas* in Madrid. Windows facing the street have double panes.

Hostal la Perla Asturiana. Plaza de Santa Cruz, 3, 28012 Madrid. ☎ **91-366-46-00.** Fax 91-366-46-08. www.perlaasturiana.com. E-mail: perlaasturiana@mundivia.es. 33 units. TV TEL. 6,200 ptas. (US$37.20) double; 8,500 ptas. (US$51) triple. MC, V. Metro: Puerta del Sol.

Ideal for those who want to stay in the heart of old Madrid (1 block off Plaza Mayor and 2 blocks from Puerta del Sol), this small family-run establishment has a courteous staff member at the desk 24 hours a day for security and convenience. You can socialize in the small, comfortable lobby that's adjacent to the reception desk. The guest rooms are clean and simple, but often cramped; fresh towels are supplied daily. Many inexpensive restaurants and tapas bars are nearby. No breakfast is served.

Hostal Residencia Americano. Puerta del Sol, 11, 28013 Madrid. ☎ **91-522-28-22.** Fax 91-522-11-92. 44 units. TV TEL. 6,500 ptas. (US$39) double; 8,500 ptas. (US$51) triple; 9,500 ptas. (US$57) quad. AE, MC, V. Metro: Puerta del Sol.

Americano, on the third floor of a five-story building, is suitable for those who want to be right in Puerta del Sol. Owner/manager A. V. Franceschi has refurbished all the guest rooms, most of them outside chambers with balconies facing the street. Mr. Franceschi promises hot and cold running water 24 hours a day. No breakfast is served.

Hostal Residencia Principado. Zorrilla, 7, 28014 Madrid. ☎ **91-429-81-87.** http://hrprincipado.turin.com. E-mail: hr.principado@wanadoo.es. 15 units. TV. 6,500 ptas. (US$39) double. AE, MC, V. Parking 2,200 ptas. (US$13.20). Metro: Sevilla or Banco de España. Bus: 5, 9, or 53.

The two-star Principado is a real find. Located in a well-kept townhouse, it is run by a gracious owner, who keeps everything clean and inviting. New tiles, attractive bedspreads, and curtains give the rooms a fresh look. Safety boxes are provided. For breakfast, you can go to a nearby cafe. English is spoken.

Hotel Francisco I. Arenal, 15, 28013 Madrid. ☎ **91-548-43-14.** Fax 91-542-28-99. 58 units. TV TEL. 12,000 ptas. (US$72) double. Rates include breakfast. AE, DC, MC, V. Parking 2,200 ptas. (US$13.20). Metro: Puerta del Sol or Ópera.

Here you can rent clean, modern rooms. There's a pleasant lounge and a bar, and on the sixth floor you'll find a comfortable, rustically decorated restaurant. The hotel was considerably modernized in 1993, with the addition of new bathrooms as well as air-conditioning in most of the guest rooms. The hotel provides 24-hour room service and laundry and valet service.

Hotel Inglés. Calle Echegaray, 8, 28014 Madrid. ☎ **91-429-65-51.** Fax 91-420-24-23. 58 units. TV TEL. 13,000 ptas. (US$78) double; 16,000 ptas. (US$96) suite. AE, DC, MC, V. Parking 1,300 ptas. (US$7.80). Metro: Puerta del Sol or Sevilla.

You'll find the Hotel Inglés on a central street lined with *tascas*, although the hotel also operates its own 24-hour cafeteria. Today it's more modern and impersonal than it was when Virginia Woolf made it her address in Madrid. Behind a redbrick facade you'll find unpretentious and contemporary guest rooms, all well maintained. The comfortable armchairs in the TV lounge are likely to be filled with avid soccer fans. The lobby is air-conditioned, although the guest rooms are not. Guests who open their windows at night are likely to hear noise from the enclosed courtyard, so light sleepers beware.

Hotel Paris. Alcalá, 2, 28014 Madrid. ☎ **91-521-64-96.** Fax 91-531-01-88. 121 units. A/C TV TEL. 13,000 ptas. (US$78) double. Rates include breakfast. AE, DC, MC, V. Metro: Puerta del Sol.

Originally built in a grandiose style in the 1870s, when it was undoubtedly more chic than it is today, this hotel occupies a prime location adjacent to the hysterical traffic of the Puerta del Sol. It contains five floors of simple but clean and comfortable guest rooms, each with parquet floors, white walls, plain furnishings, and views that extend either out over the surrounding neighborhood or over a calm and quiet courtyard. Something about the dark-paneled lobby might remind you of the old-fashioned, hot and somnolent Spain of long ago. There's a high-ceilinged dining room one floor above lobby level, serving wholesome, uncomplicated meals every day at lunch and dinner. This hotel is a good bargain for Madrid if your tastes aren't too demanding, if you're not a budding decorator, and if you want a central location.

Hotel Residencia Lisboa. Ventura de la Vega, 17, 28014 Madrid. ☎ **91-429-98-94.** Fax 91-369-41-96. E-mail: hostallisboa@inves.es. 27 units. 7,500 ptas. (US$45) double. AE, DC, MC, V. Parking 2,200 ptas. (US$13.20). Metro: Puerta del Sol.

The Lisboa, on Madrid's most famous restaurant street, can be a bit noisy, but that's our only complaint. The hotel is a neat, modernized townhouse with compact rooms and a staff that speaks five languages. The Lisboa does not serve breakfast, but budget dining rooms, cafes, and tascas surround it.

Hotel Residencia Santander. Calle Echegaray, 1, 28014 Madrid. ☎ **91-429-95-51.** Fax 91-369-10-78. 38 units. TEL. 8,000 ptas. (US$48) double. MC, V. Metro: Puerta del Sol.

A snug little hotel just off Puerta del Sol, the Santander is a refurbished 1930 house with adequate rooms, some of which contain TVs. Although it's on a teeming street, you might appreciate the nonstop local atmosphere. Restaurants and bars in the area are active day and night. No breakfast is served.

NEAR ATOCHA STATION
MODERATE

Hotel Mercátor. Calle Atocha, 123, 28012 Madrid. ☎ **91-429-05-00.** Fax 91-369-12-52. 89 units. MINIBAR TV TEL. 13,500 ptas. (US$81) double; 14,500 ptas. (US$87) suite. AE, DC, MC, V. Parking 1,740 ptas. (US$10.45). Metro: Atocha or Antón Martín.

Only a 3-minute walk from the Prado, Centro de Arte Reina Sofía, and the Thyssen-Bornemisza museums, the Mercátor is orderly, well run, and clean, with enough comforts and conveniences to please the weary traveler. The public rooms are simple, outfitted in a vaguely modern type of minimalism. Some of the guest rooms are more inviting than others, especially those with desks and armchairs. Twenty-one units are air-conditioned. The Mercátor is a *residencia*—that is, it offers breakfast only and does not have a formal restaurant for lunch and dinner; however, it has a bar and cafeteria serving light meals, such as *platos combinados* (combination plates). The hotel has a garage and is within walking distance of American Express. Laundry service is provided, plus room service 7am to 10pm.

NH Nacional. Paseo del Prado 48, 28014 Madrid. ☎ **91-429-66-29.** Fax 91-369-15-64. E-mail: nhnacional@nh-hoteles.es. 214 units. A/C MINIBAR TV TEL. 24,100 ptas. (US$151.85) double; 55,000 ptas. (US$346.50) suite. AE, DC, MC, V. Metro: Atocha.

Around 1900, this stately looking hotel was built to house the hundreds of railway passengers flooding into Madrid through the nearby Atocha railway station. In 1997, a well-respected nationwide chain, NH Hotels, ripped out much of the building's then-dowdy interior, reconstructing the public areas and bedrooms in a smooth, seamless decor that takes maximum advantage of the building's tall ceilings and large spaces. In the bedrooms the belle époque trappings of another day have been replaced with modern design and avant-garde art, giving the units a warm and welcoming ambience. Today, it's one of the three hotels that the chain is the most proud of, a destination for dozens of corporate conventions, and a cozy retreat for hundreds of visitors. On site are both a restaurant and a simple bistro-style coffee shop.

INEXPENSIVE

Hotel Residencia Cortezo. Doctor Cortezo, 3, 28012 Madrid. ☎ **91-369-01-01.** Fax 91-369-37-74. 90 units. A/C MINIBAR TV TEL. 15,000 ptas. (US$90) double; 18,000 ptas. (US$108) suite. AE, DC, MC, V. Parking 2,000 ptas. (US$12). Metro: Tirso de Molina.

Just off calle de Atocha, which leads to the railroad station of the same name, the Cortezo is a short walk from Plaza Mayor and Puerta del Sol. The accommodations are comfortable but very simply furnished, with contemporary bathrooms. The beds are springy, the colors are well chosen, and the furniture is pleasantly modern; many rooms have sitting areas with a desk and armchair. The public areas match the guest rooms in freshness. The hotel was built in 1959 and last renovated in 1989.

NEAR RETIRO/SALAMANCA
VERY EXPENSIVE

✪ **Park Hyatt Villa Magna.** Paseo de la Castellana, 22, 28046 Madrid. ☎ **800/ 223-1234** in the U.S. and Canada, or 91-587-12-34. Fax 91-431-22-86. www.madrid. hyatt.com. E-mail: hotel@villamagna.es. 182 units. A/C MINIBAR TV TEL. 72,000 ptas. (US$432) double; from 107,000 ptas. (US$642) suite. AE, DC, MC, V. Parking 2,500 ptas. (US$15). Metro: Rubén Darío.

One of the finest hotels in Europe, the nine-story Park Hyatt is faced with slabs of rose-colored granite and set behind a bank of pines and laurels on the city's most fashionable boulevard. It was already a supremely comfortable and elegant modern hotel when Hyatt International took over its management in 1990. Today it is an even finer choice than the Palace or Villa Real and is matched in luxury, ambience, and tranquillity only by the Ritz, which has a greater patina since it's much older.

The hotel was originally conceived when a handful of Spain's elite teamed up to create a setting in which their special friends, along with an array of discriminating international visitors, would be pleased to live and dine. They hired an architect, imported a French decorator (whose style is contemporary-neoclassical), planted gardens, and put the staff through an intensive training program.

Separated from the busy boulevard by a park-like garden, its has a contemporary facade. In contrast, its interior recaptures the style of Carlos IV, with paneled walls, marble floors, and bouquets of fresh flowers. Almost every film star shooting on location in Spain passes through the lobby and drawing rooms.

This luxury palace has plush but dignified guest rooms decorated in Louis XVI, English Regency, or Italian provincial style. Each comes with fresh flowers and a TV with video movies and satellite reception (including news broadcasts from the United States).

Dining/Diversions: A pianist provides entertainment in the lobby-level champagne bar. The in-house restaurant, the **Berceo,** serves international food in a glamorous setting. The hotel is known for its summer terraces, **Calalú** and Berceo, set in gardens. The former is the only terrace in Madrid where you can enjoy live jazz, performed Tuesday to Saturday.

Amenities: 24-hour room service, concierge, same-day laundry and dry cleaning, limousine service, baby-sitting, business center, health and fitness center, car rentals, barber and beauty shop, the boutique "VillaMagna," availability of both tennis and golf (15 and 25 minutes from the hotel, respectively).

✪ **The Ritz.** Plaza de la Lealtad, 5, 28014 Madrid. ☎ **800/225-5843** in the U.S. and Canada, or 91-701-67-67. Fax 91-701-67-76. www.ritz.es. E-mail: reservas@ritz.es. 158 units. A/C MINIBAR TV TEL. 60,000–85,000 ptas. (US$360–US$510) double; from 150,000 ptas. (US$900) suite. AE, DC, MC, V. Parking 4,000 ptas. (US$24). Metro: Banco de España.

An international rendezvous point of legendary renown, the Ritz is the most famous hotel in Spain and the most prestigious address in Madrid. Its name has appeared countless times in the Spanish-language tabloids that document the comings and goings of glamorous jet-setters. Encased in a turn-of-the-century shell with soaring ceilings and graceful columns, it contains all the special luxuries that world travelers have come to expect. Billions of pesetas have been spent on renovations since its acquisition in the 1980s by the British-based Forte chain. The result is a bastion of glamour where, despite modernization, great effort was expended to retain the hotel's belle époque character and architectural details.

No other Madrid hotel, except possibly the Palace, has a more varied history. One of *Les Grand Hôtels Européens,* the Ritz was built in 1908 at the command of King Alfonso XIII, with the aid of César Ritz. It looks out onto the circular Plaza de la Lealtad in the center of town, near 300-acre Retiro Park, facing the Prado, the adjacent Palacio de Villahermosa, and the Stock Exchange. The Ritz was constructed when costs were relatively low and when spaciousness, luxury, and comfort were the standard. Its facade has now been designated a historic monument.

Guest rooms contain fresh flowers, well-appointed marble bathrooms, and TVs with video movies and satellite reception. The hotel requests that male guests wear a jacket and tie after 11am in the public areas. Nonetheless, casual wear, even blue jeans, is seen at the hotel, but such guests are conspicuous by their lack of what the Spanish call *gracia.*

Dining/Diversions: The hotel maintains a formal dining room, **Restaurante Goya,** decorated in shades of cream, blue, and gold, and lined with mirrors and 16th-century Flemish tapestries. Chefs present an international menu featuring the most elaborate paella in Madrid. In time-honored Spanish tradition, guests tend to dress up here, sometimes even for breakfast. (Management stresses that this is not a resort hotel.) Guests looking for a more casual eatery usually head for the **Jardín Ritz.**

Amenities: 24-hour room service, laundry/valet, express checkout, fitness center, car-rental kiosk, business center, foreign currency exchange.

EXPENSIVE

Emperatriz. López de Hoyos, 4, 28006 Madrid. ☎ **91-563-80-88.** Fax 91-563-98-04. 158 units. A/C MINIBAR TV TEL. 26,500 ptas. (US$159) double; 65,000 ptas. (US$390) suite. AE, DC, MC, V. Metro: Rubén Darío.

This hotel is just off the wide Paseo de la Castellana. Built in the 1970s, it has been recently renovated in a combination of Laura Ashley and Spanish contemporary by Madrid's trendiest firm, Casa & Jardin. Rooms are comfortable and classically styled in cheery yellows and salmons, with pale striped wallpapers, and come with TVs that receive many different European channels. Ask for a room on the seventh floor, where you'll get a private terrace at no extra charge.

Dining/Diversions: Guests gather in the cozy lobby bar before planning their assault on Madrid for the evening. Standard Spanish and international cuisine is served in the hotel's restaurant, followed by a substantial breakfast buffet in the morning. There is also a moderately priced fixed-price lunch.

Amenities: Beauty salon, barbershop, and laundry/valet service, along with a concierge and room service.

Gran Hotel Velázquez. Calle de Velázquez, 62, 28001 Madrid. ☎ **91-575-28-00.** Fax 91-577-51-31. 146 units. A/C MINIBAR TV TEL. 21,970 ptas. (US$131.80) double; from 32,000 ptas. (US$192) suite. AE, DC, MC, V. Parking 2,200 ptas. (US$13.20). Metro: Velázquez.

Opened in 1947 on an affluent residential street near the center of town, this hotel has a 1930s-style art deco facade and a 1940s interior filled with well-upholstered furniture and richly grained paneling. Several public rooms including a bar radiate from a central oval area. As in many hotels of its era, the guest rooms vary, some large enough for entertaining, with a small but separate sitting area for reading or watching TV. All contain piped-in music. This is one of the most attractive medium-size hotels in Madrid, with plenty of comfort and convenience.

Dining/Diversions: An in-house restaurant, **Las Lanzas,** features both international and Spanish cuisine.

Amenities: Room service (8am to midnight), beauty salon, dry cleaning, laundry.

Wellington. Velázquez, 8, 28001 Madrid. ☎ **91-575-44-00.** Fax 91-576-41-64. www.hotel-wellington.com. E-mail: wellin@genio.infor.es. 288 units. A/C MINIBAR TV TEL. 38,000 ptas. (US$228) double; from 52,000 ptas. (US$312) suite. AE, DC, MC, V. Parking 2,750 ptas. (US$16.50). Metro: Retiro or Velázquez.

The Wellington, with its somber antique-tapestried entrance, is one of Madrid's more sedate deluxe hotels, built in the mid-1950s but substantially remodeled since. Set in the Salamanca residential area near Retiro Park, the Wellington offers redecorated but rather staid guest rooms, each with cable TV and movie channels, music, two phones (one in the bathroom), and combination safe. Units are furnished in English-inspired mahogany reproductions, and the bathrooms are modern and immaculate, with marble sheathing and fixtures. Doubles with private terraces (at no extra charge) are the most sought-after accommodations.

Dining/Diversions: An added bonus here is the **El Fogón** grill room, styled like a 19th-century tavern, where many of the provisions for the typically Spanish dishes are shipped in from the hotel's own ranch. The pub-style **Bar Inglés** is a hospitable rendezvous. Lighter meals are served in the **Las Llaves de Oro** (Golden Keys) cafeteria.

Amenities: 24-hour room service, same-day dry cleaning and laundry, outdoor swimming pool in summer, garage, beauty parlor.

MODERATE

✪ **Novotel Madrid.** Calle Albacete, 1 (at Avenida Badajos), 28027 Madrid. ☎ **800/ 221-4542** in the U.S. and Canada, or 91-724-76-00. Fax 91-404-11-05. www.novotel.com. 236 units. A/C MINIBAR TV TEL. 19,900 ptas. (US$119.40) double. Children 15 and under stay free in parents' room. AE, DC, MC, V. Parking 2,000 ptas. (US$12). Metro: Concepción. Exit from M-30 at Barrio de la Concepción/Parque de las Avenidas, just before reaching the city limits of central Madrid, then look for the chain's trademark electric-blue signs.

Novotel was originally intended to serve the hotel needs of a cluster of multinational corporations with headquarters 1½ miles east of the center of Madrid, but its guest rooms are so comfortable and its prices so reasonable that tourists have begun using it as well. Opened in 1986, it is located on the highway, away from the maze of sometimes confusing inner-city streets, which makes it attractive to motorists.

Bedrooms are laid out in a standardized format whose popularity in Europe has made it one of the hotel industry's most notable success stories. Each contains a well-designed bathroom, in-house movies, a radio, a TV, and soundproofing. The sofas, once their bolster pillows are removed, can be transformed into comfortable beds for children. The English-speaking staff is well versed in both sightseeing attractions and solutions to most business-related problems.

INEXPENSIVE

Gran Hotel Colón. Pez Volador, 11, 28007 Madrid. ☎ **91-573-59-00.** Fax 91-573-08-09. 359 units. A/C MINIBAR TV TEL. 19,800–23,800 ptas. (US$118.80–US$142.80) double. AE, DC, MC, V. Parking 2,000 ptas. (US$12). Metro: Sainz de Baranda.

East of Retiro Park, the Gran Hotel Colón is a few minutes from the city center by subway. Built in 1966, it offers comfortable yet reasonably priced accommodations in a modern structure. More than half of the guest rooms have private balconies, and all contain comfortably traditional furniture, much of it built-in.

Other assets include two dining rooms, a covered garage, and bingo games. One of the Colón's founders was an accomplished interior designer, which accounts for the

---

ⓘ Family-Friendly Hotels

Meliá Castilla *(see p. 148)*   Children can spend hours and all their extra energy in the hotel's swimming pool and gymnasium. On the grounds is a showroom exhibiting the latest European automobiles. Hotel services include baby-sitting.

Novotel Madrid *(see p. 144)*   Children 15 and under stay free in their parents' room, where the sofa converts into a comfortable bed. Kids delight in the open-air swimming pool and the offerings of the bountiful breakfast buffet.

Tirol *(see p. 150)*   This centrally located three-star hotel is a favorite of families seeking good comfort at moderate price. It also has a cafeteria.

---

unusual stained-glass windows and murals in the public rooms and the paintings by Spanish artists in the lounge.

Hotel Claridge. Plaza Conde de Casal, 6, 28007 Madrid. ☎ **91-551-94-00.** Fax 91-501-03-85. 150 units. A/C TV TEL. Mon–Thurs 12,800 ptas. (US$76.80), Fri–Sun 10,000 ptas. (US$60) double; Mon–Thurs 20,000 ptas. (US$120), Fri–Sun 18,000 ptas. (US$108) suite. AE, MC, V. Metro: Conde de Casal.

This contemporary building, last renovated in 1994, is beyond Retiro Park, about 5 minutes from the Prado by taxi or subway. The rooms are well organized and pleasantly styled: small and compact, with coordinated furnishings and colors. These include excellent beds and small but well-organized private bathrooms. You can take your meals in the hotel's cafeteria and also relax in the modern lounge.

SOUTH OF THE PLAZA MAYOR
INEXPENSIVE

Hotel Puerta de Toledo. Glorieta Puerta de Toledo, 4, 28005 Madrid. ☎ **91-474-71-00.** Fax 91-474-07-47. E-mail: hpto@hotel-puertodetoledo.es. 160 units. A/C MINIBAR TV TEL. 12,600–13,960 ptas. (US$79.40–US$87.95) double. AE, DC, MC, V. Metro: Puerto de Toledo.

One of the largest buildings on the square that contains it, this low-key red brick hotel was constructed in 1968. Public areas are outfitted with stone floors, angular and low-slung *moderno* furniture, and a simple decor that might remind you of the waiting lounge in a large international airport. Bedrooms are relatively small, but with big windows—most of them overlooking the square—and uncomplicated but comfortable contemporary furniture. Overall, this hotel's low prices more than compensate for its rather banal look. Only breakfast is served, but the staff will direct you to a nearby restaurant, about a block away, that's under separate management.

CHAMBERÍ
VERY EXPENSIVE

Castellana Inter-Continental Hotel. Paseo de la Castellana, 49, 28046 Madrid. ☎ **800/327-0200** in the U.S., or 91-310-02-00. Fax 91-319-58-53. 306 units. A/C MINIBAR TV TEL. 48,000–62,000 ptas. (US$288–US$372) double; from 76,500 ptas. (US$459) suite. AE, DC, MC, V. Parking 2,600 ptas. (US$15.60). Metro: Rubén Darío.

Solid, spacious, and conservatively modern, this is one of Madrid's more reliable hotels. Originally built in 1963 as the then-most-prestigious hotel on this famous boulevard, the Castellana Inter-Continental lies behind a barrier of trees within a neighborhood of apartment houses and luxury hotels. Its high-ceilinged public rooms provide a welcome refuge from the Madrileño heat and are a tribute to the art of Spanish masonry, with terrazzo floors and a large-scale collection of angular abstract murals pieced together from multicolored stones and tiles. Most of the guest rooms have private balconies and traditional furniture, each with a color TV with in-house videos and many channels from across Europe. Some rooms are in need of rejuvenation.

Dining/Diversions: The **La Ronda Bar** offers drinks near the elegant **Los Continentes Restaurant,** which serves a creative Mediterranean cuisine. In addition, **El Jardín** is the summer retreat, with candlelit dinners and live background music. Another restaurant, **El Sarracin,** provides good food at thrifty prices.

Amenities: There's a helpful concierge and a travel agent who will book theater tickets, rental cars, and airline connections; there's also 24-hour room service, laundry, baby-sitting, kiosks and boutiques, hairdresser/barbershop, business center, and top-floor gym with sauna and outdoor solarium.

Miguel Angel. Miguel Angel, 29–31, 28010 Madrid. ☎ **91-442-81-99.** Fax 91-442-53-20. 270 units. A/C MINIBAR TV TEL. 30,000–40,000 ptas. (US$180–US$240) double; from 50,000 ptas. (US$300) suite. AE, DC, MC, V. Parking 2,500 ptas. (US$15). Metro: Gregorio Maranon.

Just off Paseo de la Castellana, the sleekly modern Miguel Angel opened its doors in 1975 and has been renovated and kept up-to-date periodically ever since. It has much going for it: ideal location, contemporary styling, good furnishings, art objects, an efficient staff, and plenty of comfort. Behind its facade is an expansive sun terrace on several levels, with clusters of garden furniture surrounded by paintings of semitropical scenes.

The soundproofed guest rooms contain radios, TVs, color-coordinated fabrics and carpets, and in many cases reproductions of classic Iberian furniture.

Dining/Diversions: The **Farnesio** bar is decorated in a Spanish Victorian style, with piano music beginning at 8pm. A well-managed restaurant on the premises is the **Florencia.** Dinner is also served until around 3am in the **Zacarías Boîte,** where you can dine while watching an occasional cabaret or musical performance.

Amenities: 24-hour room service, same-day laundry/valet, indoor heated swimming pool, saunas, hairdressers, and a drugstore. Art exhibitions are sponsored in the arcade of boutiques.

✪ **Santo Mauro Hotel.** Calle Zurbano, 36, 28010 Madrid. ☎ **91-319-69-00.** Fax 91-308-54-77. E-mail: santo-mauro@itelco.es. 37 units. A/C MINIBAR TV TEL. 46,000 ptas. (US$276) double; from 60,000 ptas. (US$360) suite. AE, DC, MC, V. Parking 1,950 ptas. (US$11.70). Metro: Rubén Darío or Alonso Martínez.

This hotel opened in 1991 in what was once a neoclassical villa built in 1894 for the duke of Santo Mauro. Set within a garden and done in a French style, it's decorated with rich fabrics and art deco art and furnishings. Staff members outnumber rooms by two to one. Each of the rooms contains an audio system with a wide choice of tapes and CDs as well as many lovely details, like raw silk curtains, Persian carpets, jewel-toned colors, antique prints, and parquet floors. Rooms are of generous size and come in many combinations ranging from studios to duplex suites.

Dining/Diversions: Restaurante Belagua is reviewed separately, later in this chapter. An elegant bar is located off the main lobby, and tables are set up beneath the garden's large trees for drinks and snacks.

Amenities: 24-hour room service, laundry/valet, reception staff trained in the procurement of practically anything, indoor swimming pool, health club with sauna and massage.

EXPENSIVE

Conde Duque. Plaza Conde Valle de Súchil, 5, 28015 Madrid. ☎ **91-447-70-00.** Fax 91-448-35-69. www.hotelcondeduque.es. E-mail: condeduque@hotelcondeduque.es. 143 units. A/C MINIBAR TV TEL. 28,000 ptas. (US$168) double; from 34,000 ptas. (US$204) suite. AE, DC, MC, V. Parking 1,800 ptas. (US$10.80). Metro: San Bernardo.

The modern four-star Conde Duque, near a branch of El Corte Inglés department store, opens onto a tree-filled plaza in a residential neighborhood that's near the Glorieta Quevado. The hotel is 12 blocks north of the Plaza de España, off calle de San Bernardo, which starts at the Gran Vía. Furnishings include built-in modern headboards and reproductions of 19th-century English pieces, plus bedside lights and telephones. Rooms contain a lot of thoughtful extras, including safes, fax facilities, a tea- or coffeemaker, fireproof materials, and a fire warning system. Bathrooms contain scales, phones, hydromassage showers (suites only), and magnifying mirrors.

Dining/Diversions: The hotel operates a tearoom and cafeteria, plus a full-service restaurant serving regional and international dishes.

Amenities: Concierge, laundry/dry cleaning, and baby-sitting.

MODERATE

Hotel Escultor. Miguel Angel, 3, 28010 Madrid. ☎ **91-310-42-03.** Fax 91-319-25-84. 61 units. A/C MINIBAR TV TEL. From 15,000 ptas. (US$90) double; from 23,000 ptas. (US$138) suite. AE, DC, MC, V. Parking 2,300 ptas. (US$13.80) nearby. Metro: Rubén Darío.

This comfortably furnished hotel built in 1975 provides fewer services and offers fewer facilities than others within its category, but it compensates with larger accommodations. Each guest unit has its own charm and contemporary styling—with video films, private bathroom, and an efficient, logical layout. The hotel is fully air-conditioned, and the staff provides information about facilities in the neighborhood. There's a small but comfortable bar that's open nightly, plus a traditional restaurant, the Señorio de Erazu, which closes on Saturday at lunchtime and all day on Sunday. Room service is offered at breakfast only, 7 to 10:30am.

Residencia Bréton. Bréton de los Herreros, 29, 28003 Madrid. ☎ **91-442-83-00.** Fax 91-441-38-16. www.nh-hoteles.com. 57 units. A/C MINIBAR TV TEL. 20,400 ptas. (US$122.40) double; 30,000 ptas. (US$180) suite. AE, DC, MC, V. Parking 1,600 ptas. (US$9.60) nearby. Metro: Ríos Rosas.

You'll find this well-furnished modern hotel on a side street several blocks from Paseo de la Castellana. As a residencia, it doesn't offer a major dining room, but it does have a little bar and breakfast room adjoining the reception lounge. All guest rooms have wood-frame beds, wrought-iron fixtures, wall-to-wall curtains, comfortable chairs, and ornate tile work in the bathrooms.

INEXPENSIVE

Hostal Residencia Don Diego. Calle de Velázquez, 45, 28001 Madrid. ☎ **91-435-07-60.** Fax 91-431-42-63. 58 units. A/C TV TEL. 11,235 ptas. (US$67.40) double; 14,000 ptas. (US$84) triple. MC, V. Metro: Velázquez.

On the fifth floor of an elevator building, Don Diego is in a combination residential/commercial neighborhood that's relatively convenient to many of the city monuments. The vestibule contains an elegant winding staircase accented with iron griffin heads supporting its balustrade. The hotel is warm and inviting, filled with leather couches and comfortable, no-nonsense, angular yet attractive furniture. A bar stands at the far end of the main sitting room. The hotel's cafeteria serves breakfast 7:45 to 11am. From 7 to 11pm daily, you can also order drinks and snacks, such as sandwiches and omelettes. Laundry service is provided, and room service is available daily 8am to midnight.

CHAMARTÍN
EXPENSIVE

Cuzco. Paseo de la Castellana, 133, 28046 Madrid. ☎ **91-556-06-00.** Fax 91-556-03-72. 328 units. A/C MINIBAR TV TEL. 26,000 ptas. (US$156) double; from 33,000 ptas. (US$198) suite. AE, DC, MC, V. Parking 2,100 ptas. (US$12.60). Metro: Cuzco.

Popular with businesspeople and tour groups, Cuzco lies in a commercial neighborhood of big buildings, government ministries, spacious avenues, and the main Congress Hall. The Chamartín railway station is a 10-minute walk north, so this is a popular and convenient address.

This 15-floor structure, set back from Madrid's longest boulevard, has been redecorated and modernized many times since it was completed in 1967. The Cuzco has spacious guest rooms, with modern furnishings and patterned rugs, and each has a separate sitting area, video movies, and a private bathroom.

Dining/Diversions: There is a bilevel snack bar and cafeteria. The lounge is a forest of marble pillars and leather armchairs, its ambience enhanced by contemporary oil paintings and tapestries.

Amenities: Beauty parlor, sauna, massage, gymnasium, and cocktail bar.

Eurobuilding. Calle Padre Damián, 23, 28036 Madrid. ☎ **91-345-45-00.** Fax 91-345-45-76. 520 units. A/C MINIBAR TV TEL. 32,000 ptas. (US$192) double; from 36,000 ptas. (US$216) suite. AE, DC, MC, V. Parking 2,500 ptas. (US$15). Metro: Cuzco.

Even while the Eurobuilding was on the drawing boards, the rumor was that this five-star sensation of white marble would provide, in the architect's words, "a new concept in deluxe hotels." It is actually two hotels linked by a courtyard, away from the city center but right in the midst of apartment houses, boutiques, nightclubs, first-class restaurants, tree-shaded squares, and the modern Madrid business world.

The more glamorous of the twin buildings is the main one, named Las Estancias de Eurobuilding; it contains only suites, all of which were recently renovated in luxurious pastel shades. Ornately carved gold-and-white beds, background music, room-wide terraces for breakfast and cocktail entertaining—all are tastefully coordinated. Across the courtyard, the neighbor Eurobuilding contains less impressive, but still very comfortable, double rooms, many with views from private balconies of the formal garden and swimming pool below. All the accommodations have TVs with video movies and satellite reception, security doors, and individual safes.

Dining/Diversions: Le Relais Coffee Shop is suitable for a quick bite, while **Le Relais Restaurant** offers buffets at both breakfast and lunch. For more formal dining, **La Taberna** at both lunch and dinner features Spanish and international cuisine, specializing in seafood and various paella dishes.

Amenities: Laundry/valet, concierge, 24-hour room service, baby-sitting, health club with sauna, outdoor swimming pool.

Meliá Castilla. Calle Capitán Haya, 43, 28020 Madrid. ☎ **800/336-3542** in the U.S., or 91-567-50-00. Fax 91-567-50-51. www.solmelia.com. E-mail: melia-castilla@solmelia.com. 915 units. A/C MINIBAR TV TEL. 31,500 ptas. (US$189) double; from 59,500 ptas. (US$357) suite. AE, MC, V. Parking 2,950 ptas. (US$17.70). Metro: Cuzco.

This mammoth hotel qualifies, along with the above-recommended Palace, as one of the largest in Europe. Loaded with facilities and built primarily to accommodate huge conventions, Meliá Castilla also caters to the needs of the individual traveler. Everything is larger than life here: You need a floor plan to get around. The lounges and pristine marble corridors are vast—there's even a landscaped garden as well as an automobile showroom.

Each twin-bedded guest room comes with a private bathroom, TV, and modern furniture. Some lower rooms are quite noisy. Meliá Castilla is in the north of Madrid, about a block west of Paseo de la Castellana, a short drive from the Chamartín railway station.

Dining/Diversions: The hotel has a coffee shop, a seafood restaurant, a restaurant specializing in paella and other rice dishes, cocktail lounges, and the **Trinidad** nightclub. In addition, there's a cabaret restaurant, **Scala Meliá Castilla.**

Amenities: 24-hour room service, hairdresser/barbershop, concierge, baby-sitting, laundry/valet, swimming pool, shopping arcade with souvenir shops and bookstore, saunas, gymnasium, parking garage.

MODERATE

Aristos. Avenida Pío XII, 34, 28016 Madrid. ☎ **91-345-04-50.** Fax 91-345-10-23. 24 units. A/C TV TEL. 21,000–23,000 ptas. (US$126–US$138) double. AE, DC, MC, V. Parking 1,500 ptas. (US$9). Metro: Pío XII.

This three-star hotel is in an up-and-coming residential area of Madrid, not far from the Eurobuilding (see above). Its main advantage is a front garden where you can lounge, have a drink, or order a complete meal. The hotel's restaurant, El Chaflán, is popular with neighborhood residents. Each of the guest rooms has a small terrace and an uncomplicated collection of modern furniture.

Hotel Chamartín. Estacíon de Chamartín, 28036 Madrid. ☎ **91-323-30-87** or 91-334-49-00. Fax 91-733-02-14. www.hotelchamartin.com. E-mail: chamartin@husa.es. 396 units. A/C MINIBAR TV TEL. 21,100 ptas. (US$126.60) double; from 86,000 ptas. (US$516) suite. AE, DC, MC, V. Metro: Chamartín. Bus: 5.

This brick-sided hotel soars nine stories above the northern periphery of Madrid. It's part of the massive modern shopping complex attached to the Chamartín railway station, although once you're inside your soundproofed room, the noise of the railway station will seem far away. The owner of the building is RENFE, Spain's government railway system, but the nationwide chain that administers it is HUSA Hotels. The hotel is 15 minutes by taxi from both the airport and the historic core of Madrid and is conveniently close to one of the capital's busiest metro stops. Especially oriented to the business traveler, Chamartín offers a currency exchange kiosk, a travel agency, a car-rental office, and a lobby video screen that posts the arrival and departure of all of Chamartín's trains.

A coffee bar serves breakfast daily, and room service is available 7am to midnight. The hotel restaurant, Cota 13, serves international cuisine. A short walk from the hotel lobby, within the railway-station complex, are a handful of shops and movie theaters, a roller-skating rink, a disco, and ample parking.

ARGÜELLES/MONCLOA
EXPENSIVE

Husa Princesa. Serrano Jover, 3, 28015 Madrid. ☎ **91-542-35-00.** Fax 91-542-35-01. www.husa.es. E-mail: husaprincesa@husa.es. 275 units. A/C TV TEL. 39,300 ptas. (US$235.80) double; from 77,900 ptas. (US$467.40) suite. AE, DC, MC, V. Parking 3,500 ptas. (US$21). Metro: Argüelles.

Originally built during the mid-1970s and radically renovated after its takeover in 1991 by the nationwide chain HUSA, the Princesa is a sprawling hotel designed with a series of massive rectangular sections clustered into an angular whole. The concrete-and-glass facade overlooks busy boulevards in the center of Madrid.

Both businesspeople and groups of visiting tourists patronize the hotel; each of the guest rooms contains comfortable, contemporary furniture and a modern bathroom.

Dining/Diversions: The hotel's restaurant is called **Ricón de Argüelles.** There is also a bar, the **Bar Royal.**

Amenities: 24-hour room service, concierge, baby-sitting, large assortment of conference rooms, underground parking garage, hairdressing salon.

Meliá Madrid Princesa. Princesa, 27, 28008 Madrid. ☎ **800/336-3542** in the U.S., or 91-541-82-00. Fax 91-541-19-05. www.solmelia.com. E-mail: meliamadrid@solmelia.es. 265 units. A/C MINIBAR TV TEL. 39,600 ptas. (US$237.60) double; from 46,100–93,500 ptas. (US$276.60–US$561) suite. AE, DC, MC, V. Parking 2,500 ptas. (US$15). Metro: Ventura Rodríguez.

Here you'll find one of the most modern yet uniquely Spanish hotels in the country. Its 23 floors of wide picture windows have taken a permanent position in the capital's skyline. Each of the guest rooms is comfortable, spacious, and filled with contemporary furnishings, plus a TV with video movies and many channels from across Europe. Most units offer views over the skyline of Madrid. Chalk-white walls dramatize the flamboyant use of color accents; the bathrooms are sheathed in marble.

Dining/Diversions: Restaurante Princesa is elegant and restful; equally popular is **Don Pepe Grill.** The cuisine in both restaurants is international and includes an array of Japanese and Indian dishes. There are also three bars and a coffee shop.

Amenities: 24-hour room service, concierge, baby-sitting, hairdresser/barber, laundry, a gallery that includes souvenir shops and bookstores, health club with sauna and massage.

MODERATE

Tirol. Marqués de Urquijo, 4, 28008 Madrid. ☎ **91-548-19-00.** Fax 91-541-39-58. www.hotel-tirol.com. 95 units. A/C TV TEL. 13,800 ptas. (US$82.80) double. Rates include buffet breakfast. MC, V. Metro: Argüelles. Bus: 2 or 21.

A short walk from Plaza de España and the swank Meliá Madrid hotel (see above), the Tirol is a good choice for clean, unpretentious comfort. Furnishings in this three-star hotel are simple and functional. Eight of the guest rooms have private terraces. A cafeteria and a parking garage are on the premises.

4 Where to Dine

Even more than Barcelona, Madrid boasts the most varied cuisine and the widest choice of dining opportunities in Spain. At the fancy tourist restaurants, prices are comparable to those in New York, London, or Paris, but there are many low-cost taverns and family restaurants as well.

It's the custom in Madrid to consume the big meal of the day from 2 to 4pm. After a recuperative siesta, Madrileños then enjoy tapas—and indeed, no culinary experience would be complete without a tour of the city's many tapas bars (see "An Early-Evening Tapeo," below, and "The Best of the Tascas," at the end of this chapter).

All this nibbling is followed by a light supper in a restaurant, usually from 9:30pm to as late as midnight. Many restaurants, however, start serving dinner at 8pm to accommodate visitors from other countries who don't like to dine so late.

Many of Spain's greatest chefs have opened restaurants in Madrid, energizing the city's culinary scene. Gone are the days when mainly Madrileño food was featured, which meant Castilian specialties such as *cocido* (a chickpea-and-sausage stew) or roasts of suckling pig or lamb. Now, you can take a culinary tour of the country without ever leaving Madrid—from Andalusia with its gazpacho and braised bull's tails to Asturias with its *fabada* (a rich pork stew) and *sidra* (cider) to the Basque country, which has the most sophisticated cuisine in Spain. There is also a host of Galician and Mediterranean restaurants in Madrid. Amazingly, although Madrid is a landlocked city surrounded by a vast arid plain, you can order some of the freshest seafood in the country here.

Meals include service and tax (ranging from 7% to 12%, depending on the restaurant) but not drinks, which add to the tab considerably.

In most cases service can seem perfunctory by U.S. standards. Waiters are matter-of-fact, do not fawn over you, nor do they return to the table to ask how things are. This can seem off-putting at first, but if you observe closely you'll see that Spanish waiters typically handle more tables than American waiters and that they generally work quickly and more efficiently.

An Early-Evening Tapeo

What's more fun than a pub crawl in London or Dublin? In Madrid, it's a *tapeo,* and you can drink just as much or more than in those far northern climes. A tapeo—one of the pleasures of a visit to Madrid—is the act of strolling from one bar to another to keep yourself amused and fed before the fashionable Madrileño dining hour of 10pm.

Most of the world knows that tapas are Spain's delectable appetizers; hundreds of restaurants in England and the United States now serve them. In Madrid they're served in tabernas, tascas, bars, and cafes.

Although Madrid took to tapas with a passion, they may have originated in Andalusia, especially around Jerez de la Frontera, where they were traditionally served to accompany the sherry produced there. The first tapa (which means a cover or lid) was probably *chorizo* (a spicy sausage) or a slice of cured ham perched over the mouth of a glass to keep the flies out. Later, the government mandated bars to serve a "little something" in the way of food with each drink to dissipate the effects of the alcohol. This was important when drinking a forti-fied wine like sherry, as its alcohol content is more than 15% higher than that of normal table wines. Eating a selection of tapas as you drink will help preserve your sobriety.

Tapas can be relatively simple: toasted almonds; slices of ham, cheese, or sausage; a potato omelette; or the ubiquitous olives. They can also be more elab-orate: a succulent veal roll; herb-flavored snails; *gambas* (fried or grilled shrimp); a saucer of peppery *pulpo* (octopus); stuffed peppers; delicious *anguila* (eel); *cangrejo* (crabmeat salad); merluza (hake) salad flavored with sweet red peppers, garlic, and cumin; and even bull testicles.

Each bar in Madrid gains a reputation for its rendition of certain favorite foods. One bar, for example, specializes in very garlicky grilled mushrooms, usu-ally washed down with pitchers of sangría. Another will specialize in gambas. Most chefs in Madrid are men, but at tapas bars or *tascas,* the cooks are most often women—perhaps the mother or sister of the owner, but usually the wife.

For a selection of our favorite bars, see "The Best of the Tascas" later in this chapter. There are literally hundreds of others, many of which you'll discover on your own during your strolls around Madrid.

Follow the local custom and don't overtip. Theoretically, service is included in the price of the meal, but it's customary to leave an additional 10%.

MENÚ DEL DÍA & CUBIERTO   Order the *menú del día* (menu of the day) or *cubierto* (fixed price)—both fixed-price menus based on what is fresh at the market that day. They are the dining bargains in Madrid, although often lacking the quality of more expensive à la carte dining. Usually each will include a first course, such as fish soup or hors d'oeuvres, followed by a main dish, plus bread, dessert, and the wine of the house. You won't have a large choice. The *menú turístico* is a similar fixed-price menu, but for many it's too large, especially at lunch. Only those with big appetites will find it the best bargain.

CAFETERIAS   These usually are not self-service establishments but restaurants serving light, often American, cuisine. Go for breakfast instead of dining at your hotel, unless it's included in the room price. Some cafeterias offer no hot meals, but many

Central Madrid Dining

Alfredo's Barbacoa **29**
Alkalde **35**
Amparo **35**
Antonio Sánchez **48**
Arce **55**
Bajamar **17**
Barraca **52**
Batuecas **14**
Bocaito **54**
Bodegón **30**
Bola **11**
Cabo Mayor **15**
Café Balear **25**
Café de Oriente **7**
Caripén **12**
Casa Alberto **46**
Casa Beingna **29**
Casa Lucio **1**
Casa Mingo **13**
Casa Paco **4**
Casa Vallejo **20**
Cenador del Prado **44**
Cervecería Alemania **49**
Cervecería Santa Bárbara **23**
Chata **1**
Chez Lou Crêperie **29**
Ciao Madrid **22**
Cornugopia **9**
Cosaco **2**
Cuatro Estaciones **15**
Cuchi **5**
Cuevas de Luís Candelas **5**
Cuevas del Duque **16**
Edelweiss **41**
Errota-Zar **40**
Espejo **58**
Esquina del Real **6**
Foster's Hollywood **33**
Fuencisla **19**
Galayos **5**
Galette **36**
Gamella **37**
Goizeko Kabi **29**
Gran Café de Gijón **57**
Horcher **37**
Hylogui **43**
Inca **56**
Jockey **27**
Lhardy **42**
Mad Madrid **24**
Mentidero de la Villa **59**
Mesón Las Descalzas **10**
Museo del Jamon **45**
Nabucco **21**
Nicomedes **33**
O'Pazo **15**
Olivo Restaurant **29**
Paellería Valenciana **51**
Paloma **33**
Pedro La Rumbe **34**
Pescador **31**
Platerías Comedor **47**
Posada de la Villa **3**

Principe de Viana **29**
Príncipe y Serrano **29**
Restaurante Belagua **26**
Ríofrío **28**
San Carlo **39**
San Mamés **14**
Schotis **1**
Sobrino de Botín **5**
Suntory **29**
Taberna Carmencita **53**
Taberna del Alabardero **8**
Teatriz **32**
Terraza **50**
Tienda de Vinos **55**
Tocororo **47**
Trainera **30**
Trucha **43**
V.I.P. Gran Via **18**
Viridiana **38**
Zalacaín **25**

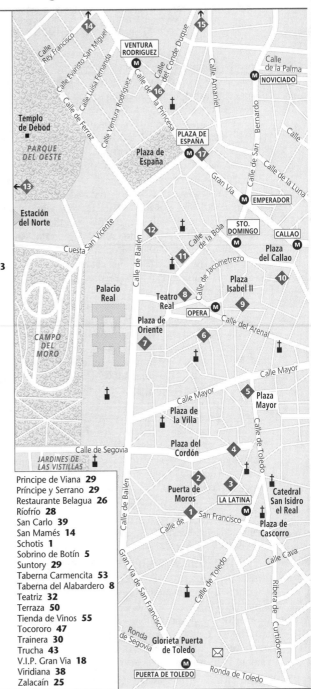

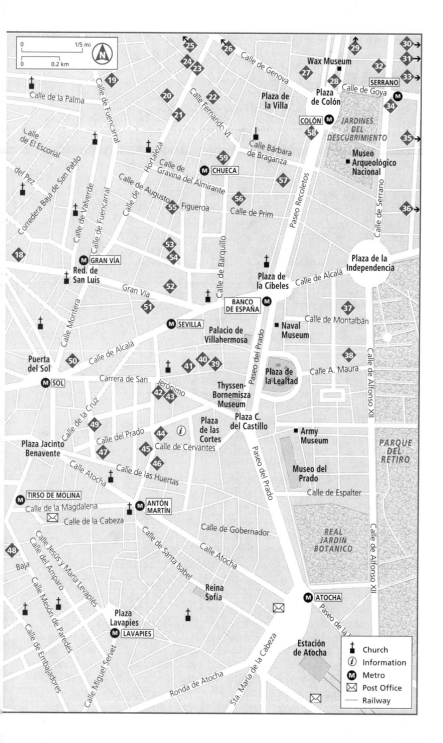

Calle de la Palma

Calle de El Escorial

del Pez

Corredera Baja de San Pablo

Calle de Fuencarral

Calle de Valverde

Calle de Fuencarral

Calle de la Palma

19

20

21

22

Calle Fernando VI

23

24

25

26

Calle de Genova

Wax Museum

27

28

29

30 →

31 →

32

33 →

Plaza de Colón

SERRANO

Calle de Goya

34

35 →

COLÓN Ⓜ

JARDINES DEL DESCUBRIMIENTO

Museo Arqueológico Nacional

Calle de Serrano

Plaza de la Villa

Calle Bárbara de Braganza

58

59

CHUECA Ⓜ

Calle de Gravina

Calle de Augusto Figueroa

Hortaleza

55

56

57

Calle de Prim

Paseo Recoletos

36 →

18

GRAN VÍA Ⓜ

Red. de San Luis

Gran Vía

53

54

52

51

Calle de Barquillo

Plaza de la Cibeles

Calle de Alcalá

Plaza de la Independencia

Calle Montera

SEVILLA Ⓜ

Palacio de Villahermosa

BANCO DE ESPAÑA Ⓜ

Naval Museum

Calle de Montalbán

37

Puerta del Sol

50

Calle de Alcalá

Carrera de San Jerónimo

41 **40** **39**

42 **43**

Thyssen-Bornemisza Museum

Plaza de la Lealtad

Calle A. Maura

38

Calle de Alfonso XII

SOL Ⓜ

Calle de la Cruz

49

Calle del Prado

44 ⓘ

Plaza de las Cortes

Plaza C. del Castillo

Calle de Cervantes

Plaza Jacinto Benavente

47

45

46

Calle Atocha

Calle de las Huertas

Army Museum

PARQUE DEL RETIRO

Museo del Prado

Paseo del Prado

TIRSO DE MOLINA Ⓜ

Calle de la Magdalena

Calle de la Cabeza

ANTÓN MARTÍN Ⓜ

Calle de Santa Isabel

Calle de Atocha

Calle de Gobernador

Museo del Prado

Calle de Espalter

48

Baja

Calle Jesús y María

Calle del Amparo

Calle Mesón de Paredes

Calle de Embajadores

Levapiés

Plaza Lavapies

LAVAPIES Ⓜ

Calle Miguel Servet

Reina Sofía

REAL JARDÍN BOTANICO

Calle de Alfonso XII

ATOCHA Ⓜ

Estación de Atocha

Paseo de la...

Ronda de Atocha

Sta. María de la Cabeza

†	Church
ⓘ	Information
Ⓜ	Metro
⊠	Post Office
—	Railway

feature combined plates of fried eggs, French fries, veal, and lettuce-and-tomato salad, which make adequate fare, or snacks like hot dogs and hamburgers.

NEAR THE PLAZA DE LAS CORTÉS
MODERATE

El Espejo. Paseo de Recoletos, 31. ☎ **91-308-23-47.** Reservations required. *Menú del día* 3,050 ptas. (US$18.30). AE, DC, MC, V. Sun–Fri 1–4pm; daily 9pm–midnight. Metro: Colón. Bus: 27. INTERNATIONAL.

Here you'll find good food and one of the most perfectly crafted art nouveau decors in Madrid. If the weather is good, you can choose one of the outdoor tables, served by a battery of uniformed waiters who carry food across the busy street to a green area flanked with trees and strolling pedestrians. We prefer a table inside, within view of the tile maidens with vines and flowers entwined in their hair. Upon entering, you'll find yourself in a charming cafe/bar, where many visitors linger before walking down a hallway toward the spacious dining room. Dishes include grouper ragout with clams, steak tartare, guinea fowl with Armagnac, and lean duck meat with pineapple. Profiteroles with cream and chocolate sauce make a delectable dessert.

Errota-Zar. Jovellanos, 3, 1st floor. ☎ **91-531-24-64.** Reservations recommended. Main courses 2,800–3,000 ptas. (US$16.80–US$18); *menu completo* 5,000 ptas. (US$30). AE, DC, MC, V. Mon–Sat 1–4pm and 9pm–midnight. Closed Aug 15–30. Metro: Banco España and Sevilla. BASQUE.

Next to the House of Deputies and the Zarzuela Theater, this old building is called "Basque House." Errota-Zar, which means "old mill," is a nostalgic reference to the Basque country, home of the Olano family, owners of the restaurant.

A small bar at the entrance displays a collection of fine cigars and wines, and the blue-painted walls are adorned with original paintings of Basque landscapes. The restaurant has only about two dozen tables; they fill up easily with discerning diners. The deliciously prepared food features an array of sun-kissed bounty from the fields and rivers of Spain. Try such appetizers as the rare *tolosa* kidney bean or fried anchovies. Many Basques begin their meal with a *tortilla de bacalao,* salt cod omelette. For main dishes, sample the delights of *chuleton de buey* (oxtail), along with grilled vegetables, or *kokotxas de merluza en aceite,* the cheeks of the hake fish cooked in the finest virgin olive oil. Hake cheeks may not sound appetizing, but Spaniards and many foreigners praise this dish. You might opt instead for *foie al Pedro Jimenez* (duck liver grilled and served with a sweet wine sauce). The best homemade desserts are *cuajada de la casa,* a thick yogurt made from sheep's milk, or *tarta de limon,* a lemon cake. You might also try, as an oddity, rice ice cream in prune sauce.

La Trucha. Manuel Fernandez Gonzalez, 3. ☎ **91-429-58-33.** Reservations recommended. Main courses 1,800–3,200 ptas. (US$10.80–US$19.20). AE, MC, V. Mon–Sat 12:30–4pm and 7:30pm–midnight. Metro: Sevilla. SPANISH/SEAFOOD.

With its Andalusian tavern ambience, La Trucha boasts a street-level bar and small dining room with arched ceiling and whitewashed walls. The decor is made festive with hanging braids of garlic, dried peppers, and onions. On the lower level the walls of a second bustling area are covered with eye-catching antiques, bullfight notices, and other bric-a-brac. There's a complete à la carte menu including *trucha* (trout), *verbenas de ahumados* (a selection of smoked delicacies), a glorious stew called *fabada* (made with beans, Galician ham, black sausage, and smoked bacon), and a *comida casera rabo de toro* (home-style oxtail). No one should miss nibbling on the *tapas variadas* in the bar.

If this branch turns out to be too crowded, there's another **Trucha** at Núñez de Arce, 6 (☎ **91-532-08-82**).

INEXPENSIVE

Edelweiss. Jovelianos, T. ☎ **91-521-03-26.** Reservations recommended. Main courses 1,400–2,800 ptas. (US$8.40–US$16.80); fixed-price lunch 2,500 ptas. (US$15). AE, MC, V. Daily 1–4pm and Mon–Sat 8pm–midnight. Closed Aug. Metro: Cibeles. Bus: 5. GERMAN.

This German standby has provided good-quality food and service at moderate prices since World War II. Here you will be served hearty portions of food, mugs of draft beer, and fluffy pastries; that's why there's always a wait.

Start with Bismarck herring, then dive into goulash with spaetzle or *Eisbein* (pigs' knuckles) with sauerkraut and mashed potatoes, the most popular dish at the restaurant. Finish with the homemade apple tart. The decor is vaguely German, with travel posters and wood-paneled walls. Edelweiss is air-conditioned in summer.

NEAR PLAZA DE LA CIBELES
MODERATE

✪ **Bocaito.** Calle Libertad, 4–6 (two blocks north of *Las Cibeles*). ☎ **91-532-12-19.** Reservations recommended. Main courses 2,000–2,800 ptas. (US$12–US$16.80). MC, V. Mon–Fri 1–4pm and 8:30pm–midnight, Sat 8:30pm–midnight. Closed last 2 weeks Aug. Metro: Banco De España. SPANISH/TAPAS.

Behind a double horseshoe bar the staff cooks and prepares some of the most appreciated tapas in Madrid. Inside the 150-year-old house, four original columns of wood encircle the high ceiling, and bullfighting posters adorn the white-tile walls. The selection of tapas ranges from simple delights such as *ajos tiernos en aceite* (tender garlic in olive oil), cured Serrano ham, *gambas fritas* (fried shrimp) and green asparagus in scrambled eggs to some very sophisticated delicacies such as *bacalao con caviar* (salt cod pâté with caviar). The famous *mejimecha* (mussels marinated with ham and onions in béchamel sauce) is sublime, as are the anchovies of the house and tasty croquettes. The prices for the tapas range from 900 to 1,200 pesetas (US$5.40 to US$7.20). Don Miguel Benavente, the chef and owner for more than three decades, recommends the plato combinado (a combination platter of all tapas) which, together with a glass of very palatable Rioja wine, is available at a cost of 1,500 pesetas (US$9). A selection of the many culinary treats on offer includes the *plato de cuchara* (daily specials), lentils with *chorizo* (sausage), *merluza* (hake), *osso bucco al horno* (braised veal shank), and a number of more typical Andalusian and Castilian dishes.

Tocororo. Calle del Prado, 3 (at the corner of Echegaray). ☎ **91-369-40-00.** Reservations required Thurs–Sat. Main courses 2,500–3,500 ptas. (US$15–21); fixed-price menu 1,500 ptas. (US$9). AE, DC, MC, V. Tues–Wed 1:30–4pm and 8:30pm–1:30am. Closed last 2 weeks Feb and last week Aug, first week Sept. Metro: Sevilla. CUBAN.

This Cuban restaurant opened in 1998 by a native of that country. The nostalgia is evident in the pictures of Old Havana Varadero Beach and Cienfuegos, and in the paintings of famous artists such as Lam y Mattos which adorn the walls. The waitstaff is as lively as the pop Cuban music playing on the stereo. Typical dishes are *ceviche* (marinated fish), *ropa vieja* (shredded meat served with black beans and rice), or lobster *enchilade* or grilled. If you prefer a simpler, more rustic repast, try a selection of *empanada y tamales* (fried potato pastries and plantain dough filled with onions and ground meat). Among the specials of the house are the cocktails *mojito* (rum, mint, and a hint of sugar) and daiquiris. In winter there is live Cuban music. With a discreet but pleasant ambience, this restaurant is located in the zone of *La Marcha* (most of the bars and discos are in this area) and enjoys limited competition (there are only six other Cuban restaurants in the whole city).

NEAR THE PLAZA DE ESPAÑA
EXPENSIVE

Bajamar. Gran Vía, 78. ☎ **91/559-59-03.** Reservations recommended. Main courses 3,200–8,000 ptas. (US$19.20–US$48). AE, DC, MC, V. Daily 1–4pm and 8pm–midnight. Metro: Plaza de España. SEAFOOD.

Bajamar, one of the best fish houses in Spain, is right in the heart of the city. Both fish and shellfish are flown in fresh daily, the prices depending on what the market charges. Lobster, king crab, prawns, and soft-shell crabs are all priced according to weight. There is a large array of reasonably priced dishes as well. The service is smooth and professional and the menu is in English. For an appetizer order the half-dozen giant oysters or rover crayfish. The special seafood soup is a most satisfying meal in itself; the lobster bisque is also worth trying. Some of the noteworthy main courses include turbot Gallego style, seafood paella, and baby squid cooked in its ink. The simple desserts include the chef's custard.

MODERATE

La Bola. Calle de la Bola, 5. ☎ **91-547-69-30.** Reservations required. Main courses 2,075–3,000 ptas. (US$12.45–US$18); fixed-price menu 3,800 ptas. (US$22.80). No credit cards. Mon–Sat 1–4pm and 9pm–midnight. Metro: Plaza de España or Ópera. Bus: 1 or 2. MADRILEÑA.

This is a taberna in which to savor the 19th century. Just north of the Teatro Real, it's one of the few restaurants (if not the only one) left in Madrid with a blood-red facade; at one time, nearly all fashionable restaurants were so coated. La Bola hangs on to tradition like a tenacious bull. Time has passed, but not inside this restaurant: The soft, traditional atmosphere, the gentle and polite waiters, the Venetian crystal, the Carmen-red draperies, and the aging velvet preserve the 1870 ambience. Grilled sole, fillet of veal, and roast veal are regularly featured. Basque-style hake and grilled salmon also are well recommended. Refreshing dishes to begin your meal include grilled shrimp, red-pepper salad, and lobster cocktail.

Las Cuevas del Duque. Princesa, 16. ☎ **91-559-50-37.** Reservations required. Main courses 2,000–2,500 ptas. (US$12–US$15); fixed-price menu 3,800 ptas. (US$22.80). AE, DC, MC, V. Mon–Fri 1–4pm; daily 8pm–midnight. Metro: Ventura Rodríguez. Bus: 1, 2, or 42. SPANISH.

Located in front of the Duke of Alba's palace, a short walk from Plaza de España, Las Cuevas del Duque has an underground bar and a small, 20-table dining room. Specialties include such simple Spanish fare as roast suckling pig (on which its reputation was built), sirloin, tiny grilled lamb cutlets, and a few seafood dishes, including hake in garlic sauce and sole cooked in cider. In fair weather a few tables are set outside, beside a tiny triangular garden. Other tables line the calle de la Princesa side and make an enjoyable roost for an afternoon drink.

ON OR NEAR THE GRAN VÍA
EXPENSIVE

Arce. Augusto Figueroa, 32. ☎ **91-522-59-13.** Reservations recommended. Main courses 2,800–5,750 ptas. (US$16.80–US$34.50). AE, DC, MC, V. Mon–Fri 1:30–4pm, Mon–Sat 9pm–midnight. Closed the week before Easter and Aug 15–31. Metro: Colón. BASQUE.

Arce has brought some of the best modern interpretations of Basque cuisine to the palates of Madrid, thanks to the enthusiasm of owner/chef Iñaki Camba and his wife, Theresa. Within a comfortably decorated dining room, you can enjoy dishes made of the finest ingredients using natural flavors designed to dominate your taste buds. Examples include a salad of fresh scallops and an oven-baked casserole of fresh boletus mushrooms, seasoned lightly so the woodsy vegetable taste comes through. Look for unusual preparations of hake and seasonal variations of such game dishes as pheasant and woodcock.

MODERATE

El Mentidero de la Villa. Santo Tomé, 6. ☎ **91-308-12-85.** Reservations required. Main courses 1,950–2,540 ptas. (US$11.70–US$15.25); menú del día 2,200 ptas. (US$13.20). MC, V. Mon Fri 1:30 4:30pm, Mon Sat 9pm midnight. Closed last 2 weeks of Aug. Metro: Alonso Martínez, Colón, or Gran Vía. Bus: 37. SPANISH/FRENCH.

The Mentidero ("Gossip Shop" in English) is certainly a multicultural experience. The owner describes the cuisine as "modern Spanish with Japanese influence and a French cooking technique." That may sound confusing, but the result is an achievement; each ingredient in every dish manages to retain its distinct flavor. The kitchen plays with such adventuresome combinations as veal liver in sage sauce, a spring roll filled with fresh shrimp and leeks, noisettes of veal with tarragon, fillet steak with a sauce of mustard and brown sugar, and medallions of venison with purée of chestnut and celery. One especially notable dessert is sherry trifle. The postmodern decor includes softly trimmed trompe l'oeil ceilings, exposed wine racks, ornate columns with unusual lighting, and a handful of antique carved horses from long-defunct merry-go-rounds.

La Barraca. Reina, 29–31. ☎ **91-532-71-54.** Reservations recommended. Main courses 1,800–3,200 ptas. (US$10.80–US$19.20). AE, DC, MC, V. Daily 1–4pm and 8:30pm–midnight. Metro: Gran Vía or Sevilla. Bus: 1, 2, or 74. VALENCIAN.

La Barraca is like a country inn right off the Gran Vía, and it's a longtime local favorite. The food, frankly, used to be better, but perhaps our tastes have changed since our student days. This Valencian-style restaurant is a well-managed establishment recommended for its tasty Levante cooking. There are four different dining rooms, three of which lie one flight above street level; they're colorfully cluttered with ceramics, paintings, photographs, Spanish lanterns, flowers, and local artifacts. The house specialty, paella a la Barraca, is made with pork and chicken. Specialties in the appetizer category include *desgarrat* (a salad of codfish and red peppers), mussels in a white-wine sauce, and shrimp sautéed with garlic. In addition to the recommended paella, you can select at least 16 rice dishes, including black rice and queen paella. Main-dish specialties include brochette of angler fish and prawns and rabbit with fines herbes. Lemon-and-vodka sorbet brings the meal to a fitting finish.

San Carlo. Barquillo, 10. ☎ **91-522-79-88.** Reservations recommended. Main courses 2,600–3,000 ptas. (US$15.60–US$18); menu deluxe 6,000 ptas. (US$36); fixed-price menu 2,500 ptas. (US$15). AE, DC, MC, V. Tues–Sat 1:30–4pm and 9pm–midnight, Sun 1:30–4pm. Closed Aug 14–19. Metro: Banco de España. ITALIAN.

In the center of Madrid, this winning choice is located in a 19th-century building whose interior evokes the Teatro San Carlo in Naples. Pastel-colored walls are adorned with paintings and photographs of famous artists who have appeared here. On weekends there is live musical entertainment. The restaurant aspires to fill a gap in the Madrid market for quality Italian food sold at affordable prices, and succeeds admirably in its goal. If you want only a light pizza, opt for the front room. But if you desire more authentic Italian cuisine, head for the rear. Here you will find the cutting edge in cuisine, using local products to create dishes of flavor and goodness. Try pasta with prawns and mushrooms or delectable lasagna with fresh eggplant and basil. One of the finest meat dishes is fillet of veal with fresh asparagus and a mushroom known as *colmenillas*. Among the fish selections, sample *lubina con tomato seco al vino blanco*, or whitefish perfectly prepared with sun-dried tomatoes in a white-wine sauce. Finish with a tiramisu perfumed in Amaretto.

INEXPENSIVE

Paellería Valenciana. Caballero de Gracia, 12. ☎ **91-531-17-85.** Reservations recommended. Main courses 1,250–2,800 ptas. (US$7.50–US$16.80); fixed-price menu 1,600 ptas. (US$9.60). AE, MC, V. Mon–Sat 1:30–4:30pm. Metro: Gran Vía. SPANISH.

This lunch-only restaurant ranks as one of the best values in the city. The specialty is paella, which you must order by phone in advance. Once you arrive, you might begin with a homemade soup or the house salad, then follow with the rib-sticking paella, served in an iron skillet for two or more only. Among the desserts, the chef's special pride is razor-thin orange slices flavored with rum, coconut, sugar, honey, and raspberry sauce. A carafe of house wine comes with the set menu, and after lunch the owner comes around dispensing free cognac.

V.I.P. Gran Vía, 43. ☎ **91-559-64-57.** Main courses 950–1,500 ptas. (US$5.70–US$9). AE, DC, MC, V. Daily 9am–3am. Metro: Callao. FAST FOOD.

This place looks like a bookstore emporium from the outside, but in back it's a cafeteria serving fast food. There are more than a dozen VIPs scattered throughout Madrid, but this is the most central one. You might begin with a cup of soothing gazpacho. Hamburgers are the rage here, but the service leaves a lot to be desired.

NEAR THE PUERTA DEL SOL
VERY EXPENSIVE

Lhardy. Carrera de San Jéronimo, 8. ☎ **91-521-33-85.** Reservations recommended in the upstairs dining room. Main courses 7,000–9,000 ptas. (US$42–US$54). AE, DC, MC, V. Mon–Sat 1–3:30pm and 9–11:30pm. Closed Aug. Metro: Puerta del Sol. SPANISH/INTERNATIONAL.

Lhardy has been a Madrileño legend since it opened in 1839 as a gathering place for the city's literati and political leaders. In 1846 it entertained Dumas (father, not son). On street level is what might be the most elegant snack bar in Spain. Within a dignified and antique setting of marble and varnished hardwoods, cups of steaming consommé are dispensed from silver samovars into delicate porcelain cups, and rows of croquettes, tapas, and sandwiches are served to stand-up clients who pay for their food at a cashier's kiosk near the entrance. A ground-floor deli and take-out service is open daily 9am to 3pm and 5 to 9:30pm.

The real culinary skill of the place, however, is found on Lhardy's second floor, where you'll find a formal restaurant decorated in the ornate belle époque style of Isabel Segunda. Specialties of the house include fish, pork and veal, tripe in a garlicky tomato and onion wine sauce, and *cocido,* the celebrated chickpea stew of Madrid. *Soufflé sorpresa* (baked Alaska) is the dessert specialty.

Terraza. Alcala, 15. ☎ **91-521-87-00.** Main courses 3,500–4,000 ptas. (US$21–US$24); fixed-price menu 9,000 ptas. (US$54). AE, DC, MC, V. Mon–Fri 1–3:30pm, 9–11:30pm; Sat 9–11pm. Closed Aug. Metro: Sevilla. SPANISH/INTERNATIONAL.

Glamorous in its neo-baroque casino location, and with a mouthwatering menu, this restaurant is a perfect example of postmodern Spanish cuisine. The fifth-floor restaurant provides a panoramic view of the heart of Madrid and can either be reached by an elevator or by a sweeping 19th-century staircase designed to impress. The decor is classically restrained, with high ceilings and crystal chandeliers. The delicious fresh food reinterprets Spanish dishes. An example is *raya* (ray) in oil and saffron with parsley purée and nuts on a bed of finely diced fries. More traditional dishes include the succulent *merluza a la Gallega* (Galician hake), *crema de la fabada asturiana* (creamed Asturian bean soup), and the steeply priced *jamon jabugo* (cured ham from acorn-fed pigs) served with a *menestra* (mixed vegetables) al dente. Only French champagne and

---

ⓕ   Family-Friendly Restaurants

Children visiting Spain will delight in patronizing any of the restaurants at the Parque de Atracciones in the **Casa de Campo** (see "Especially for Kids" in chapter 6). Another good idea is to go on a picnic (see "Picnics, Madrid Style," later in this chapter).

For a taste of home, there are always the fast food chains: McDonald's, Burger King, and Kentucky Fried Chicken are everywhere. Remember, however, that the burgers and chicken will have a slightly different taste from those served back home.

Try taking the family to a local *tasca,* where children are bound to find something they like from the wide selection of tapas.

Foster's Hollywood *(see p. 167)* (see p. 167)   This restaurant has juicy hamburgers, plus lots of fare familiar to American kids.

V.I.P. *(see p. 158)* (see p. 158)   This chain spread across Madrid serves fast food, hamburgers, and other foodstuffs that kids go for in a big way, especially the ice cream concoctions.

Spanish wines are listed and one of the best is the rounded woody red, the Ribeira de Duero from the province of Valladolid.

EXPENSIVE

Caripén. Plaza de la Marina Española, 4. ☎ **91-541-11-77.** Reservations recommended on weekends. Main courses 3,500–4,000 ptas. (US$21–US$24). MC, V. Mon–Sat 9pm–3am. Closed Aug. Metro: Opera/Santo Domingo. ITALIAN/FRENCH.

In a historic district near the Royal Opera House and the Spanish Senate, this restaurant was once El Tablao, the flamenco club of Lola Flores, one of the most famous of all Spanish dancers. Its art deco decor is still basically intact but, instead of flamenco, you get the inspired French bistro cookery of Daniel Boute. At his little 25-table restaurant, diners sample some of the finest fare in the Spanish capital. The restaurant is especially popular with the "*gatos*" of Madrid, because it serves until 3am when most other quality establishments are shuttered. (Local residents are called gatos because they like to roam about at night.) Exceptional products are prepared with a finely honed technique. Go for the *mejillones de roca* (mussels in white-wine and cream sauce) or a perfectly prepared steak tartare. The pasta is homemade, and one exceptional dish is foie gras with mushrooms. Skate in black butter is one of the menu's finest choices, and you can finish off with such desserts as tiramisu, freshly made fruit tarts, or crepes.

Platerías Comedor. Plaza de Santa Ana, 11. ☎ **91-429-70-48.** Reservations recommended. Main courses 2,500–5,000 ptas. (US$15–US$30). AE, DC, MC, V. Mon–Fri 1:30–4pm and 8:30pm–midnight; Sat 9pm–midnight. Metro: Puerta del Sol. SPANISH.

One of the most charming dining rooms in Madrid, Platerías Comedor has richly brocaded walls evocative of 19th-century Spain. Busy socializing may take place on the plaza outside, but this serene oasis makes few concessions to the new generation in its food, decor, or formally attired waiters. Specialties include beans with clams, stuffed partridge with cabbage and sausage, duck liver with white grapes, tripe à la Madrid, veal stew with snails and mushrooms, and guinea hen with figs and plums. Follow up any of these with the passion fruit sorbet. Many restaurants have sprouted up in recent years that serve better food, but Platerías Comedor continues to thrive as a culinary tradition; its old-fashioned atmosphere is hard to come by.

MODERATE

✪ Café de Oriente. Plaza de Oriente, 2. ☎ **91-541-39-74.** Reservations recommended in restaurant only. Restaurant, main courses 1,900–4,000 ptas. (US$11.40–US$24). Cafe, tapas 600–1,200 ptas. (US$3.60–US$7.20); coffee 650 ptas. (US$3.90). AE, DC, MC, V. Daily 1–4pm and 9pm–midnight. Metro: Ópera. FRENCH/SPANISH.

The Oriente is a cafe-and-restaurant complex, the former being one of the most popular in Madrid. From the cafe tables on its terrace, there's a spectacular view of the Palacio Real (Royal Palace) and the Teatro Real. The dining rooms—Castilian upstairs, French Basque downstairs—are frequented by royalty and diplomats. Typical of the refined cuisine are vichyssoise, fresh vegetable flan, and many savory meat and fresh-fish offerings. Service is excellent. Most visitors, however, patronize the cafe, trying if possible to get an outdoor table. The cafe is decorated in turn-of-the-century style, with banquettes and regal paneling, as befits its location. Pizza, tapas, and drinks (including Irish, Viennese, Russian, and Jamaican coffees) are served.

✪ Casa Paco. Plaza Puerta Cerrada, 11. ☎ **91-366-31-66.** Reservations required. Main courses 1,100–3,800 ptas. (US$7.20–US$22.80); fixed-price menu 4,000 ptas. (US$24). DC. Mon–Sat 1:30–4pm and 8:30pm–midnight. Closed Aug. Metro: Puerta del Sol, Ópera, or La Latina. Bus: 3, 21, or 65. STEAK.

Madrileños defiantly name Casa Paco, just beside the Plaza Mayor, when someone dares to denigrate Spanish steaks. They know that here you can get the thickest, juiciest, tastiest steaks in Spain. Señor Paco was the first in Madrid to sear steaks in boiling oil before serving them on plates so hot that the almost-raw meat continues to cook, preserving the natural juices. Located in the Old Town, this two-story restaurant has three dining rooms, but reservations are imperative. Steaks are priced according to weight. If you face a long wait, while away the time sampling the tapas at the bar in front.

Casa Paco isn't just a steakhouse. You can start with fish soup and proceed to grilled sole, baby lamb, or *Casa Paco cocido,* the house version of Madrid's famous chickpea and pork soup. You might top it off with one of the luscious desserts, but know that Paco no longer serves coffee. It made customers linger, keeping tables occupied while potential patrons had to be turned away.

Cornucopia en Descalzas. Calle Flora, 1. ☎ **91/547-6465.** Reservations recommended. Main courses 1,800–2,600 ptas. (US$10.80–US$15.60); fixed-price lunch (Tues–Fri only) 1,600 ptas. (US$9.60). AE, MC, V. Tues–Sun 1:30–4pm and 8:30–11:30pm. Closed 1 week in Aug. Metro: Ópera or Callao. EURO-AMERICAN.

Set on a narrow side street adjacent to the medieval Plaza de Descalzas Reales, this restaurant occupies the mezzanine level of what was originally built in the 19th century as a private palace. Its glamour and allure derive from its ownership by four partners, two of whom (North Carolina-born Jennifer Cole and Kimberly Manning) are American; the others include French-born François and Spanish-born Fernando. Within a pair of elegant and airy dining rooms whose gleaming parquet floor remains intact from the original decor, you can admire a roster of frequently changing paintings, any of which is available for sale. Menu items include marinated salmon, marinated and grilled tuna served with couscous, duck breast with barbecue sauce, scallops served in a wine-and-cream sauce, and a succulent version of grilled *calamares* with garlicky aioli. Desserts are sumptuous and might include a dollop of such original homemade ice creams as *morito.* Named after a traditional Cuban cocktail, it's flavored with mint, lemon, and rum. All the food is capably prepared, the ingredients are fresh, and the staff is among the more inviting in Madrid.

✪ **El Cenador del Prado.** Prado, 4. ☎ **91-429-15-61.** Reservations recommended. Jackets and ties are recommended for men. Main courses 1,500–2,600 ptas. (US$9–US$15.60); fixed-price menu 3,350 ptas. (US$20.10). AE, DC, MC, V. Mon–Fri 1:45–4pm; Mon–Sat 9pm–midnight. Closed Aug 12–19. Metro: Puerta del Sol. INTERNATIONAL.

This restaurant is deceptively elegant. In the simple anteroom, an attendant will check your coat and packages in an elaborately carved armoire and the maître d' will usher you into one of a trio of rooms. Two of the rooms, done in tones of peach and sepia, have cove moldings and English furniture, as well as floor-to-ceiling gilded mirrors. A third room, the most popular, is ringed with lattices and flooded with sun from a skylight.

The imaginative and creative food reflects a basically French influence, with the occasional Asian flourish. You can enjoy such well-flavored specialties as crepes with salmon and Iranian caviar, a salad of crimson peppers and salted anchovies, a casserole of snails and oysters with mushrooms, a ceviche of salmon and shellfish, potato-leek soup studded with tidbits of hake and clams, sea bass with candied lemons, veal scallopini stuffed with asparagus and garlic sprouts, and medallions of venison served with pepper-and-fig chutney.

La Esquina del Real. Calle Unon, 18. ☎ **91-559-43-09.** Reservations recommended on weekends. Main courses 2,300–2,800 ptas. (US$13.80–US$16.80). AE, V. Mon–Fri 2–4pm and 9pm–midnight, Sat 9pm–midnight. Closed last 2 weeks of Aug. Metro: Opera/Sol. FRENCH.

Next to the Teatro Real you'll find this restaurant in an impressive 17th-century building with an ancient stone facade, thick granite walls, and the original wooden beams supporting old ceilings. This place has a sophisticated atmosphere yet prices are very reasonable. One Madrid food critic recently labeled this place one of the Spanish capital's "best kept" culinary secrets. The hospitable owner and chef, Marcel Magossian, extends a hearty welcome to patrons—domestic and foreign—and feeds them well. Fresh ingredients are transformed into such tasty concoctions as large prawns with a delicate raspberry vinaigrette or roast oxtail with mashed potatoes and fresh mushrooms. Even a rather common dish, veal fricassee in mushroom sauce, is transformed into something sublime. To end your dinner, you might opt for a combination platter of warm cheese, or else the tart tatin, ice cream with crunchy caramel sauce, brought right to the table for a flambé.

INEXPENSIVE

Casa Alberto. Huertas, 18. ☎ **91-429-93-56.** Reservations recommended. Main courses 1,000–2,500 ptas. (US$6–US$15). AE, DC, MC, V. Tues–Sat 1–4pm; Tues–Sun 8:30pm–midnight. Metro: Antón Martín. CASTILIAN.

One of the oldest tascas in the neighborhood, Casa Alberto was originally established in 1827, and has thrived ever since. It lies on the street level of the house where Miguel de Cervantes lived briefly in 1614, and contains an appealing mixture of bullfighting memorabilia, engravings, and reproductions of Old Master paintings. Many visitors opt only for the tapas, which are continually replenished from platters on the bar, but there's also a sit-down dining area for more substantial meals. Specialties include fried squid, shellfish in vinaigrette sauce, *chorizo* (sausage) in cider sauce, and several versions of baked or roasted lamb.

✪ **Mad Madrid.** Calle Virgin de los Peligros, 4. ☎ **91-532-62-28.** Reservations recommended. Main courses 1,600–2,100 ptas. (US$10.70–US$14.05); fixed-price menu (at lunch only) 1,500 ptas. (US$10.05). AE, DC, MC, V. Mon–Wed 1–4pm and 9:30pm–3am; Thurs–Sat 1–4pm and 9:30pm–4am. Dinner served until 12:30am. Metro: Sevilla, Gran Vía. INTERNATIONAL.

This restaurant bar in the very center of Madrid is a hot spot. Done all in gray and red in stark minimalism (sort of a tongue-in-cheek Soviet style), there's also a garden where you can enjoy a cocktail on a summer night. Taking her inspiration from around the Mediterranean, chef Belen Laguía changes the menu every three months. Staple menu items include starters such as goat cheese on caramelized onions and corral salad, which is comprised of wild chicken marinated in vinegar and cream on four types of lettuce. Other dishes to savor are marinated salmon with dill and golden caviar, which is black, and comes from an inland sea in the dry southern province of Murcia. This is served with Japanese seaweed and fresh seasonal vegetables presented al dente. Desserts include apple tart, not too sweet and topped with egg yolk.

Mesón las Descalzas. Postigo San Martín, 3. ☎ **91-522-72-17.** Reservations recommended. Main courses 1,600–3,000 ptas. (US$9.60–US$18); fixed-price menu 1,200 ptas. (US$7.20). AE, DC, MC, V. Daily 1–4pm and 8pm–midnight. Metro: Callao. SPANISH.

Las Descalzas, a recommended tavern-style restaurant, has a massive tapas bar that's often crowded at night. Behind a glass-and-wood screen is the restaurant section, its specialties including kidneys with sherry, *sopa castellana* (seafood soup), Basque-style hake, crayfish, shrimp, oysters, clams, and paella with shellfish. There is folk music for entertainment.

Museo del Jamon. Carrera de San Jerónimo, 6 (1 block east of Puerta del Sol). ☎ **91-521-03-46.** *Menú del día* 950–1,600 ptas. (US$5.70–US$9.60); *platos combinados* 500–750 ptas. (US$3–US$4.50). MC, V. Daily 8:30am–1am. Metro: Puerta del Sol. SPANISH/TAPAS.

The displays on the walls of this unique establishment explain the bewildering name: "The Museum of Ham." As in an art exhibition, large amounts of different kinds of hams—cured by a variety of methods—hang from the ceilings. The popular *chorizos* are hooked in rows that remind one of those scenes in the "Golden Age" paintings. This is indeed a real museum of the most celebrated fast food in Spain. On certain nights the tavern offers live entertainment in the dining area upstairs, often a guitarist. The *paella* for two is reasonably priced. The aged *jamon Serrano* or Serrano ham is a great delicacy now highly prized at tapas bars throughout Spain, Europe, and North America. You might try it in small sandwiches known as *bocattas* or in the always-available tapas. The daily menu is varied and served in generous portions. Service is efficient if not too friendly, but customers don't seem to mind.

Taberna del Alabardero. Felipe V, 6. ☎ **91-547-25-77.** Reservations required for restaurant only. Bar: tapas 450–1,500 ptas. (US$2.70–US$9); glass of house wine 200 ptas. (US$1.20). Restaurant: main courses 1,900–2,500 ptas. (US$11.40–US$15). AE, DC, MC, V. Daily 8am–1am. Metro: Ópera. BASQUE/SPANISH.

In close proximity to the Royal Palace, this little Spanish classic is known for its selection of tasty tapas, ranging from squid cooked in wine to fried potatoes dipped in hot sauce. Photographs of famous former patrons, including Nelson Rockefeller and the race-car driver Jackie Stewart, line the walls. The restaurant in the rear is said to be one of the city's best-kept secrets. Decorated in typical tavern style, it serves savory Spanish and Basque cuisine made from market-fresh ingredients.

RETIRO/SALAMANCA
EXPENSIVE

Alkalde. Jorge Juan, 10. ☎ **91-576-33-59.** Reservations required. Main courses 2,000–5,300 ptas. (US$12–US$31.80); fixed-price menu from 6,000 ptas. (US$36). AE, DC, MC, V. Daily 1:15–4pm and 8:30pm–midnight. Closed Sat–Sun in July–Aug. Metro: Retiro or Serrano. Bus: 8, 20, 21, or 53. BASQUE.

For decades, Alkalde has been known for serving top-quality Spanish food in an old tavern setting. Decorated like a Basque inn, it has beamed ceilings with hams hanging from the rafters. Upstairs is a large typical tavern; downstairs is a maze of stone-sided cellars that are pleasantly cool in summer (though the whole place is air-conditioned).

Basque cookery is the best in Spain, and Alkalde honors that noble tradition. Begin with the cream of crabmeat soup, followed by *gambas a la plancha* (grilled shrimp) or *cigalas* (crayfish). Other recommended dishes include *mero salsa verde* (brill in a green sauce), trout Alkalde, stuffed peppers, and chicken steak. The dessert specialty is copa *Cardinal* (ice cream topped with fruit).

✪ **El Amparo.** Callejón de Puigcerdá, 8 (at corner of Jorge Juan). ☎ **91-431-64-56.** Reservations required. Main courses 2,950–4,500 ptas. (US$17.70–US$27). AE, MC, V. Mon–Fri 1:30–3:30pm, Mon–Sat 9:30–11:30pm. Metro: Goya. Bus: 21 or 53. BASQUE.

Behind the cascading vines on El Amparo's facade is one of Madrid's most elegant gastronomic enclaves. Inside this converted carriage house three tiers of roughly hewn wooden beams surround tables set with pink napery and glistening silver for a touch of cosmopolitan glamour. A sloping skylight floods the interior with sun by day; at night, pinpoints of light from the high-tech hanging lanterns create intimate shadows. Polite, uniformed waiters serve well-prepared nouvelle cuisine versions of cold marinated salmon with a tomato sorbet, cold cream of vegetable and shrimp soup, bisque of shellfish with Armagnac, ravioli with crayfish dressed with balsamic vinegar and vanilla-scented oil, roast lamb chops with garlic purée, breast of duck, ragout of sole, steamed fish of the day, roulades of lobster with soy sauce, and steamed hake with pepper sauce.

El Pescador. Calle José Ortega y Gasset, 75. ☎ **91-402-12-90.** Reservations required. Main courses 6,000–15,000 ptas. (US$36–US$90); fixed-price menu 6,500 ptas. (US$39). MC, V. Mon–Sat 1:30–4pm and 8:30pm–midnight. Closed Aug. Metro: Lista. SEAFOOD.

El Pescador is a popular fish restaurant that has become a favorite of Madrileños who appreciate the more than 30 kinds of fish served, all prominently displayed in a glass case. Many of these are unknown in North America, and some originate off the coast of Galicia. The management air-freights them in and prefers to serve them grilled (*a la plancha*).

You might precede your main course with spicy fish soup and accompany it with one of the many good wines from northeastern Spain. If you're not sure what to order (even the English translations might sound unfamiliar), try one of the many varieties and sizes of shrimp. These go under the names *langostinos, cigalas, santiaguinos,* and *carabineros.* Many of them are expensive and priced by the gram, so be careful when you order.

✪ **Horcher.** Alfonso XII, 6. ☎ **91-532-35-96.** Reservations required. Jackets and ties required for men. Main courses 3,500–8,000 ptas. (US$21–US$48). AE, DC, MC, V. Mon–Fri 1:30–4pm; Mon–Sat 8:30pm–midnight. Metro: Retiro. GERMAN/INTERNATIONAL.

Horcher originated in Berlin in 1904. In 1943, prompted by a tip from a high-ranking German officer that Germany was losing the war, Herr Horcher moved his restaurant to Madrid. For years, it was known as the best dining room in the city, until culinary competition overtook that stellar position. Nevertheless, the restaurant has continued its grand European traditions, including excellent service.

Where to start? You might try the skate or shrimp tartare or the distinctive warm hake salad. Both the venison stew with green pepper and orange peel and the crayfish with parsley and cucumber are typical of the elegant fare served with impeccable style. Spanish aristocrats often come here in autumn to sample game dishes, including venison, wild boar, and roast wild duck. Other main courses include veal scallopini in tarragon and sea bass with saffron. For dessert, the house specialty is crêpes Sir Holden, prepared at your table with fresh raspberries, cream, and nuts.

⭘ **La Gamella.** Alfonso XII, 4. ☎ **91-532-45-09.** Reservations required. Main courses 2,300–4,500 ptas. (US$13.80–US$27). AE, DC, MC, V. Mon–Fri 1:30–4pm, Mon–Sat 9pm–midnight. Metro: Retiro. Bus: 19. CALIFORNIAN/CASTILIAN.

La Gamella established its gastronomic reputation shortly after it opened several years ago in less imposing quarters in another part of town. In 1988 its Illinois-born owner, former choreographer Dick Stephens, moved his restaurant into the 19th-century building where the Spanish philosopher Ortega y Gasset was born. The prestigious Horcher, one of the capital's legendary restaurants (see above), is just across the street—but the food here at La Gamella is better. The russet-colored, high-ceilinged design invites customers to relax. Mr. Stephens has prepared his delicate and light-textured specialties for the king and queen of Spain, as well as for Madrid's most talked-about artists and merchants, many of whom he knows and greets personally between sessions in his kitchen.

Typical menu items include a ceviche of Mediterranean fish, sliced duck liver in truffle sauce, a dollop of goat cheese served over caramelized endive, duck breast with peppers, and an array of well-prepared desserts, among them an all-American cheese-cake. Traditional Spanish dishes such as chicken with garlic have been added to the menu, plus what has been called "the only edible hamburger in Madrid." Because of the intimacy and the small dimensions of the restaurant, reservations are important.

La Trainera. Calle Lagasca, 60. ☎ **91-576-80-35.** Reservations recommended. Main courses 5,000–7,000 ptas. (US$30–US$42). AE, DC, MC, V. Mon–Sat 1–4pm and 8pm–midnight. Metro: Serrano. SEAFOOD.

This restaurant is more expensive, and more chic, than its sprawling, paneled interior might imply. Suitable for up to 300 diners at a time, it occupies a quartet of dining rooms within a turn-of-the-century building in the glamorous shopping neighborhood of Serrano. Look for vaguely Basque-inspired platters of very fresh seafood, which arrive steaming hot and drizzled with subtle combinations of herbs, wines, and olive oils. No meat of any kind is served here. Instead, you'll find spicy and garlic-enriched versions of fish soup, an *escabeche of bonita* served as an appetizer, fillet of sole prepared in any of several different versions, Cantabrian crayfish, and well-conceived versions of a *salpicon de mariscos* (a platter of shellfish). Other fish include red mullet, swordfish with capers, monkfish, and virtually anything else that swims. Any of these can be preceded with a heaping platter of shellfish set atop a bed of artfully arranged seaweed. Succulent shellfish, including lobster, shrimp, crab, and mussels, plus an array of other items, is market-priced by weight.

Pedro Larumbe. Serrano, 61. ☎ **91-575-11-12.** Reservations required. Main course 2,800–3,000 ptas. (US$16.80–US$18); *menú completo* 6,500 ptas. (US$39). AE, DC, MC, V. Mon–Fri 1:30–4pm and 9pm–midnight, Sat 9pm–midnight. Closed Aug 15–30. Metro: Ruben Dario and Nuñez de Balboa. BASQUE/FRENCH.

In an opulent section of La Castellana, very close to Plaza de Colón, this century-old building was once the headquarters of the famous newspaper ABC. Today it is the elegant restaurant of National Gastronomic Award-winner, Pedro Larumbe. There are three dining areas, each as elegantly impressive as the others: the classic *Salon Pompeyano,* the art deco *Salon Fundador,* and the beautifully tiled *Patio Andalus.* This Navarrese chef not only likes a fin-de-siècle decor, he prefers turn-of-the-century cookery as well. His specialties are often from the tried-and-true recipes of yesterday, as evoked by his *solomillo à la mostaza* (steak with mustard sauce). He also specializes in hake in green sauce with mussels, a favorite dish of the Basque country. One of his specialties is *ensalada de bocavante con salsa de almendras,* lobster salad with almond dressing, a true delight. The service is impeccable, the wine list well chosen, and the desserts something to write home about: tiramisu with a sweet wine and caramel sauce or "tear drops" of chocolate—rich, dark, tear-shaped chocolate pieces.

Suntory. Paseo Castellana, 36. ☎ **91-577-37-34.** Reservations recommended. *Menú completo* 6,500 ptas. (US$39). AE, DC, MC, V. Mon–Sat 1:30–3:30pm. Metro: Rubén Dario. JAPANESE.

Already acclaimed for its chain restaurants around the world, Suntory has invaded an attractive section of La Castellana, and is winning converts to its impeccably prepared Japanese cuisine. Decorated in the minimalist style evocative of other Japanese restaurants around the world, this is the domain of Ken Sato, acclaimed as the finest Japanese chef in Spain. There are three dining areas, including the Teppan Yaki, the Shabu-Shabu, and a sushi bar. The finest and freshest fish and shellfish is served here. Visiting Japanese praise the quality of fish found in Spanish waters. Try some of the exquisite sushi or the Mediterranean prawn tempura. The red tuna sashimi is our favorite. Finish these delicacies with a tempura *helado* (cake with vanilla icing).

Viridiana. Juan de Mena, 14. ☎ **91-531-52-22.** Reservations recommended. Main courses 3,000–4,500 ptas. (US$18–US$27). AE, MC, V. Mon–Sat 1:30–4pm and 9pm–midnight. Closed 1 week at Easter and in Aug. Metro: Banco. INTERNATIONAL.

Viridiana—named after the 1961 Luis Buñuel classic film—is praised as one of the up-and-coming restaurants of Madrid, known for the creative imagination of its chef and part-owner, Abraham García, who has lined the walls with stills from Buñuel films. He is also a film historian, not just a self-taught chef. Menu specialties are usually contemporary adaptations of traditional recipes, and they change frequently according to the availability of the ingredients. Examples of the highly individualistic cooking include a salad of exotic lettuces served with smoked salmon, chicken laced with cinnamon, baby squid with curry served on a bed of lentils, roasted lamb served in puff pastry with fresh basil, and the choicest langostinos from Cádiz. The food here is sublime, and the inviting ambience encourages you to relax as you sit back to enjoy dishes that often dazzle the eye, notably venison and rabbit arranged on a plate with fresh greens to evoke an autumnal scene in a forest.

MODERATE

Gran Café de Gijón. Paseo de Recoletos, 21. ☎ **91-521-54-25.** Reservations required for restaurant. Main courses 3,000–5,000 ptas. (US$18–US$30); fixed-price menu 1,800 ptas. (US$10.80). AE, DC, MC, V. Mon–Fri and Sun 7am–1:30am; Sat 7am–2am. Metro: Banco de España, Colón, or Recoletos. SPANISH.

Each of the old European capitals has a coffeehouse that traditionally attracts the literati—in Madrid it's the Gijón, which opened in 1888 in the heyday of the city's belle époque. Artists and writers still patronize this venerated old cafe, many of them spending hours over one cup of coffee. Open windows look out onto the wide paseo, and the large terrace is perfect for sun worshippers and bird-watchers. Along one side of the cafe is a stand-up bar, and on the lower level is a restaurant. Food is prepared the way it used to be in Madrid. Patrons liked it then, and they come back for the same dishes enjoyed in their youth. In summer you can sit in the garden to enjoy a *blanco y negro* (black coffee with ice cream) or a mixed drink.

CHAMBERÍ
VERY EXPENSIVE

✪ **Jockey.** Amador de los Ríos, 6. ☎ **91-319-24-35.** Reservations required. Main courses 3,500–6,750 ptas. (US$21–US$40.50). AE, DC, MC, V. Mon–Fri 1–4pm and Mon–Sat 9pm–midnight. Closed Aug. Metro: Colón. INTERNATIONAL.

For decades this was the premier restaurant of Spain, though that title is more hotly contested today. A favorite of international celebrities, diplomats, and heads of state, it was once known as the Jockey Club, although "Club" was eventually dropped because it suggested exclusivity. The restaurant, with tables on two levels, isn't large. Wood-paneled walls and colored linen provide a cozy ambience. Against the paneling are a dozen prints of jockeys mounted on horses—hence the name of the place.

Since Jockey's establishment shortly after World War II, each chef who has come along has prided himself on coming up with new and creative dishes. You can still order Beluga caviar from Iran, but might settle happily for the goose-liver terrine or slices of Jabugo ham. Cold melon soup with shrimp is soothing on a hot day, especially when followed by grill-roasted young pigeon from Talavera or sole fillets with figs in chardonnay. Stuffed small chicken Jockey style is a specialty, as is *tripa Madrileña*, a local dish. Desserts are sumptuous.

EXPENSIVE

La Fuencisla. San Mateo, 4, 28004. ☎ **91-521-61-86.** Reservations recommended. Main courses 2,500–2,800 ptas. (US$15–US$16.80); *menú completo* 6,000 ptas. (US$36). AE, M, V. Mon–Sat 2–4pm and 9pm–1am. Closed Aug. Metro: Tribunal. SPANISH.

This small but comfortable restaurant has been serving meals in the most traditional Spanish style for nearly half a century. A family business, La Fuencisla (named as an offering to the Virgin of Segovia) has seen Señor and Señora De Frutos attending to their customers since its opening. He greets the visitors in the front while she creates tasty homemade meals in the kitchen. The dishes are typical of the Segovia, prepared with fresh ingredients according to time-tested recipes. No dish is more typical than the grilled chops of milk-fed lamb, an offering praised by gastronomes. Begin with fresh asparagus in country butter and aromatic garlic or else savory mussels in a marinara sauce. Fillet of tuna freshly baked in the oven is another palate pleaser. For desserts, the cooks always prepare homemade tarts, which are especially good when the fresh fruit comes in. Otherwise you might opt for the rice pudding or *flan de coco* (coconut pudding).

La Paloma. Jorge Juan, 39. ☎ **91-576-86-92.** Reservations recommended. Main courses 2,800–3,200 ptas. (US$16.80–US$19.20); *menú completo* 7,500 ptas. (US$45). AE, DC, MC, V. Mon–Sat 1:30–4pm and 9pm–midnight. Metro: Vergara. BASQUE/FRENCH.

In the exclusive Salamanca neighborhood, this small but comfortable restaurant is the showcase for the culinary talents of chef-owner Segundo Alonso, who made a stellar reputation for himself at the more exclusive El Amparo. Many of his fans followed him here and have since become regulars. His restaurant is in a nostalgic old restored house with high ceilings and wooden beams. His French and Basque dishes are some of the finest of their kind in Madrid. His food is robust, and he's known for what are called variety meats, especially his pigs' trotters. Even if you have never sampled this dish before, dare try it here. You might be glad you did. You could settle instead for his equally celebrated wood pigeon stuffed with foie gras. He also does an excellent lasagna with crab meat, spinach, and leeks, and also a fine *rabo de toro* or bull's tail stewed in red-wine sauce. The best fish dishes are grilled turbot with tomato paste and thyme and sea urchin gratineed and served with quail eggs. For dessert, try fresh dates with chantilly cream or order a velvety almond mousse with cinnamon ice cream.

✪ **Las Cuatro Estaciones.** General Ibáñez Ibero, 5. ☎ **91-553-63-05.** Reservations required. Main courses 2,100–5,000 ptas. (12.60–US$30); fixed-price dinner 6,500 ptas. (US$39). AE, DC, MC, V. Mon–Fri 1:30–4pm and Mon–Sat 9–11:30pm. Closed Aug. Metro: Guzmán el Bueno. MEDITERRANEAN.

Las Cuatro Estaciones is placed by gastronomes and horticulturists alike among their favorite Madrid dining spots, and it's a neck-and-neck rival with the prestigious

Jockey. In addition to superb food, the establishment prides itself on the masses of flowers that change with the season. Depending on the time of year, mirrors surrounding the multilevel bar near the entrance reflect thousands of hydrangeas, chrysanthemums, or poinsettias. Even the napery matches whichever colors the resident florist has chosen as the seasonal motif. Each person involved in food preparation spends a prolonged apprenticeship at restaurants in France before returning home to test their talents on the taste buds of aristocratic Madrid.

Representative specialties include crab bisque, a *petite marmite* of fish and shellfish, a salad of eels, fresh asparagus and mushrooms in puff pastry with parsley-butter sauce, and a nouvelle cuisine version of blanquette of monkfish so tender that it melts in your mouth. The desserts include any specials the chef has concocted that day, a selection of which is brought temptingly to your table.

✪ **Restaurante Belagua.** In the Hotel Palacio Santo Mauro, calle Zurbano, 36. ☎ **91-319-69-00.** Reservations recommended. Main courses 2,900–3,800 ptas. (US$17.40–US$22.80). AE, DC, MC, V. Daily 1:30–3:30pm and 8:30–11:30pm. Closed national holidays. Metro: Rubén Darío or Alonso Martínez. BASQUE.

This glamorous restaurant was originally built in 1894 as a small palace in the French neoclassical style. In 1991 Catalán designer Josep Joanpere helped transform the building into a carefully detailed hotel (the Santo Mauro), which we've recommended separately (see above). On the hotel premises is this highly appealing postmodern restaurant, today one of the capital's finest.

Assisted by the well-mannered staff, you'll select from a menu whose inspiration and ingredients change with the seasons. Examples include watermelon-and-prawn salad, light cream of cold ginger soup, haddock baked in a crust of potatoes tinted with squid ink, fillet of monkfish with prawn-and-zucchini sauce, and duck with honey and black cherries. Depending on the selection that day, dessert might include miniature portions of flan with strawberry sauce plus an array of the day's pastries. The restaurant's name, incidentally, derives from a village in Navarre known for its natural beauty.

MODERATE

Teatriz. Calle Hermossila, 15. ☎ **91-577-53-79.** Reservations recommended. Main courses 2,000–2,400 ptas. (US$12–US$14.40); *menú completo* 4,500 ptas. (US$27). AE, DC, MC, V. Daily noon–3am. Closed Aug. Metro: Serrano. ITALIAN.

Decorated by the famed French architect and designer Philippe Starck, this old theater has been transformed into a topnotch Italian restaurant in the prosperous Serrano area. Theater seats have long given way to dining tables, but Starck kept many of the old theater elements. As you head for the restroom, you encounter a stunning fountain of marble, silver, and gold, everything bathed in a bluish light that makes it look like a nightclub. The kitchen closes at midnight but the bar remains open until 3am. Dishes are genuine and cleverly crafted, if not too inventive. Launch yourself with fresh mozzarella with tomatoes in virgin olive oil or perhaps raw salmon and turbot flavored with fresh dill. One of the best pastas is tortellini filled with Parmesan-flavored ground meat. Desserts are worth saving room for, including cannelloni stuffed with dark chocolate or fresh cheese mousse with mango ice cream. There is also a velvety-smooth tiramisu.

INEXPENSIVE

Foster's Hollywood. Velázquez, 80. ☎ **91-435-61-28.** Main courses 950–2,950 ptas. (US$5.70–US$17.70). AE, DC, MC, V. Sun–Thurs 1pm–midnight, Fri–Sat 1pm–2am. Metro: Quevedo. AMERICAN.

When Foster's opened its doors in 1971, it was not only the first American cuisine restaurant in Spain, but also one of the first in Europe. Since those early days it has grown to 15 restaurants in Madrid, and has even opened branches in Florida. A popular hangout for both locals and visiting Yanks, it offers a choice of dining venues, ranging from classical club American to a studio, the latter evoking a working movie studio with props. The varied menu includes Tex-Mex selections, ribs, steaks, sandwiches, freshly made salads, and, as its signature product, hamburgers grilled over natural charcoal in many variations. The *New York Times* once claimed that it had "probably the best onion rings in the world."

Other locations include Paseo de la Castellana, 116-118 (☎ **91-564-63-08**) and Princesa, 13 (☎ **91-559-19-14**), near Plaza de España.

Ríofrío. Centro Colón; Plaza de Colón, 1. ☎ **91-319-29-77.** Main courses 700–3,200 ptas. (US$4.20–US$19.20); fixed-price menu 2,500 ptas. (US$15); sandwiches 525–900 ptas. (US$3.15–US$5.40). AE, DC, MC, V. Daily 7:30am–2am. Metro: Colón. Bus: 5, 14, 21, 27, or 45. INTERNATIONAL.

Overlooking Madrid's version of New York's Columbus Circle, this is a sort of all-purpose place for drinking, eating, dining, or nightclubbing. The least-expensive way to eat here is to patronize one of two self-service cafeterias, where average meals run from 1,200 to 1,800 pesetas (US$8.40 to US$12.60). There's also a large restaurant serving international cuisine, with meals averaging 3,500 pesetas (US$24.50), plus yet another dining room for informal lunches, dinners, snacks, or apéritifs. The spacious glassed-in terrace, open year-round, is known for serving some of the best paella in Madrid. Finally, there's even a nightclub, El Descubrimiento, should you desire to make an evening of it. The club serves dinner costing from 4,500 pesetas (US$31.50), which includes not only the meal but also a show to follow. Sandwiches are available throughout the day if you'd like just a light bite in the hot Madrid sun.

NEAR ALONSO MARTINEZ
MODERATE

Café Balear. Calle Sagunto, 18. ☎ **91/447-9115.** Reservations recommended. Main courses 1,600–5,500 ptas. (US$9.60–US$33). AE, MC, V. Daily 1:30–4pm, Tues–Sat 8:30–11:30pm. Metro: Iglesia. PAELLA/SEAFOOD.

Only a handful of other restaurants in Madrid focus as aggressively as this one on the national dish of Spain, paella, which here comes in 14 different versions, including permutations that might surprise even the most jaded aficionado of Spanish cuisine. Within a yellow-and-white dining room loaded with verdant potted plants, you can order any of several *calderas* (casseroles) that bubble with all kinds of fish and shellfish. Paella here includes versions with shellfish, with chicken and shellfish, with pork, with crabs, with lobster, and with an all-black version that's tinted with squid ink for extra flavor. There's even a vegetarian version sans fish. Your fellow diners represent many of the creative arts of Spain, with lots of journalists, writers, poets, and artists who seem to have adopted the place.

Casa Vallejo. Calle San Lorenzo, 9. ☎ **91-308-61-58.** Reservations recommended. Main courses 1,600–4,000 ptas. (US$9.60–US$24); fixed-price menu (available Mon–Fri only) 1,800 ptas. (US$10.80). MC, V. Mon–Sat 2–4pm; Tues–Sat 9:30pm–midnight. Metro: Tribunale or Alonso Martinez. SPANISH.

This hardworking bistro with a not-terribly-subtle staff has less exposure to international clients than do some of its competitors. But despite that, you'll find a sense of culinary integrity that's based on a devotion to fresh ingredients and a rigid allegiance to time-tested Spanish recipes. It occupies a turn-of-the-century building and contains room for only 42 diners at a time. Menu items include garlic soup; tartlets layered with tomatoes, zucchini, and cheese; a ragout of clams and artichokes; croquettes of chicken; fillet of pork; duck breast in orange or prune sauce; and creamy desserts. Budget gourmets in Madrid praise the hearty flavors, the robust cookery, and the prices.

Ciao Madrid. Calle Apodaca, 22 (☎ **91-447-00-36;** metro: Tribunal); and calle Argensola 7 (☎ **91-308-25-19;** metro: Alonso Martínez). Reservations recommended. Pastas 1,200–1,600 ptas. (US$7.20–US$9.60); main courses 1,600–2,500 ptas. (US$9.60–US$15). AE, DC, MC, V. Mon–Fri 1:30–3:45pm; Mon–Sat 9:30pm–midnight. The branch at calle Apodaca is closed in Sept; branch at calle Argensola is closed in Aug. ITALIAN.

These are two highly successful all-Italian restaurants established and maintained by extended members of the Laguna family. The older of the two is the branch on Apodaca, established about a dozen years ago; the second came on the scene in the early 1990s. Both maintain the same hours, prices, menu, and interior inspired by the tenets of minimalist Milanese decor. Good-tasting items include risottos and pastas such as ravioli or tagliatelle with wild mushrooms. No one will mind if you order a pasta as a main course (lots of clients here do, accompanying it with a green salad). If you're in the mood for a more substantial meal, consider osso bucco, veal scallopini, chicken or veal parmigiana, and any of several kinds of fish.

CHAMARTÍN
VERY EXPENSIVE

✪ **Zalacaín.** Alvarez de Baena, 4. ☎ **91-561-48-40.** Reservations required. Main courses 9,500–12,000 ptas. (US$57–US$72). AE, DC, MC, V. Mon–Fri 1:15–4pm; Mon–Sat 9–11:45pm. Closed week before Easter and in Aug. Metro: Rubén Darío. INTERNATIONAL.

Outstanding in both food and decor, Zalacaín opened in 1973 and introduced nouvelle cuisine to Spain. It is reached by an illuminated walk from Paseo de la Castellana and housed at the garden end of a modern apartment complex. In fact, it's within an easy walk of such deluxe hotels as the Castellana and the Miguel Angel. The name of the restaurant comes from the intrepid hero of Basque author Pío Baroja's 1909 novel, *Zalacaín El Aventurero*. Zalacaín is small, exclusive, and expensive. It has the atmosphere of an elegant old mansion: The walls are covered with textiles, and some are decorated with Audubon-type paintings.

The menu features many Basque and French specialties, often with nouvelle cuisine touches. It might offer a superb sole in a green sauce, but it also knows the glory of grilled pig's feet. Among the most recommendable main dishes are oysters with caviar and sherry jelly; crepes stuffed with smoked fish; ravioli stuffed with mushrooms, foie gras, and truffles; Spanish bouillabaisse; and veal escalopes in orange sauce. For dessert, we'd suggest one of the custards, perhaps raspberry or chocolate.

EXPENSIVE

El Bodegón. Pinar, 15. ☎ **91-562-88-44.** Reservations required. Main courses 3,500–5,200 ptas. (US$21–US$31.20). AE, DC, MC, V. Mon–Fri 1:30–4pm, Mon–Sat 9pm–midnight. Closed holidays and Aug. Metro: Rubén Darío. INTERNATIONAL/BASQUE/SPANISH.

El Bodegón is imbued with the atmosphere of a gentleman's club for hunting enthusiasts. International globetrotters are attracted here, especially in the evening, as the restaurant is near such deluxe hotels as the Castellana and the Miguel Angel. King Juan Carlos and Queen Sofía have dined here.

Waiters in black and white, with gold braid and buttons, bring dignity to the food service. Even bottled water is served champagne-style, chilled in a silver floor stand. There are two main dining rooms, both conservative and oak-beamed in the country-inn style. We recommend starting with cream of crayfish bisque or velvety vichyssoise. Main-course selections include grilled filet mignon with classic béarnaise sauce and venison bourguignonne. Other choices include shellfish au gratin Escoffier, quails

Fernand Point, tartare of raw fish marinated in parsley-enriched vinaigrette, and smoked salmon.

✪ **El Cabo Mayor.** Juan Ramón Jiménez, 37. ☎ **91-350-87-76.** Reservations recommended. Main courses 2,800–3,900 ptas. (US$16.80–US$23.40). AE, DC, MC, V. Mon–Fri 1:30–4pm and Mon–Sat 8:45–11:45pm. Closed 1 week at Easter and in Aug. Metro: Cuzco. SPANISH.

In the prosperous northern edges of Madrid, El Cabo Mayor is not far from Chamartín Station. This is one of the best, most popular, and most stylish restaurants in Madrid, attracting on occasion the king and queen. An open-air staircase leading to the entranceway descends from a manicured garden on a quiet side street. A battalion of uniformed doormen stands ready to greet arriving taxis. The restaurant's decor is a nautically inspired mass of hardwood panels, brass trim, old-fashioned pulleys and ropes, a tile floor custom-painted with sea-green and blue waves, and hand-carved models of fishing boats. In brass replicas of portholes, some dozen bronze statues honoring fishers and their craft are displayed in illuminated positions of honor.

Menu choices include paprika-laden peppers stuffed with fish, a salad composed of Jabugo ham and foie gras of duckling, Cantabrian fish soup, stewed sea bream with thyme, asparagus mousse, salmon in sherry sauce, and loin of veal in cassis sauce. Desserts include such selections as a rice mousse with pine-nut sauce.

✪ **El Olivo Restaurant.** General Gallegos, 1. ☎ **91-359-15-35.** Reservations recommended. Main courses 2,950–3,700 ptas. (US$17.70–US$22.20); fixed-price menus 3,500–5,950 ptas. (US$21–US$35.70). AE, DC, MC, V. Tues–Sat 1–4pm and 9pm–midnight. Closed Aug 15–31 and 4 days around Easter. Metro: Plaza de Castilla. MEDITERRANEAN.

Locals praise the success of a non-Spaniard (in this case, French-born Jean Pierre Vandelle) in recognizing the international appeal of two of Spain's most valuable culinary resources, olive oil and sherry. His likable restaurant, located in northern Madrid, pays homage to the glories of the Spanish olive. Designed in tones of green and amber, it is the only restaurant in Spain that wheels a trolley stocked with 40 regional olive oils from table to table. From the trolley, diners select a variety to soak up with chunks of rough-textured bread that is, according to your taste, seasoned with a dash of salt.

Menu specialties include grilled fillet of monkfish marinated in herbs and olive oil, then served with black-olive sauce over a compote of fresh tomatoes, and four preparations of codfish arranged on a single platter and served with a *pil-pil* sauce. (Named after the sizzling noise it makes as it bubbles on a stove, *pil-pil* sauce is composed of codfish gelatin and herbs that are whipped into a mayonnaise-like consistency with olive oil.) Dessert might be one of several different chocolate pastries. A wide array of reasonably priced Bordeaux and Spanish wines can accompany your meal.

A final note: Many clients deliberately arrive early as an excuse to linger within El Olivo's one-of-a-kind sherry bar. Although other drinks are offered, the bar features more than a hundred brands of *vino de Jerez*, more than practically any other establishment in Madrid. Priced at 250 to 750 pesetas (US$1.75 to US$5.25) per glass, they make the perfect apéritif.

Goizeko Kabi. Comandante Zorita, 27. ☎ **91-533-01-85.** Reservations recommended. Main courses 1,800–5,000 ptas. (US$10.80–US$30). AE, DC, V. Mon–Sat 1–4pm, 8:30pm–midnight. Metro: Alvarado. BASQUE.

This restaurant serves some of the best Basque dishes in Madrid in a small, intimate, and understated interior. Particularly delicious is the starter of *boquerones*, almost sweet anchovies marinated in garlic and olive oil. We also loved the *bacalao pil-pil vizcaina* (cod in a Basque garlic sauce) and the wonderfully juicy king prawns. Dessert lovers will revel in the orange mousse with a coating of bitter chocolate or the more experimental black bread ice cream with coffee sauce.

✪ **O'Pazo.** Calle Reina Mercedes, 20. ☎ **91-553-23-33.** Reservations required. Main courses 2,200–5,350 ptas. (US$13.20–US$32.10). MC, V. Mon–Sat 1–4pm and 8:30pm–midnight. Closed Aug. Metro: Nuevos Ministerios or Alvarado. Bus: 3 or 5. GALICIAN/SEAFOOD.

O'Pazo is a deluxe Galician restaurant, viewed by local cognoscenti as one of the top seafood places in the country. The fish is flown in daily from Galicia and much of it is priced by weight, depending on market rates. In front is a cocktail lounge and bar, all polished brass, with low sofas and paintings. Carpeted floors, cushioned Castilian furniture, soft lighting, and colored-glass windows complete the picture.

The fish and shellfish soup is delectable, although others gravitate to the seaman's broth as a beginning course. Natural clams are succulent, as are *cigalas* (a kind of crayfish), spider crabs, and Jabugo ham. Main dishes range from baby eels to sea snails, from Galician style scallops to *zarzuela* (a seafood casserole).

✪ **Principe de Viana.** Calle Manuel de Falla, 5. ☎ **91-457-15-49.** Reservations required. Main courses 1,800–3,200 ptas. (US$10.80–US$19.20). AE, DC, MC, V. Mon–Fri 1–4pm, 9–11:30pm; Sat 9–11:30pm. Closed in Aug. Metro: Lima. BASQUE.

This place has gotten rave reviews. The decor is neutral yet classical in style. Fish is of course the most important staple of Basque cuisine, and there is a wide selection from which to choose. You might go the traditional route, with *bacalao ajoarriera* (cod with red peppers and tomatoes) or *merluza en salsa verde* (hake in parsley, garlic, and olive oil sauce). There are also more adventurous modern concoctions such as a salad with *chipirones* (baby squid) and *mojellas* (sweet meats) in a soya vinaigrette. Those with a sweet tooth will be more than satisfied with the dessert of cream cheese and mango sorbet. From the many Spanish and occasional foreign wines to choose from, the Albirino from Galicia is particularly recommended.

INEXPENSIVE

Alfredo's Barbacoa. Juan Hurtado de Mendoza, 11. ☎ **91-345-16-39.** Reservations recommended. Main courses 700–2,500 ptas. (US$4.20–US$15). AE, DC, MC, V. Mon–Sat 1–4:30pm and 8:30pm–midnight (Fri and Sat until 1am). Metro: Cuzco. AMERICAN.

Alfredo's is a popular rendezvous for Americans longing for home-style food. Al himself arrives at his bar/restaurant wearing boots, blue jeans, and a 10-gallon hat; his friendly welcome has made the place a center for both his friends and newcomers to Madrid. You *can* have hamburgers here, but they are of the barbecued variety, and you might prefer the barbecued spareribs or chicken. The salad bar is an attraction. And it's a rare treat to be able to have corn on the cob in Spain.

The original **Alfredo's Barbacoa,** Lagasca, 5 (☎ **91-576-62-71;** metro: Retiro), is still in business, and also under Al's auspices.

CHUECA
INEXPENSIVE

El Inca. Gravina, 23. ☎ **91-532-77-45.** Reservations required on weekends. Main courses 2,800–3,600 ptas. (US$16.80–US$21.60); fixed-price dinner 2,800 ptas. (US$16.80). AE, DC, V. Tues–Sun 1:30–4pm and Tue–Sat 9am–12:30am. Closed Aug. Metro: Chueca. PERUVIAN.

For a taste of South America, try El Inca, decorated with Incan motifs and artifacts. Since it opened in the early 1970s, it has hosted its share of diplomats and celebrities, although you're more likely to see families and local office workers. The house cocktail is a deceptively potent *pisco* sour—the recipe comes straight from the Andes. Many of the dishes contain potatoes, the national staple of Peru. The salad of potatoes and black olives is given unusual zest with a white-cheese sauce. Other specialties are the *ceviche de merluza* (raw hake marinated with onions) and *aji de gallina* (a chicken-and-rice dish made with peanut sauce), a Peruvian favorite.

Nabucco. Calle Hortaleza, 108. ☎ **91-310-06-11.** Reservations recommended. Pizza 755–1,000 ptas. (US$4.55–US$6); main courses 950–1,600 ptas. (US$5.70–US$9.60). AE, DC, MC, V. Mon–Sat 1:30–4pm, Sun–Thurs 8:45pm–midnight, Fri–Sat 8:45pm–1am. Metro: Alonso Martínez. Bus: 7 or 36. ITALIAN.

In a neighborhood of Spanish restaurants, the Italian trattoria format here comes as a welcome change. The decor resembles a postmodern update of an Italian ruin, complete with trompe l'oeil walls painted like marble. Roman portrait busts and a prominent bar lend a dignified air. Menu choices include cannelloni, a good selection of veal dishes, and such main courses as osso bucco. You might begin your meal with a selection of antipasti.

○ **Taberna Carmencita.** Libertad, 16. ☎ **91-531-66-12.** Reservations recommended. Main courses 1,800–2,800 ptas. (US$10.80–US$16.80); fixed-price menu 1,500 ptas. (US$9) available only at lunch. AE, DC, MC, V. Mon–Fri 1–4pm; Mon–Sat 9pm–midnight. Metro: Chueca or Banco de España. SPANISH/BASQUE.

Carmencita, founded in 1840 and exquisitely restored, is a street-corner enclave of old Spanish charm, filled with 19th-century detailing and tile work. It was a favorite hangout for the poet Federico García Lorca, as well as a meeting place for intelligentsia in the pre–Civil War days. Meals might include entrecôte with green pepper sauce, escalope of veal, braised mollusks with port, fillet of pork, codfish with garlic, and Bilbao-style hake. Every Thursday the special dish is a complicated version of Madrid's famous cocido. Patrons wax lyrical over this regional stew and the chefs have had decades to get it right.

Tienda de Vinos. Augusto Figueroa, 35. ☎ **91-521-70-12.** Main courses 850–2,500 ptas. (US$5.10–US$15). No credit cards. Mon–Sat 1–4pm and 9pm–midnight. Metro: Chueca. SPANISH.

Officially this restaurant is known as Tienda de Vinos (the Wine Store), but ever since the 1930s Madrileños have called it "El Comunista" (The Communist). Its now-deceased owner was a fervent Communist, and many locals who shared his political beliefs patronized the establishment. This rickety old wine shop with a few tables in the back is quite fashionable with actors and journalists looking for Spanish fare without frills. There is a menu, but no one ever looks at it—just ask what's available. Nor do you get a bill; you're just told how much to pay. Guests sit at simple wooden tables with wooden chairs and benches; walls are decorated with old posters, calendars, pennants, and clocks. Start with garlic or vegetable soup or lentils, followed by lamb chops, tripe in a spicy sauce, or meatballs and soft-set eggs with asparagus.

OFF THE PLAZA MAYOR
MODERATE

Casa Lucio. Cava Baja, 35. ☎ **91-365-32-52.** Reservations recommended. Main courses 2,500–3,600 ptas. (US$15–US$21.60). AE, DC, MC, V. Sun–Fri 1–4pm; daily 9pm–midnight. Closed Aug. Metro: La Latina. CASTILIAN.

Set on a historic street whose edges once marked the perimeter of Old Madrid, this is a venerable tasca with all the requisite antique accessories. Dozens of cured hams hang from hand-hewn beams above the well-oiled bar. Among the clientele is a stable of sometimes surprisingly well-known public figures—perhaps even the king. The two dining rooms, each on a different floor, have whitewashed walls, tile floors, and exposed brick. A well-trained staff offers classic Castilian food, which might include Jabugo ham with broad beans, shrimp in garlic sauce, hake with green sauce, several types of roasted lamb, and a thick steak served sizzling hot on a heated platter, called *churrasco de la casa*.

El Cuchi. Calle de Cuchilleros, 3. ☎ **91-366-44-24.** Reservations required. Main courses 2,500–3,500 ptas. (US$15–US$21). AE, DC, MC, V. Mon–Sat 1pm–midnight, Sun 1–4pm and 8pm–midnight . Metro: Puerta del Sol. MEXICAN/SPANISH.

A few doors down from Sobrino de Botín (see below), El Cuchi defiantly claims "Hemingway never ate here." However, just about everybody else has, attracted by both its low prices and its labyrinth of dining rooms. A European link in Mexico's famous Carlos 'n' Charlie's chain, the Madrid restaurant, a true tourist joint but amazingly popular, stands off a corner of Plaza Mayor. Ceiling beams and artifacts suggest rusticity. Specialties include black-bean soup, ceviche, guacamole, stuffed trout, and roast suckling pig (much cheaper than that served at Botín). You've had all this before, and probably in better versions, but the collection of beers from all over the globe and the rainbow-colored margaritas are unequaled in Madrid.

El Schotis. Cava Baja, 11. ☎ **91-365-32-30.** Reservations recommended. Main courses 1,200–2,900 ptas. (US$7.20–US$17.40); fixed-price menu 3,250 ptas. (US$19.50). AE, DC, MC, V. Daily 1–4pm, Mon–Sat 8:30–midnight. Metro: Puerta del Sol or La Latina. SPANISH.

El Schotis was established in 1962 within a solid stone building on one of Madrid's oldest and most historic streets. A series of large and pleasingly old-fashioned dining rooms is the setting for an animated crowd of Madrileños and foreign visitors, who receive ample portions of conservative, well-prepared vegetables, salads, soups, fish, and above all, meat. Specialties of the house include roasted baby lamb, grilled steaks and veal chops, shrimp with garlic, fried hake in green sauce, and traditional desserts. Although one reader found everything but the gazpacho "ho-hum," this local favorite pleases thousands of diners annually. There's a bar near the entrance for tapas and before- or after-dinner drinks.

La Posada de la Villa. Cava Baja, 9. ☎ **91-366-18-60.** Reservations recommended. Main courses 1,850–3,000 ptas. (US$11.10–US$18). AE, MC, V. Daily 1–4:30pm, Mon–Sat 8pm–midnight. Closed Aug. Metro: La Latina. SPANISH.

This historic inn, founded in 1642, offers a modern, more sanitized derivation of the earthy, grilled cuisine that fed the stonemasons who built the thick walls around you. Within a trio of dining rooms whose textured plaster and old stonework absolutely reeks of Old Castile, you'll find a hardworking staff and a menu that focuses on a time-honored specialty—roasted baby lamb—that's ordered more often than anything else on the menu. Other excellent choices include different versions of hake; Madrid-style tripe, and the rich, savory stew (*cocida Madrileño*) that many local residents remember fondly from the days of their childhood.

Las Cuevas de Luís Candelas. Calle de Cuchilleros, 1. ☎ **91-366-54-28.** Reservations required. Main courses 1,600–4,000 ptas. (US$9.60–US$24). DC, MC, V. Daily 1–4pm and 7:30pm–midnight. Metro: Puerta del Sol. SPANISH/INTERNATIONAL.

Right down the steps from the popular but very touristy Mesón del Corregidor, a competitor restaurant, is the even-better-known and also kitschy Las Cuevas de Luís Candelas, housed in a building dating from 1616. Enter the restaurant, which opened its doors at the turn of the century, through a doorway under an arcade, on steps leading to the calle de Cuchilleros—the nightlife center of Madrid that teems with restaurants, flamenco clubs, and rustic taverns. The restaurant with its hokey Spanish decor is named after Luís Candelas, an 18th-century bandit who's sometimes known as the Spanish Robin Hood. He is said to have hidden out in this maze of *cuevas* (dens). Although the menu is in English, the cuisine is authentically Spanish (but often overcooked). Specialties include the chef's own style of hake. To begin your meal, you might try another house dish, *sopa de ajo Candelas* (garlic soup). As in the other restaurants on the Plaza Mayor, roast suckling pig and roast lamb are featured, but we prefer these two dishes at Botín (see below). In spite of the tourist-trap overtures of this atmospheric place, so many readers report such hilarious fun here we've included it among our recommendations. It's not truly Spanish, but with all that hand-kissing of the ladies, music, and festive food and drink, it's still a fun night in Old Madrid for those not seeking authenticity.

Los Galayos. Calle Botoneras, 5. ☎ **91-366-30-28.** Reservations recommended. Main courses 1,400–4,000 ptas. (US$8.40–US$24). AE, DC, MC, V. Daily 1pm–midnight. Metro: Puerta del Sol. SPANISH.

Its location is among the most desirable in the city, on a narrow side street about three steps from the arcades of Plaza Mayor. Within two separate houses, the restaurant has flourished on this site since 1894. In summer, cascades of vines accent a series of tables and chairs on the cobblestones outside, perfect for tapas-sampling and people-watching. Some visitors consider an evening here among the highlights of their trip to Spain.

The ambience inside evokes Old Castile, with vaulted or beamed ceilings in several dining rooms. The Grande family, your multilingual hosts, prepares traditional versions of fish, shellfish, pork, veal, and beef in time-tested ways. Suckling pig, baby goat, and roasted lamb are almost always featured.

✪ **Sobrino de Botín.** Calle de Cuchilleros, 17. ☎ **91-366-42-17.** Reservations required. Main courses 1,015–7,690 ptas. (US$6.10–US$46.15); fixed-price menu 4,430 ptas. (US$26.60). AE, DC, MC, V. Daily 1–4pm and 8pm–midnight. Metro: La Latina or Ópera. SPANISH.

Ernest Hemingway made this restaurant famous. In the final two pages of his novel *The Sun Also Rises,* Jake invites Brett to Botín for the Segovian specialty of roast suckling pig, washed down with Rioja Alta.

By merely entering its portals, you step back to 1725, the year the restaurant was founded. You'll see an open kitchen with a charcoal hearth, hanging copper pots, an 18th-century tile oven for roasting the suckling pig, and a big pot of regional soup whose aroma wafts across the tables. Painter Francisco Goya was once a dishwasher here. Your host, Don Antonio, never loses his cool—even when he has 18 guests standing in line waiting for tables.

The two house specialties are roast suckling pig and roast Segovian lamb. From the à la carte menu, you might try the fish-based "quarter-of-an-hour" soup. Good main dishes include baked Cantabrian hake and filet mignon with potatoes. The dessert list features strawberries (in season) with whipped cream. You can wash down your meal with Valdepeñas or Aragón wine, although most guests order sangría.

INEXPENSIVE

El Cosaco. Plaza de la Paja, 2. ☎ **91-365-35-48.** Reservations recommended. Main courses 850–1,975 ptas. (US$5.10–US$11.85). AE, MC, V. Daily 9pm–midnight, Sun 1:30–3:30pm. Metro: La Latina. RUSSIAN.

One of the few Russian restaurants in Madrid sits adjacent to one of the most charming, historic, and evocative squares in town. Inside, you'll find a trio of dining rooms outfitted with paintings and artifacts from what used to be known as the Soviet Union. The food seems to taste best when preceded with something from a long list of vodkas, many of them from small-scale distilleries that you might not immediately recognize. Items include rich and savory cold-weather dishes that seem a bit disjointed from the sweltering heat of Madrid, but which you might interpret as satisfying alternatives from the all-Spanish restaurants that lie within the same neighborhood.

Examples include beef Stroganoff; quenelles of perch with fresh dill; thin-sliced smoked salmon or smoked sturgeon that's artfully arranged with capers, chopped onions, and chopped hard-boiled eggs. Red or white versions of borscht make a worthy debut, and blinis, stuffed with caviar or paprika-laced beef, are always excellent.

La Chata. Cava Baja, 24. ☎ **91-366-14-58.** Reservations recommended. Main dishes 1,600–2,300 ptas. (US$9.60–US$13.80). AE, MC, V. Daily 12:30–5pm; Mon–Sat 8pm–midnight. Metro: La Latina. SPANISH.

The cuisine here is Castilian, Galician, and northern Spanish. Set behind a heavily ornamented tile facade, the place has a stand-up tapas bar at the entrance and a formal restaurant in a side room. Many locals linger at the darkly paneled bar, which is framed by hanging Serrano hams, cloves of garlic, and photographs of bullfighters. Full meals might include such dishes as roast suckling pig, roast lamb, *calamares en su tinta* (squid in its own ink), grilled fillet of steak with peppercorns, and omelettes flavored with strips of eel.

IN THE ARTURO SORIA DISTRICT
MODERATE

Nicomedes. Moscatelar, 18. ☎ **91-388-78-28.** Reservations recommended. Main courses 2,000–2,300 ptas. (US$12–US$13.80). AE, DC, MC, V. Tues–Sat 1:30–4pm and 9:30pm–midnight, Sun 1:30–4pm. Closed Aug. Metro: Esperanza and Arturo Soria. ESTREMADURAN.

This colonial-style building has been refurbished by the charming Suárez sisters into a modern-looking château with bay windows covering the full height of this impressive edifice. The atmosphere is one of openness combined with friendly hospitality. The interior is beige decorated stucco complemented by tropical plants. In fine weather, patrons often dine on the terrace. The dishes from the western province of Estremadura are showcased. Goat cheese with glazed onions is a tasty opener, as are *bolsitas rellenas de gamba y queso fresco* (crispy pasta balls stuffed with shrimp and fresh cheese). *Rape al horno con habitas y ajetes* (baked monkfish with beans and garlic) is a savory offering, though *solomillo de buey* (fondue of ox steak) is more typical of the region. For dessert, try the homemade cake of the day or a special sweet "biscuit" made with prunes and served with caramel sauce. The house wine is Marti de la Costa from 1996.

NEAR PLAZA REPÚBLICA ARGENTINA
MODERATE

Casa Benigna. Benigno Soto, 9. ☎ **91-413-33-56.** Reservations required. Main courses 3,500–4,000 ptas. (US$21–US$24); *menú sorpresa* 6,500 ptas. (US$39). AE, DC, MC, V. Mon–Sat 1:30–3:30pm and 9–11pm, Sun 1:30–4pm. Closed Aug 7–21. Metro: Concha Espina. MEDITERRANEAN/SCANDINAVIAN.

This small bistro in the northern sector of Madrid has been run by the family of Jorge Garcia for more than a decade. It is decorated in a typical but inviting Mediterranean style, with blue walls along with murals of rural landscapes, even a library of books. The restaurant is the only one in Madrid that blends the cuisine of the far north of Europe with that of the sunny Mediterranean countries. The family has a close relative in Norway who contributes to their Scandinavian recipes. Their dishes are exquisitely prepared and based on the finest ingredients. Here you can order everything from Norwegian herring in delectable marinades to *arroz abanda,* a variation of traditional paella using different varieties of seafood. One especially good dish is *mamoncillo de cordero mechado,* or roast ribs of tender baby lamb. Many vegetarians and others appreciate their *parillada de verduras,* or grilled fresh vegetables. For dessert, opt for the Norwegian cookies with wild berries or freshly made crepes with apple sauce.

Príncipe y Serrano. Serrano, 240. ☎ **91-458-86-76.** Reservations recommended. Main courses 1,700–3,500 ptas. (US$10.20–US$21); *menú completo* 6,500 ptas. (US$39). AE, DC, MC, V. Mon–Fri 1:30–4pm and 8:30pm–midnight; Sat 8:30pm–midnight. Closed Aug. Metro: Colombia and Concha Espino. CASTILIAN.

This classic restaurant exudes distinction. Its sophisticated dining areas on both floors offer a warm and cozy atmosphere, and the outside lawns and flowered patios (one of them resembling a miniature golf course with small swimming pools) make you forget you are in the center of a big city. There is the big *salon central,* two small dining areas for more private dinners, plus a bar downstairs. The cooking is simple yet cosmopolitan and is always done under the close supervision of the two daughters of the famed Salvador Gallego, who is known as the master of haute Spanish cuisine in the Sierra of Madrid. The cookery is classic but also inventive, as evoked by an especially good dish—roast potatoes with mussels. Based on the sea's bounty, try the *merluza al estilo abuela Salvadora* (baked hake with onions gratinee and ham) or the *manitas de Iberico rellenas de morcilla* (pork filled with chorizo, that spicy Spanish sausage). We take delight in the freshly made apple tart with prune sauce or the crepes filled with mango and served in a fancy caramel cream sauce.

INEXPENSIVE

La Atalaya. Joaquin Costa, 31. ☎ **91-562-87-45.** Reservations recommended. Main courses 2,300–2,600 ptas. (US$13.80–US$15.60); fixed-price menu 1,600 ptas. (US$9.60). AE, DC, MC, V. Tues–Sat 1:30–4pm and 9pm–midnight; Sun 1:30–4pm. Closed Aug. Metro: República de Argentina. CANTABRIAN.

The owner of this pleasant restaurant, Gena Sanchez, hails from Santander in Northern Spain and, in the typical style of her hometown, has decorated the yellow walls of her establishment with modern paintings. The food is also typical of Spain's green northern coast, with an emphasis on fresh fish. Every Thursday and Saturday the chefs prepare the most typical dish of Santander, hearty cabbage soup. Called *cocido montanés,* it is also made with sausage, green beans, and black pudding. *Caracoles marucas* or clams Santander style, prepared in a spicy sauce, is another good offering, as is *sopa de pescado,* or fish soup, one of the finest of its kind in Madrid. You might also opt for a *torta de queso caliente,* a warm cheese soufflé. For dessert, traditional regional puddings are served.

NEAR CIUDAD UNIVERSITARIA
EXPENSIVE

San Mamés. Bravo Murillo, 88. ☎ **91-534-50-65.** Reservations recommended. Fixed-price menus 5,000–6,000 ptas. (US$30–US$36). AE, DC, MC, V. Mon–Fri 1:30–4pm and 8:30–11:30pm; Sat 1:30–4pm. Closed Aug. Metro: Cuatro Caminos. BASQUE/MADRILEÑA.

Situated in the north of the city in an historic building, this restaurant has been in the hands of the Garcia family more than 50 years. The tasca is decorated with colorful ceramic tiles and photographs of the celebrities who have dined here over the years. It is considered something of a "secret" address. Only two rooms, it has an atmosphere of intimacy and good cheer, almost homelike. The style of cookery offers some of the best cuisine from both the Madrid and Basque kitchens. The owners shop carefully for their ingredients, which they use to prepare a repertoire of very tasty and well-flavored dishes. The fare is simple but good. Their most typical dish is *callos a la madrileña,* tripe stew with meat and chick peas, beloved by regulars. Otherwise, you might opt for *bacalao aquarido,* salt cod prepared with green peppers, tomatoes, and onions. Another dish favored in the Basque country is *cocochas de merluza,* which are hake cheeks served with bread sauce. For dessert, the owners recommend their *requeson con pasas* (cheesecake with raisins) or a hearty pudding called *tocino de cielo.*

INEXPENSIVE

Las Batuecas. Avenida Reina Victoria, 17, 28033 Madrid. ☎ **91-554-04-52.** Reservations required. Main courses 1,800–2,200 ptas. (US$10.80–US$13.20); fixed-price menu 1,300 ptas. (US$7.80); *menú completo* 3,000 ptas. (US$18). No credit cards. Mon–Fri 1–4pm and 9–11pm; Sat 1–4pm. Closed Aug. Metro: Guzmán El Bueno and Cuatro Caminos. SPANISH.

This restaurant unpretentiously calls itself *a casa de comidas,* or "meal house." Since 1954, the little restaurant of José Pascual and his family has been located near the university. Many of their customers originally came here as students, and over the years have become devotees of the homemade Spanish food, which is wholesome and good without being pretentious. The decoration is plain, with old paintings and newspaper articles intermixed with cartoons and reviews by travel and food magazines in different languages. It has two floors with tables, all in the rustic style. But no one comes here for decor. The food is the attraction. Come here with a big appetite and launch yourself into a fine meal with such dishes as *tortilla de callos* (omelette with tripe), or perhaps squid cooked in its ink. You can also try fresh artichokes cooked with white-wine and ham or *berenjenas rebosadas* (batter-fried sliced eggplant). One of the tastiest main dishes is a perfectly done shoulder flank of lamb roast. Desserts include cakes made from almonds, chocolate, or vanilla, or else a fine selection of puddings.

Chez Lou Crêperie. Pedro Munguruza, 6. ☎ **91-350-34-16.** Reservations required on weekends. Crepes 1,000–1,900 ptas. (US$6–US$11.40). No credit cards. Mon–Sat 1:30–4pm and 8:30pm–1am. Metro: Plaza de Castilla. Bus: 27 or 147. FRENCH.

Near the Eurobuilding in the northern sector of Madrid, Chez Lou stands near the huge mural by Joan Miró. Come here if you're seeking a light supper when it's too hot for one of those table-groaning Spanish meals. In this intimate setting, you get well-prepared and reasonably priced French food. The restaurant serves pâté as an appetizer, then a large range of crepes with many different fillings. Folded envelope style, the crepes aren't tearoom size, and they're perfectly adequate as a main course. We've sampled several variations, finding the ingredients nicely blended yet distinct enough to retain their identity. A favorite is the large crepe stuffed with minced onions, cream, and smoked salmon. The ham-and-cheese crepe is also tasty.

NEAR RECOLETOS

La Galette. Conde de Aranda, 11. ☎ **91-576-06-41.** Reservations recommended. Main courses 1,200–2,000 ptas. (US$7.20–US$12); fixed-price lunch 1,200–1,900 ptas. (US$7.20–US$11.40). AE, DC, MC, V. Mon–Sat 2–4pm and 9pm–midnight. Metro: Retiro. VEGETARIAN/INTERNATIONAL.

La Galette was one of Madrid's first vegetarian restaurants, and it remains one of the best. Small and charming, it lies in a residential and shopping area in the exclusive Salamanca district, near Plaza de la Independencia and the northern edge of Retiro Park. There is a limited selection of meat dishes, but the true allure lies in this establishment's imaginative preparation of vegetables. Examples include baked stuffed peppers, omelettes, eggplant croquettes, and even vegetarian hamburgers. Some of the dishes are macrobiotic. The place is also noted for its mouth-watering pastries. The same owners also operate La Galette II, in the same complex.

THE BEST OF THE TASCAS

Don't starve waiting around for Madrid's fashionable 9:30 or 10pm dinner hour. Throughout the city you'll find tascas, bars that serve wine and platters of tempting

---

Picnics, Madrid Style

On a hot day, do as the Madrileños do: Secure the makings of a picnic lunch and head for Casa de Campo (metro: El Batán), those once-royal hunting grounds in the west of Madrid across the Manzanares River. Children delight in this adventure, as they can also visit a boating lake, the Parque de Atracciones, and the Madrid zoo.

Your best choice for picnic fare is **Rodilla,** Preciados, 25 (☎ **91-522-57-01;** metro: Callao), where you can find sandwiches, pastries, and take-out tapas. Sandwiches, including vegetarian, meat, and fish versions, begin at 100 pesetas (US60¢). It's open Monday to Saturday 8:30am to 12:30am, Sunday 8:30am to 11pm.

---

hot and cold hors d'oeuvres known as tapas: mushrooms, salads, baby eels, shrimp, lobster, mussels, sausage, ham, and, in one establishment at least, bull testicles. Below we've listed our favorite tapas bars. Keep in mind that you can often save pesetas by ordering at the bar rather than occupying a table.

Antonio Sánchez. Mesón de Parades, 13. ☎ **91-539-78-26.** Tapas (in the bar) 300–800 ptas. (US$1.80–US$4.80); main courses 800–2,500 ptas. (US$4.80–US$15); fixed-price lunch (Mon–Fri only) 1,100 ptas. (US$6.60). MC, V. Daily 1–4pm; Mon–Sat 8pm–midnight. Metro: Tirso de Molina. TAPAS.

Named in 1850 after the founder's son, who was killed in the bullring, Antonio Sánchez is full of bullfighting memorabilia, including the stuffed head of the animal that gored young Sánchez. Also featured on the dark paneled walls are three works by the Spanish artist Zuloaga, who had his last public exhibition in this restaurant near Plaza Tirso de Molina. A limited array of tapas, including garlic soup, are served with Valdepeñas wine drawn from a barrel—though many guests ignore the edibles in favor of smoking cigarettes and arguing the merits of this or that bullfighter. A restaurant in the back serves Spanish food with a vaguely French influence.

✪ **Casa Mingo.** Paseo de la Florida, 2. ☎ **91-547-79-18.** Main courses 550–1,200 ptas. (US$3.30–US$7.20). No credit cards. Daily 11am–midnight. Metro: Norte, then a 15-min. walk. SPANISH/TAPAS.

Casa Mingo has been known for decades for its Asturian cider, both still and bubbly. The perfect accompanying tidbit is a piece of the local Asturian *cabrales* (goat cheese), but the roast chicken is the specialty of the house, with an unbelievable number of helpings served daily. There's no formality here, since customers share big tables under the vaulted ceiling in the dining room. In summer the staff sets up tables and wooden chairs out on the sidewalk. This is not so much a restaurant but a bodega/taverna that serves food.

Cervecería Alemania. Plaza de Santa Ana, 6. ☎ **91-429-70-33.** Beer 200–400 ptas. (US$2.40); tapas 300–2,000 ptas. (US$1.80–US$12). No credit cards. Sun–Thurs 11am–12:30am, Fri–Sat 11am–2am. Metro: Alonso Martín or Tirso de Molina. TAPAS.

This place earned its name because of long-ago German clients. Opening directly onto one of the liveliest little plazas in Madrid, it clings to its turn-of-the-century traditions. Young Madrileños are fond of stopping in for a mug of draft beer. You can sit at one of the tables, leisurely sipping beer or wine, since the waiters make no attempt to hurry you along. To accompany your beverage, try the fried sardines or a Spanish omelette.

Many of the tascas on this popular square are crowded and noisy—often with blaring loud music—but this one is quiet and a good place to have a conversation.

Cervecería Santa Bárbara. Plaza de Santa Bárbara, 8. ☎ **91-319-04-49.** Beer 150–300 ptas. (US$.90–US$1.80); tapas 350–4,000 ptas. (US$2.10–US$24). V. Daily 11:30am–midnight. Metro: Alonzo or Martínez. Bus: 3, 7, or 21. TAPAS.

Unique in Madrid, Cervecería Santa Bárbara is an outlet for a beer factory, and the management has spent a lot to make it modern and inviting. Hanging globe lights and spinning ceiling fans create an attractive ambience, as does the black-and-white checkerboard marble floor. You go here for beer, of course: *cerveza negra* (black beer) or *cerveza dorada* (golden beer). The local brew is best accompanied by homemade potato chips or by fresh shrimp, lobster, crabmeat, or barnacles. You can either stand at the counter or go directly to one of the wooden tables for waiter service.

Taberna Toscana. Ventura de la Vega, 22. ☎ **91-429-60-31.** Beer 140 ptas. (US85¢); glass of wine 110 ptas. (US65¢); tapas 250–4,000 ptas. (US$1.50–US$24). V. Tues–Sat noon–4pm and 8pm–midnight. Closed Aug. Metro: Puerta del Sol or Sevilla. TAPAS.

Many Madrileños begin their nightly tasca crawl here. The aura is that of a village inn that's far removed from 20th-century Madrid. You sit on crude country stools, under sausages, peppers, and sheaves of golden wheat that hang from the age-darkened beams. The long, tiled bar is loaded with tasty tidbits, including the house specialties: *lacón y cecina* (boiled ham), *habas* (broad beans) with Spanish ham, and chorizo (a sausage of red peppers and pork)—almost meals in themselves. Especially delectable are the kidneys in sherry sauce and the snails in hot sauce.

6

Exploring Madrid

In recent years Madrid has changed drastically. No longer is it fair to say that one should only go there for the Prado and as a base for exploring Toledo or El Escorial. Those are still important draws, of course. But as you'll discover, Madrid has something to amuse and delight everyone.

1 The Major Museums

✪ **Museo del Prado.** Paseo del Prado. ☎ **91-330-28-00.** Admission 500 ptas. (US$3). Tues–Sat 9am–7pm, Sun and holidays 9am–2pm. Closed Jan 1, Good Friday, May 1, and Dec 25. Metro: Banco de España or Atocha. Bus: 10, 14, 27, 34, 37, or 45.

With more than 7,000 paintings, the Prado is one of the most important repositories of art in the world. It began as a royal collection and was enlarged by the Hapsburgs, especially Charles V, and later the Bourbons. In paintings of the Spanish school the Prado has no equal; on your first visit, concentrate on the Spanish masters (Velázquez, Goya, El Greco, and Murillo).

Major Italian works are exhibited on the ground floor. You'll see art by Italian masters—Raphael, Botticelli, Mantegna, Andrea del Sarto, Fra Angelico, and Correggio. The most celebrated Italian painting here is Titian's voluptuous Venus being watched by a musician who can't keep his eyes on his work.

The Prado is a trove of the work of El Greco (c. 1541–1614), the Crete-born artist who lived much of his life in Toledo. You can see a parade of "The Greek's" saints, Madonnas, and Holy Families—even a ghostly *John the Baptist.*

You'll find a splendid array of works by the incomparable Diego Velázquez (1599–1660). The museum's most famous painting, in fact, is his *Las Meninas,* a triumph in the use of light effects. The faces of the queen and king are reflected in the mirror in the painting itself. The artist in the foreground is Velázquez, of course.

The Flemish painter Peter Paul Rubens (1577–1640), who met Velázquez while in Spain, is represented by the peacock-blue *Garden of Love* and by the *Three Graces.* Also noteworthy is the work of José Ribera (1591–1652), a Valencia-born artist and contemporary of Velázquez whose best painting is the *Martyrdom of St. Philip.* The Seville-born Bartolomé Murillo (1617–82)—often referred to as the "painter of Madonnas"—has three *Immaculate Conceptions* on display.

The Prado has an outstanding collection of the work of Hieronymus Bosch (1450?–1516), the Flemish genius. *The Garden of Earthly Delights,* the best-known work of "El Bosco," is here. You'll also see his *Seven Deadly Sins* and his triptych *The Hay Wagon.* See also *The Triumph of Death,* by another Flemish painter, Pieter Breughel the Elder (1525?–69), who carried on Bosch's ghoulish vision.

Francisco de Goya (1746–1828) ranks along with Velázquez and El Greco in the trio of great Spanish artists. Hanging here are his unflattering portraits of his patron, Charles IV, and his family, as well as the *Clothed Maja* and the *Naked Maja.* You can also see the much-reproduced *Third of May* (1808), plus a series of Goya sketches (some of which, depicting the decay of 18th-century Spain, brought the Inquisition down on the artist) and his expressionistic "black paintings."

✪ **Thyssen-Bornemisza Museum.** Palacio de Villahermosa, Paseo del Prado, 8. ☎ **91-369-01-51.** Admission 700 ptas. (US$4.20) adults, 400 ptas. (US$2.40) students and seniors, free for children 11 and under. Tues–Sun 10am–7pm. Metro: Banco de España. Bus: 1, 2, 5, 9, 10, 14, 15, 20, 27, 34, 45, 51, 52, 53, 74, 146, or 150.

Until around 1985, the contents of this museum virtually overflowed the premises of a legendary villa near Lugano, Switzerland. One of the most frequently visited sites of Switzerland, the collection had been laboriously amassed over a period of about 60 years by the Thyssen-Bornemisza family, scions of a century-old shipping, banking, mining, and chemical fortune with roots in Holland, Germany, and Hungary. Experts had proclaimed it as one of the world's most extensive and valuable privately owned collections of paintings, rivaled only by the legendary holdings of Queen Elizabeth II.

For tax and insurance reasons, and because the collection had outgrown the boundaries of the lakeside villa that contained it, the works were discreetly marketed in the early 1980s to the world's major museums. Amid endless intrigue, a litany of glamorous supplicants from eight different nations came calling. Among them were Margaret Thatcher and Prince Charles; trustees of the Getty Museum in Malibu, California; the president of West Germany; the duke of Badajoz, brother-in-law of King Carlos II; even emissaries from Walt Disney World in Orlando, Florida, all hoping to acquire the collection for their respective countries or entities.

Eventually, thanks partly to the lobbying by Baron Hans Heinrich Thyssen-Bornemisza's fifth wife, a Spanish-born beauty (and former Miss Spain) named Tita, the collection was awarded to Spain for US$350 million. Controversies over the public cost of the acquisition raged for months. Despite the brouhaha, various estimates have placed the value of this collection between US$1 billion and US$3 billion.

To house the collection, an 18th-century building adjacent to the Prado, the Villahermosa Palace, was retrofitted with the appropriate lighting and security devices, and renovated at a cost of US$45 million. Rooms are arranged numerically so that by following the order of the various rooms (no. 1 through 48, spread out over three floors), a logical sequence of European painting can be traced from the 13th through the 20th centuries. The nucleus of the collection consists of 700 world-class paintings. They include works by, among others, El Greco, Velázquez, Dürer, Rembrandt, Watteau, Canaletto, Caravaggio, Hals, Memling, and Goya.

Unusual among the world's great art collections because of its eclecticism, the Thyssen group also contains goodly numbers of 19th- and 20th-century paintings by many of the notable French impressionists, as well as works by Picasso, Sargent, Kirchner, Nolde, and Kandinsky—artists whose previous absence within Spanish museums had become increasingly obvious.

In addition to European paintings, major American works can also be viewed here, including paintings by Thomas Cole, Winslow Homer, Jackson Pollock, Mark

Central Madrid Attractions

Aquápolis **11**
Biblioteca Nacional **26**
Campo del Moro **10**
Casa de Lope de Vega **31**
Casón del Buen Retiro **34**
Catedral de la Almudena **4**
Convento de la
  Encarnacion **17**
Monasterio de las
  Descalzas Reales **7**
Museo de América **14**
Museo Arqueológico
  Nacional **25**
Museo de Cera
  de Madrid **28**
Museo de Cerralbo **15**
Museo de la Real Academia
  de Bellas Artes de
  San Fernando **30**
Museo de las Figuras
  de Cera **23**
Museo del Ejército **33**
Museo del Prado **35**
Museo Lázarp Galdiano **22**
Museo Municipal **20**
Museo Nacional Centro de
  Arte Reina Sofía
  ("The Sofidou") **39**
Museo Nacional de Artes
  Decorativas **27**
Museo Naval **29**
Museo Romántico **19**
Museo Sorolla **21**
Museo Taurino **24**
Museo Tifológico **18**
Palacio Real **9**
Palacio Senado **16**
Panteón de Goya **11**
Parque de Atracciones **12**
Planetarium **38**
Plaza Mayor **6**
Rastro **2**
Real Basílica de San
  Francisco el Grande **3**
Real Fábrica de Tapices **37**
Real Jardín Botánico **36**
San Isidro el Real **1**
San Nicolás **5**
Teatro Real **8**
Teleferico **11**
Templo de Debod **13**
Thyssen-Bornemisza
  Museum **32**
Zoo Aquarium de la Casa
  de Campo **11**

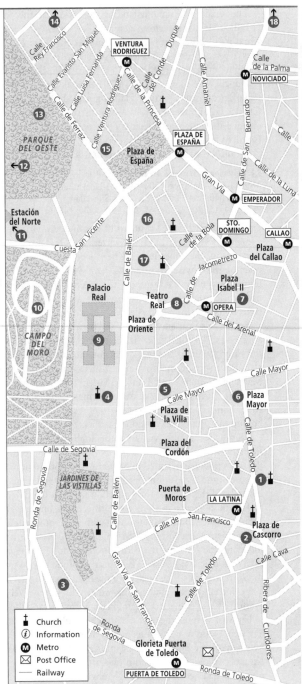

†	Church
ⓘ	Information
Ⓜ	Metro
✉	Post Office
—	Railway

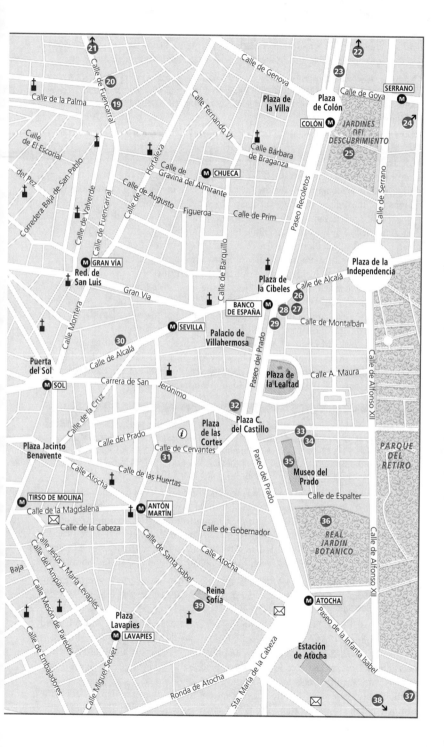

Rothko, Edward Hopper, Robert Rauschenberg, Stuart Davis, and Roy Lictenstein. There is also an agreeable and moderately priced cafeteria and restaurant on site.

✪ **Museo Nacional Centro de Arte Reina Sofía.** Santa Isabel, 52. ☎ **91-467-50-62.** Admission 500 ptas. (US$3); free after 2:30pm on Sat and all day Sun. Mon and Wed–Sat 10am–9pm, Sun 10am–2:30pm. Free guided tours Mon and Wed at 5pm, Sat at 11am. Metro: Atocha.

Filling for the world of modern art the role that the Prado has filled for traditional art, the "MOMA" of Madrid (its nickname) is the greatest repository of 20th-century art in Spain. Set within the echoing, futuristically renovated walls of the former General Hospital, originally built between 1776 and 1781, the museum is a sprawling, high-ceilinged showplace named after the Greek-born wife of Spain's present king. Once designated "the ugliest building in Spain" by Catalán architect Oriol Bohigas, the Reina Sofía has a design that hangs in limbo somewhere between the 18th and the 21st centuries. It incorporates a 50,000-volume art library and database, a cafe, a theater, a bookstore, Plexiglas-sided elevators, and systems that calibrate security, temperature, humidity, and the quality of light surrounding the exhibits.

Special emphasis is paid to the great artists of 20th-century Spain: Juan Gris, Salvador Dalí, Joan Miró, and Pablo Picasso (the museum has been able to acquire a handful of his works). What many critics feel is Picasso's masterpiece, *Guernica,* now rests at this museum after a long and troubling history of traveling. Banned in Spain during Franco's era (Picasso refused to have it displayed here anyway), it hung until 1980 at New York's Museum of Modern Art. The fiercely antiwar painting immortalizes the town's shameful blanket bombing by the German Luftwaffe, fighting for Franco during the Spanish Civil War. Guernica was the cradle of the Basque nation, and Picasso's canvas made it a household name around the world.

2 Near the Plaza Mayor & Puerta del Sol

Museo de la Real Academia de Bellas Artes de San Fernando (Fine Arts Museum). Alcalá, 13. ☎ **91-522-14-91.** Tues–Sat admission 400 ptas. (US$2.40) adults, 200 ptas. (US$1.20) students; free for children 17 and under. Tues–Fri 9am–7pm, Sat–Mon 9am–2pm. Metro: Puerta del Sol or Sevilla. Bus: 15, 20, 51, 52, 53, or 150.

An easy stroll from Puerta del Sol, the Fine Arts Museum is located in the restored and remodeled 17th-century baroque palace of Juan de Goyeneche. The collection—more than 1,500 paintings and 570 sculptures, ranging from the 16th century to the present—was started in 1752 during the reign of Fernando VI (1746–59). It emphasizes works by Spanish, Flemish, and Italian artists. You can see masterpieces by El Greco, Rubens, Velázquez, Zurbarán, Ribera, Cano, Coello, Murillo, Goya, and Sorolla.

✪ **Palacio Real (Royal Palace).** Plaza de Oriente, calle de Bailén, 2. ☎ **91-454-87-00.** Admission 850 ptas. (US$5.10) adults, 350 ptas. (US$2.10) students and children. Mon–Sat 9am–6pm, Sun 9am–3pm. Metro: Ópera or Plaza de España.

This huge palace was begun in 1738 on the site of the Madrid Alcázar, which burned to the ground in 1734. Some of its 2,000 rooms—which that "enlightened despot" Charles III called home—are open to the public; others are still used for state business. The palace was last used as a royal residence in 1931, before King Alfonso XIII and his wife, Victoria Eugénie, fled Spain.

Highlights of a visit include the Reception Room, the State Apartments, the Armory, and the Royal Pharmacy. To get an English-speaking guide, say *"Inglés"* to the person who takes your ticket.

The Reception Room and State Apartments should get priority here if you're rushed. They include a rococo room with a diamond clock; a porcelain salon; the Royal Chapel; the Banquet Room, where receptions for heads of state are still held; and the Throne Room.

The rooms are literally stuffed with art treasures and antiques—salon after salon of monumental grandeur, with no apologies for the damask, mosaics, stucco, Tiepolo ceilings, gilt and bronze, chandeliers, and paintings.

If your visit falls on the first Wednesday of the month, look for the changing of the guard ceremony, which occurs at noon and is free to the public.

In the Armory, you'll see the finest collection of weaponry in Spain. Many of the items—powder flasks, shields, lances, helmets, and saddles—are from the collection of Carlos V (Charles of Spain). From here, the comprehensive tour takes you into the Pharmacy.

You may want to visit the **Museo de las Carruajes (Carriage Museum),** also at the Royal Palace, to see some of the grand old relics used by Spanish aristocrats. Afterward, stroll through the Campo del Moro, the gardens of the palace.

Real Basílica de San Francisco el Grande. Plaza de San Francisco el Grande, San Buenaventura, 1. ☎ **91-365-38-00.** Admission 50 ptas. (US30¢). Tues–Sat 10am–1pm and 4–6:30pm. Metro: La Latina or Puerta del Toledo. Bus: 3, 60, C, or M4.

Ironically, Madrid, the capital of cathedral-rich Spain, does not itself possess a famous cathedral—but it does have an important church, with a dome larger than that of St. Paul's in London. This 18th-century church is filled with a number of ecclesiastical works, notably a Goya painting of St. Bernardinus of Siena. A guide will show you through.

3 Along Paseo del Prado

Museo Arqueológico Nacional. Serrano, 13. ☎ **91-577-79-12.** Admission 500 ptas. (US$3), free for children and adults over 65; free for everyone Sat 2:30–8:30pm and Sun. Tues–Sat 9:30am–8:30pm, Sun 9:30am–2:30pm. Metro: Serrano or Retiro. Bus: 1, 9, 19, 51, 74, or M2.

This stately mansion is a storehouse of artifacts from the prehistoric to the baroque. One of the prime exhibits here is the Iberian statue *The Lady of Elche,* a piece of primitive carving (from the 4th century B.C.), discovered on the southeastern coast of Spain. Finds from Ibiza, Paestum, and Rome are on display, including statues of Tiberius and his mother, Livia. The Islamic collection from Spain is outstanding. There are also collections of Spanish Renaissance lusterware, Talavera pottery, Retiro porcelain, and some rare 16th- and 17th-century Andalusian glassware.

Many of the exhibits are treasures that were removed from churches and monasteries. A much-photographed choir stall from the palace of Palencia dates from the 14th century. Also worth a look are the reproductions of the Altamira cave paintings (chiefly of bison, horses, and boars), discovered near Santander in northern Spain in 1868.

Museo del Ejército (Army Museum). Méndez Núñez, 1. ☎ **91-522-89-77.** Admission 100 ptas. (US60¢) adults, free for children 18 and under and adults over 65. Tues–Sun 10am–2pm. Metro: Banco de España, or Retiro. Bus: 10, 19, 27, or 34.

This museum, in the Buen Retiro Palace, houses outstanding exhibits from military history, including El Cid's original sword. In addition, you can see the tent used by Carlos V in Tunisia, relics of Pizarro and Cortés, and an exceptional collection of armor. Look for the piece of the cross that Columbus carried when he landed in the

New World. The museum had a notorious founder: Manuel Godoy, who rose from relative poverty to become the lover of Maria Luisa of Parma, wife of Carlos IV.

Museo Nacional de Artes Decorativas. Calle de Montalbán, 12. ☎ **91-532-64-99.** Admission 400 ptas. (US$2.40) adults; 200 ptas. (US$1.20) students, children, and seniors. Tues–Fri 9:30am–3pm, Sat–Sun 10am–2pm. Metro: Banco de España. Bus: 14, 27, 34, 37, or 45.

In 62 rooms spread over several floors, this museum, near the Plaza de la Cibeles, displays a rich collection of furniture, ceramics, and decorative pieces. Emphasizing the 16th and 17th centuries, the eclectic collection includes Gothic carvings, alabaster figurines, festival crosses, elaborate dollhouses, elegant baroque four-poster beds, a chapel covered with leather tapestries, and even kitchens from the 18th century. Two new floors focusing on the 18th and 19th centuries have recently been added.

Museo Naval. Paseo del Prado, 5. ☎ **91-379-52-99.** Free admission. Tues–Sun 10:30am–1:30pm. Closed Aug. Metro: Banco de España. Bus: 2, 14, 27, 40, 51, 52, or M6.

The history of nautical science and the Spanish navy, from the time of Isabella and Ferdinand until today, comes alive at the Museo Naval. The most fascinating exhibit is the map made by the first mate of the *Santa María* to show the Spanish monarchs the new discoveries. There are also souvenirs of the Battle of Trafalgar.

4 Near the Gran Vía & Plaza de España

⊙ Monasterio de las Descalzas Reales. Plaza de las Descalzas Reales, s/n. ☎ **91-542-00-59.** Admission 650 ptas. (US$3.90) adults, 350 ptas. (US$2.10) children. Sat and Tues–Thurs 10:30am–12:30pm and 4–5pm, Fri 10:30am–12:30pm, Sun 11am–1:15pm. Bus: 1, 2, 5, 20, 46, 52, 53, 74, M1, M2, M3, or M5. From Plaza del Callao, off the Gran Vía, walk down Postigo de San Martín to Plaza de las Descalzas Reales; the convent is on the left.

In the mid–16th century, aristocratic women—either disappointed in love or "wanting to be the bride of Christ"—stole away to this convent to take the veil. Each brought a dowry, making this one of the richest convents in the land. By the mid–20th century it sheltered mostly poor women. True, it still contained a priceless collection of art treasures, but the sisters were forbidden to auction anything; in fact, they were literally starving. The state intervened, and the pope granted special dispensation to open the convent as a museum. Today the public can look behind the walls of what had been a mysterious presence on one of the most beautiful squares in Old Madrid.

An English-speaking guide will show you through. In the Reliquary are the noblewomen's dowries, one of which is said to contain bits of wood from Christ's Cross; another, some of the bones of St. Sebastian. The most valuable painting is Titian's *Caesar's Money.* The Flemish Hall shelters other fine works, including paintings by Hans de Beken and Breughel the Elder. All of the tapestries were based on Rubens's cartoons, displaying his chubby matrons.

Templo de Debod. Paseo de Rosales. ☎ **91-366-74-15.** Admission 300 ptas. (US$1.80) adults, 150 ptas. (US90¢) children under 16; free on Wed and Sun. Apr 1–Sept 30, Mon–Fri 10am–2pm and 6–8pm; Oct 1–Mar 31, Mon–Fri 9:45am–1:45pm and 4:15–6:15pm; Sat and Sun 10am–1pm year-round. Metro: Plaza de España or Ventura Rodríguez. Bus: 25, 33, 39, 46, or 74.

This Egyptian temple near Plaza de España once stood in the Valley of the Nile, 19 miles from Aswan. When the new dam threatened the temple, the Egyptian government dismantled and presented it to Spain. Taken down stone by stone in 1969 and 1970, it was shipped to Valencia and taken by rail to Madrid, where it was reconstructed and opened to the public in 1971. Photos upstairs depict the temple's long history.

Taking the Bull by the Horns

Madrid draws the finest matadors in Spain. If a matador hasn't proven his worth in the **Plaza Monumental de Toros de las Ventas,** Alcalá, 237 (☎ **91-356-22-00;** metro: Ventas), he hasn't been recognized as a top-flight artist. The major season begins during the Fiestas de San Isidro, patron saint of Madrid, on May 15. This is the occasion for a series of fights, during which talent scouts are in the audience. Matadors who distinguish themselves in the ring are signed up for Majorca, Málaga, and other places.

The best way to get tickets to the bullfights is to go to the stadium's box office (open Friday to Sunday 10am to 2pm and 5 to 8pm). Concierges for virtually every upper-bracket hotel can also acquire tickets. Alternatively, you can contact one of Madrid's best ticket agents, **Localidades Galicia,** Plaza del Carmen, 1 (☎ **91-531-27-32;** metro: Puerto del Sol), open Tuesday to Saturday 9:30am to 1:30pm and 4:30 to 7:30pm, Sunday 9:30am to 1:30pm. Tickets to bullfights are 2,000 to 20,000 pesetas (US$12 to US$120), depending on the event and the position of your seat. Front-row seats are *barreras. Delanteras*—third-row seats—are available in both the *alta* (high) and the *baja* (low) sections. The cheapest seats, *filas,* afford the worst view and are in the sun (*sol*) the whole time. The best seats are in the shade (*sombra*). Bullfights are held on Sundays and holidays throughout most of the year, and every day during certain festivals, which tend to last around three weeks, usually in the late spring. Starting times are adjusted according to the anticipated hour of sundown on the day of a performance, usually 7pm from March to October and 5pm during late autumn and early spring. Late-night fights by neophyte matadors are sometimes staged under spotlights on Saturday around 11pm.

5 In Chamartín, Chueca & Salamanca

✪ **Museo Lázaro Galdiano.** Serrano, 122. ☎ **91-561-60-84.** Admission 500 ptas. (US$3). Tues–Sun 10am–2pm. Closed holidays and Aug. Metro: Rubén Darío, Núñez de Balboa. Bus: 9, 16, 19, 27, 45, 51, 61, 89, or 114.

Imagine 37 rooms in a well-preserved 19th-century mansion bulging with artworks—including many by the most famous old masters of Europe. Visitors usually take the elevator to the top floor and work down, lingering over such artifacts as 15th-century handwoven vestments, swords and daggers, royal seals, 16th-century crystal from Limoges, Byzantine jewelry, Italian bronzes from ancient times to the Renaissance, and medieval armor.

One painting by Bosch evokes his own peculiar brand of horror, the canvas peopled with creepy fiends devouring human flesh. The Spanish masters are the best represented—among them El Greco, Velázquez, Zurbarán, Ribera, Murillo, and Valdés-Leal.

One section is devoted to works by the English portrait and landscape artists Reynolds, Gainsborough, and Constable. Italian artists exhibited include Tiepolo and Guardi. Salon 30—for many, the most interesting—is devoted to Goya and includes paintings from his "black period."

This off-the-beaten track museum is a gem and usually enjoyably underpopulated, a nice contrast to the overcrowded Prado, Thyssen, and Reina Sofía museums.

Museo Municipal. Fuencarral, 78. ☎ **91-588-86-74.** Admission 300 ptas. (US$1.80) adults, 150 ptas. (US90¢) seniors and children under 18; free Wed and Sun. Tues–Fri 9:30am–8pm, Sat–Sun 10am–2pm. Metro: Bilbao or Tribunal. Bus: 3, 21, 40, 147, or 149.

After years of restoration, the Museo Municipal displays collections on local history, archaeology, and art, with an emphasis on the Bourbon Madrid of the 18th century. Paseos with strolling couples are shown on huge tapestry cartoons. Paintings from the royal collections are here, plus period models of the best-known city squares and a Goya that was painted for the Town Hall.

Museo Romántico. San Mateo, 13. ☎ **91-448-10-71.** Admission 400 ptas. (US$2.40) adults, 200 ptas. (US$1.20) students and children, free for seniors over 65 years. Tues–Sat 9am–3pm, Sun 10am–2pm. Closed Aug. Metro: Alonso Martínez.

Geared toward those seeking the romanticism of the 19th century, the museum is housed in a mansion decorated with numerous period pieces—crystal chandeliers, faded portraits, oils from Goya to Sorolla, opulent furnishings, and porcelain. Many exhibits date from the days of Isabella II, the high-living, fun-loving queen who was forced into exile and eventual abdication.

Museo Sorolla. General Martínez Campos, 37. ☎ **91-310-15-84.** Admission 400 ptas. (US$2.40). Tues–Sat 10am–3pm, Sun 10am–2pm. Metro: Iglesia or Rubén Darío. Bus: 5, 16, 61, 40, or M3.

From 1912, painter Joaquín Sorolla and his family occupied this elegant Madrileño townhouse off Paseo de la Castellana. His widow turned it over to the government, and it is now maintained as a memorial. Much of the house remains as Sorolla left it, right down to his stained paintbrushes and pipes. The museum wing displays a representative collection of his works.

Although Sorolla painted portraits of Spanish aristocrats, he was essentially interested in the common people, often depicting them in their native dress. On view are the artist's self-portrait and the paintings of his wife and their son. Sorolla was especially fond of painting beach scenes of the Costa Blanca.

6 Outside the City Center

Museo de América (Museum of the Americas). Avenida de los Reyes Católicos, 6. ☎ **91-549-2641.** Free admission. Tues–Sat 10am–3pm, Sun 10am–2:30pm. Metro: Moncloa.

This museum near the university campus houses an outstanding collection of pre-Columbian, Spanish-American, and Native American art and artifacts. Various exhibits chronicle the progress of the inhabitants of the New World, from the Paleolithic period to the present day. One exhibit, "Groups, Tribes, Chiefdoms, and States," focuses on the social structure of the various peoples of the Americas. Another display outlines the various religions and deities associated with them. Also included is an entire exhibit dedicated to communication, highlighting written as well as nonverbal expressions of art.

Museo Taurino (Bullfighting Museum). Plaza de Toros de las Ventas, Alcalá, 237. ☎ **91-725-18-57.** Free admission. Mar–Oct, Tues–Fri and Sun 9:30am–2:30pm; Nov–Feb, Mon–Fri 9:30am–2:30pm. Metro: Ventas. Bus: 12, 21, 38, 53, 146, M1, or M8.

This museum might serve as a good introduction to bullfighting for those who want to see the real event. Here you'll see the death costume of Manolete, the *traje de luces* (suit of lights) that he wore when he was gored to death at age 30 in Linares's bullring.

Other memorabilia evoke the heyday of Juan Belmonte, the Andalusian who revolutionized bullfighting in 1914 by performing close to the horns. Other exhibits include a Goya painting of a matador, as well as photographs and relics that trace the history of bullfighting in Spain from its ancient origins to the present day.

Museo Tiflológico. La Coruña, 18. ☎ **91-589-42-00.** Free admission. Tues–Fri 10am–2pm and 5–8pm, Sat 10am–2pm. Metro: Estrecho. Bus: 3, 42, 43, 64, or 124.

This museum is designed for sightless and sight-impaired visitors. Maintained by Spain's National Organization for the Blind, it's one of the few museums in the world that emphasizes tactile appeal. All the exhibits are meant to be touched and felt; to that end, the museum provides audiotapes, in English and Spanish, to guide visitors as they move their hands over the object on display. It also offers pamphlets in large type and Braille.

One section of the museum features small-scale replicas of such architectural wonders as the Mayan and Aztec pyramids of Central America, the Eiffel Tower, and the Statue of Liberty. Another section contains paintings and sculptures created by blind artists, such as Miguel Detrel and José António Braña. A third section outlines the status of blind people throughout history, with a focus on the sociology and technology that led to the development of Braille during the 19th century.

Panteón de Goya (Goya's Tomb). Glorieta de San Antonio de la Florida, s/n. ☎ **91-542-07-22.** Admission 300 ptas. (US$1.80); free on Wed and Sun. Tues–Fri 10am–2pm and 4–8pm, Sat–Sun 10am–2pm (in summer daily 10am–2pm only). Metro: Norte. Bus: 41, 46, 75, or C.

In a remote part of town beyond the North Station lies Goya's tomb, containing one of his masterpieces—an elaborately beautiful fresco depicting the miracles of St. Anthony on the dome and cupola of the little hermitage of San Antonio de la Florida. This has been called Goya's Sistine Chapel. Already deaf when he began the painting, Goya labored dawn to dusk for 16 weeks, painting with sponges rather than brushes. By depicting common street life—stone masons, prostitutes, and beggars—Goya raised the ire of the nobility who held judgment until the patron, Carlos IV, viewed it. When the monarch approved, the formerly outrageous painting was deemed acceptable.

The tomb and fresco are in one of the twin chapels (visit the one on the right) that were built in the latter part of the 18th century. Discreetly placed mirrors will help you see the ceiling better.

Real Fábrica de Tapices (Royal Tapestry Factory). Fuenterrabía, 2. ☎ **91-434-05-51.** Admission 250 ptas. (US$1.50). Mon–Fri 9am–2pm. Closed Aug and holidays. Metro: Menéndez Pelayo. Bus: 10, 14, 26, 32, 37, C, or M9.

At this factory, the age-old process of making exquisite (and very expensive) tapestries is still carried on with consummate skill. Nearly every tapestry is based on a cartoon of Goya, who was the factory's most famous employee. Many of these patterns, such as *The Pottery Salesman,* are still in production today. (Goya's original drawings are in the Prado.) Many of the other designs are based on cartoons by Francisco Bayeu, Goya's brother-in-law.

7 Parks & Gardens

For a touch of green in Madrid's sprawling gray urban expanse, visit one of the following:

Casa de Campo (metro: Lago or Batán) is the former royal hunting grounds—miles of parkland lying south of the Royal Palace across the Manzanares River. You can see the gate through which the kings rode out of the palace grounds, either on horseback or in carriages, on their way to the tree-lined park. A lake in the park is usually filled with rowers. You can have drinks and light refreshments around the water or go swimming in a municipally operated pool. Children will love both the zoo and the Parque de Atracciones (see "Especially for Kids," below). The Casa de Campo can be visited daily 8am to 9pm.

❂ **Parque de Retiro** (metro: Retiro), originally a playground for the Spanish monarchs and their guests, extends over 350 acres. The huge palaces that once stood here were destroyed in the early 19th century; only the former dance hall, the Cáson del Buen Retiro (housing the modern works of the Prado), and the building containing the Army Museum remain. The park boasts numerous fountains and statues, plus a large lake. There are also two exposition centers, the Velásquez and Crystal palaces (built to honor the Philippines in 1887), and a lakeside monument, erected in 1922 in honor of King Alfonso XII. In summer, the rose gardens are worth a visit, and you'll find several places for inexpensive snacks and drinks. The park is open daily 24 hours, but it is safest from 7am to about 8:30pm.

Across calle de Alfonso XII, at the southwest corner of Parque de Retiro, is the **Real Jardín Botánico (Botanical Garden)** (tel. **91-420-30-17;** metro: Atocha; bus: 10, 14, 19, 32, or 45). Founded in the 18th century, the garden contains more than 104 species of trees and 3,000 types of plants. Also on the premises are an exhibition hall and a library specializing in botany. The park is open daily 10am to 9pm except in August; admission is 200 pesetas (US$1.20).

8 Especially for Kids

Museo de Cera de Madrid (Wax Museum). Paseo de Recoletos, 41. ☎ **91-319-26-49.** Admission 1,500 ptas. (US$9) adults, 1,000 ptas. (US$6) children, free for children 3 and under. Daily 10am–2pm and 4–8pm. Metro: Colón. Bus: 27, 45, or 53.

The kids will enjoy seeing a lifelike wax Columbus calling on Ferdinand and Isabella, as well as Marlene Dietrich checking out Bill and Hillary Clinton. The 450 wax figures also include heroes and villains of World War II. Two galleries display Romans and Arabs from the ancient days of the Iberian Peninsula; a show in multivision gives a 30-minute recap of Spanish history from the Phoenicians to the present.

Parque de Atracciones. Casa de Campo. ☎ **91-463-29-00.** Admission 600 ptas. (US$3.60). Apr–May Tues–Fri noon–8pm, Sat–Sun noon–10pm; June–Aug Tues–Fri 6pm–1am, Sat 6pm–2am, Sun noon–1am; Sept Tues–Sun (variable hours; call to check before going); Oct–Mar Sat noon–8pm (sometimes 9pm), Sun 11am–8pm (sometimes 9pm). Take the Teleférico cable car (see below); at the end of this ride, microbuses take you the rest of the way. Alternatively, take the suburban train from Plaza de España and stop near the entrance to the park (Entrada de Batán).

The park was created in 1969 to amuse the young at heart with an array of rides and concessions. The former include a toboggan slide, a carousel, pony rides, an adventure into outer space, a walk through a transparent maze, a visit to a jungle, a motor-propelled series of cars disguised as a tail-wagging dachshund puppy, and a gyrating whirligig clutched in the tentacles of an octopus named El Pulpo. The most popular rides are a pair of roller coasters named "7 Picos" and "Jet Star." The park also has many diversions for adults. See "Madrid After Dark," later in this chapter, for details.

Teleférico. Paseo del Pintor Rosales, s/n. ☎ **91-541-74-50.** Fare 375 ptas. (US$2.25) one-way, 520 ptas. (US$3.10) round-trip. Apr–Sept, daily 11am–9pm; Oct–Mar, Sat–Sun noon–9pm. Metro: Plaza de España or Argüelles. Bus: 74.

Strung high above several of Madrid's verdant parks, this cable car was originally built in 1969 as part of a public fairgrounds (Parque de Atracciones) modeled vaguely along the lines of Disneyland. Today, even for visitors not interested in visiting the park, the *teleférico* retains an allure of its own as a high-altitude method of admiring the cityscape of Madrid. The cable car departs from Paseo Pintor Rosales at the eastern edge of Parque del Oeste (at the corner of calle Marqués de Urquijo) and carries you high above two parks, railway tracks, and over the Manzanares River to a spot near a picnic ground and restaurant in Casa de Campo. Weather permitting, there are good views of the Royal Palace along the way. The ride takes 11 minutes.

Zoo Aquarium de la Casa de Campo. Casa de Campo. ☎ **91-512-37-70.** Admission 1,600 ptas. (US$9.60) adults, 1,300 ptas. (US$7.80) seniors and children 3–8, free for children 2 and under. Daily 10am–sunset. Metro: Batán. Bus: 33.

This modern well organized facility allows you to see about 3,000 animals from five continents. Most are in simulated natural habitats, with moats separating them from the public. There's a petting zoo for the kids and a show presented by the Chu-Lin band. The zoo/aquarium complex includes a 520,000-gallon tropical marine aquarium, a dolphinarium, and a parrot club.

9 Special-Interest Sightseeing

FOR THE LITERARY ENTHUSIAST

Casa de Lope de Vega. Cervantes, 11. ☎ **91-429-92-16.** Admission 200 ptas. (US$1.20). Mon–Fri 10am–2pm, Sat 10am–1:30pm. Closed Aug. Metro: Anton Martín.

Felix Lope de Vega, a prolific Madrid-born author, dramatized Hapsburg Spain as no one had before, earning a lasting position in Spanish letters. A reconstruction of his medieval house stands on a narrow street—ironically named for Cervantes, his competitor for the title of the greatest writer of the golden age of Spain. The dank, dark house is furnished with relics of the period, although one can't be sure that any of the furnishings or possessions actually belonged to this 16th-century genius.

HEMINGWAY HAUNTS

Chicote. Gran Vía, 12. ☎ **91-532-67-37.** Beer 550 ptas. (US$3.30), whiskey and soda 1,000 ptas. (US$6). Mon–Sat 8am–3am. Metro: Gran Vía.

Ernest Hemingway used Chicote as a setting for his only play, *The Fifth Column.* He would sit here night after night, gazing at the *putas* (it was a famed hooker bar back then) as he entertained friends with such remarks as "Spain is a country for living and not for dying." The bar still draws a lively crowd.

Museo del Prado. Paseo del Prado. ☎ **91-330-28-00.**

Of the Prado, A. E. Hotchner wrote in his *Papa Hemingway:* "Ernest loved the Prado. He entered it as he entered cathedrals." More than any other, one picture held him transfixed, Andrea del Sarto's *Portrait of a Woman.* (For further details about the Prado, see "The Major Museums," earlier in this chapter.)

Sobrino de Botín. Cuchilleros, 17. ☎ **91-366-42-17.**

In the final two pages of Hemingway's novel *The Sun Also Rises,* Jake invites Brett here for roast suckling pig and red wine. In another book, *Death in the Afternoon,* Hemingway told his mythical "Old Lady": "I would rather dine on suckling pig at Botín's than sit and think of casualties my friends have suffered." Since that time, thousands upon thousands of Americans have eaten at Botín (see "Where to Dine" in chapter 5 for details), a perennial favorite of all visiting Yankees.

ARCHITECTURAL STANDOUTS

✪ **Plaza Mayor.** Metro: Puerta del Sol.

In the heart of Madrid, this famous square was known as the Plaza de Arrabal during medieval times, when it stood outside the city wall. The original architect of Plaza Mayor itself was Juan Gómez de Mora, who worked during the reign of Philip III.

Under the Hapsburgs, the square rose in importance as the site of public spectacles, including the abominable autos-da-fé, in which heretics were burned. Bullfights, knightly tournaments, and festivals were also staged here.

Three times the buildings on the square burned—in 1631, 1672, and 1790—but each time the plaza bounced back. After the last big fire, it was completely redesigned by Juan de Villanueva.

Nowadays a Christmas fair is held around the equestrian statue of Philip III (dating from 1616) in the center of the square. On summer nights the Plaza Mayor becomes the virtual living room of Madrid, as tourists sip sangría at the numerous cafes and listen to the music performances, many of which are spontaneous.

Puerta de Toledo. Metro: Puerta de Toledo.

Puerta de Toledo is one of the two surviving town gates (the other is Puerta de Alcalá). Constructed during the brief and unpopular rule of Joseph I Bonaparte, this one marks the spot where citizens used to set out for the former imperial capital of Toledo. On an irregularly shaped square, it stands at the intersection of the Ronda de Toledo and calle de Toledo. Its original purpose was a triumphal arch to honor Napoléon Bonaparte. In 1813 it became a symbol of Madrid's fierce independence and the loyalty of its citizens to their Bourbon rulers, who had been restored to the throne in the wake of the Napoleonic invasion.

Walking Tour—Hapsburg Madrid

Start: Southeastern corner of the Palacio Real.
Finish: Calle del Arenal.
Time: 3 hours.
Best Times: Saturday or Sunday, when you can also visit the flea market of El Rastro.
Worst Times: Monday to Saturday 7:30 to 9:30am and 5 to 7:30pm—because of heavy traffic.

This tour encompasses 16th- and 17th-century Madrid, including the grand plazas and traffic arteries that the Hapsburg families built to transform a quiet town into a world-class capital.

The tour begins at the:

1. **Palacio Real (Royal Palace),** at the corner of Calle de Bailén and Calle Mayor. The latter was built by Philip II in the 1560s to provide easy access from the palace to his preferred church, San Jerónimo el Real.

   Walk east on:

2. **Calle Mayor,** on the south side of the street. Within a block, you'll reach a black bronze statue of a kneeling angel, erected in 1906 to commemorate the aborted assassination of King Alfonso XIII (grandfather of the present king, Juan Carlos).

   Across the street from the kneeling angel is the:

3. **Palacio de Abrantes,** Calle Mayor, 86, today occupied by the Italian Institute of Culture.

   On the same side of the street as the kneeling angel, to the statue's left, is the:

4. **Palacio de Uceda,** Calle Mayor, 79, today the headquarters of the Spanish military (their version of the U.S. Pentagon). Both of these palaces are among the best examples of 17th-century civil architecture in Madrid.

   Walk half a block east, crossing to the north side of Calle Mayor and detouring about 20 yards to the left, down narrow Calle de San Nicolás. You'll come to the somber facade of the oldest church in Madrid, the 12th-century:

Walking Tour—Hapsburg Madrid

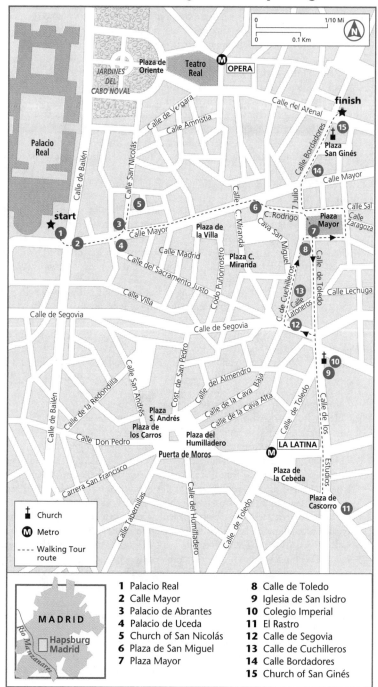

1 Palacio Real
2 Calle Mayor
3 Palacio de Abrantes
4 Palacio de Uceda
5 Church of San Nicolás
6 Plaza de San Miguel
7 Plaza Mayor

8 Calle de Toledo
9 Iglesia de San Isidro
10 Colegio Imperial
11 El Rastro
12 Calle de Segovia
13 Calle de Cuchilleros
14 Calle Bordadores
15 Church of San Ginés

5. **Church of St. Nicolás,** Plaza de San Nicolás. Only a brick tower remains from the original building, one of the few examples of the Mudéjar style in the capital. The reredos at the high altar is the work of Juan de Herrera, also the architect of El Escorial.

Retrace your steps to Calle Mayor. Turn left and continue to walk east. You'll pass Plaza de la Villa on your right, and, one block later:

6. **Plaza de San Miguel,** an iron-canopied meat-and-vegetable market. You might stock up on ingredients for a picnic here. (The market is open Monday to Friday 9am to 2pm and 5 to 8pm, Saturday 9am to 2pm.)

Leave Plaza de San Miguel by Ciudad Rodrigo (there might not be a sign), which leads under a soaring granite archway and up a sloping street to the northwestern corner of:

7. **Plaza Mayor,** the landmark square that is at the heart of Old Madrid.

> ☕ **TAKE A BREAK**   **Café Bar Los Galayos,** Plaza Mayor, 1 (☎ **91-366-30-28**), has long been one of the best places for tapas along this square. If you're taking the walking tour during the day, you may want to return to this cafe/bar at night, when it is most lively. In summer you can select one of the outdoor tables for your drinks and tapas. The cafe is open daily noon to 1am.

Stroll through Plaza Mayor, crossing it diagonally and exiting at the closer of its two southern exits. A dingy steep flight of stone stairs leads down to the beginning of the:

8. **Calle de Toledo.** Note in the distance the twin domes of the yellow-stucco and granite:

9. **Iglesia de San Isidro,** legendary burial place of Madrid's patron saint and his wife, Santa Maria de la Cadeza. The church lost its status as a cathedral in 1992, when the honor went to the larger Church of La Almudena.

Adjacent to San Isidro is the baroque facade of the:

10. **Colegio Imperial,** which was also run by the Jesuits. Lope de Vega, Calderón, and many other famous men studied at this institute.

If your tour takes place on a Saturday or Sunday before 3pm, visit:

11. **El Rastro,** Madrid's world-famous flea market. Continue along Calle de Toledo, then fork left onto Calle Estudios and proceed to Plaza de Cascorro, named after a hero of the Cuban wars. El Rastro begins here. If your tour takes place Monday to Friday, skip the Rastro neighborhood. Instead, turn right onto:

12. **Calle de Segovia,** which intersects Calle de Toledo just before it passes in front of the Catedral de San Isidro. Walk one block and turn right onto the first street:

13. **Calle de Cuchilleros.** Follow it north past 16th- and 17th-century stone-fronted houses. Within a block, a flight of granite steps forks to the right. Climb the steps (a sign identifies the new street as Calle Arco de Cuchilleros) and you'll pass one of the most famous *mesones* (typical Castilian restaurants) of Madrid, the Cueva de Luís Candelas.

Once again you will have entered Plaza Mayor, this time on the southwestern corner. Walk beneath the southernmost arcade and promenade counterclockwise beneath the arcades, walking north underneath the square's eastern arcade. Then walk west beneath its northern arcade. At the northwest corner, exit through the archway onto Calle 7 de Julio. Fifty feet later, cross Calle Mayor and take the right-hand narrow street before you. This is:

14. **Calle Bordadores,** which during the 17th century housed Madrid's embroidery workshops, staffed exclusively by men.

As you proceed, notice the 17th-century brick walls and towers of the:

15. Church of San Ginés, Arenal, 15. The church of one of Madrid's oldest parishes owes its present look to the architects who reconstructed it after a devastating fire in 1872.

At the end of this tour, you'll find yourself on traffic-congested Calle del Arenal, at the doorstep of many interesting old streets.

10 Organized Tours

A large number of agencies in Madrid book organized tours and excursions to sights and attractions both within and outside the city limits. Although your mobility and freedom might be somewhat hampered, some visitors appreciate the ease and convenience of being able to visit so many sights in a single efficiently organized day.

Many of the city's hotel concierges, and all of the city's travel agents, will book anyone who asks for a guided tour of Madrid or its environs with one of Spain's largest tour operators, **Pullmantours,** Plaza de Oriente, 8 (☎ **91-541-18-07**). Regardless of their destination and duration, virtually every tour departs from the Pullmantours terminal, at that address. Half-day tours of Madrid include an artistic tour priced at 5,250 ptas. (US$31.50) per person, which includes entrance to a selection of the city's museums, and a panoramic half-day tour for 3,000 ptas. (US$18).

Toledo is the most popular full-day excursion outside the city limits. Trips cost 8,700 ptas. (US$52.20). These tours (including lunch) depart daily at 9:45am from the above-mentioned departure point, last all day, and include ample opportunities for wandering at will through the city's narrow streets. You can, if you wish, take an abbreviated morning tour of Toledo, without stopping for lunch, for 5,600 ptas. (US$33.60).

Another popular tour stops briefly in Toledo and continues on to visit both the monastery at El Escorial and the Valley of the Fallen (*Valle de los Caídos*) before returning the same day to Madrid. With lunch included, this all-day excursion costs 12,000 ptas. (US$72).

The third major destination of bus tours from Madrid's center to the city's surrounding attractions is Pullmantours' full-day guided excursion to Ávila and Segovia, which takes in a heady dose of medieval and ancient Roman monuments that are really very interesting. With lunch included, the price per person is 9,000 ptas. (US$54).

The hop-off, hop-on **Madrid Vision Bus** lets you set your own pace and itinerary. A scheduled panoramic tour lasts a half-hour, provided that you don't get off the bus. Otherwise, you can opt for an unlimited number of stops, exploring at your leisure. The Madrid Vision makes four complete tours daily, two in the morning and two in the afternoon; on Sunday and Monday buses depart only in the morning. Check with **Trapsa Tours** (☎ **91-767-17-43**) for departure times, which are variable. The full-day tour, with unlimited stops, costs 2,200 ptas. (US$13.20). You can board the bus at the Madrid tourist office.

11 Shopping

Seventeenth-century playwright Tirso de Molina called Madrid "a shop stocked with every kind of merchandise," and it's true—an estimated 50,000 stores sell everything from high-fashion clothing to flamenco guitars to art and ceramics.

If your time is limited, go to one of the big department stores (see below). They all carry a bit of everything.

THE SHOPPING SCENE

SHOPPING AREAS   The Center   The sheer diversity of shops in Madrid's center is staggering. Their densest concentration lies immediately north of the Puerta del Sol, radiating out from calle del Carmen, calle Montera, and calle Preciados.

Calle Mayor & Calle del Arenal   Unlike their more stylish neighbors to the north of Puerta del Sol, shops in this district to the west tend toward the small, slightly dusty enclaves of coin and stamp dealers, family-owned souvenir shops, clock makers, sellers of military paraphernalia, and an abundance of stores selling musical scores.

Gran Vía   Conceived, designed, and built in the 1910s and 1920s as a showcase for the city's best shops, hotels, and restaurants, the Gran Vía has since been eclipsed by other shopping districts. Its art nouveau/art deco–glamour still survives in the hearts of most Madrileños, however. The bookstores here are among the best in the city, as are outlets for fashion, shoes, jewelry, furs, and handcrafted accessories from all regions of Spain.

El Rastro   It's the biggest flea market in Spain, drawing collectors, dealers, buyers, and hopefuls from throughout Madrid and its suburbs. The makeshift stalls are at their most frenetic on Sunday morning. For more information, refer to the "Flea Markets" section under "Shopping A to Z," below.

Plaza Mayor   Under the arcades of the square itself are exhibitions of lithographs and oil paintings, and every weekend there's a loosely organized market for stamp and coin collectors. Within three or four blocks in every direction you'll find more than the average number of souvenir shops.

On calle Marqués Viudo de Pontejos, which runs east from Plaza Mayor, is one of the city's headquarters for the sale of cloth, thread, and buttons. Also running east, on calle de Zaragoza, are silversmiths and jewelers. On calle Postas you'll find housewares, underwear, soap powders, and other household items.

Near the carrera de San Jerónimo   Several blocks east of Puerta del Sol is Madrid's densest concentration of gift shops, crafts shops, and antiques dealers—a decorator's delight. Its most interesting streets include calle del Prado, calle de las Huertas, and Plaza de las Cortés. The neighborhood is pricey, so don't expect bargains here.

Northwest Madrid   A few blocks east of Parque del Oeste is an upscale neighborhood that's well stocked with luxury goods and household staples. Calle de la Princesa, its main thoroughfare, has shops selling shoes, handbags, fashion, gifts, and children's clothing. Thanks to the presence of the university nearby, there's also a dense concentration of bookstores, especially on calle Isaac Peral and calle Fernando el Católico, several blocks north and northwest, respectively, from the subway stop of Argüelles.

Salamanca District   It's known throughout Spain as the quintessential upper-bourgeois neighborhood, uniformly prosperous, and its shops are correspondingly exclusive. They include outlets run by interior decorators, furniture shops, fur and jewelry shops, several department stores, and design headquarters whose output ranges from the solidly conservative to the high-tech. The main streets of this district are calle de Serrano and calle de Velázquez. The district lies northeast of the center of Madrid, a few blocks north of Retiro Park. Its most central metro stops are Serrano and Velázquez.

HOURS   Major stores are open (in most cases) Monday to Saturday 9:30am to 8pm. Many small stores take a siesta between 1:30 and 4:30pm. Of course, there is never any set formula, and hours can vary greatly from store to store, depending on the idiosyncrasies and schedules of the owner.

SHIPPING   Many art and antiques dealers will crate and ship bulky objects for an additional fee. Whereas it usually pays to have heavy objects shipped by sea, in some cases it's almost the same price to ship crated goods by airplane. Of course, it depends on the distance your crate will have to travel overland to the nearest international port, which, in many cases for the purposes of relatively small-scale shipments by individual clients, is Barcelona. Consequently, it might pay to call two branches of **Emery Worldwide** from within Spain to explain your particular situation, and receive comparable rates. For information about sea transit for your valuables, call **Emery Worldwide Ocean Services** at their only Spanish branch, in Barcelona (☎ 93-479-30-50). For information about **Emery Worldwide Air Freight,** call their main Spanish office in Madrid (☎ 91-747-56-66) for advice on any of the dozen air-freight pickup stations they maintain throughout Spain. These include, among many others, Barcelona, Alicante, Málaga, Bilbao, and Valencia. For more advice on this, and the formalities that you'll go through in clearing U.S. customs after the arrival of your shipment in the United States, call **Emery Worldwide** in the United States at ☎ 800/488-9451.

For most small- and medium-sized shipments, air freight isn't much more expensive than ocean shipping. **Iberia's Air Cargo Division** (☎ 800/221-6002 in the U.S.) offers air-freight service from Spain to New York, Chicago, Miami, or Los Angeles. What will you pay for this transport of your treasured art objects or freight? Here's a rule of thumb: For a shipment under 100 kilos (220 pounds), from either Barcelona or Madrid to New York, the cost is approximately 734 pesetas (US$4.40) per pound. The per-pound price goes down as the weight of the shipment increases, declining to, for example, 254 pesetas (US$1.50) per pound for shipments of more than 1,000 kilos (2,200 pounds). Regardless of what you ship, there's a minimum charge of 8,500 pesetas (US$51).

For an additional fee, Iberia or one of its representatives will also pick up your package. For a truly precious cargo, ask the seller to build a crate for it. For information within Spain about air-cargo shipments, call Iberia's cargo division at Madrid's Barajas Airport (☎ 91-587-33-07) or at Barcelona's airport (☎ 93-401-34-26).

Remember that your air-cargo shipment will need to clear Customs after it's brought into the United States. This involves some additional paperwork, costly delays, and in some cases a trip to the airport where the shipment first entered the United States. It's usually easier (and in some cases, much easier) to hire a commercial customs broker to do the work for you. **Emery Worldwide,** a division of CF Freightways, can clear most shipments of goods for around US$138, which you'll pay in addition to any applicable duty you owe your home government. For information, you can call ☎ 800/443-6379 within the United States.

TAX & HOW TO RECOVER IT   If you are not a European Union resident and you make purchases in Spain worth more than 15,000 pesetas (US$105), you can get a tax refund. (The internal tax, known as VAT in most of Europe, is called IVA in Spain.) Depending on the goods, the rate usually ranges from 7% to 16% of the total worth of your merchandise. Luxury items are taxed at 33%.

To get this refund, you must complete three copies of a form that the store will give you, detailing the nature of your purchase and its value. Citizens of non-EU countries show the purchase and the form to the Spanish Customs Office. The shop is supposed to refund the amount due you. Inquire at the time of purchase how they will do so and discuss in what currency your refund will arrive.

TRADITIONAL SALES   The best sales are usually in summer. Called *rebajas,* they start in July and go through August. As a general rule, merchandise is marked down even more in August to make way for the new fall wares in most stores.

DUTY-FREE—WORTH IT OR NOT?   Before you leave home, check the regular retail price of items that you're most likely to buy. Duty-free prices vary from one country to another and from item to item. Sometimes you're better off purchasing an item in a discount store at home. If you don't remember prices back home, you can't tell when you're getting a good deal.

BARGAINING   The days of bargaining are, for the most part, long gone. Most stores have what is called *precio de venta al público* (PVP), a firm retail price not subject to negotiation. With street vendors and flea markets, it's a different story because haggling *a la española* is expected. However, you'll have to be very skilled to get the price reduced a lot, as most of these street-smart vendors know exactly what their merchandise is worth and are old hands at getting that price.

SHOPPING A TO Z

Spain has always been known for its craftspeople, many still working in the time-honored and labor-intensive traditions of their grandparents. It's hard to go wrong if you stick to the beautiful handcrafted Spanish objects—hand-painted tiles, ceramics, and porcelain; handwoven rugs; handmade sweaters; and intricate embroideries. And, of course, Spain produces some of the world's finest leather. Jewelry, especially gold set with Majorca pearls, represents good value and unquestioned luxury.

Some of Madrid's art galleries are known throughout Europe for discovering and encouraging new talent. Antiques are sold in highly sophisticated retail outlets. Better suited to the budgets of many travelers are the weekly flea markets.

Spain continues to make inroads into the fashion world. Its young designers are regularly featured in the fashion magazines of Europe. Excellent shoes are available, some highly fashionable. But be advised that prices for shoes and quality clothing are generally higher in Madrid than in the United States.

ANTIQUES

In addition to the following shops, you might want to visit the flea market (see El Rastro, below).

Centro de Anticuarios Lagasca. Lagasca, 36. No phone. Metro: Serrano or Velázquez.

You'll find about a dozen antiques shops here, clustered into one covered arcade. They operate as individual businesses, although by browsing through each you'll find an impressive assemblage of antique furniture, porcelain, and whatnots. Open Monday to Saturday 10am to 1:30pm and 5 to 8pm.

Galeria de Arte del Lubre. Serrano, 5. ☎ **91-576-96-82.** Metro: Retiro. Bus: 9 or 15.

Housed in a mid-19th-century building are several unusual antiques dealers (and a large carpet emporium as well) many of whom specialize in antique, sometimes monumental paintings. Each establishment maintains its own schedule, although the center itself has overall hours. Open Monday to Saturday 10am to 2pm and 5 to 8:15pm.

ART GALLERIES

✪ **Galería Kreisler.** Hermosilla, 6. ☎ **91-431-42-64.** Metro: Serrano. Bus: 27, 45, or 150.

One successful entrepreneur on Madrid's art scene is Ohio-born Edward Kreisler, whose gallery, now run by his son Juan, specializes in figurative and contemporary paintings, sculptures, and graphics. The gallery prides itself on occasionally displaying and selling the works of artists who are critically acclaimed and displayed in museums in Spain. Open Monday to Saturday 10:30am to 2pm and 5 to 9pm. Closed in August and on Saturday afternoons July 15 to September 15.

CAPES

Capas Seseña. Cruz, 23. ☎ **91-531-68-40.** Metro: Sevilla or Puerta del Sol. Bus: 5, 51, or 52.

Founded shortly after the turn of the century, this shop manufactures and sells wool capes for both women and men. The wool comes from the mountain town of Béjar, near Salamanca. Celebrities who have been spotted donning Seseña capes include Picasso, Hemingway, Miró, and recently, First Lady Hillary Clinton and daughter Chelsea. Open Monday to Friday 10am to 1:30pm and 5 to 8pm, Saturday 10am to 1:30pm.

CARPETS

Ispahan. Serrano, 5. ☎ **91-575-20-12.** Metro: Retiro. Bus: 1, 2, 9, or 15.

In this 19th-century building, behind bronze handmade doors, are three floors devoted to carpets from around the world, notably Afghanistan, India, Nepal, Iran, Turkey, and the Caucasus. One section features silk carpets. Open Monday to Saturday 10am to 2pm and 4:30 to 8:30pm.

CERAMICS

✪ **Antigua Casa Talavera.** Isabel la Católica, 2. ☎ **91-53-16-840.** Metro: Santo Domingo. Bus: 1, 2, 46, 70, 75, or 148.

"The first house of Spanish ceramics" has wares that include a sampling of regional styles from every major area of Spain, including Talavera, Toledo, Manises, Valencia, Puente del Arzobispa, Alcora, Granada, and Seville. Sangría pitchers, dinnerware, tea sets, plates, and vases are all handmade. Inside one of the showrooms is an interesting selection of tiles, painted with reproductions of scenes from bullfights, dances, and folklore. There's also a series of tiles depicting famous paintings in the Prado. At its present location since 1904, the shop is only a short walk from Plaza de Santo Domingo. Open Monday to Friday 10am to 1:30pm and 5 to 8pm, Saturday 10am to 1:30pm.

CRAFTS

El Arco de los Cuchilleros Artesania de Hoy. Plaza Mayor, 9 (basement level). ☎ **91-365-26-80.** Metro: Puerta del Sol or Ópera.

Set within one of the 17th-century vaulted cellars of Plaza Mayor, this shop is entirely devoted to unusual craft items from throughout Spain. The merchandise is one of a kind and in most cases contemporary; it includes a changing array of pottery, leather, textiles, wood carvings, glassware, wickerwork, papier-mâché, and silver jewelry. The hardworking owners deal directly with the artisans who produce each item, ensuring a wide inventory of handcrafts. The staff is familiar with the rituals of applying for tax-free status of purchases here, and speaks several different languages. Open January to September, Monday to Saturday 11am to 8pm; October to December, Monday to Saturday 11am to 9pm.

DEPARTMENT STORES

El Corte Inglés. Preciados, 3. ☎ **91-379-80-00.** Metro: Puerta del Sol.

This flagship of the largest department-store chain in Madrid sells hundreds of souvenirs and Spanish handcrafts, such as damascene steelwork from Toledo, flamenco dolls, and embroidered shawls. Some astute buyers report that it also sells glamorous fashion articles, such as Pierre Balmain designs, for about a third less than equivalent items in most European capitals. Services include interpreters, currency-exchange windows, and parcel delivery either to a local hotel or overseas. Open Monday to Saturday 10am to 9pm.

EMBROIDERIES

Casa Bonet. Núñez de Balboa, 76. ☎ **91-575-09-12.** Metro: Núñez de Balboa.

The intricately detailed embroideries produced in Spain's Balearic Islands (especially Majorca) are avidly sought for bridal chests and elegant dinner settings. A few examples of the store's extensive inventory are displayed on the walls. Open Monday to Friday 9:45am to 2pm and 5 to 8pm, Saturday 10:15am to 2pm.

ESPADRILLES

Casa Hernanz. Toledo, 18. ☎ **91-366-54-50.** Metro: Puerta del Sol, Ópera, or La Latina.

A brisk walk south of Plaza Mayor delivers you to this store, in business since the 1840s. In addition to espadrilles, they sell shoes in other styles, as well as hats. Open Monday to Friday 9am to 1:30pm and 4:30 to 8pm, Saturday 10am to 2pm.

FANS & UMBRELLAS

Casa de Diego. Puerta del Sol, 12. ☎ **91-522-66-43.** Metro: Puerta del Sol.

Here you'll find a wide inventory of fans, ranging from plain to fancy, from plastic to exotic hardwood, from cost-conscious to lavish. Some fans tend to be a bit overpriced; shopping around may increase your chances of finding a real bargain. Now open year-round, Monday to Saturday 9:45am to 8pm.

FASHIONS FOR MEN

For the man on a budget who wants to dress reasonably well, the best outlet for off-the-rack men's clothing is one of the branches of the Corte Inglés department-store chain (see above). Most men's boutiques in Madrid are very expensive and may not be worth the investment.

FASHIONS FOR WOMEN

Herrero. Preciados, 7. ☎ **91-521-29-90.** Metro: Puerta del Sol or Callao.

The sheer size and buying power of this popular retail outlet for women's clothing make it a reasonably priced emporium for all kinds of feminine garb as well as various articles for gentlemen. An additional outlet lies on the same street at no. 16 (☎ **91-521-15-24**). Both are open Monday to Saturday 10:30am to 8pm; some Sundays noon to 8pm.

Modas Gonzalo. Gran Vía, 43. ☎ **91-547-12-39.** Metro: Callao or Puerta del Sol.

This boutique's baroque, gilded atmosphere evokes the 1940s, but its fashions are strictly up-to-date, well made, and intended for stylish adult women. Open Monday to Saturday 10am to 1:30pm and 4:30 to 8pm.

FLEA MARKETS

✪ **El Rastro.** Plaza Cascorro and Ribera de Curtidores. Metro: La Latina. Bus: 3 or 17.

Foremost among markets is El Rastro (translated as either flea market or thieves' market), occupying a roughly triangular district of streets and plazas a few minutes' walk south of Plaza Mayor. Its center is Plaza Cascorro and Ribera de Curtidores. This market will delight anyone attracted to a mishmash of fascinating junk interspersed with bric-a-brac and paintings. *Note:* Thieves are rampant here (hustling more than just antiques), so secure your wallet carefully, be alert, and proceed with caution. Insofar as scheduling your visit to El Rastro, bear in mind that this is a flea market involving hundreds of merchants who basically pull up their display tables and depart whenever their goods are sold or they get fed up with the crowds. In theory, vendors hawk their wares every day 9:30am to 1:30pm, and after a leisurely lunch, again 5 to 8pm. But the best day for scheduling a visit here is Sunday morning, when the neighborhood has a higher percentage of merchants and salespersons than any other time of the week.

FOOD & WINE

Mallorca. Velázquez, 59. ☎ **91-431-99-09.** Metro: Velázquez.

Madrid's best-established gourmet shop opened in 1931 as an outlet selling a pastry called *ensaimada,* and this is still one of the store's most famous products. Tempting arrays of cheeses, canapés, roasted and marinated meats, sausages, and about a dozen kinds of pâté accompany a spread of tiny pastries, tarts, and chocolates. Don't overlook the displays of Spanish wines and brandies. A stand-up tapas bar is always clogged with clients three deep, sampling the wares before they buy larger portions to take home. Tapas cost from 150 to 400 pesetas (US90¢ to US$2.40) per *ración* (portion). Open daily 9:30am to 9pm.

HATS & HEADGEAR

Casa Yustas. Plaza Mayor, 30. ☎ **91-366-50-84.** Metro: Puerta del Sol.

Founded in 1894, this extraordinary hat emporium is very popular. Want to see yourself as a Congo explorer, a Spanish sailor, an officer in the kaiser's army, or even Napoléon? Open Monday to Saturday 9:30am to 9:30pm, Saturday 11am to 9pm.

LEATHER

✪ **Loewe.** Gran Vía, 8. ☎ **91-522-68-15.** Metro: Banco de España or Gran Vía.

Since 1846 this has been the most elegant leather store in Spain. Its gold medal–winning designers have always kept abreast of changing tastes and styles, but the inventory still retains a timeless chic. The store sells luggage, handbags, and jackets for men and women (in leather or suede). Open Monday to Saturday 9:30am to 8pm.

PERFUMES

Perfumería Padilla. Preciados, 17. ☎ **91-522-86-29.** Metro: Puerta del Sol.

This store sells a large and competitively priced assortment of Spanish and international scents for women. They also maintain a branch at calle del Carmen, 8 (☎ **91/ 522-66-83**). Both branches are open Monday to Saturday 10am to 2pm and 5 to 8:30pm.

Oriental Perfumeries. Mayor, 1. ☎ **91-521-59-05.** Metro: Puerta del Sol.

Located at the western edge of the Puerta del Sol, this time-tested shop carries one of the most complete stocks of perfume in Madrid—both national and international brands. It also sells gifts, souvenirs, and costume jewelry. Open Monday to Saturday 10am to 8:30pm.

PORCELAIN

Lasarte. Gran Vía, 44. ☎ **91-521-49-22.** Metro: Callao.

This imposing outlet is devoted almost exclusively to Lladró porcelain; the staff can usually tell you about new designs and releases the Lladró company is planning for the near future. Open Monday to Friday 9:30 to 8pm, Saturday 10am to 8pm.

SHOPPING MALLS

ABC Serrano. Serrano, 61 or Castellane, 34. Metro: Serrano.

Set within what used to be the working premises of a well-known Madrileño newspaper (*ABC*), this is a complex of about 85 upscale boutiques that emphasize fashion, housewares, cosmetics, and art objects. Although each of the outfitters inside are independently owned and managed, most of them maintain hours of Monday to Saturday 10am to midnight. On the premises, you'll find cafes and restaurants to keep you fed between bouts of shopping, lots of potted and flowering shrubbery, and acres and acres of Spanish marble and tile.

12 Madrid After Dark

Madrid abounds in dance halls, tascas, cafes, theaters, movie houses, music halls, and nightclubs. You'll have to proceed carefully through this maze, as many of these offerings are strictly for residents or for Spanish-speakers.

Because dinner is served late in Spain, nightlife doesn't really get under way until after 11pm, and it generally lasts until around 3am—Madrileños are so fond of prowling around at night that they are known around Spain as *gatos* (cats). If you arrive at 9:30pm at a club, you'll have the place all to yourself, if it's even open.

In most clubs a one-drink minimum is the rule: Feel free to nurse one drink through the entire evening's entertainment.

In summer Madrid becomes a virtual free festival because the city sponsors a series of plays, concerts, and films. Pick up a copy of the *Guía del Ocio* (available at most newsstands) for listings of these events. This guide also provides information about occasional discounts for commercial events, such as the concerts that are given in Madrid's parks. Also check the program of *Fundación Juan March,* calle Castello, 77 (☎ **91-435-42-40;** metro: Núñez de Balboa). Tapping into funds that were bequeathed to it by a generous financier (Sr. Juan March), it stages free concerts of Spanish and international classical music within a concert hall at its headquarters at calle Castello, 77. In most cases, these are 90-minute events that are presented every Monday and Saturday at noon, and every Wednesday at 7:30pm.

Flamenco in Madrid is geared mainly to prosperous tourists with fat wallets, and nightclubs are expensive. But since Madrid is preeminently a city of song and dance, you can often be entertained at very little cost—in fact, for the price of a glass of wine or beer, if you sit at a bar with live entertainment.

Like flamenco clubs, discos tend to be expensive, but they often open for what is erroneously called afternoon sessions (from 7 to 10pm). Although discos charge entry fees, at an afternoon session the cost might be as low as 500 pesetas (US$3), rising to 2,000 pesetas (US$12) and beyond for a night session—that is, beginning at 11:30pm and lasting until the early morning hours. Therefore, go early, dance until 10pm, then proceed to dinner (you'll be eating at the fashionable hour).

Nightlife is so plentiful in Madrid that the city can be roughly divided into the following "night zones."

Plaza Mayor/Puerta del Sol The most popular areas from the standpoint of both tradition and tourist interest, they can also be dangerous, so explore them with caution, especially late at night. They are filled with tapas bars and *cuevas* (drinking caves). Here it is customary to begin a tasca crawl, going to tavern after tavern, sampling the wine in each, along with a selection of tapas. The major streets for such a crawl are Cava de San Miguel, Cava Alta, and Cava Baja. You can order *pinchos y raciónes* (tasty snacks and tidbits).

Gran Vía This area contains mainly cinemas and theaters. Most of the after-dark action takes place on little streets branching off the Gran Vía.

Plaza de Isabel II/Plaza de Oriente Another area much frequented by tourists, many restaurants and cafes flourish here, including the famous Café de Oriente.

Chueca   Along such streets as Hortaleza, Infantas, Barquillo, and San Lucas, this is the gay nightlife district, with dozens of clubs. Cheap restaurants, along with a few female striptease joints, are also found here. This area can also be dangerous at night, so watch for pickpockets and muggers. As of late, there has been greater police presence at night.

Argüelles/Moncloa   For university students, this part of town sees most of the action. Many dance clubs are found here, along with ale houses and fast-food joints. The area is bounded by Pintor Rosales, Cea Bermúdez, Bravo Murillo, San Bernardo, and Conde Duque.

THE PERFORMING ARTS

Madrid has a number of theaters, opera companies, and dance companies. To discover where and when specific cultural events are being performed, pick up a copy of *Guía del Ocio* at any city newsstand. The sheer volume of cultural offerings can be staggering; for a concise summary of the highlights, see below.

Tickets to dramatic and musical events usually range in price from 700 to 3,000 pesetas (US$4.20 to US$18), with discounts of up to 50% granted on certain days of the week (usually Wednesday and matinees on Sunday).

The concierges at most major hotels can usually get you tickets to specific concerts, if you are clear about your wishes and needs. They charge a considerable markup, part of which is passed along to whichever agency originally booked the tickets. You'll save money if you go directly to the box office to buy tickets. In the event your choice is sold out, you may be able to get tickets (with a reasonable markup) at **Localidades Galicia** at Plaza del Carmen, 1 (☎ **91-531-27-32;** metro: Puerta del Sol). This agency also markets tickets to bullfights and sporting events. It is open Tuesday to Saturday 9:30am to 1:30pm and 4:30 to 7:30pm, Sunday 9:30am to 1:30pm.

Here follows a grab bag of nighttime diversions that might amuse and entertain you. First, the cultural offerings:

MAJOR PERFORMING-ARTS COMPANIES

For those who speak Spanish, the **Compañía Nacional de Nuevas Tendencias Escénicas** is an avant-garde troupe that performs new and often controversial works by undiscovered writers. On the other hand, the **Compañía Nacional de Teatro Clásico,** as its name suggests, is devoted to the Spanish classics, including works by the ever-popular Lope de Vega and Tirso de Molina.

Among dance companies, the national ballet of Spain—devoted exclusively to Spanish dance—is the **Ballet Nacional de España.** Their performances are always well attended. The national lyrical ballet company is the **Ballet Lírico Nacional.**

World-renowned flamenco sensation Antonio Canales and his troupe, **Ballet Flamenco Antonio Canales,** offer spirited high-energy performances. Productions are centered on Canales's impassioned *Torero,* his interpretation of a bullfighter and the physical and emotional struggles within the man. For tickets and information, you can call Madrid's most comprehensive ticket agency, the previously recommended **Localidades Galicia,** Plaza del Carmen, 1 (☎ **91-531-27-32**), for tickets to cultural events and virtually any other event in Castile. Other agencies include **Casa de Catalunya** (☎ **91-538-33-33**) and **Corte Ingles** (☎ **91-432-93-00**). Both Casa de Catalunya and Cortes Ingles have satellite offices located throughout Madrid.

Madrid's opera company is the **Teatro de la Ópera,** and its symphony orchestra is the outstanding **Orquesta Sinfónica de Madrid.** The national orchestra of Spain— widely acclaimed on the continent—is the **Orquesta Nacional de España,** which pays particular homage to Spanish composers.

CLASSICAL MUSIC

Auditorio del Parque de Atracciones. Casa de Campo. Metro: Lago or Batán.

The schedule of this 3,500-seat facility might include everything from punk-rock musical groups to the more high-brow warm-weather performances of visiting symphony orchestras. Check with Localidades Galicia to see what's on at the time of your visit (see above).

Auditorio Nacional de Música. Príncipe de Vergara, 146. ☎ **91-337-01-00.** Tickets 1,000–6,000 ptas. (US$6–US$36). Metro: Cruz del Rayo.

Sheathed in slabs of Spanish granite, marble, and limestone and capped with Iberian tiles, this hall is the ultramodern home of both the National Orchestra of Spain and the National Chorus of Spain. Standing just north of Madrid's Salamanca district, it ranks as a major addition to the competitive circles of classical music in Europe. Inaugurated in 1988, it is devoted exclusively to the performances of symphonic, choral, and chamber music. In addition to the Auditorio Principal (Hall A), whose capacity is almost 2,300, there's a hall for chamber music (Hall B), as well as a small auditorium (seating 250) for intimate concerts.

Fundación Juan March. Castelló, 77. ☎ **91-435-42-40.** Metro: Núñez de Balboa.

This foundation sometimes holds free concerts at lunchtime. The advance schedule is difficult to predict, so call for information.

La Fidula. Calle Huerta S, 57. ☎ **91-429-29-47.** Cover 500–700 ptas. (US$3–US$4.20). Metro: Antón Martín.

Serving as a bastion of civility in a sea of rock-and-roll and disco chaos, this club was converted from an 1800s grocer. Today it presents chamber music concerts nightly at 11:30pm with an additional show at 1am on weekends. The club offers the prospect of a tranquil, cultural evening on the town, at a moderate price. They take performances here seriously—late arrivals may not be seated for concerts. It is open Monday to Thursday and Sunday 7pm to 3am, Friday and Saturday 7pm to 4am.

Teatro Cultural de la Villa. Plaza de Colón. ☎ **91-575-60-80.** Tickets, depending on event, 1,300–4,500 ptas. (US$7.80–US$27). Metro: Serrano or Colón.

Spanish-style ballet along with *zarzuelas* (musical reviews), orchestral works, and theater pieces, are presented at this cultural center. Tickets go on sale 5 days before the event of your choice, and performances are usually presented at 2 evening shows (8 and 10:30pm).

✪ Teatro Real. Plaza Isabel II. ☎ **91-516-06-60.** Tickets 4,000–32,000 ptas. (US$24–US$192). Metro: Ópera.

Reopened in 1997 after a massive US$157 million renovation, this theater is one of the world's finest stage and acoustic settings for opera. Its extensive state-of-the-art equipment affords elaborate stage designs and special effects. Luis Antonio García Navarro, the internationally heralded maestro from Valencia, is the musical and artistic director of the Royal Opera House, at least until 2002, and he works with leading Spanish lyric talents, including Plácido Domingo. Today, the building is the home of the Compania del Teatro Real, a company specializing in opera, and is also a major venue for classical music. On November 19, 1850, under the reign of Queen Isabel II, the Royal Opera House opened its doors with Donizetti's *La Favorita*.

THEATER

Madrid offers many different theater performances, useful to you only if you are very fluent in Spanish. If you aren't, check the *Guía del Ocia* for performances by

English-speaking companies on tour from Britain or select a concert or subtitled movie instead.

In addition to the major ones listed below, there are at least 30 other theaters, including one devoted almost entirely to children's plays, the **Sala la Bicicleta,** in the Ciudad de los Niños at Casa de Campo. Nonprofessional groups stage dozens of other plays in such places as churches.

Teatro Calderón. Atocha, 18. ☎ **91 429 52 38.** Tickets 3,000 8,000 ptas. (US$18 US$48). Metro: Tirso de Molina.

This is the largest theater in Madrid, with a seating capacity of 2,000. Although in the past this venue included everything from dramatic theater to flamenco, in recent years it has moved to a more serious approach that focuses mostly on opera, with performances beginning most evenings at 8pm. A long-running favorite is Bizet's *Carmen,* whose setting within Spain partly justified its enduring popularity among Madrileños.

Teatro de la Comedia. Príncipe, 14. ☎ **91-521-49-31.** Tickets 1,300–2,600 ptas. (US$7.80–US$15.60); 50% discount on Thurs. Metro: Sevilla. Bus: 15, 20, or 150.

This is the home of the Compañía Nacional de Teatro Clásico. Here, more than anywhere else in Madrid, you're likely to see performances from the classic repertoire of such great Spanish dramatists as Lope de Vega and Calderón de la Barca. There are no performances on Wednesday, and the theater is closed during July and August. The box office is open daily 11:30am to 1:30pm and 5 to 6pm, and for about an hour before the performances.

Teatro Español. Príncipe, 25. ☎ **91-429-62-97.** Tickets 2,300–4,000 ptas. (US$13.80–US$24); 50% discount on Wed. Metro: Sevilla.

This company is funded by Madrid's municipal government, its repertoire a time-tested assortment of great and/or favorite Spanish plays. The box office is open daily 11:30am to 1:30pm and 5 to 6pm.

Teatro Lírico Nacional de la Zarzuela. Jovellanos, 4. ☎ **91-524-54-00.** Tickets 1,200–4,500 ptas. (US$7.20–US$27). Metro: Sevilla.

Near Plaza de la Cibeles, this theater of potent nostalgia produces ballet and an occasional opera in addition to zarzuela. Show times vary. The box office is open daily noon to 5pm.

Teatro María Guerrero. Tamayo y Baus, 4. ☎ **91-310-29-49.** Tickets 1,600–2,600 ptas. (US$9.60–US$15.60). Metro: Banco de España or Colón.

Also funded by the government, the María Guerrero (named after a much-loved Spanish actress) works in cooperation with the Teatro Español (see above) for performances of works by such classic Spanish playwrights as Lope de Vega and García Lorca. The box office is open daily 11:30am to 1:30pm and 5 to 6pm.

Teatro Nuevo Apolo. Plaza de Tirso de Molina, 1. ☎ **91-369-14-67.** Cover usually 2,800 ptas. (US$16.80). Metro: Tirso de Molina.

Nuevo Apolo is the permanent home of the renowned Antología de la Zarzuela company. It is on the restored site of the old Teatro Apolo, where these musical variety shows have been performed since the 1930s. Prices and times depend on the show. The box office is open daily 11:30am to 1:30pm and 5 to 6pm.

CABARET

Madrid's nightlife is no longer steeped in prudishness, as it was (at least officially) during the Franco era. You can now see glossy cabaret acts and shows with lots of nudity.

Café del Foro. Calle San Andres, 38. ☎ **91-445-37-52.** No cover (but may be imposed for a specially booked act). Metro: Bilbao. Bus: 40, 147, 149, or N19.

This old-time favorite in the Malasaña district has suddenly in the 1990s become one of the most fashionable places in Madrid to hang out after dark. Patronizing the club are members of the literati along with a large student clientele. You never know exactly what the show for the evening will be, although live music of some sort generally starts at 11:30pm. Cabaret is often featured, along with live merengue, bolero, and salsa. There's a faux starry sky above the stage area, plus Roman colonnades that justify the name Café del Foro. Open daily 7pm to 3am.

Scala Meliá Castilla. Calle Capitán Haya, 43 (entrance at Rosario Pino, 7). ☎ **91-571-44-11.** Cover 5,500 ptas. (US$33), including first drink. Metro: Cuzco.

Madrid's most famous dinner show is a major Las Vegas–style spectacle, with music, water, light, and color. The program is varied, including international or Spanish ballet, magic acts, ice skaters, whatever. Most definitely a live orchestra will entertain you. It is open Tuesday to Saturday 8:30pm to 3am. Dinner is served beginning at 9pm; the show is presented at 10:45pm. The show with dinner costs 10,500 pesetas (US$63), and if you partake you don't have to pay the cover charge above, as it's included in the show/dinner price. Reservations are essential.

FLAMENCO

Café de Chinitas. Torija, 7. ☎ **91-559-51-35.** Dinner and show 10,250 ptas. (US$61.50); show without dinner (but includes one drink) 4,550 ptas. (US$27.30). Metro: Santo Domingo. Bus: 1 or 2.

One of the best flamenco clubs in town, Café de Chinitas is set one floor above street level in a 19th-century building midway between the Ópera and the Gran Vía. It features an array of (usually) gypsy-born flamenco artists from Madrid, Barcelona, and Andalusia, with acts and performers changing about once a month. You can arrange for dinner before the show, although many Madrileños opt for dinner somewhere else and then arrive just for drinks and the flamenco. Open Monday to Saturday, with dinner served 9 to 11pm and the show lasting 10:30pm to 2am. Reservations are recommended.

Casa Patas. Calle Cañizares, 10. ☎ **91-369-04-96.** Admission 3,000 ptas. (US$18). Metro: Tirso de Molina.

This club is now one of the best places to see "true" flamenco as opposed to the more tourist-oriented version presented at Corral de la Morería (see below). It is also a bar and restaurant, with space reserved in the rear for flamenco. Shows are presented midnight on Thursday, Friday, and Saturday and during Madrid's major fiesta month of May. The best flamenco in Madrid is presented here: Proof of the pudding is that flamenco singers and dancers often hang out here after hours. Tapas are priced at 450 to 2,500 pesetas (US$2.70 to US$15) and are available at the bar. The club is open daily 8pm to 3am.

Corral de la Morería. Morería, 17. ☎ **91-365-84-46.** Dinner and show 11,000 ptas. (US$66); show without dinner (includes one drink) 4,300 ptas. (US$25.80). Metro: La Latina or Puerta del Sol.

In the old town, the Morería (meaning where the Moors reside) sizzles with flamenco. Colorfully costumed strolling performers warm up the audience around 11pm; a flamenco show follows, with at least 10 dancers. It's much cheaper to eat somewhere else first, then pay only the one-drink minimum. Open daily 9pm to 3am.

The Sultry Sound of Flamenco

The lights dim and the flamenco stars clatter rhythmically across the dance floor. Their lean bodies and hips shake and sway to the music. The word *flamenco* has various translations, meaning everything from "gypsified Andalusian" to "knife," and from "blowhard" to "tough guy."

Accompanied by stylized guitar music, castanets, and the fervent clapping of the crowd, dancers are filled with tension and emotion. Flamenco dancing, with its flash, color, and ritual, is evocative of Spanish culture, although its origins remain mysterious.

Experts disagree as to where it came from, but most claim Andalusia as its seat of origin. Although its influences were both Jewish and Islamic, it was the gypsy artist who perfected both the song and the dance. Gypsies took to flamenco like "rice to paella," in the words of the historian Fernando Quiñones.

The deep song of flamenco represents a fatalistic attitude toward life. Marxists used to say it was a deeply felt protest of the lower classes against their oppressors, but this seems unfounded. Protest or not, over the centuries rich patrons, often brash young men, liked the sound of flamenco and booked artists to stage *juergas* or fiestas where dancer-prostitutes became the erotic extras. By the early 17th century, flamenco was linked with pimping, prostitution, and lots and lots of drinking, both by the audience and the artists.

By the mid–19th century, flamenco had gone legitimate and was heard in theaters and *café cantantes*. By the 1920s, even the pre-Franco Spanish dictator, Primo de Rivera, was singing the flamenco tunes of his native Cádiz. The poet Federico García Lorca and the composer Manuel de Falla preferred a purer form, attacking what they viewed as the degenerate and "ridiculous" burlesque of *flamenquismo*, the jazzed-up, audience-pleasing form of flamenco. The two artists launched a Flamenco Festival in Grenada in 1922. Of course, in the decades since, their voices have been drowned out, and flamenco is more *flamenquismo* than ever.

In his 1995 book *Flamenco Deep Song,* Thomas Mitchell draws a parallel to flamenco's "lowlife roots" and the "orgiastic origins" of jazz. He notes that early jazz, like flamenco, was "associated with despised ethnic groups, gangsters, brothels, free-spending bluebloods, and whoopee hedonism." By disguising their origins, Mitchell notes, both jazz and flamenco have entered the musical mainstream.

DANCE CLUBS

The Spanish dance club takes its inspiration from those of other Western capitals. In Madrid most clubs are open from around 6pm to 9pm, later reopening around 11pm. They generally start rocking at midnight or thereabouts.

Joy Eslava. Arenal, 1. ☎ **91-366-37-33.** Cover 2,000 ptas. (US$14), including first drink. Metro: Puerta del Sol.

Near the Puerta del Sol, this place has survived the passing fashions of Madrileño nightlife with more style than many of its (now-defunct) competitors. Virtually everyone in Madrid is likely to show up here, ranging from traveling sales reps in town from Düsseldorf to the youthful members of the Madrileño *movida*. Open nightly 10pm to 6:30am. Drinks are 1,500 ptas. (US$9) each.

Kapital. Atocha, 125. ☎ **91-420-29-06.** Cover 2,000 ptas. (US$12), including first drink. Metro: Antón Martín.

This is the most sprawling, labyrinthine, and multicultural disco in Madrid at the moment. Set within what was originally a theater, it has seven different levels, each sporting at least one bar and an ambience that's often radically different from the one you just left on a previous floor. Voyeurs of any age can take heart—there's a lot to see at the Kapital, with a mixed crowd that pursues whatever form of sexuality seems appropriate at the moment. Open Thursday to Sunday 11:30pm to 5:30am. Second drinks cost from 1,000 pesetas (US$6) each.

Kathmandu. Señores de Luzón, 3. No phone. Cover 1,200 ptas. (US$7.20), including first drink. Metro: Puerta del Sol.

This is Madrid's club of the moment, where cutting-edge music echoes through the night—reggae, jungle, hip-hop, jazzy funk. At this alternative disco, be prepared for a dizzy psychedelic experience. The club would feel right at home among the dives in New York's SoHo. Decidedly androgynous, it's an Oriental-inspired, ultramodern scoff at normalcy. The bar on the top floor is a curious retreat with Tibetan textiles draped from the ceiling. Nepalese art decorates part of the downstairs. At times the floor becomes so overcrowded you think the club will sink, but it carries on with wild abandon. Open Thursday 11am to 5am, Friday and Saturday 10am until 6am.

Long Play. Plaza Vasquez de Mella, 2. ☎ **93-532-90-69.** Cover 1,200 ptas. (US$7.20), including first drink. Metro: Gran Vía.

Catering to crowds of all ages, Long Play manages to combine disco music with long stretches of bars, comfortable tables and chairs, and a crowd with seemingly nothing to do but dance, dance, dance. Recorded music sometimes gives way to live bands. Open Friday to Saturday midnight to 6am.

Pachá. Calle Barcelo, 11. ☎ **91-446-01-37.** Cover 2,000 ptas. (US$12), including first drink. Metro: Tribunal.

The carefully contrived setting is pseudo-opulent, and the drinks sometimes hard to get because of the milling crowds. Despite that, Pachá thrives as one of the late-night staples in Madrid for the mid-20s to late-40s clientele (a crowd that often segregates itself by age into distinctly different areas of the place). More than other nightclubs in Madrid, this has been the subject of complaints from neighbors about late-night noise. Open Tuesday to Sunday 11pm to 5am.

JAZZ

✪ **Café Central.** Plaza del Angel, 10. ☎ **91-369-41-43.** Cover 1,300 ptas. (US$7.80); prices can vary depending on the show. Metro: Antón Martín.

Off the Plaza de Santa Ana, beside the famed Gran Hotel Victoria, the Café Central has a vaguely turn-of-the-century art deco interior, with an unusual series of stained-glass windows. Many of the customers read newspapers and talk at the marble-top tables during the day, but the ambience is far more animated during the nightly jazz sessions, which are ranked among the best in Spain and often draw top artists. Open Sunday to Thursday 1:30pm to 2:30am, Friday and Saturday 1:30pm to 3:30am; live jazz is offered daily 10pm to midnight. Beer costs 400 pesetas (US$2.40).

Café Populart. Calle Huertas, 22. ☎ **91-429-84-07.** Metro: Antón Martín or Sevilla. Bus: 6 or 60.

This club is known for its exciting jazz groups, which encourage the audience to dance. It specializes in Brazilian, Afro-bass, reggae, and new wave African music.

When the music starts, usually around 11pm, the prices of drinks are nearly doubled. Open daily 6pm to 2 or 3am. Beer costs 350 pesetas (US$2.10), whisky with soda 600 pesetas (US$3.60). After the music begins, beer costs 600 pesetas (US$3.60), whisky with soda 950 pesetas (US$5.70).

Clamores. Albuquerque, 14. ☎ **91-445-79-38.** Cover Tues–Sat usually 600–1,200 ptas. (US$3.60–US$7.20), but varies with act; Sun–Mon no cover. Metro: Bilbao.

With dozens of small tables and a huge bar in its dark and smoky interior, Clamores, which means noises in Spanish, is the largest and one of the most popular jazz clubs in Madrid. Established in the early 1980s, it has thrived because of the diverse roster of American and Spanish jazz bands that have appeared here. The place is open daily 6pm to around 3am, but jazz is presented only Tuesday to Saturday. Tuesday to Thursday, performances are at 11pm and again at 1am; Saturday, performances begin at 11:30pm, with an additional show at 1:30am. There are no live performances on Sunday or Monday nights, when the format is recorded disco music. Regardless of the night of the week you consume them, drinks begin at around 700 pesetas (US$4.20) each.

BARS & PUBS

Balmoral. Hermosilia, 10. ☎ **91-431-41-33.** Metro: Serrano.

Its exposed wood and comfortable chairs evoke a London club. The clientele tends toward journalists, politicians, army brass, owners of large estates, bankers, diplomats, and the occasional literary star. *Newsweek* magazine dubbed it one of the "best bars in the world." No food other than tapas is served. Open Monday to Saturday noon to midnight or 1am. Beer is 500 pesetas (US$3); drinks are from 900 pesetas (US$5.40).

Balneario. Juan Ramón Jiménez, 37. ☎ **91-350-87-76.** Metro: Cuzco.

Clients enjoy potent drinks in a setting with fresh flowers, white marble, and a stone bathtub that might have been used by Josephine Bonaparte. Near Chamartín Station on the northern edge of Madrid, Balneario is one of the most stylish and upscale bars in the city. It is adjacent to and managed by one of Madrid's most elegant and prestigious restaurants, El Cabo Mayor, and often attracts that dining room's clients for apéritifs or after-dinner drinks. Tapas include endive with smoked salmon, asparagus mousse, and anchovies with avocado. Open Monday to Saturday noon to 2:30am. Drinks are 650 to 1,000 pesetas (US$3.90 to US$6); tapas cost 650 to 1,800 pesetas (US$3.90 to US$10.80).

Bar Cock. De la Reina, 16. ☎ **91-532-28-26.** Metro: Gran Vía.

This bar on two floors attracts some of the most visible artists, actors, models, and filmmakers in Madrid. The name comes from the word *cocktail,* or so they say. The decor is elaborate and unique, in contrast to the hip clientele; the martinis are Madrid's best. Open daily 7pm to 3am; closed December 24 to 31. Drinks are 1,000 pesetas (US$6).

A Little Bit of Everything

The four-story **Bagëlus,** calle María de Molina, 25 (☎ **91-561-61-00;** metro: Avenida America), is a bit of an oddity in Madrid, providing entertainment and shopping 24 hours a day. A Spanish version of the American mall, here you'll find restaurants, cafes, bookstores, discos, and more. Sip on a drink, book your next vacation at the travel agency, enjoy live music from cabaret to flamenco, or just sit back and observe Madrid's version of yuppies hustling from shop to shop.

○ **Chicote.** Gran Vía, 12. ☎ **91-532-67-37.** Metro: Gran Vía.

This is Madrid's most famous cocktail bar. It's classic retro chic, with the same 1930s interior design it had when the foreign press came to sit out the Spanish Civil War, although the sound of artillery shells along the Gran Vía could be heard at the time. Long a favorite of artists and writers, the bar became a haven for prostitutes in the late Franco era. No more. It's back in the limelight again, a sophisticated and much-frequented rendezvous. Open daily 8am to 3am. Drink prices can be high—from 1,000 pesetas (US$6)—but the waiters serve them with such grace you don't mind.

Hispano Bar/Buffet. Paseo de la Castellana, 78. ☎ **91-411-48-76.** Metro: Nuevos Ministerios.

This establishment does a respectable lunch trade every day for members of the local business community, who crowd in to enjoy the amply portioned *platos del día*. These might include a platter of roast duck with figs or orange sauce, or a supreme of hake. After around 5pm, however, the ambience becomes that of a busy after-office bar, patronized by stylishly dressed women and many local entrepreneurs. The hubbub continues on into the night. Open daily from 1:30pm to 1:30am. Full meals at lunchtime cost from around 4,500 to 5,000 pesetas (US$27 to US$30), while beer costs from 300 pesetas (US$1.80).

La Venencia. Calle Echegaray, 7. ☎ **91-429-73-13.** Metro: Sevilla.

On one of the traditional tasca streets in Old Madrid, this tavern has a distinct personality. It is dedicated to the art of serving Spain's finest sherry—and that's it. Don't come in here asking for an extra-dry martini. Our favorite remains Manzanilla, a delicate fino with just a little chill on it. If Luis Buñuel were to need extras in a film, surely the patrons here would be ideal. To go with all that sherry, the waiters (a little rough around the edges) will serve tapas, especially those garlicky marinated olives, *majoama* (cured tuna), and blue-cheese canapés. Barrels form the decor, along with antique posters long turned tobacco-gold from the cigarette smoke. Open daily from 7pm to 1:30am.

Los Gabrieles. Echegaray, 17. ☎ **91-429-62-61.** Metro: Tirso de Molina.

Located in the heart of one of Madrid's most visible warrens of narrow streets, in a district that pulsates with after-dark nightlife options, this historic bar served throughout most of the 19th century as the sales outlet for a Spanish wine merchant. Its cellar was once a fabled gypsy bordello. In the 1980s its two rooms were transformed into a bar and cafe, where you can admire lavishly tiled walls with detailed scenes of courtiers, dancers, and Andalusian maidens peering from behind mantillas and fans. Open Monday to Friday from 2:30pm to 2am, Saturday and Sunday from noon to 3am. Beer costs 300 to 400 pesetas (US$1.80 to US$2.40).

○ **Palacio Gaviria.** Calle del Arenal, 9. ☎ **91-526-60-69.** Cover 2,000 ptas. (US$12), including first drink. Metro: Puerta del Sol or Ópera.

Its construction in 1847 was heralded as the architectural triumph of one of the era's most flamboyant aristocrats, the Marqués de Gaviria. Famous as one of the paramours of Queen Isabella II, he outfitted his palace with the ornate jumble of neoclassical and baroque styles that later became known as *Isabelino*. In 1993, after extensive renovations, the building was opened to the public as a concert hall for the occasional presentation of classical music and as a late-night cocktail bar. Ten high-ceilinged rooms now function as richly decorated, multipurpose areas for guests to wander in, drinks in hand, reacting to whatever, or whomever, happens to be there at the time. (One room is discreetly referred to as having been the bedroom-away-from-home of the queen herself.) No food is served, but the libations include a stylish list of cocktails and wines. The often-dull music doesn't match the elegance of the decor. Dance nights are usually Thursday through Saturday, everything from the tango to the waltz. Cabaret is usually featured on most other nights. Open Monday to Friday from 9pm to 3am, Saturday and Sunday from 9pm to 5am. Second drinks start at 1,200 pesetas (US$7.20).

Teatriz. Hermosilla, 15. ☎ **91.577.53.79.** Metro: Serrano.

Part of its function is as a restaurant where soft lighting and a decor by world-class decorator Philippe Starck create one of the most stylish environments in Madrid. A meal averages around 3,000 pesetas (US$18) at lunch and 4,000 pesetas (US$24) in the evening, but if it's just a drink you're looking for, consider an extended session at any of the site's three bars. Here, within a setting not quite like a disco, but with a sound system almost as good, you'll find a music bar environment where stylish folk of all persuasions enjoy drinks and the gossip that often seems to originate at places like this. The restaurant is open daily from 1:30 to 4pm and 9am to 1pm. The bars are best appreciated every night from 9pm to 3am.

✪ **Viva Madrid.** Manuel Fernández y González, 7. ☎ **91-429-36-40.** Metro: Antón Martín.

A congenial and sudsy mix of students, artists, and foreign tourists cram into the turn-of-the-century interior here, where antique tile murals and blatant belle époque nostalgia contribute to an undeniable charm. In the good old days (the 1950s, that is) the fabled beautiful people showed up here, notably Ava Gardner with the bullfighter Manolete when they couldn't take their hands off each other. But Orson Welles or even Louis Armstrong used to pop in as well. Crowded and noisy, it's a place where lots of beer is swilled and spilled. It's set within a neighborhood of antique houses and narrow streets near the Plaza de Santa Ana. Open Friday from noon to 1am, Saturday from noon to 2am. Beer costs 500 pesetas (US$3); whisky begins at 900 pesetas (US$5.40).

CAVE CRAWLING

To capture a peculiar Madrid joie de vivre of the 18th century, visit some mesones and cuevas, many found in the barrios bajos. From Plaza Mayor, walk down the Arco de Cuchilleros until you find a gypsy-like cave that fits your fancy. Young people love to meet in the taverns and caves of Old Madrid for communal drinking and songfests. The sangría flows freely, the atmosphere is charged, and the room is usually packed; the sounds of guitars waft into the night air. Sometimes you'll see a strolling band of singing students going from bar to bar, colorfully attired, with ribbons fluttering from their outfits.

Mesón de la Guitarra. Cava de San Miguel, 13. ☎ **91-559-95-31.** Metro: Puerta del Sol or Ópera.

Our favorite cueva in the area, Mesón de la Guitarra is loud and exciting on any night of the week, and it's as warmly earthy as anything you'll find in Madrid. The decor combines terra-cotta floors, antique brick walls, hundreds of sangría pitchers clustered above the bar, murals of gluttons, old rifles, and faded bullfighting posters. Like most things in Madrid, the place doesn't get rolling until around 10:30pm, although you can stop in for a drink and tapas earlier. Don't be afraid to start singing an American song if it has a fast rhythm—60 people will join in, even if they don't know the words. Open daily from 7pm to 1:30am. Beer is 250 pesetas (US$1.50); wine is from 125 pesetas (US75¢); tapas are 800 to 1,000 pesetas (US$4.80 to US$6).

Mesón del Champiñón. Cava de San Miguel, 17. No phone. Metro: Puerta del Sol or Ópera.

In English the name of this place means "mushroom," and that is exactly what you'll see depicted in various sizes along sections of the vaulted ceilings. The bartenders keep a brimming bucket of sangría behind the long stand-up bar as a thirst quencher for the crowd. A more appetizing way to experience a *champiñón* is to order a *ración* of grilled, stuffed, and salted mushrooms, served with toothpicks. Two tiny, slightly dark rooms in the back are where Spanish families go to hear organ music performed. Unless you want to be exiled to the very back, don't expect to get a seat. Practically everybody prefers to stand. Open daily 6pm to 2am.

Sesamo. Príncipe, 7. ☎ **91-429-65-24.** Metro: Sevilla or Puerta del Sol.

In a class by itself, this cueva, dating from the early 1950s, draws a clientele of young painters and writers with its bohemian ambience. Hemingway was one of those early visitors (a plaque commemorates him). At first you'll think you're walking into a tiny snack bar—and you are. But proceed down the flight of steps to the cellar. Here, the walls are covered with contemporary paintings and quotations. At squatty stools and tables, an international assortment of young people listens to piano music and sometimes piano or guitar playing. Open daily 6:30pm to 2am. A pitcher of sangría (for four) is 1,200 pesetas (US$7.20); beer costs 300 pesetas (US$1.80).

GAY & LESBIAN BARS

Black and White. Gravina (at the corner of Libertad). ☎ **91-531-11-41.** Metro: Chueca.

This is the major gay bar of Madrid, in the center of the Chueca district. A guard will open the door to a large room—painted, as you might expect, black and white. There's a disco in the basement, but the street-level bar is the premier gathering spot, featuring drag shows beginning at 3am Thursday to Sunday, male striptease, and videos. Old movies are shown against one wall. Open Monday to Friday 8pm to 5am, Saturday and Sunday 8pm to 6am. Beer is 500 pesetas (US$3); whisky costs 850 pesetas (US$5.10).

Cruising. Perez Galdos, 5. ☎ **91-521-51-43.** Metro: Chueca.

One of the predominant gay bars of Madrid, a center for gay consciousness-raising and gay cruising (though they say the name refers to automobile driving), this place has probably been visited at least once by every gay male in Castile. There are practically no women inside, but always a hustler looking for a tourist john. It doesn't get crowded or lively until late at night. Open Monday to Friday 8pm to 3:30am, Saturday and Sunday 8pm to 4:30am. Beer costs from 400 to 500 pesetas (US$2.40 to US$3).

Isis. Plaza de Chueca. No phone. Metro: Chueca.

This is one of the few exclusively women's bars in Madrid. Men, often of the flamboyant variety, occasionally show up, but it's mainly a place where ladies meet. The decor is a bit campy with flaming torches but the spotlight is on the patrons. Shunned during the Franco era, lesbians are asserting a more aggressive presence on the Madrid *la noche* scene. Patrons range from young lipstick beauties to older women who'd like to break in the new arrivals.

Refugio. Calle Doctor Cortezo, 1. ☎ **91-369-40-38.** Cover 1,000 ptas. (US$6). Metro: Tirso de Molina.

This is one of the best-established gay discos in Madrid, with a strong emphasis on dancing, drinking, and dialogue, or simply standing and cruising whenever it feels appropriate. The interior is like a grotto with nude gladiator statues, equaled only by the caged dancing boys stirring up libidos. Larger than many of its gay competitors within Madrid, it sometimes hosts theme nights (golden oldies night, merengue night), that regrettably, don't really get going until very, very late. Open nightly midnight to 5am.

Rick's. Calle Clavel, 8. No phone. Metro: Chueca.

Rick's takes its name from "Everybody Comes to Rick's," the original title of the Bogie classic *Casablanca*. Many gay bars in the Chueca barrio are sleazy, but this is a classy joint—just like the fictional Rick's in Morocco. It's decorated with Bogie paraphernalia, including marble floors and gilt columns. The only thing missing is a piano player singing "As Time Goes By"—and Bergman, of course. Gay men patronize the place, with the occasional woman showing up, too. Incongruously it has a foosball table in the bar but lavender walls. Open daily 11:30pm "until some time in the early morning."

A CASINO

Casino Gran Madrid is at kilometer 29 along the carretera La Coruña (the A6 highway running between Madrid and La Coruña), Apartado, 62 (☎ **91-856-11-00**). The largest place for gambling in Madrid, it appeals to nongamblers with a well-choreographed roster of dining and entertainment facilities, including two restaurants, four bars, and a nightclub. And if you happen to enjoy gambling, there are facilities for French and American roulette, blackjack, punto y banco, baccarat, and chemin de fer. Presentation of a passport at the door is essential—without it, you won't be admitted. Entrance costs 500 pesetas (US$3), although that fee is often waived for residents of some of Madrid's larger hotels who arrive with a ticket that's sometimes provided gratis by the hotel's management. The casino and all of its facilities are open daily 4pm to 5am.

An à la carte restaurant in the French Gaming Room offers international cuisine, with dinners costing from 7,000 pesetas (US$42). A buffet in the American Gaming Room will cost around 3,000 pesetas (US$18). The restaurants are open 9:15pm to 2am.

The casino is about 18 miles (29km) northwest of Madrid. If you don't feel like driving, the casino has buses that depart from Plaza de España, 6, every afternoon and evening at 4:30, 6, 7:30, and 9pm. Note that between October and June, men must wear jackets and ties; T-shirts and tennis shoes are forbidden in any season.

7

Side Trips from Madrid

Madrid makes an ideal base for excursions because it's surrounded by some of Spain's major attractions. The day trips listed below to both New Castile and Old Castile range from 9 to 54 miles (14 to 91km) outside Madrid, allowing you to leave in the morning and be back by nightfall. In case you choose to stay overnight, however, we've included a selection of hotels in each town.

The satellite cities and towns around Madrid include Toledo, with its El Greco masterpieces; the wondrous El Escorial monastery; Segovia's castles that float in the clouds; and the Bourbon palaces at La Granja.

1 Toledo

42 miles (68km) SW of Madrid, 85 miles (137km) SE of Ávila

If you have only one day for an excursion outside Madrid, go to Toledo—a place made special by its Arab, Jewish, Christian, and even Roman and Visigothic elements. A national landmark, the city that so inspired El Greco in the 16th century has remained relatively unchanged. You can still stroll through streets barely wide enough for a man and his donkey—much less for an automobile.

Surrounded on three sides by a bend in the Tagus River, Toledo stands atop a hill overlooking the arid plains of New Castile—a natural fortress in the center of the Iberian Peninsula. It was a logical choice for the capital of Spain, though it lost its political status to Madrid in the 1500s. Toledo has remained the country's religious center, as the seat of the Primate of Spain.

If you're driving, the much-painted skyline of Toledo will come into view about 3½ miles (6km) from the city. When you cross the Tagus River on the 14th-century Puente San Martín, the scene is reminiscent of El Greco's moody, storm-threatened *View of Toledo,* which hangs in New York's Metropolitan Museum of Art. The artist reputedly painted that view from a hillside that is now the site of Parador Nacional de Conde Orgaz. If you arrive at the right time, you can enjoy an apéritif on the parador's terrace and watch one of the famous violet sunsets of Toledo (see "Where to Stay," below).

Another Toledan highlight is the **Carretera de Circunvalación,** the route that threads through the city and runs along the Tagus. Clinging to the hillsides are rustic dwellings, the cigarrales of the Imperial City, immortalized by 17th-century dramatist Tirso de Molina, who named his trilogy *Los Cigarrales de Toledo.*

Madrid Environs

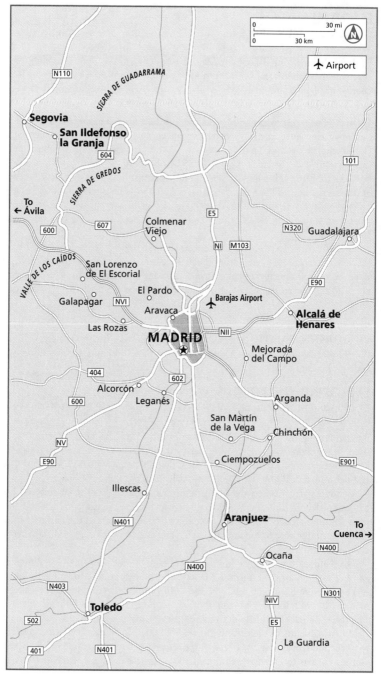

ESSENTIALS

GETTING THERE   By Train   RENFE trains run here frequently every day. Those departing Madrid's Atocha Railway Station for Toledo run daily 7am to 9:50pm; those leaving Toledo for Madrid run daily 7am to 9pm. Traveling time is approximately 2 hours. RENFE also runs two express trains a day to and from Toledo, taking only 1 hour and making a stop at Aranjuez. For train information in Madrid call ☎ **91-328-90-20;** in Toledo call ☎ **925-22-30-99.**

By Bus   Bus transit between Madrid and Toledo is faster and more convenient than travel by train. Buses are maintained by several companies, the largest of which include Continental or Galiano. They depart from Madrid's Estación Sur de Autobuses (South Bus Station), calle Méndez Alvaro (☎ **91-468-42-00** for information), every day between 6:30am and 10pm at 30-minute intervals. The fastest leave Monday to Friday on the hour. Those that depart weekdays on the half hour, and those that run on weekends, take a bit longer. Travel time, depending on whether the bus stops at villages en route, is between 1 hour and 1 hour 20 minutes. One-way transit costs 590 pesetas (US$3.55).

Once you reach Toledo, you'll be deposited at the Estación de Autobuses, which lies beside the river, about ¾ mile from the historic center. Although many visitors opt to walk, be advised that the ascent is steep. Bus numbers 5 and 6 run from the station uphill to the center, charging 115 pesetas (US70¢) for the brief ride. Pay the driver directly.

By Car   Exit Madrid via Cibeles (Paseo del Prado) and take the N-401 south.

VISITOR INFORMATION   The **tourist information office** is at Puerta de Bisagra (☎ **925-22-08-43**). It's open Monday to Friday 9am to 6pm, Saturday 9am to 7pm, and Sunday 9am to 3pm.

EXPLORING THE TOWN

✪ **Cathedral.** Arco de Palacio. ☎ **925-22-22-41.** Cathedral, free; Treasure Room, 500 ptas. (US$3). Daily 10:30am–1:30pm and 3:30–6pm. Bus: 5 or 6.

Ranked among the greatest Gothic structures, the cathedral actually reflects several styles, since more than 2½ centuries elapsed during its construction (1226–1493). Many historic events transpired here, including the proclamation of Joanna the Mad and her husband, Philip the Handsome, as heirs to the throne of Spain.

Among its art treasures, the transparente stands out—a wall of marble and florid baroque alabaster sculpture overlooked for years because the cathedral was too poorly lit. Sculptor Narciso Tomé cut a hole in the ceiling, much to the consternation of Toledans, and now light touches the high-rising angels, a *Last Supper* in alabaster, and a Virgin in ascension.

The 16th-century Capilla Mozárabe, containing works by Juan de Borgona, is another curiosity of the cathedral. Mass is still held here using Mozarabic liturgy.

The Treasure Room has a 500-pound 15th-century gilded monstrance—allegedly made with gold brought back from the New World by Columbus—that is still carried through the streets of Toledo during the feast of Corpus Christi.

Other highlights of the cathedral include El Greco's *Twelve Apostles and Spoliation of Christ* and Goya's *Arrest of Christ on the Mount of Olives*. The cathedral shop, where you buy tickets to enter, is well organized and stocks a variety of quality souvenirs, including ceramics and damascene.

Alcázar. Calle General Moscardó, 4, near the Plaza de Zocodover. ☎ **925-22-30-38.** Admission 200 ptas. (US$1.20) adults, free for children under 10. Tues–Sun 10am–2pm and 4–6pm (6:30pm July–Sept). Bus: 5 or 6.

The Alcázar, located at the eastern edge of the old city, dominates the Toledo skyline. It became world famous at the beginning of the Spanish Civil War, when it underwent a 70-day siege that almost destroyed it. Today it has been rebuilt and turned into an army museum, housing such exhibits as a plastic model of what the fortress looked like after the Civil War, electronic equipment used during the siege, and photographs taken during the height of the battle. A walking tour gives a realistic simulation of the siege. Allow an hour for a visit.

✪ **Museo de Santa Cruz.** Calle Miguel de Cervantes, 3. ☎ **925-22-14-02.** Free admission. Mon–Sat 10am–6pm, Sun 10am–2pm. Bus: 5 or 6. Pass beneath the granite archway on the eastern edge of the Plaza de Zocodover and walk about 1 block.

Today a museum of art and sculpture, this was originally a 16th-century Spanish Renaissance hospice, founded by Cardinal Mendoza—"the third king of Spain"—who helped Ferdinand and Isabella gain the throne. The facade is almost more spectacular than any of the exhibits inside. It's a stunning architectural achievement in the classical plateresque style. The major artistic treasure inside is El Greco's *The Assumption of the Virgin,* his last known work. Paintings by Goya and Ribera are also on display along with gold items, opulent antique furnishings, Flemish tapestries, and even Visigoth artifacts. In the patio of the museum you'll stumble across various fragments of carved stone and sarcophagi lids. One of the major exhibits is of a large Astrolablio tapestry of the zodiac from the 1400s. In the basement you can see artifacts, including elephant tusks, from various archaeological digs throughout the province.

Casa y Museo de El Greco. Calle Samuel Leví, 3. ☎ **925-22-40-46.** Admission 200 ptas. (US$1.20) adults, free for children under 10. Tues–Sat 10am–2pm and 4–6pm, Sun 10am–2pm. Bus: 5 or 6.

Located in Toledo's *antiguo barrio judio* (the old Jewish quarter, a labyrinth of narrow streets on the old town's southwestern edge), the House of El Greco honors the great master painter, although he didn't actually live here. In 1585 the artist moved into one of the run-down palace apartments belonging to the Marquís of Villena. Although he was to live at other Toledan addresses, he returned to the Villena palace in 1604 and remained there until his death. Only a small part of the original residence was saved from decay. In time, this and a neighboring house became the El Greco museum; today it's furnished with authentic period pieces.

You can visit El Greco's so-called studio, where one of his paintings hangs. The museum contains several more works, including a copy of *A View of Toledo* and three portraits, plus many pictures by various 16th- and 17th-century Spanish artists. The garden and especially the kitchen also merit attention, as does a sitting room decorated in the Moorish style.

Monasterio de San Juan de los Reyes. Calle Reyes Católicos, 17. ☎ **925-22-38-02.** Admission 150 ptas. (US90¢) adults, free for children 8 and under. Winter, daily 10am–1:45pm and 3:30–6pm; summer, daily 10am–1:45pm and 3:30–7pm. Bus: 2.

Founded by King Ferdinand and Queen Isabella to commemorate their triumph over the Portuguese at Toro in 1476, the church was started in 1477 according to the plans of architect Juan Guas. It was finished, together with the splendid cloisters, in 1504, dedicated to St. John the Evangelist, and used from the beginning by the Franciscan friars. An example of Gothic-Spanish-Flemish style, San Juan de los Reyes was restored after the damage caused during Napoléon's invasion and after its abandonment in 1835; since 1954 it has been entrusted again to the Franciscans. The church is located at the extreme western edge of the old town, midway between the Puente (bridge) of San Martín and the Puerta (gate) of Cambron.

Toledo

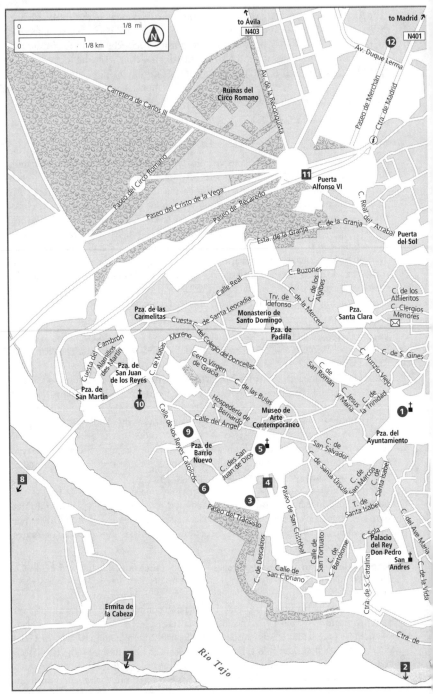

Ruinas del
Circo Romano

to Ávila
N403

to Madrid
N401

Av. Duque Lerma

Paseo de Merchán

Ctra. de Madrid

Carretera de Carlos III

Paseo del Circo Romano

Av. de la Reconquista

11 Puerta
Alfonso VI

C. Real del Arrabal

Puerta
del Sol

Paseo del Cristo de la Vega

Paseo de Recaredo

Esta. de la Granja

C. de la Granja

C. Buzones

Calle Real

C. de Santa Leocadia

Trv. de
Ildefonso

C. de la Merced

C. de los Algibes

Pza. de las
Carmelitas

Cuesta C. del Colegio del Doncellas

Monasterio de
Santo Domingo

Pza. de
Padilla

Pza.
Santa Clara

C. de los
Afileritos

C. Clergios
Menores

C. de S. Gines

Cuesta del Cambrón

Alamillos
des Martín

Pza. de
San Juan
de los Reyes

C. de Matías Moreno

Cerro Virgen
de Gracia

C. de las Bulas

C. de
San Román

C. Nunzio Viejo

C. de
Jesús
y María

C. de
la Trinidad

1

Pza. de
San Martín

10

Calle de los Reyes Católicos

Hospedería de
S. Bernardo

Calle del Ángel

Museo de
Arte
Contemporáneo

9

Pza. de
Barrio
Nuevo

C. des San
Juan de Dios

5

6

3

4

Paseo de San Cristóbal

C. de San Salvador

C. de Santa Úrsula

C. de
San Marcos

Pza. del
Ayuntamiento

T. de
Santa Isabel

C. de
Santa Isabel

C. de S. Sola

Palacio
del Rey
Don Pedro

San
Andres

C. del Ave María

C. de la Vida

8

Paseo del Tránsito

C. de Descalzos

Calle de
San Cipriano

Calle de
San Tortuato

C. de
S. Bartolomé

Ctra. de S. Catalina

Ermita de
la Cabeza

Río Tajo

7

2

Ctra. de

0   1/8 mi
0   1/8 km

12

N

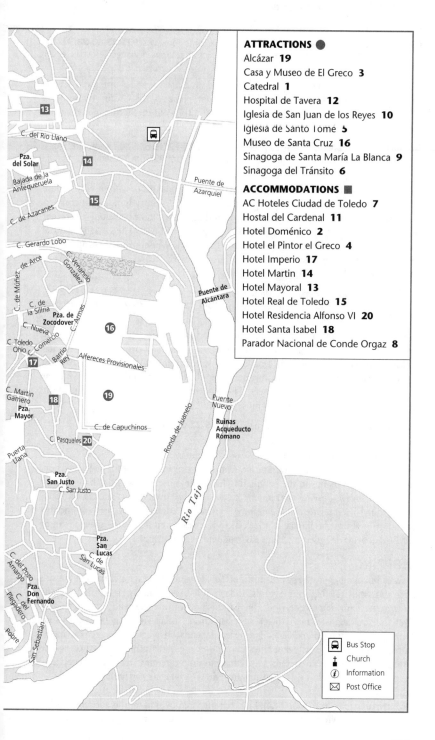

ATTRACTIONS ●
Alcázar **19**
Casa y Museo de El Greco **3**
Catedral **1**
Hospital de Tavera **12**
Iglesia de San Juan de los Reyes **10**
Iglesia de Santo Tomé **5**
Museo de Santa Cruz **16**
Sinagoga de Santa María La Blanca **9**
Sinagoga del Tránsito **6**

ACCOMMODATIONS ■
AC Hoteles Ciudad de Toledo **7**
Hostal del Cardenal **11**
Hotel Doménico **2**
Hotel el Pintor el Greco **4**
Hotel Imperio **17**
Hotel Martin **14**
Hotel Mayoral **13**
Hotel Real de Toledo **15**
Hotel Residencia Alfonso VI **20**
Hotel Santa Isabel **18**
Parador Nacional de Conde Orgaz **8**

Bus Stop
† Church
ⓘ Information
⊠ Post Office

☉ **Iglesia de Santo Tomé.** Plaza del Conde, 4, Vía Santo Tomé. ☎ **925-25-60-98.** Admission 200 ptas. (US$1.20). Daily 10am–6:45pm (closes at 5:45pm in winter). Closed Dec 25 and Jan 1.

This modest little 14th-century chapel, situated on a narrow street in the old Jewish quarter, might have been overlooked had it not possessed El Greco's masterpiece *The Burial of the Count of Orgaz*, created in 1586. To avoid the hordes, go when the chapel first opens.

Sínagoga del Tránsito. Calle Samuel Leví. ☎ **925-22-36-65.** Admission 400 ptas. (US$2.40). Tues–Sat 10am–1:45pm and 4–5:45pm, Sun 10am–1:45pm. Closed Jan 1, May 1, Dec 24–25, and Dec 31. Bus: 2.

One block west of the El Greco home and museum stands this once-important house of worship for Toledo's large Jewish population. A 14th-century building, it is noted for its superb stucco Hebrew inscriptions, including psalms inscribed along the top of the walls and a poetic description of the Temple on the east wall. The synagogue is the most important part of the **Museo Sefardí** (Sephardic Museum), which opened in 1971 and contains art objects as well as tombstones with Hebrew epigraphy, some of which are dated before 1492.

Sínagoga de Santa María La Blanca. Calle Reyes Católicos, 2. ☎ **925-22-72-57.** Admission 150 ptas. (US90¢). Apr–Sept, daily 10am–2pm and 3:30–7pm; Oct–Mar, daily 10am–2pm and 3:30–6pm. Bus: 2.

In the late 12th century, the Jews of Toledo erected an important synagogue in the *almohada* style, which employs graceful horseshoe arches and ornamental horizontal moldings. Although by the early 15th century it had been converted into a Christian church, much of the original remains, including the five naves and elaborate Mudéjar decorations, mosquelike in their effect. The synagogue lies on the western edge of the city, midway between the El Greco museum and San Juan de los Reyes.

Hospital de Tavera. Hospital de Tavera, 2. ☎ **925-22-04-51.** Admission 500 ptas. (US$3). Daily 10:30am–1:30pm and 3:30–6pm.

This 16th-century Greco-Roman palace north of the medieval ramparts of Toledo was originally built by Cardinal Tavera; it now houses a private art collection. Titian's portrait of Charles V hangs in the banqueting hall. The museum owns five paintings by El Greco: *The Holy Family, The Baptism of Christ,* and portraits of St. Francis, St. Peter, and Cardinal Tavera. Ribera's *The Bearded Woman* also attracts many viewers. The collection of books in the library is priceless. In the nearby church is the mausoleum of Cardinal Tavera, designed by Alonso Berruguete.

SHOPPING

In swashbuckling days, the swordsmiths of Toledo were world renowned. They're still here and still turning out swords today. Toledo is equally renowned for its *damasquinado,* or damascene work, the Moorish art of inlaying gold, even copper or silver threads, against a matte black steel backdrop. Today Toledo is filled with souvenir shops hawking damascene. The price depends on whether the item is handcrafted or machine made. Sometimes machine-made damascene is passed off as the more expensive handcrafted item, so you have to shop carefully. Bargaining is perfectly acceptable in Toledo, but if you get the price down, you can't pay with a credit card—only cash.

Marzipan (called *mazapán* locally) is often prepared by nuns and is a local specialty. Many shops in town specialize in this treat made of sweet almond paste.

The province of Toledo is also renowned for its pottery, which is sold in so many shops at competitive prices that it's almost unnecessary to recommend specific branches hawking these wares. However, over the years we've found that the prices at the large roadside emporiums on the outskirts of town on the main road to Madrid often have better bargains than the shops within the city walls, where rents are higher.

Better yet, for the best deals, and if you're interested in buying a number of items, consider a trip to Talavera la Reina, 47 miles (76km) west of Toledo, where most of the pottery is made. Since Talavera is the largest city in the province, it is hardly a picture-postcard little potter's village. Most of the shops lie along the main street of town, where you'll find store after store selling this distinctive pottery in multi-colored designs.

Pottery hunters also flock to Puente del Arzobispo, another ceramic center, known for its green-hued pottery. From Talavera drive west on the N-V to Oropesa, then south for 9 miles (14km) to a fortified bridge across the Tagus. In general, ceramics here are cheaper than those sold in Toledo.

Just past Oropesa at the turnoff to Lagartera is the village where the highly sought-after embroidery of La Mancha originates. Virtually every cottage displays samples of this free-form floral stitching, shaped into everything from skirts to tablecloths. Of course, shops in Toledo are also filled with samples of this unique embroidery.

Casa Bermejo. Calle Airosas, 5. ☎ **925-28-53-67.**

Established in 1910, this factory and store employs almost 50 artisans, whom you can observe at work as part of a visit to its premises. The outlet carries a wide array of damascene objects fashioned into Toledo's traditional Mudéjar designs. These include swords, platters, pitchers, and other gift items. Don't think, however, that everything this place manufactures follows the inspiration of the medieval Arabs. The outfit engraves many of the ornamental swords that are awarded to graduates of West Point in the United States, as well as the decorative, full-dress military accessories used by the armies of various countries of Europe, including France. Open Monday to Friday 9am to 1pm and 3 to 6pm, Saturday 8am to 1pm. Closing times are later in July and August, determined solely by business traffic.

Casa Telesforo. Plaza de Zocodover, 13. ☎ **925-22-33-79.**

Many long-time residents of Toledo remember this place as the supplier of the marzipan consumed at their childhood birthday parties and celebrations. A specialist in the almond-and-sugar confection whose origins go back to the year 1806, it sells the best marzipan in town, cunningly made into such whimsical shapes as hearts, diamonds, flowers, and fish. Open daily 9am to 9pm, later in summer, depending on the crowds.

Felipe Suarez. Paseo de los Canónigos, 19. ☎ **925-22-56-15.**

Established in the 1920s, this outfit has manufactured damascene work in various forms ranging from unpretentious souvenir items to art objects of rare museum-quality beauty that sell for as much as 2 million pesetas (US$14,000). You'll find swords, straight-edged razors, pendants, fans, and an array of pearls. The shop maintains extended hours throughout the year, daily 9:30am to 7pm.

Santiago Sanchez Martín. Calle Rio Llano, 15. ☎ **925-22-77-57.**

This is one of the most painstaking and prestigious manufacturers of damascene work in Toledo. It specializes in the elaborately detailed arabesques whose techniques are as old as the Arab conquest of Iberia. Look for everything from decorative tableware (platters, pitchers), to mirror frames, jewelry, letter openers, and ornamental swords. Open Monday to Friday 9am to 2pm and 5 to 7pm.

WHERE TO STAY
EXPENSIVE

☼ **AC Hoteles Ciudad de Toledo.** Crta. De Circumvalación, 15, 41005 Toledo. ☎ **925/ 28-51-25.** Fax 925/28-47-00. www.ac-hoteles.com. E-mail: ciud.resep@ac-hoteles.com. 49 units. A/C MINIBAR TV TEL. 20,000 ptas. (US$120) double; 25,000 ptas. (US$150) suite. AE, MC, V. Free parking. Bus: 5.

Opened in 1998, this is the first hotel in years that has emerged as a superior choice to the government-run parador. If El Greco were painting his *A View of Toledo* today, he would surely have come to this site instead of the parador location. On a beltway south of the city—follow the directions to the Parador Nacional de Conde Orgaz— this deluxe property is a member of a chain which also includes the swanky **Santo Mauro** in Madrid. The epitome of luxury living and contemporary lines, this hotel across the river from Toledo is entered at the third floor. You move down through the spiraling architectural design to reach the rest of the hotel. Bedrooms are spacious and luxuriously furnished, all in contemporary styling, each with tiled bathrooms. The suites have oversize bathtubs and hydromassage.

Dining/Diversions: The food is excellent, with both regional and international specialties featured. In addition to the main restaurant, a 24-hour cafeteria is also open.

Amenities: Laundry, dry cleaning, concierge, room service, baby-sitting.

☼ **Parador Nacional de Conde Orgaz.** Cerro del Emperador, 45002 Toledo. ☎ **925- 22-18-50.** Fax 925-22-51-66. www.parador.es. 76 units. A/C MINIBAR TV TEL. 21,000 ptas. (US$126) double; 26,000 ptas. (US$156) suite. AE, DC, MC, V. Free parking. Drive across Puente San Martín and head south for 2½ miles (4km).

You'll have to make reservations well in advance to stay at this parador, which is built on the ridge of a rugged hill where El Greco is said to have painted his *View of Toledo*. That view is still here, and it is without a doubt one of the grandest in the world. The main living room/lounge has fine furniture—old chests, brown leather chairs, and heavy tables—and leads to a sunny terrace overlooking the city. On chilly nights you can sit by the public fireplace. The guest rooms are the most luxurious in all of Toledo, far superior to those at Maria Cristina (see below). Spacious and beautifully furnished, they contain private bathrooms and reproductions of regional antique pieces.

Dining/Diversions: The cuisine is enhanced by one of the most panoramic views from any restaurant in Europe. A bar with a full view of Toledo is across the lobby from the restaurant. It's worth it to taxi out here just to have a drink on the terrace and absorb the panorama.

Amenities: Room service, laundry/valet, outdoor swimming pool.

MODERATE

☼ **Hostal del Cardenal.** Paseo de Recaredo, 24, 45003 Toledo. ☎ **925-22-49-00.** Fax 925-22-29-91. www.cardenal.macom.es. E-mail: cardenal@macom.es. 27 units. A/C TV TEL. 12,600 ptas. (US$75.60) double; 17,150 ptas. (US$102.90) suite. AE, DC, MC, V. Bus: 2 from rail station.

Although long acclaimed as the best restaurant in Toledo (see below), the fact that this establishment has rooms available is still a well-kept secret. They're not as grand as those at the Parador, but they are choice nevertheless, sought by those wanting to capture an old Toledan atmosphere. The entrance to this unusual hotel is set into the stone fortifications of the ancient city walls, a few steps from the Bisagra Gate. To enter the hotel, you must climb a series of terraces to the top of the crenellated walls of the ancient fortress. Here, grandly symmetrical and very imposing, is the hostal, the former residence of the 18th-century cardinal of Toledo, Señor Lorenzana. Just beyond the entrance, still atop the city wall, you'll find flagstone walkways, Moorish fountains, rose gardens, and cascading vines. The establishment has tiled walls; long, narrow salons; dignified Spanish furniture; and a smattering of antiques. Each room has a private bathroom. The only parking is what's available free on the street. A member of the hotel staff will call you a taxi if you don't want to walk the steep ascent (on narrow to nonexistent sidewalks) into the historic district.

Hotel Doménico. Cerro del Emperador, 45002 Toledo. ☎ **925-28-01-01.** Fax 925-28-02-03. 50 units. A/C MINIBAR TV TEL. 16,380–18,075 ptas. (US$98.30–US$108.45) double; 26,075 ptas. (US$156.45) suite. AE, MC, V. Free parking. Bus: 7.

A four-star hotel, one of the finest in Toledo, Doménico is located among Los Cigarrales, the typical country houses lying south of the city and offering panoramic views. The building, though modern, is constructed in a classic and traditional style. Launched in 1993, the hotel is only a 5-minute drive to the historic core of Toledo. Bedrooms are medium in size and comfortably furnished. Some of the rooms have windows in the roof for greater light. The beds have excellent mattresses, and amenities include private safes and hair dryers. The second- and third-floor rooms have terraces opening onto the swimming pool or views of the city. A terrace restaurant offers a fine national and international cuisine, and there is also a cafeteria bar. Room service is available until 10:30pm, and other services include a concierge and laundry.

۞ Hotel El Pintor El Greco. Alamillos del Tránsito, 13, 45002 Toledo. ☎ **925-28-51-91.** Fax 925-21-58-19. www.hotelpintorgreco.com. E-mail: info@hotelpintorgreco.com. 33 units. A/C TV TEL. 14,700–18,000 ptas. (US$88.20–US$108) double. AE, DC, MC, V. Parking 800 ptas. (US$4.80).

In the old Jewish quarter, one of the most traditional and historic districts of Toledo, this hotel was converted from a typical *casa Toledana,* which had once been used as a bakery. With careful restoration, especially of its ancient facade, it was transformed into one of Toledo's best and most atmospheric small hotels—the only one to match the antique charm of Hostal del Cardenal (see above), although, it too, seems relatively unknown. Decoration in both the public rooms and bedrooms is in a traditional Castilian style. Phones, piped-in music, air-conditioning, satellite TV, and individual security boxes have been added to the immaculately kept bedrooms. Bedrooms come in a variety of shapes and sizes, as befits a building of this age, but all are equipped with firm mattresses and small bathrooms with stall showers and adequate shelf space. At the doorstep of the hotel are such landmarks as the Monasterio de San Juan de los Reyes, Sínagoga de Santa María la Blanca, Sínagoga del Tránsito, Casa y Museo de El Greco, and Iglesia de Santo Tomé. Public parking is available for 800 pesetas (US$4.80) per day.

Hotel María Cristina. Marqués de Mendigorría, 1, 45003 Toledo. ☎ **925-21-32-02.** Fax 925-21-26-50. www.hotelesmayoral.com. E-mail: @hotelesmayoral.com. 63 units. A/C MINIBAR TV TEL. 13,900 ptas. (US$83.40) double; 22,925 ptas. (US$137.55) suite. AE, DC, MC, V. Parking 1,000 ptas. (US$6).

Adjacent to the historic Hospital de Tavera and near the northern perimeter of the old town, this stone-sided, awning-fronted hotel resembles a palatial country home. If you're willing to forgo the view from the Parador and the charm of Hostal del Cardenal, this hotel is generally cited as *numero segundo* in Toledo. Originally built as a convent in 1560 and later used as a hospital, it was transformed into this comfortable hostelry in the late 1980s. Sprawling, historic, and generously proportioned, it contains clean, amply sized, attractively furnished guest rooms, each with a private bathroom. Amenities include 24-hour room service, laundry, concierge, and babysitting. On site is the very large and well-recommended restaurant, El Abside, where fixed-price lunches and dinners are served, ranging in price from 1,825 to 2,500 pesetas (US$10.95 to US$15). There's also a bar. The food is much better, however, at Hostal del Cardenal.

INEXPENSIVE

Hotel Imperio. Cadena, 5, 45001 Toledo. ☎ **925-22-76-50.** Fax 925-25-3183. www. teleline.es/personal/himperio/. E-mail: himperio@teleline.es. 21 units. A/C TV TEL. 6,200 ptas. (US$37.20) double. AE, DC, MC, V.

Long a budget favorite, this modest hotel is a few yards from the Alcazar and Cathedral. Built in the '80s, the hotel was recently renovated (and just in time), adding more comfort to the small rooms. The furnishings are in a rather severe style, but the beds are comfortable and the mattresses renewed. However, for the price this is one of the city's best choices. Rooms on the second floor have balconies overlooking the street. A snack bar is on site, but some fine restaurants lie just outside the door. The only parking available is on the street, and room service is offered until 10pm. Other amenities include laundry and a concierge.

Hotel Martin. Calle Covachuela, 12, 45003 Toledo. ☎ and fax **925-22-17-33.** E-mail: hotelmartin@pyme.com. 17 units. A/C MINIBAR TV TEL. 6,750 ptas. (US$40.50) double. MC, V. Parking 1,000 ptas. (US$6).

A good, serviceable choice, the two-story Martin opened in 1992 in the vicinity of the Bisagra Gate, the main medieval doorway to the city of Toledo. It's only a 10-minute walk to the historic center. The hotel possesses a homelike atmosphere you feel as soon as you enter its precincts behind a red-brick facade with old street lights and vertical windows. The interior is decorated in wood and soft, pastel colors. The rooms are medium in size and furnished comfortably and unpretentiously. Bathrooms are impeccably maintained with showers and hair dryers. Amenities include room service until 11pm, plus a laundry. A continental breakfast is served in the coffee bar.

Hotel Mayoral. Avenida de Castilla-La Mancha, 3, 45003 Toledo. ☎ **925-21-60-00.** Fax 925-21-69-54. 110 units. A/C MINIBAR TV TEL. 12,500 ptas. (US$75) double. AE, DC, MC, V. Parking 1,000 ptas. (US$6). Bus: 5 or 6.

In front of the walls of Toledo, next to the bus station, this hotel was inaugurated in 1989 and met with instant approval. A rather formal entrance followed by a severe hallway leads to comfortable, well-furnished, and medium-size bedrooms that offer good beds with well-maintained bathrooms equipped with hair dryers. Most of the accommodations open onto balconies with views of interior patios, although a few have a panoramic view of Toledo. Mayoral maintains an excellent restaurant serving both a Spanish and international cuisine, plus a cozy bar. A buffet breakfast is served daily, and other amenities include room service, laundry, and a concierge.

Hotel Real de Toledo. Calle Real del Arrabal, 4, 45003 Toledo. ☎ **925-22-93-00.** Fax 925-22-87-67. www.socranet.com/hotelreal. 54 units. A/C TV TEL. 11,000 ptas. (US$66) double. AE, DC, MC, V. Parking 1,000 ptas. (US$6). Bus: 5 or 6.

This 19th-century building, located within the ancient city walls between Bisagra and the Sun Gates, has been a hotel since 1991. The facade is made from Castilian brick and is dotted with old large-framed windows. Despite the age of the building, the interior is modern and comfortable. The walls are decorated in beige and finished with pinewood. Many of the rooms open onto a view. Although each is comfortable and well equipped, some don't get enough light. Bathrooms are small and well maintained. Amenities include laundry and a concierge. There is no room service or a restaurant, but the hotel does have a small on-site cafeteria.

Hotel Residencia Imperio. Calle de las Cadenas, 5, 45001 Toledo. ☎ **925-22-76-50.** Fax 925-25-31-83. www.teleline.es/personal/himperio. E-mail: himperio@teleline.es. 21 units. A/C TV TEL. 6,800 ptas. (US$40.80) double. AE, DC, MC, V.

Just off calle de la Plata, one block west of Plaza de Zocodover, the Imperio is the best bet for those on a tight budget. The rooms are clean and comfortable but small and lackluster, showing the wear of their years. Most overlook a little church with a wall overgrown with wisteria. Parking is available on the street.

WHERE TO DINE
MODERATE

✪ **Asador Adolfo.** La Granada, 6. ☎ **925-22-73-21.** Reservations recommended. Main courses 2,800–3,600 ptas. (US$16.80–US$21.60); fixed-price menu 5,500–6,500 ptas. (US$33–US$39). AE, DC, MC, V. Daily 1–4pm, Mon–Sat 8pm–midnight. Bus: 5 or 6. SPANISH.

Less than a minute's walk north of the cathedral, at the corner of calle Hombre de Palo behind an understated sign, Asador Adolfo is one of the finest restaurants in town (though we prefer the Hostal del Cardenal). Sections of the building were first constructed during the 1400s, although the thoroughly modern kitchen has recently been renovated. Massive beams support the dining room ceilings, and here and there the rooms contain faded frescoes dating from the original building.

Game dishes are a house specialty; such choices as partridge with white beans and venison consistently rate among the best anywhere. Other offerings include hake flavored with local saffron as well as a wide array of beef, veal, or lamb dishes. To start, try the *pimientos rellenos* (red peppers stuffed with pulverized shellfish). The house dessert is marzipan, prepared in a wood-fired oven and noted for its lightness.

✪ **Hostal del Cardenal.** Paseo de Recaredo, 24. ☎ **925-22-08-62.** Reservations required. Main courses 1,200–2,800 ptas. (US$7.20–US$16.80); fixed-price menu 2,080 ptas. (US$12.50). AE, DC, MC, V. Daily 1–4pm and 8:30–11:30pm. Bus: 2 from rail station. SPANISH.

Treat yourself to Toledo's best-known restaurant, owned by the same people who run Madrid's Sobrino de Botín (see chapter 5). The chef prepares regional dishes with flair and originality. Choosing from a menu very similar to that of the fabled Madrid eatery, begin with "quarter of an hour" (fish) soup or white asparagus, then move on to curried prawns, baked hake, filet mignon, or smoked salmon. Roast suckling pig is a specialty, as is partridge in casserole. Arrive early to enjoy a sherry in the bar or in the courtyard.

La Abadía. Plaza de San Nicolás, 3. ☎ **925-25-07-46.** Reservations recommended. Main courses 1,500–2,500 ptas. (US$9–US$15); set menu 3,475 ptas. (US$20.85). DC, MC, V. Fri–Sat noon–3pm; daily 8pm–midnight. CASTILIAN.

The "Abbey" (its English name) started life as a cerveceria or alehouse before it was turned into a convivial restaurant and tapas bar. Next to San Nicolás church, it stands at the intersection of Núñez de Arce and calle de Alfileteros. It is ideal for a huge Castilian meal or else for wine drinking and tapas eating. The decor is a tasteful combination of modern and rustic styles, and the interior is separated into two sections—both a restaurant and a bar area. In honor of its old function as a cerveceria, a wide variety of international beers is offered. The menu is composed of fresh ingredients deftly handled by the kitchen staff. One of the best dishes—and beloved by Toledans—is a partridge casserole with white-wine, bay leaves, and onions. Fillet of venison in a mushroom sauce is another worthy choice, as is *ensalada de verdura a la parilla* (a salad of freshly grilled vegetables). Some of the most delightful tapas include croquettes, roasted red peppers, a selection of cheese, and such meats as venison and Serrano ham. The most unusual dessert is an ice cream made of Manchego cheese.

Mesón Aurelio. Calle Sínagoga, 6. ☎ **925-22-20-97.** Reservations recommended. Main courses 2,500–4,000 ptas. (US$15–US$24); fixed-price menu 3,500 ptas. (US$21). AE, DC, MC, V. Daily 1–4:30pm and 8–11:30pm. Bus: 5 or 6. CASTILIAN.

Established in the late 1940s, Mesón Aurelio occupies two separate but neighboring dining rooms, with two separate entrances, near the northern edge of the cathedral. It's one of the restaurant staples of Toledo, with its generous portions, Castilian ambience, and efficient service. Traditional versions of *sopa castellana,* grilled hake, *lubina à la sal* (whitefish cooked in salt), fresh salmon, and roast lamb are on the menu. Note that whereas the main outlet of this restaurant (calle Sinagoga, 6) is usually closed every Wednesday, the smaller of the restaurant's two branches (calle Sinagoga, 1) remains open, opting instead to close every Monday. Despite their different closing days, the food items and prices within the two branches are identical.

Parador Nacional de Conde Orgaz. Cerro del Emperador. ☎ **925-22-18-50.** Reservations not accepted. Main courses 1,600–2,800 ptas. (US$9.60–US$16.80); fixed-price menu 4,000 ptas. (US$24). AE, DC, MC, V. Daily 1–4pm and 8:30–11pm. Drive across Puente San Martín and head south for 2½ miles (4km). CASTILIAN.

Sturdy Castilian cuisine is enhanced by one of the most panoramic views from any restaurant in Europe. Located in a fine parador (recommended above), this restaurant is on the crest of a hill—said to be the spot that El Greco chose for his *View of Toledo.* The place is tourist-trodden, and the food doesn't quite match the view, but it's a worthy choice, nonetheless. The fixed-price meal might include tasty Spanish tapas, hake, then perhaps either veal or beef grilled on an open fire, and dessert. If you're dining lightly, try a local specialty, *tortilla española con magra* (potato omelette with ham or bacon). There is a bar on the upper level.

INEXPENSIVE

El Catavinos. Avenida Reconquista, 10. ☎ **925-22-22-56.** Reservations recommended. Main courses 900–2,000 ptas. (US$5.40–US$12); set menu 1,275 ptas. (US$7.65); *menú de degustación* 3,500 ptas. (US$21). AE, DC, MC, V. Tues–Sat noon–midnight, Sun 8pm–midnight. SPANISH/CASTILIAN.

El Catavinos means wine taster in Spanish, and indeed this charming restaurant started its life as a wine cellar. On the periphery of the center, a 10-minute walk from the Puerta de Bisagra, the restaurant has a convivial bar downstairs and a restaurant upstairs, decorated with old photographs of Peru. In fair weather, guests often eat on the terrace. The menu is filled with exciting and reasonably priced dishes, including such delicacies as partridge salad, bell peppers with a stuffing of hare, and grilled venison and veal meatballs in a savory tomato sauce. The *menu de degustación* is a cornucopia of seven different platters, each accompanied by one of seven different wines. The desserts offered include a cheesecake made from goat milk with a sweet white-wine.

El Emperador. Carretera del Valle, 1. ☎ **925-22-46-91.** Reservations recommended. Main courses 1,200–3,500 ptas. (US$7.20–US$21); fixed-price menu 3,000 ptas. (US$18). V. Daily 1–4pm and Mon–Sat 8–11pm. Bus: Carretera Valle. SPANISH.

A circa-1974 restaurant on the outskirts of Toledo, 1 mile southwest of the historic core of the town, near the parador, El Emperador is reached via an arched bridge. Its terraces overlook the river and the towers of Toledo; the tavern-style interior has leather-and-wood chairs, heavy beams, and wrought-iron chandeliers. Service at this family-owned establishment is attentive. The fixed-price menu might include a choice of soup (beef, vegetable, or noodle), followed by a small steak with French fries, then fresh fruit, plus wine. Although the dishes are decently prepared from fresh ingredients, it is the economical prices that make this an appealing choice.

La Parilla. Horno de los Bizcochos, 8. ☎ **925-21-22-45.** Main courses 2,100–2,600 ptas. (US$12.60–US$15.60); fixed-price menu 1,500 ptas. (US$9). AE, DC, MC, V. Daily 1–4pm and 8–10:30pm. Bus: 5 or 6. SPANISH.

Go here for some real Franco-era dishes. This classic Spanish restaurant, within a thick-walled medieval building, stands on a cobbled street near the Hotel Alfonso VI, just east of the cathedral. The menu offers no surprises, but it's reliable. Likely inclusions on the bill of fare are roast suckling pig, spider crabs, Castilian baked trout, stewed quail, baked kidneys, and La Mancha rabbit. This is the type of heavy fare so beloved by Castilians, who still frequent the place in great numbers.

La Perdiz. Calle Reyes Católicos, 7. ☎ **925-21-46-58.** Reservations recommended. Main courses 1,500–2,000 ptas. (US$9–US$12); set menu 2,500 ptas. (US$15). AE, MC, V. Tues–Sat noon–11pm, Sun noon–4pm. CASTILIAN.

La Perdiz is named from the favorite dish of Toledans—partridge. That bird is best showcased here in a dish called *perdiz estofada a la toledano,* partridge stew with white-wine, bay leaf, and onions. Another excellent choice is venison in a mushroom sauce. The menu also has some imaginative offerings such as a fresh fried cheese tossed in an orange dressing.

   The best dessert is that local favorite, marzipan, here served as a tart with almond biscuits. On occasion a roast suckling pig is featured. The location is in the center of the old Jewish ghetto, about midpoint between two synagogues, Santa Maria la Blanca and Tránsito. The restaurant has two floors with views of the historic district, and walls are of wood and brick. Locals, and with good reason, cite the place for its good quality cuisine at affordable prices. The same people who run **La Perdiz** also operate **Asador Adolfo,** Toledo's premier restaurant. But prices at **La Perdiz** are far more reasonable.

La Tarasca. Calle Hombre de Palo, 6. ☎ **925-22-43-42.** Reservations not required. Main courses 1,500–2,600 ptas. (US$9–US$15.60); set menu 2,200 ptas. (US$13.20). MC, V. Daily 7:30am–11pm. CASTILIAN.

This restaurant, the domain of the Martin brothers, serves good food but it's mainly recommended for its convenience, as it lies only a couple of blocks north of the cathedral. With two dining rooms and a cafeteria, it is also open throughout the day, even serving breakfast. The decor, although plain, still evokes a 19th-century aura. Walls are painted in green with wood paneling resting under beams, and the rooms are joined by archways. The cuisine consists of the hearty, robust fare that Toledans feast on, including the traditional opener, *sopa castellana,* a hearty soup made with various meats and beans. You can opt for such standard dishes as grilled steak and potatoes, but braised game hen would be more traditional, as would trout caught in local waters. One of our favorite dishes is *pimientos rellenos,* stuffed peppers, or else *cordoniz a la toledana,* roasted quail with savory brown sauce. All desserts, including the puddings, are homemade.

TOLEDO AFTER DARK

Before your nighttime crawl through Toledo, begin with a stopover at **Bar Ludena,** Plaza de la Horn Madelena, 13, Corral de Don Diego, 10 (☎ **925-22-33-84**), where a loyal clientele come for the delectable tapas served here. Glasses of wine are sometimes passed through a small window to clients who are standing outside, enjoying the view of the square. The bar is little more than a narrow corridor, serving *raciónes* of tapas that are so generous they make little meals, especially when served with bread. The roasted red peppers in olive oil are quite tasty, along with the stuffed crabs and *calamares* (squid). Huge dishes of pickled cucumbers, onions, and olives are available.

They also have a tiny dining room behind a curtain at the end of the bar, serving inexpensive fare.

Despite the many tourists that throng through its streets during the day, Toledo is quiet, dignified, and sleepy at night, with fewer dance clubs than you'd expect from a town of its size. If you want to hear some recorded music, head for **Bar La Abadia,** calle Núñez de Arce, 5 (☎ **925-25-11-40**), where crowds of local residents, many of them involved in the tourism industry, crowd elbow to elbow for pints of beer, glasses of wine, and access to the music of New York, Los Angeles, or wherever. A roughly equivalent competitor is **Bar Camelot,** calle Cristo de la Luz, s/n (no phone), which occupies an old, stone-sided building within the historic core of Toledo. Both are open nightly 9pm to around 4am.

2 Aranjuez

29 miles (47km) S of Madrid, 30 miles (48km) NE of Toledo

This Castilian town, at a confluence of the Tagus and Jarama Rivers, was once home to Bourbon kings in the spring and fall. With the manicured shrubbery, stately elms, fountains, and statues of the Palacio Real and surrounding compounds, Aranjuez remains a regal garden oasis in what is otherwise an unimpressive agricultural flatland known primarily for its strawberries and asparagus.

ESSENTIALS

GETTING THERE   By Train   Trains depart about every 20 minutes from Madrid's Atocha Railway Station to make the 50-minute trip to Aranjuez. Twice a day you can take an express train from Madrid to Toledo, which makes a brief stopover at Aranjuez. This trip takes only 30 minutes. Trains run less often along the east-west route to and from Toledo (a 40-minute ride). The Aranjuez station lies about a mile outside town. For information and schedules, call ☎ 91-891-02-02. You can walk it in about 15 minutes, but taxis and buses line up on calle Stuart (2 blocks from the city tourist office). The bus that makes the run from the center of Aranjuez to the railway station is marked "N-Z."

By Bus   Buses for Aranjuez depart every 30 minutes from 7:30am to 10pm from Madrid's Estación Sur de Autobuses, calle Méndez Alvaro. In Madrid, call ☎ 91-468-42-00 for information. Buses arrive in Aranjuez at the City Bus Terminal, calle Infantas, 8 (☎ 91-891-01-83).

By Car   Driving is easy; it takes about 30 minutes once you reach the southern city limits of Madrid. To reach Aranjuez, follow the signs to Aranjuez and Granada, taking highway N-IV.

VISITOR INFORMATION   The **tourist information office** is at Plaza de San Antonio, 9 (☎ 91-891-04-27), open Monday to Friday 10am to 2pm and 4 to 6pm.

SEEING THE SIGHTS

✪ **Palacio Real.** Plaza Palacio. ☎ **91-891-13-44.** Admission 650 ptas. (US$3.90) adults, 250 ptas. (US$1.50) students and children. Apr–Sept, Wed–Mon 10am–6:15pm; Oct–Mar, Wed–Mon 10am–5:15pm. Bus: Routes from the rail station converge at the square and gardens at the westernmost edge of the palace.

Since the beginning of a united Spain, the climate and natural beauty of Aranjuez have attracted Spanish monarchs: Ferdinand and Isabella; Philip II, when he managed to tear himself away from El Escorial; Philip V; and Charles III.

The structure you see today dates from 1778 (the previous buildings were destroyed by fire). The palace is lavishly and elegantly decorated: Salons show the opulence of a bygone era, with room after room of royal extravagance. Especially notable are the dancing salon, the throne room, the ceremonial dining hall, the bedrooms of the king and queen, and a remarkable Salon de Porcelana (Porcelain Room). Paintings include works by Lucas Jordan and José Ribera. A guide conducts you through the huge complex (a tip is expected).

Jardín de la Isla. Directly northwest of the Palacio Real. No phone. Free admission. Apr–Sept, daily 8am–8:30pm; Oct–Mar, daily 8am–6:30pm.

After the tour of the Royal Palace, wander through the Garden of the Island. Spanish impressionist Santiago Rusiñol captured its evasive quality on canvas, and one Spanish writer said that you walk here "as if softly lulled by a sweet 18th-century sonata." A number of fountains are remarkable: the "Ne Plus Ultra" fountain, the black-jasper fountain of Bacchus, the fountain of Apollo, and the ones honoring Neptune (god of the sea) and Cybele (goddess of agriculture).

You may also stroll through the Jardín del Parterre, located in front of the palace. It's much better kept than the Garden of the Island, but not as romantic.

Casita del Labrador. Calle Reina, Jardín del Príncipe. ☎ **91-891-03-05.** Admission 550 ptas. (US$3.30) adults, 225 ptas. (US$1.35) students and children. May–Sept, Tues–Sun 10am–6:30pm; Oct–Apr, Tues–Sun 10am–5:30pm.

"The Little House of the Worker," modeled after the Petit Trianon at Versailles, was built in 1803 by Charles IV, who later abdicated in Aranjuez. The queen came here with her youthful lover, Godoy (whom she had elevated to the position of prime minister), and the feeble-minded Charles didn't seem to mind a bit. Surrounded by beautiful gardens, the "bedless" palace is lavishly furnished in the grand style of the 18th and 19th centuries. The marble floors represent some of the finest workmanship of that day; the brocaded walls emphasize the luxurious lifestyle; and the royal toilet is a sight to behold (in those days, royalty preferred an audience). The clock here is one of the treasures of the house. The casita lies half a mile east of the Royal Palace; those with a car can drive directly to it through the tranquil Jardin del Príncipe.

WHERE TO STAY

Hostal Castilla. Carretera Andalucia, 98, 28300 Aranjuez. ☎ **91-891-26-27.** 17 units. TV TEL. 7,500 ptas. (US$45) double. AE, DC, MC, V.

On one of the town's main streets north of the Royal Palace and gardens, the Castilla consists of the ground floor and part of the first floor of a well-preserved early 18th-century house. Most of the accommodations overlook a courtyard with a fountain and flowers. Owner Joaquin Suárez, who speaks English fluently, suggests that reservations be made at least a month in advance. There are excellent restaurants nearby, and the hostal has an arrangement with a neighboring bar to provide guests with an inexpensive lunch. This is a good location from which to explore either Madrid or Toledo on a day trip. Parking is available along the street.

WHERE TO DINE

✪ **Casa José.** Calle Abastos, 32. ☎ **91-891-14-88.** Reservations recommended. Main courses 1,800–3,000 ptas. (US$10.80–US$18). AE, DC, MC, V. Tues–Sun 1–4pm and Tues–Sat 9pm–midnight. SPANISH/INTERNATIONAL.

Set near Town Hall and the Church of Antonio, this well-managed restaurant occupies two ground-floor rooms of a 300-year-old house in the heart of town; it's the premier restaurant of the entire area, and local gastronomes drive for miles around to dine here. The regionally based repertoire of food is prepared with an intelligent association of flavors. Any of the daily offerings is well worth ordering. Menu items focus on fresh ingredients that the staff buys every morning at the town markets. Look for a menu that changes at least four times a year, with an emphasis on pork, veal, fish, chicken, and shellfish. Of special note are braised lamb chops in a fresh tomato and cilantro sauce; Jabugo ham with broad beans; shrimp in garlic sauce; hake with green sauce; and thick juicy steaks.

Casa Pablo. Almibar, 42. ☎ **91-891-14-51.** Reservations recommended. Main courses 2,000–2,600 ptas. (US$12–US$15.60); 4-course fixed-price menu 3,000 ptas. (US$18). AE, MC, V. Daily 1–4:30pm and 8pm–midnight. Closed Aug. SPANISH.

An unpretentious and well-managed restaurant near the bus station in the town center, Casa Pablo was established in 1941. At tables set outside beneath a canopy, you can dine while enjoying red and pink geraniums along the tree-lined street; in cooler weather you can eat either upstairs or in the cozy rear dining room. The fixed-price menu includes four courses, a carafe of wine, bread, and gratuity. If it's hot out and you don't feel like having a heavy dinner, try a shrimp omelette or half a roast chicken; once we ordered just a plate of asparagus in season, accompanied by white-wine. If you want a superb dish, try a fish called *mero* (Mediterranean pollack of delicate flavor), grilled over an open fire.

La Rana Verde. Reina, 1. ☎ **91-891-32-38.** Reservations recommended. Main courses 1,200–2,500 ptas. (US$7.20–US$15); fixed-price menu 1,500–3,900 ptas. (US$9–US$23.40). MC, V. Daily 9pm–midnight. SPANISH.

"The Green Frog," just east of the Royal Palace and next to a small bridge spanning the Tagus, is still the traditional choice for many. Opened in 1905 by Tomás Díaz Heredero, it is owned and run by a third-generation member of his family, who has decorated it in a 1920s style. The restaurant looks like a summerhouse, with its high-beamed ceiling and soft ferns drooping from hanging baskets. The preferred tables are in the nooks overlooking the river. As in all the restaurants of Aranjuez, asparagus is a special feature. Game, particularly partridge, quail, and pigeon, can be recommended in season; fish, too, including fried hake and fried sole, makes a good choice. Strawberries are served with sugar, orange juice, or ice cream.

3 San Lorenzo de El Escorial

30 miles (48km) W of Madrid, 32 miles (52km) SE of Segovia

Aside from Toledo, the most important excursion from Madrid is to the austere royal monastery of San Lorenzo de El Escorial. Philip II ordered the construction of this granite-and-slate behemoth in 1563, two years after he moved his capital to Madrid. Once the haunt of aristocratic Spaniards, El Escorial is now a resort where hotels and restaurants flourish in summer, as hundreds come to escape the heat of the capital. Aside from the appeal of its climate, the town of San Lorenzo itself is not very noteworthy. But because of the monastery's size, you might decide to spend a night or two at San Lorenzo—or more if you have the time.

San Lorenzo makes a good base for visiting nearby Segovia, the royal palace at La Granja, and the Valley of the Fallen.

ESSENTIALS

GETTING THERE By Train More than 2 dozen trains depart daily from Madrid's Atocha, Nuevos Ministerios, and Chamartín train stations. Trip time is little more than an hour. During the summer extra coaches are added. For schedules and information, call ☎ **91-328-90-20.**

The railway station for San Lorenzo de El Escorial is located about a mile outside of town along Ctra. Estación (☎ 91-890-07-14). The Herranz bus company meets all arriving trains with a shuttle bus that ferries arriving passengers to and from the Plaza Virgen de Gracia, about a block east of the entrance to the monastery.

By Bus   The Office of Empresa Herranz, calle Reina Victoria, 3, in El Escorial (☎ 91-890-41-22 or 91-890-41-25), runs some 40 buses per day back and forth between Madrid and El Escorial. On Sunday, service is curtailed to 10 buses. Trip time is an hour, and a round-trip fare costs 750 pesetas (US$4.50). The same company also runs one bus a day to El Valle de los Caídos. It leaves El Escorial at 3:15pm with a return at 5:30pm. The ride takes only 15 minutes, and a round-trip fare is 870 pesetas (US$5.20), El Valle only.

By Car   Follow the N-VI highway (marked on some maps as A-6) from the northwest perimeter of Madrid toward Lugo, La Coruña, and San Lorenzo de El Escorial. After about a half hour, fork left onto the C-505 toward San Lorenzo de El Escorial. Driving time from Madrid is about an hour.

VISITOR INFORMATION   The **tourist information office** is at Floridablanca, 10 (☎ 91-890-15-54). It is open Monday to Friday 10am to 2pm and 3 to 5pm, Saturday 10am to 2pm.

SEEING THE SIGHTS

✪ **Real Monasterio de San Lorenzo de El Escorial.** Calle San Lorenzo de El Escorial, 1. ☎ **91-890-59-03.** Comprehensive ticket 850 ptas. (US$5.10) adults, 350 ptas. (US$2.10) children. Guided tour 950 ptas. (US$5.70). Apr–Sept, Tues–Sun 10am–7pm; Oct–Mar, Tues–Sun 10am–6pm.

This huge granite fortress houses a wealth of paintings and tapestries and also serves as a burial place for Spanish kings. Foreboding both inside and out because of its sheer size and institutional look, El Escorial took 21 years to complete, a remarkably short time considering the bulk of the building and the primitive construction methods of the day. After his death, the original architect, Juan Bautista de Toledo, was replaced by Juan de Herrera, the greatest architect of Renaissance Spain, who completed the structure.

Philip II, who collected many of the paintings exhibited here in the New Museums, did not appreciate El Greco and favored Titian instead. But you'll still find El Greco's *The Martyrdom of St. Maurice,* rescued from storage, and his *St. Peter.* Other superb works include Titian's *Last Supper* and Velázquez's *The Tunic of Joseph.*

The Royal Library houses a priceless collection of 60,000 volumes—one of the most significant in the world. The displays range from the handwriting of St. Teresa to medieval instructions on playing chess. See, in particular, the Muslim codices and a Gothic *Cantigas* from the 13th-century reign of Alfonso X ("The Wise").

You can also visit the Philip II Apartments; these are strictly monastic, and Philip called them the "cell for my humble self" in this "palace for God." Philip became a religious fanatic and requested that his bedroom be erected overlooking the altar of the 300-foot-high basilica, which has four organs and whose dome is based on Michelangelo's drawings for St. Peter's. The choir contains a crucifix by Cellini. By comparison, the Throne Room is simple. On the walls are many ancient maps. The Apartments of the Bourbon Kings are lavishly decorated, in contrast to Philip's preference for the ascetic.

Under the altar of the church you'll find one of the most regal mausoleums in the world, the Royal Pantheon, where most of Spain's monarchs—from Charles I to Alfonso XII, including Philip II—are buried. In 1993 Don Juan de Borbón, the count of Barcelona and the father of King Juan Carlos (Franco passed over the count and never allowed him to ascend to the throne) was interred nearby. On a lower floor is the "Wedding Cake" tomb for children.

Allow at least three hours for a visit. The guided tour doesn't take you to all the sites, but you are free to explore on your own afterward.

Casa de Príncipe (Prince's Cottage). Calle Reina, s/n. ☎ **91-891-03-05.** Admission included in comprehensive ticket to El Escorial, see above. Apr–July and Sept, Sat–Sun and holidays 10am–5:45pm; Aug, Tues–Sun 10am–5:45pm; Oct–Mar, Sat–Sun and holidays 10am–6:45pm.

This small but elaborately decorated 18th-century palace near the railway station was originally a hunting lodge built for Charles III by Juan de Villanueva. Most visitors stay in El Escorial for lunch, visiting the cottage in the afternoon.

El Valle de los Caídos (Valley of the Fallen). ☎ **91-890-56-11.** Admission 650 ptas. (US$3.90) adults, 250 ptas. (US$1.50) students and children. Apr–Sept, Tues–Sun 10am–6pm; Oct–Mar, Tues–Sun 10am–6pm. Bus: Tour buses from Madrid usually include an excursion to the Valley of the Fallen on their 1-day trips to El Escorial (see "By Bus," above). By Car: Drive to the valley entrance, about 5 miles (8km) north of El Escorial in the heart of the Guadarrama Mountains. Once here, drive 3½ miles (6km) west along a wooded road to the underground basilica.

This is Franco's El Escorial, an architectural marvel that took two decades to complete, dedicated to those who died in the Spanish Civil War. Its detractors say that it represents the worst of neofascist design; its admirers say they have found renewed inspiration by coming here.

A gargantuan cross nearly 500 feet high dominates the Rock of Nava, a peak of the Guadarrama Mountains. Directly under the cross is a basilica with a vault in mosaic, completed in 1959. Here José Antonio Primo de Rivera, the founder of the Falange party, is buried. When this Nationalist hero was buried at El Escorial, many, especially influential monarchists, protested that he was not a royal. Infuriated, Franco decided to erect another monument. Originally it was slated to honor the dead on the Nationalist side only, but the intervention of several parties led to a decision to include all the *caídos* (fallen). In time the mausoleum claimed Franco as well; his body was interred behind the high altar.

A funicular extends from near the entrance to the basilica to the base of the gigantic cross erected on the mountaintop above (where there's a superb view). The fare is 350 pesetas (US$2.10), and the funicular runs daily from 10:30am to 1:15pm and 4 to 6pm.

On the other side of the mountain is a Benedictine monastery that has sometimes been dubbed "the Hilton of monasteries" because of its seeming luxury.

WHERE TO STAY
MODERATE

Hotel Botánico. Calle Timoteo Padros, 16, 28200 San Lorenzo de El Escorial. ☎ **91-890-78-79.** Fax 91-890-81-58. 20 units. 15,000 ptas. (US$90) double; 19,300–30,000 ptas. (US$115.80–US$180) suite. AE, V. Free parking.

True to its name, the hotel stands in a lovely manicured garden consisting of both indigenous and exotic shrubbery. Although the building is traditionally Castilian, the decor seems vaguely alpine, with wood paneling and beams in the reception rooms. The clean, well-lit rooms are large and comfortable, with especially good beds. There is a restaurant inside the hotel, which specializes in rice and fish dishes. Main courses range from 1,500 to 2,500 pesetas (US$9 to US$15) and there is a fixed-price menu at 5,000 pesetas (US$30).

Hotel Victoria Palace. Calle Juan de Toledo, 4, 28200 San Lorenzo de El Escorial. ☎ **91-896-98-90.** Fax 91-896-98-96. E-mail: victoria@iies.es. 96 units. TV TEL. 12,500–18,600 ptas. (US$75–US$111.60) double. AE, MC, V. Parking 1,800 ptas. (US$10.80).

The Victoria Palace, with its view of El Escorial, is the finest hotel in town, a traditional establishment that has been modernized without losing its special aura of style and comfort. It is surrounded by beautiful gardens and has an outdoor swimming pool. The rooms (some with private terraces) are well furnished and maintained. The rates are reasonable enough, and a bargain for a four-star hotel. The dining room serves some of the best food in town.

INEXPENSIVE

✪ **Hostal Cristina.** Juan de Toledo, 6, 28200 San Lorenzo de El Escorial. ☎ **91-890-19-61.** Fax 91-890-12-04. www.jazzviajeros.com/. E-mail: hcristina@jazzviajeros.com. 16 units. TV TEL. 6,500 ptas. (US$39) double. MC, V.

An excellent budget choice, this hotel is run by the Delgado family, who opened it in the mid-1980s. It doesn't pretend to compete with the comfort and amenities of the Victoria Palace or even the Miranda & Suizo (see below), but it has its devotees nonetheless. About 50 yards from the monastery, it stands in the center of town, offering clean and comfortable but simply furnished rooms. The helpful staff will direct you to the small garden. Since the food served in the restaurant is both good and plentiful, many Spanish visitors prefer to book here for a summer holiday. Parking is available along the street.

Miranda & Suizo. Calle Floridablanca, 20, 28200 San Lorenzo de El Escorial. ☎ **91-890-47-11.** Fax 91-890-43-58. www.mirandasuizo.com. E-mail: mirandasuizo@mirandasuizo. com. 52 units. TV TEL. 12,000 ptas. (US$72) double; 16,000–20,000 ptas. (US$96–US$120) suite. AE, DC, MC, V.

On a tree-lined street in the heart of town, within easy walking distance of the monastery, this excellent middle-bracket establishment ranks as a leading two-star hotel. It is the second choice in town, with rooms not quite as comfortable as those at the Victoria Palace. The Victorian-style building, nevertheless, has good guest rooms, some with terraces; 10 have TVs. The furnishings are comfortable, the beds often made of brass; sometimes you'll find fresh flowers on the tables. In summer, there is outside dining. Parking is available nearby for 1,000 pesetas (US$6) per day.

WHERE TO DINE
MODERATE

Charolés. Calle Floridablanca, 24. ☎ **91-890-59-75.** Reservations required. Main courses 2,800–3,800 ptas. (US$16.80–US$22.80). AE, DC, MC, V. Daily 1–4pm and 9pm–midnight. SPANISH/INTERNATIONAL.

The thick and solid walls of this establishment date, according to its managers, "from the monastic age"—and probably predate the town's larger and better-known monastery of El Escorial. The restaurant contained within was established around 1980, and has been known ever since as the best dining room in town. It has a flower-ringed outdoor terrace for use during clement weather. The cuisine doesn't quite rate a star, but chances are you'll be satisfied. The wide choice of menu items based entirely on fresh fish and meats includes such dishes as grilled hake with green or hollandaise sauce, shellfish soup, pepper steak, a *pastel* (pie) of fresh vegetables with crayfish, and herb-flavored baby lamb chops. Strawberry or kiwi tart is a good dessert choice.

Mesón la Cueva. San Antón, 4. ☎ **91-890-15-16.** Reservations recommended. Main courses 1,500–2,800 ptas. (US$9–US$16.80); *menú del día* 2,000 ptas. (US$12); *menú especial* (chef's special menu of the day) 3,700 ptas. (US$22.20). AE, MC, V. Tues–Sun 1–4pm and 8:30–11:30pm. CASTILIAN.

Founded in 1768, this restaurant captures the world of Old Castile, and it is only a short walk from the monastery. A *mesón típico* built around an enclosed courtyard, "the Cave" boasts such nostalgic accents as stained-glass windows, antique chests, a 19th-century bullfighting collage, faded engravings, paneled doors, and iron balconies. The cooking is on target, and the portions are generous. Regional specialties include Valencian paella and *fabada asturiana* (pork sausage and beans), but the fresh trout broiled in butter is the best of all. The menu's most expensive items are Segovian roast suckling pig and roast lamb (tender inside, crisp outside). Off the courtyard through a separate doorway is La Cueva's tasca, filled with Castilians quaffing their favorite before-dinner drinks.

NEAR THE VALLEY OF THE FALLEN

Hosteleria Valle de los Caídos. Valle de los Caídos. ☎ **91-890-55-11.** Reservations not accepted. Fixed-price menu 1,500 ptas. (US$9). No credit cards. Daily 9–10am, 2–3:30pm, and 9–10pm. Closed Dec 15–Jan 15. SPANISH.

There aren't a lot of dining options around the Valley of the Fallen, and of the few that exist, this is about as good a bet as you'll get. Built in 1956, it's set amid a dry but dramatic landscape halfway along the inclined access road leading to Franco's monuments, reachable only by car or bus. It's a mammoth modern structure with wide terraces and floor-to-ceiling windows. The *menú del día* usually includes such dishes as cannelloni Rossini, pork chops with potatoes, a dessert choice of flan or fruit, and wine. The typical fare of roast chicken, roast lamb, shellfish, and paella is somewhat cafeteria-style in nature.

EL ESCORIAL AFTER DARK

No longer the dead place it was during the long Franco era, the town comes alive at night, fueled mainly by the throngs of young people who pack into the bars and taverns, especially those along calle Rey and calle Floridablanca. Some of our favorite bars, offering vats of wine or kegs of beer, include the **Piano Bar Regina,** Floridablanca (☎ **91-890-68-43**); **Gurriato,** Leindro Rubio, 3 (☎ **91-890-47-10**); and **Don Felipe II,** Floridablanca (☎ **91-896-07-65**). The hottest disco is **Move it,** Plaza de Santiago, 11 (☎ **91-890-54-91**), which rarely imposes a cover unless some special group is featured.

4 Segovia

54 miles (91km) NW of Madrid, 42 miles (68km) NE of Ávila

Less commercial than Toledo, Segovia, more than anywhere else, typifies the glory of Old Castile. Wherever you look, you'll see reminders of a golden era—whether it's the most spectacular Alcázar on the Iberian Peninsula or the well-preserved, still-functioning Roman aqueduct.

Segovia lies on the slope of the Guadarrama Mountains, where the Eresma and Clamores Rivers converge. This ancient city stands in the center of the most castle-rich part of Castile. Isabella herself was proclaimed queen of Castile here in 1474.

The narrow, winding streets of this hill city must be covered on foot to fully view the Romanesque churches and 15th-century palaces along the way.

ESSENTIALS

GETTING THERE   By Train   Fifteen trains leave Madrid's Chamartín Railway Station every day and arrive two hours later in Segovia, where you can board bus no. 3, which departs every quarter-hour for the Plaza Mayor. The trains that leave from Chamartín first travel through Atocha Station, making it closer to some travelers' hotels. The station at Segovia lies on the Paseo Obispo Quesada, s/n (☎ 921-42-07-74), a 20-minute walk southeast of the town center.

By Bus   Buses arrive and depart from the Estacionamiento Municipal de Autobuses, Paseo de Ezequile González, 10 (☎ 921-42-77-25), near the corner of the Avenida Fernández Ladreda and the steeply sloping Paseo Conde de Sepúlveda. There are 10 to 15 buses a day to and from Madrid (which depart from Paseo de la Florida, 11; metro: Norte), and about four a day traveling between Ávila, Segovia, and Valladolid. One-way tickets from Madrid cost around 765 pesetas (US$4.60).

By Car   Take the N-VI (on some maps it's known as the A-6) or the Autopista del Nordeste northwest from Madrid, toward León and Lugo. At the junction with Route 110 (signposted Segovia), turn northeast.

VISITOR INFORMATION   The **tourist information office** is at Plaza Mayor, 10 (☎ 921-46-03-34). It is open daily 10am to 2pm and 5 to 8pm. There is an additional tourist office at plaza del Azoguejo (☎ 921-46-29-06), at the foot of the aqueduct. Coming from the train station, you'll encounter this office first.

SEEING THE SIGHTS

✪ **El Alcázar.** Plaza de La Reina Victoria Eugenia. ☎ **921-46-07-59.** Admission 400 ptas. (US$2.40) adults, 250 ptas. (US$1.50) children 8–14, free for children 7 and under. Apr–Sept, daily 10am–7pm; Oct–Mar, daily 10am–6pm. Bus: 3. Take either calle Vallejo, calle de Velarde, calle de Daoiz, or Paseo de Ronda.

If you've ever dreamed of castles in the air, then all the fairy-tale romance of childhood will return when you view the Alcázar. Many have waxed poetic about it, comparing it to a giant boat sailing through the clouds. View the Alcázar first from below, at the junction of the Clamores and Eresma Rivers. It's on the west side of Segovia, and you may not spot it when you first enter the city—but that's part of the surprise.

The castle dates from the 12th century, but a large segment, which contained its Moorish ceilings, was destroyed by fire in 1862. Restoration has continued over the years.

Royal romance is associated with the Alcázar. Isabella first met Ferdinand here, and today you can see a facsimile of her dank bedroom. Once married, she wasn't foolish enough to surrender her royal rights, as replicas of the thrones attest—both are equally proportioned. Philip II married his fourth wife, Anne of Austria, here as well.

Walk the battlements of this once-impregnable castle, from which its occupants hurled boiling oil onto the enemy below. Or ascend the hazardous stairs of the tower, originally built by Isabella's father as a prison, for a panoramic view of Segovia.

✪ **Roman Aqueduct (Acueducto Romano).** Plaza del Azoguejo.

This architectural marvel was built by the Romans nearly 2,000 years ago. Constructed of mortarless granite, it consists of 118 arches, and in one two-tiered section it soars 95 feet to its highest point. The Spanish call it El Puente. It spans the Plaza del Azoguejo, the old market square, stretching nearly 800 yards. When the Moors took Segovia in 1072, they destroyed 36 arches, which were later rebuilt under Ferdinand and Isabella in 1484.

○ Cabildo Catedral de Segovia. Plaza Catedral, Marqués del Arco. ☎ **921-43-53-25.** Free admission to cathedral; cloisters, museum, and chapel room 300 ptas. (US$1.80) adults, 50 ptas. (US30¢) children. Spring and summer, daily 9am–7pm; off-season, daily 9:30am–6pm.

Constructed between 1515 and 1558, this is the last Gothic cathedral built in Spain. Fronting the historic Plaza Mayor, it stands on the spot where Isabella I was proclaimed queen of Castile. Affectionately called *la dama de las catedrales,* it contains numerous treasures, such as the Blessed Sacrament Chapel (created by the flamboyant Churriguera), stained-glass windows, elaborately carved choir stalls, and 16th- and 17th-century paintings, including a reredos portraying the deposition of Christ from the cross by Juan de Juni. The cloisters are older than the cathedral, dating from an earlier church that was destroyed in the so-called War of the Communeros. Inside the cathedral museum you'll find jewelry, paintings, and a collection of rare antique manuscripts.

Iglesia de la Vera Cruz. Carretera de Zamarramala. ☎ **921-43-14-75.** Admission 200 ptas. (US$1.20). Apr–Sept, Tues–Sun 10:30am–1:30pm and 3:30–7pm; Oct–Mar, Tues–Sun 10:30am–1:30pm and 3:30–6pm.

Built in either the 11th or the 12th century by the Knights Templar, this is the most fascinating Romanesque church in Segovia. It stands in isolation outside the walls of the old town, overlooking the Alcázar. Its unusual 12-sided design is believed to have been copied from the Church of the Holy Sepulchre in Jerusalem. Inside you'll find an inner temple, rising two floors, where the knights conducted nightlong vigils as part of their initiation rites.

Monasterio del Parral. Subida del Parral, 2 (across the Eresma River). ☎ **921-43-12-98.** Free admission. Mon–Sat 10am–2:30pm and 4–6:30pm; Sun 10–11:30am, 4–6:30pm. Take Ronda de Sant Lucía and cross the Eresma River.

The restored "Monastery of the Grape" was established for the Hieronymites by Henry IV (1425–74), a Castilian king known as "The Impotent." The monastery lies across the Eresma River about a half mile north of the city. The church is a medley of styles and decoration—mainly Gothic, Renaissance, and plateresque. The facade was never completed, and the monastery itself was abandoned when religious orders were suppressed in 1835. Today it's been restored and is once again the domain of the *jerónimos,* Hieronymus priests and brothers. Inside, a robed monk will show you the various treasures of the order, including a polychrome altarpiece and the alabaster tombs of the Marquis of Villena and his wife—all the work of Juan Rodríguez.

Esteban Vicente Contemporary Art Museum. Plazuela de las Bellas. ☎ **921-46-20-10.** Admission 400 ptas. (US$2.40) adults, 200 ptas. (US$1.20) seniors and students, free for children under 12. Mon–Sat 11am–2pm and 4–7pm, Sun 11am–2pm.

In the heart of the city, in a newly renovated 15th-century palace, a permanent collection of some 142 works by the Abstract Expressionist artist, Esteban Vicente, has opened. The Spanish-born artist, now in his late 90s, has described himself as "an American painter, with very deep and loving Spanish roots." Born in a small town outside Segovia in 1903, he remained in Spain until 1927, eventually (since 1936) residing in New York, where he played a pivotal role in the development of American abstract art. Today, he is one of the last surviving members of the New York School, whose members include Rothko, de Kooning, and Pollock. Vicente's paintings and collages convey his sense of structure and feelings of luminous serenity with colors of astonishing vibrancy, brilliance, and range. His paintings are shown at the Metropolitan Museum of Art, the Museum of Modern Art, and the Whitney, all in New York—and now Segovia.

WHERE TO STAY
EXPENSIVE

✪ **Parador de Segovia.** Carretera Valladolid, s/n (N-601), 40003 Segovia. ☎ **921-44-37-37.** Fax 921-43-73-62. www.parador.es. 120 units. A/C MINIBAR TV TEL. 21,000 ptas. (US$126) double; from 32,000 ptas. (US$192) suite. AE, DC, MC, V. Covered parking 1,000 ptas. (US$6), free outside.

This 20th-century tile-roofed parador sits on a hill 2 miles (3km) northeast of Segovia (take the N-601). It stands on an estate called El Terminillo, which used to be famous for its vines and almond trees, a few of which still survive. If you have a car and can get a reservation, book here; the comfort level dwarfs that found at either Los Arcos or Los Linajes. The guest rooms are deluxe, containing such extras as private safes and tiled bathrooms. Furnishings are tasteful (often in blond pieces), and large windows open onto panoramic views of the countryside. Some of the older rooms here are a bit dated, however, with a lackluster decor.

Dining/Diversions: The parador has one of the better restaurants in Segovia; its windows open onto a panoramic view of the mountains of Sierra de Guadarrama. A complete meal here, of both regional specialties and international dishes, costs around 3,700 pesetas (US$22.20). The hotel also offers a bar.

Amenities: The vast lawns and gardens contain two lake-like swimming pools; there is also an indoor pool, plus a sauna and tennis courts.

MODERATE

Hotel Infanta Isabel. Plaza Mayor, 40001 Segovia. ☎ **921-46-13-00.** Fax 921-46-22-17. E-mail: hinfanta@teleline.es. 27 units. A/C MINIBAR TV TEL. 12,700–15,000 ptas. (US$76.20–US$90) double. AC, DC, MC, V. Parking 1,000 ptas. (US$6).

Named after Queen Isabel, the great-grandmother of the present-day king, the hotel stands overlooking the charming central square and is within a stone's throw of the majestic cathedral. This is where she would stay when on her way to the nearby summer palace of La Granja. The present owners have modernized the interior considerably but a good deal of the building's 19th-century grandeur, such as the staircase, remain. Each room is decorated in its own style, and each is furnished with an eye to comfort. Despite its style, the hotel has every convenience; satellite TV and modern bathrooms strike a reassuring 20th-century note.

Hotel Los Linajes. Dr. Velasco, 9, 40003 Segovia. ☎ **921-46-04-75.** Fax 921-46-04-79. 53 units. A/C TV TEL. 11,000–13,000 ptas. (US$66–US$78) double; 14,900–16,900 ptas. (US$89.40–US$101.40) suite. AE, DC, V. Parking 1,100 ptas. (US$6.60). Bus: 1.

In the historical district of St. Stephen at the northern edge of the old town stands this hotel, the former home of a Segovian noble family. While the facade dates from the 11th century, the interior is modern, except for some Castilian decorations. Following a 1996 renovation, the hotel looks a bit brighter and fresher than Los Arcos (see below). One of the best choices in town, Los Linajes offers gardens and patios where guests can enjoy a panoramic view over the city. The hotel also has a bar/lounge, coffee shop, disco, and garage.

Los Arcos. Paseo de Ezequiel González, 26, 40002 Segovia. ☎ **800/528-1234** in the U.S., or 921-43-74-62. Fax 921-42-81-61. 59 units. A/C MINIBAR TV TEL. 15,500 ptas. (US$93) double. AE, DC, MC, V. Parking 1,000 ptas. (US$6).

This concrete-and-glass five-story structure opened in 1987 and is generally cited as the best in town, although you may prefer Los Linajes instead (see above). Well run and modern, it attracts the business traveler, although tourists frequent the place in droves as well. Rooms are generally spacious but furnished in a standard international bland way, except for the beautiful rug-dotted parquet floors. Built-in furnishings and tiny bathrooms are part of the offering, along with private safes. Rooms are well kept, although some furnishings look worn.

Even if you don't stay here, consider dining at the hotel's La Cocina de Segovia, which is the only hotel dining room that competes successfully with Mesón de Cándido (see below). As at the nearby competitors, roast suckling pig and roast Segovia lamb—perfectly cooked in specially made ovens—are the specialties. There's also a tavernlike cafe and bar. In all, it's a smart, efficiently run, and pleasant choice, if not a terribly exciting one.

INEXPENSIVE

Las Sirenas. Juan Bravo, 30, 40001 Segovia. ☎ **921-46-26-63.** Fax 921-46-26-57. 39 units. A/C TV TEL. 8,500 ptas. (US$51) double. AE, DC, MC, V.

Standing on the most charming old plaza in Segovia, opposite the Church of St. Martín, this hotel was built around 1950, and has been renovated several times. However, it has long since lost its Franco-era supremacy to Los Arcos (see above). It is modest and well maintained, and decorated in a conservative style. Each bedroom is filled with functional, simple furniture. Breakfast is the only meal served, but the staff at the reception desk can direct clients to cafes and tascas nearby.

WHERE TO DINE

El Bernardino. Cervantes, 2. ☎ **921-46-24-74.** Reservations recommended. Main courses 1,400–2,500 ptas. (US$8.40–US$15); fixed-price menu 2,800 ptas. (US$16.80). AE, DC, MC, V. Daily 1–4pm and 8:30–11pm. CASTILIAN.

El Bernardino, a 3-minute walk west of the Roman aqueduct, is built like an old tavern. Lanterns hang from beamed ceilings, and the view over the red-tile rooftops of the city is delightful. The *menú del día* might include a huge paella, roast veal with potatoes, flan or ice cream, plus bread and wine. You might begin your meal with *sopa castellana* (made with ham, sausage, bread, egg, and garlic). The roast dishes are exceptional here, including roast suckling pig, from a special oven, and roast baby lamb. You can also order grilled rib steak or stewed partridge.

José María. Cronista Lecea, 11. ☎ **921-46-11-11.** Reservations recommended. Main courses 1,500–2,500 ptas. (US$9–US$15); fixed-price menu 4,000–6,000 ptas. (US$24–US$36). AE, DC, MC, V. Daily 1–4pm and 8–11:30pm. SEGOVIAN.

This centrally located bar and restaurant, 1 block east of the Plaza Mayor, serves quality regional cuisine in a rustic stucco-and-brick dining room. Before dinner, locals crowd in for tapas at the bar, then move into the dining room for such Castilian specialties as roast suckling pig, rural-style conger eel, and freshly caught sea bream. Try the cream of crabmeat soup, roasted peppers, salmon with scrambled eggs, house-style hake, or grilled veal steak. For dessert, a specialty is ice cream tart with a whisky sauce.

✪ **Mesón de Cándido.** Plaza del Azoguejo, 5. ☎ **921-42-59-11.** Reservations recommended. Main courses 2,000–4,000 ptas. (US$12–US$24); fixed-price menu 3,500 ptas. (US$21). AE, DC, MC, V. Daily 12:30–4:30pm and 8–midnight. CASTILIAN.

For years this beautiful old Spanish inn, standing on the eastern edge of the old town, has maintained a monopoly on the tourist trade. Apart from the hotel restaurants—specifically La Cocina de Segovia at the Los Arcos—it is the town's finest dining choice. The Cándido family took it over in 1905, and fourth- and fifth-generation family members still run the place, having fed, over the years, everybody from Hemingway to Nixon. The oldest part of the restaurant dates from 1822, and the place has gradually been enlarged since then. The proprietor of the House of Cándido is known as *mesonero mayor de Castilla* (the major innkeeper of Castile). He's been decorated with more medals and honors than paella has grains of rice. The restaurant's popularity can be judged by the crowds of hungry diners who fill every seat in the six dining rooms. The à la carte menu includes those two regional staples: *cordero asado* (roast baby lamb) and *cochinillo asado* (roast suckling pig). Some of the seating areas are cramped and confining. Opt for a table on the second floor, facing the Aqueduct, or else one of the outdoor cafe tables in front.

Mesón Duque. calle Cervantes, 12. ☎ **921-46-24-87.** Reservations recommended. Main courses 850–2,500 ptas. (US$5.10–US$15). AE, DC, MC, V. Daily 12:30–5pm and 8–11:30pm. CASTILIAN.

Set on the street that links Segovia's ancient Roman aqueduct with the city's medieval core, this restaurant was established in 1895, and has fed many successive generations of local residents ever since. The severely dignified interior looks almost unchanged since it was built. The decor includes heavy ceiling beams, exposed stone, rough-textured plaster, and battered 19th-century artifacts from long-ago farms. Come here for the kind of cuisine that was in vogue when the restaurant was built, with very few concessions to modern cuisine. There's an excellent version of cream of crabmeat soup; roasted suckling pig slow-cooked on a spit; savory roasted lamb with aromatic rosemary, thyme, and garlic; and different preparations of grilled chicken, veal, beef, and pork. An excellent accompaniment for any of these might include kidney beans cooked with chunks of salted cod, fresh spinach, and mounds of mashed potatoes or rice.

AN EASY EXCURSION TO LA GRANJA

To reach La Granja, 7 miles (11km) southeast of Segovia, you can take a 20-minute bus ride from the center of the city. Six to ten buses a day leave from Paseo Conde de Sepulveda at Avenida Fernández Ladreda. A one-way fare costs 105 pesetas (US65¢). For information, call ☎ **921-42-77-25.**

✪ **Palacio Real de La Granja.** Plaza de España, 17, San Ildefonso (Segovia). ☎ **921-47-00-19.** Admission 650 ptas. (US$3.90) adults, 250 ptas. (US$1.50) children 5–14, free for children 4 and under. Apr–May, Mon–Fri 10am–1:30pm and 3–5pm, Sat–Sun 10am–6pm; June–Sept, daily 10am–6pm; Oct–Mar, Mon–Sat 10am–1:30pm and 3–5pm, Sun 10am–2pm.

San Ildefonso de la Granja was the summer palace of the Bourbon kings of Spain, who replicated the grandeur of Versailles in the province of Segovia. Set against the snow-capped Sierra de Guadarrama, the slate-roofed palace dominates the village that grew up around it (which, these days, is a summer resort).

The founder of La Granja was Philip V, grandson of Louis XIV and the first Bourbon king of Spain (his body, along with that of his second queen, Isabel de Fernesio, is interred in a mausoleum in the Collegiate Church). Philip V was born at Versailles on December 19, 1683, which may explain why he wanted to re-create that atmosphere at Segovia.

Before the palace was built in the early 18th century, a farm stood here—hence the totally incongruous name *la granja,* meaning "the farm" in Spanish. Inside you'll find valuable antiques (many in the Empire style), paintings, and a remarkable collection of tapestries based on Goya cartoons from the Royal Factory in Madrid.

Most visitors, however, seem to find a stroll through the gardens more pleasing, so allow adequate time for that. The fountain statuary is a riot of cavorting gods and nymphs, hiding indiscretions behind jets of water. The gardens are studded with chestnuts and elms. A spectacular display takes place when the water jets are turned on.

SEGOVIA AFTER DARK

Some of the most spontaneous good times can be created around the Plaza Mayor, Plaza Azagejo, and the busy calle del Carmen that runs into the Plaza Azagejo. Each of those sites contains a scattering of simple bars and cafes that grow more crowded at night as the days grow hotter. If you want to go dancing, two of the most popular discos are **Mansion,** calle de Juan Bravo (no phone), which is open nightly from 11pm till dawn for dancing, drinking, and flirting with the 20- to 30-year-old crowd; and its somewhat more stylish competitor, **Bar Ginasio,** Paseo del Salon (no phone), which is open nightly from 8pm till dawn, a bit more atmospheric and frequented by persons from ages 25 to around 50.

Seville 8

Sometimes a city becomes famous simply for its beauty and romance. Seville (called Sevilla in Spain), the capital of Andalusia, is such a place. In spite of its sultry heat in summer and its many problems, such as rising unemployment and street crime, it remains one of the most charming Spanish cities.

Don Juan and Carmen—aided by Mozart and Bizet—have given Seville a romantic reputation. Because of the acclaim of *Don Giovanni* and *Carmen,* not to mention *The Barber of Seville,* debunkers have risen to challenge this reputation. But if a visitor can see only two Spanish cities in a lifetime, they should be Seville and Toledo.

All the images associated with Andalusia—orange trees, mantillas, lovesick toreros, flower-filled patios, and castanet-rattling gypsies— come to life in Seville. But it's not just a tourist city; it's a substantial river port, and it contains some of the most important artistic works and architectural monuments in Spain.

Unlike most Spanish cities, Seville has fared rather well under most of its conquerors—the Romans, Arabs, and Christians. Pedro the Cruel and Ferdinand and Isabella held court here. When Spain entered its 16th-century golden age, Seville funneled gold from the New World into the rest of the country and Columbus docked here after his journey to America.

Be warned, however, that driving here is a nightmare: Seville was planned for the horse and buggy rather than for the car, and nearly all the streets run one way toward the Guadalquivir River. Locating a hard-to-find restaurant or a hidden little square will require patience and luck.

1 Orientation

GETTING THERE
BY PLANE Iberia (☎ **800/772-4642** in the U.S. or 902/400-500 toll free in Spain) flies several times a day between Madrid (and elsewhere via Madrid) and Seville's Aeropuerto San Pablo, calle Almirante Lobo (☎ **95-44-90-23**). It also flies several times a week to and from Alicante, Grand Canary Island, Lisbon, Barcelona, Palma de Majorca, Tenerife, Santiago de Compostela, and (once a week) Zaragoza. The airport lies about 6 miles (9.6km) from the center of the city, along the highway leading to Carmona.

BY TRAIN   Train service into Seville is now centralized into the Estación Santa Justa, Avenida Kansas City, s/n (☎ **95-454-02-02** for information and reservations, or 95-454-03-03 for information). Buses C1 and C2 take you from this train station to the bus station at Prado de San Sebastián, and bus EA runs to and from the airport. The high-speed AVE train has reduced travel time from Madrid to Seville to 2½ hours. The train makes 17 trips daily, with a stop in Córdoba. Sixteen trains a day connect Seville and Córdoba; the AVE train takes 45 minutes and a TALGO takes 1½ hours. Three trains a day run to Málaga, taking 3 hours; there are also three trains per day to Granada (4 hours).

BY BUS   Although Seville confusingly has several satellite bus stations servicing small towns and nearby villages of Andalusia, most buses arrive and depart from the city's largest bus terminal, on the southeast edge of the old city, at Prado de San Sebastián, calle José María Osborne, 11 (☎ **95-441-71-11**). Several different companies make frequent runs to and from Córdoba (2½ hours), Málaga (3½ hours), Granada (4 hours), and Madrid (8 hours). For information and ticket prices, call Alsina Graells at ☎ **95-441-88-11.** A newer bus station is at Plaza de Armas (☎ **95-490-80-40**), but it usually services destinations beyond Andalusia, including Portugal.

BY CAR   Seville lies 341 miles (540km) southwest of Madrid and 135 miles (217km) northwest of Malága. Several major highways converge on Seville, connecting it with the rest of Spain and Portugal. During periods of heavy holiday traffic, the N-V (E-90) from Madrid through Extremadura—which, at Mérida, connects with the southbound N630 (E-803)—is usually less congested than the N-IV (E-5) through eastern Andalusia.

VISITOR INFORMATION

The tourist office, **Oficina de Información del Turismo,** at Avenida de la Constitución, 21B (☎ **95-422-14-04**), is open Monday to Saturday 9am to 7pm, Sunday and holidays 10am to 2pm.

CITY LAYOUT

The heart of Seville lies along the east bank of the Guadalquivir River. This **old town,** or *centro histórico,* is a fairly compact area and can be explored on foot—the only real way to see it. Once this part of Seville was enclosed by walls. Today nearly all the sights lie between two of the major bridges of Seville: the Puente de San Telmo, to the south, and the Puente de Isabel II (also known as the Puente de Triana), an Eiffel Tower-like structure from the mid-1800s. Near Puente de San Telmo are such sights as the Torre del Oro, the University of Seville, and the Parque de María Luisa. Near the Puente de Isabel II are the Maestranza bullring, the major shopping streets, and the Museo de Bellas Artes. In the middle of the centro histórico rises the cathedral and its adjoining Giralda tower, the Alcázar, and the colorful streets of the old Jewish quarter, the Barrio de Santa Cruz.

MAIN STREETS, SQUARES & ARTERIES   The old **Paseo de Colón** is that part of Seville's historic core that opens onto the Guadalquivir River. Any number of streets, including Santander, lead to **Avenida de la Constitución,** where you'll find the major attractions of Seville, including the Alcázar and the cathedral. To the east of both the Alcázar and the cathedral lies the Barrio de Santa Cruz. Major historic squares include Plaza Nueva, Plaza de El Salvador, Plaza de Jerez, and Plaza de Triunfo. From Plaza del Duque, the Museo de Bellas Artes is reached by heading west toward the river along calle Alfonso XII. The best place to start your exploration of Seville is Plaza Virgen de los Reyes. From here many of the major attractions, including the Giralda, the Patio de los Naranjos, and the Archivo de Indias, are all close at hand. Directly south of the plaza is the Alcázar—the whole area, in fact, is historic Seville in a nutshell.

FINDING AN ADDRESS   Most of Seville's streets run one way, usually toward the Guadalquivir River. Individual buildings are numbered with odd addresses on one side of the street and even numbers on the opposite side, so no. 14 would likely fall opposite no. 13 and 15. Many addresses are marked *s/n*, which means the building has no number (*sin número*). When this occurs, be sure to obtain the name of a cross street as a reference point.

MAPS   Arm yourself with a detailed street map, not the general overview often handed out free at tourist offices. Even if you're in Seville for only a day or two, you'll still need a detailed street map to find such attractions as the Museo de Bellas Artes. The best street maps of Seville are those published by **Euro City,** available at local newsstands and in bookstores. These maps contain not only a detailed street index, but also provide tourist information, places of interest, and even locations of vital SOS services (such as the police station) on the map. Regrettably, no one seems to have come up with an adequate map to get you through the intricate maze of the Barrio de Santa Cruz, so you can more or less count on getting lost there. There is, however, a sketch map provided by the tourist office to help get you around the area.

Neighborhoods in Brief

CENTRO HISTÓRICO   This is the heart of historic Seville, with its most imposing sights, of which the massive cathedral is the dominant attraction. This is the area where you'll want to spend the most time, and it's also where you'll find the finest hotels and restaurants.

BARRIO DE SANTA CRUZ   This is an area of wrought-iron *cancelas* (gates), courtyards with Andalusian tiled fountains, art galleries, restaurants, cafes, tabernas, flowerpots of geraniums, and winding narrow alleyways. The former ghetto of Seville's Jews, it's today named after a Christian saint, and is the single most colorful part of the city for exploring, which is best done during the day (at night, muggings might be a danger). Filled with interesting sights, such as Casa Murillo and some fascinating churches, it's one of the architectural highlights of Andalusia.

LA MACARENA   Thought to be named for a Roman, Macarios, and the site of his former estate, this is a famous quarter of Seville that seems sadly neglected by visitors, who spend most of their time in the two quarters discussed above. The name also describes a popular rumba. It's filled with interesting attractions such as the Convento de Santa Inés (reached along calle María Coronel). According to legend, King Pedro the Cruel was so taken with Inés's beauty that he pursued her constantly—until she poured boiling oil over her face to disfigure herself.

TRIANA & EL ARENAL   These two districts were immortalized by Cervantes, Quevedo, and Lope de Vega, the fabled writers of Spain's golden age. They were the rough-and-tough seafaring quarters when Seville was a thriving port in the 1600s. In El Arenal, the 12-sided Torre del Oro, or "gold tower," built by the Almohads in 1220, overlooks the river on Paseo Cristobal Colón. You can take the riverside esplanade, Marqués de Contadero, which stretches along the banks of the river from the tower. The Museo Provincial de Bellas Artes is also found here, containing Spain's best collection of Seville's painters, notably Murillo. Across the river, Triana was once the gypsy quarter but has now been gentrified.

2 Getting Around

BY BUS

You can actually walk most everywhere in Seville, although there are buses, used mainly for visiting the environs, which have little interest for tourists. If you use a bus for getting around the city, you'll find that most lines converge at Plaza de la Encarnación, Plaza Nueva, or in front of the cathedral on Avenida de la Constitución. Bus service is daily from 6am to 11:15pm. The city tourist office will provide a booklet outlining bus routes. You can purchase a 10-trip bonobús to save money. The best buses for circling through the center of town include C1 and C2 (*circulares interiores*).

BY TAXI

This is quite a viable means of getting around, especially at night, when streets are dangerous because of frequent muggings. Call **Tele Taxi** (☎ **95-462-22-22**) or **Radio Taxi** (☎ **95-458-00-00**). Cabs are metered and charge 52 pesetas (US30¢) per kilometer.

BY CAR

Chances are you arranged to rent a car before you got to Seville (rates are lower that way). However, if you didn't, you'll find offices of Avis and Hertz at the airport as well as in the city: **Avis** maintains offices at the airport (☎ **95-444-91-21**), and at the train station (☎ **95-453-78-61**). **Hertz** has three Seville offices: at the airport (☎ **95-451-47-20**), at Vía Santa Justa near the train station (☎ **95-442-61-56**), and in the city at Luis Montato, 63 (☎ **95-457-00-55**).

BY BICYCLE

Although Seville is intensely hot in summer, bike rentals are possible, even though spring and autumn are better times—at least cooler—for cycling around. Rentals are available at **El Ciclismo,** Paseo Catalina de Ribera, 2 (☎ **95-441-19-59**), in Puerta de la Carne, at the northern end of the Jardines de Murillo. It's open Monday to Friday 10am to 1:30pm and 5 to 8pm, Saturday 10am to 1:30pm.

Fast Facts: Seville

American Express The American Express office in Seville is in the Hotel Inglaterra, Plaza Nueva, 7 (☎ **95-421-16-17**). Hours are Monday to Friday 9:30am to 1:30pm and 4:30 to 7:30pm, Saturday 10am to 1pm.

Business Hours Most banks in Seville are open Monday to Friday 9am to 2pm and on Saturday 9am to noon. (Always conceal your money before walking out of a bank in Seville.) Shops are generally open Monday to Saturday 9:30am to 1:30pm and 4:30 to 8pm. Most department stores are open Monday to Saturday 10am to 8pm.

Bus Information The Central Bus Station, Prado de San Sebastián, calle José María Osborne, 11 (☎ **95-441-71-11**), is the place to go for bus information, or you can call daily 7am to 9pm.

Consulates The **U.S. Consulate** is at Paseo de las Delicias, 7 (☎ **95-423-18-85**), open Monday to Friday 10am to 1pm and 2 to 4:30pm. The **United Kingdom Consulate** is at Plaza Nueva, 8 (☎ **95-422-88-75**), open Monday to Friday 8am to 3pm.

Hospital   For medical emergencies, go to the Hospital Universitario y Provincial, Avenida Doctor Fedriani, s/n (☎ 95-455-74-00).

Internet Access   Try the **Cibercenter** at Calle Julio Cesar, 8 (☎ 954-22-88-99), off Calle Reyes Católicos. It is open daily 9am to 9pm.

Laundry   Lavandería Roma, calle Sánchez Bedoya, 18 (☎ 95-421-05-35), is open Monday to Friday 10am to 2pm and 5 to 8pm, Saturday 10am to 2pm.

Police   The police station is located on Paseo de las Delicias (☎ 95-461-54-50).

Post Office   The post office is at Avenida de la Constitución, 32 (☎ 95-421-64-76). It's open Monday to Friday 8:30am to 8:30pm, Saturday 9:30am to 2pm.

Safety   With massive unemployment, the city has been hit by a crime wave in recent years. María Luisa Park is especially dangerous, as is the highway leading to Jerez de la Frontera and Cádiz. Dangling cameras and purses are especially vulnerable. Don't leave cars unguarded with your luggage inside. Regrettably, some daring attacks are made—as they are in U.S. cities—when passengers stop for traffic signals.

Taxis   See "Getting Around," earlier in this section.

Telephone & Telex   The telephone office is at calle Sierpes, 11 (for telephone service information, call ☎ 003). To send wires by phone, call ☎ 95-422-20-00.

3 Where to Stay

During Holy Week and the Seville Fair, hotels often double, even triple, their rates. Price increases are often not announced until the last minute. If you're going to be in Seville at these times, arrive with an ironclad reservation and an agreement about the price before checking in.

VERY EXPENSIVE

✪ **Hotel Alfonso XIII.** San Fernando, 2, 41004 Sevilla. ☎ **800/221-2340** in the U.S. and Canada, or 95-422-28-50. Fax 95-421-60-33. www.luxurycollection.com/alfonsoxiii. 146 units. A/C MINIBAR TV TEL. 48,000–64,000 ptas. (US$288–US$384) double; 90,000–115,000 ptas. (US$540–US$690) suite. AE, DC, MC, V. Parking 2,750 ptas. (US$16.50).

Set at the southwestern corner of the gardens that front Seville's famous Alcázar, in the historic heart of town, this five-story rococo building is one of the three or four most legendary hotels in Spain. As such, it is obviously the premier address in Seville. Built as an aristocratic shelter for patrons of the Iberoamerican Exposition of 1929 and named after the then-king of Spain, it reigns as a super-ornate and super-expensive bastion of glamour. Constructed in the Mudéjar/Andalusian-revival style, it contains hallways that glitter with hand-painted tiles, acres of marble and mahogany, antique furniture embellished with intricately embossed leather, and a spaciousness nothing short of majestic.

Dining/Diversions: The **San Fernando** restaurant offers Italian and continental cuisine. A lobby bar features midday coffee amid potted palms and memorials to another age, its blue, white, and yellow tiles reflecting the colors of Seville.

Amenities: 24-hour room service, laundry/valet, concierge, car rentals with or without drivers, baby-sitting, spectacular garden, outdoor pool, tennis courts, shops, arcade-enclosed courtyard with potted flowers and splashing fountain.

Hotel Tryp Colón. Canalejas, 1, 41001 Sevilla. ☎ **800/387-8842** in the U.S., or 95-422-29-00. Fax 95-422-09-38. www.tryp.es. E-mail: colon@trynet.com. 228 units. A/C MINIBAR TV TEL. 36,300-50,820 ptas. (US$217.80–US$304.90) double; 81,600-124,100 ptas. (US$489.60–US$744.60) suite. Rates include breakfast. AE, DC, MC, V. Parking 2,400 ptas. (US$14.40).

Set about a quarter mile northwest of the Giralda and about 2 blocks southeast of the Fine Arts Museum (*Museo Provincial de Bellas Artes*), this hotel is Seville's closest rival in prestige and architectural allure to the legendary Alfonso XIII. Originally built around the turn of the century and overhauled in 1988, it retains such features as a massive stained-glass dome stretching over the lobby, baronial staircases, formal service, and all the niceties of an expensive hotel. The guest rooms, all with private bathrooms, are conservative and traditional, although some are in need of an overhaul.

Dining/Diversions: El **Burladero** restaurant serves lunches and dinners (see "Where to Dine," below). There's also a bar that seems to be favored by visiting bullfighters, journalists, and politicians.

Amenities: 24-hour room service, concierge, baby-sitting, laundry/valet, sauna, car-rental facilities, shopping boutiques.

EXPENSIVE

Al-Andalus Palace. Avenida Palmera, s/n, 43012 Sevilla. ☎ **95-423-66-15.** Fax 95-423-02-00. 328 units. A/C MINIBAR TV TEL. 35,375 ptas. (US$212.25) double; 45,000 ptas. (US$270) suite. AE, DC, MC, V. Parking 1,200 ptas. (US$7.20). Bus: 34.

No hotel in Seville has a more avant-garde modern design than this four-star choice lying 5 minutes from the center in the Heliopolis district, an upscale residential area. Front public rooms are suspended by cable, and the glass facade reflects both the blue skies of Seville and the marble floors. Bedrooms are large and elegantly appointed, and brightly lit because of their large windows. They are well equipped with excellent mattresses, and some have balconies overlooking the hotel swimming pool. Decor and furnishings are in a minimalist style—functional but modern with neutral, muted color schemes. Many accommodations have small living rooms and suites with their own breakfast bars. Bathrooms are finished in marble and have large tubs and mirrors; the suites also contain a hydromassage.

Dining/Diversions: The top rated El **Patgio** has an international à la carte menu. A buffet restaurant called **Guadalquivir** is also on site, as is a chic cocktail bar, **Pigalle.**

Amenities: Swimming pool and garden, gym, sauna, massage, steam baths, tennis courts, 24-hour room service, laundry, facilities for persons with disabilities, and golf course nearby.

✪ **Bécquer.** Calle Reyes Católicos, 4, 41001 Sevilla. ☎ **95-422-89-00.** Fax 95-421-44-00. www.hotel-becquer.com. E-mail: becquer@hotelbecquer.com. 118 units. A/C TV TEL. 23,000 ptas. (US$138) double. AE, DC, MC, V. Parking 1,600 ptas. (US$9.60). Bus: 21, 24, 30, or 31.

A short walk from the action of the Seville bullring (Maestranza) and only 2 blocks from the river, Bécquer lies on a street of cafes where you can order tapas and drink Andalusian wine. The Museo Provincial de Bellas Artes is also nearby. Built in the 1970s, the hotel was enlarged and much renovated in the late 1980s. It occupies the site of a mansion and retains many objets d'art rescued before the building was demolished. Guests register in a wood-paneled lobby before being shown to one of the bedrooms, which are functionally furnished, well kept, and reasonably comfortable—in all, a good value in a pricey city. All units have private bathrooms.

Dining/Diversions: Only breakfast is served, but you'll find a bar and lounge.

Amenities: Laundry, concierge, room service, baby-sitting.

✪ **Casa Imperial.** Calle Imperial, 29, 41003 Sevilla. ☎ **954-50-03-00.** Fax 954-50-03-30. www.casaimperial.com. E-mail: info@casaimperial.com. 24 units. A/C MINIBAR TV TEL. 30,781 ptas. (US$184.70) double; 36,650 ptas. (US$219.90) suite. Rates include breakfast buffet. Free parking.

Seville Accommodations

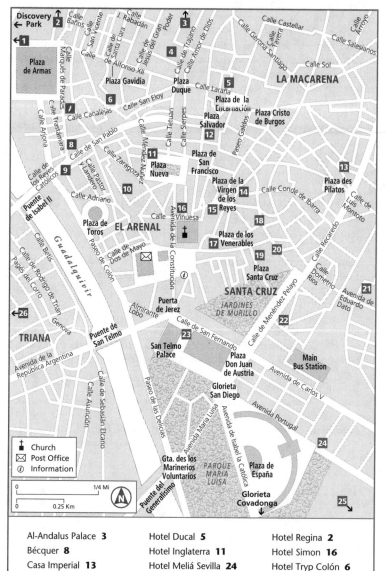

Al-Andalus Palace **3**
Bécquer **8**
Casa Imperial **13**
Grand Hotel Barcelo **1**
Hacienda Benazuza **25**
Hostal Goya **17**
Hotel Alcázar **22**
Hotel Alfonso XIII **23**
Hotel América **4**
Hotel Doña María **15**

Hotel Ducal **5**
Hotel Inglaterra **11**
Hotel Meliá Sevilla **24**
Hotel Murillo **19**
Hotel Occidental
  Porta Coeli **21**
Hotel Monte Triana **26**
Hotel Los Seises **14**
Hotel Plaza de Armas **7**
Hotel la Rabida **10**

Hotel Regina **2**
Hotel Simon **16**
Hotel Tryp Colón **6**
La Casa de la
  Juderia **20**
Las Casas de los
  Mercaderes **12**
Puerta de Triana **9**
Residencia
  Fernando III **18**

In the historic center of Seville, this hotel is one of charm and grace. Launched in the mid-90s, the casa stands near Casa Pilatos, and dates from the 15th century, when it was the home of the butler to the Marquis of Tarifa. The interior is refined and elegant, and there are four Andalusian patios, adorned with exotic plants and a tasteful decor. The beamed ceilings are from the original construction, and sparkling chandeliers hang from the ceilings. The bedrooms are large—many have small kitchens, plus ample terraces and private baths. The bathrooms are tastefully decorated with luxurious tubs, some of which are antiques.

Dining/Diversions: There's a passable restaurant serving international food, plus a cozy bar.

Amenities: 24-hour room service, laundry, concierge, free access to a nearby health club with a swimming pool.

Grand Hotel Barcelo. Isla de la Cartuja, 41018 Sevilla. ☎ **95-446-22-22.** Fax 95-446-04-28. 295 units. A/C MINIBAR TV TEL. 14,500–18,500 ptas. (US$87–US$111) double; 45,000–55,000 ptas. (US$270–US$330) suite. AE, DC, MC, V. Parking 1,500 ptas. (US$9).

This hotel was built expressly to house the surge of visitors at the Seville Expo of 1992. The only hotel located on the former site of Expo itself, facing the Guadalquivir River, it lies a 5-minute taxi ride from the center of Seville. The location seems a bit isolated and sad now that the excitement of Expo is long gone; the hotel is often underbooked. It was designed in three hypermodern ring-shaped modules, each four stories tall and all interconnected by passageways leading to the public rooms. Designated as a five-star luxury hotel, this hotel was reserved during Expo for visiting dignitaries and heads of state. Its designers intended its perpetual use, at the end of the party, as one of the city's most visible hotels—sort of a modern-day counterpart to the Alfonso XIII (which was designed for use by dignitaries during Seville's International Exposition of 1929).

Dining/Diversions: The **Restaurante Colón** serves gourmet versions of regional cuisine. A lobby bar and the **Cartura Bar** offer soothing libations, sometimes to live piano music.

Amenities: 24-hour room service, concierge, laundry/valet, limousine pickups, baby-sitting, business center, conference facilities, outdoor swimming pool, in-house florist, shops, currency exchange, car rentals, multilingual TV channels, health club with sauna, massage, gymnasium, squash courts.

✪ Hotel Inglaterra. Plaza Nueva, 7, 41001 Sevilla. ☎ **95-422-49-70.** Fax 95-456-13-36. 116 units. A/C TV TEL. Jan–Mar and May–Dec, 19,000–22,000 ptas. (US$114–US$132) double; Apr, 23,000–25,000 ptas. (US$138–US$150) double. AE, DC, MC, V. Parking 1,500 ptas. (US$9).

Established in 1857 and since modernized into a comfortably glossy seven-story contemporary design, this eminently respectable and rather staid hotel lies a 5-minute walk southwest of the cathedral, occupying one entire side of a palm-fringed plaza. Much of its interior is sheathed with acres of white or gray marble, and the furnishings include ample use of Spanish leather and floral-patterned fabrics. Despite their modernity, the bedrooms nonetheless evoke old-fashioned touches of Iberian gentility. The best rooms are on the fifth floor.

Dining/Diversions: One floor above street level, overlooking the mosaic pavements of Plaza Nueva, the hotel's sunny restaurant serves well-prepared fixed-price meals from a frequently changing international menu. There's also an in-house cocktail lounge favored by local businesspeople.

Amenities: 24-hour room service, laundry/valet service, concierge, baby-sitting, car-rental facilities.

ⓗ   Family-Friendly Hotels

Hotel Doña María *(see p. 250)*   Located behind the cathedral and the Giralda, this is one of the most gracious hotels in the old quarter of Seville. The garden courtyard and the rooftop pool delight adults and children alike. Rooms contain wide beds and bathrooms with dual sinks, and some rooms are large enough for the entire family.

Hotel Meliá Sevilla *(see p. 249)*   On the outskirts of town, this 11-story structure offers many facilities appreciated by families, including a pool, fitness center, squash court, and parking garage. Families enjoy dining on a terrace alfresco, and there's also a snack bar on the grounds. Housekeeping in the guest rooms is good.

Residencia y Restaurante Fernando III *(see p. 253)*   This hotel lies in the medieval Barrio de Santa Cruz, the old Jewish quarter. The helpful and polite staff speak English and are welcoming to families, offering some guest rooms large enough to accommodate those traveling with children.

✪ **Hotel Meliá Sevilla.** Doctor Pedro de Castro, 1, 41004 Sevilla. ☎ **800/336-3542** in the U.S., or 95-442-15-11. Fax 95-442-16-08. www.solmelia.com. 366 units. A/C MINIBAR TV TEL. 24,900 ptas. (US$149.40) double; from 43,000 ptas. (US$258) suite. AE, DC, MC, V. Parking 1,700 ptas. (US$10.20).

Located a short walk east of the Plaza de España, near the Parque María Luisa, this is the most elegant, tasteful, and international of the modern skyscraper hotels of Seville. It opened in 1987, rising 11 floors. It incorporates acres of white marble as well as several dozen shopping boutiques and private apartments into its L-shaped floor plan. Bedroom decor is contemporary and comfortable, and each unit offers a private bathroom, though rooms in the back lack a view. The Meliá was a favorite of the planners of the massive Expo, which transformed the face of both Seville and Andalusia. The hotel lacks the personal touch provided by the staff at Alfonso XIII, but its rooms are superior to those at the Inglaterra.

Dining/Diversions: The **Giralda Restaurant** serves three-course fixed-price lunches and dinners. There's also a large and stylish piano bar, **Corona,** plus an informal coffee shop, **Las Salinas.**

Amenities: 24-hour room service, laundry, baby-sitting, business center, car rentals, outdoor swimming pool with a section reserved for children, sauna, arcade of shops and boutiques, several flowering outdoor terraces.

Hotel Occidental Porta Coeli. Eduardo Dato, 49, 41018 Sevilla. ☎ **954-53-35-00.** Fax 954-53-2342. E-mail: reservas-portacoeli@occidental-hoteles.com. 244 units. A/C MINIBAR TV TEL. 25,000 ptas. (US$150) double; 45,000 ptas. (US$270) suite. AE, DC, MC, V. Parking 1,500 ptas. (US$9). Bus: 2 or 3.

Don't come here to recapture the romance and legend of old Seville. In fact, the facade of this modern hotel, a 10-minute walk from the city center, is so impersonal and bland you might think you've landed in Iran. But once inside, you'll find grand comfort and even style. In business since the mid-80s, the hotel was last renovated in 1999. A courteous and efficient staff welcome you to an interior that is both inviting and avant-garde. The spacious rooms are furnished in a medley of classical and contemporary and most open onto balconies. Bathrooms are state of the art, with such conveniences as hair dryers.

Dining/Diversions: The **Florencia Restaurant,** the hotel's most formal choice, always hires top chefs and offers an international menu but also emphasizes regional specialties. There's also an English style pub, **Farnecio,** plus a cafeteria.

Amenities: Indoor swimming pool, patio garden for sunbathing, 24-hour room service, laundry, concierge, guided tours arranged.

Las Casas del Rey de Baeza. Calle Santiago, Plaza Jesus de la Redencion, 2, 41003 Sevilla. ☎ **95-456-14-96.** Fax 95-456-14-41. http://lascasas.zoom.es. E-mail: baeza@zoom.es. 44 units. A/C MINIBAR TV TEL. 20,000 ptas. (US$120) double; 23,000 ptas. (US$138) suite. AE, DC, MC, V. Parking 2,000 ptas. (US$12).

Less luxurious than its sibling, La Casa de la Judería, this antique hotel is still a winning choice. With its stone floors and 19th-century Andalusian architecture, it's close to the Casa de Pilatos. A hotel since 1998, it has an interior patio surrounded by a cozy coterie of rooms and a long Andalusian balcony. Some of the beautifully furnished bedrooms have living rooms, and the decor is finely honed in marble and wood with comfortable furnishings. Bathrooms contain the usual amenities such as excellent plumbing along with such features as hair dryers.

Amenities: Breakfast is the only meal served, but amenities include a concierge, room service, and laundry.

✪ Taverna del Alabardero. Zaragoza, 20, 41001 Sevilla. ☎ **95-456-06-37.** Fax 95-456-36-66. www.esh.es. E-mail: hotel.alabardero@esh.es. 7 units. A/C MINIBAR TV TEL. 19,800 ptas. (US$118.80) double; 28,000 ptas. (US$168) suite. Rates include continental breakfast. AE, DC, MC, V. Parking 2,000 ptas. (US$12).

This tavern not only houses one of the two best restaurants in Seville, but is perhaps the single most charming place to stay in the city. Close to the bullring and a 5-minute walk from the cathedral, this is a restored 19th-century mansion. There is a spectacular central patio, and, in all, a romantic atmosphere prevails. The units on the third floor have balconies overlooking street scenes as well as whirlpool baths. All the bedrooms are spacious and comfortable, each individually decorated in a specific regional style. Bathrooms are well appointed and contain such amenities as hair dryers.

Dining/Diversions: The second-floor restaurant is reviewed below. On warm days, guests can relax on the patio or terrace, ordering drinks or desserts.

Amenities: 24-hour room service, laundry, concierge.

MODERATE

Hotel Alcázar. Menéndez y Pelayo, 10, 41004 Sevilla. ☎ **95-441-20-11.** Fax 95-442-16-59. 100 units. A/C TV TEL. 13,500–17,000 ptas. (US$81–US$102) double. Rates include breakfast. AE, DC, MC, V. Parking 1,500 ptas. (US$9).

On the wide and busy Boulevard Menéndez y Pelayo, across from the Jardines de Alcázon, this pleasantly contemporary hotel is sheltered behind a facade of brown brick. Built in 1964, the hotel was last renovated in 1991. Slabs of striated gray marble cool the reception area in the lobby, next to which you'll find a Spanish restaurant and bar. Above, three latticed structures resemble a trio of *miradores*. The medium-size guest rooms have functional modern furniture and private bathrooms.

Hotel Doña María. Don Remondo, 19, 41004 Sevilla. ☎ **95-422-49-90.** Fax 95-421-95-46. 69 units. A/C TV TEL. Jan–Feb and July–Aug 14,000 ptas. (US$84) double; Mar–June and Sept–Dec 20,000–28,000 ptas. (US$120–US$168) double. AE, DC, MC, V. Parking 2,000 ptas. (US$12).

Staying at this four-star, four-story hotel is a worthwhile investment, partly because of the tasteful Iberian antiques in the stone lobby and upper hallways. Also, its location a few steps from the cathedral creates a dramatic view from the Doña María's rooftop terrace. An ornate neoclassical entryway is offset with a pure white facade and iron balconies, which hint at the building's origin in the 1840s as a private villa. Amid the flowering plants on the upper floor, you'll find a swimming pool ringed with garden-style lattices and antique wrought-iron railings. Each of the one-of-a-kind rooms offers a private bathroom and is well furnished and comfortable, although some are rather small. A few have four-poster beds, others a handful of antique reproductions. Light sleepers might find the noise of the church bells jarring. Breakfast is the only meal served.

Hotel Los Seises. Calle Segovias, 6, 41004 Sevilla. ☎ **954-22-94-95.** Fax 954-22-43-34. www.sol.com/hotel-los-seises. E-mail: seises@jet.es. 42 units. A/C MINIBAR TV TEL. 18,000 ptas. (US$108) double. AE, DC, MC, V. Parking 2,200 ptas. (US$13.20).

Immediately behind the cathedral in the old Jewish quarter of Santa Cruz, this three-story hotel opened in 1992. It was once the 16th-century palace of the archbishop of Seville. Renovations have added modern concepts but many of the old Andalusian touches have been retained as well. In this category of antique hotels, we still prefer the Casa Imperial (see above), but what you get here isn't bad. At least it was the Pope's choice when he visited Seville. Traditional stucco walls are adorned with modern paintings, which are a contrast to the antique tiles. Rooms range from small to spacious, and each is equipped with good beds and restored bathrooms, each containing a hair dryer. The restaurant serves standard Andalusian meals. One of the most stunning aspects of this hotel is the panoramic vista of La Giralda you can enjoy while sunbathing next to the rooftop pool. Amenities include limited room service, laundry, and a concierge.

Hotel Monte Triana. Clara de Jesús Montero, 24, 41010 Sevilla. ☎ **954-34-1832.** Fax 954-34-3328. E-mail: hmtventas@cli.ccs.es. 116 units. A/C MINIBAR TV TEL. 15,000 ptas. (US$90). AE, DC, MC, V. Parking 1,000 ptas. (US$6). Bus: 43.

In the Triana district, this three-star hotel lies a 15-minute walk from the commercial center and the historic monuments. A hotel since 1991, the building rises four floors behind a dull facade with large windows. Business travelers are more attracted to the hotel than tourists, although it is perfectly acceptable for both. Most of the rooms are on the interior, away from street noises, and connected to a pleasant patio. The decor is not inspired but rather functional, although there is comfort here. The housekeeping is first rate and the bathrooms are well equipped, including hair dryers and complimentary toiletries. A cafeteria serves breakfast and assorted dishes throughout the day, and amenities include room service until 11pm, laundry, and private safes in the bedrooms.

Hotel Plaza de Armas. Avenida Marqués de Paradas, s/n, 41001 Sevilla. ☎ **954-490-19-92.** Fax 954-90-1832. www.nh-hoteles.es. 262 units. A/C MINIBAR TV TEL. 15,500 ptas. (US$93) double; 19,500 ptas. (US$117) suite. AE, DC, MC, V.

This three-star hotel of glass and steel is in direct contrast to the antique casas of Seville which have been converted into hotels. It was built in 1992, and is the city's most modern-looking structure lying in the center close to the Plaza de Armas, La Giralda, and the cathedral. The interior design consists of architectural lines of almost Japanese simplicity, intermixed with steel and wood. The rooms are airy and colorful in a severe contemporary style, with oversize beds and comfortable mattresses, plus roomy bathrooms fully equipped with such features as hair dryers. There's a bar and formal restaurant serving Mediterranean cuisine. Amenities include a swimming pool, solarium, room service until 11pm, laundry, and facilities for persons with disabilities.

Hotel Regina. Calle San Vicente, 97, 41002 Sevilla. ☎ **854-490-75-62.** Fax 954-90-7562. 72 units. A/C MINIBAR TV TEL. 19,000 ptas. (US$114) double; 21,500 ptas. (US$129) duplex. AE, DC, MC, V. Parking 1,200 ptas. (US$7.20).

Right in the historic center, facing the Parque de la Cartuga and close to the Museo de Bellas Artes, this inviting hotel was constructed in 1992 in anticipation of the Seville Exposition. Its rooms are spacious and decorated in pastels with light woods. The bedrooms are comfortable, with firm beds; the bathrooms immaculate and filled with such amenities as hair dryers. The hotel staff can arrange guided tours of the city. On site is a cafeteria offering breakfasts and light meals daily until 11pm. Amenities include laundry and private safes in the rooms.

✪ **Hotel Simon.** Calle Garcia de Vinuesa, 190, 41001 Sevilla. ☎ **954-22-66-60.** Fax 954-22-66-15. www.sol.com/hotel-simon. E-mail: hotel-simonjet.es. 29 Units. A/C TV TEL. 12,000 ptas. (US$72) double. AE, DC, MC, V.

This two-story, former 18th-century mansion next to the cathedral in the Arenal district is a bargain hunter's delight. For a hotel rated only one star by the government, it is a cozy nest of charm and comfort. Within, there's a beautiful and ornate staircase with a patio of tropical plants. The social areas are chic and comfortable, and the TV lounge displays bric-a-brac belonging to the original mansion. Reservations are recommended as far in advance as possible, because the word is out that this is a relatively stylish establishment charging low prices. The rooms are medium size to large and each is individually decorated in keeping with the history of this place. Many antiques grace the rooms. Walls are adorned with paintings. On site is a cafeteria serving informal fare, and other amenities include a laundry and concierge.

✪ **La Casa de la Judería.** Plaza Santa Maria la Blanca, Callejon de Dos Hermanas, 7, 41004 Sevilla. ☎ **95-442-21-70.** Fax 95-442-21-70. www.zoom.es. E-mail: juderia.zoom.es. 104 units. A/C MINIBAR TV TEL. 18,000 ptas. (US$108) double; 29,000 ptas. (US$174) suite. AE, DC, MC, V. Parking 2,000 ptas. (US$12).

In the Santa Cruz district, the old Jewish barrio of Seville, this hotel is installed in a palace from the 1600s that was once owned by the Duke of Beja, a great character in the history of Spain's aristocracy and known as the patron of Cervantes. Within easy walking distance of the cathedral and other sights of historic interest, the building has been a hotel since 1991. It's now one of the best places to stay in Seville, offering an excellent bang for your peseta. The bedrooms, all medium in size, are individually decorated and furnished in an antique style, sometimes with four-poster beds with top-quality mattresses. All the accommodations have balconies, some facing street scenes and others opening onto one of the four interior patios in the classic Andalusian style. Many units also have living rooms, and all the suites contain a whirlpool. Bathrooms are beautifully maintained, with complimentary toiletries and hair dryers. Amenities include 24-hour room service, laundry, gym, and a concierge, plus guided tours to the historical center. The hotel also offers a cafeteria and a cozy piano bar at night.

✪ **Las Casas de los Mercaderes.** Calle Alvarez Quinteero, 9–13, 41004 Sevilla. ☎ **95-422-58-58.** Fax 95-422-98-84. http: //lascasas.zoom.es. E-mail: mercaderes.zoom.es. 47 units. A/C MINIBAR TV TEL. 17,500 ptas. (US$105) double. AE, DC, MC, V. Parking 1,000 ptas. (US$6).

In the business center of Seville, the restored mansion lies close to the cathedral between the squares of San Francisco and Salvador. Its name reflects the history of the area which was once home to many immigrant merchants. Its 19th-century precincts have been fully renovated—at the time an 18th-century patio was discovered. Much of the original style and grace notes were retained, and now it's one of the leading choices in town. Most of the medium-size rooms have balconies and classical Spanish furnishings. Bathrooms are modern and well equipped, with all the expected facilities such as hair dryers. Amenities include limited room service, laundry, and concierge, plus a coffee bar where breakfast is served.

Puerta de Triana. Reyes Católicos, 5, 41001 Sevilla. ☎ **954-21-54-04.** Fax 954-21-54-01. 62 units. A/C TV TEL. 18,000 ptas. (US$108) double. AE, DC, MC, V.

This five story budgeteer's dream is only a 5-minute walk from the cathedral in the Paseo Colón district. Last renovated in 1992, it was constructed in the early '70s in a neoclassic style. The interior is surprisingly elegant and tasteful for an establishment charging such low prices. Antique styles are mixed with modern features. Rated two stars by the government, the hotel offers bedrooms that are simply but comfortably furnished, each immaculately maintained. The bedrooms have none of the ornateness of the public rooms but are welcoming nonetheless. If you're driving to this location near the Plaza de Toros, you can ask the staff to direct you to one of the nearby garages where discounts for hotel guests are available.

✪ Residencia y Restaurante Fernando III. San José, 21, 41001 Sevilla. ☎ **95-421-77-08.** Fax 95-422-02-46. E-mail: fernandoiii@altos.com. 157 units. A/C TV TEL. 16,000–17,000 ptas. (US$96–US$102) double. AE, DC, MC, V. Parking 1,800 ptas. (US$10.80).

You'll find the Fernando III on a narrow, quiet street at the edge of the Barrio de Santa Cruz, near the northern periphery of the Murillo Gardens. Its vast lobby and baronial dining hall are reminiscent of a luxurious South American hacienda. The building is modern, constructed around 1970 with marble and hardwood detailing, and is sparsely furnished with leather chairs, plants, and wrought-iron accents. Many of the accommodations—medium in size, comfortably furnished, and well maintained—offer balconies filled with cascading plants; all have private bathrooms. There is a TV salon as well as a paneled bar. The hotel's restaurant features regional Andalusian cuisine.

INEXPENSIVE

Hostal Goya. Mateus Gago, 31, 41004 Sevilla. ☎ **95-421-11-70.** Fax 95-456-29-88. 20 units (10 with bathroom). Jan–Mar and May–Dec, 6,500 ptas. (US$39) double without bathroom, 7,000 ptas. (US$42) double with bathroom; Apr, 8,000 ptas. (US$48) double without bathroom, 9,000 ptas. (US$54) double with bathroom. No credit cards.

Its location in a narrow-fronted townhouse in the oldest part of the barrio is one of the Goya's strongest virtues. The building's gold-and-white facade, ornate iron railings, and picture-postcard demeanor are all noteworthy. Bedrooms are cozy and simple, without phones or TVs. Guests congregate in the marble-floored ground-level salon, where a skylight floods the couches and comfortable chairs with sunlight. No meals are served. Reserve well in advance. Parking is often available along the street.

Hotel América. Jesús del Gran Poder, 2, 41002 Sevilla. ☎ **95-422-09-51.** Fax 95-421-06-26. 100 units. A/C MINIBAR TV TEL. 12,000 ptas. (US$72) double; 15,000 ptas. (US$90) triple. AE, DC, MC, V. Parking 1,125 ptas. (US$6.75) nearby.

Built in 1976 and partially renovated in 1994, this hotel contains rather small bedrooms but the maids keep the place spick-and-span. Superior features include wall-to-wall carpeting and, in winter, individual heat control that works. Relax in the TV lounge or order a drink in the Duque Bar. Near the hotel is a parking garage for 600 cars. There isn't a major restaurant, but the América does offer a tearoom, snack bar, and cafeteria that serves regional and international cuisine. The hotel is set on the northern side of the Plaza del Duque. One of Spain's major department stores, El Corte Inglés, opens onto the same square.

Hotel Ducal. Plaza de la Encarnación, 19, 41003 Sevilla. ☎ **95-421-51-07.** Fax 95-422-89-99. 51 units. A/C TEL. 7,075–11,995 ptas. (US$42.45–US$71.95) double. AE, DC, MC, V. Parking 1,800 ptas. (US$10.80) nearby.

In this fairly modern hotel the guest rooms are modest but comfortable, with provincial and utilitarian furnishings and central heating for those Sevillian winters. A continental breakfast can be brought to your room, but no other meals are served. The location, near El Corte Inglés department store, is handy to many specialty shops.

Hotel La Rabida. Calle Castelar, 24, 41001 Sevilla. ☎ **94-422-09-60.** Fax 95-422-73-45. www.sol.com/hotel-rabida. E-mail: hotel-rabida@sol.com. 105 units. A/C MINIBAR TV TEL. 9,300 ptas. (US$55.80) double. AE, MC, V.

This former 19th-century mansion once belonged to one of Seville's most aristocratic families. The four-story building, a hotel for half a century, lies in the Arenal district, a 5-minute walk from the cathedral. Modestly renovated in 1998, the hotel offers small but clean and modernized bedrooms, each renovated in 1998, with the plumbing renewed. The hotel's most attractive feature is a lobby patio crowned by a stained-glass skylight. Amenities are limited to laundry and an on-site cafeteria.

Hotel Murillo. Calle Lope de Rueda, 7–9, 41004 Sevilla. ☎ **95-421-60-95.** Fax 95-421-96-16. www.sol.com/hotel-murillo. E-mail: murillo@nexo.es. 57 units. TEL. 7,100–8,900 ptas. (US$42.60–US$53.40) double; 8,800–11,200 ptas. (US$52.80–US$67.20) triple. AE, DC, MC, V. Parking 2,000 ptas. (US$12) nearby.

Tucked away on a narrow street in the heart of Santa Cruz, the old quarter, the Residencia Murillo (named after the artist who used to live in this district) is almost next to the gardens of the Alcázar. Inside, the lounges harbor some fine architectural characteristics and antique reproductions; behind a grilled screen is a retreat for drinks. Many of the rooms we inspected were cheerless and gloomy, so have a look before checking in. Like all of Seville's hotels, the Murillo is in a noisy area. You can reach this *residencia* from the Menéndez y Pelayo, a wide avenue west of the Parque María Luisa, where a sign will take you through the Murillo Gardens on the left. Motorists should try to park in Plaza de Santa Cruz. Then walk two blocks to the hotel, which will send a bellhop back to the car to pick up your suitcases. If there are two in your party, station a guard at the car, and if you're going out at night, call for an inexpensive taxi to take you instead of strolling through the streets of the old quarter—it's less romantic but a lot safer.

NEARBY

✪ **Hacienda Benazuza.** Calle Virgen de las Nieves, s/n, 41800 Sanlúcar la Major, Sevilla. ☎ **95-570-33-44.** Fax 95-570-34-10. www.hbenazuza.com. E-mail: hbenazuza@arrakis.es. 44 units. A/C MINIBAR TV TEL. 40,000–59,000 ptas. (US$240–US$354) double; 54,000–175,000 ptas. (US$324–US$1,050) suite. AE, DC, MC, V. Closed Aug. Free parking. From Seville, follow the signs for Huelva and head south on the A-49 highway, taking exit no. 6.

Set on a hillside above the agrarian hamlet of Sanlúcar la Mayor, 12 miles (19km) south of Seville, this legendary manor house is surrounded by 40 acres of olive groves and its own farmland. Its ownership has been a cross-section of every major cultural influence that has swept through Andalusia since the Moors laid its foundations in the 10th century. In 1992 the property was bought by Basque-born entrepreneur Rafael Elejabeitia, who transformed the premises into one of Andalusia's most charming hotels. Careful attention was paid to preserving the ancient Moorish irrigation system, whose many reflecting pools nourish the gardens. All but a few of the guest rooms lie in the estate's main building, and each is individually furnished with Andalusian antiques and Moorish trappings.

4 Where to Dine

VERY EXPENSIVE

✪ Egaña Oriza. San Fernando, 41. ☎ **95-422-72-11.** Reservations required. Main courses 2,800–5,900 ptas. (US$16.80–US$35.40); fixed-price menus 6,800–10,200 ptas. (US$40.80–US$61.20). AE, DC, MC, V. Restaurant, Mon–Fri 1:30–3:30pm, Mon–Sat 9–11:30pm. Bar, daily 9am–midnight. Closed Aug. BASQUE/CONTINENTAL.

Seville's most stylish and best restaurant is set within the conservatory of a restored mansion adjacent to the Murillo Gardens. Much of its reputation stems from its role as one of the few game specialists in Andalusia—a province that is otherwise devoted to seafood. The restaurant was established by Basque-born owner and chef José Mari Egaña, who managed to combine his passion for hunting with his flair for cooking. Many of the ingredients that go into the dishes presented on the menu were trapped or shot within Andalusia, a region whose potential for sports shooting is underused, according to Sr. Egaña. The view from the dining room encompasses a garden and a wall that formed part of the fortifications of Muslim Seville.

The availability of many specialties depends on the season, but might include ostrich carpaccio, gazpacho with prawns, steak with foie gras in grape sauce, casserole of wild boar with cherries and raisins, quenelles of duck in a potato nest with apple purée, stewed mountain sheep cooked with figs, rice with stewed thrush, and woodcock flamed in Spanish brandy. The wine list provides an ample supply of hearty Spanish reds to accompany these dishes. Dessert might feature a chocolate tart slathered with freshly whipped cream. Sr. Egaña's wife, Mercedes, runs the establishment's two-story dining room.

EXPENSIVE

Casa Robles. Calle Alvarez Quintero, 58. ☎ **95-421-31-50.** Reservations recommended. Main courses 1,500–2,500 ptas. (US$9–US$15); fixed-price menus 4,800–10,500 ptas. (US$28.80–US$63). AE, DC, MC, V. Daily 1–4:30pm and 8pm–1am. ANDALUSIAN.

Praised by local residents as well as by visitors, this restaurant began its life as an unpretentious bar and bodega in 1954. Over the years, thanks to a staff directed by owner-chef Juan Robles and his children, it developed into a courteous and bustling restaurant scattered over two floors of a building a short walk from the cathedral. Amid an all-Andalusian decor, you can enjoy such dishes as fish soup in the Andalusian style, *lubina con naranjas* (whitefish with Sevillana oranges), hake baked with strips of Serrano ham, and many kinds of fresh fish. The dessert list is long, diverse, and very tempting.

✪ El Burladero. In the Hotel Tryp Colón, Canalejas, 1. ☎ **95-422-29-00.** Reservations recommended. Main courses 2,000–4,000 ptas. (US$12–US$24); fixed-price menus 5,500–6,000 ptas. (US$33–US$36). AE, DC, MC, V. Daily 1:30–4:30pm and 9–midnight. Closed Aug. CONTINENTAL.

Set within one of Seville's most prominent hotels, this restaurant is awash with the memorabilia and paraphernalia of the bullfighting trade. The interior wall tiles were removed from one of the pavilions at the 1929 Seville World's Fair, and the photographs adorning the walls are a veritable history of bullfighting. (The restaurant, incidentally, is named after the wooden barricade—*el burladero*—behind which bullfighters in an arena can escape from the charge of an enraged bull.) The restaurant boasts a popular bar, where a wide assortment of Sevillanos meet and mingle before their meals.

Menu specialties include upscale interpretations of local country dishes, with an attractive mix of items from other regions of Spain as well. Examples include *bacalao*

ⓘ Family-Friendly Restaurants

El Puerto *(see p. 259)*   Down by the river, onto which its terraces open, this is a good and inexpensive family seafood restaurant, offering one of the most reasonably priced cubiertos (fixed-price menus) in Seville. It's ideal for the family on a tight budget.

Pizzería El Artesano   Near the cathedral, this is an ideal place for lunch if you're touring the heart of Seville, viewing the Alcázar and other attractions. The pizzas are good here, and the staff starts serving them at 12:30pm—so you don't have to wait around with hungry children until many restaurants open at 1:30pm.

Río Grande *(see p. 259)*   This is the best place to go for a classic Sevillian meal. It can turn into a real family affair if you order a big platter of paella, studded with chicken and shellfish. The restaurant sits against the bank of the Guadalquivir River, and there's also a snack bar if you're lunching light.

---

al horno con patatas (baked salt cod with potatoes and saffron sauce); roasted shoulder of lamb stuffed with a deboned bull's tail and served in a richly aromatic sauce; clams with white kidney beans; a local version of *cocido,* a boiled amalgam of sausages, meats, chickpeas, and vegetables; and a stew of eel meat heavily laced with garlic and spices. Dishes from other parts of Europe might include truffled fillet steak in puff pastry, duck liver, and salmon cooked in lemon-flavored dill sauce.

La Dehesa. Calle Luis de Morales, 2. ☎ **954-57-62-04.** Reservations required. Main courses 2,500–3,000 ptas. (US$15–US$18); set menu 5,500 ptas. (US$33). AE, DC, MC, V. Daily 1:30–4pm and 8:30pm–midnight. ANDALUSIAN.

One of the leading restaurants of Seville, La Dehesa is known for its regional decor. It lies in the center of town, 5 minutes from the train station and a 20-minute walk from the cathedral. The restaurant has been serving gastronomes in Seville since the early '90s and is owned by the Meliá hotel chain. It is decorated like an elegant bodega or wine tavern with stucco walls and windows containing potted plants. Each corner is a shrine to a particular bullfighter, all of whom have donated memorabilia. The menu specializes in grilled meats but does all dishes exceedingly well. Try the flavor-filled *ensaladita de la Dehesa* (shrimp, avocado, and a green leaf salad) or else tender grilled lamb cutlets or fresh hake, also perfectly grilled. You might begin in the classic local style with an Andalusian gazpacho. Desserts are all homemade, including tarts and an especially delightful platter of crêpes stuffed with nuts and banana ice cream.

La Albahaca. Plaza de Santa Cruz, 12. ☎ **95-422-07-14.** Reservations recommended. Main courses 2,600–3,000 ptas. (US$15.60–US$18); fixed-price menus 4,500–5,500 ptas. (US$27–US$33). AE, DC, MC, V. Mon–Sat noon–4pm and 8pm–midnight. BASQUE/FRENCH.

Located on a prominent square in the Barrio de Santa Cruz, this restaurant with an open-air terrace offers a limited but savory menu that has become a favorite of Sevillians. Specialties include a salad of carpaccio of codfish with fresh asparagus and herbs, seafood soup, shellfish bisque, grilled lamb chops, partridge braised in sherry, salmon wrapped in parchment, and chocolate pudding for dessert. The restaurant is in a manor home built in 1929.

Seville Dining

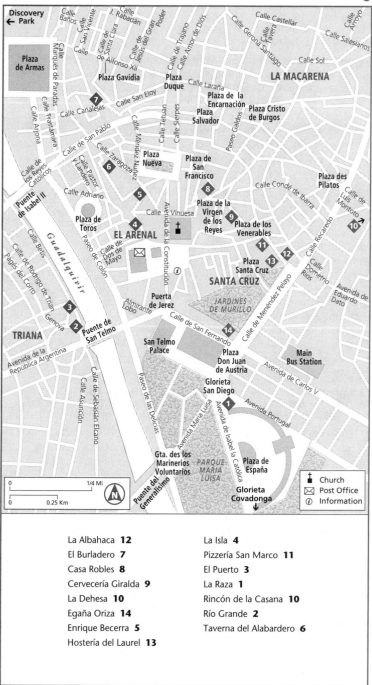

La Albahaca **12**

El Burladero **7**

Casa Robles **8**

Cervecería Giralda **9**

La Dehesa **10**

Egaña Oriza **14**

Enrique Becerra **5**

Hostería del Laurel **13**

La Isla **4**

Pizzería San Marco **11**

El Puerto **3**

La Raza **1**

Rincón de la Casana **10**

Río Grande **2**

Taverna del Alabardero **6**

✪ **La Isla.** Arfe, 25. ☎ **95-421-26-31.** Reservations recommended. Main courses 5,000–6,500 ptas. (US$30–US$39). AE, DC, MC, V. Daily 1–5pm and 8pm–midnight. Closed Aug. SPANISH/ANDALUSIAN.

In two large dining rooms designed in Andalusian fashion (thick plaster walls, tile floors, and taurine memorabilia), this air-conditioned restaurant was established shortly after World War II and has done a thriving business ever since. Its seafood is trucked or flown in from either Galicia, in northern Spain, or Huelva, one of Andalusia's major ports, and is almost always extremely fresh. Menu items include *merluza a la primavera* (hake with young vegetables), *solomillo a la Castellana* (grilled beefsteak with strips of Serrano ham), chicken croquettes, and shellfish soup. The restaurant lies a short walk from the cathedral, within a very old building erected, the owners say, on foundations laid by the ancient Romans.

Rincón de la Casana. Santo Domingo de la Calzada, 13. ☎ **95-453-17-10.** Reservations required. Main courses 1,900–2,900 ptas. (US$11.40–US$17.40); set menu 1,950 ptas. (US$11.70). AE, DC, MC, V. Daily 1–4:30pm and Mon–Sat 8pm–12:30am. ARGENTINEAN/ANDALUSIAN.

Close to the old town, this landmark restaurant has existed since the mid-80s, and seems to win new followers every year. Converted from an old building, it has a main door of intricate carving and craftsmanship, and its roof is red tiled in the traditional style. The two-story interior has one of the most interesting decors in the city, with antique tiles and typical Andalusian artifacts. At the entrance is the mounted head of the last bull killed by the famous matador, José Luís Vasquez. The chefs know their Andalusian ingredients right down to the last olive. On our last visit we savored such creations as *chuleton de buey* (ox steak) and *carne con chimichuri* (steak with chopped parsley and garlic dressing in virgin olive oil). Desserts are freshly made every day, including traditional puddings and tasty tarts, most often with fresh fruit.

✪ **Taverna del Alabardero.** Calle Zaragoza, 20. ☎ **95-456-06-37.** Fax 95-456-36-66. Reservations recommended. Main courses 1,600–2,800 ptas. (US$9.60–US$16.80). AE, DC, MC, V. Daily 1–3:30pm and 8pm–midnight. Closed Aug. Bus: 13, 25, 26. ANDALUSIAN.

One of Seville's most prestigious and well-recommended restaurants occupies a 19th-century townhouse near Plaza Nueva, 3 blocks from the cathedral. A favorite of nearly every politician and diplomat who visits Seville, it has recently hosted the king and queen of Spain, the king's mother, the Spanish president and members of his cabinet, and dozens of well-connected affluent visitors. Amid a collection of European antiques and oil paintings, you'll dine in any of two main rooms or three private ones, and perhaps precede your meal with a drink or tapas on the building's flowering patio. There's a garden in back with additional tables. Menu items include spicy peppers stuffed with pulverized thigh of bull, an Andalusian fish (*urta*) set on a compote of aromatic tomatoes with coriander, a tournedos of codfish with essence of red peppers, and Iberian beefsteak with *foie gras* and green peppers.

MODERATE

✪ **Enrique Becerra.** Gamazo, 2. ☎ **95-421-30-49.** Reservations recommended. Main courses 2,200–2,600 ptas. (US$13.20–US$15.60). AE, DC, MC, V. Mon–Sat 1–5pm and 8pm–midnight. ANDALUSIAN.

This is a cozy, snug retreat in a whitewashed house with wrought-iron window grilles near the cathedral and its home-cooked dishes are among the city's finest. The restaurant takes its name from its owner, a smart and helpful host, who installed it in a late 19th-century building. A popular tapas bar and Andalusian dining spot, it offers an intimate setting and a hearty welcome that makes you feel that your business is really appreciated.

Food on the Run

Directly east of the cathedral, ✪ **Cervecería Giralda,** calle Mateus Gago, 1 (☎ **95-422-74-35**), is one of the least expensive dining spots near the cathedral, Alcázar, and Giralda Tower. Residents and tourists alike eat here. You can make a meal from the selection of tapas, ranging from 275 to 325 pesetas (US$1.65 to US$1.95). The tavern is open daily 9am to midnight.

Lying on the opposite side of the Guadalquivir, away from the throngs of tourists, is the Barrio de Triana. This used to be its own little village community until Seville burst its seams and absorbed it. It is still the place to go to escape the high food tariffs on the cathedral side of the river.

✪ **El Puerto,** Betis, s/n (☎ **95-427-17-25**), stands next door to the famed Río Grande restaurant. It has a multilevel alfresco terrace opening onto the river. You can get fresh seafood here, but the special buy is the chef's *cubierto* (menu of the house), costing 1,500 pesetas (US$10.50); tapas range from 250 to 750 pesetas (US$1.50 to US$4.50). At the cafeteria bar, you serve yourself; inside is an inexpensive restaurant with waiter service. It's open Tuesday to Sunday 1 to 4pm and 8pm to midnight (closed in January). Bus: 41 or 42.

Another way to enjoy quick meals is to eat at one of the tapas bars recommended below under "Seville After Dark." Portions, called *raciónes,* are usually generous, and many tourists on the run often eat standing at the bar, making a full meal out of two orders of tapas.

While perusing the menu, you can sip dry Tío Pepe and nibble herb-cured olives with lemon peel. The gazpacho here is among the city's best, and the sangría is served ice cold. Specialties include hake real, sea bream Bilbao style, and a wide range of meat, fish, and vegetarian dishes. The wine list is one of the best in Seville.

✪ **Río Grande.** Calle Betis, 1/n. ☎ **95-427-39-56.** Reservations required. Main courses 1,600–5,000 ptas. (US$9.60–US$30); fixed-price menu 3,250 ptas. (US$19.50). AE, DC, MC, V. Daily 1–4:30pm and 8pm–12:30am. Bus: 41 or 42. ANDALUSIAN.

This classic Sevillian restaurant is named for the Guadalquivir River, which its panoramic windows overlook. It sits against the bank of the river near Plaza de Cuba in front of the Torre del Oro. Some diners come here just for a view of the city monuments. A meal might include stuffed sweet pepper *flamenca,* fish-and-seafood soup seaman's style, the chef's fresh salmon, chicken-and-shellfish paella, bull tail Andalusian, and garlic chicken. You can also have a selection of fresh shellfish that's brought in daily. Large terraces contain a snack bar, the Río Grande Pub, and a bingo room. You can often watch sports events on the river in this pleasant (and English-speaking) spot.

INEXPENSIVE

✪ **Hostería del Laurel.** Plaza de los Venerables, 5. ☎ **95-422-02-95.** Reservations recommended. Main courses 950–2,500 ptas. (US$5.70–US$15). AE, DC, MC, V. Daily noon–4pm and 7:30pm–midnight. ANDALUSIAN.

Located in one of the most charming buildings on tiny, difficult-to-find Plaza de los Venerables in the labyrinthine Barrio de Santa Cruz, this hideaway restaurant has iron-barred windows stuffed with plants. Inside, amid Andalusian tiles, beamed ceilings, and more plants, you'll enjoy good regional cooking. Many diners stop for a drink and tapas at the ground-floor bar before going into one of the dining rooms. The hostería is attached to a three-star hotel.

La Raza. Isabel la Católica, 2. ☎ **95-423-38-30.** Reservations recommended. Main courses 1,300–2,300 ptas. (US$7.80–US$13.80). AE, DC, MC, V. Daily noon–5pm and 8pm–midnight. ANDALUSIAN.

A terrace restaurant in Parque María Luisa, La Raza is known for both its setting and its tapas. It has seen better days, but the staff is attentive and the food very good. Begin with gazpacho, then go on to one of the meat dishes, or perhaps an order of the savory paella. On Friday and Saturday there is often music to entertain guests, many of whom are American and Japanese tourists.

✪ **Pizzería San Marco.** Calle Mesón de Moro, 6. ☎ **95-421-43-90.** Reservations recommended. Main courses 825–1,500 ptas. (US$4.95–US$9). MC, V. Tues–Sun 1:30–4:30pm and 8:30pm–12:30am. ITALIAN.

Despite the informality implied by its name, this is actually a well-managed restaurant with sit-down service and bilingual waiters. Pizza is only one of the many items featured on the menu, and often is relegated to a secondary role, as clients usually opt for any of several kinds of pastas, salmon salad, duck in orange sauce, osso bucco, chicken Parmesan, and several forms of scaloppini. There's also a congenial corner for drinking, named Harry's Bar in honor of grander role models in Venice and elsewhere.

Despite the allure of the food, the real interest of the place is its setting. It lies within what was originally an Arab bathhouse, more than 1,000 years ago. Its interior reminds some visitors of a secularized mosque, despite the presence of a modern wing added around 1991 in anticipation of increased business from Seville's Expo celebration. The establishment lies within the Barrio de Santa Cruz, on an obscure side street running into calle Mateus Gago.

5 Exploring Seville

Seville has a wide range of palaces, churches, cathedrals, towers, and historic hospitals. Since it would take a week or two to visit all of them, we have narrowed the sights down to the very top attractions. The only way to explore Seville is on foot, with a good map in hand—but remember to be alert to muggers.

THE TOP ATTRACTIONS

✪ **Catedral.** Plaza del Triunfo, Avenida de la Constitución. ☎ **95-421-49-71.** Admission (including visit to Giralda Tower) 700 ptas. (US$4.20) adults, 200 ptas. (US$1.20) children and students. Daily 11am–5pm.

The largest Gothic building in the world, and the third-largest church in Europe after St. Peter's in Rome and St. Paul's in London, this church was designed by builders with a stated goal—that "those who come after us will take us for madmen." Construction began in the late 1400s and took centuries to complete.

Built on the site of an ancient mosque, the cathedral claims to contain the remains of Columbus, with his tomb mounted on four statues.

Works of art abound, many of them architectural, such as the 15th-century stained-glass windows, the iron screens (*rejas*) closing off the chapels, the elaborate 15th-century choir stalls, and the Gothic reredos above the main altar. During Corpus Christi and Immaculate Conception observances, altar boys with castanets dance in front of the high altar. In the Treasury are works by Goya, Murillo, and Zurbarán as well as a touch of the macabre in a display of skulls. After touring the dark interior, emerge into the sunlight of the Patio of Orange Trees, with its fresh citrus scents and chirping birds.

Warning: Shorts and T-shirts are not allowed.

○ **Giralda Tower.** Plaza del Triunfo. Admission included in admission to cathedral (above). Same hours as cathedral (above).

Just as Big Ben symbolizes London, La Giralda conjures up Seville. This Moorish tower, next to the cathedral, is the city's most famous monument. Erected as a minaret in the 12th century, it has seen later additions, such as 16th-century bells. To climb it is to take the walk of a lifetime. There are no steps—you ascend an endless ramp. If you can make it to the top, you'll have a dazzling view of Seville. Entrance is through the cathedral.

Alcázar. Plaza del Triunfo, s/n. ☎ **95-50-23-23.** Admission 600 ptas. (US$4.20). Oct–Mar, Tues–Sat 9:30am–6pm, Sun 9:30am–2:30pm; Apr–Sept, Tues–Sat 9:30am–8pm, Sun 9:30am–6pm.

Pedro the Cruel built this magnificent 14th-century Mudéjar palace, north of the cathedral. It is the oldest royal residence in Europe still in use: On visits to Seville, King Juan Carlos stays here. From the Dolls' Court to the Maidens' Court through the domed Ambassadors' Room, it contains some of the finest work of Sevillian artisans. In many ways, it evokes the Alhambra at Granada. Ferdinand and Isabella, who at one time lived in the Alcázar and influenced its architectural evolution, welcomed Columbus here on his return from America. On the top floor, the Oratory of the Catholic Monarchs has a fine altar in polychrome tiles made by Pisano in 1504. The well-kept gardens, filled with beautiful flowers, shrubbery, and fruit trees, are alone worth the visit.

Hospital de la Santa Caridad. Calle Temprado, 3. ☎ **95-422-32-32.** Admission 400 ptas. (US$2.40). Mon–Sat 9:30am–1:30pm and 3:30–6pm, Sun 9am–1pm.

This 17th-century hospital is intricately linked to the legend of Miguel Manara, portrayed by Dumas and Mérimée as a scandalous Don Juan. It was once thought that he built this institution to atone for his sins, but this has been disproved. The death of Manara's beautiful young wife in 1661 caused such grief that he retired from society and entered the "Charity Brotherhood," burying corpses of the sick and diseased as well as condemned and executed criminals. Today the members of this brotherhood continue to look after the poor, the old, and invalids who have no one else to help them. Nuns will show you through the festive orange-and-sienna courtyard. The baroque chapel contains works by the 17th-century Spanish painters Murillo and Valdés-Leál. As you're leaving the chapel, look over the exit door for the macabre picture of an archbishop being devoured by maggots.

Torre del Oro. Paseo de Cristóbal Colón. ☎ **95-422-24-19.** Admission 100 ptas. (US60¢); free on Tues. Tues–Fri 10am–2pm, Sat–Sun 11am–2pm.

The 12-sided Tower of Gold, dating from the 13th century, overlooks the Guadalquivir River. Originally it was covered with gold tiles, but someone long ago made off with them. Recently restored, the tower has been turned into a maritime museum, Museo Náutico, displaying drawings and engravings of the port of Seville in its golden heyday.

○ **Casa de Pilatos.** Plaza Pilatos, 1. ☎ **95-422-50-55.** Museum, 1,000 ptas. (US$6); patio and gardens, 500 ptas. (US$3). Museum, daily 10am–2pm and 4–6pm. Patio and gardens, daily 9am–7pm.

This 16th-century Andalusian palace of the dukes of Medinaceli recaptures the splendor of the past, combining Gothic, Mudéjar, and plateresque styles in its courtyards, fountains, and salons. According to tradition, this is a reproduction of Pilate's House in Jerusalem. Don't miss the two old carriages or the rooms filled with Greek and Roman statues. The collection of paintings includes works by Carreño, Pantoja de la

Cruz, Sebastiano del Piombo, Lucas Jordán, Batalloli, Pacheco, and Goya. The museum's first floor is seen by guided tour only, but the ground floor, patios, and gardens are self-guided. The palace is about a 7-minute walk northeast of the cathedral on the northern edge of Barrio de Santa Cruz, in a warren of labyrinthine streets whose traffic is funneled through the nearby calle de Aguilas.

Archivo General de Indias. Avenida de la Constitución, s/n. ☎ **95-421-12-34.** Free admission. Mon–Fri 10am–1pm.

The great architect of Philip II's El Escorial, Juan de Herrera, was also the architect of this building next to the cathedral, originally the *Lonja* (Stock Exchange). Construction on the Archivo General de Indias lasted from 1584 to 1646. In the 17th century it was headquarters for the Academy of Seville, which was founded in part by the great Spanish artist Murillo.

In 1785, during the reign of Charles III, the building was turned over for use as a general records office for the Indies. That led to today's Archivo General de Indias, said to contain some four million antique documents, even letters exchanged between patron Queen Isabella and explorer Columbus (he detailing his discoveries and impressions). These very rare documents are locked in air-conditioned storage to keep them from disintegrating. Special permission has to be acquired before examining some of them. Many treasure hunters come here hoping to learn where Spanish galleons laden with gold went down off the coasts of the Americas. On display in glass cases are fascinating documents in which the dreams of the early explorers come alive again.

✪ **Museo Provincial de Bellas Artes de Sevilla.** Plaza del Museo, 9. ☎ **95-422-18-29.** Admission 250 ptas. (US$1.50), free for students. Tues 3–8pm, Wed–Sat 9am–8pm, Sun 9am–2pm. Bus: C3, C4, 13, or 14.

This lovely old convent off calle de Alfonso XII houses one of the most important Spanish art collections. A whole gallery is devoted to two paintings by El Greco, and works by Zurbarán are exhibited; however, the devoutly religious paintings of the Seville-born Murillo are the highlight. An entire wing is given over to macabre paintings by the 17th-century artist Valdés-Leál. His painting of John the Baptist's head on a platter includes the knife—lest you miss the point. The top floor, which displays modern paintings, is less interesting.

MORE ATTRACTIONS

✪ **Barrio de Santa Cruz** What was once a ghetto for Spanish Jews, who were forced out of Spain in the late 15th century in the wake of the Inquisition, is today the most colorful district of Seville. Near the old walls of the Alcázar, winding medieval streets with names like *Vida* (Life) and *Muerte* (Death) open onto pocket-sized plazas. Flower-filled balconies with draping bougainvillea and potted geraniums jut out over this labyrinth, shading you from the hot Andalusian summer sun. Feel free to look through numerous wrought-iron gates into patios filled with fountains and plants. In the evening it's common to see Sevillians sitting outside drinking icy sangría under the glow of lanterns.

Although the district as a whole is recommended for sightseeing, seek out in particular the **Casa de Murillo (Murillo's House),** Santa Teresa, 8 (☎ **95-421-75-35**). Bartolomé Esteban Murillo, the great Spanish painter known for his religious works, was born in Seville in 1617. He spent his last years in this house in Santa Cruz, dying in 1682. Five minor paintings of the artist are on display. The furnishings, although not owned by the artist, are period pieces. Admission is 250 pesetas (US$1.75), and the house is open Tuesday to Saturday 10am to 2pm and 6 to 8pm. At press time, the house was closed for renovations; check its status with the tourist office before heading here.

Seville Attractions

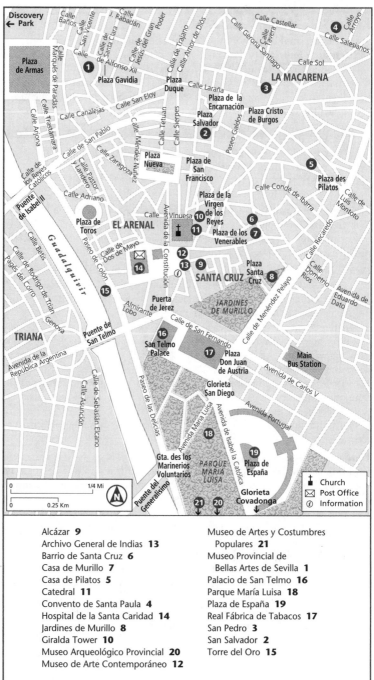

Alcázar **9**
Archivo General de Indias **13**
Barrio de Santa Cruz **6**
Casa de Murillo **7**
Casa de Pilatos **5**
Catedral **11**
Convento de Santa Paula **4**
Hospital de la Santa Caridad **14**
Jardines de Murillo **8**
Giralda Tower **10**
Museo Arqueológico Provincial **20**
Museo de Arte Contemporáneo **12**

Museo de Artes y Costumbres
  Populares **21**
Museo Provincial de
  Bellas Artes de Sevilla **1**
Palacio de San Telmo **16**
Parque María Luisa **18**
Plaza de España **19**
Real Fábrica de Tabacos **17**
San Pedro **3**
San Salvador **2**
Torre del Oro **15**

Taking the Bull by the Horns

From Easter until late October, some of the best bullfighters in Spain appear at the **Maestranza bullring,** on Paseo de Colón (☎ 95-422-35-06). One of the leading bullrings in Spain, the stadium attracts matadors whose fights often receive TV and newspaper coverage throughout Iberia. Unless there's a special festival going on, bullfights (*corridas*) occur on Sunday. The best bullfights are staged during April Fair celebrations. Tickets tend to be pricey and should be purchased in advance at the ticket office (*despacho de entradas*) on calle Adriano, beside the stadium. You'll also find many unofficial kiosks selling tickets placed strategically along the main shopping street, calle Sierpes. However, they charge a 20% commission for their tickets—a lot more if they think they can get it.

To enter the Barrio Santa Cruz, turn right after leaving the Patio de Banderas exit of the Alcázar. Turn right again at Plaza de la Alianza, going down calle Rodrigo Caro to Plaza de Doña Elvira. Use caution when strolling through the area, particularly at night; many robberies have occurred here.

Parque María Luisa   This park, dedicated to María Luisa, sister of Isabella II, was once the grounds of the Palacio de San Telmo. The palace, whose baroque facade is visible behind the deluxe Alfonso XIII Hotel, today houses a seminary. The former private royal park is now open to the public.

Running south along the Guadalquivir River, the park attracts those who want to take boat rides, walk along paths bordered by flowers, jog, or go bicycling. The most romantic way to traverse it is by rented horse and carriage, but this can be expensive, depending on your negotiation with the driver.

In 1929 Seville was to host the Spanish American Exhibition, and many pavilions from other countries were erected here. The worldwide depression put a damper on the exhibition, but the pavilions still stand.

Exercise caution while walking through this park, as many muggings have been reported.

Plaza de América   Another landmark Sevillian square, Plaza de América represents city planning at its best: Here you can walk through gardens planted with roses, enjoying the lily ponds and the fountains and feeling the protective shade of the palms. And here you'll find a trio of elaborate buildings left over from the world exhibition that never materialized—in the center, the home of the government headquarters of Andalusia; on either side, two minor museums worth visiting only if you have time to spare.

Museo Arqueológico Provincial, Plaza de América, s/n (☎ 95-423-24-01), contains many artifacts from prehistoric times and the days of the Romans, Visigoths, and Moors. It's open Tuesday to Sunday 10am to 2:30pm. Admission is 250 pesetas (US$1.50) for adults and free for students and children. Buses 30, 31, and 34 go there.

Nearby is the **Museo de Artes y Costumbres Populares,** Plaza de América, s/n (☎ 95-423-25-76), displaying folkloric costumes, musical instruments, cordobán saddles, weaponry, and farm implements that document the life of the Andalusian people. It's open Tuesday to Saturday 9am to 2:30pm, but closed on holidays. Admission is 250 pesetas (US$1.50) for adults and free for children and students.

Plaza de España   The major building left from the exhibition at the Parque María Luisa (see above) is a half-moon-shaped structure in Renaissance style, set on this landmark square of Seville. The architect, Anibal González, not only designed but also supervised the construction of this immense structure; today it is a government office building. At a canal here you can rent rowboats for excursions into the park, or you can walk across bridges spanning the canal. Set into a curved wall are alcoves, each focusing on characteristics of one of Spain's 50 provinces, as depicted in tile murals.

Real Fábrica de Tabacos   When Carmen waltzed out of the tobacco factory in the first act of Bizet's opera, she made its 18th-century original in Seville world famous. This old tobacco factory was constructed between 1750 and 1766, and 100 years later it employed 10,000 *cigarreras,* of which Carmen was one in the opera. (She rolled cigars on her thighs.) In the 19th century, these tobacco women made up the largest female workforce in Spain. Many visitors arriving today, in fact, ask guides to take them to "Carmen's tobacco factory." The building, the second largest in Spain and located on calle San Fernando near the city's landmark luxury hotel, the Alfonso XIII, is still here. But the Real Fábrica de Tabacos is now part of the Universidad de Sevilla. Look for signs of its former role, however, in the bas-reliefs of tobacco plants and Indians over the main entrances. You'll also see bas-reliefs of Columbus and Cortés. Then you can wander through the grounds for a look at student life, Sevillian style. The factory is directly south of the Alcázar gardens.

6 Especially for Kids

The greatest thrill for kids in Seville is climbing **La Giralda,** the former minaret of the Great Mosque that once stood here. The view from this 20-story bell tower is certainly worth the climb, but most kids delight in the climb itself. With some inclined ramps and some steps, the climb was originally designed to be ridden up on horseback. Little gargoyle-framed windows along the way allow you to preview the skyline of Seville.

With your family in tow, head for **Plaza de España;** you'll find rowboats as well as *pedaloes* (pedal boats) to rent. A collection of Andalusian donkey carts here adds to the fun, and there are ducks to feed on the Isla de los Patos. If your children take to that, they'll enjoy feeding the pigeons as well.

The tourist office (see above) will give advice on how to rent pedaloes or canoes for trips along the Guadalquivir River. Or you can go to the riverbanks near the Torre del Oro and make your own rental arrangements with **Cruceros Turisticos Torre del Oro,** Paseo Marqués de Contadero (☎ **95-421-13-96**).

Finally, to cap your family trip to Seville, take one of the **horse-and-buggy rides** that leave from Plaza Virgen de los Reyes on Adolfo Rodríguez Jurado, or from the Parque de María Luisa at Plaza de España. Rates are government controlled at 4,000 pesetas (US$24), but prices rise during April Fair and Holy Week.

Walking Tour—The Old City

Start: At the Giralda by the cathedral.
Finish: At the Hospital de los Venerables in the Barrio de Santa Cruz.
Time: 4 hours, including rapid visits to the interiors.
Best Times: Early morning (from 7 to 11am) and late afternoon (from 3 to 7pm).
Worst Times: After dark or during the heat of midday.

Seville is so loaded with architectural and artistic treasures that this brisk overview of the central zone doesn't begin to do justice to its cultural wealth. Although this walking tour includes the city's most obvious (and spectacular) monuments, such as the Giralda and the cathedral, it also includes lesser-known churches and convents—

whose elaborate decorations were paid for by gold imported from the New World during Spain's Age of Exploration. It also features promenades through the city's most desirable shopping district, and meanders through the labyrinthine alleyways of the Barrio de Santa Cruz.

Begin with a visit to the:

1. **Cathedral,** a Gothic structure so enormous that even its builders recognized the folly and fanaticism of their dreams. Its crowning summit, the Giralda, one of Europe's most famous towers, was begun in the late 1100s by the Moors and raised even higher by the Catholic monarchs in 1568. Because of the position of these connected monuments near the summit of a hill overlooking the Guadalquivir, some scholars nostalgically refer to the historic neighborhood around them as the Acropolis.

After your visit, walk to the cathedral compound's northeastern corner for a visit to the:

2. **Palacio Arzobispal (Archbishop's Palace),** a 16th-century building resting on 13th-century foundations, with a 17th-century baroque facade of great beauty. Although conceived to house the overseer of the nearby cathedral, it was sometimes pressed into service to house secular visitors. One of these was Napoléon's representative, Maréchal Soult, after he conquered Seville in the name of the Bonaparte family and France early in the 19th century.

From here, walk across the street, heading south, to Plaza Virgin de los Reyes, for a visit to the:

3. **Convento de la Encarnación (Convent of the Incarnation).** Its origins date from the 1300s, shortly after the Catholic reconquest of Seville. Part of its architectural curiosity includes the widespread use of the lobed, horseshoe-shaped arches and windows traditionally used in mosques.

Exit from the church, then walk eastward across Plaza del Triunfo into the entrance of one of the most exotic palaces in Europe, the:

4. **Reales Alcázar (Royal Alcázar).** The oldest royal seat in Spain, it was begun for the Moorish caliphs in A.D. 712 as a fortress, then enlarged and embellished over the next thousand years by successive generations of Moorish and, beginning in 1248, Christian rulers. Its superimposed combination of Arab and Christian Gothic architecture creates one of the most interesting monuments in Iberia. Lavish gardens, as exotic as what you'd expect in the Old Testament, sprawl in an easterly direction in back. More than any other monument on this tour, with the exception of the cathedral, the Alcázar deserves a second visit after the end of this walking tour.

Exit from the Alcázar back onto Plaza del Triunfo. At the plaza's southwestern edge rises the imposing bulk of the:

5. **Archivo General de Indias (Archive of the Indies).** It was designed in the 1580s by Juan de Herrera, whose rectilinear austerity at El Escorial appealed to the religious fanaticism of Philip II. Built as a commodities exchange, it was abandoned for a site in Cádiz when that port replaced Seville as the most convenient debarkation point for ships coming from the New World. In 1758 it was reconfigured as the repository for the financial records and political and cultural archives of anything concerning the development of the Western Hemisphere. Its closets and storerooms contain more than four million dossiers—many bureaucratic and tedious, but some of passionate interest to scholars and academics.

From here, walk half a block west to the roaring traffic of Avenida de la Constitución, then turn north, bypassing the facade of the already-visited cathedral.

Walking Tour—The Old City

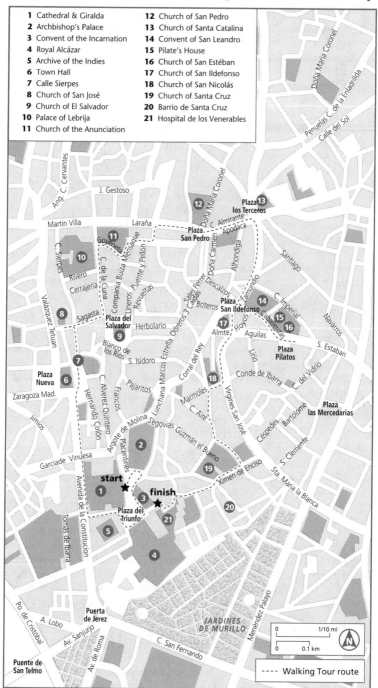

1 Cathedral & Giralda
2 Archbishop's Palace
3 Convent of the Incarnation
4 Royal Alcázar
5 Archive of the Indies
6 Town Hall
7 Calle Sierpes
8 Church of San José
9 Church of El Salvador
10 Palace of Lebrija
11 Church of the Anunciation

12 Church of San Pedro
13 Church of Santa Catalina
14 Convent of San Leandro
15 Pilate's House
16 Church of San Estéban
17 Church of San Ildefonso
18 Church of San Nicolás
19 Church of Santa Cruz
20 Barrio de Santa Cruz
21 Hospital de los Venerables

- - - - Walking Tour route

The avenida will end within 2 blocks at the ornate bulk of Seville's:

6. **Ayuntamiento (Town Hall).** Begun in 1527, and enlarged during the 19th century, it's the city's political showcase. For a view of its most interesting (plateresque) facade, turn right (east) when you reach it, then flank the building's eastern edge for a view of the medallions and allegorical figures that kept teams of stonemasons busy for generations.

The Town Hall's northeastern facade marks the beginning of Seville's most famous and desirable shopping street:

7. **Calle Sierpes,** which stretches north from the Town Hall. The street's southern terminus, where you're standing, was once the site of a since-demolished debtor's prison where Miguel de Cervantes languished for several years, laying out the plot and characters of his innovative masterpiece *Don Quixote*.

Walk along the western edge of this famous street, turning left (west) after 2 blocks onto calle Jovellanos for a view of the:

8. **Iglesia (Church) de San José.** Named in honor of a famous carpenter (St. Joseph, husband of the Virgin), this lavish baroque chapel functioned as the seat of the carpenter's guild after its completion in 1747.

Retrace your steps along calle Jovellanos to calle Sierpes, traverse its busy traffic, and continue walking due east along calle Sagasta. Within a block, calle Sagasta will deposit you in Plaza del Salvador, in front of the elaborate facade of the:

9. **Iglesia del Salvador (Savior).** One of the grandest churches of Seville, preferred by many visitors to the rather chilly pomposity of the previously visited cathedral, this enormous building was begun in 1674 on the site of one of the Muslim world's holiest sites, the mosque of Ibn Addabas. Beneath the Catholic iconography you can still make out the base of the Moorish minaret (converted long ago into a Christian belfry) and the Moorish layout of the building's courtyard.

After your visit, walk 3 blocks north along calle Cuna (a wide boulevard that Sevillanos usually refer to simply as "Cuna") for an exterior view of one of the most-envied private homes in town, the:

10. **Palacio de Lebrija or Casa de la Condesa de Lebrija,** at calle Cuna, 18. Austere on the outside, lavish and Mudéjar on the inside, it was built in the 1400s and managed to incorporate a series of ancient mosaics, dug up from the excavations in the nearby town of Itálica, for incorporation into its floors. Although it's closed to casual visits, it's the most visible vestige of an aristocratic way of life that's rapidly fading.

From here, walk 2 short blocks east along calle de Goyeneta for a view of the:

11. **Iglesia de la Anunciación.** Built in 1565 with profits from the New World, and associated for many centuries with both the Jesuits and the city's university, it contains a cold, rather macabre-looking crypt (Panteón de Sevillanos Ilustres) where the bodies of many of the city's governors and their families are buried.

From here, head east, passing through Plaza de la Anunciación onto calle del Laraña Imagen for a short 2 blocks. Rising ahead of you from its position beside Plaza de San Pedro is the:

12. **Iglesia de San Pedro.** Built in the Mudéjar style in the 1300s, with some of its portals and towers added during the 1600s and 1700s, it's famous as the site where Spain's greatest painter, Velázquez, was baptized in 1599. Coffered ceilings rise above the building's main sanctuary and its eight shadowy chapels. The site is available for visits only during mass, during which visitors should remain as

quiet and discreet as possible.

From Plaza de San Pedro, adjacent to the church's eastern entrance, walk east for 2 blocks along calle del Almirante Apodaca until you reach the:

13. **Iglesia de Santa Catalina,** a 14th century Gothic-Mudéjar monument that has endured many alterations and additions during its life span. Most significant of these is a simple Gothic portal that was moved into its present position in 1930 from another church. Make it a point to walk around this medieval hybrid for views of horseshoe (lobed) arches that attest to the strong influence of Moorish design on its past.

After your visit, walk south for a block along calle Carrión, whose name will change after a block to calle Francisco Mejías. The massive and severe-looking building that rises in about a block is the:

14. **Convento de San Leandro.** Although the building you see today was begun around 1580, it replaced a much older 13th-century church that was the first to be constructed in Seville after the Christian reconquest in 1248. Severe and simple, with a single barrel vault covering its single aisle, it's open only during early morning (7am) mass and on some holy festival days.

Immediately to the southeast, opening off Plaza de Pilatos, is the grandest and most ornate palace that's open to view in Seville, the:

15. **Casa de Pilatos (Pilate's House).** One of the city's most frequently visited museums, it was built in 1521 by the marquis de Tarifa after his trip to the Holy Land where, according to legend, he was inspired by the ruined house in Jerusalem from which Pontius Pilate is said to have governed. The main entrance, modeled after an ancient Roman triumphal arch, is fashioned from bronze, jasper, and Carrara marble, and the overall effect is one of imperial Roman grandeur.

After your visit, walk less than a block southeast for a view of the:

16. **Iglesia de San Estéban.** It's one of the finest examples of Mudéjar-Gothic architecture in Andalusia. Constructed during the late 1300s and early 1400s, it combines Moorish-style coffered ceilings with Gothic ribbed vaulting in ways beloved by students of the history of Spanish architecture.

From here, retrace your steps back to Plaza de Pilatos, then fork right onto calle Caballerizas for a block until you reach Plaza de San Ildefonso. Flanking its edge rises the:

17. **Iglesia de San Ildefonso.** It's one of the most charming baroque churches in Seville, a colorful and graceful small-scale structure filled with artistic treasures partly paid for with profits from the New World. Regrettably, it's open only during the hours of mass, during which discreet visitors can admire the interior.

From here, walk west for 2 short blocks south along calle Virgenes until you reach the:

18. **Iglesia de San Nicolás de Bari.** Although the church was built in the 1700s, long after the departure of the Moors, the forest of red-marble columns that support the five aisles of its interior evoke some aspects of a mosque. The eclectic, and somewhat cluttered, aspect of its baroque interior is particularly charming.

From here, walk south for a block along calle de Federico Rubio until you reach the soaring walls of a building usually described as the gateway to one of Seville's most colorful antique neighborhoods, the:

19. **Iglesia de Santa Cruz (Holy Cross).** Originally built between 1665 and 1728, and conceived as the parish church of the Barrio de Santa Cruz, which you'll visit shortly, it's prefaced with a relatively new facade that was added in 1929. This is a particularly active church, servicing the spiritual needs of a congested neigh-

borhood, and is normally open only during the hours of mass.

At this point your tour will become less rigidly structured, and will allow you to wander through the narrow and labyrinthine alleyways of the:

20. Barrio de Santa Cruz. Before 1492, when the Jews were driven from Spain by the repressive edicts of Ferdinand and Isabella, this was the Jewish ghetto of Seville. Today it's highly desirable real estate—thick-walled houses, window boxes studded with flowers, severe exteriors opening onto private patios that ooze Andalusian charm. Wander at will through the neighborhood, and don't be surprised if you quickly get lost in the maze of twisting streets. Know that your final destination lies uphill (to the southwest) at a point near the cathedral (discreet signs indicate its direction).

We recommend that you walk southwest along the relatively wide calle Ximénes de Enriso, ducking into side alleyways at your whim for views of the streets that radiate out from there. At the barrio's southwestern edge, beside Plaza de los Venerables, you'll want to visit one of the barrio's greatest monuments, the:

21. Hospital de los Venerables (Hospice of the Venerable Ones). It was founded in 1675 as a retirement home for aged priests, was completed 12 years later, and is maintained today as a museum.

☕ **TAKE A BREAK**   One of the best places in this barrio to have a drink and take tapas is **Casa Román,** on Plaza de los Venerables (☎ **95-421-64-08**). This bygone-era bar has some of the finest tapas in the old quarter, and you can make your selection at a deli counter. It's also a good place to stop for a pick-me-up glass of regional wine.

From here, you're only a very short walk from the point near the cathedral where you initiated this walking tour several hot and dusty, but artistically rewarding, hours ago.

7 Organized Tours

CITY TOURS

One of the best ways to navigate your way around the labyrinth of a complicated, traffic-clogged city like Seville is to take a city tour that offers a historical and geographical overview. A local outfit that handles only the briefest of bus tours is **Transvías de Sevillas,** Plaza de Colón (☎ **95-450-20-99**). Tours of Seville depart every hour, on the hour, year-round, beginning at 10am, with the last departure scheduled for 6pm. The commentary is jaded and a bit blasé, and the overview is fairly superficial, but the cost of 1,500 pesetas (US$9) per person is reasonable. Know that during the hour-long tour, you'll never emerge from the bus. Reservations aren't necessary. Departures are from in front of the Transvías office, opposite the Bullring (Maestranza) on Plaza de Colón.

More appealing are the 4-hour city tours conducted twice-daily by **Visitour,** Avenida de los Descubrimientos, s/n, Isla de la Cartuja (☎ **95-446-36-29**). Morning and afternoon tours are conducted daily at 9am, 9:30am, 3:45pm, 4pm, 4:30pm, 8pm, and 8:30pm, costing 4,900 to 5,750 pesetas (US$29.40 to US$34.50) each. Morning tours include a visit to the cathedral, two museums, and the Santa Cruz district, whereas the afternoon tour is a boat trip around the city and a visit to one museum. The morning tour is the more expensive of the two.

ANDALUSIAN EXCURSIONS

In addition to being loaded with monuments of consuming historic and cultural interest, Seville makes a worthy base for explorations of Andalusia. The best of the tours are offered by **Visitour,** Avenida de los Descubrimientos, s/n, Isla de la Cartuja (☎ **95-446-36-29**). A company formed in 1995 from a corps of experienced travel professionals, they are well versed in the charm and lore of the region. Their buses, holding between 8 and 48 passengers, offer some of the best guided tours in Andalusia, always with the option of retrieving and redepositing clients at their hotels. Reservations a day in advance are strongly recommended. Two of the company's most popular tours depart daily. A tour of Granada leaves Seville at 7am, explores all that city's major monuments and neighborhoods, and returns to Seville around 7pm. The price is 13,750 pesetas (US$82.50). A tour of Córdoba departs from Seville at 8:30am and 9am, returning around 6pm and 6:30pm, costing 11,500 pesetas (US$69) per person.

Two other worthy tours depart 3 or 4 days a week, depending on the season. A visit to Jerez de la Frontera and Cádiz includes a visit to the riding school at Jerez, a tour of one of the city's most interesting wine bodegas, lunch in an Andalusian village (Puerto de Santa María), and a boat ride that begins on the Guadalete River and ends in Cádiz's Atlantic harbor. The tour, departing at 9am and 9:30am and returning at 6pm and 6:30pm, costs 11,900 pesetas (US$71.40) per person. If at all possible, try to schedule your participation for a Thursday (or, during June and July, for Thursday or Saturday), as participants attend a riding exhibition in Jerez that's conducted only on those days. A visit to the historic hamlet of Ronda, conducted several times a week, departing at 9am and 9:30am, returning at 6pm and 6:30pm, costs 13,500 pesetas (US$81) per person.

8 Shopping

SHOPPING A TO Z
ART GALLERIES
Rafael Ortíz. Marmolles, 12. ☎ **95-421-48-74.**

This is one of the most respected art galleries in Seville, specializing in contemporary paintings, usually from Iberian artists. Exhibitions change frequently, and because of canniness of this emporium's judgments, inventories sell out quickly. It's open Monday to Saturday 10am to 1:30pm and 4:30 to 8pm.

BOOKS
The English Bookshop. Eduardo Dato, 36. ☎ **95-465-57-54.**

Smaller than many of the other book emporiums in Seville, this is the kind of place where you can find tomes on gardening, political discourse, philosophy, and pop fiction, all gathered into one cozy place. Open Monday to Saturday 10am to 1:45pm and 4:30 to 8:30pm.

Librería Vértice. San Fernando, 33. ☎ **95-421-16-54.**

Set conveniently close to Seville's university, this store stocks books in a polyglot of languages. Inventory ranges from the esoteric and professorial to Spanish romances of the soap-opera genre. Open Monday to Saturday 10am to 1:30pm and 4:30 to 8:30pm.

CERAMICS
El Postigo. Arfe, s/n. ☎ **95-456-00-13.**

Set in the town center near the cathedral, this shop contains one of the biggest selections in town of Andalusian ceramics. Some of the pieces are much, much too big to fit into your suitcase; others, especially the hand-painted tiles, make charming souvenirs that can easily be transported. Open Monday to Saturday 10am to 2pm, Monday to Friday 5 to 8pm.

Martian. Calle Sierpes, 74. ☎ **95-421-34-13.**

Set close to Seville's Town Hall, this outfit sells a wide array of painted tiles and ceramics, the kind that invariably look better when transported away from the store and displayed within your home. The inventory includes vases, plates, cups, serving dishes, and statues, all made in or near Seville. Many of the pieces exhibit ancient geometric patterns of Andalusia. Other floral motifs are rooted in Spanish traditions of the 18th century. Open Monday to Saturday 10am to 1:30pm and 4:30 to 8:30pm.

DEPARTMENT STORES

El Corte Inglés. Plaza Duque, 10. ☎ **95-422-09-31.**

This is the best of the several department stores clustered in Seville's commercial center. A well-accessorized branch of a nationwide chain, it features multilingual translators and rack after rack of every conceivable kind of merchandise for the well-stocked home, kitchen, and closet. If you're in the market for the brightly colored *feria* costumes worn by young girls during Seville's holidays, there's an impressive selection of the folkloric accessories that make Andalusia memorable. Open Monday to Saturday 10am to 9pm.

   Marks & Spencer, Plaza Duque, 6 (☎ **95-456-36-56**), is the Seville branch of a gigantic chain of middle-of-the-road department stores based in England. It caters to British expatriates and retirees based in the hills around Seville, so expect conservative, well-made clothes. Open Monday to Saturday 10am to 9pm.

FANS

Casa Rubio. Sierpes, 56. ☎ **95-422-68-72.**

Carmen fluttered her fan and broke hearts in ways that Andalusian maidens have done with their *caballeros* for centuries. Casa Rubio stocks one of the city's largest supplies, ranging from the austere and dramatic to some of the most florid and fanciful aids to coquetry available in Spain. Open Monday to Saturday 10am to 1:45pm and 5 to 8pm.

FASHION

Iconos. Avenida de la Constitución. ☎ **95-422-14-08.**

This is an excellent example of a small, idiosyncratic boutique loaded with fashion accessories that can be used by everyone from teenage girls to mature women. Silk scarves, costume jewelry, and an assortment of T-shirts with logos lettered in varying degrees of tastelessness—it's all here. Much of the merchandise represents the new, youthful perceptions of post-*movida* Spain. Open Monday to Saturday 10am to 2pm, Monday to Friday 5 to 8pm.

Nicole Miller. Albareda, 16. ☎ **95-456-36-14.**

This is one of the best addresses in Seville for women who want to avoid the anonymity of El Corte Inglés, benefit from a solicitous staff, and gain access to fashion statements from Spain and the rest of Europe. Open Monday to Saturday 10am to 2pm, Monday to Friday 5 to 8pm.

Perdales. Cuna, 23. ☎ **95-421-37-09.**

One of the most prestigious purveyors of flamenco dresses and feria costumes in Seville, this shop outfits many professional performers. Much of its merchandise is akin to couture; other items are less expensive and sold off the rack. Open Monday to Saturday 10am to 2pm, Monday to Friday from 5 to 8pm.

Victorio & Lucchino. Sierpes, 87. ☎ **95-422-79-51.**

This outfit has gained a reputation as a purveyor of stylish clothing, often based on Italian models, to well-heeled women of Andalusia. If you've already exhausted the inventories of the boutiques within El Corte Inglés and not found the alluring garment you're looking for, this place will probably have it. Open Monday to Saturday 10am to 2pm, Monday to Friday 5 to 8pm.

GIFTS

Artesania Textil. Sierpes, 70. ☎ **95-456-28-40.**

This shop specializes in the nubby and rough textiles that reflect the earthiness of contemporary Spanish art. Weavings—some using linen, others the rough fibers of Spanish sheep—are the specialty here. Examples include place mats, tablecloths, blankets, shawls, and wall hangings. Open Monday to Saturday 10am to 2pm, Monday to Friday 5 to 8pm.

Matador. Avenida de la Constitución, 28. ☎ **95-422-62-47.**

Souvenirs of the city, T-shirts, hammered wrought-iron whatnots, and ceramics—this store carries these and about a dozen other types of unpretentious gift items you might want to display in your private space back home. Open Monday to Saturday 10am to 2pm, Monday to Friday 5 to 8:30pm.

Venecia. Cuna, 51. ☎ **95-422-99-94.**

The venue here is upscale, and the inventory includes lots of items you can certainly do without—but might not want to. Crystal, art objects, and fanciful accoutrements to the good life as envisioned by bourgeois Spain can all be found here. Open Monday to Saturday 10am to 2pm, Monday to Friday 5 to 8:30pm.

JEWELRY

Joyero Abrines. Sierpes, 47. ☎ **95-427-84-55.**

This is the kind of place where grooms have bought engagement and wedding rings for their brides for generations, and where generations of girlfriends have selected watches and cigarette lighters for the *hombre* of their dreams. There's another branch of this well-known store at calle de la Asunsión, 28 (☎ **95-427-42-44**). Both are open Monday to Saturday 10am to 1:30pm, Monday to Friday 5 to 8:30pm.

MUSIC

Virgin Megastore. Sierpes, 81. ☎ **95-421-21-11.**

This is one of the few stores in Seville that favors the rock-and-roll motif of the rest of Europe and North America without entirely rejecting the Andalusian aesthetic. If you're looking for anything from an esoteric and obscure recording of a 19th-century *zarzuela* to the punk-rock electronic vibes of an underground band in London, this place is likely to have it. It also sells computer games (having brought Nintendo to Andalusia) and a limited roster of books. Open Monday to Friday 10am to 2pm, Saturday 10am to 9pm.

RIDING GEAR

Arcab. Paseo Cristobal Colon, 8. ☎ **95-456-14-21.**

Few other cities in Spain identify their holidays and traditions with horse riding as closely as Seville does. If you're passionately interested in horses (or know someone who is), this place can provide an array of Andalusian-style riding costumes, harnesses, saddles, bridles, and buckles that will make you and your mount feel like direct descendants of the conquistadors. Open Monday to Friday 10am to 2pm, Saturday 10am to 9pm.

9 Seville After Dark

Everyone from Lord Byron to Jacqueline Onassis has appreciated the unique blend of heat, rhythm, and sensuality that interconnect into nightlife in Seville. If you're looking for a theme to define your nightlife wanderings, three of the most obvious possibilities might involve a bacchanalian pursuit of sherry, wine, and well-seasoned tapas. After several drinks, you might venture to a club whose focus revolves around an appreciation of flamenco as a voyeuristic insight into another era and the melding of the Arab and Christian aesthetic. And when you've finished with that, and if you're not wilted from the heat and the crowds, there's always the possibility of learning the intricate steps of one of southern Spain's most addictive dances, La Sevillana.

To keep abreast of what's happening in the arts and after dark in Seville, pick up a copy of the free monthly leaflet *El Giraldillo,* or consult listings in the local press, *Correo de Andalucía, Sudoeste, Nueva Andalucía,* or *ABC Sevilla.* Everything is listed here from jazz venues to classical music concerts and from art exhibits to dance events. You can also call the cultural hot line at ☎ 010 to find out what's happening. Most of the staff at the other end speak English.

Keep an eye out for classical concerts that are sometimes presented in the cathedral of Seville, the church of San Salvador, and the Conservatorio Superior de Música at Jesús del Gran Poder. Variety productions, including some plays for the kids, are presented at **Teatro Alameda,** Crédito (☎ 95-438-83-12). The venerable **Teatro Lope de Vega,** Avenida María Luisa (☎ 95-423-45-46), is the setting for ballet performances and classical concerts, among other events. Near Parque María Luisa, this is the leading stage of Seville, but knowledge of Spanish is necessary.

OPERA

✪ **Teatro de la Maestranza.** Paseo de Colón, 22. ☎ 95-422-65-73.

It wasn't until the 1990s that Seville got its own opera house, but it quickly became one of the world's premier venues for operatic performances. Naturally, the focus is on works inspired by Seville itself, including Verdi's *La Forza del destino* or Mozart's *Marriage of Figaro.* Jazz, classical music, and even the quintessentially Spanish *zarzuelas* (operettas) are also performed here. The opera house can't be visited except during performances. Tickets (which vary in price, depending on the event staged) can be purchased daily 10am to 2pm and from 5 to 8pm at the box office in front of the theater.

FLAMENCO

When the moon is high in Seville and the scent of orange blossoms is in the air, it's time to wander the alleyways of Santa Cruz in search of the sound of castanets. Or take a taxi, to be on the safe side.

El Arenal. Calle Rodo, 7. ☎ 95-421-64-92. Cover 3,700 ptas. (US$22.20), including first drink.

The singers clap, the guitars strum, the tension builds, and the room here feels the ancient and mysterious magic of the flamenco. It's performed at two shows nightly, every evening at 9:30 and 11:30pm. No food is served, but drinks are brought to the minuscule tables in a sweltering back room that's endlessly evocative of Old Andalusia.

❂ El Patio Sevillano. Paseo de Cristóbal Colón, 11. ☎ **95-421-41-20.** Cover 3,800 ptas. (US$22.80), including first drink.

In central Seville on the riverbank between two historic bridges, El Patio Sevillano is a showcase for Spanish folk song and dance, performed by exotically costumed dancers. The presentation includes a wide variety of Andalusian flamenco and songs, as well as classical pieces by such composers as de Falla, Albéniz, Granados, and Chueca. From March to October, there are three shows nightly, at 7:30, 10, and 11:45pm. From November to February, there are two shows nightly, at 7:30 and 10pm.

Los Gallos. Plaza de Santa Cruz, 11. ☎ **95-421-69-81.** Cover 3,500 ptas. (US$21), including first drink.

Negotiating through the labyrinth of narrow streets of the Barrio de Santa Cruz seems to contribute to the authenticity of reaching this intimate and high-energy flamenco club, devoted to the preservation of the venerable art form. No food is served during the shows, which begin every night at 9 and 11:30pm.

DANCE CLUBS
Disco Antigüedades. Calle Argote de Molina. No phone. Cover 650 ptas. (US$3.90), including first drink.

If you're interested in a more universal kind of dance step (disco fever), this is Seville's most popular dance emporium. Set about 2 blocks north of the cathedral, within an antique, much-renovated building, it opens nightly at 11pm; its closing hour varies, depending on business. Expect lots of salsa and merengue in addition to more international tunes that derive from such cities as Los Angeles, London, and Madrid.

DRINKS & TAPAS
Casa Román. Plaza des los Venerables. ☎ **95-421-64-08.**

Tapas are said to have originated in Andalusia, and this old-fashioned bar, incongruously named Román, looks as if it has been dishing them up since day one (actually since 1934). Definitely include this place on your tasca-hopping through the old quarter of the Barrio de Santa Cruz. At the deli counter in front you can make your selection; you might even pick up the fixings for a picnic in the Parque María Luisa. Open Monday to Friday 9am to 3pm and 5:30pm to 12:30am, Saturday and Sunday 10am to 3pm and 6:30pm to 12:30am. Tapas are priced from 550 pesetas (US$3.30).

❂ El Rinconcillo. Gerona, 40. ☎ **95-422-31-83.**

El Rinconcillo has a 1930s ambience, partly because of its real age and partly because of its owners' refusal to change one iota of the decor—this has always been one of the most famous bars in Seville. Actually, it may be the oldest bar in Seville, with a history that dates from 1670. Amid dim lighting, heavy ceiling beams, and iron-based,

Dancing the Sevillana

Flamenco is danced in solitary grandeur, but everyone joins in with the communal but complicated dance steps of the *sevillana.* The best place to check it out is **El Simpecao,** calle Bertis, s/n (no phone). Beginning at 11pm every night of the year, recorded music presents four distinctly different facets of the complicated and old-fashioned dance steps in which dozens of everyday folk strut their Andalusian style in a way you'll rarely see outside of Spain. The setting is modern and just a wee bit battered. Entrance is free; bottled beer costs from around 300 ptas. (US$1.80) each.

marble-topped tables, you can enjoy a beer or a full meal along with the rest of the easygoing clientele. The bartender will mark your tab in chalk on a well-worn wooden countertop. El Rinconcillo is especially known for its salads, omelettes, hams, and selection of cheeses. Look for the art-nouveau tile murals. El Rinconcillo is at the northern edge of the Barrio de Santa Cruz, near the Santa Catalina Church. It's open Thursday to Tuesday 1pm to 2am. A complete meal will cost around 3,000 pesetas (US$18).

La Alicantina. Plaza de El Salvador, 2. ☎ **95-422-61-22.**

What is reported to be the best seafood tapas in town are served against a typically Sevillian, glazed-tile decor. Both the bar and the sidewalk tables are always filled to overflowing. The owner serves generous portions of clams marinara, fried squid, grilled shrimp, fried codfish, and clams in béchamel sauce. Located about 5 blocks north of the cathedral, La Alicantina is open daily 11:30am to 3:30pm and 7:30 to 11:30pm. Tapas range upward from 300 pesetas (US$1.80).

Modesto. Cano y Cueto, 5. ☎ **95-441-68-11.**

At the northern end of Murillo Gardens, opening onto a quiet square with flower boxes and an ornate iron railing, Modesto serves fabulous seafood tapas. The bar is air-conditioned, and you can choose your appetizers just by pointing. Upstairs there's a good-value restaurant, offering a meal for 2,000 pesetas (US$14), including such dishes as fried squid, baby sole, grilled sea bass, and shrimp in garlic sauce. Modesto is open daily 8pm to 2am. Tapas are priced from 500 pesetas (US$3).

A SPECIAL BAR
✪ **Abades.** Abades, 1. ☎ **95-422-56-22.**

A converted mansion in the Barrio de Santa Cruz has been turned into a rendezvous that's been compared to "a living room in a luxurious movie set." One member of the Spanish press labeled it "wonderfully decadent, similar to the ambience created in a Visconti film." In the heart of the Jewish ghetto, it evokes the style of the Spanish Romantic era. The house dates from the 19th century, when it was constructed around a central courtyard with a fountain. It became notorious as a love den in Franco's era. Drinks and low-key conversations are the style here, and since its opening in 1980 all the visiting literati and glitterati have put in an appearance. Young men and women in jeans also patronize the place, enjoying the comfort of the sofas and wicker armchairs.

The ingredients of a special drink called *aqua de Sevilla* are a secret, but we suspect sparkling white-wine, pineapple juice, and eggs (the whites and yolks mixed in separately, of course). Classical music is played in the background. Take a taxi to get here at night, as it might not be safe to wander late along the narrow streets of the barrio. In summer, it's open daily 9pm to 4am; in winter, daily 8pm to 2:30am.

GAY BARS
Seville has a large gay and lesbian population, much of it composed of foreigners and of Andalusians who fled here for a better life, escaping smaller, less tolerant towns and villages. Gay life thrives in such bars as **Isbiliyya Café-Bar,** Paseo de Colón (☎ **95-421-04-60**), which is usually open in summer daily from 8pm to 5am (winter hours are daily 6pm to 4am). The bar is found across the street from the Puente Isabel II bridge. Outdoor tables are a magnet in summer. Another option on the gay scene is **Poseidon,** calle Marqués de Parades, 30 (☎ **95-421-31-92**). This bar and dance club—mercifully air-conditioned in summer—draws not only a mixed crowd but also

an assortment of ages, although most patrons tend to be under 30. It jumps Thursday to Saturday from 10:30pm to 5am.

10 Side Trips from Seville

CARMONA

21 miles (34km) E of Seville

An easy hour-long bus trip from the main terminal in Seville, Carmona is an ancient city dating from Neolithic times. It grew in power and prestige under the Moors, establishing ties with Castile in 1252.

Surrounded by fortified walls, Carmona has three Moorish fortresses—one a parador, the other two the **Alcázar de la Puerta de Córdoba** and **Alcázar de la Puerta de Sevilla.** The top attraction is **Seville Gate,** with its double Moorish arch, opposite St. Peter's Church. Note too, **Córdoba Gate** on calle Santa María de Gracia, which was attached to the ancient Roman walls in the 17th century.

The town itself is a virtual national landmark, filled with narrow streets, white-washed walls, and Renaissance mansions. **Plaza San Fernando** is the most important square, with many elegant 17th-century houses. The most important church is dedicated to **Santa María** and stands on the calle Martín López. You enter a Moorish patio before exploring the interior with its 15th-century white vaulting.

At Jorge Bonsor there's a **Roman amphitheater** as well as a **Roman necropolis** containing the remains of 1,000 families that lived in and around Carmona 2,000 years ago. Of the two important tombs, the Elephant Vault consists of three dining rooms and a kitchen. The other, the Servilia Tomb, was the size of a nobleman's villa. On site is a **Museo Arqueológico** (☎ **95-414-08-11**), displaying artifacts found at the site. From April to October, hours are Tuesday to Saturday 9am to 2pm and 4 to 6pm; off-season, Tuesday to Friday 10am to 2pm, Saturday and Sunday 10am to 2pm. Admission is 250 pesetas (US$1.50).

If you're driving to Carmona, exit from Seville's eastern periphery onto the N-V superhighway, following the signs to the airport, then to Carmona on the road to Madrid. The Carmona turnoff is clearly marked.

WHERE TO STAY & DINE

✪ **Casa de Carmona.** Plaza de Lasso, 1, 41410 Carmona (Sevilla). ☎ **95-419-10-00,** or 212/686-9213 for reservations within North America. Fax 95-419-01-89. www.casadecarmona. com. E-mail: reservations@casadecarmona.com. 30 units. A/C MINIBAR TV TEL. 23,000–32,000 ptas. (US$138–US$192) double; 90,000 ptas. (US$540) suite. Add about 30% for Feria de Sevilla and Easter (Semana Santa). AE, DC, MC, V. Free parking.

One of the most elegant and intimate hotels in Andalusia, this plushly furnished hideaway was originally built as the home of the Lasso family during the 1500s. Several years ago, a team of entrepreneurs added the many features required for a luxury hotel, all the while retaining the marble columns, massive masonry, and graceful proportions of the building's original construction. The most visible public room still maintains vestiges of its original function as a library. Each bedroom is a cozy enclave of opulent furnishings, with distinct decor inspired by ancient Rome, medieval Andalusia, or Renaissance Spain.

On the premises is an outdoor restaurant whose culinary inspiration derives from modern interpretations of Andalusian and international cuisine, with meals served daily 1 to 4pm and from 9 to 11:30pm and priced from around 4,000 pesetas (US$24) each. Amenities include concierge, room service, laundry/dry cleaning, newspaper delivery, baby-sitting, and currency exchange. Set at the edge of the village,

the hotel also offers an outdoor swimming pool with a flowery terrace, an inner courtyard covered against the midsummer heat with canvas awning, and a small exercise
room.

ITÁLICA

5½ miles (9km) NW of Seville

Lovers of Roman history will flock to Itálica (☎ 95-599-73-76), the ruins of an
ancient city northwest of Seville on the major road to Lisbon, near the small town of
Santiponce.

After the battle of Ilipa, Publius Cornelius Scipio Africanus founded Itálica in 206
B.C. Two of the most famous of Roman emperors, Trajan and Hadrian, were born
here. Indeed, master builder Hadrian was to have a major influence on his hometown.
During his reign, the **amphitheater,** the ruins of which can be seen today, was among
the largest in the Roman Empire. Lead pipes that carried water from the Guadalquivir
River still remain. A small **museum** displays some of the Roman statuary found here,
although the finest pieces have been shipped to Seville. Many mosaics, depicting
beasts, gods, and birds, are on exhibit, and others are constantly being discovered. The
ruins, including a Roman theater, can be explored for 250 pesetas (US$1.50). The site
is open April through September, Tuesday to Saturday 9am to 6:30pm and Sunday
9am to 3pm. From October through March, it's open Tuesday to Saturday 9am to
5:30pm and Sunday 10am to 4pm.

If you're driving, exit from the northwest periphery of Seville, following the signs
for highway E-803 in the direction of Zafra and Lisbon. If you don't have a car, take
the bus marked "calle de Santiponce" leaving from calle Marqués de Parada near the
railway station in Seville. Buses depart every hour for the 30-minute trip.

JEREZ DE LA FRONTERA

54 miles (87km) S of Seville

The charming little Andalusian town of Jerez made a name for itself in England for
the thousands of casks of golden sherry it shipped there over the centuries. More than
3,000 years old, Jerez is nonetheless a modern, progressive town with wide boulevards,
although it does have an interesting old quarter. Busloads of visitors pour in every year
to get free drinks at one of the bodegas where wine is aged and bottled.

The name of the town is pronounced "Her-*ez*" or "Her-*eth*," in Andalusian or
Castilian, respectively. The French and the Moors called it various names, including
Heres and Scheris, which the English corrupted to Sherry.

ESSENTIALS

GETTING THERE   By Plane   Iberia and Avianco offer flights to Jerez every
Monday to Friday from Barcelona and Zaragoza; daily flights from Madrid; and several flights a week to and from Valencia, Tenerife, Palma de Majorca, and Grand
Canary Island. No international flights land at Jerez. The airport at Ctra. Jerez-Sevilla
lies about 7 miles (11km) northeast of the city center (follow the signs to Seville). Call
☎ 956-15-00-00 for information.

By Train   Trains from Madrid arrive daily. The trip from Madrid to Jerez on the
TALGO costs 7,600 to 8,800 pesetas (US$45.60 to US$52.80) and lasts 4½ hours.
The railway station in Jerez is at Plaza de la Estación (☎ 956-34-23-19), at the east-
ern end of calle Medina.

By Bus   Bus connections are more frequent than train connections, and the location
of the bus terminal is also more convenient. You'll find it on calle Cartuja, at the

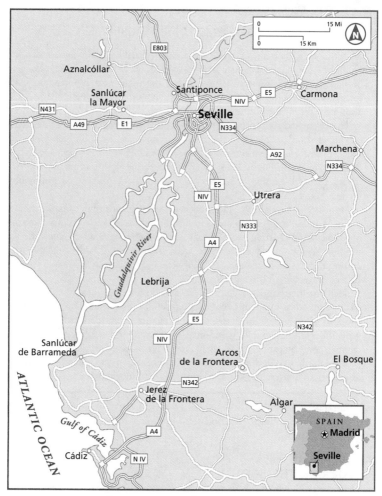

corner of the calle Madre de Díos, a 12-minute walk east of the Alcázar. About 17 buses arrive daily from Cádiz (1 hour away) and 3 per day travel from Ronda (2¾ hours). Seven buses a day arrive from Seville (1½ hours). Phone ☎ **956-34-52-07** for more information.

By Car   Jerez lies on the highway connecting Seville with Cádiz, Algeciras, Gibraltar, and the ferryboat landing for Tangier, Morocco. There's also an overland road connecting Jerez with Granada and Málaga.

VISITOR INFORMATION   The **tourist information office** is at calle Larga, 39 (☎ **956-33-11-50**). To reach it from the bus terminals, take calle Medina to calle Honda and continue along as the road turns to the right. The English-speaking staff can provide directions, transportation suggestions, open hours, and so on, for any bodega you might want to visit. You will also be given a map pinpointing the location of various bodegas. Open April through October, Monday to Friday 9am to 2pm and

---

The Legacy of al-Andalus

The Moors who once occupied Andalusia—notably Seville, Granada, and Córdoba—left more than such architectural treasures as the Giralda Tower in Seville, the great mosque in Córdoba, and the Alahambra in Granada. Their intellectual and cultural legacy still influence modern life, not only in Spain, but also in the rest of the Western world.

The celebrated Arab princesses and sultans with their harems are long gone, encountered today only in the tales of Washington Irving and others. Yet from A.D. 711, the Moors (Muslims who were an ethnic mixture of Berbers, Hispano-Romans, and Arabs) occupied southern Spain for nearly 8 centuries and turned it into a seat of learning. It was a time of soaring achievements in philosophy, medicine, and music.

Moorish rule brought the importation of the eggplant and the almond, as well as the Arabian steed—not to mention such breakthroughs in academia as astronomy (including charting the positions of the planets) and a new and different view of Aristotle. Arab numerals replaced the more awkward Roman system, and from the Arabs came the gift of algebra. Ibn Muadh of Jaén wrote the first European treatise on trigonometry.

Such intellectual giants emerged as the Córdoba-born Jewish philosopher Maimonides. It is said that Columbus evolved his theories about a new route to the East after hours and hours of studying the charts of Idrisi, an Arabian geographer who drew up a world map as early as 1154. Arabs relied upon the compass as a navigational aid long before its use among Portuguese explorers.

Córdoba desired to shine brighter than Baghdad as a center of science and the arts. In time it attracted Abd ar-Rahman II, who introduced the fifth string to

---

5 to 8pm, Saturday 9am to 2pm; off-season, Monday to Saturday 8am to 3pm and 5 to 7pm.

EXPLORING THE AREA

✪ **TOURING THE BODEGAS**   Jerez is not surrounded by vineyards, as you might expect. The vineyards lie to the north and west of Jerez, within the "Sherry Triangle" marked by Jerez, Sanlúcar de Barrameda, and El Puerto de Santa María (the latter two towns on the coast). This is where top-quality *albariza* soil is to be found, the highest quality containing an average of 60% chalk—ideal for the cultivation of grapes used in sherry production, principally the white *Palomino de Jerez*. The ideal time to visit is September. However, visitors can count on the finest in hospitality year-round, since Jerez is widely known for the warm welcome it bestows.

There must be more than a hundred bodegas in and around Jerez where you not only can see how sherries are made, bottled, and aged, but also can get free samples. Among the most famous producers are Sandeman, Pedro Domecq, and González Byass, the maker of Tío Pepe.

On a typical visit to a bodega, you'll be shown through several buildings in which sherry and brandy are manufactured. In one building, you'll see grapes being pressed and sorted; in another, the bottling process; in a third, thousands of large oak casks. Then it's on to an attractive bar where various sherries—amber, dark gold, cream, red, sweet, and velvety—can be sampled. If either is offered, try the very dry La Ina sherry or the Fundador brandy, one of the most popular in the world.

the Arab lute, leading to the development of the six-string guitar. He also ordained the way food should be eaten at mealtimes, a legacy that lives to this day. Before, everybody just helped himself or herself randomly to whatever had been prepared; but he devised a method where courses were served in a regimented order, ending with dessert, fruit, and nuts. Today, Andalusian chefs are reviving many of the old recipes from the Arab cupboard, such as lamb cooked with honey.

Of course, on the entertainment scene, the art form of flamenco can claim significant Middle Eastern influences as well. In his book *In Search of the Firedance,* James Woodall writes, "The music, the literature, the folklore, even religion, but above all the people themselves, speak of it [the epoch of al-Andalus]. It is a matter of attitude, or mentality, and it will be encountered again and again in flamenco."

Arab poetry may have inspired the first ballads sung by European troubadours, which had an enormous impact on later Western literature. Also, many Spanish words today have their origins in the Arabic language, including *alcázar* for fortress, *arroz* for rice, *naranja* for orange, and *limón* for lemon.

The Moors brought an irrigation system to Andalusia, which increased crop production; many of today's systems follow those 1,000-year-old channels. And paper first arrived in Europe through Córdoba.

Although the fanatical Isabella la Católica may have thrown a fit at the heretical idea, it was really a trio of peoples that shaped modern Spain as a nation: the Jews, the Christians, and most definitely the Arabs. The Arabs and the Jews may have been ousted by Isabella and Ferdinand at the close of the 15th century, but their influence still lingers.

Warning: These drinks are more potent than you might expect.

Most bodegas are open Monday to Friday only, 10:30am to 1:30pm. Regrettably, many of them are closed in August, but many do reopen by the third week of August to prepare for the wine festival in early September.

Of the dozens of bodegas you can visit, the most popular are listed below. Some of them charge an admission fee and require a reservation.

A favorite among British visitors is **Harveys of Bristol,** calle Arcos, 57 (☎ **956-15-10-02**), which doesn't require a reservation. An English-speaking guide leads a 2-hour tour year-round, except during the first 3 weeks of August. Visit Monday to Friday for tours at noon, costing 300 pesetas (US$1.80).

You'll definitely want to visit **Williams & Humbert Limited,** Nuño de Cañas, 1 (☎ **956-34-45-39**), which offers tours at noon and 1:30pm Monday to Friday, charging 300 pesetas (US$1.80). Their premium brands include the world-famous Dry Sack Medium Sherry, Canasta Cream, Fino Pando, and Manzanilla Alegría, in addition to Gran Duque de Alba Gran Reserva Brandy. It is wise to reserve in advance.

Another famous name is **González Byass,** Manuel María González, 12 (☎ **956-34-00-00**); admission is 500 pesetas (US$3), and reservations are required. Tours depart at 10am, 11am, noon, and 1pm Monday to Friday. Equally famous is **Domecq,** calle San Ildefonso, 3 (☎ **956-35-70-00**), requiring a reservation but charging no admission. Tours depart at 10am, 11am, and noon Monday to Friday.

THE DANCING HORSES OF JEREZ   A rival of sorts to Vienna's famous Spanish Riding School is the **Escuela Andaluza del Arte Ecuestre (Andalusian School of**

Plan B

Since many people go to Jerez specifically to visit a bodega, August or weekend closings can be very disappointing. If this happens to you, head to the nearby village of Lebrija, about halfway between Jerez and Seville, 8½ miles (14km) west of the main highway. This local winemaking center, where some very fine sherries originate, offers a good glimpse of rural Spain. At one small bodega, that of Juan García, you're courteously escorted around by the owner. Local citizens will gladly point out the several other area bodegas as well. It's all very casual, lacking the rigidity and formality attached to the bodegas of Jerez.

Equestrian Art), Avenida Duque de Abrantes, 11 (☎ **956-30-77-98**). In fact, the long, hard schooling that brings horse and rider into perfect harmony originated in this province. The Viennese school was started with Hispano-Arab horses sent from this region, the same breeds you can see today. Every Thursday at noon, crowds come to admire the Dancing Horses of Jerez as they perform in a show that includes local folklore. Numbered seats sell for 2,400 pesetas (US$14.40), with unnumbered seats going for 1,500 pesetas (US$9). When performances aren't scheduled, you can visit the stables and tack room, observing as the elegant horses are being trained. Hours are Monday to Wednesday and Friday 11am to 1pm; admission is 450 pesetas (US$2.70). Bus 18 goes here.

WHERE TO STAY

Expensive

Hotel Avenida Jerez. Avenida Alcalde Álvaro Domecq, 10, 11405 Jerez de la Frontera. ☎ **956-34-74-11.** Fax 956-33-72-96. www.nh-hoteles.es. E-mail: nh@nh-hoteles.es. 95 units. A/C MINIBAR TV TEL. 18,900 ptas. (US$113.40) double; 26,000 ptas. (US$156) suite. AE, DC, MC, V. Parking 1,500 ptas. (US$9).

Close to the commercial heart of Jerez, this hotel occupies a modern balconied structure of seven stories and is the best hotel within Jerez itself, although Montecastillo (see below) on the outskirts is a serious challenger. Inside, cool floors of polished stone, leather armchairs, and a variety of potted plants create a restful haven. The good-size rooms are discreetly contemporary and decorated in neutral colors, with big windows, comfortable beds, and private bathrooms equipped with hair dryers.

    Dining/Diversions: The hotel maintains a pleasant cafeteria providing coffee shop–style snacks and platters of Spanish food. There's also a bar.

    Amenities: Room service (daily 7am to 11pm), baby-sitting, concierge, laundry/valet, car-rental desk.

Hotel Royal Sherry Park. Avenida Alcalde Álvaro Domecq, 11 Bis, 11405 Jerez de la Frontera. ☎ **956-31-76-14.** Fax 956-31-13-00. www.travelcom.es/sherry. E-mail: reservas@sherryparkhotel.com. 170 units. A/C MINIBAR TV TEL. 18,250 ptas. (US$109.50) double; 28,000–32,000 ptas. (US$168–US$192) suite. AE, DC, MC, V. Free parking.

Especially noted for its setting in a palm-fringed garden and for its large pool, this is one of the best modern hotels in Jerez. Located on a wide and verdant boulevard north of the historic center of town, it contains a marble-floored lobby, efficiently modern public rooms, and fairly standard but comfortable bedrooms, each with a private tiled bathroom. The uniformed staff lays out a copious breakfast buffet and serves drinks at several hideaways, both indoors and in the garden.

    Dining/Diversions: El Abaco Restaurant, which spills over onto an outdoor terrace, serves flavorful international cuisine. A bar with a good selection of sherries and whiskeys lies nearby.

Amenities: Room service (available daily from 8am to midnight), laundry/valet, concierge, baby-sitting, outdoor pool, car rentals, shopping boutiques.

Montecastillo. Carrertera N-342, 11406 Jerez de la Frontera. ☎ **956-15-12-00.** Fax 956-15-12-09. 120 units. A/C MINIBAR TV TEL. 19,000–26,000 ptas. (US$114–US$156) double; 62,500–125,000 ptas. (US$375–US$750) suite. AE, DC, MC, V. Free parking.

Giving Hotel Avenida Jerez serious competition is this deluxe country club in the rolling hills of the sherry wine country. The most tranquil retreat in the area, it has rooms with scenic-view balconies overlooking a Jack Nicklaus–designed 18-hole golf course. Just a 10-minute ride from the center of Jerez, the hotel is elegantly furnished and professionally run. The spacious guest rooms are decorated in a provincial French style with elegant fabrics, beautiful linens, and large beds fitted with quality mattresses. The marble baths boast plush towels, toiletries, and hair dryers.

Dining/Diversions: At the **Montecastillo Restaurant,** favorite regional meals are combined with traditional Spanish and international dishes for some of the best cuisine in the area.

Amenities: Room service, laundry/dry cleaning, baby-sitting. In addition to the golf course, there are pools and a sauna. Horseback riding and tennis are available nearby, and there are paddle tennis facilities at the adjacent and exclusive Montecastillo Country Club.

Moderate

La Cueva Park. Carretera de Arcos km 6,5 Apartado 536, 11406 Jerez de la Frontera. ☎ **956-18-9120.** Fax 956-18-9121. www.madeinspain.net/hotelcadiz/lacuevapark. 58 units. A/C MINIBAR TV TEL. 18,000 ptas. (US$108) double; 40,000 ptas. (US$240) suite. AE, DC, MC, V. Parking 1,000 ptas. (US$6).

This charming hotel in a century-old building lies 4 miles from the center of town, attracting motorists, though it's also half a mile from the bus station. The architecture is typical of Andalusia, with a tiled roof overhanging thick brick walls. Gardens surround the hotel. All the medium-size units have a classical decor and are comfortably furnished. There are also nine white-walled bungalow-style apartments, classified as suites, each with its own cooking area, living room, and terrace. The hotel restaurant, Mesón la Cueva, serves high-quality Andalusian and international dishes. There's also a cafeteria, an outdoor pool, and laundry service.

Inexpensive

El Coloso. Pedro, Alonso 13, 11402 Jerez de la Frontera. ☎ or fax **956-34-90-08.** E-mail: martaorden@hotmail.com. 25 units. A/C TV TEL. 7,500 ptas. (US$45) double; 22,000 ptas. (US$132) suite. Rates include breakfast buffet. MC, V. Parking 800 ptas. (US$4.80).

A few steps from the Plaza de la Angustias in the historic center, this is one of the best bargains in town, modest but recommendable in its unpretentious way. The decor is in the conventional local style, with white-washed walls and a trio of Andalusian-style patios with balconies opening onto street scenes of Jerez. The hotel opened in 1969, and was last renovated in 1998. Bedrooms are a bit cramped but beautifully maintained with good beds. Breakfast is the only meal served. Even though low budget, it does not sacrifice comfort and cleanliness.

Hotel Serit. Higueras, 7, 11402 Jerez de la Frontera. ☎ **956-34-07-00.** Fax 956-34-07-16. E-mail: hotelsedit@redicom.es. 35 units. A/C TV TEL. 8,000–10,000 ptas. (US$48–US$60) double. AE, DC, MC, V. Parking 1,000 ptas. (US$6).

The modern three-star Hotel Serit, near Plaza de la Angustias, offers rooms that are functionally furnished and comfortable at a good price. Ranging in size from small to medium, rooms are equipped with firm mattresses resting on good Spanish beds, and small but well-maintained private bathrooms, each with a shower stall and a hair dryer. There's a pleasant bar downstairs, plus a modern breakfast lounge. Laundry and room service are provided.

WHERE TO DINE

El Bosque. Alcalde Álvaro Domecq, 26. ☎ **95-631-31-00.** Reservations required. Main courses 3,000–5,000 ptas. (US$18–US$30). AE, DC, MC, V. Mon–Sat 1:30–5pm and 8:30pm–2am. SPANISH/INTERNATIONAL.

Less than a mile northeast of the city center, the city's most elegant restaurant was established just after World War II. A favorite of the sherry-producing aristocracy, it retains a strong emphasis on bullfighting memorabilia, which makes up most of the decor.

Order the excellent *rabo de toro* (bull's-tail stew) if you want to be a true native. You might begin with a soothing Andalusian gazpacho, then try one of the fried fish dishes, such as hake Seville style. Rice with king prawns and baby shrimp omelettes are deservedly popular dishes. Occasionally, Laguna duck in honey with chestnuts and pears is featured. Desserts, including pistachio ice cream, are usually good.

Gaitán. Calle Gaitán, 3. ☎ **956-34-58-59.** Reservations recommended. Main courses 1,000–2,500 ptas. (US$6–US$15); fixed-price menu 2,500 ptas. (US$15). AE, DC, MC, V. Daily 1–4:30pm, Mon–Sat 8:30–11:30pm. ANDALUSIAN.

Juan Hurtado, who has won acclaim for the food served here, owns this small restaurant near Puerta Santa María. Surrounded by walls displaying celebrity photographs, you can enjoy such Andalusian dishes as garlic soup, various stews, duck à la Sevillana, and fried seafood. One special dish is lamb cooked with honey, based on a recipe so ancient it goes back to the Muslim occupation of Spain. For dessert, the almond tart is a favorite.

۞ Mesa Redonda. Manuel de la Quintana, 3. ☎ **956-34-00-69.** Reservations required. Main courses 1,800–2,000 ptas. (US$10.80–US$12); set menu 4,500 ptas. (US$27). AE, DC, MC, V. Mon–Sat 1:30–4pm and 9–11pm. Closed last week in July and first 3 weeks in Aug. TRADITIONAL SPANISH.

This restaurant is a rare treat. For the last 15 or so years, the owner and chef, José Antonio Romero and his wife, Margarita, have sought out the traditional recipes that were once served in the private homes of the aristocratic sherry dons of Jerez. They present these to you in winning and tasty combinations in a setting that is like visiting someone's private residence, complete with a library. In the library are many old recipe books and literature about food and wine. Only 10 tables are offered nightly, and these are easily filled. The menu is ever changing, as is the culinary repertoire of this couple. The cookery has wise simplicity and a superb technique. Try *albondiguillas marineras* or fish balls in a shellfish sauce and most definitely *hojaldre de rape y gambas* (a pastry filled with monkfish and prawns). Most recommendable are the *filetes de lenguado con zetas* (fillet of sole with mushrooms) and *cordero asado* (grilled lamb). For dessert, there is nothing finer than the lemon and almond cake.

Restaurante Tendido 6. Calle Circo, 10. ☎ **956-34-48-35.** Reservations required. Main courses 550–2,000 ptas. (US$3.30–US$12). AE, DC, MC, V. Mon–Sat 1–4pm and 8pm–midnight. SPANISH.

This combination restaurant and tapas bar has loyal clients who come from many walks of life. The chef creates a dignified regional cuisine that includes grilled rump steak, fish soup, and a wide array of Spanish dishes, including Basque and Castilian cuisine. There's nothing really exciting here, but the long-tested recipes are filled with flavor and the place is a good value. The Tendido is on the south side of Plaza de Toros.

Appendix A: Barcelona, Madrid & Seville in Depth

Before you arrive in Barcelona, Madrid, or Seville, a little background information goes far to enrich the experience. Each completely different, each a fascination unto itself, these three cities are the most intriguing that Spain has to offer, packed with the greatest artistic and culinary treasures.

This appendix will cover the basic background and makeup of these cities, with essays on history, the bullfight, culture, art, architecture, food, and wine.

1 The Cities Today

BARCELONA

As residents of Barcelona move into the 21st century, they are both nostalgic for the past and eager to embrace the future. Barcelona suffered the harsh effects of both war and economic stagnation, but leaves the 20th century as a modern, progressive city and as Spain's figurative second capital.

Hardworking Barcelona enjoys the most diversified and prosperous economy of any region in the country (it claims 6% of Spain's land, but produces 20% of its GNP). Among the roster of natives and long-time residents, past and present, are Antoni Gaudí, Pablo Picasso, Salvador Dalí, Joan Miró, and singer Montserrat Caballé, all of whose work has helped redefine their respective art forms.

Unlike many cities that have struggled through post-Olympic slumps, Barcelona has reaped residual benefits from the 1992 games: a slew of impressive new hotels, top-notch sporting facilities now available for public use, and a glittering airport that funnels 18 million visitors into Catalonia and the rest of Spain every year.

In Barcelona, the "new" is actually a return to the "old." Miles of grimy industrial waterfront have been returned to clean and sandy beaches. Flower stalls, bird cages, and decorative pavements along Les Rambles have been rejuvenated, and a state-of-the-art transportation network carries visitors past discreetly restored Gothic and Romanesque buildings and city monuments that just might look better now than when they were first erected 800 years ago. Unlike either of its landlocked competitors, Seville and Madrid, Barcelona can (and does) welcome a growing tourist phenomenon, the cruise-ship industry. And despite the city's burgeoning population, and the unfortunate increase in both drug addiction and street crime, access to the city is easier than ever: Construction of ring roads in the early 1990s has alleviated downtown traffic problems and lowered pollution.

In the last decades of the 20th century the defiant artistic hegemony of Barcelona has begrudgingly given way to the rise of Madrid as superstar of Spain's large cities. The change has exacerbated the traditional cultural and economic rivalry between the cities, and has added a greater sense of passion to the football (soccer) games that lock all of Spain into their obsessive grip whenever a match between the country's two biggest cities is broadcast. But despite Madrid's successful efforts to gradually redefine its allure, visitors who favor Barcelona prefer it with a passion deeper than simple nostalgia. Barcelona—grander, older, more poignant, and more evocative than the brasher and more bureaucratic Madrid—says it best in its civic motto, *Barcelona Es Teva* (Barcelona Belongs to You).

If you decide you love Barcelona, you won't be alone. Nearly 40% of visitors to Spain go to Catalonia. The fact that about 90% of those visitors have trod on Catalonian soil at least twice before speaks well of the region's depth and allure, and of Barcelona's continuing ability to attract them.

MADRID

Madrid's passionate colors and frenetic lives may have already been revealed to you in the films of Pedro Almodóvar. But there's nothing like coming and seeing for yourself the cultural renaissance of Spain's once repressed capital, formerly mired in a long and lingering dictatorship that stifled creativity.

The city of Madrid lies landlocked on a windswept and often arid plain, beneath a sky that has been described as "Velázquez blue." Certain poets have even labeled Madrid the "gateway to the skies." It's populated by adopted sons and daughters from virtually every region of Spain, a demographic fact that adds to its cosmopolitan gloss. Despite its influence as the cultural beacon of the Spanish-speaking world and its quintessentially Spanish nature, the city lacks such all-important Iberian features as a beach, an ancient castle and cathedral, and an archbishop. To compensate, the always-practical Madrileños long ago learned to substitute lazy strolls through the city's verdant parks and along its paseos. They built an airy and elegant palace (which the Spanish king and queen use mainly for ceremonial purposes) and erected countless churches, many glistening with baroque ornamentation and gilt. As for an archbishop, Madrileños are content with falling under the jurisdiction of the archbishop in nearby Toledo.

Madrid, seemingly led at times by its student population of 200,000 or more, is a city to be experienced on its streets and in its cafes, which are filled with more *joie de vivre* than anywhere else in Europe, including Paris. Unemployment may be high, but the youth of Madrid—at least for the moment—seem hopeful about themselves and the future of their city. Almost everyone you meet in Madrid today is an immigrant or a foreign tourist: It's like searching for a native New Yorker in New York.

Known as a melting pot for individualists, which Spain seems to produce in profusion, Madrid moves into the millennium as a world-class capital. Gone are the censorship, the fears, the armed guards, and the priggish morality of the years of Franco, whose influence often impelled Spain's artists, such as Picasso, to ply their crafts in neighboring countries.

Today, artists and writers gravitate to the newly revitalized Madrid, whose allures, freedoms, and promises of acclaim and fiscal recognition pull them into one of the most fertile artistic climates in the world. Whether or not you agree with its expression—artists and art movements, like discos, come and

I thought that I should never return to the country I love more than any other, except for my own.

—Ernest Hemingway

Three Spaniards, four opinions.

—Old Spanish Proverb

go—Madrid is alive, passionate, and richly able to spearhead the *movida* ("action") of a newly liberated Spanish culture.

The legendary propensity of Spaniards to celebrate their nightlife is observed with something approaching passion in Madrid, as Madrileños stay awake till the wee hours, perhaps congregating in the very early morning over hot chocolate and *churros* (fried fingerlike doughnuts). Standing at the same countertop with them might be representatives of the hundreds of business-people and bankers whose zeal and imagination have revitalized the business landscape, transforming hypermodern office towers into well-respected and often feared entrepreneurial forces. For despite Madrid's many pleasures, Madrileños recognize that their city is a place for work as well as for play, as evidenced by the spate of emerging industries, services, and products.

Its inhabitants are enormously proud of their well-endowed city. If you approach it with indulgence, affection, and a sense of humor, you'll be richly rewarded. The capital of the Spanish-speaking world and the object of travel fantasies for thousands of residents of Central and South America, Madrid is at the same time a monolithic big city and a tapestry of small villages that have developed individual identities throughout the various expansions of the capital. Each neighborhood offers countless subcultures that thrive within its precincts. The result is an almost inexhaustible supply of diversions and distractions, some potent enough to justify spending almost all your Spanish vacation in Madrid.

SEVILLE

No less an authority than Santa Teresa called Seville "the work of the devil." But matadors and flamenco artists pay no heed to this long-ago utterance, and continue to preserve the traditions and passions of this remarkable city, the fourth largest in Spain. The Romans, Phoenicians, Greeks, Carthaginians, and Moors all came to conquer, but those hordes have now given way to thousands of foreign visitors, who come to see what all the excitement is about. In the 14th century, shortly after the city was ripped away from its domination by the Moors, a Castilian folk saying entered mainstream Iberian usage: *"Qui non ha visto Sevilla non ha visto maravilla"* ("He who hasn't seen Seville has missed something marvelous").

Seville has more folktales and pithy phrases associated with it than virtually any other city in Spain, and to many visitors it encapsulates all the clichés anyone ever imagined about Iberia. Its sights are more colorful, its *ferias* more uninhibited and garish, its bejeweled wooden Virgins that are carried through the streets during Holy Week more surreal, its bullfights more emotional, and its equestrian grandeur more haughty and aristocratic than anywhere else in Spain.

If you persevere through the blistering heat (the Spaniards refer to it as *La Manzanilla de Espana*—the Frying Pan of Spain), the corrosive sense of poverty and petty crime, and the traffic generated by a city of more than

800,000 inhabitants, Seville will present wonders to you. Jean Cocteau referred to Seville, along with Venice and Beijing, as one of the world's most magical cities. Bizet and Mozart used it as the setting for *Carmen* and *Don Giovanni*, and few visitors can remain immune to the charms of its endless palm trees and orange blossoms, its winning combinations of Moorish and Christian architecture.

Set around a medieval Moorish core, a sweltering 70 miles inland from the sea, on the banks of the Guadalquivir, Seville is graced with an architecture whose style was fueled both by the zeal of the Catholic monarchs to strengthen their grip on Andalusia and by floods of gold pouring into its port from the New World.

Today its prominence as a seaport has declined immeasurably, thanks to the deeper drafts of oceangoing vessels and to the fact that the Guadalquivir contains more silt, and is a lot less mighty, than when the Castilians selected the city as the capital of Catholic Andalusia. Dredging efforts have opened the river somewhat to barge traffic, although its volume will never be comparable to that of the burgeoning seaport of Barcelona or even its prime Andalusian competitor, Cádiz.

Seville has compensated in other ways, however. Few cities have reinvented themselves as aggressively as Seville during the 1990s. Although the city's distinctive traditions were retained with something approaching religious fervor, far-reaching changes were initiated as part of the 1992 Expo festival that celebrated the 500th anniversary of Columbus's departure from Seville for the colonization of the New World. Thanks partly to the fact that Spain's once-powerful prime minister, Felipe González Márquez, was born and reared in Seville, funds poured into the city for the development of the Expo site on an island in the Guadalquivir, Isla de La Cartuja. Seven new bridges were built across the Guadalquivir, and miles of riverfront esplanade, new rail and bus stations, renovated or rebuilt terminals at the local airport, refurbished museums, more than 20 new hotels, a new opera house (Teatro de la Maestranza), and a new convention center were all created in anticipation of the event.

Although the movida that has transformed the ambience of Madrid is less intense in Seville, there's a renewed sense of vigor to the syncopated clapping of the flamenco, the crowds milling around the city's legendary tapas bars, and the teenage Carmen clones that appear during ferias wearing polka-dot dresses and rattling their castanets. Crime, the heat, and the exhaust fumes put a damper on all aspects of tourism to the city. But despite those ills, Seville continues to arouse passion in its visitors, a pale reflection of the violence that drove the jealous protagonist of *Carmen* to plunge a knife into her heart.

2 A Look at the Past

Dateline

- **11th c. B.C.** Phoenicians settle Spain's coasts.
- **650 B.C.** Greeks colonize the east.
- **600 B.C.** Celts cross the Pyrenees and settle in Spain.
- **6th–3rd c. B.C.** Carthaginians make Cartagena their colonial capital, driving out the Greeks.

continues

ANCIENT TIMES

Ancestors of the Basques may have been the first settlers in Spain 10,000 to 30,000 years ago, followed, it is believed, by Iberians from North Africa. They, in turn, were followed by Celts, who crossed the Pyrenees around 600 B.C. These groups evolved into a Celtic-Iberian people who inhabited central Spain.

Others coming to the Iberian Peninsula in ancient times were the Phoenicians, who took over coastal areas on the Atlantic beginning in the 11th century B.C. Cádiz, originally the Phoenician settlement of Gades, is perhaps the oldest town in Spain. The Greeks came roughly 500 years after the Phoenicians, lured by the peninsula's wealth of gold and silver. The Greeks established colonies that were later conquered by Carthaginians from North Africa.

Around 200 B.C. the Romans vanquished the Carthaginians and laid the foundations of the present Latin culture. Traces of Roman civilization can still be seen today. By the time of Julius Caesar, Spain (Hispania) was under Roman law and began a long period of peace and prosperity.

BARBARIAN INVASIONS, THE MOORISH KINGDOM & THE RECONQUEST

When Rome fell in the 5th century, Spain was overrun, first by the Vandals and then by the Visigoths from eastern Europe. The chaotic rule of the Visigothic kings lasted about 300 years, but the barbarian invaders did adopt the language of their new country and tolerated Christianity as well.

In A.D. 711 Moorish warriors led by Tarik crossed over into Spain and conquered the disunited country. By 714 they controlled most of it, except for a few mountain regions around Asturias. For 8 centuries the Moors occupied their new land, which they called *al-Andalus,* or Andalusia, with Córdoba as the capital. A great intellectual center, Córdoba became the scientific capital of Europe; notable advances were made in agriculture, industry, literature, philosophy, and medicine. The Jews were welcomed by the Moors, often serving as administrators, ambassadors, and financial officers. But the Moors quarreled with one another, and soon the few Christian strongholds in the north began to advance south.

The Reconquest, the name given to the Christian efforts to rid the peninsula of the Moors, slowly reduced the size of the Muslim holdings, with Catholic monarchies forming in northern areas. The three powerful kingdoms of Aragón, Castile, and León were joined in 1469, when Ferdinand of Aragón married Isabella of Castile. Catholic kings, as they were called, launched the final attack on the Moors and completed the Reconquest in 1492 by capturing Granada.

That same year Columbus, the Genoese sailor, landed on the West Indies, laying the

- **2nd c. B.C.–A.D. 2nd c.** Rome controls most of Iberia. Christianity spreads.
- **218–201 B.C.** Second Punic War: Rome defeats Carthage.
- **5th c. A.D.** Vandals, then Visigoths, invade Spain.
- **8th c.** Moors conquer most of Spain.
- **1214** More than half of Iberia is regained by Catholics.
- **1469** Ferdinand of Aragón marries Isabella of Castile.
- **1492** Catholic monarchs seize Granada, the last Moorish stronghold. Columbus lands in the New World.
- **1519** Cortés conquers Mexico. Charles I is crowned Holy Roman Emperor, as Charles V.
- **1556** Philip II inherits throne and launches the Counter-Reformation.
- **1588** England defeats Spanish Armada.
- **1700** Philip V becomes king. War of Spanish Succession follows.
- **1713** Treaty of Utrecht ends war. Spain's colonies reduced.
- **1759** Charles III ascends throne.
- **1808** Napoléon places brother Joseph on the Spanish throne.
- **1813** Wellington drives French out of Spain; the monarchy is restored.
- **1876** Spain becomes a constitutional monarchy.
- **1898** Spanish-American War leads to Spain's loss of Puerto Rico, Cuba, and the Philippines.
- **1923** Primo de Rivera forms military directorate.
- **1930** Right-wing dictatorship ends; Primo de Rivera exiled.
- **1931** King Alfonso XIII abdicates; Second Republic is born.
- **1933–35** Falange party formed.

- **1936–39** Civil War between the governing Popular Front and the Nationalists led by General Francisco Franco.
- **1939** Franco establishes dictatorship, which will last 36 years.
- **1941** Spain technically stays neutral in World War II, but Franco favors Germany.
- **1955** Spain joins the United Nations.
- **1969** Franco names Juan Carlos as his successor.
- **1975** Juan Carlos becomes king. Franco dies.
- **1978** New, democratic constitution initiates reforms.
- **1981** Coup attempt by right-wing officers fails.
- **1982** Socialists gain power after 43 years of right-wing rule.
- **1986** Spain joins the European Community (now the European Union).
- **1992** Barcelona hosts the Summer Olympics; Seville hosts 1992 Expo.
- **1996** A conservative party defeats Socialist party, ending 13-year rule. José María Aznar chosen prime minister.
- **1998** Two cultural milestones for Spain: the inauguration of the controversial Guggenheim Museum at Bilbao and the reopening of Madrid's opera house, Teatro Real.
- **1999** Spain falls under the Euro umbrella.
- **2000** Economy goes on an upswing as the siesta begins to become obsolete.

foundations for a far-flung empire that brought wealth and power to Spain during the 16th and 17th centuries.

The Spanish Inquisition, begun under Ferdinand and Isabella, sought to eradicate all heresy and secure the primacy of Catholicism. Non-Catholics, Jews, and Moors were mercilessly persecuted, and many were driven out of the country.

THE GOLDEN AGE & LATER DECLINE

Columbus's voyage to America and the conquistadors' subsequent exploration of that land ushered Spain into its golden age.

In the first half of the 16th century, Balboa discovered the Pacific Ocean, Cortés seized Mexico for Spain, Pizarro took Peru, and a Spanish ship (initially commanded by the Portuguese Magellan, who was killed during the voyage) circumnavigated the globe. The conquistadors took Catholicism to the New World and shipped cargoes of gold back to Spain. The Spanish Empire extended all the way to the Philippines. Charles V, grandson of Ferdinand and Isabella, was the most powerful prince in Europe—King of Spain and Naples, Holy Roman Emperor and Lord of Germany, Duke of Burgundy and the Netherlands, and ruler of the New World territories.

But much of Spain's wealth and human resources was wasted in religious and secular conflicts. First Jews, then Muslims, and finally Catholicized Moors were driven out—and with them much of the country's prosperity. When Philip II ascended the throne in 1556, Spain could indeed boast vast possessions: the New World colonies; Naples, Milan, Genoa, Sicily, and other portions of Italy; the Spanish Netherlands (modern Belgium and the Netherlands); and portions of Austria and Germany. But the seeds of decline had already been planted.

Philip, a fanatic Catholic, devoted his energies to subduing the Protestant revolt in the Netherlands and to becoming the standard-bearer for the Counter-Reformation. He tried to return England to Catholicism, first by marrying Mary I ("Bloody Mary") and later by wooing her half sister, Elizabeth I, who rebuffed him. When, in 1588, he resorted to sending the Armada, it was ignominiously defeated; and that defeat symbolized the decline of Spanish power.

In 1700 a Bourbon prince, Philip V, became king, and the country fell under the influence of France. Philip V's right to the throne was challenged by a Hapsburg archduke of Austria, thus giving rise to the War of the Spanish

Succession. When it ended, Spain had lost Flanders, its Italian possessions, and Gibraltar (still held by the British today).

During the 18th century, Spain's direction changed with each sovereign. Charles III (1759–88) developed the country economically and culturally. Charles IV became embroiled in wars with France, and the weakness of the Spanish monarchy allowed Napoléon to place his brother Joseph Bonaparte on the throne in 1808.

THE 19TH & 20TH CENTURIES

Although Britain and France had joined forces to restore the Spanish monarchy, the European conflicts encouraged Spanish colonists to rebel. Ultimately, this led the United States to free the Philippines, Puerto Rico, and Cuba from Spain in 1898.

In 1876 Spain became a constitutional monarchy. But labor unrest, disputes with the Catholic Church, and war in Morocco combined to create political chaos. Conditions eventually became so bad that the Cortés, or parliament, was dissolved in 1923, and General Miguel Primo de Rivera formed a military directorate. Early in 1930 Primo de Rivera resigned, but unrest continued.

On April 14, 1931, a revolution occurred, a republic was proclaimed, and King Alfonso XIII and his family were forced to flee. Initially the liberal constitutionalists ruled, but soon they were pushed aside by the socialists and anarchists, who adopted a constitution separating church and state, secularizing education, and containing several other radical provisions (for example, agrarian reform and the expulsion of the Jesuits).

The extreme nature of these reforms fostered the growth of the conservative Falange party (*Falange española*, or Spanish Phalanx), modeled after Italy's and Germany's fascist parties. By the 1936 elections, the country was divided equally between left and right, and political violence was common. On July 18, 1936, the army, supported by Mussolini and Hitler, tried to seize power, igniting the Spanish Civil War. General Francisco Franco, coming from Morocco to Spain, led the Nationalist (rightist) forces in the three years of fighting that ravaged the country. Towns were bombed and atrocities were committed in abundance. Early in 1939, Franco entered Barcelona and went on to Madrid; thousands of republicans were executed. Franco became chief of state, remaining so until his death in 1975.

Although Franco adopted a neutral position during World War II, his sympathies obviously lay with Germany and Italy, and Spain as a nonbelligerent assisted the Axis powers. This action intensified the diplomatic isolation into which the country was forced after the war's end—in fact, it was excluded from the United Nations until 1955.

Before his death, General Franco selected as his successor Juan Carlos de Borbón y Borbón, son of the pretender to the Spanish throne. After the 1977 elections, a new constitution was approved by the electorate and the king; it guaranteed human and civil rights, as well as free enterprise, and canceled the status of the Roman Catholic Church as the church of Spain. It also granted limited autonomy to several regions, including Catalonia and the Basque provinces, both of which, however, are still clamoring for complete autonomy.

In 1981, a group of right-wing military officers seized the Cortés and called upon Juan Carlos to establish a Francoist state. The king, however, refused, and the conspirators were arrested. The fledgling democracy overcame its first test. Its second major accomplishment—under the Socialist administration of Prime Minister Felipe González, the country's first leftist government since

1939—was to gain Spain's entry into the European Community (now Union) in 1986.

Further proof that the new Spain had been fully accepted by the international community came in 1992. Spain was designated by the European Union (EU) as the Cultural Capital of Europe for the year; but more significant, the Summer Olympics were held successfully in Barcelona and the world's fair, Expo '92, was mounted in Seville, in Andalusia.

In March 1996, more than 78% of Spain's 32 million registered voters cast ballots and ended the 13-year rule of the scandal-plagued Socialist party of Prime Minister Felipe González. A conservative party with roots in the Franco dictatorship was swept into power, led by José Maria Aznar, leader of the Popular party, who pledged to represent "all Spain." González took the defeat bitterly, alleging that the vote "was a step back to the fascist dictatorship of Franco."

That dire prediction has not proved accurate, as Spain forged ahead to integrate itself more fully into the European economy, taking stringent measures to streamline its economy to meet the requirements necessary for that step.

In January 1999, Spain joined 10 other EU countries in adopting the euro as its new currency, although it will be going through a transitional period until January 1, 2002. Until that time, the peseta and the euro will continue to exist side by side.

In the meantime, the economy continues to boom, but some beloved traditions, such as the siesta, seem fated to go the way of the dodo bird.

3 Architecture 101

FROM THE ROMANS TO THE MOORS

Architectural roots in Spain date from the Romans, who built aqueducts and more than 12,000 miles of roads and bridges as a means of linking their assorted Iberian holdings. The greatest of these, Via Augusta, followed the Costa Brava, Costa Blanca, and Costa del Sol to transport armies and supplies between Cádiz and the Pyrenees.

This Hispano-Roman style involves prolific use of the vault and the arch—obvious in such marvels as the **aqueduct at Segovia,** the triumphal **arch at Tarragona,** and the rectilinear, carefully planned community at **Mérida** (whose Roman monuments are among the best preserved in Europe).

Historians cite A.D. 409 as the end of the Roman age in Iberia, the beginning of political anarchy, and the migration into Spain of thousands of immigrants (Vandals, Alans, Suevians, and Visigothic tribespeople) from Central Europe. The newcomers, recent converts to some kind of Christianity, built crude chapels and fortresses based on a mishmash of aesthetic ideals from northern Europe and Byzantium, using engineering principles copied from the ancient Romans.

Spain's Romanesque style began to develop around A.D. 800, derived from the legacy of these crude Visigothic buildings (see below). Meanwhile, a major new aesthetic was forcibly imposed upon Spain from the south.

HISPANO-MOORISH ARCHITECTURE

The Moors gained control of the Iberian Peninsula in the 8th century, and their 600-year rule left an architectural legacy that is among the most exotic and colorful in Europe. Regrettably, only a handful of *alcázares* (palaces), *alcazabas* (fortresses), and converted mosques remain intact today. Moorish buildings tended to be relatively flimsy and heavily accented with decorations.

Many have collapsed (or were deliberately destroyed) in the Catholic zeal to "re-Christianize" Iberia.

The most visible traits of the Saracenic style included the use of forests of (sometimes mismatched) columns within mosques, each of which was used to support a network of horseshoe-shaped arches. These interconnected to support low, flat roofs. Some arches were scalloped, then decorated with geometric designs or calligraphic inscriptions from the Koran.

MOZARABIC ARCHITECTURE

Mozárabes were Christian Spaniards who retained their religion under the Muslim rule. They successfully blended Gothic and Moorish styles in their art and architecture. The few structures that remain intact from this period can be found in Toledo and include the **Monastery of El Cristo de la Luz,** originally built in the 900s as a mosque; a 12th-century synagogue, now the church of **Santa María de la Blanca;** and the churches of **Santiago del Arrabal** and **San Román.** A secular example of the style in Toledo is the **Puerto del Sol,** an ornate gate built into the walls that surround the old city. Constructed around 1200, about 150 years after Toledo's reconquest by Christian forces, it combines the distinctive Moorish horseshoe arch with feudal battlements and Christian iconography.

MUDÉJAR ARCHITECTURE

Equivalent in some ways to the above-mentioned Mozárabe style (with which it is frequently confused), Mudéjar refers to the architectural and decorative style developed by Spanish Muslims living in Christian territories after the Reconquista. A mix of Gothic and Moorish influences, it reached its peak between 1275 and 1350, made frequent use of brick instead of stone, and specialized in elaborate woodcarvings that merged the Moorish emphasis on geometrics and symmetry with Christian themes. Regrettably, after the final Moorish stronghold fell to the Christians in 1492, Spanish monarchs did everything they could to purge any artistic legacy left by the Moors. Mudéjar influences, however, still cropped up in rural pockets of Spain until the middle of the 18th century, and, in some cases, even merged subtly with ornate features of the baroque.

PRE-ROMANESQUE & ROMANESQUE ARCHITECTURE

Ensconced in Asturias, feudal rulers of the Christian Visigothic tribes refined their architectural tastes. Stonework became better crafted than the crude models of the previous two centuries, and arches became more graceful. Under the rule of Alfonso the Chaste (791–842), dozens of pre-Romanesque churches were built in Oviedo, and a body believed to be that of Saint James was discovered, miraculously, in a field in Galicia. Thus was born **Santiago de Compostela** (St. James of the Field), the eventual site of a great cathedral and one of the most famous pilgrimage sites in the Christian world.

From these beginnings, and based on money and cultural influences from the floods of pilgrims pouring in from Italy, France, and other parts of Europe, a trail of Romanesque churches, shelters, monasteries, and convents sprang up across northern Spain, especially along the pilgrim route in Catalonia, Aragón, and northern Castile. The style is known for semicircular arches, small windows, crude but evocative carvings, and thick walls. It is best represented in the **church of San Gil** in Zaragoza and the **cloisters of San Pedro,** near Pamplona in the town of Estella.

The Spectacle of Death

For obvious reasons, many people consider bullfighting cruel and shocking. But as Ernest Hemingway pointed out in *Death in the Afternoon:* "The bullfight is not a sport in the Anglo-Saxon sense of the word, that is, it is not an equal contest or an attempt at an equal contest between a bull and a man. Rather it is a tragedy: the death of the bull, which is played, more or less well, by the bull and the man involved and in which there is danger for the man but certain death for the bull." Hemingway, of course, was an aficionado.

When the symbolic drama of the bullfight is acted out, some believe it reaches a higher plane, the realm of art. Some people argue that it is not a public exhibition of cruelty at all, but rather a highly skilled art form that requires will to survive, courage, showmanship, and gallantry. Regardless of how you view it, the spectacle is an authentic Spanish experience and, as such, reveals much about the character of the land and its people.

The *corridas* (bullfights) season lasts from early spring until around mid-October. Fights are held in a *plaza de toros* (bullring), which include the oldest ring in remote Ronda to the big-time Plaza de Toros in Madrid. Sunday is corrida day in most major Spanish cities, although Madrid and Barcelona may also have fights on Thursday.

Tickets fall into three classifications, and prices are based on your exposure to the famed Spanish sun: *sol* (sun), the cheapest; *sombra* (shade), the most expensive; and *sol y sombra* (a mixture of sun and shade), the medium-price range.

The corrida begins with a parade. For many viewers, this may be the high point of the afternoon's festivities, as all the bullfighters are clad in their *trajes de luce,* or luminous suits.

SPANISH GOTHIC

This style surged across provinces adjacent to the French border (Catalonia and Navarre) beginning around 1250. By the late 1200s, churches that had been initiated in the Romanesque style (such as the **Burgos cathedral**) were completed as sometimes flamboyant Gothic monuments. During the 1300s and 1400s, bishops in León, Toledo, and Burgos even imported architects and masons from Gothic strongholds in other parts of Europe to design their cathedrals. In Spain, the Gothic style included widespread use of the ogive (high-pointed) arches and vaults, clustered pilasters, and an opening up of walls to incorporate large, usually stained-glass, windows.

THE RENAISSANCE

After the expulsion of the Moors from Iberia, and Columbus's first landings in the New World in 1492, Spain found itself caught up in a vivid, emphatic sense of its own manifest destiny. Searching for a national style of architecture, the Spanish monarchs adapted the aesthetic trends of Renaissance Italy into a "Hispanicized" style. Foremost among these was the 16th-century plateresque, which emulated in stone the finely worked forms that a silversmith might have hammered into silver plate. The style is best viewed in the exterior of the

Bullfights are divided into thirds. The first is the *tercio de capa* (cape), during which the matador tests the bull with various passes and gets acquainted with it. The second portion, the *tercio de varas* (sticks), begins with the lance-carrying *picadores* on horseback, who weaken, or "punish," the bull by jabbing it in the shoulder area. The horses are sometimes gored, even though they wear protective padding, or the horse and rider may be tossed into the air by the now-infuriated bull. The picadores are followed by the *banderilleros*, whose job it is to puncture the bull with pairs of boldly colored darts.

In the final *tercio de muleta* the action narrows down to the lone fighter and the bull. Gone are the fancy capes. Instead, the matador uses a small red cloth known as a muleta, which, to be effective, requires a bull with lowered head. (The picadores and banderilleros have worked to achieve this.) Using the muleta as a lure, the matador wraps the bull around himself in various passes, the most dangerous of which is the natural; here, the matador holds the muleta in his left hand, the sword in his right. Right-hand passes pose less of a threat, since the sword can be used to spread out the muleta, making a larger target for the bull. After a number of passes, the time comes for the kill, the moment of truth. A truly skilled fighter may dispatch the bull in one thrust.

After the bull dies, the highest official at the ring may award the matador an ear from the dead bull, or perhaps both ears, or ears and tail. For a truly extraordinary performance, the hoof is sometimes added. Spectators cheer a superlative performance by waiving white handkerchiefs, imploring the judge to award a prize. The bullfighter may be carried away as a hero, or if he has displeased the crowd, he may be jeered and chased out of the ring by an angry mob. At a major fight, usually six bulls are killed by three matadors in one afternoon.

University of Salamanca and the Chapel of the New Kings inside the **cathedral at Toledo.**

CLASSICAL SPANISH ARCHITECTURE

The austere regime of Philip II not only welcomed but demanded a less ornate national style from the country's architects. Fervently religious and obsessively ambitious for the advancement of Spanish interests, he embraced the austere ancient Roman forms that had been revived during Italy's late Renaissance. The style's most megalomaniacal manifestation within Spain came with Juan de Herrera's gargantuan, brooding, and military-looking monastery and palace at **El Escorial** (1563–84) on an isolated and windswept plateau outside Madrid. Philip II considered the style an appropriate manifestation of the stern principles of the Counter-Reformation and the new Inquisition that followed.

Later during the Renaissance, Herrera's rectilinear gridirons were replaced with the curved lines of the baroque. This style was avidly embraced by the Jesuits, one of the most powerful religious orders in Spain at the time, whose austere religious bent stood in marked contrast to their flamboyant architectural tastes. The baroque style appears at its most ornate in Andalusia, a region enjoying a building boom at the time thanks to the wealth that poured into its ports from the gold mines of Mexico and Peru.

Ironically, baroque was the style most enthusiastically embraced by the Spanish colonies in South America. Spain's interpretation of Italian baroque architecture is sometimes referred to as Churrigueresque, after José Churriguera (1665–1725), designer to the kings of Spain and architect of Salamanca's New Cathedral. The style is characterized by its dense concentrations of busy ornamentation that often completely disguised the basic form of the building itself. An example of baroque style in Spain is the wedding-cake facade of the **Murcia cathedral.**

FROM BAROQUE TOWARD MODERN

Under the Spanish Bourbon rulers of the 18th century, the favored style embraced the baroque and neoclassical influences of aristocratic France. **El Pardo, Riofrio,** and **Aranjuez** were all built as Europeanized hideaways. Even the design of the **Royal Palace in Madrid** was modeled after Versailles.

In the 19th century the Romantic age encouraged a revolt against the ideals of balance and reason that had defined upscale European architecture during the late 1700s. Spanish architecture throughout the 19th century was torn between the value of the individual architect's eclectic, personalized, and sometimes flamboyant vision, and the inevitable reactions that swung the pendulums of public taste back toward greater restraint and symmetry. There developed a new respect for the Gothic, as many 500-year-old Gothic cathedrals were adapted or altered with neo-Gothic alterations that modern art historians sometimes view with horror.

Out of this tension emerged one of Spain's most widely recognized architectural giants, **Antoni Gaudí** (1852–1926). His idiosyncratic, organic style, called Catalan Art Nouveau, or *modernisme,* coincided neatly with the most intense building boom ever experienced within his hometown of Barcelona. Gaudí succeeded in fusing regional aesthetics and forms with a style that still challenges architectural thinking. He created curiously curved and sinuous, "organic-looking" buildings in protest against the rising anonymity of the industrial age and dull architecture without soul that would reach its most grotesque form in Nazi Germany long after Gaudí's death. One of the best examples of his ideas can be seen in **Barcelona's Casa Milá.**

ARCHITECTURE TODAY

Other than occasional models of genuine inspiration, such as the whimsical and surrealist buildings devised by Salvador Dalí, much of modern Spain's architecture is derived from the older, tried-and-true sources that span the country's distinguished range of architectural traditions. When it comes to recycling the feudal or Renaissance monuments of yesteryear, Spain has no equal, as evidenced by the country's network of historic paradors (government-run hostelries). Regrettably, some areas of modern Spain, including many neighborhoods of Madrid and long stretches of the Costa del Sol, have bristled with high-rise, concrete-and-glass apartment houses. Few boast any distinguishing features, provoking laments from traditionalists.

One example of genuine inspiration, however, is the work of **Rafael Moneo,** who lives in Madrid and has designed mainly in Spain with such exceptions as the Davis Museum and Cultural Center at Wellesley, Massachusetts, in 1993. One of his most notable designs is the Museo Nacional de Arte Roman in Mérida. In 1996 he won the Pritzker Architecture Prize, viewed as the Oscar for architects. The Spanish architect **Santiago Calatrava** has been hailed as one of Europe's most innovative architects, although he trained as an

engineer and sculptor. He seeks to build a bridge between architecture and art.
In Barcelona, his Bach de Roda-Felipe II Bridge spans the rail tracks that run
from north to south, linking the ocean and city itself. Other projects include
the Bilbao Airport Terminal and the "City of Sciences" in Valencia.

Although Spain has a lot of homegrown talent, it also turns to foreign architects, especially for flashy signature projects. The most famous example of this
is **Frank Gehry's Guggenheim Museum at Bilbao,** hailed as the first great
building of the 21st century. One critic said that Gehry has "repudiated Modernist sanctity, symmetry, and right-angled geometrics in his own fearless way,
taking them apart and putting them back together with a rollicking, cockeyed
brilliance."

4 The Cuisine: Tapas, Paella & Sangría

Barcelona, Madrid, and, to a much lesser extent, Seville manage to incorporate
within their borders a gastronomic sampling of each of the country's best-loved
dishes. The cities' highly varied cuisines seem to hold one thing in common:
immense portions. Whenever possible, try to sample some of Spain's regional
specialties, offered at restaurants throughout the city. Many of these, such as
Andalusian **gazpacho** and Valencian **paella,** have become great dishes of the
world. You may want to simply order the *menú del día,* which is the menu of
the day or the chef's specially featured menu of the day.

MEALS

BREAKFAST In Spain the day starts with a continental breakfast of coffee,
hot chocolate, or tea, with assorted rolls, butter, and jam. Spanish breakfast
might also consist of *churros* (fried fingerlike doughnuts) and hot chocolate
that is very sweet and thick. However, a majority of Spaniards, it seems, simply have coffee. The coffee is usually strong and black, served with hot milk:
either a *café con leche* (half coffee, half milk) or *cortado* (a shot of espresso "cut"
with a dash of milk). If you find it too strong and bitter for your taste, you
might ask for a *café americano.*

LUNCH The most important meal of the day in Spain, lunch is comparable to the farm-style noonday dinner in America. It usually includes three or
four courses, beginning with a choice of soup or several dishes of hors d'oeuvres called *entremeses.* Often a fish or egg dish is served after this, then a meat
course with vegetables. Wine is always part of the meal. Dessert is usually pastry, custard, or fruit—followed by coffee. Lunch is normally served 1 to 4pm,
with "rush hour" at 2pm.

TAPAS After the early evening promenade, many Spaniards head for their
favorite *tascas,* bars where they drink wine and sample assorted *tapas,* or snacks,
such as bits of fish, eggs in mayonnaise, or olives.

Because many Spaniards eat very late, they often have an extremely light
breakfast, certainly coffee and perhaps a pastry. However, by 11am they are
often hungry and lunch might not be until 2pm or later. Many Spaniards fill
the emptiness in their stomachs with a late-morning snack, often at a cafeteria. Favorite items to order are a *tortilla* (Spanish omelette with potatoes) and
even a beer. Many request a large tapa served with bread.

DINNER Most tourists have their most extravagant meal of the day at din-
nertime. A typical meal starts with a bowl of soup, followed by a second
course, often a fish dish, and by another main course, usually veal, beef, or
pork, accompanied by vegetables. Again, desserts tend to be fruit, custard, or
pastries.

Naturally, if one had a heavy and late lunch and stopped off at a tapas bar or two before dinner, supper might be much lighter, perhaps some cold cuts, sausage, a bowl of soup, or even a Spanish omelette made with potatoes. Wine is always part of the meal. Afterward, you might have a demitasse and a fragrant Spanish brandy. The chic dining hour, even in one-donkey towns, is 10 or 10:30pm. In most middle-class establishments, people dine around 9:30pm. (In Madrid's well-touristed regions and in hardworking Catalonia, you can usually dine at 8pm, though you still may find yourself alone in the restaurant. Dining is usually later in the south—perhaps 10pm in Seville.)

DINING CUSTOMS   Many restaurants in Spain close on Sunday, so be sure to check ahead. Hotel dining rooms are generally open 7 days, and there's always someplace open in such big cities as Madrid and Barcelona or such well-touristed areas as the Costa del Sol.

Generally, reservations are not necessary, except at popular, top-notch restaurants.

THE CUISINE

SOUPS & APPETIZERS   Soups are usually served in big bowls. Cream soups, such as asparagus and potato, can be fine; sadly, however, they are too often made from powdered envelope soups such as Knorr and Liebig. Served year-round, chilled **gazpacho,** on the other hand, is tasty and particularly refreshing during the hot months. The combination is pleasant: olive oil, garlic, ground cucumbers, and raw tomatoes with a sprinkling of croutons. Spain also offers several varieties of fish soup (*sopa de pescado*) in all its provinces, and many of these are superb.

In top restaurants in all three cities, as many as 15 tempting hors d'oeuvres might be offered, often among the best of their kind anywhere. In lesser-known places, including restaurants without an active turnover of clients or inventories, avoid these *entremeses,* which often consist of last year's sardines and shards of sausage left over from the Moorish conquest.

EGGS   These are served in countless ways. A **Spanish omelette,** a *tortilla española,* is made with potatoes and usually onions. A simple omelette is called a *tortilla francesa.* A *tortilla portuguesa* is similar to the American Spanish omelette.

FISH   Spain's fish dishes tend to be outstanding and vary from province to province. Restaurants in both Madrid and Barcelona seek out the raw ingredients and the regional recipes for some of the finest fish dishes in Spain. One of the most common varieties is sweet white hake (*merluza*). *Langosta,* a variety of lobster, is seen everywhere—it's a treat but terribly expensive. The Portuguese in particular, but some Spaniards, too, go into raptures at the mention of barnacles (*mejillones*). Gourmets relish their seawater taste; others find them tasteless. *Rape* (pronounced *rah*-pay) is the Spanish name for monkfish, a sweet, wide-boned ocean fish with a scallop-like texture. Also try a few dozen half-inch baby eels. They rely heavily on olive oil and garlic for their flavor, but they taste great. Squid cooked in its own ink is suggested only to those who want to go native. Charcoal-broiled sardines, however, are a culinary delight— a particular treat in the Basque provinces but occasionally available in Madrid or Barcelona. Trout Navarre is one of the most popular fish dishes, usually stuffed with bacon or ham.

PAELLA   You can't go to Spain without trying its celebrated paella. Flavored with saffron, paella is an aromatic rice dish usually topped with shellfish, chicken, sausage, peppers, and local spices. Served authentically, it comes steaming hot from the kitchen in a metal pan called a *paellera.* (Incidentally, what is known in America as Spanish rice isn't Spanish at all. If you ask an English-speaking waiter for Spanish rice, you'll be served paella.)

MEATS Don't expect Kansas City steak, but do try the spit-roasted suckling pig, so sweet and tender it can often be cut with a fork. The veal is also good, and the Spanish *lomo de cerdo,* loin of pork, is unmatched anywhere. Tender chicken is most often served in the major cities and towns today, and the Spanish are adept at spit-roasting it until it turns a delectable golden brown. However, in more remote spots of Spain "free-range" chicken is often stringy and tough.

VEGETABLES & SALADS Through more sophisticated agricultural methods, Spain now grows more of its own vegetables, which are available year-round, unlike days of yore, when canned vegetables were used all too frequently. Both potatoes and rice are a staple of the Spanish diet, the latter a prime ingredient, of course, in the famous paella originating in Valencia. Salads don't usually get the attention they do in California, and are often made simply with just lettuce and tomatoes.

DESSERTS The Spanish do not emphasize dessert, often opting for fresh fruit. Flan, an egg custard, appears on all menus—sometimes with a burnt-caramel sauce. Ice cream appears on nearly all menus as well. But the best bet is to ask for a basket of fruit, which you can wash at your table. Homemade pastries are usually moist and not too sweet. As a dining oddity, many restaurants serve fresh orange juice for dessert—though it's not odd at all to Spaniards. Madrileños love it!

OLIVE OIL & GARLIC Olive oil is used lavishly in Spain, the largest olive grower on the planet. Despite its well-documented health effects, you may not want it in all dishes. If you prefer your fish grilled in butter, the word is *mantequilla.* In some instances, you'll be charged extra for the butter. Garlic is also an integral part of the Spanish diet, and even if you love it, you may find the Spaniard loves it more than you do and uses it in the oddest dishes.

WHAT TO DRINK

WATER Tap water is generally safe to drink in Barcelona, Madrid, and Seville. Despite that, many frequent travelers opt to drink bottled water instead, simply because it usually tastes better. If you're traveling in remote areas, play it safe and drink bottled water. One of the most popular non-carbonated bottled waters in Spain is Solares. Nearly all restaurants and hotels have it. Bubbly water is *agua mineral con gas;* non-carbonated, *agua mineral sin gas.* Note that bottled water in some areas may cost as much as the regional wine.

SOFT DRINKS In general, avoid the carbonated citrus drinks on sale everywhere. Most of them never saw an orange, much less a lemon. If you want a citrus drink, order old, reliable Schweppes. An excellent non-carbonated drink for the summer is called Tri-Naranjus, which comes in lemon and orange flavors. Your cheapest bet is a liter bottle of *gaseosa,* which comes in various flavors. In summer you should also try a drink that we've never had outside Spain, *horchata*—a nutty, sweet milk-like beverage made of tubers called *chufas.*

COFFEE Even if you are a dedicated coffee drinker, you may find the *café con leche* (coffee with milk) a little too strong. We suggest *leche manchada,* a little bit of strong, freshly brewed coffee in a glass that's filled with lots of frothy hot milk.

MILK In the largest cities you can get bottled milk, but it loses a great deal of its flavor in the process of pasteurization. In all cases, avoid untreated milk and milk products. Lauki is about the best brand of fresh milk.

From Vineyards to the Bodegas

Wines were first cultivated in Spain more than 2,000 years ago by ancient Greeks and Romans. Great emphasis came to be placed on the export of wines for both the orgies of the late Roman Empire and the celebration of communion during the early years of the Christian church.

Some of the country's vintages have been acknowledged as superb since the turn of the century, when vintners from Bordeaux, fleeing the phylloxera epidemic that had devastated many of the vineyards of France, carried their expertise to such regions as La Rioja, Navarre, and Catalonia. Beginning about a century earlier, others, most notably the vintners of such Andalusian regions as Jerez, grew rich on exporting sherries to the dinner tables of faraway Britain.

Today, Spain devotes more acreage to the cultivation of vineyards than any other nation in the world. For many years, however, because of trade restrictions and economic stagnation during the Franco regime, the output from many of these acres was not considered the equivalent of top wines from such competing regions as France, Italy, Chile, and California. Connoisseurs, when faced with a Spanish wine list, tended to focus rather narrowly on the wines of Jerez, La Rioja, and the Penedés region of Catalonia.

Thanks to some of the most aggressive and enlightened marketing in Europe, however, all of that is changing. Beginning in the 1990s, based partly on subsidies and incentives from the European Union, Spanish vintners have scrapped most of the country's obsolete wine-making equipment, hired new talent, and poured time and money into the improvement and promotion of wines from even high-altitude or arid regions not previously suitable for the drink's production. Thanks to irrigation, improved grape varieties, technological developments, and the expenditure of billions of pesetas, bodegas and vineyards are sprouting up throughout the country, opening their doors to visitors interested in how the stuff is grown, fermented, and bottled. These wines are now earning awards at wine competitions around the world for their quality and bouquet.

Interested in impressing a newfound Spanish friend over a wine list? Consider bypassing the usual array of Riojas, sherries, and sparkling Catalonian cavas in favor of, say, a Galician white from Rias Baixas, which some connoisseurs consider the perfect accompaniment for seafood. Among reds, make a beeline for vintages from the fastest-developing wine region of Europe, the arid, high-altitude district of Ribera del Duero, near Burgos, whose alkaline soil, cold nights, and sunny days have earned unexpected praise from wine makers (and encouraged massive investments) in the past 5 years.

For more information about these and others of the 10 wine-producing regions of Spain (and the 39 officially recognized wine-producing *Denominaciones de Origen* scattered across those regions), contact **Wines from Spain,** c/o the Commercial Office of Spain, 405 Lexington Ave., 44th Floor, New York, NY 10174-0331 (☎ **212/661-4959**).

BEER   Although not native to Spain, beer (*cerveza*) is now drunk everywhere. Domestic brands include San Miguel, Mahou, Águila, and Cruz Blanca.

WINE   Sherry (*vino de Jerez*) has been called "the wine with a hundred souls." Drink it before dinner (try the topaz-colored *finos,* a dry and very pale sherry) or whenever you drop in to some old inn or bodega for refreshment; many of them have rows of kegs with spigots. *Manzanilla,* a golden-colored medium-dry sherry, is extremely popular. The sweet cream sherries (Harvey's Bristol Cream, for example) are favorite after-dinner wines (called *olorosos*). While the French may be disdainful of Spanish table wines, they can be truly noble, especially two leading varieties, Valdepeñas and Rioja, both from Castile. If you're not too exacting in your tastes, you can always ask for the *vino de la casa* (wine of the house) wherever you dine. The Ampurdán of Catalonia is heavy. From Andalusia comes the fruity Montilla. There are also some good local champagnes (*cavas*) in Spain, such as Freixenet. One brand, Benjamín, also comes in individual-sized bottles.

Spanish wines are hardly what they cost in Franco's day; however, even those sold in restaurants (some restaurant owners mark the wine up 100% or more) are still relatively inexpensive. But if you start out with a bottle costing the owner between 710 and 1,150 pesetas (US$5 and US$8), even with the markup it's still a worthwhile purchase for a diner.

SANGRÍA   The all-time favorite refreshing drink in Spain, sangría is a red-wine punch that combines wine with oranges, lemons, seltzer, and sugar. Be careful, however; many joints that do a big tourist trade produce a sickly sweet Kool-Aid version of sangría for unsuspecting visitors.

WHISKEY & BRANDY   Imported whiskeys are available at most Spanish bars but at a high price. If you're a drinker, switch to brandies and cognacs, where the Spanish reign supreme. Try Fundador, made by the Pedro Domecq family in Jerez de la Frontera. If you're seeking a smooth cognac, ask for the "103" white label.

Appendix B:
Basic Phrases & Vocabulary

English	Spanish	Pronunciation
Hello	**Buenos días**	bway-noss dee-ahss
How are you?	**¿Como está usted?**	koh-moh ess-tah oo-steth
Very well	**Muy bien**	mwee byen
Thank you	**Gracias**	gra-theeahss
Good-bye	**Adiós**	ad-dyohss
Please	**Por favor**	pohr fah-bohr
Yes	**Sí**	see
No	**No**	noh
Excuse me	**Perdóneme**	pehr-doh-neh-may
Give me	**Deme**	day-may
Where is . . .?	**¿Donde está?**	dohn-day ess-tah
the station	**la estación**	la ess-tah-thyohn
a hotel	**un hotel**	oon oh-tel
a restaurant	**un restaurante**	oon res-tow-rahn-tay
the toilet	**el servicio**	el ser-vee-thee-o
To the right	**A la derecha**	ah lah day-ray-chuh
To the left	**A la izquierda**	ah lah eeth-kyehr-duh
Straight ahead	**Adelante**	ah-day-lahn-tay
I would like . . .	**Quiero**	kyehr-oh
to eat	**comer**	ko-mayr
a room	**una habitación**	oo-nah ah-bee-tah-thyon
How much?	**¿Cuánto?**	kwahn-toh
The check	**La cuenta**	la kwen-tah
When	**¿Cuándo?**	kwan-doh
Yesterday	**Ayer**	ah-yeyr
Today	**Hoy**	oy
Tomorrow	**Mañana**	mah-nyah-nah
Breakfast	**Desayuno**	deh-sai-yoo-noh
Lunch	**Comida**	ko-mee-dah
Dinner	**Cena**	thay-nah

NUMBERS

1	**uno** (*oo*-noh)	15	**quince** (keen-thay)
2	**dos** (dose)	16	**dieciséis** (dyeth-ee-sayss)
3	**tres** (trayss)	17	**diecisiete** (dyeth-ee-sye-tay)
4	**cuatro** (kwah-troh)	18	**dieciocho** (dyeth-ee-oh-choh)
5	**cinco** (theen-koh)	19	**diecinueve** (dyeth-ee-nyway-bay)
6	**seis** (sayss)	20	**veinte** (bayn-tey)
7	**siete** (syeh-tay)	30	**treinta** (trayn-tah)
8	**ocho** (oh-choh)	40	**cuarenta** (kwah-ren-tah)
9	**nueve** (nway-bay)	50	**cincuenta** (theen-kwhen-tah)
10	**diez** (dyeth)	60	**sesenta** (say-sen-tah)
11	**once** (ohn-thay)	70	**setenta** (say-ten-tah)
12	**doce** (doh-thay)	80	**ochenta** (oh-chayn-tah)
13	**trece** (tray-thay)	90	**noventa** (noh-ben-tah)
14	**catorce** (kah-tor-thay)	100	**cien/ciento** (thyen/thyen-toe)

Appendix C: Menu Savvy

Arroz Rice
Bacalao al ajo arriero Cod-and-garlic dish named after Leonese mule drivers
Bacalao al pil-pil Cod with garlic and chile peppers
Bajoques farcides Peppers stuffed with rice, pork, tomatoes, and spices
Butifarra Catalonian sausage made with blood, spices, and eggs
Caldereta Stew or a stew pot
Caseolada Potato-and-vegetable stew with bacon and ribs
Chanfaina salmantina Rice, giblets, lamb sweetbreads, and pieces of *chorizo*
Chilindrón Sauce made from tomatoes, peppers, garlic, and *chorizo*
Chorizo Spicy pork sausage
Cochifrito navarro Small pieces of fried lamb
Cocido español Spanish stew
Cocido madrileño Chickpea stew of Madrid, with potatoes, cabbage, turnips, beef, marrow, bacon, *chorizo,* and black pudding
Empanada Crusted pie of Galicia, with a variety of fillings
Escudella Catalan version of chickpea stew
Fabada White-bean stew of Asturias
Habas a la catalana Stew of broad beans, herbs, and spices
Lacón con grelos Salted ham with turnip tops
Magras con tomate Slices of slightly fried ham dipped in tomato sauce
Merluza a la gallega Galician hake with onion, potatoes, and herbs
Merluza a la sidra Hake cooked with cider
Morcilla Black (blood) sausage akin to black pudding
Paella alicantina Rice dish made with chicken and rabbit
Pato a la naranja Duck with orange, an old Valencian dish
Pinchito Small kebab
Pisto manchego Vegetable stew from La Mancha
Pollos a la chilindrón Chicken cooked in a tomato, onion, and pepper sauce
Salsa verde Green sauce
Sangría Drink made with fruit, brandy, and wine
Sopa de ajo castellana Garlic soup with ham, bread, eggs, and spices
Tapas Small dishes or appetizers served with drinks at a tavern
Tortilla de patatas Spanish omelette with potatoes
Trucha a la navarra Trout fried with a piece of ham
Turrón Almond paste
Zarzuela Fish stew

Index

See also Accommodations and Restaurant indexes below.

GENERAL INDEX

Accommodations
Aranjuez, 229
Barcelona, 7–8, 49–62
Madrid, 10–12, 131–150
Seville, 14–15, 245–254
Toledo, 222–224
Acueducto Romano (Segovia), 235
Aeropuerto San Pablo (Seville), 241
Airfares, 31–34
Airlines, 29–30
to Barcelona, 38
Airports
Barcelona, 38
Madrid, 122
Seville, 241
Alcázar (Segovia), 235
Alcázar (Seville), 261
Alcázar (Toledo), 216
Alcázar de la Puerta de Sevilla (Carmona), 277
All Saints' Day (Seville), 25
American Express, 21
Barcelona, 46
Madrid, 125
Seville, 244
Amusement parks
Barcelona, 94
Madrid, 190
Andalusia, 270, 280, 289
Andalusian School of Equestrian Art (Jerez de la Frontera), 282
Antiques
Barcelona, 23, 102, 104
Madrid, 198
Aquarium
Barcelona, 91
Madrid, 191
Aranjuez, 228–230
Archaeological museums
Carmona, 277
Museo Arqueológico Nacional (Madrid), 185
Museo Arqueológico Provincial (Seville), 264
Archbishop's Palace (Seville), 266
Architecture, 292–297
Barcelona, 94–95

Archivo General de Indias (Seville), 262, 266
ARCO (Madrid's International Contemporary Art Fair) (Madrid), 23
Argüelles/Moncloa (Madrid), 124
accommodations, 149–150
nightlife, 203
Army Museum (Madrid), 185
Art galleries
Barcelona, 103
Madrid, 198
Seville, 271
Art museums, 89
Casa y Museo de El Greco (Toledo), 217
Esteban Vicente Contemporary Art Museum (Segovia), 236
Fundació Antoni Tàpies (Barcelona), 87
Fundació Joan Miró (Barcelona), 89
Museo de América (Madrid), 188
Museo de la Real Academia de Bellas Artes de San Fernando (Madrid), 184
Museo de Santa Cruz (Toledo), 217
Museo Lázaro Galdiano (Madrid), 187
Museo Municipal (Madrid), 187
Museo Nacional Centro de Arte Reina Sofía (Madrid), 184
Museo Nacional de Artes Decorativas (Madrid), 186
Museo Provincial de Bellas Artes de Sevilla, 262
Museo Romántico (Madrid), 188
Museo Sorolla (Madrid), 188
Museo Tiflológico (Madrid), 188
Museu Barbier-Mueller Art Precolombí (Barcelona), 87
Museu Cau Ferrat (Sitges), 116

Museu d'Art Contemporani de Barcelona, 86
Museu d'Art Modern (Barcelona), 88
Museu de les Arts Decoratives (Barcelona), 92
Museu de Montserrat, 119
Museu Egipci de Barcelona, 88
Museu Frederic Marés (Barcelona), 96
Museu Maricel (Sitges), 116
Museu Nacional d'Art de Catalunya (Barcelona), 89
Museu Picasso (Barcelona), 2
Panteón de Goya (Madrid), 189
Prado Museum (Madrid), 4, 180
Thyssen-Bornemisza Museum (Madrid), 181
Arxiu de la Carona d'Aragó (Barcelona), 98
ATMs, 20
Atocha Station (Madrid), 122, 129
accommodations near, 141
Auditorio Nacional de Música (Madrid), 204
Autumn Festival (Madrid), 24
Ayuntamiento (Seville), 268

Baby-Sitters
Barcelona, 46
Madrid, 128
Barajas Airport (Madrid), 122
Barcelona card, 43
Barceloneta. *See* La Barceloneta
Bargaining, 198
Barri de la Ribera (Barcelona), 41
Barri Gòtic (Barcelona), 2, 40–41
accommodations, 49
sights and attractions, 83
walking tour, 96–98
Barri Xinés (Barrio Chino; El Raval) (Barcelona), 40–41
Barrio de Santa Cruz (Seville), 5, 262, 270

Bars and pubs
  Barcelona, 110–113
  Madrid, 209–213
  Seville, 275–276
  Sitges, 118
  Toledo, 227
Beaches, Sitges, 115
Blues. *See* Jazz and blues
Bodega Bohemia (Barcelona), 3
Bodegas, Jerez de la Frontera, 280, 281
Bookstores
  Barcelona, 46
  Seville, 271
Bosch, Hieronymus, 181
Breughel, Pieter, the Elder, 181
Bucket shops, 31
Bullfighting Museum (Madrid), 188
Bullfights, 23, 294–295
  Barcelona, 89
  Madrid, 3, 187
  Seville, 264
Bus travel
  in Barcelona, 43
  to Barcelona, 39
  in Madrid, 125
  to Madrid, 122
  to Spain, 34

Cabaret, Barcelona, 109
Cabildo Catedral de Segovia (Segovia), 236
Cable car
  Barcelona, 46
  Madrid, 190
Cafes, Madrid, 4
Calendar of events, 23–25
Calle Sierpes (Seville), 6, 268
Capilla de Santa Llúcia (Barcelona), 96
Car travel, 39
  in Barcelona, 44
  in Madrid, 125
  to Madrid, 122
  to Spain, 35
Cardona, 120
Carmona, 277
Carnaval
  Madrid, 23
  Sitges, 114
Carrer de la Tapineria (Barcelona), 100
Casa Amatller (Barcelona), 95
Casa Batlló (Barcelona), 95
Casa de Campo (Madrid), 189
Casa de L'Ardiaca (Barcelona), 96
Casa de la Ciutat/Ayunta-miento (Barcelona), 95
Casa de la Condesa de Lebrija (Seville), 268

Casa de Lope de Vega (Madrid), 191
Casa de Murillo (Seville), 262
Casa de Pilatos (Seville), 6, 261, 269
Casa de Príncipe (San Lorenzo de El Escorial), 232
Casa del Canonge (Barcelona), 98
Casa Lleó Morera (Barcelona), 95
Casa Milà (Barcelona), 95
Casa-Museu Gaudí (Barcelona), 93
Casinos
  Barcelona, 114
  Madrid, 213
Casita del Labrador (Aranjuez), 229
Catalonia, 37
Catedral (Seville), 260, 266
Catedral de Barcelona, 86
Cathedrals. *See* Churches and cathedrals
Cavas, 2, 120
Cave Crawling in Madrid, 211
Center of Contemporary Culture of Barcelona (CCCB), 86
Ceramics. *See* Pottery and porcelain
Cervantes, Miguel de, 6
Chamartín (Madrid), 122, 129
  accommodations near, 147–149
  sights and attractions, 187–188
Charles III, 4, 184, 228, 232, 291
Charles IV, 181
Charles V, 180, 220, 290
Charter flights, 31
Chicote (Madrid), 5
Children
  accommodations
    Madrid, 145
    Seville, 249
  restaurants
    Barcelona, 71
    Seville, 256
  sights and attractions
    Barcelona, 94
    Madrid, 190
    Seville, 265
Chueca (Madrid), 124
  nightlife, 203
  restaurants, 171
  sights and attractions, 187–188
Church of St. Nicolás (Madrid), 194

Churches and cathedrals
  Cabildo Catedral de Segovia (Segovia), 236
  Capilla de Santa Llúcia (Barcelona), 96
  Catedral (Seville), 260, 266
  Catedral de Barcelona, 86
  Church of St. Nicolás (Madrid), 194
  Iglesia de la Anunciación (Seville), 268
  Iglesia de la Vera Cruz (Segovia), 236
  Iglesia de San Estéban (Seville), 269
  Iglesia de San Ildefonso (Seville), 269
  Iglesia de San Isidro (Madrid), 194
  Iglesia de San José (Seville), 268
  Iglesia de San Nicolás de Bari (Seville), 269
  Iglesia de San Pedro (Seville), 268
  Iglesia de Santa Catalina (Seville), 269
  Iglesia de Santa Cruz (Seville), 269
  Iglesia de Santo Tomé (Toledo), 220
  Iglesia del Salvador (Seville), 268
  La Sagrada Família (Barcelona), 3, 88
  Real Basílica de San Francisco el Grande (Madrid), 185
  Sant Vicenç de Cardona, 120
  Toledo Cathedral, 216
Ciutat Vella (Barcelona), 2. *See also* Barri Gòtic
  accommodations, 49, 52–56
  restaurants, 63, 66–71
  sights and attractions, 83, 86–87
Classical music
  Barcelona, 107
Climate, 22
Club and music scene
  Barcelona, 109–110
  Madrid, 205–209
  Seville, 275
Codorníu, 120
Columbus, Christopher, 87, 90, 190, 280, 290
  Monument (Mirador de Colón; Barcelona), 40, 42
Consulates
  Barcelona, 46
  Madrid, 128
  Seville, 244

Convent of the Incarnation (Seville), 266
Convento de la Encarnación (Seville), 266
Convento de San Leandro (Seville), 269
Corpus Christi, 24
Córdoba, 280, 289
Crafts
 Madrid, 199
 Toledo, 221
Credit cards, 22
Cuisine, 297–299
Currency, 20
Currency exchange
 Barcelona, 46
 Madrid, 128
Customs regulations, 19

Dalí, Salvador, 184, 296
Dance clubs and discos
 Barcelona, 109
 Madrid, 207
 Seville, 275
Dentists
 Barcelona, 47
 Madrid, 128
Department stores
 Barcelona, 102
 Madrid, 199
 Seville, 272
Día de los Santos Inocentes (Seville), 25
Diada (Barcelona), 24
Disabilities, travelers with, 26
Día de los Reyes (Barcelona), 23
Doctors, 25
 Madrid, 128
Drinks, 299
Drugstores
 Barcelona, 47
 Madrid, 128

Eixample (Barcelona), 40, 42
 accommodations, 49
 sights and attractions, 87
El Alcázar (Segovia), 235
El Alcázar (Seville), 261
El Arenal (Seville), 6
El Greco, 116, 119, 180–184, 187, 214–217, 220, 231, 262
 Casa y Museo de El Greco (Toledo), 217
El Rastro (Madrid), 194, 196, 200
El Raval (Barcelona). See Barri Xinés
El Valle de los Caídos (San Lorenzo de El Escorial), 232
Embassies
 Madrid, 128

Emergencies
 Barcelona, 47
Entry requirements, 18
Escolanía (Montserrat), 119
Escuela Andaluza del Arte Ecuestre (Jerez de la Frontera), 282
Estació de França (Barcelona), 38
Esteban Vicente Contemporary Art Museum (Segovia), 236

Fashion
 Barcelona, 103
 Madrid, 200
 Seville, 272
Fast food and picnic fare
 Barcelona, 81
 Madrid, 178–179, 201
Ferdinand of Aragón, 87, 190, 217, 228, 235, 241, 261, 270, 289
Feria de Sevilla, 23
Ferries
 to the Balearic Islands (Majorca and Minorca), 39
Festival Internacional de Jazz de Barcelona, 25
Festivals and special events, 23–25
Fiesta de la Mercé (Barcelona), 24
Fiesta de San Isidro (Madrid), 24
Fiestas of Lavapiés and La Paloma (Madrid), 24
Fine Arts Museum (Madrid), 184
Fira del Libre de Barcelona, 24
Flamenco, 5, 281
 Barcelona, 108
 Seville, 274
Flea markets, Madrid, 4, 200
Franco, Francisco, 291
Fuentes Luminosas (Barcelona), 93
Fundació Antoni Tàpies (Barcelona), 87
Fundació Joan Miró (Barcelona), 89
Funicular, 119
 Barcelona, 44, 93

Galería Olímpica (Barcelona), 89
Gardens. See Parks and gardens
Gaudí y Cornet, Antoni, 3, 95, 296
 Casa-Museu Gaudí (Barcelona), 93

La Sagrada Família (Barcelona), 88
Gay men and lesbians, 27
 Barcelona, 113
 Madrid, 212–213
 Seville, 276
 Sitges, 116, 118
Genet, Jean, 40
Giralda Tower (Seville), 261
Gothic Quarter (Barcelona). See Barri Gòtic
Goya, Francisco de, 181–185, 187–189, 216–217, 239, 260, 262
 Panteón de Goya (Goya's Tomb) (Madrid), 189
Gran Teatre del Liceu (Barcelona), 41
Gran Vía (Madrid), 124
 accommodations on or near, 136–138
 attractions near, 186
 nightlife, 202
 shopping, 196
Grape Harvest Festival (Madrid), 25
Gris, Juan, 184

Harbor Front (Barcelona), 3, 42
Health concerns, 25
Hemingway, Ernest, 191
History, 288–292
Holidays, 22
Holy Week (Seville), 5, 23
Hospital de la Santa Caridad (Seville), 261
Hospital de los Venerables (Seville), 270
Hospital de Tavera (Toledo), 220
Hospitals and clinics
 Barcelona, 47
 Madrid, 129
 Seville, 245

Iglesia de la Anunciación (Seville), 268
Iglesia de la Vera Cruz (Segovia), 236
Iglesia de San Estéban (Seville), 269
Iglesia de San Ildefonso (Seville), 269
Iglesia de San Isidro (Madrid), 194
Iglesia de San José (Seville), 268
Iglesia de San Nicolás de Bari (Seville), 269
Iglesia de San Pedro (Seville), 268
Iglesia de Santa Catalina (Seville), 269

Iglesia de Santa Cruz
(Seville), 269
Iglesia de Santo Tomé
(Toledo), 220
Iglesia del Salvador (Seville),
268
Information sources, 17
Aranjuez, 228
Barcelona, 39
Madrid, 123
San Lorenzo de El Escorial,
231
Segovia, 235
Seville, 242
Toledo, 216
Insurance, 25
Internet access
Barcelona, 47
Madrid, 129
Seville, 245
Isabella I, 87, 190, 217, 228,
234–236, 241, 261–262,
270, 281, 289–290
Isabella II, 210
Itálica, 278
IVA (value-added tax), 48

Jardín de la Isla (Aranjuez),
229
Jazz and blues, in Barcelona,
25, 110
Jerez de la Frontera, 278–284
Jews, 281, 290
Seville, 5
Toledo, 217, 220
Juan Carlos, 291

L'Aquarium de Barcelona, 90
La Barceloneta (Barcelona),
40, 42
restaurants, 77–79
sights and attractions, 90
La Giralda (Seville), 6, 265
La Granja, 239
La Macarena (Seville), 243
La Sagrada Família
(Barcelona), 3, 88
Las Murallas (Barcelona), 100
Laundry and dry cleaning,
129
Barcelona, 47
Seville, 245
Leather goods
Barcelona, 104
Madrid, 201
Les Rambles (Barcelona), 2,
40–41
Lope de Vega, Felix, 194, 203,
205, 243
Casa de Lope de Vega
(Madrid), 191
Luggage storage and lockers,
129

Magazines
Barcelona, 47

Madrid, 129
Maps
Barcelona, 41
Madrid, 123
Seville, 243
Marathon Catalunya
(Barcelona), 23
Markets, Barcelona, 104
Meals, 297
Mercat de la Boquería
(Barcelona), 10
Metro (subway)
Barcelona, 43
Madrid, 124
Mirador de Colón
(Barcelona), 90
Miró, Joan, 2, 41, 184
Fundació (Barcelona), 89
Parc de (Barcelona), 93
Modernisme movement, 42,
95
Monasterio de las Descalzas
Reales (Madrid), 186
Monasterio de San Juan de
los Reyes (Toledo), 217
Monasterio del Parral
(Segovia), 236
Monastery at Montserrat,
118–119
Monestir de Pedralbes
(Barcelona), 92
Money, 20–21
Montjuïc, 81
Montjuïc (Barcelona), 40, 42,
44–46, 93
Montserrat, 118–119
Moors, 235, 280–281,
289–290, 292–293
Mosques, in Seville, 6
Movida, in Madrid, 5
Murillo, Bartolomé Esteban,
180, 184, 187, 243,
261–262
Casa de Murillo (Seville),
262
Museo Arqueológico
(Carmona), 277
Museo Arqueológico Nacional
(Madrid), 185
Museo Arqueológico
Provincial (Seville), 264
Museo de América (Madrid),
188
Museo de Artes y Costumbres
Populares (Seville), 264
Museo de Cera de Madrid,
190
Museo de la Real Academia
de Bellas Artes de San
Fernando (Madrid), 184
Museo de las Carruajes
(Madrid), 185
Museo de Santa Cruz
(Toledo), 217
Museo del Ejército (Madrid),
185

Museo del Prado. *See* Prado
Museum (Madrid)
Museo Lázaro Galdiano
(Madrid), 187
Museo Municipal (Madrid),
187
Museo Nacional Centro de
Arte Reina Sofía (Madrid),
184
Museo Nacional de Artes
Decorativas (Madrid), 186
Museo Naval (Madrid), 186
Museo Provincial de Bellas
Artes de Sevilla, 262
Museo Romántico (Madrid),
188
Museo Sorolla (Madrid), 188
Museo Taurino (Madrid), 188
Museo Tiflológico (Madrid),
188
Museu Arqueològic de
Catalunya (Barcelona), 89
Museu Barbier-Mueller Art
Precolombí (Barcelona), 87
Museu Cau Ferrat (Sitges),
116
Museu d'Art Contemporani
de Barcelona, 41, 86
Museu d'Art Modern
(Barcelona), 88
Museu d'Història de la Ciutat
(Barcelona), 86
Museu de la Ciència
(Barcelona), 91, 94
Museu de les Arts Decoratives
(Barcelona), 92
Museu de Montserrat, 119
Museu del Calçat Antic
(Barcelona), 100
Museu Egipci de Barcelona,
88
Museu Frederic Marés
(Barcelona), 86, 96
Museu Maricel (Sitges), 116
Museu Marítim (Barcelona),
91
Museu Nacional d'Art de
Catalunya (Barcelona), 89
Museu Picasso (Barcelona), 2,
41, 88
Museu Romàntic, 116
Music. *See* Jazz and blues;
Club and music scene;
Classical music; Flamenco
Muslims. *See* Moors

Newspapers
Barcelona, 47
Madrid, 129
Nightlife. *See also* Bars and
pubs; Club and music
scene; Performing arts
Barcelona, 106–113
Madrid, 202–213
San Lorenzo de El Escorial,
234

General Index

Segovia, 240
Seville, 274–276
Sitges, 118
Toledo, 227
Norte Diagonal (Barcelona)
accommodations, 62
restaurants, 75, 77

Old City (Barcelona). *See*
Ciutat Vella
Olympic Village (Barcelona).
See Vila Olímpica
Opera, in Seville, 6, 274
Organized tours. *See* Tours
Madrid, 195

Palacio Arzobispal (Seville),
266
Palacio de Lebrija (Seville),
268
Palacio Real (Aranjuez), 228
Palacio Real (Madrid), 184,
192
Palacio Real de La Granja (La
Granja), 239
Palatine Chapel of Santa
Agata (Barcelona), 98
Palau de la Generalitat
(Barcelona), 98
Palau de Pedralbes
(Barcelona), 42
Palau Reial (Barcelona), 87
Panteón de Goya (Madrid),
189
Parc d'Atraccions (Montjuïc)
(Barcelona), 94
Parc d'Atraccions (Tibidabo)
(Barcelona), 94
Parc de Joan Miró
(Barcelona), 93
Parc de la Ciutadella
(Barcelona), 81, 93
sights and attractions in
and around, 88
Parc de Montjuïc
sights and attractions in
and around, 89
Parc Güell (Barcelona), 92
Parc Zoologic (Barcelona), 94
Parks and gardens
Barcelona, 92–93
Madrid, 189–190
Seville, 264
Parque de Atracciones
(Madrid), 190
Parque de Retiro (Madrid), 4,
123, 190
accommodations near,
142–144
Parque María Luisa (Seville),
264
Paseo del Prado (Madrid),
124
attractions along, 185
Passeig del Moll de la Fusta
(Barcelona), 40, 42, 77

Passports, 18
Pedralbes (Barcelona), 42
Penedés wineries, 120
Performing arts
Barcelona, 107–108
Madrid, 203–205
Seville, 274
Peseta, 20
Philip II, 192, 228, 230–231,
235, 290, 295
Philip IV, 3–4
Philip V, 239, 290
Picasso, Pablo, 2, 184
Museu Picasso (Barcelona),
2, 41, 88
Plaça de la Seu (Barcelona),
96
Plaça de Ramón Berenguer el
Gran (Barcelona), 100
Plaça de Sant Jaume
(Barcelona), 41, 98
Plaça de Sant Just
(Barcelona), 99
Plaça del Rei (Barcelona), 98
Plaça Nova (Barcelona), 96
Plaça Reial (Barcelona), 40
Playas del Muerto (Sitges),
115
Plaza de América (Seville),
264
Plaza de España (Madrid),
123–124
accommodations near, 133
attractions near, 186
Plaza de España (Seville),
264–265
Plaza de las Cortés (Madrid)
accommodations near,
132–133
Plaza Mayor (Madrid),
123–124, 191, 196
accommodations south of,
145
attractions near, 184–185
nightlife, 202
Poble Espanyol (Barcelona),
42, 90, 94
Porcelain. *See* Pottery and
porcelain
Post offices
Barcelona, 47
Madrid, 129
Seville, 245
Pottery and porcelain
Barcelona, 105
Madrid, 201
Seville, 271
Prado Museum (Madrid), 4,
180, 191
Puerta de Toledo (Madrid),
192
Puerta del Sol (Madrid),
123–124
accommodations near,
138–141
attractions near, 184–185
nightlife, 202

Radio
Barcelona, 47
Madrid, 129
Rambles (Ramblas). *See* Les
Rambles (Barcelona)
Rastro (Madrid), 4
Real Basílica de San Francisco
el Grande (Madrid), 185
Real Fábrica de Tabacos
(Seville), 265
Real Fábrica de Tapices
(Madrid), 189
Real Jardin Botánico
(Madrid), 190
Real Monasterio de San
Lorenzo de El Escorial, 231
Reales Alcázar (Seville), 266
Reconquest, 289
Rest rooms
Barcelona, 47
Madrid, 129
Restaurants
Barcelona, 9, 10, 63–81
family-friendly, 71
Madrid, 12–13, 150–178
Seville, 15–16, 255–260
Toledo, 225–227
Retiro Park (Madrid), 4, 123,
190
accommodations near,
142–144
Ribera, José, 180, 184, 187,
217–220, 229
Roman amphitheater and
necropolis (Carmona), 277
Roman Aqueduct (Segovia),
235
Roman ruins
Barcelona, 41, 83–86,
96–100
Carmona, 277
Itálica, 278
Segovia, 235
Roman Walls (Barcelona),
100
Romans, 289, 292
Royal Alcázar (Seville), 266
Royal Palace (Aranjuez), 228
Royal Palace (Barcelona), 87
Royal Palace (Madrid), 184,
192
Rubens, Peter Paul, 180

Safety
Barcelona, 48
Madrid, 130
Seville, 245
Sagrada Família (Barcelona),
3, 88
Sala Parés (Barcelona), 2
Salamanca (Madrid), 124,
196
sights and attractions,
187–188
San Lorenzo de El Escorial,
230–234

Sant Jeroni (Montserrat), 119
Sant Sadurní d'Anoia, 120
Sant Vicenç de Cardona, 120
Santa Cova (near
    Montserrat), 119
Sardana, in Barcelona, 2, 86
Science Museum (Barcelona),
    91
Seasons, 22
Segovia, 234–239
Semana Santa (Seville), 5, 23
Seniors, 27–28
Sevillana, 275
Seville, 241–284
Seville Fair, 23
Seville Gate (Carmona), 277
Shipping, 197
Shopping
    Barcelona, 101–106
    Madrid, 195–201
    Seville, 271–273
    Toledo, 220–221
Shopping centers & malls
    Barcelona, 105
    Madrid, 202
Sitges, 114–118
Sínagoga de Santa María La
    Blanca (Toledo), 220
Sínagoga del Tránsito
    (Toledo), 220
Spanish Civil War, 114
Students, 28–29
Subway (metro)
    Barcelona, 43
    Madrid, 124
Sur Diagonal (Barcelona)
    accommodations, 57–62
    restaurants, 72–75

Tapas, 297. *See also* Tascas
    Madrid, 4
Tàpies, Fundació Antoni
    (Barcelona), 87
Tarragona, 37, 292
Tascas
    Barcelona, 80
    Madrid, 4
Taxes, 48
Taxis
    Barcelona, 44
    Madrid, 125
Teatro Calderón (Madrid),
    205
Teatro Real (Madrid), 204
Teleférico (Madrid), 190
Telegrams and telex,
    Barcelona, 48
Telephone
    Barcelona, 48
    Madrid, 130
    Seville, 245
Television
    Barcelona, 47
    Madrid, 129
Templo de Debod (Madrid),
    186

Theater
    Barcelona, 107
    Madrid, 204–205
Three Kings Day (Barcelona),
    23
Thyssen-Bornemisza Museum
    (Madrid), 181
Tibidabo (Barcelona), 40, 42,
    44, 93
Tipping
    Barcelona, 48
Toledo, 214–217, 220–228
Torre de Collserola
    (Barcelona), 92
Torre del Oro (Seville), 261
Tourist information, 17
Tours
    Andalusia, 271
    Barcelona, 100–101
    Madrid, 195
    organized, 35–36
    Seville, 270
Train travel
    in Barcelona, 44
    to Barcelona, 38
    to Madrid, 122
    to Spain, 34
Transportation
    Barcelona, 43–44
    Madrid, 124–125
    Seville, 244
Traveler's checks, 21
Traveling
    to Barcelona, 38–39
    to Madrid, 122
    to San Lorenzo de El
        Escorial, 230
    to Segovia, 235
    to Seville, 241
    to Spain, 29–36
    to Toledo, 216
Triana (Seville), 6

Valley of the Fallen (San
    Lorenzo de El Escorial),
    232
Value-added tax (IVA), 48
Velázquez, Diego, 3,
    180–184, 187, 231, 268
Veranos de la Villa (Madrid),
    24
Verbena de Sant Joan
    (Barcelona), 24
Vila Olímpica (Barcelona), 42
    accommodations, 62
Visitor information. *See*
    Information sources

Water, drinking, 299
Wax Museum (Madrid), 190
Web sites, travel, 17
Wineries
    Penedés, 120
Wines, 300

Xampanyerías (champagne
    bars), in Barcelona, 2

Zoo
    Barcelona, 94
    Madrid, 191
Zoo Aquarium de la Casa de
    Campo (Madrid), 191

BARCELONA ACCOMMODATIONS

Abat Cisneros (Montserrat),
    119
Avenida Palace, 7, 59
Barcelona Hilton, 7, 57
Claris, 7, 57
Duques de Bergara, 53
Gran Hotel Havana, 59
Granvía, 54
Hostal Levante, 8, 55
Hostal Neutral, 55
Hotel Arts, 7, 9, 62
Hotel Astoria, 61
Hotel Balmes, 61
Hotel Calípolis (Sitges), 116
Hotel Colón, 7, 52, 54
Hotel Condes de Barcelona,
    60
Hotel Continental, 8, 55
Hotel Cortés, 55
Hotel Derby/Hotel Gran
    Derby, 61
Hotel España, 55
Hotel Hespería, 54, 62
Hotel Lleó, 53
Hotel Majestic, 60
Hotel Meliá Barcelona Sarrià,
    60
Hotel NH Calderón, 52
Hotel Platjador (Sitges), 117
Hotel Princesa Sofía, 54, 58
Hotel Regencia Colón, 8, 54
Hotel Ritz, 7, 58
Hotel San Agustín, 56
Hotel Suizo, 56
Hotel Wilson, 62
Le Meridien Barcelona, 8, 52
Mesón Castilla, 56
Montecarlo, 54
Parador Nacional Duques de
    Cardona, 120
Princesa Sofía, 8
Rey Juan Carlos I, 9, 59
Rialto, 56
Rivoli Ramblas, 53
San Sebastián Playa (Sitges),
    117
Turín, 56

MADRID ACCOMMODATIONS

AC Hoteles Ciudad de
    Toledo, 222
Anaco, 137
Aristos, 149
Best Western Villa de Barajas,
    133
Casón del Tormes, 136

Castellana Inter-Continental Hotel, 12, 145
Conde Duque, 146
Crowne Plaza Madrid City Centre, 12, 133
Cuzco, 147
Emperatriz, 143
Eurobuilding, 148
Gran Hotel Colón, 11, 144
Gran Hotel Reina Victoria, 12, 138
Gran Hotel Velázquez, 143
Green Hotel El Prado, 137
Hostal Alcázar Regis, 137
Hostal Buenos Aires, 137
Hostal Castilla (Aranjuez), 229
Hostal Cervantes, 11, 133
Hostal Cristina (San Lorenzo de El Escorial), 233
Hostal del Cardenal (Toledo), 222
Hostal la Macarena, 139
Hostal la Perla Asturiana, 139
Hostal Nuevo Gaos, 138
Hostal Residencia Americano, 140
Hostal Residencia Don Diego, 147
Hostal Residencia Principado, 140
Hostal-Residencia Continental, 11, 138
Hotel Atlántico, 136
Hotel Botánico (San Lorenzo de El Escorial), 232
Hotel Chamartín, 149
Hotel Claridge, 145
Hotel Doménico (Toledo), 223
Hotel El Pintor El Greco (Toledo), 223
Hotel Escultor, 147
Hotel Francisco I, 140
Hotel Gaudí, 136
Hotel Imperio (Toledo), 224
Hotel Infanta Isabel (Segovia), 237
Hotel Inglés, 140
Hotel Los Linajes (Segovia), 237
Hotel María Cristina (Toledo), 223
Hotel Martin (Toledo), 224
Hotel Mayoral (Toledo), 224
Hotel Mercátor, 141
Hotel Nuria, 138
Hotel Opera, 139
Hotel Paris, 140
Hotel Puerta de Toledo, 145
Hotel Real de Toledo, 224
Hotel Residencia Cortezo, 141
Hotel Residencia Imperio (Toledo), 225
Hotel Residencia Lisboa, 141

Hotel Residencia Santander, 141
Hotel Santo Domingo, 136
Hotel Victoria Palace (San Lorenzo de El Escorial), 233
Hotel Villa Real, 11, 132
Husa Princesa, 149
Las Sirenas (Segovia), 238
Los Arcos (Segovia), 237
Meliá Castilla, 12, 145, 148
Meliá Madrid Princesa, 149
Miguel Angel, 146
Miranda & Suizo (San Lorenzo de El Escorial), 233
NH Nacional, 141
Novotel Madrid, 11, 144–145
Palace, 132
Palace Hotel, 11
Parador de Segovia, 237
Parador Nacional de Conde Orgaz (Toledo), 226
Park Hyatt Villa, 11
Park Hyatt Villa Magna, 142
Residencia Bréton, 147
Residencia Liabeny, 137
Ritz, 10, 12
Santo Mauro Hotel, 11, 146
The Ritz, 142
Tirol, 145, 150
Tryp Ambassador, 139
Wellington, 144

SEVILLE ACCOMMODATIONS

Al-Andalus Palace, 246
Bécquer, 15, 246
Casa de Carmona, 277
Casa Imperial, 15, 246
El Coloso (Jerez de la Frontera), 283
Grand Hotel Barcelo, 15, 248
Hacienda Benazuza, 14, 254
Hostal Goya, 253
Hotel Alcázar, 250
Hotel Alfonso XIII, 14, 245
Hotel América, 253
Hotel Avenida Jerez (Jerez de la Frontera), 282
Hotel Doña María, 14, 249–250
Hotel Ducal, 254
Hotel Inglaterra, 15, 248
Hotel La Rabida, 254
Hotel Los Seises, 251
Hotel Meliá Sevilla, 15, 249
Hotel Monte Triana, 251
Hotel Murillo, 254
Hotel Occidental Porta Coeli, 249
Hotel Plaza de Armas, 251
Hotel Regina, 252
Hotel Royal Sherry Park (Jerez de la Frontera), 282

Hotel Serit (Jerez de la Frontera), 283
Hotel Simon, 252
Hotel Tryp Colón, 245
La Casa de la Judería, 252
La Cueva Park (Jerez de la Frontera), 283
Las Casas de los Mercaderes, 252
Las Casas del Rey de Baeza, 250
Montecastillo (Jerez de la Frontera), 283
Murillo, 14
Puerta de Triana, 253
Residencia y Restaurant Fernando III, 14
Residencia y Restaurante Fernando III, 249, 253
Taverna del Alabardero, 15, 250

BARCELONA RESTAURANTS

7 Portes, 10, 79
Abat Cisneros (Montserrat), 119
Agua, 78
Agut, 66
Agut d'Avignon, 63
Alt Heidelberg, 80
Bar del Pi, 80
Bar Turò, 80
Beltxenea, 9, 72
Biocenter, 68
Bodega la Plata, 80
Bodegueta, 80
Botafumeiro, 9, 75
Brasserie Flo, 67
Ca La María, 75
Café de L'Academia, 69
Café Viena, 81
Can Costa, 9, 77
Can Culleretes, 67
Can Isidre, 73
Can Majó, 78
Can Pescallunes, 67
Casa Alfonso, 80
Casa Calvet, 73
Casa Leopoldo, 63
Casa Tejada, 81
Chez Jeanette (Sitges), 117
Chicago Pizza Pie Factory, 81
Dulcinea, 71, 82
Egipte, 67
El Caballito Blanco, 75
El Duc, 69
El Túnel, 78
El Velero (Sitges), 117
Els Quatre Gats, 10
Els Quatre Gats (Sitges), 68, 117
Gaig, 76
Garduña, 9, 69, 71
Jaume de Provença, 10, 72

La Balsa, 79
La Buena Brasa, 73
La Cuincta, 60
La Dama, 9, 72
La Dentellière, 70
La Jarra, 81
La Llauna, 79
La Rosca, 70
Las Campanas, 82
L'Olive, 74
Los Caracoles, 9, 68
Mercat de la Boquería, 81
Mesón del Café, 99
Neichel, 10, 76
Nou Celler, 70
Pitarra, 70
Pla de la Garsa, 71
Poble Espanyol, 71
Quo Vadis, 66
Ramonet, 78
Reno, 77
Restaurant Hoffmann, 66
Restaurant Hofmann, 10
Restaurante Diana, 73
Rey de la Gamba, 82
Roig Robí, 77
Rosalert, 74
Senyor Parellada, 71
Talaia Mar, 74
Tragaluz, 75
Via Veneto, 77

MADRID RESTAURANTS

Alfredo's Barbacoa, 171
Alkalde, 162
Antonio Sánchez, 178
Arce, 156
Asador Adolfo (Toledo), 225
Bajamar, 156
Bocaito, 155
Café Balear, 168
Café Bar Los Galayos, 194
Café de Oriente, 13, 160
Caripén, 159
Casa Alberto, 161
Casa Benigna, 175
Casa José (Aranjuez), 229
Casa Lucio, 172
Casa Pablo (Aranjuez), 230
Casa Paco, 14, 160
Casa Vallejo, 168
Charolés (San Lorenzo de El Escorial), 233
Chez Lou Crêperie, 177
Ciao Madrid, 169
Cornucopia en Descalzas, 160
Edelweiss, 155
El Amparo, 12, 163
El Bernardino (Segovia), 238
El Bodegón, 169
El Bosque (Jerez de la Frontera), 284
El Cabo Mayor, 13, 170
El Catavinos (Toledo), 226

El Cenador del Prado, 161
El Cosaco, 174
El Cuchi, 173
El Emperador (Toledo), 226
El Espejo, 154
El Inca, 171
El Mentidero de la Villa, 13, 157
El Olivo Restaurant, 170
El Pescador, 163
El Schotis, 173
Errota-Zar, 154
Foster's Hollywood, 13, 159, 167
Gaitán (Jerez de la Frontera), 284
Goizeko Kabi, 170
Gran Café de Gijón, 165
Horcher, 14, 163
Hostal del Cardenal (Toledo), 225
Hosteleria Valle de los Caídos (Valley of the Fallen), 234
Jockey, 12, 165
José María (Segovia), 238
La Abadia (Toledo), 225
La Atalaya, 176
La Barraca, 157
La Bola, 156
La Chata, 175
La Esquina del Real, 161
La Fuencisla, 166
La Galette, 177
La Gamella, 13, 164
La Paloma, 166
La Parilla (Toledo), 227
La Perdiz (Toledo), 227
La Posada de la Villa, 173
La Rana Verde (Aranjuez), 230
La Tarasca (Toledo), 227
La Trainera, 164
La Trucha, 154
Las Batuecas, 177
Las Cuatro Estaciones, 13, 166
Las Cuevas de Luís Candelas, 173
Las Cuevas del Duque, 156
Lhardy, 158
Los Galayos, 13, 174
Mad Madrid, 161
Mesa Redonda (Jerez de la Frontera), 284
Mesón Aurelio (Toledo), 226
Mesón de Cándido (Segovia), 238
Mesón Duque (Segovia), 239
Mesón la Cueva (San Lorenzo de El Escorial), 234
Mesón las Descalzas, 162
Museo del Jamon, 162
Nabucco, 172
Nicomedes, 175
O'Pazo, 171
Paellería Valenciana, 158

Parador Nacional de Conde Orgaz (Toledo), 226
Pedro Larumbe, 164
Platerías Comedor, 159
Príncipe de Viana, 171
Príncipe y Serrano, 176
Restaurante Belagua, 167
Restaurante Tendido 6 (Jerez de la Frontera), 284
Ríofrío, 168
San Carlo, 157
San Mamés, 176
Sobrino de Botín, 14, 174, 191
Suntory, 165
Taberna Carmencita, 172
Taberna del Alabardero, 162
Teatriz, 167
Terraza, 158
Tienda de Vinos, 172
Tocororo, 155
V.I.P., 158–159
Viridiana, 165
Zalacaín, 13, 169

SEVILLE RESTAURANTS

Casa de Carmona, 277
Casa Robles, 255
Casa Román, 270
Cervecería Giralda, 16, 259
Egaña Oriza, 15
El Burladero, 16, 255
El Puerto, 16, 256, 259
Enrique Becerra, 15, 258
Hostería del Laurel, 16, 259
La Albahaca, 256
La Dehesa, 256
La Isla, 16, 258
La Raza, 260
Pizzería El Artesano, 256
Pizzería San Marco, 15–16, 260
Rincón de la Casana, 258
Río Grande, 16, 256, 259
Taverna del Alabardero, 16, 258